Portrait of a Yeshva Boy by Isidor Kaufmann, oil on board, c. 1895-1915.

Image provided by the Jewish Museum, New York.

An Eternal Light: Brody, in Memoriam (Ukraine)

Translation of
Ner Tamid: Yizkor leBrody

Original Yizkor Book

Editor-in-chief: Aviv Meltzer

Organization of former Brody Residents in Israel

Published in Jerusalem, Israel, 1994

Published by JewishGen

An Affiliate of the Museum of Jewish Heritage - A Living Memorial to the Holocaust New York

An Eternal Light: Brody, in Memoriam
Translation of *Ner Tamid: Yizkor leBrody*

First Printing: June 2018, Sivan 5778
Second Printing: March 2019, Adar II, 5779

Translation Project Coordinator: Moshe Kutten
Translation Project Coordinator Emerita: Marjorie Stamm Rosenfeld
Layout: Joel Alpert
Formatting: Lynn Mercer
Cover Design: Nina Schwartz

Published by JewishGen, Inc.
An Affiliate of the Museum of Jewish Heritage
A Living Memorial to the Holocaust
36 Battery Place, New York, NY 10280

"JewishGen, Inc. is not responsible for inaccuracies or omissions in the original work and makes no representations regarding the accuracy of this translation. Digital images of the original book's contents can be seen online at the New York Public Library Web site."

The mission of the JewishGen organization is to produce a translation of the original work and we cannot verify the accuracy of statements or alter facts cited.

Printed in the United States of America by Lightning Source, Inc.

Library of Congress Control Number (LCCN): 2018946888
ISBN: 978-1-939561-61-9 (hard cover: 736 pages, alk. paper)

JewishGen and the Yizkor-Books-in-Print Project

This book has been published by the **Yizkor-Books-in-Print Project,** as part of the **Yizkor Book Project** of **JewishGen, Inc**.

JewishGen, Inc. is a non-profit organization founded in 1987 as a resource for Jewish genealogy. Its website [www.jewishgen.org] serves as an international clearinghouse and resource center to assist individuals who are researching the history of their Jewish families and the places where they lived. JewishGen provides databases, facilitates discussion groups, and coordinates projects relating to Jewish genealogy and the history of the Jewish people. In 2003, JewishGen became an affiliate of the **Museum of Jewish Heritage - A Living Memorial to the Holocaust** in New York.

The **JewishGen Yizkor Book Project** was organized to make more widely known the existence of Yizkor (Memorial) Books written by survivors and former residents of various Jewish communities throughout the world. Later, volunteers connected to the different destroyed communities began cooperating to have these books translated from the original language—usually Hebrew or Yiddish—into English, thus enabling a wider audience to have access to the valuable information contained within them. As each chapter of these books was translated, it was posted on the JewishGen website and made available to the general public.

The **Yizkor-Books-in-Print Project** began in 2011 as an initiative to print and publish Yizkor Books that had been fully translated, so that hard copies would be available for purchase by the descendants of these communities and also by scholars, universities, synagogues, libraries, and museums.

These Yizkor books have been produced almost entirely through the volunteer effort of researchers from around the world, assisted by donations from private individuals. The books are printed and sold at near cost, so as to make them as affordable as possible. Our goal is to make this important genre of Jewish literature and history available in English in book form, so that people can have the personal histories of their ancestral towns on their bookshelves for themselves and for their children and grandchildren.

A list of all published translated Yizkor Books in the project with prices and ordering information can be found at:

http://www.jewishgen.org/Yizkor/ybip.html

Lance Ackerfeld, Yizkor Book Project Manager

Joel Alpert, Yizkor-Book-in-Print Project Coordinator

JewishGen
Yizkor Book Project

This book is presented by the
Yizkor Books in Print Project
Project Coordinator: Joel Alpert

Part of the
Yizkor Books Project of JewishGen, Inc.
Project Manager: Lance Ackerfeld

These books have been produced solely through volunteer effort of individuals from around the world. The books are printed and sold at near cost, so as to make them as affordable as possible.

Our goal is to make this history and important genre of Jewish literature available in English in book form so that people can have the near-personal histories of their ancestral towns on their bookshelves for themselves and for their children and grandchildren.

Any donations to the Yizkor Books Project are appreciated.

Please send donations to:
Yizkor Book Project
JewishGen
36 Battery Place
New York, NY 10280

JewishGen, Inc. is an affiliate of the
Museum of Jewish Heritage
A Living Memorial to the Holocaust

About *An Eternal Light*

The city of Brody – now in Ukraine but in Austrian Galicia in the 19th century and in Poland between the two world wars--boasted a Jewish presence for almost 400 years. A Jewish community was documented there as early as 1588 and endured until 1943, when the last Jews were deported from Brody for extermination in a Nazi death camp. A number of survivors who had miraculously escaped the Nazi death machine ended up in Israel. There, in 1955, Nathan-Michael Gelber's Toldot Yehudei Brody 1584-1943 (Brody: A History of the Jews of Brody 1584-1943) was published by Mosad HaRav Kook in Jerusalem as part of a series about towns in Europe which had been home to Jews. Meanwhile, other Brody survivors dreamed of a second book to commemorate and perpetuate their mother city. What they envisioned was a spirited collection containing historical essays, remembrances, testimonies, even poems, about what life had been like in Brody. Out of this dream was born the volume Ner Tamid: Yizkor LeBrody (An Eternal Light: Brody, in Memoriam), published by the Organization of Former Brody Residents in Israel in 1994.

Marjorie Stamm Rosenfeld
(Project Coordinator emerita)

Translator's Foreword

My father, Aharon Kutten, ran away from his home in Brody when he was 16 years old, jumping, at the spur of a moment, on a train that took young members of a Zionist organization, for whom he was counselor, on their way to Palestine. While the young kids were sent by their parents to Palestine, he left without any documentation and with only his shirt on his back. He made it to Palestine, after stealing borders on the train and living on the streets of Trieste, Italy for two years. He went back to visit his parents in Brody in winter 1938, but they could not or would not leave with him. He left Europe just in time before WW II broke out and was able to build a home, a family, as well as a successful and extremely productive career in Israel. My grandparents, Khana and Moshe Kutten, perished in the Holocaust along with the six million Jewish martyrs.

My parents, Aharon and Sonia Kuten, did not talk to us much about their childhood and about their family life in their hometowns. Being young and busy with our own lives and family we were not smart enough to interrogate them until it was too late.

I found out that my father's story and the stories of his siblings, who also escaped Europe in time, were not unique when I started reading the "Ner Tamid–Brody Yizkor" book, in search for more information on the Jewish life in Brody. I learned so much about the culturally rich Jewish life in Brody before the war and the events during Holocaust from this book that it drove me to translate it to English, so that my children and my descendants would be able to read it when they start to ask questions.

I am also thankful for the opportunity presented to me, to be able to do my small part in making sure that the Holocaust and the rich Jewish life in Europe would never be forgotten.

Moshe Kutten
Pennsylvania, USA

From the Book Cover Sleeve:

This book tells about Brody's Jews during a period of 400 years of the existence of their community: about the changes they went through, the days of flourishing and glory and the days of lowliness and poverty, and the way Brody came to be called "Jerusalem of Galitzia", until its destruction during the Holocaust.

The first part of the book, authored by the historian N. M. Gelber z"l, along with the entry "Brody" from "*Pinkas Ha'Kehilot*", embodies the history of the community from its establishment until its destruction (1588 - 1943).

The second part of the book - which is the main part - contains the description of the community between the two World Wars, until its destruction during the Second World War. Presented are testimonies and memories from the Holocaust (chapter three and four), which complement the original details of the history of the community and its tragic and cruel end during the period of the Holocaust.
The fifth chapter of the book - "Images and Eulogies" ends with a list of the "Righteous of the Nations of the World", who saved a few of our Brody's community Jews.

The Yizkor chapter, containing the list of our community martyrs who were killed during the Holocaust at the hands of evil gentiles "For the sanctification of the Name," is actually a realization of the idea of the publication of a memorial book for those who were buried in mass graves in foreign soil, those who were not given a Jewish burial and those whose burial location is unknown.

The following lists were added to the Yizkor chapter: A list of Brody's young people who fought against the Nazis and were killed during the years 1939 - 1945, a list of Brody's natives who passed away in Israel and a list of Brody's natives and their descendants who were killed during the Israel campaigns.
Two appendices were added at the end of the book: an appendix in English and the article "We the Polish Jews" by Julian Tuvim.

Front cover of the Original Yizkor Book- painted by the artist Shmuel Lamm

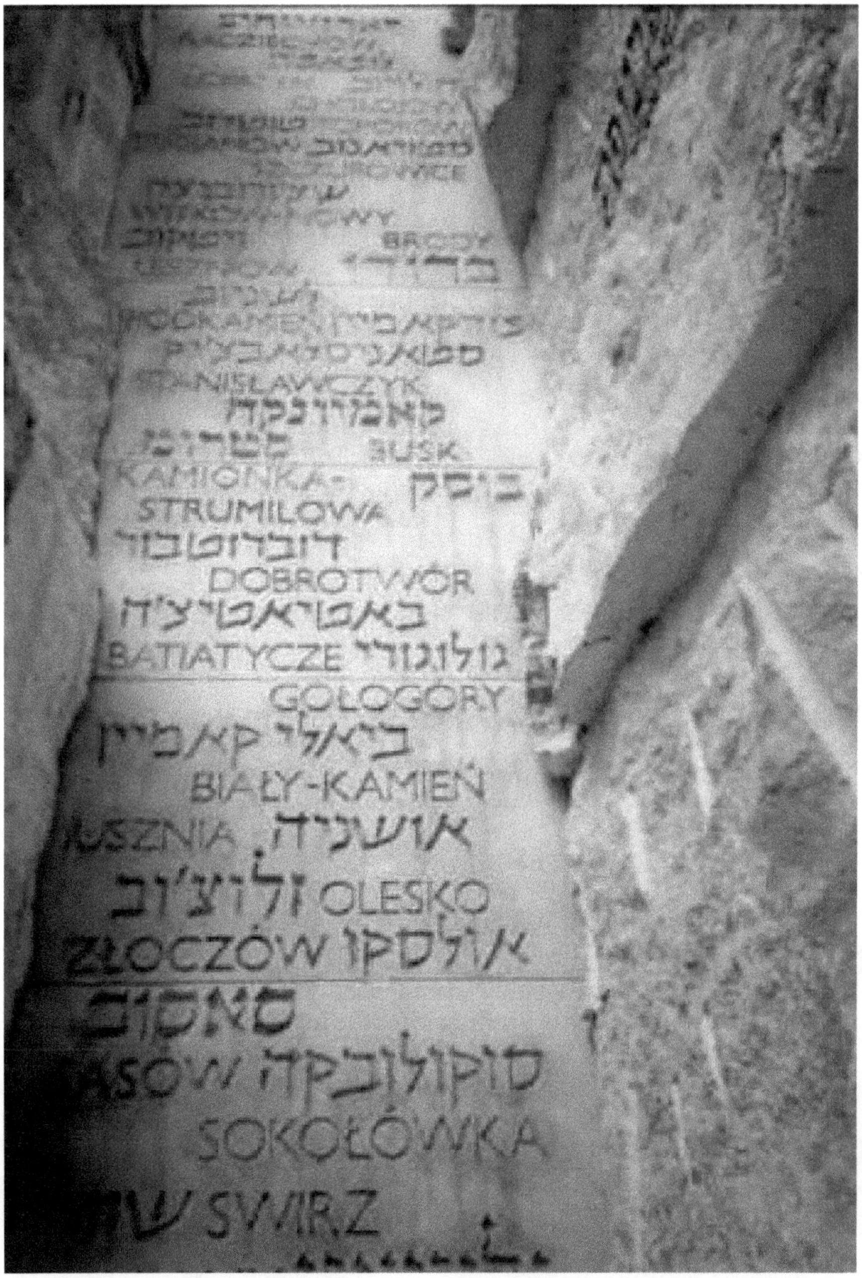

Back cover of the Original Yizkor Book - Memorial in “Yad Vashem”

The Founders of the Organization of Former Brody and its Vicinity Residents in Israel

Uri Gasthalter
David Hammermann, of blessed memory
Nathan Meirsohn
Josef Parvari-Leiner, of blessed memory
Alexander-Olek Podmerner
Moshe Rosenblum, of blessed memory
Naphtali Jacob Rotmann
Haya Shahar-Donner
Moshe Shalmi-Stadtmauer
Haim Shmuszkin
Mendel Singer, of blessed memory
Anshel Stromwasser, of blessed memory

The Former Brody and its Vicinity Residents Committee

Naphtali Harash
Hermann Lilian
Dov Pestes (chairman)
Alexander-Olek Podmerner
Zipora Rom
Haya Shahar-Donner
Moshe Shalmi-Stadtmauer
Raphael Shlinger-Shalev
Haim Shmuszkin
Eliezer Tolmacz
Jacob Tomashower
Isaac Zohar-Zorne

The Memorial Book's Committee

David Altmann
Josef Ettinger, of blessed memory
Bianka Lilian
Malwina Lilian-Dembinski
Dov Pestes
Zipora Rom
Zehava Shmuszkin
Isaac Zohar-Zorne

The Editorial Board

Yehoshua-Shiko Mandel
Aviv Meltzer (editor-in-chief)
Josef Parvari-Leiner, of blessed memory
Sarah-Samith Shmuszkin-Rubinstein

Eternal memorial to Brody's martyrs in Holon cemetery

Geopolitical Information:

Alternate names for the town are: Brody [Pol, Ger, Ukr, Rus], Brod [Yid], Prode

Period	Town	District	Province	Country
Before WWI (c. 1900):	Brody	Brody	Galicia	Austrian Empire
Between the wars (c. 1930):	Brody	Brody	Tarnopol	Poland
After WWII (c. 1950):	Brody			Soviet Union
Today (c. 2000):	Brody			Ukraine

Brody, Ukraine is located at: 50°05' N, 25°09' E

Nearby Jewish Communities:

Radyvyliv 6 miles NE
Leshniv 11 miles NNW
Stanislavchyk 12 miles WNW
Pidkamin 13 miles SE
Shchurovychi 14 miles NNW
Sokolivka 14 miles WSW
Olesko 14 miles SW
Pochayev 15 miles ESE
Lopatyn 16 miles NW
Sasiv 17 miles SSW
Zavidche 18 miles NNW
Stremil'che 18 miles NNW
Berestechko 18 miles N
Kozin 19 miles NE
Bilyi Kamin 19 miles SW
Toporiv 19 miles W

MAP OF UKRAINE IN 2014

Notes to the Reader:

We apologize ahead of time for the poor quality of images in the book. Often these images had been scanned from the original Yizkor books which were of poor quality to begin with, being copies of old photographs. Each transfer results in loss of quality. We have done the best we could given the original material and the resources and technology at hand. Even though images often appear of higher quality on computer screens, that does not transfer to high quality images in print. A reader can view the original scans on the web sites listed below.

Within the text the reader will note "{34}" standing ahead of a paragraph. This indicates that the material translated below was on page 34 of the original book. However, when a paragraph was split between two pages in the original book, the marker is placed in this book after the end of the paragraph for ease of reading.

Also please note that all references within the text of the book to page numbers, refer to the page numbers of the original Yizkor Book.

In order to obtain a list of all Shoah victims from Brody, the reader should access the Yad Vashem web site listed below; one can also search for specific family names using family name option. These lists are continually updated by Yad Vashem, so it is worthwhile to periodically search these lists.

There is much valuable information available on this web site, including the Pages of Testimony, etc.

http://yvng.yadvashem.org

A list of this book and all books available in the Yizkor-Book-In-Print Project along with prices is available at:

http://www.jewishgen.org/Yizkor/ybip.html

Nowy Cmentarz Żydowski
11
Cmentarz Katolicki
JAZŁOWCZYK
FOLWARKI MAŁE
Leszniowska
ZAMEK
Podzamcze
Słoneczna
Krupnicza
Goldhabera
Podwale Dolne
Jurydyka
WAŁY SZPITALINE
Podwale Górne
Ruska
Szkolna
Nowa
Szpital
Tow. Muz.
Muzyczna
Cerkiewna
Gim. Żeń.
Długa
Zamkowa
Średnia
Owocowa
Kalira
RYNEK C
RYNEK B
RYNEK A
RYNEK D
Zukra
Szpitalna
Krechowieckich (Złota)
Witosławskiego
Sokół
Kasa Chorych
Bzowa
FOLWARKI WIELKIE
Wały Gimnazjalne
Kołodziejska
Żelazna
Klasztorna
Łazienna
Bożnicza
Ormiańska
Plac Sobieskiego
Korzeniowskiego
Sz. Żyd. Wesoła
Magistrat
Gim. Pań.
Okrężna
GETTO
Kolejowa
Zyblikiewicza
SMOLNO
Łamana
Gęsia
Cicha
Zamknięta
Mickiewicza (Lwowska)
Stary Cmentarz Żydowski
Starocmentarna
Miodowa
Kowalska
PLAN MIASTA
BRODY
1 old synagogue
2 new synagogue
3 jewish municipality house
4 jewish school
5 jewish hall
6 orphanage
7 cinema "palas"
8 home for aged
9 jewish hospital
10 musical association
11 new cemetry
12 old cemetry
13 catholic church
TARGOWICA (Park Miejski)
SUCHOWÓLKA
STARE BRODY
Dwór Schnella
Stacja Towarowa
Dworzec
Stacja Kolejowa
SZWABY
Do Lwowa Przez Krasne
Linia Kolejova Równe - Lwów
Do Radziwiłowa
SKREŚLIŁ: PARWARI JÓZEF (LEINER)

Table of Contents

Chapter Five: Images and Eulogies

Chapter Six: Memorial Pages

English Section

Addendum

List of Pictures

Translated by Moshe Kutten

[All Pictures are top to bottom or clockwise from top left]

Page numbers are page numbers of the original book, not the page numbers of this translation.

[English page 11] [Hebrew page 1]*

Preface

Retyped by Genia Hollander

The flow of books dedicated to the memory of the Jewish communities obliterated in the Holocaust during World War II – which began essentially in the nightmarish days when the mournful news started to reach the free world – did not abate but grew stronger in the fifties and sixties of our century. And even today, nearly half a century after the War's end, the urgent desire of the survivors of those communities to erect a "Yad Vashem" (a memorial) to the martyred victims annihilated by the Nazi foe, may his name and memory be blotted out, has neither ceased nor weakened.

Actually gravestones cannot be erected on the "mass fraternal graves" thousands of kilometres from the State of Israel where the few survivors have basically concentrated. In most of the European Jewish communities, even the graveyards and their tombstones have disappeared, nor is there even place to erect a memorial for, in most instances, construction occurred at the Jewish cemetery sites – streets were widened, homes were built or public gardens were planted.

After the war, a few of "the brands plucked from the fire" gathered in some of the Jewish towns, emerging from the camps and places of hiding – refugees returning from the former Soviet Union and released prisoners-of-war. And they remained there until they fenced in the cemeteries and raised up the tombstone fragments – the memorial stones. But after this holy work was done, the last remnants of the communities left where they had lived and scattered throughout the world. One may assume that these tombstones too, will not long survive, for who will guarantee us that these cemetery areas will not be used for additional construction needs. For, after all, these places no longer have Jewish communal bodies to worry about their maintenance.

Attempts were made after the war to erect memorial monuments not necessarily where the bodies or their ashes were interred. Gravestones were also put up for individual Jews cremated at Treblinka. Stone monuments for entire communities were set up in Israel and outside it by organizations of cooperating people who came from those communities. Our community's survivors in Israel as well have erected, in the cemetery near Holon, a memorial gravestone to the martyrs of Brody; it was consecrated on 19th Iyyar 5747 (1987).

[Page 12]*

However, this way of commemorating the communities has not been the sole answer; and the publication of memorial volumes dedicated to select communities that are no longer has become a more common phenomenon. It seems that symbols, stones, memorials and joint memorial monuments were an inadequate answer for the aching hearts, the burden-laden memories and the grief. The physically and emotionally stricken hearts sought relief by reducing to writing their oppressing thoughts, their impressions and their dark memories, and this outpouring of the soul brings a modicum of relief.

Therefore, among the remaining few, the new style has spread of perpetuating in writing the memory of the communities – the cities, the towns and their surroundings that were destroyed during the German conquest. The surviving members of the communities have organized. They are continuing the existence of the communities as it were through a world of memories. It may be that this characteristic of people up in years, and the remaining few are such today. And they so long to return to their memories and find relief in writing memorial books that, occasionally, after an organization has published a memorial volume, it develops the desire to go further, to issue an additional volume, just so the thread of memories of days past not be torn, that the heart's ties to the holy and pure who were murdered by bestial human beings no be sundered.

These activities of perpetuation that have become a movement among the organizations of survivors of the destroyed communities have also revealed a variety of concomitant phenomena. It happens not infrequently that perpetuation activists voice their opinions loudly and try to influence without themselves being involved in the actual doing. On the other hand, there are in the "Landsmanshaftn" individuals devoted with all their might and energy to realizing the idea of perpetuating the memory of their community and its martyrs and do not turn the publication into an instrumentality for private gain. We are fortunate that we, too, among our Brody brethren, have such an extraordinary person about whose like Maimonides wrote: "were it not for the obsessed, the world would remain desolate". The reference is to Joseph Parvari-Leiner, of blessed memory. He conceived the idea of perpetuating the community of Brody even before the guns of World War II were silenced, when the first bitter news began to arrive about the total destruction of the Jews of Europe. He dreamed of a monument that would withstand the ravages of time, a memorial that would be very long lasting!

At the very outset of the process of organizing a committee of former Brody residents in Israel in the early fifties, various ideas were raised for perpetuating the memory of the destroyed community. Year-after-year, when the former residents of Brody in Israel gathered to honour their community and honour the memory of its martyrs, the outstanding intellectuals of Brody: - Dov Sadan, Aryeh Tartakover and Medel Zinger, all of blessed memory – continued to stress that a memorial-volume is the preferred response suited to the memory of "The Jerusalem of Galicia". Already in 1953, at one of the first memorial ceremonies, Jacob Nethaneli-Rothman spoke of: "the perpetuation of the Brody community".

[Page 13]

Since then, for thirty-eight years, the concept of a memorial-volume was caught up in the tangle of rhetoric. Mendel Zinger sought to advance the implementation of the perpetuation concept and Dov Sadan, at the start of 1955, responded: "....and if you are talking (apart from the volume written by Nathan Michael Gelber, *Brody: A History of the Jews of Brody 1584-1943, 1955*) of another volume, larger, more comprehensive, more varied and primarily more lively, in which one could sense the city's air which we breathed – I will join you wholeheartedly.

Thereafter, there were another number of attempts to breathe a fresh spirit into the work of perpetuation, but in vain. The years passed and the dreamers seemed to be moving farther from publishing the volume. The last push to pave the way and recruit all those Brody-ites prepared to make a supreme effort to advance the publication of the Brody Memorial volume was made by Joseph Leiner, who issued an impassioned call through the pages of Brody – A 'Mother-City' of the Jewish People, (Av 5729). Here is what he wrote: “Dear Brody-ites, Let us get straight to the point. We are the last generation who come from Brody a 'mother-city' of the Jewish people, which enriched our people with scholars and famous Rabbis; with pioneers of the Enlightenment and the early shoots of our national rebirth: with renewers of the Hebrew language and with the best of the builders of this country; and it is our duty to establish a monument to the martyrs who perished there in the days of the Nazi conquest. If we do not do this for ourselves, for our children, for the following generations and history, no one else will do it and the memory of the city will be erased forever!” His words were written with great emotion and sacred awe at the magnitude of the undertaking which he saw as his life's work and the fulfilment of his mission (see his sons' comments, pp.360-361). But because of insignificant matters, it never succeeded. In the meantime, Joseph Parvari-Leiner was summoned to the Court on high and never saw his dream realized.

Incidentally, these were difficult and trying times for the concerned Brody-ites in the country who were left with only a gleam of hope and an unquestioned faith that the matter would indeed come to pass. The connection that had been established between Yitzhak Zorne and Hayyim-Szmusz-kin led to a meeting of the Brody-ites in the winter of 1987 in the home of Berta Klenberg-Margulies. Those present declared their desire to become part of the effort and assist in preparing the volume for print. But from then till now, another six years elapsed in which the ranks of the workers dwindled and those who remained felt a moral obligation to prepared the testimonies, the memoirs and the impressions that had been gathered over the long years and to publish them in a memorial volume worthy of the community's glorious past and the memory of its martyrs.

[Page 14]*

Joseph Leiner's zealousness to continue the project of perpetuating the community of Brody was justified, but the struggles of writing, editing and publishing books in general and memorial books in particular are difficult. How great were the troubles and the confrontations! The sages of Rome have already said: "habent sua fata libelli", i.e. "Books have their own fate". This was said of books that saw the light of day, how much the more so books that are in the process of preparation, of coming into being. And with Joseph's death, his words took on even greater strength, the strength of a last will and testament which made it incumbent upon us, the lone survivors who, like him, had been miraculously saved, to continue that sublime goal of his labour, to perpetuate the memory of the community's martyrs murdered by the Nazi. And indeed, the perpetuation project was not interrupted – and, behold, the volume is in our hands.

This volume relates the deeds of the Jews of Brody through the nearly four hundred years of its existence; the transformations it underwent; its days of prosperity and glory, of depression and poverty; and the ways the Jews of Brody earned it the title of the "Jerusalem of Galicia".

The first part of the volume was written by Dr. Nathan Michael Gelber, of blessed memory, a historian of repute among the scholars of the history of Zionism in Galicia and its communities. He described the history of the city of Brody and its Jewish community from the day of its establishment to that of its destruction (1588-1943).

The period between the two World Wars (1918-1939) received a comprehensive and in-depth study and Dr. Gelber used most of the primary sources at his disposal to the fullest. A description of this period from the various aspects of the continuous history of our community occupies the second part of the volume before us. It is actually a portrait of a city and its community on the threshold of World War II, that is, on the eve of the Holocaust.

Many are the points of view and great is the importance of the chapters presented in the memorial volume, which covers the history of our community in the distant past and in the brief twenty-year period under the rule of an independent Poland. But first and foremost, the book is to be seen as a memorial monument, a book of testimonies and remembrances which are the original and complementary data of the history of the community in the days of its tragic and brutal decline in the Holocaust period. Every refugee and survivor who managed to escape this danger that was lying in ambush to take his life, everyone who fled his pursuers, those who emerged from the forests and left while there was still time before the deeds of hatred and annihilation burst forth against them and every researcher and person of ordinary intelligence who will open the memorial book, will find comfort in its perusal.

[Page 15]*

Let us say a few words about the nature of this special literature – "the Landschaften literature" – which has already acquired its place among other genres of history books. We must point out at once that the attitude of the professional critics of memorial volumes is not unambiguous. There are those who are sceptical about this sort of literature and even this is sometimes an understatement. This is not to say that their attitude to it is absolutely negative, but they indicate its lacks, the greatest of which is that the memorial volumes do not depend upon official documents or printed books and periodicals but primarily upon the memory of the writers.

But from this point of view, an important advantage of the memorial volumes "accused" of not being scientific should be emphasized: their importance lies precisely in the fact that their authors are not professional historians who must use the proper "jargon" in their work and follow the scientific regimen to handle the topic along set lines and include a long list of bibliographical and other notes. On the other hand, the memorial volumes have a particular charm lacking in the scientific history books: their form is simple, their language and style less severe and pedantic and sometimes, they are not free of distortions of various sorts – but this is precisely what assures the writer's naiveté and honesty. More than other volumes, the memorial books contain an abundance of information that helps one understand the spirit of the nation and its characteristics, information whose significance is unquestioned: but in spite of this, their echo is weak and unheard in the professional literature.

There remains only one aspect that can clarify the difference between our community and the great majority of the communities in which our brothers were annihilated. The Holocaust was not the first destruction in the history of our people but while most of the persecutions of the past were connected in our memory with the "sanctification of the Name", i.e. with martyrdom, the circumstances of this destruction caused the prevailing opinion about it to be of a phenomenon in which an entire nation was seized with an enormous paralyzing fear. The truth, however, is that no one of the other nations conquered, ruled and persecuted by the Nazi was there greater display of heroism than among the Jewish people.

[Page 16]*

Who has not heard of the Warsaw Ghetto uprising; the Bialystok Ghetto uprising? But only a few know of resistance movements in the other small ghettos across conquered Poland. Alongside the terrible Holocaust chapters in our city – the seven fires of Gehenna, the tortures of Tophet, starvation, plagues, killing and throttling – chapters have been recorded of awesome heroism; the glory of some of Brody's youth who did not hesitate to take up arms and use them against the best of prey. The friends of our youth: Joseph Berger, Shlomo Halberstadt, Shmuel Weiler, Yaakov Linder, the engineer Feuerstein (a relative newcomer), Arthur Klepper and others, of blessed memory, fought at the risk of their lives in the forests and as part of the guerrilla (partisan) warfare, not in order to be victorious – for the difference between the forces allowed no such hope – but to save the honour of their depressed and demeaned people. They simply did not want their armed force to be missing from the field of battle against the Nazi legions.

Dr. Joseph Karmish deals with this important topic in the last chapter of his study: "The Holocaust of the Jews of Galicia" (Heb), (in "Pirkei Galicia" [chapters on Galicia] in the Dr. Abraham Zilberstein Memorial Volume, edited by Israel Cohen and Dov Sadan, Tel-Aviv, Am Oved, 1957). It becomes clear that in the small far-flung places, a desire beat in the breasts of the Jewish youth to rebel and strike at the Nazi foe.

The rebels knew that they had no chance of success but their desire was strong to at least die with honour. In his description of these resistance movements in the ghettos and outside them, the author balances the Jewish and German sources - on the one hand, the testimony gathered from the Holocaust survivors and, on the other hand, the official German documents. A comparison of the information on the resistance movements of the Jewish youth in the city of Brody transmitted by Shmuel Weiler, one of the members of "The Battling Jewish organization" in our city, (see: The Underground Movement in the Ghettos and Camps, Material and Documents [in Polish], 1948, edited by Betty Ajzensztajn), with the report of the murderer, Katzmann, on the extermination of "the gang members" in "the Jerusalem of Galicia", is an example of balancing the historical sources. It also indicates how the memorial volume literature can be of assistance along with documentation.

About fifty years - two generations - from the day the ghetto was annihilated and the approximately 3,000 last Jews of Brody were taken on their last road, the Brody Community Memorial Volume is appearing, the last wish of the survivors of the city's Jewish community that had numbered almost 20,000 souls; of the survivors of the Jews of the surrounding area who had lived in the towns of Lopatyn, Leszniow, Podkamien, Bialy Kamien, Olesko, Sasow and the villages of the entire region; and of the survivors of the considerable number of Jewish refugees from western Poland who had fled to Brody from September 1939 on, ahead of the Nazi hordes.

[Page 17]*

The city of Brody, a mother city in Israel, is no longer. "In the city of Brody, the lights have gone out". The holy and pure of our city, along with the rest of the masses of Jews in conquered Europe, also trod that blood-soaked course through the fires of the Nazi Hell to their horrible, tragic end.

How the people of Brody were murdered; to how many horrifying tortures they were subjected; by what strange deaths they were killed - these are what the "brands rescued from the flames" recounted, and these things are what have been recorded in blood in the memorial volume and the scroll of lamentations that is before us.

Joseph Parvari-Leiner, of blessed memory, by his deeds in paving the way to realizing the publication of this volume, earned the right to head the list of those who brought the command of our dear ones, of blessed memory, to bring this book to press. And may he who continued his work, Joseph Ettinger, be remembered for good – the keeper of the archives of the Committee of Brody-ites in Israel. Both, to our great distress, departed this life before seeing the fulfilment of this exalted goal of the highest order; to establish a memorial to the city of our birth and its martyrs, may their memory be a blessing!

Our thanks and appreciation to the members of the Editorial Board, may they have a long life, which gave of their time and effort to realize the perpetuation idea and assisted in bringing the book's manuscript to press. Dr. Sarah Szmuszkin-Rubinstein's pioneering labour of classifying and sifting the testimonies and the memories contributed very greatly to the first crystallization of the volume and its design, and she accompanied the different stages of its preparation for printing. The Committee Chairman, our dear friend Dov Pestes, took upon himself the heavy burden of being the liaison person providing the contact between the Brody-ites in Israel and thus assuring the maximum cooperation of all of us in advancing the book and bringing it to satisfactory conclusion. Thanks to his patience and his pleasant manner, a pleasant atmosphere was assured, making it possible for the work, devotion and meticulousness to prepare the infrastructure for the table of names of our dear ones who perished where they dwelt or were sent to extermination camps. Shmuel Stoianover, one "snatched from the fire", the "last Mohican" from Brody, just recently made Aliyah with his household. Thanks to his marvelous memory and expertise in the household groupings of the Jews of Brody and their origin, he tripled the number of names of the deceased included in the Memorial Table that appears in this volume.

[Page 18]*

In addition, the Editorial Board considers it to be its pleasant duty to extol the manifold activities of Yitzchak Zohar-Zorne, Naftali Harash, and Alexander Olek Podmerner, Joseph Leiner's colleague in bearing the administrative burden of the Organization, Zipora Rom-Spodek,

Raphael-Fulu Shalev-Shlinger and Hayyim Szmuszkin on behalf of the community of those in Israel who came from Brody.

And last but very far from least that deserves thanks, Dr. Aviv Meltzer, who, with a sense of mission laboured diligently and bestowed a language of grace upon the collective creativity of the remnant of the Brody Diaspora.

In conclusion, many thanks to all those – and the list is long! – who, by deed and with material, assisted the members of the Memorial Volume Committee and the Editorial Board in the various stages of preparing the book and readying it for the press, and especially for their complete faith that the awaited volume would indeed see the light of day, thus tangibly realizing the perpetuation process begun about fifty years ago.

Yehoshu'a-Shiko Mandel, son of Shina and Gershon Mandel
Israel, in straits, between 17th Tammuz and 9th Ab 5753.

[Page 9]

At the Outset

We are faced with a single task: To ensure that the memory of the status and the fate of the Jewish community of Brody will remain with us in this generation, and for generations to come.

Aryeh Tartakover

[Page 11]

On the Character of the Brody Community

by Aryeh Tartakover

Translation by Moshe Kutten

Edited by Yocheved Klausner

From the speech during the assembly in memory of the destruction of Jewish Brody, 21st May 1951, Herzliya High–School, Tel Aviv, Israel

The place occupied by the Brody Jewish community in the history of the Jewish nation and of the human society in general cannot be defined by standard social concepts. There were more the a few phenomena in this community, which one cannot find in other places in Poland or in other countries.

We should start with the most prominent phenomenon, which is unique in itself. Brody was known to be one of the wealthiest and well established communities in the history of the Jewish nation, both economically and as a center of Jewish culture and creativity. It was also considered, for many generations, to be one of the largest centers of Jewish Zionism and nationalism. Such a triple combination is rare in the history of the Jewish nation and in other nations of world. It is customary among nations that one city is considered to be the economical center, then another – the political center and a third city the cultural and spiritual center. An important and characteristic example is the English nation: Its capital – London, serves as its political center, the economical center is Manchester, and its cultural and spiritual center is Oxford (or Cambridge). This is the situation in most other countries. There are cases where the same place serves as a political and economic center, or as a political and cultural center. However, cases where a location serves as a triple center are very rare.

Brody was one of the exceptions to this rule. Not only was Brody a city where an immense Jewish wealth was accumulated, but it was also home to people like Nachman Krochmal, Shlomo Yehuda Rapoport, Yehoshua Heshel Shor, Zvi Peretz Chayut and others, who helped to establish the city as the center of Jewish thought. At the same time, the city played a highly important role as a Zionist city and one of the centers of the national Jewish movement in the Habsburg Empire. Brody not only sent a representative to the state parliament, but some prominent Jewish figures excelled in their service to the Jewish nation and served in pioneering national roles. An example would be the banker Natan Kalir, who was bestowed a title of nobility by the emperor due to his significant achievements in the field of economy. At the same time, Kalir acted vigorously toward the fulfillment of his dream of Jewish agriculture in Galicia, although at the end he did not succeed – mainly due to the internal Jewish resistance itself.

How can we explain the mystery behind the city's special status? People tried to explain it using various directions of reasoning, all of them logical. It would be worthwhile to summarize them in a few words, before we find the most important factor, which was probably decisive in the way things have developed.

It is possible to claim, that the special status of the Brody community was achieved, because the Jewish population of Brody was a majority of the general population, most of the time. There were not many other places in the world where this majority status was as prominent as in Brody. Brody was essentially a Jewish city where the non-Jews represented small minorities. The Jews were living almost independently (outwardly, this could be observed particularly during the Sabbath and holidays, when the city took on a festive atmosphere and the economic life came to a halt). Thus, because of numerical advantage and internal unity, the Jewish influence grew in all aspects of life. There is probably a significant measure of truth in this assumption; population homogeneity would have paved the road for important achievements, and probably played a major role in determining the special character of the Jewish population from the days it first appeared on the stage of history until today.

[Page 12]

There is also another explanation. Not only were the Jews a majority among the city population, but they were not subjected to the influence of the non-Jewish population which was itself divided - both nationally and culturally. Brody was one of the few places in Galicia where the German language had an important status among the non-Jews, over the Polish and Ukrainian languages. In time, however, the German language was gradually rejected by the Polish language, which in turn began to feel the rivalry of the Ukrainian language; in happened particularly at the time when Ukrainian nationalism started to thrive among the Ukrainian population, which was a majority in eastern Galicia. However, competition between the languages reduced the circle of influence of all three languages, particularly since the groups who used these languages were far from maintaining friendly relations with one another; instead of interaction among these cultures, rivalry and antagonism prevailed. Under these conditions, the process of social and national-cultural assimilation was limited, and every group - and in our case, the Jewish group - was able to keep its independence and capabilities.

There is also a third explanation, which, like the other two explanations holds some truth in it: The feeling of distinguished status in the people's minds and souls, as well as the wealth, wisdom, and Zionist spirit of the Brody Jewish community prevailed not only during one or two generations in the last two centuries. These values were acquired over many generations, during which the standing of the community as one of the most respected communities of the Jewish nation was crystalized. Brody's Jews wanted to preserve this distinguished status regardless of the external circumstances. They succeeded to do so even during the first half of this century, when the conditions that enabled the economic growth of the city changed, when the "Golden Age" of the Galicia scholarship, of which Brody was the center, was over and when - particularly after the First World War - the center of the national Zionist movement started to shift more and more toward other regions of Poland and Western Europe. Even under these changes, Brody knew how to preserve its status in which it found a great deal of moral support.

All these explanations are valid to a certain extent. However, even with the historic perspective we now have, when accepting these explanations we are neglecting one major reason. This exceptional phenomenon of the triple social importance of Brody's community cannot be explained just by demographic or ecological reasons, may their weight be as it may. The reasons for these phenomena are, without a doubt, much deeper. We need to uncover them, as only then can we see the full picture.

It would be beneficial if we present the big dispute about the foundations of the social life during last two centuries. These were the centuries during which the development of the social philosophy transpired.

[Page 13]

We are all aware of the brilliant definition (albeit a one-sided one) by the founder of modern socialism, Karl Marx, according to which the economy is the basis of all phenomena of the social life, including cultural and political phenomena. This materialistic view of the world that found its strongest expression in Karl Marx's thinking, succeeded to conquer the hearts and the brains of common people and the elites, and many favor it even today. However, it encountered a strong resistance, the signs of which were revealed even before the final realization of materialism. In particular, the signs were discovered as part of the Utopian Socialism at the end of the last century (in which ethics and faith were the essence). Utopian Socialism's main interpretation can be attributed to the greatest German sociologist (also one of the world's greatest) - Max Weber. According to Weber, the economy is not the basis of social life, but the other way around - the economy is a result of various social factors, first and foremost - faith. This is where Weber's explanation of the growth of modern Capitalism came from. In his opinion, Capitalism grew from the depths of the Christian consciousness of the Protestants and Puritans. God's spirit that burnt in the souls of these people motivated them to increase their efforts in all facets of life including the economic facet. According to Weber, work was loaded on man's shoulder by the command of God, and therefore man cannot enjoy the benefits of his work. According to

God's commandment man needs to live a modest and somber life and thus his income becomes an instrument for the amplification of the economic life. According to Weber, this is how capitalism was born.

These are, briefly, the main elements of Weber's philosophy, which also, as stated above, was notable in its one–sidedness and subject to corrections by many. The main claim against this philosophy was that it was impossible to visualize it as applicable in all circumstances and for all nations; it was claimed that there is an abundant number of examples in which the application of Weber's theory is doubtful. This is where it becomes relevant to our case. If there is any nation in the world, where this theory could be superbly applied, the Jewish nation would be one of the first. Weber himself, in his book about the growth of the modern capitalism, mentioned the Jews as comparable to the Puritans and the Protestants. There is no doubt that there are similarities between these groups, the same way that there is no doubt about the preeminence of the Jews in this matter. It seems that what happened to the Protestants and the Puritans during the transitional period between the middle–ages and modern time, happened to the Jews at the beginning of their existence, and even more when they were scattered among other nations, while preserving their special way of life, concentrated around their tradition and worship of God. Their economic activity grew significantly, but it was strongly affected, like other facets of their life, by their faith.

Here is, probably, where the road leads us to the true explanation of the unique character of Jewish Brody. Its soaring economy had, from the start, a special character, seemingly unparalleled to what happened in other nations under similar circumstances (except in the case of the Puritans and the Protestants mentioned above), including Western European Jews under similar circumstances. There was in Brody a deep association between economy and faith (maybe even more correct to say, between the economy and the traditional Jewish culture). This traditional culture was also linked to political phenomena in the Jewish society. As there was no partition between the secular and sacred life, as life was organized according to God's instructions, so there was also no partition between the culture and the economy or between the culture and the political phenomena.

[Page 14]

In this respect, the Brody Jewish community was one of the most typical in the history of the nation during the last two hundred years. Not in all places, the coupling of economic, cultural and political aspects thrived as much as in the case of Brody, since opportunities for Jewish initiative were not as widely available in other places. We know of only one similar case, although it involved a much smaller community – the Jewish community of Lodz, in Congress Poland. In this community, similar to what happened in Brody, the tremendous soaring in the economic life was coupled by the prominent cultural standing (mainly in education but also in the Hebrew and Yiddish creativeness). At the same time, Lodz was one of hubs for the Zionist activity in Poland and the entire Jewish nation. There is a great distance between these two communities, in space and time, as the Lodz community reached its prime while Brody has already accumulated hundreds of years of important achievements. However, Lodz continued in its full momentum thrust forward right until the holocaust, while in Brody, the signs of decline appeared already during the period between the two World Wars. Despite the distance, the similarity between these two cities remained deeply rooted, and both symbolize the Jewish ingenuity.

On these foundations the entire structure of social life – the affirmation of life – was established; not just life, but life based on ideology, the ideology that was centered around the phrase: "I shall not die but live, to tell about God's acts". This was the foundation of the Jewish economic activity as well, which was more a mission than just an activity, and of a deep–rooted, large–scale and multifaceted culture. This culture was expressed by the tradition (the "golden chain" of the Brody Rabbis), by the Enlightenment Movement, that won numerous accomplishments here, or by the New Culture movement (Secular Judaism) with its various branches. The Zionist movement blossomed here as well, conquering the hearts of the Brody Jews like an exploding storm, and the Jewish nationalism was established. It drew the conclusions from the Krakov

Conference of 1906 very quickly, and made the slogan of "conquering the communities to achieve fulfillment of national rights in various institutions" into reality, with far reaching results.

This was the miracle of the Jewish community of Brody. At the beginning of the century [20th century,MK], when you walked through the streets and open areas of the city, most of them ancient with seemingly strange names (The Golden Street, The Catholic Church Street, Yuridika Street, Ravik Park - named after the noble upon whose land the embankment park was built); when you passed through one of the alleys near the "Old" Synagogue, one of the most magnificent synagogues in Poland, where, according to tradition, Baal Shem Tov prayed, or near the "New" Synagogue, which was in itself an ancient building; when you walked by the Commerce and Industry Bureau, one of the three of this kind in the whole Galicia (the others were in Lvov and Krakow), probably the oldest one, and passed near the Community House that served as the National and Zionist center, always crowded with people at assemblies, meetings and lectures; when you passed by the government High-School, which changed its teaching language from German to Polish, and all of its Jewish students observed the Jewish holidays and most of them joined the clandestine Zionist youth-movement "Zion's Flowers", despite the risk of being expelled from the school for this "sin"; when, at least while it was still possible, you saw the house where Yehoshua Heshel Schor edited his newspaper "the Pioneer" and Natan Kalir conducted his big businesses and dreamed of Jewish agriculture - then you would have understood the secret of the greatness of Brody's community despite the fact that it was not always possible to explain these phenomena according to ordinary logic, as the unordinary was above the ordinary here.

[Page 15]

Only the memories are left from these great days that passed. The decline of Brody's community actually started during the twenties of this century (20th centuryMK]. Even during Austrian Galicia, where poverty ruled, and much more when Brody was part of Poland that was bankrupt between the two World Wars, it was difficult to preserve the economic prominence of that community. It was also very difficult to preserve the cultural reputation, even though great effort was invested and some very important accomplishments have been attained. The worthy goal of the Enlightenment was successfully sustained by people like Chaim Tartakover, may his memory be blessed, and Nathan Michael Gelber, Mendel Zinger, Dov Sadan and others, may they live long. Although they were all born and educated in Brody, they carried its prominence to other places as well, and at the end to our free homeland. Whatever was left in Brody was destroyed during the Holocaust, as the entire Jewish-life was destroyed in Poland by the villains.

Today our responsibility is to make sure that the memory of the prominence and greatness of the Brody Jewish community will stay with us and with future generations. This is not only a matter of emotions, although emotions are important. There is also the lesson that we can learn from our experience in Brody, for the benefit of our future. If we know how to keep the deep-rooted foundations, from which all of these phenomena grew in the Brody community, melted into one unified concept, then our old tradition will come alive again and become the guide toward a future of honor. This would bring in its footsteps the salvation of our nation, and would have an impact on all those created in the Image of God. This is the commandment by which we all need to act.

[Page 16]

The Great Old Synagogue

The entrance to the New Synagogue
In the background part of the Old Synagogue

Snail, Emerge from Your Shell!

by Simon Sauber

Translation by Moshe Kutten

Our memorial day ceremony is approaching. It is now 25 years that I prepare for this day every year.

The hall is always full. However, the change that occurs from one year to another is that our guests are getting old... and not only that.

Every year, we are being told that a certain person or an unknown person separated from us forever. Every such news is saddening and gloomy. It is thinning our lines and they would never fill up again.

We are all representing one generation. Although Brody still exists on the geographic map, it is not the same Brody and its residents are not the same residents. Therefore, I see the unique value in the meetings of Brody natives who live in Israel, sometimes with the participation of Brody natives who are scattered in all corners of the worlds, and all of whom are attracted to these meetings and they fill an emotional need for them.

This is the place to mention the arduous work invested by our comrades, especially by our friend Mr. Yosef Leiner (Parvary), who devote a good part of their private life to the organization of the meetings.

Despite of that, I feel sometimes a certain coolness and formality in these meetings. What is the reason for that? Are we fed up with these meetings? Do the worries of the daily life and daily events dull our memories? ...and what memories! These are memories from our childhood and youth, which would never return - memories from the days of school, the images of our teachers, our classroom boyfriends and girlfriends, and of course the images of our closest relatives – our family members. Then there were those first steps in the Zionist youth movements and our songs, which were not very successful I may add, not very successful I may add, to our first loves.

Did we forget all of these memories?

Perhaps we are too burdened with our life experiences, or maybe because of our social status we do not want to return to the days in the past even in our memories. What a pity! This is too bad!

We often do not even recognize each other! It is possible that my old time friend, even my brother, with whom I lost contact forty years ago, is sitting in the same row and we simply do not recognize each other? Perhaps the passing years and our experiences are the cause or perhaps the cause is the fact that we changed our surnames or the authorities of the countries that our fate led us to changed them.

The irony of fate!

It is possible that my surname or my first name have been forgotten. However, my nickname from the school days, "White Sauber", or "Philosopher" were certainly etched in the memory of people who were close to me. It is possible that people can't remember the name Pestes, but they do certainly remember who was "the orphan without a grandfather".

[Page 18]

Perhaps the school I went to, or my home address or my work can remind people who I am? Perhaps there are fortunate people among us who possess group pictures from those days? What an idea! We have to revive these old pictures from the period of our youth, in our heart and in our memory!

This idea does not force anybody to stick a sign on the forehead, a note on the wall will suffice, or perhaps, it is preferable that our organizers would publish a booklet or pamphlet where everybody can describe and record a portrayal of oneself, and where old pictures from those years can be copied and published. I am convinced that such picture booklet would revive in our heart and memory everything that we have lost and was gone into oblivion, and will provide us satisfaction, happiness and the possibility to cling to our past and our youth that have been robbed away from us. Let this project cost as much as it would – it is a worthwhile thing to do!

I recall the last "memorial service". I was sitting in one of the rows. My wife was sitting by me, and several people, whose company I join to attend all the memorial services, were sitting around me. There were

Polak, Vilner, Pestes, Shweibish and several others who are my friends from my youth. Who are all of the rest of Brody people who fill this hall to capacity?

At a certain moment, my wife turned to me and asked: "Tell me Shimon, Brody was not such a big city, the Jews were only part of the population and the people sitting here are all about the same age as yours, so why aren't you recognizing each other?"

How could I answer her question? I did provide some answer, but the stone she threw at me hit a very sensitive point in my consciousness. If I ignore the fact that drove me through different and strange roads and trails, I did spend my childhood and youth in that city among the people who gathered here.

From that point on, I could no longer listen to the talk given by the lecturer, or the stories, told by my friends around me, about their children and grandchildren. I immersed myself in my memories, and my eyes scanned the faces of the people around me with excitement and great suspension. How could I visualize these old people, whose hair turned gray, as my friends from my youth? How can one return to events and experiences that happened fifty years before?

Not everything has been forgotten!

I do remember our little apartment in the backyard of Gross on Kolejowa Street, along with the statue of Little Jesus, the fruit trees, and the cellar, in which ice was stored during the winter. I do remember vividly the cowsheds in the neighboring yard of the Grosskopf's. I see in my mind the barn attic above the cowshed, where we, the little ones, established a "hospital" as a game. I do recall that I always wanted to be a "doctor" rather than a "patient".

I ask myself: "who among the people present in this hall, was a participant in these games?" Perhaps the tall woman, sitting in the third row, is Henia Grosskopf? ...and that little woman, sitting near me, is she the daughter of the Gross's? At her wedding, which took place at the Kelper Restaurant, I tried for the first time the bitter taste of the alcohol...as a close neighbor, almost a family member, I was asked by old Mr. Gross to collect the empty wine bottles from the tables. I was a ten years old boy at the time and I executed that mission with an exaggerated diligence.

[Page 19]

I did not forget to drink what remained of the wine at the bottom of the bottles. As a result, my parents found me, after a long search, deep asleep, under one of the tables.

That person with the gray hair, who is sitting in the first row, looks so similar to Sheinholtz, our religion teacher. It is true that whoever was fortunate to study under the other Hebrew teacher, Mr. Lerner, learned Hebrew properly; however, with Mr. Sheinholtz we studied the history of the Jewish nation, in Polish. I even remember his catchphrases: “When the Israelites won – the Amalekites ran away” (the phrase rhymes in Polish – and it sounds amusing). The phrase is stuck in my memory as if I heard it yesterday. Therefore I ask – is that man, sitting there, him? ...or if not, who is he?

Memories follow memories. We moved to an apartment on 3 Rynek Street, where the Ponikova Beer warehouses were located above the apartment of Rabbi Popper. I have joyful and fascinating memories from there, formed on the joyous and lovely Jewish holidays at the Rabbi's house who celebrated them with all of his Hassidim.

There are also the delightful memories of first love of the thirteen years old Don Juan to my neighbor Papka Bel'or, and later on to her cousin Lola Frenkel. I recall the answer of that twelve years old “dame” to me: ”Jak Kuba Bogu, tak Bog Kubie” (literally – “whatever Jacob did to G-d, G-d would do to Jacob”; meaning “Do unto others as you would have them do unto you”). Perhaps these girls are sitting here among the attendees.

...and perhaps, my other neighbor, Shveibish is here? She lent me her blue underwear for my appearance on the school's stage playing the part from “Guralu Chi Chi Nie Z'al?” (“Native of mountain-land, aren't you sad?” – the opening of a popular folk song). I am not sure whether I looked like a “native of mountain-land” on that stage, but I do remember vividly the spectators' surprised and astonished face expressions to the blue “feminine” underwear. Perhaps these Brody's beauties are here, at this moment, in this hall. ...and you, my good friends from the meetings of the Zionist youth movement, do you remember our trips to the forest in Radzivilov and the beautiful songs we used to sing? Are you here among us now? I think yes. At least some of you are sitting here. The only thing is that we changed so much until we do not recognize each other anymore. Everybody closed themselves in their own home, and the years that passed blurred the rest of signs.

I do not think that you are indifferent to the memories from those happy days, which were certainly etched deep in your heart, like in mine. Therefore, I have a request: throw away your titles, honor and seriousness. Go back to the past for a moment. I promise you that this would be an unforgettable experience. We can sit here in a circle, as we used to sit in Ostrovchio, or in Radzivilov Forest, and you would be seen as you were in your youth. Even you, my friend, who thought once that the wealth of your father distinguishes you from the others, children of the poor, come and break the barrier you built to be different. Believe me, when we went to the public bath on Fridays with our grandfathers, we exposed our shiny behinds, over there on the upper rack, and they all seemed to be amazingly similar.

...and you, my city Brody's native, who this days “sits on the top of Olympus” in Tel Aviv, Haifa or Jerusalem, and chooses to participate with us solemnly in this memorial ceremony by sending wishes through the telephone or via a telegram – wake up! Throw away, just for one day, your titles, and your status halo, come down and sit down with us, for one evening, on this hard bench in this hall. Forget about the fact that you are a professor, doctor or manager and remember that you are the same Khayim, Moshe or Avram, who is made of the same diaspora material and who came from the same small town like the rest of us.

[Page 20]

Do you remember how we played football in Ostrovchik, and how as small children, we carried on our shoulders the shoes of the Jewish football players, Bumza and Kantor, in order to be able to get into the stadium for free? ...or perhaps you joined me once when we jumped the fences over to my neighbor's orchard to steal some apples off the trees, and like everybody else returned home with apples in your shirts and a hole in your pants.

Believe me that it is worthwhile to forget, for one day, the daily hardships and go back to memories from the old days. Those days would never return, but these memories would remind you about unforgettable experiences among people who were also born in Brody.

[Page 19 - English] [Page 23 - Hebrew]*

Chapter One:
The History of the City of Brody and the Jewish Community

On the Start of the Jewish Settlement in Brody

By Natan Michael Gelber

...from his History of the Jews of Brody: "Jewish Mother Cities," Vol. 6, Mosad HaRav Kook, Jerusalem (1955) , pp 13-14

The entry" "brody, The Jewish Settlement of Brody from its Beginnings until its annihilation",; from "Pinkas Ha'kehilot", Jerusalem (1979-80), pp 121-134

Brody, which was an unknown village in the Olesko district, was awarded in 1441, along with the city of Olesko, by the Polish king Władysław Warneńczyk to the noble Jan Sieniński The "Satrost" [leader in Polish] from Sandz, as gratitude for his great role in the defense Reisyn [the city of Rusyanyi or Belarus] from the attacks by the Tatars. The small village, was surrounded by pine-forests and swamps and that is where its name comes from – Brody (Brodit in the Slavic language means turbid water).

After the death of Sieniński in 1477, his son Piotr inherited the city of Olesko and its district which included the village of Brody. His daughters divided the estate and Brody became the property of his daughter Yedevga, who was married to Marczin Kamieniecki, the "Voivode" (head of the district) of Kamenets Podolsk. In 1578, the estate was divided again among the three son of Kamieniecki's – Jan, Woiczik and

Stanislow. Brody was handed over to the two brothers Jan and Woiczik along with the city of Olesko and several other towns in the area.

However, the brothers were not able to manage the affairs of estate affairs and were forced to sell their estate to Belz's Voivoda, Stanisław Żółkiewski. He recognized the importance of location value, and put his mind and effort to developed it, since he realized that Brody is located on the main road – Reisyn-Podolia-Vohlyn. He decided to build a fort there and establish a new city which he named Lubicz [Lyubeshov].

The Polish king Stephen Báthory, issued a special certificate in Warsaw on 22 August, 1584 allowing to build the private city ("miastto prywatne" of Lubicz between the villages of Brody and Lahodov, in an area located among the swamp region of Ostrov based on the Magneburg Law (ius tecutonicum Magdeburgense). According that the privilege stated in the law, which exempts the city residents for some taxes, the city was planned to be a commerce center, where fairs would take place three times a year, and two market days, twice weekly. Based on that privilege, Żółkiewski issued licenses to build buildings, to be privately owned by their builders, on his lands in that area. In that way, Żółkiewski hoped to attract many residents to settle in the new city. Most of the populate that settled in the new city were Ruthenes [Ukrainians in Polish] as well as Polish and Jews.

The first evidence confirming the existence of Jews in the city, is from a certificate about a Jew by the name of Moshe that appeared before the city council to testify that he had bought a house from a residence by the name of Bogadnova Zelikovitz for 11 Guilders. A list from 30 June of the same year, documenting a court case of a Jew by the name of Barukh who was accused of slandering a Ruthenian by the name of Stechko. The accused was sentenced to "ask the accuser for forgiveness".

[Page 24 - Hebrew]

The number of Jewish residents, who concentrated in the "The Street of the Jews" (Ulica Zydowska), grew quickly. In a certificate from 26 March 1596, the name of the town – Lubicz, is mentioned, headed by the village head (wojt) Mikolai Tribokh. However, a few months later, he signed a document as "Miklolai Tribokh, Head of the Village of Brody".

That is how we learn about the resolution to change the name of the city to Brody.

The existence of the "Jewish Street" proves the fact that, as early as the beginning of the 16th century, there was Jewish population who was organized in some form. Although, the documents from the archive of the Berandine's [Church], in Lvov, tell us only about the occupations of the city Jews, it is reasonable to assume that a Jewish community had already existed then. In any case, the son of the community's Rabbi by the name of Avraham Rabinovitz, is mentioned in one of the documents

The Jewish Community in Brody from its Beginning until its Destruction in WW II*

Brody, Sub-District of Brody, Ternopol District

Year	Total Population	Jews
1618	(?)	About 400
1765	(?)	7,627
1783	13,609	11,137
1799	16,401	14,105
1820	18,627	16,392
1830	18,604	16,000
1880	20,071	15,316
1890	17,515	12,751
1900	17,361	11,912
1910	18,055	12,188
1921	10,800	7,202
1931	(?)	8,288

** From "Pinkas Hekehilot – the encyclopedia of Jewish settlements from their establishment until after WW II. The second volume (Eastern Galitsia), Brody, Yad Vashem, Jerusalem, 5740 [1979/80-], pp. 121-134.*

1. From its Beginnings Until 1919

A. From its founding until 1772

Brody was established in 1584 by an overlord, the Nobleman Stanislav Zolkiewski, and in that same year the king gave it the status of a city. After a while, the city became known as Lyubeshov. Until the separation of Poland in 1772, it changed ownership among several different noble families, and in 1682 even belonged to the heir-apparent Jakub Ludwig Sobieski. He subsequently sold it to a representative of the Potocki family in 1704.

[Page 25 - Hebrew]

Important stages in the economic development of Brody were, among others, in 1633, the granting of the right of "emporium" by the king (the mandatory overnight storage of items in-transit, and preferential right of purchase for the inhabitants of the city); the building of a castle and fortifications around the city in 1630-1635; and the construction of a factory to weave silk and woolen fabrics, for which purpose Scots, Armenians and Greeks were brought to settle in the city. However, Brody's development was impeded by the Cossack siege in 1648 and the plague which followed it; by the great fires of 1696 and 1742, which burned down whole quarters of the city; and by the invasions of the Russian and Tartar armies in the early years of the 18th century. Nonetheless, the city's geographically advantageous position and its continuous improvement by the overlords who were among the most important families of the Polish nobility, made it one of the region's most important and best developed cities at the time both in population and economy.

The Jews settled in Brody from its establishment as a city, and documents from 1588 list its first Jewish inhabitants. In the 1590's, the "Street of the Jews" is already mentioned as well as the name of Abraham, the son of Brody's Rabbi. In their concern for the development of the city, Brody's overlords granted the Jews rights almost on a par with those granted other settlers (Poles, Ruthenians, Armenians, and even Scots) and, as a result, the number of Jewish settlers increased. Many of the Jews in the town fell victim to the plague of 1648, and its survivors were again harmed in the Tartar invasion of 1651. The number of Jewish settlers increased again during the 1670's as a result of the influx of Jewish refugees flowing from neighboring Podolia in the wake of the war with the Turks, and from areas in the Ukraine which were given over to the Cossacks. The tenuous stability was again rocked by Turkish invasions in 1696, and by a fire in the same year which consumed in its path dozens of Jewish houses. Lost in the devastation was also the Community Council Building with its archives in which were the charters attesting to the rights and privileges granted the Jews until that time.

Responding to their request, in 1699 the city's then-overlord presented the Jewish community with a new charter which reiterated both older and more recent rights granted pertaining to various areas. This charter was authorized by the city's overlords from then on until the partition of Poland in 1772. According to the charter, the Jews were permitted to live, buy or build homes and open businesses in all parts of the city, as well as to deal in any type of business - on condition that these ventures did not violate the privileges that had been granted to the Christian guilds. The Jews were exempted from surcharges exacted on behalf of the city and fortress, except those related to fire-fighting or against enemy attack. They were obligated to pay a third of the city's expenses as well as Royal Treasury taxes including head-tax. Brody's Jews were permitted to vote for city officers; knowledge and consent of community representatives was required both for taxation by the city and for selection of officials responsible for supervising the marketplace and the weights and measures. The privileges noted above also included rights regarding freedom of religion, the autonomy of the Jewish religious courts, etc., and over all, ranked Brody's Jewry about equally with the rest of the population in legal matters. This was a phenomenon rare during this period, compared to the majority of Jewish communities in other cities – whether privately-owned (by overlords) or part of the royal jurisdiction.

[Page 26 - Hebrew]

However, the Jews of Brody were not allowed to live in peace. At the beginning of the 18th century they were sorely hurt by the invasions of the Tartar and Russian armies and by the general anarchy that reigned in all of Poland at the time, to the extent that a number of Jewish families were forced to uproot and move to Germany. Attacks on Jews also increased, the most notorious occurring during the mass riots of 1718.

An expression of the Catholic reaction that was widespread in Poland was the attempt of the Bishop of Lutsk, Bishop Kobielski, to "create souls for the Church" in Brody as well as in other cities. In 1743, a religious disputation a la Middle Ages was forced upon the community leaders. The definitive answer was given on questions about "the coming of the Savior" and other such topics by the rabbis and community leaders. [Something in the original was apparently omitted here.] The replies were apparently drafted by the doctor of the community**, Dr. Abraham Uziel**, a Talmudist and scholar. The Bishop produced other missionizing pastoral letters, aided by a similar letter of 1751 by the Pope. But when it became apparent that this missionary attempt was in vain, the Bishop then influenced the overlord of the city, Potocki, who jailed Brody's community leaders and even those of other Polish towns who had convened to offer whatever assistance [was] possible during this difficult period. The prisoners were released only after a large ransom was paid to the overlords of the city. (This event was like a foreshadowing of the storm that ravaged Reisen on the heels of the Frankist scandal.)

However, the status of the Jews of Brody was not diminished, and on the eve of the partition the Jewish community of Brody numbered the largest in all of Poland.

At the beginning of their settlement in Brody, the Jews supported themselves mostly by lending money (with interest and against security) to local merchants and manual laborers (not necessarily Jewish), and from real estate leasing and purchase for resale. In 1620-1633 alone, the number of home purchases within the city proper reached 30 in number, with 13 resales. In addition, the Jews also sold and built homes in the outlying areas and within the estates of the nobility of the surrounding area. In documents of this period, the Jews are mentioned as major moneylenders and leasers (of taxes, manors, forests, breweries). Generally, and particularly in the days of the anti-Jewish decrees of 1648-49, most Jews supported themselves through trade and the crafts. After their major competitors left the city – the Scots in 1648 and the Armenians in the 1740's – their chances for success really improved. In the latter half of the 17th century, Jews were counted among the city's manual laborers, as tailors, furriers, and butchers – but also as metal smiths, Turkish belt makers, fabric dyers, saddlers, and pharmacists.

From the beginning of the 18th century, great changes took place in the financial structure of the Jewish community of Brody. First and foremost, Brody's concentration on foreign trade increased. Jewish merchants from Brody were among the regular visitors at the fairs of Leipzig and Breslau. After the conflagrations of 1742 and 1748, the overlord Potocki shored up the Jews of Brody by allowing them considerable credit and giving them partial exemption from tax payments, thus allowing them to rehabilitate themselves and even advance their economic position. The overlords guaranteed the supply of their goods, did not adhere stringently to the road taxes and protected them from the oppression of the nobility. Wielding the power of their authority as lords of vast manors, and even using the aid of mercenaries, they were able to force other merchants within their manors to visit the trade fairs of Brody on their way to Lvov. For the most part, the Jews were the leasing agents and business managers of the many manors of members of the Potocki family. Many merchants, wholesalers, shopkeepers and laborers found their livelihood under the auspices of the leasing agents. Toward the end of the Polish sovereignty, unlike any other Jewish community in the Reisen region, the Jewish position in Brody was based on solid economic underpinnings.

[Page 27 - Hebrew]

In Brody proper and in its 14 dependent settlements there were, in 1765, 15 leasing agents, 3 distillery owners, 4 taverners. Of 737 providers (50% heads-of-households, the remainder apparently were sons-in-laws living with their in-laws, elderly or unskilled people), 147 were in trade, with a hand in practically every branch of business in Brody at that time (such as marketing, wines and liquors, grain and flour, iron, furs, horses and cattle, fabrics, spices, books and more), 5 in industry (of whom 4 manufactured soap, and one candles); in crafts – 326, represented in every kind of craft.

The standing of the 136 tailors in town was special in that there was not a non-Jew among them. The Tailors' Union that was started in Brody at the beginning of the 18th century wielded great influence in the community; they appointed their own rabbi, who was highly respected within the Rabbinic circle. Decorators and jewelers were organized into guilds, the only ones of their kind in the city. The flour merchants also banded together into a merchant fellowship, and they too had their own rabbi.

Throughout the region, the reputation of Jewish cordmakers and construction workers created a demand for their work. Eighty-nine people found their employment as workers and assistants, and 18 wagon-drivers served the transport needs in town and inter-city. Others in service professions included 15 classified as sundry professionals (including musicians, waiters for religious celebrations, general waiters and others). Testimony to the solidarity of the financial standing of the Brody community is the fact that it was able to support 163 working men or independent professionals: 5 rabbis – one for the city and 4 who served other townships but lived in Brody, 27 City Council clerks; 3 community scribes; 9 cantors; 2 *ba'alei tefillah* (prayer leaders), 7 teachers and their assistants, 2 *maggidim* (popular preachers), 6 Torah scribes, 11 medical specialists, 12 healers and barbers, 19 pharmacists, and 1 tax collector.

The latter part of the 16th century, the period of the earliest Jewish settlement in Brody, saw the start of its Jewish community organization. In 1599 we already find mention of a synagogue, cemetery and *mikveh* (ritual bath), and not long thereafter, the remaining institutions of the Jewish community were established. In 1612 the overlords gave the Jewish community financial support to develop these institutions. The first synagogue went up in flames in 1742 and, in its place, a fortress-style mansion was built that stood until the Second

World War. [The 1742 date may represent an error introduced in translating or type-setting Gelber's original. The *Encyclopedia Judaica* refers to the fortress-style synagogue as a 17th-century structure.] Beside the synagogue, a *bait midrash* (house of study) was erected which was apparently rebuilt in 1801 and called "the New Synagogue." The *hekdesh* (community shelter) is already mentioned in 1699 as the "Jewish Hospital." The earliest headstones in the old cemetery, used by the Jews until 1831, date from the start of the 17th century. The *Hevra Kadisha* (Jewish Burial Society) was founded in the 1680's. The *Bikkur Holim* (Society for Visiting the Sick) maintained its own doctor who was known as "*the Bikkur Holim doctor.*" At the same time other charitable organizations and educational institutions were founded, e.g., *Talmud Torah* Society, *Mishna* Society, *Azdatha* Society, and others.

[Page 28 - Hebrew]

At the beginning, the community was headed by four *parnassim* (an honorary title given to community leaders). In the second half of the 17th century, we know their names: **Yechiel b. (son of) Moses Isaac, Abraham Hirsch from Preislav, Ziskind b. Obadiah Lechwitzer,** and **Yeruham b. Yehuda-Leib.** They were counted among the Regional Councilmen in Lvov.

As the strength of [the] Brody community grew, so did its influence in the Council of the State of Reisen as well as the Council of the Four Lands. Brody was one of nine independent communities that belonged to the Lvov Region. After the anti-Jewish decrees of 1648 and 1649, when the prestige of Lvov had waned, the Brody community (together with a few other communities) came out against Lvov, the chief community, with the aim of limiting its status. From then on, the importance of the Brody community increased on the Reisen State Council.

In 1677 **Menachem-Mendel b. Nathan of Brody** participated in the meeting of the Council of the Four Lands in Poland, and in 1700 he was still a member of the Lvov Regional Council.

In the beginning of the 18th century, the role of **Jacob Abraham b. Isaac** is outstanding among the *parnassim*, serving as head of the Lvov Council in 1717-18.

Mordecai ABa"D of Brody fulfills an important role on the Council of the Four Lands as a trustee in 1724. Among other responsibilities, it falls upon him to distribute the quotas of the head tax to the Jewish communities in all of Poland.

In the Regional Council of 1740 held in *Brze zany* (Buchach), the permanent make-up of the Council was set at 13 members, of whom 4 were representatives of the Brody community.

As a major Jewish center, Brody was also home to some of the generation's greatest rabbis. We have no records of the earliest rabbis of the community. The first rabbi known to us was **Rabbi Saul Katzenellenbogen b. Rabbi Moses b. Meir,** the rabbi of Chelm. Rabbi Katzenellenbogen was appointed rabbi for the community in 1664, and retained the position until the late 70's. From Brody he went to officiate in Chelm, and left there for *Pinchev* (Pinczow) in 1784.

Of the rabbis who followed him, the majority of whom served as Heads of the Rabbinical Court of Brody and the region, the best known are:

Rabbi Isaac b. Issachar-Berish, who was known as "Cracower" (after his birthplace), a leader of the Council of the Four Lands and the grandson of Rabbi Heschel of Cracow, Rabbi Isaac headed the Brody community in the years 1690-1704. As a mark of respect and esteem, his children were known as "children of the 'ABa"D,' the *Av Bait Din* (Head of the Rabbinic Court), or 'B"ABa"D' (*B'nai' Av' Bait Din*); and in Polish documentation - Rabinovitz, that is, son of the Rabbi. (The Babad family attained great importance in the life of the Brody community and achieved similar standing in the autonomous Jewish institutions throughout Poland.)

Two years later **Rabbi Abraham Cahana b. Rabbi Shalom Shachna,** a *parnas* of the Cracow community, was elected. He presided in Brody until 1718 when he was called to preside over *Ostrog* (Ostraha). However, he was forced to leave when an overlord of the city coveted his daughter. Rabbi Abraham returned temporarily to Brody, and in 1725 he was invited to serve as Rabbi in Dubno, where he died in 1731.

The position then passed to **Rabbi Eliezer Rokeach,** who had previously (1714-1718) served as a judge in Brody. Rabbi Eliezer was known as a staunch opponent of Shabbateanism (among other measures, he agreed to the banning of the books of **Rabbi Moses Hayyim Luzzatto,** who was suspected of Shabbateanism). In 1735, Rabbi Eliezer was invited to preside over the Ashkenazi community in Amsterdam. Because of strife in the city, he subsequenty left and emigrated to Eretz Israel in 1740. He died there in 1745.

[Page 29 - Hebrew]

Some of Rabbi Eliezer's published writings are: "Ma'asei Rokeach" on the Mishnayol, "Ma'asei Rokeach" on the Torah; "Arba'ah Turei Even" including 24 responsa, and a commentary on the Haggadah of Passover.

Rabbi Jacob-Jokel Horowitz headed the Rabbinate of Brody for 11 years starting in 1736. Due to the rabbi's verdict against the daughter of an important family, who had been charged with adultery before a civil court, Rabbi Jacob was forced to leave Brody and moved to Glogau, where he served as rabbi from 1747.

Thereafter, **Rabbi Nathan-Note b. Rabbi Arieh,** the rabbi of Slutsk, served. Luck also did not shine upon him, and after initiating the Rabbinical Congress of 1756 in Brody, at which the excommunication order against Jacob Frank and his followers was imposed, he was compelled by the authorities to renounce his post. He did not take a rabbinical appointment in any other Jewish community, but rather continued to live in Brody supported by the community.

In 1760, the son of Rabbi Jacob-Jokel**, Rabbi Isaac Ha-Levi Horowitz,** nicknamed "Hamburger", was appointed as rabbi. After five years, following the death **of Rabbi Jonathan Eybeschuetz,** he was appointed Rabbi of the Hamburg communities (*'AH" W'* – Altona, Hamburg, Wandsbeck).

Rabbi Joseph Shatzkes, who was vice-president of the Lvov Region, was appointed after him.

After Shatzkes's death in 1771**, Rabbi Zvi Hirsch b. Rabbi Benjamin Buska** was appointed as Head of the Rabbinical Court in Brody. He continued in that position until 1785, when he moved to Glogau (where he also ran a *Yeshiva* for advanced students). In 1801 he was accepted as Rabbi of the Hamburg community, serving there until his death in 1806.

In addition to the above-mentioned rabbis, who for the most part held the position *of ABa"D* for Brody and the region, there were in Brody in the 18th century 4 groups of rabbinical judges led by the Heads of the Rabbinical Court. Along with the judges there were outstanding scholars, who were famous not only in Brody but throughout Poland and beyond. **Rabbi Ezekiel Landau,** author of the *"Noda bi- Yehudah",* and **Rabbi Meir Margoliouth,** author of the *"Meir Netivim",* were among those who served as judges.

Brody was also renowned for its *maggidim.* Among the more noted were: **Rabbis Meyer of Oskol, Moses Osterer, Menachem-Mendel Zholkever, Peretz b. Moses, Eliezer-Fishel of Chishinau (Kishinev),** and **Shiomo Kluger.** Many of them had their *drashot* (teaching lectures) put into written form, and they were quite well-known in their time.

One of the more interesting chapters, both in the history of the community of Brody and of the scholars and scholarship in all of Poland at the time, is that of the "Wise Men of the *Kloiz* of the Holy Community of Brody."

Over a period of almost 80 years (from the 1730's to the end of the 18th century) the learned of Brody, or rabbis and scholars from the towns of the area, sat learning steadily, from Sabbath to Sabbath, in the large *bait midrash* called a *"kloiz:"* (a smaller, more informal house of worship and study), near the old synagogue. These scholars enhanced the honor of the Torah through their writings and by dint of study, debate, and exchange of opinions with the greatest Torah scholars in the world of their time. Among the scholars were those who knew *Kabbalah,* and they had their own *shtibl* (small house of prayer) near the *kloiz.* The community of Brody took care of the material needs of the scholars of the *kloiz,* establishing a fund for this purpose from contributions by the rich men of Brody. Of the dozens of scholars of the *kloiz,* we will note but a few. **Rabbi Hayyim b. Menahem Zanzer** (1720-1783), whose knowledge of "the revealed" and "the hidden" surpassed the rabbis of Brody and the surrounding area. In matters of religious law, he was among the most stringent. In the Emden-Eybeschuetz[a] argument he sided with Rabbi Jacob Emden, and was one of the organizers of the Rabbinical Congress of Brody in 1752, that banned the *Koach Ha-Kameiot* and other Eybeschuetz writings. Some of Rabbi Hayyim's many writings: *"Neder Bar Kodesh"* – about the Ethics of our

Fathers; *"Hod Tehilla"* – on *Hanukkah* topics, were published posthumously.

[Page 30 - Hebrew]

Rabbi Nathan b. Levi, a famous Hasid, was known as a vigorous opponent of Shabbateanism and Frankism. It was his opinions that shifted the balance against the writings of Rabbi Jonathan Eybeschuetz in 1752, having them declared "absolute heresy."

Rabbi Ezekiel Landau, author of the *"Nuda bi-Yehudah",* settled and studied in Brody for a few years. He differed with most of the scholars of the *kloiz* concerning Rabbi Eybeschuetz, and attempted to prevent the banning of his works.

At about the same time, **Rabbi Abraham Gershon Kitover,** the **Ba'al Shem Tov's** brother in-law, came from his native town of Dubno to live in Brody and be part of the *kloiz.* Kitover served for many years as substitute rabbi **to Moses Osterer b. Hillel of Zamosc.** He achieved fame with his book *"Arugot Ha-Bosem".* Rabbi Kitover emigrated from Brody to Eretz Israel in 1747 and died in 1784.

The brother of Rabbi Nathan b. Levi (noted above), **Rabbi Naftali b. Levi,** author *of "Bait Levi"* and *"Ateret Shlomo",* was also outstanding among the scholars of the *kloiz* in Brody.

(Also in Brody was the *bait midrash,* a kind of "small *kloiz",* founded by *parnas* **Rabbi Jacob Babad,** where scholars of Brody and learned men from the surrounding cities also immersed themselves in Torah study.)

Brody was a community that blended both a large economically stable Jewish population, influential in the region and country, and Torah. (The generation's greatest scholars settled in Brody or streamed to it.) Is it any wonder, then, that its *parnassim,* rabbis and the best of its scholars would respond to every attempt to breach the walls of what was acceptable in thought and deed within the Polish Jewish community of that time?

In Brody on June 13, 1756, an excommunication and curse was pronounced on "The Sinners" (the members of the Jacob Frank cult) as well as upon their families and those who followed or protected them. The excommunication notice was distributed throughout the Jewish communities, and was repeated a year later at the Four Lands Council in Konstantynow, thus it received general acceptance and compliance throughout Poland. The Frankists had no following in Brody before their conversion.

[Page 31 - Hebrew]

The character of the Brody community did not help Hasidism strike roots, from the first Hasidism at the time of the **Ba'al Shem Tov** or immediately following. Even **Rabbi Gershon Kitover** and **Rabbi Mechi of Zlochev** did not succeed in gaining adherents for this new movement, even though they lived in Brody for some time. As a result of the excommunication of the Hasidim in 1772 by the *Vilna* (Vilnius) community, the Jews of Brody also excommunicated them that same year. Unlike Vilna, however, the Brody community did not go to extremes. The Jews of Brody did not declare the "sect" of the Hasidim as outside of the community of Israel, but limited their rights and their expansion. And yet, in spite of Hasidism's gains in many communities from the end of the 18th to the beginning of the 19th centuries, it did not take hold in Brody.

B. The Jewish Community During the Period of the Austrian Conquest (1772 – 1918)

When Brody entered its Austrian period, the majority of its residents were Jews and its economy was unique to the region because of its diversified economic ties with the East (as far as Persia, Russian Siberia and China); the West (Breslau, Leipzig, Frankfort-am-Main and am-Oder, and England); the North (Danzig); and the South (the lands of the Austrian Empire). In spite of the chaos of armies passing through the city in 1771-1772 and in the Kosciuszko rebellion of 1794, and in the period of the Napoleonic Wars until the Viennese Congress in 1815, the residents knew how to cope with difficulties and even continue with their businesses, crafts and development of the city.

The Austrian authorities who knew the importance of the city, did come to their aid, established the regional government there, and in 1779 declared it an "Open City". Still, as was done in the other cities of Galicia, so also in Brody, Empress Maria Theresa's policy toward the

Jews and the "Edict of Toleration" of Tsar Josef the Second were put into effect as an expression of the "official Europeanization" of the Jews – and "to increase their efficiency." The truth is that heavy special taxes were levied on the Jews, the authority of their autonomous institutions was revoked, and even their natural procreation was restricted.

The city's overlord, Count Potocki, also attempted to force the Jews from the manufacture and sale of beverages, and also refused to cancel the taxes he had till then levied on the Jewish settlers of the city as its overlord, even though the Austrian Constitution did not recognize the rights that stemmed from the private ownership of cities. When the Jews refused to pay these taxes, the overlord resorted to harsh measures. He impounded their properties and even ordered the imprisonment of those who refused to pay.

The municipality as well saw this as an opportune time to harm the Jews, who were a thorn in the side of a part of the new Austrian administration. In 1780, the representatives of the Jewish community presented a complaint to the authorities in Vienna and requested of them a "letter of protection" in order to defend their long-standing rights. However, it was not the kindness of the authorities but the Jews' standing in the economy of the city that enabled them to overcome the obstacles put in their way.

In 1799, the number of Jews in Brody increased to 14,105, representing 86% of the city's population. In 1784, the volume of trade of the city increased to 4,226,000 florins with the Jews having played a decisive role. The wealth of many Jews merchants topped 10,000 florins or even 20,000 florins and there were some whose wealth was larger than 50,000 florins. Of the city's 79 wholesalers doing high-volume business in the years 1795-1797, there were three Christians; the rest were Jews. The Jewish agents of Brodian commerce worked out of Warsaw, Vienna and other places. At the same time, the standing of the Brody's Jewish manual laborers improved. As a result of the contacts between the Jews of Brody and the outside world, there arose within the Jewish community in Brody a number of "worldly-wise" people, and even truly enlightened ones, and they were the ones who found their way to the civil courts, and defended the rights of the entire Jewish settlement.

[Page 32 - Hebrew]

At that time, the Jewish community of Brody gained its reputation as "the Jewish Amsterdam of the East". In fact, in 1820, there were 1,134 Jewish merchants, a large majority of the city's merchants, among whom there were 113 grain and food merchants, 137 haberdashers, 110 lingerie dealers, 41 spice merchants, 9 textile dealers, 8 fur merchants, 7 preservatives manufacturers, 7 taverners, 214 wholesalers and 343 store keepers and peddlers. Dealing in credit and money changing at that time there were 9 bankers and 36 money-changers. In Brody that same year, there were 393 Jewish crafts-men (this number does not include repairmen of various sorts, but only those with workshops), and they represented practically all the professions. They included 110 tailors, 14 cordmakers, 47 gold and silver smiths, 5 watchmakers, 9 cabinet makers, 20 construction carpenters, 4 tinsmiths, 11 glaziers, 4 engravers, 13 strapmakers, 7 toolers of brass, 4 painters, 2 artists, 1 gold-designer, 30 butchers, 9 sundry professionals and 118 furriers. In the ensuing years the number of furriers grew even more when Brody became a world center for the trade of furs, imported to Brody from the Ural Mountains and Siberia by way of Odessa and then reexported to the fairs at Leipzig – the world fur trading center from then on up to the Second World War.

Among the pioneers on a global scale in this trade was the Jewish Hermelein family of Brody, especially Jacob Hermelein who, in 1825, established a large trading house in Leipzig and a fur factory in Brody. In 1830, his son Mordecai was named as chief agent of the fur fair in Leipzig. Both the trading house and factory that they established in Brody survived until the end of the 1870's, while the trading house in Leipzig was in operation until the Nazis came to power in 1933.

In the 1820's, the number of Jews from Brody settling in Odessa increased, and their presence contributed significantly to the rise of that city as a commercial center. They established a school in 1826 where, in addition to Hebrew, Russian and German were also taught, and in its opening year about 200 students were enrolled. At the same time, a number of families from Brody also settled in Vienna, in spite of the prohibition against Galician Jews settling there.

The financial prosperity of the Jewish settlement in Brody continued until the end of the 1880's. In 1879, the status of Brody as an "open city" was canceled, among other things due to the building of the rail line to Russia via Podolsk, thus changing the status of Brody to a transit station for goods imported from and exported to Russia. From then on Brody declined until it became just another of the poor cities on the northern border of Galicia. The number of wholesalers dwindled and, perforce, the situation of the various brokers, money changers, clerks and hired help also declined, along with that of the craftsmen who earned their income through their association with the big businessmen. The vast transit traffic became, occasionally, ventures in smuggling. Then a mass out-migration of the Jews began, especially of the merchants, to Lvov and even overseas.

[Page 33 - Hebrew]

The crises that marked the beginning of the 20th century made the financial plight of the Jews of Brody even worse. Such employment as was available was in plants that had been originally established by Jewish entrepreneurs: the flour mill, the rice mill, a ceramics painting factory, two sawmills and a plant for producing liqueurs and whiskeys. The hundreds of the most impoverished then found a meager livelihood plucking feathers and processing them at home.

In the first half of the 19th century there was some improvement in the political status of the Jews of Brody. This found expression in the altitude of the municipality and the local Jews. Meir Kalir, who headed the enlightened circles and was known as a community activist, was elected member of the City Council in 1834 and did much for the development of the city. In 1843, the authorities also elected him to the Court of Trade and Contracts, and here, too, he advanced the development of business in Brody.

The Jews of Brody reacted enthusiastically to the events of the revolution of 1848 by increasing their lobbying not just for themselves but for the whole of Galician Jewry. In a memo presented to the Emperor already in 1847, they requested the abolition of the restrictions placed upon Jews, and primarily the special tax. In the revolutionary period, the Poles showed friendship to their Jewish compatriots, as in the rest of Galicia, out of their desire to win the Jews as allies in their own struggle to broaden their rights in an autonomous Galicia.

However, quickly enough Jewish hopes for equal rights were quashed; the special taxes were not repeated, and in recognition of the community's growth, a decree came through of conscription to the army. This last was enforced with much cruelty: when the Jews resisted the recruitment notice, military units came into the city, with soldiers dragging some 300 Jewish men to the recruitment office by force, regardless of whether or not they were recruitable.

After a number of years, the Jews of Brody finally made their peace with the decree, and a sizable number of Brody's Jews even became career officers in the Austrian army. A National Guard was established in the city, most of whose members were Jewish, a fact which roused the anger of municipal officials.

For the first Galician *Sejm,* which was announced in April 1848, the only delegate elected to represent Brody, receiving both Jewish and Christian votes, was **Meir Kalir.**

In their fight for equal rights, which continued until 1868, the Jews of Brody, particularly the intellectuals, adopted a pro-German centralist orientation of the *Shomer Yisrael* organization, in contrast to the pro-Polish orientation which gained strength among the Jews in other cities, such as Lvov and Cracow. The Jewish representatives of Brody to the Galician *Sejm* generally joined the Constitutional Party.

In the elections for the Viennese Parliament, most of the Jews of Brody supported candidates representing the German Centralist position, therefore to the Poles and to the pro-Polish assimilating Jews Brody was considered a "nest of Germanization" in Galicia. It may be that this aided the Jews of Brody in overcoming the municipal election by-laws of 1867, according to which Jews in all the cities were allotted a maximum of a third of the elected municipal positions. In March of 1867 the Kaiser approved the Galician *Sejm's* decision granting the

Jews of Brody permission to receive not a third but as much as half of the City Council positions.

[Page 34 - Hebrew]

With its annexation to Austria, the Jewish community of Brody continued its important role in the lives of the Jewish public in Galicia. Appointed as Chief Rabbi to oversee Jewish affairs in Galicia was **Rabbi Arieh Leib Bernstein** of Brody, although from the outset, his personality and the nature of his position – which basically served as a vehicle through which the authorities could implement governmental mandates – stirred up great opposition among the Jews of Brody and in Galicia itself. The man himself was known for his corruption and the exploitation of his position for his own personal benefit (the imposition of taxes as he saw fit, exploiting leasing contracts, etc.). Under the pressure of the Community Councils and in consideration of the unrest that had been created, the authorities eliminated the position in 1786.

The Kehillah of Brody wrestled with difficult problems such as removing the Community debts that had accumulated over the years, army recruitment or the ransoming of draftees with Community funds, and the settlement of Jewish families in the village according to the government plan of 1785 for the "productivization" of the Jews. The quota placed upon the Jews of Brody was 128 families for agricultural settlement. Until 1803, the Brody Community managed to fill its quota and settle the entire 128 families on the land. However, over the years only a few of the governmentally motivated settlers continued to farm, and the rest went back to live and earn their livings in the cities.

At that time, opponents of the Community Council from among the tenant-farmers clashed with it, and every now and then there was even "informing" to the authorities. With the rise of the influence of the *Maskilim* (the "Enlightened") in the 30's of the 19th century, they gained control of the Community Council in Brody and their rule was uncontested, even though the Ultra-Orthodox and the Hasidim from time to time ventured to seize the reins of leadership (especially in the 80's of that century), but only with the growing strength of the Zionist Movement at the beginning of the 20th century did changes occur in the composition of the Community Council. In 1912, 4 Zionist representatives were elected to the Council, and in the First World War years the Zionist writer Nachman Gelber headed the Council, which had an absolute Zionist majority.

The seat of the Rabbinate in Brody, as stated, was held by well-known Rabbis. After **Rabbi Zvi Hirsch Bushka** left Brody for Glogau, there were two candidates:

Rabbi Ya'akovke Landau (son of the "Noda Bi-Yehudah", a community worker and intercessor who more than once represented the Brody community before the authorities in Lvov and in the capital, Vienna.

Rabbi Meir Kristianpoller b. Rabbi Moses, the "Rabad" in Lvov, was the rival candidate. The latter was chosen as Rabbi and served in his post from 1785 until his death in 1815.

Chosen to succeed him was **Rabbi Aryeh Leib Teomim,** the grandson of the *"Noda Bi-Yehudah"* and author *of "Ayyelet Ahavim"* and the *"Ya'alat Chen"*. He served until 1831.

During his tenure**, Rabbi Moses Kluger,** a well-known scholar, was engaged as *"Rabad"*.

Along with Rabbi Aryeh Leib Teomim, **Rabbi Eliezer Landau** also served, but he did not live long and died of the cholera plague in 1831.

He was succeeded in the Rabbinate by the son of Rabbi Meir Kristianpoller, **Rabbi Yechiel Mechl Benzion,** who held the post until 1863.

After his death, the post was occupied for a prolonged period in Brody by a team *of dayyanim* (rabbis who served as religious court judges).

(From 1867-1903 **Rabbi Menahem Mendel Schor,** author *of "Torat Mena-hem"*, was added).

In 1894, **Rabbi Yitzhak Hayyot,** son of Rabbi Zvi Hirsch Hayyot, was appointed.

In 1908 **Rabbi Abraham Mendel Ha-Levi Steinberg** was chosen and continued in that post until 1928.

[Page 35 - Hebrew]

In the first quarter of the 19th century a concerted effort was made to improve the condition of the Community and its institutions. The New Synagogue was built in 1801; study conditions were improved in the *Talmud Torah* (religious elementary school) that existed since 1762; a curriculum was firmed up that included, in addition to religious studies, the study of writing and arithmetic. An organized Jewish hospital, well-equipped for its time, was built in 1815. At approximately the same time, a "Poor House" was erected where the indigent coming from outside the city could have food and lodging, and supplies for the road when they left.

All the aforementioned institutions were maintained by the Community and private contributors; well-known among them were the Nathanson and Kalir families. Especially prominent was Meir Kalir (died in 1875), who was one of the first to take the initiative to establish welfare institutions in Brody, and with his funding these institutions were set up and maintained. In addition to the hospital, through his initiative the Old Age Home, the Free Loan Society, and the community Soup Kitchen were established. In the 50's of the century, he established a Fund for scholarships for students of the general Jewish school to continue their education and training in various trades, and a Society for the Clothing of School Children and for providing them with school books free of charge.

In the 40's, a Society for Dealing with Poor Orphans was set up. Their number had grown especially after the cholera epidemic of 1830. After a while, an orphanage for boys and girls was established. In 1860, a charitable organization to support the ill, Hesed Ve Emet (Loving-kindness and Truth) was established, and in 1871 – the Tomchei Almanot (Society for the Support of Widows).

In 1867 a great fire broke out in the city; about 800 homes went up in smoke, mostly Jewish, and there is no need to say that many of the "burned out" needed immediate support from the Community. The Public Kitchen was erected in 1878 and provided free meals to the city's indigent.

From the 80's till the end of the period the Brody Community bore a heavy burden bound up with caring for the Russian refugees. Brody was a transit station on the journey overseas, even a stopping-off place for a number of years. This was a matter of hundreds and thousands of refugees who were in need of shelter and life-sustaining basics, and in these years the sources of livelihood for the people of Brody themselves had lessened and even many of them needed help. Eight hundred fifteen [people] borrowed from it [?].

The unique status of Jewish Brody among the communities of the region was also shaped by its having been the center of Jewish scholars and Torah greats in the 18th century, and the center of the Enlightenment and the Maskilim in the 19th century. Already in the 18th century, the Jews of Brody were the first among the Jews of Galicia to be attracted to general education and what it could offer. The pioneers of "Europeanization" came from the ranks of the large merchants, their children and their functionaries who came in touch with the outside world and needed to know its wisdom and its foreign languages – as well as from the physicians, graduates of European colleges who settled in Brody.

Israel from Zamoshtz, Moses Mendelssohn's teacher, lived in Brody (1752-1772), as did **Mendel Lapin Satanover** (at the start of the 19th century), **Isaac Ber Levinsohn** (1817-1820), **Jacob Samuel Bick** (1770-1831), **Isaac Erter** (1818-1825), **Nachman Krochmal, S. I. Rapaport** and others, who were considered the pillars of the Enlightenment in their generation. In the mid-19th century there lived in Brody the well-known Maskilim **Dov-Ber Blumenfeld** and **Yehoshua Heschel Schorr,** in 1852-1899 the owner and publisher of *"Hechalutz"*, a Zionist periodical. Many of the Brody *Maskilim* were among the pioneers of Hebrew and Yiddish literature in Galicia.

[Page 36 - Hebrew]

Brody was the cradle of the first Yiddish theater groups. The "Brody Singers" groups were the world pioneers of the Yiddish theater. In 1862, the "Society for the Seekers of the Hebrew Language" was established in Brody (with an affiliated social club), its purpose being to develop Hebrew literature and the Hebrew language as a living, spoken tongue. In addition to **Y. H. Schorr's** *"Hechalutz",* **Baruch Werber,** in 1865, established the Hebrew weekly *"Ivri Anokhi"* (I am a Hebrew), which appeared with brief interruptions until 1890.

Many of Brody's *Maskilim* were the disseminators of Enlightenment throughout Galicia, and even beyond it, after they left the city of their birth and settled in other places. Many born in Brody were active in the realms of non-Jewish science and literature, such as: the Orientalist **Dr. Marcus Landau; Prof. Jacob Goldenthal;** the writers **Leo Hertzberg-Fraenkel** and his son, **Prof. Sigmund Hertzberg-Fraenkel** (historian, and in 1905-1906 Rector of Chernowitz University), **Hermann Menkes, Dr. Mark Wischnitzer** and others. Among them, **Prof. Dov Sadan,** author and research scholar, should be noted.

The Zionist idea came up in the circles of the Hebrew language enthusiasts and grew particularly strong under the influence of the Russian refugees who reached Brody in the 80's. In 1890 the Zionist Organization was established in Brody and, in the course of time, was known to have had a decided influence upon the youth. It began its activity by organizing lectures and lessons in the Hebrew language. In 1899 the Organization had about 200 active members.

In 1903, the first Zionist group of high school graduates and practitioners of the free trades, *"Techiyyah"*, was organized, and it continued to exist until the outbreak of World War II. That same year, a branch of the *Po'alei Zion* (Zionist Workers) was organized in Brody and, in 1908, an organization of pioneer workers. This last group had been proceeded by the *Halutzei Zion* (Pioneers of Zion) organization (established in 1905-1906), under the leadership of the teacher and writer **Yoseph Aharonovitch.** Most of the organization's members immigrated to the Land of Israel with Aharonovitch or after him. In 1908 the *Ivriah* Society was established in Brody, one of the first in Galicia, and in 1909 the Center ("Bait Ha'am") built by the Zionist Organization was dedicated with festivity.

Through the influence of the student members of *Techiyyah*, the *Ha-Shah-ar* organization was established. Its purpose was to "infect" the students of the *batei midrashim* (the religious-studies schools) with the Zionist Idea and organize them to study the Hebrew language and general sciences. Within the framework of the Zionist Organization in

Brody there were active Zionist Women's and Youth groups. In 1911, a youth group called *Tze'irei Tzion* was established. In those years, the activity and influence of the Zionists continued to grow and their movement became a mass endeavor. The Brody Zionists faced strong competition from the assimilationist-enlightened with a tradition of scores of years of influence upon the Jewish institutions and an uncontested right as the Jewish representation in the municipal institutions and the Galician *Sejm.*

[Page 37 - Hebrew]

In 1907, Adolf Stand, the Zionist leader in Galicia, was elected to the Galician *Sejm* from Brody. In 1912, 3 Zionists were elected to the City Council and 4 to the Jewish Community Council. In 1910-1914, the Jewish Community head was the Zionist activist and author, **Nachman Gelber.** Also active in Brody at that time were *Agudat Ha-Poalim,* a branch of the Polish Socialist Party (P.P.S.), and a branch of the Jewish Socialist Party (Z.P.S.), but the number of their members was very small and their influence on the life of the Jewish community was minimal.

The assimilationist Jewish intelligentsia centered around the *"Kidmah"* club, founded in the early 90's of the 19th century, but because of the decline of the general assimilationist status at that time, its functions had been curtailed.

The Ultra-Orthodox *"Machzikei Ha-Dat"* faced opposition from the radical Ultra-Orthodox on the one hand, and from the Zionists and the Labor Parties on the other. Its main political activity was during the elections for the Community or City Councils, through joint electoral machinations with the assimilationists.

Among the important merchants the influence of the Enlightenment since the 18th century was evidenced, among other things, in the tendency to provide their children with a general education. Since there was no school in Brody to provide it, they turned to private teachers. Even in Brody, an **H. Homberg** school that had been set up there failed, as it had elsewhere in Galicia, and the school was closed in 1806. In 1818, after many attempts, the *Maskilim* in Brody succeeded in receiving a permit from the authorities to establish a Jewish general studies (academic) school (a high school with two classes). The Ultra-

Orthodox opposed the establishment of this school and set up a *Yeshiva,* but this was closed by order of the authorities after the *Maskilim* informed against the school's principal, **Rabbi Zvi Hirsh Ha-Levi,** and he was expelled from Brody. The aforementioned school wrestled with budgetary difficulties for years and had but a small number of students. Its condition was also not improved by the establishment, in 1823, of a kind of pre-high school (also of two classes), intended to prepare its students to enter the general studies school.

In 1854, a Jewish "public" school for boys and girls was opened following the program of the school set up by **Joseph Perl** in Tarnopol. **Hirsh Reitman,** a former teacher in Perl's school in Tarnopol, was put in charge. In 1855 the school had 416 children (248 boys and 168 girls), and in 1905 - 1,132 children (543 boys and 589 girls). From 1910 on, a pro-Polish assimilationist headed the school and a "Poland first" tendency came to dominate this institution. The school existed until World War II and was a major source of upset to the Ultra-Orthodox, who continued to send their children to the traditional institutions of learning only. In 1894, in Brody there were 14 *heders* (traditional elementary schools), ten teachers, and 413 pupils; and in 1905 - 24 *heders,* 48 teachers and 574 pupils. As was the practice in Galicia, the pupils of these elementary schools continued their studies in the many *batei midrashim* and *kloizen,* about 30 in number, under the supervision of the *dayyanim* or regular teachers.

In 1905, a Hebrew supplementary school in which the language of instruction was Hebrew was established, called *"Safah Hayyah"* (Living Language), and had some tens of students. Instruction in the Hebrew language for the children and the teenagers, however, was for the most part via Hebrew lessons at the Zionist parties and their clubhouses.

That also was the case with other activities of a cultural nature. In 1904, a "Toynbee-Halle" club was established in Brody in which many different sorts of activities to disseminate popular science and literature took place, for the benefit of the masses, for the most part conducted by the Zionist intelligentsia. Libraries, groups, and clubs for enthusiasts of drama, literature, and other interests also existed at the Jewish Socialist parties, at the craftsmen's organization "Arm of the Diligent" and in the

Jewish Vendors' Association. In 1907, the music group "Ha-Zamir" was established. In 1904, in Brody, a Jewish sports organization was set up and, in 1912, a branch of the "Dror" exercise association of Lvov.
[Page 38 - Hebrew]

C. Brody and the Jewish Community During World War I

Two weeks after the outbreak of World War I, on the 14th of August, 1914, the Russian forces took Brody. Upon entering the city, the Cossacks began to run wild, looting and plundering Jewish possessions, and there were many instances of women raped. A libel was circulated that the daughter of the owner of the Hotel Harash shot a Cossack. On this pretext the daughter was murdered and the Cossacks set fire to the Jewish Quarter. Many homes went up in smoke and the large synagogue was severely damaged. Almost all the Jews of substance left the city, and only the poor remained.

The Community Council, headed by **Nachman Gelber,** was faced with the difficult task of providing assistance to those in need. With the help of the *Va'ad Ha-Hatzalah Ha-Yehudi* (the Jewish Rescue Committee) of Kiev a public kitchen was set up to assist with food and clothing, mainly for the children. At that time, tens of thousands of Austrian prisoners of war, Jews among them, passed through Brody. The residents came to their aid with food and clothing and sometimes even succeeded in hiding them from the Russians until the danger passed, in spite of what could be expected from the police and the army if detected. When the Russians held the city, many of its Jews were deported to the interior of Russia.

In July 1915, the Austrian Army entered the city, but the situation of the local Jews was little improved because of the nearby battlefront which prevented normal living conditions. Nevertheless, even under these circumstances, the political parties resumed their activity, though on a limited scale of course. Among the rest, the *Tze'irei Tzion* Youth, which served as the basis for *Ha-Shomer Ha-Tza'ir* after the war, resumed its activity.

II. Brody between the Two World Wars

After the collapse of the Austrian regime, from the beginning of November 1918 until the end of June 1919, Brody was part of the Western Ukrainian Republic. The National Jewish Committee, headed by the Zionist leader, **Dr. Abraham Glasberg,** was set up there. The Ukrainian District Governor, the retired Judge Harassimovitz, was an out and out antisemite. In spite of the Ukrainian government's recognition of the National Jewish Committee, he refused to acknowledge it, schemed against the Jews at every opportunity, and even threatened them with riots.

In the face of the many needs of the impoverished Jewish community, the Committee was helpless and unable to worry about the many unemployed and the many with no means of support, and could not even provide any support whatever to the social institutions such as the orphanage, hospital, old-age home and community kitchen. In April 1919 many Jews and Poles were recruited for labor battalions.

At that same time, attacks on traveling Jews by Ukrainian soldiers were common. Four Jews were murdered, many beaten, and there were instances of rape. Jewish homes and stores were looted.

[Page 39 - Hebrew]

In June 1919, 22 Jews were imprisoned; most of them respected members of the community, including Committee Chairman **Glasberg.** They were put in a railroad car to be transported to the East, but after intervention with the Chief of Police, and apparently a considerable ransom paid, the prisoners were released.

It should be noted that the Jews of Brody, even though they themselves were in distress, helped their Polish fellow citizens whose condition was also difficult. At that time, some social and cultural activity was evidenced by the Zionist parties in Brody, mainly by the *Po'alei Zion* and the *Ha-Shomer Hatza'ir.* In August 1920, Brody was temporarily captured by the Red Army. After three days had passed relatively quietly, goods in the stores and even in private homes began to be confiscated. It should be noted that when the Polish priest was incarcerated, the Jews interceded for his release with the Soviet authorities and actually achieved it.

With the stabilization of the Polish regime in August 1920, the city quieted down and its inhabitants started rebuilding its financial and public life. But if in the 1880's there were already signs of the city's decline which continued till the outbreak of World War I, now in wartime the decline became even sharper and, by World War II, Brody had not yet fully recovered. The Jewish population (as did the city's general population) declined some 40% compared to its number in 1910.

The economic plight of the Jews was serious. The wholesale transfer of goods almost came to a halt because the city was cut off from the markets of Russia, Germany, and the vast Austrian Empire which had crumbled. Brody completely lost its standing as a commercial city situated on an important east-west and north-south crossroad. The extent of the local trade dwindled because of the decreasing population, the economic decline that affected all of Poland (the inflation and the crises), and the constant decline in the prices of the agricultural products that were the mainstay of the livelihood of those living around Brody. Only small businesses and peddling in the surrounding villages remained for the Jews, and even those seeking such a livelihood had stiff competition from the Ukrainian and Polish cooperatives that were established in the early twenties. Antisemitic attempts to boycott Jewish trade in the years before the outbreak of World War II also hurt the Jews.

On the heels of the decline in trade, the sources of livelihood of the Jewish craftsmen and small Jewish manufacturing were limited. In 1921, there were 229 Jewish workshops and factories in Brody, of which 92 were in clothing (tailor shops and haberdashery), 12 in leather goods, and 54 in food. Most serious was the plight of the Jewish workers (156 men, 85 women and 38 children): generally speaking, their workday was of undefined length; they had no health or unemployment insurance and therefore they were dismissed in the "dead" seasons or times of crisis. A significant percent of the providers of Brody were regularly unemployed and were supported by their families abroad or by the public dole. This economic situation worsened during the great crisis of 1929-1930, and the stagnation that followed continued until the Second World War.

[Page 40 - Hebrew]

In the years immediately following World War I, the **Joint Distribution Committee** came to the aid of the needy. It gave financial assistance to those whose homes and workshops had been damaged during the war. With its support, a "Small Credit Union" was established which, in 1925, had 561 members. That year, the Union granted its members 696 loans totaling 90,592 *zloties.* 56 [sic] The J.D.C. also supported the National Bank and the Free Loan Society. After the J.D.C.'s flow of support funds stopped, in 1931-33, the Free Loan Society distributed loans in the amount of 80,000 *zloties* to about 2,000 borrowers. Smaller funds for financial support also existed alongside the "Jewish Merchants Union," the "Arm of the Industrious" and the "Vita Jewish Citizens Union."

The social aid institutions which had existed in Brody for many years or had been reestablished between the two World Wars, coped with the problem of the constant shortages of the allocations needed to function properly. The Jewish Hospital, which had existed in Brody for about a hundred years, renovated its building in the 20's with the help of J.D.C. money and, in 1931, an infirmary was established from public donations in which about 100 sick people, not all of whom were Jewish, received daily care. To improve the health conditions, the "TOZ" (= Towarzystwo Ochrany Zdrowia) organization increased its activity in the late 30's. That same year, the organization held a summer camp for 100 children. The orphanage with its 30 charges, the old age home and the home for the crippled (about 40 people) were also supported till the end of the 20's by J.D.C. funds.

When the support was stopped, funding from the *Kehillah* and the municipality was insufficient, thus budget difficulties were overcome by public contributions and improvised aid activities. To increase the income for social assistance, a movie theater was established in 1929 whose entire proceeds were dedicated to the support of the above-mentioned social institutions. In 1938, the craftsmen's guild *"Kidmah"* contributed all its income to the Free Loan Society and those social organizations named above. "The Council to Aid Poor Children" (founded in 1936), the WIZO Organization, the student organization *"Achvah"*, and the Parents Council of the Jewish School also were busy with welfare and charitable activities. The latter daily distributed breakfasts and lunches to the needy and also supplied them with clothing and shoes in the winter time. The *Kehillah* Council, whose annual budget lessened from year to year, found it ever more difficult to maintain its institutions and allocated very little to welfare needs, mainly for Passover alms for the poor. In the 30's, the number of petitioners continued to increase.

Heading the Council (until the 30's, mostly appointed by the authorities) were assimilated Jews close to the Polish regime, i.e., the 'Senation' (**Bloch** and after him **Benjamin Kotin, Leon Kotin** and **Deodad-David Levin**). In 1938, the Zionist **Dr. Abraham Glasberg** was elected as Head of the *Kehillah* and, as his assistant, **Dr. Shlomo Shapira,** also a Zionist. After the death of **Rabbi Abraham Mendel Ha-Levi Steinberg** in 1928, two contenders vied for the position of Rabbi of the city: the son of the deceased, **R. Moses Steinberg,** and **R. Yosef Poppers-Babad** who also had a strong claim. In the elections held in 1929 the votes were even, therefore **Rabbi Yosef Poppers** was chosen by lottery. Influenced by the supporters of **R. Moses Steinberg,** the authorities voided the elections and the dispute continued until 1934. In that year, R. Moses was appointed as President of the Rabbinic Court (Av Bait Din). His rival served then as Senior President of the Rabbinic Court (Rosh Av Bait Din) until the period of the Holocaust, in which he perished.

[Page 41 - Hebrew]

Until 1929, a Commissar appointed by the civil authorities governed in Brody. In the elections held that year, of the total of 48 Council representatives elected, 30 were Jewish. To "keep the peace," the Jewish Councilmen voted for a Pole, Franchishek Gorka, for Mayor. Not only was he unfit for the position but he even misappropriated public funds. In the 1933 elections, under the new election law, of the total of 24 Councilmen, 10 Jews were elected and they only received the position of Vice Mayor. In 1939 no elections were held, and by inter-party agreement, City Council appointees were 7 Jews, 4 Ukrainians and 13 Poles. This time, too, the Jews received the post of Vice Mayor.

If for the *Kehillah* Council or for the City Council, the Jewish Zionist representatives had to compete with the Ultra-Orthodox and assimilated Jews, in the vote for the *Sejm* the Zionists received a decisive portion of the vote: in 1922, they received 2,794 votes out of a total of 3,741 Jewish votes, and in 1928 – 1,956 votes against only 392 votes *for Agudat Israel.*

As mentioned, in the period of the Western Ukrainian Republic, the Zionist parties that had existed till then renewed their activities. As time passed, most of the branches of all of the Zionist parties existing in Galicia were organized (General Zionists, *Hit'achdut, Po'alei Zion,* the *Mizrachi,* and the Revisionists), as well as the youth organizations (*Ha-Shomer Ha-Tz-a'ir, Ha-No'ar Ha-Zioni, Ha-Shomer Ha-Dati, Beitar* and *Brith Ha-Hayyal,* the General Zionists, and *Achvah*). Aside from these organizations, WIZO, *He-Halutz* and *Ezra* were also active. *He-Halutz* and *Beitar* maintained training [for] *kibbutzim* in the city.

The relative sizes of the Zionist organizations in the elections to the Zionist Congress were as follows:

Number of Votes in Party or List	**1931**	**1935**
General Zionists	78	256
Mizrachi	106	286
Hit'achdut	103	-
Eretz Yisrael Ha-Ovedet	-	508
Revisionists	37	-
State Party	-	126
Ha-Shachar	-	22
Radical Zionists	1	-

In the city there was a branch of Agudat Israel founded on the pre-World War I Ultra-Orthodox organizational base. What remained of the assimilationists gathered around the "Kidmah" club and the Organization of Jewish Women.

[Page 42]

The members of the Communist Party and the Communist Youth Organization showed lively activity in the dissemination of information, whether legal or not. In 1933, a number of Jewish Party members from Brody were expelled from Poland. In 1937, 4 Jews, including a girl, were sentenced to 3-7 years imprisonment for belonging to the Communist Party. In 1938, again, 3 Jews from Brody were tried and sentenced to imprisonment. The community of Brody, which in the 19th century had earned the leadership of the *Haskalah*[5] movement in Galicia by establishing modern schools, clubs for the dissemination of science, and drama and music groups, lost its standing in the period between the two World Wars. However, the public school for Jewish children founded in the mid-19th century continued to exist, and even grew from 4 to 7 classes (with 664 pupils in 1938) – but its Jewish subjects were limited to the "Religion of Moses" only. Because of budgetary constraints, a complementary Hebrew School with up to 100 pupils at times existed off and on. In the *"Tarbut"* (Culture) kindergarten, established in 1925, there were at most another 40 children. In 1920, the "Tzisha" children's home was established, with 30 pupils. In 1933, WIZO founded a handicrafts school with 40 pupils.

Available to the local branches of the Zionist parties were libraries, and lectures were held in their clubs. The academicians' organization, *"Achvah"*, evidenced lively activity in the cultural field. Of the two organizations fostering music – The Jewish Music Organization and the *"Zamir"* – the first, which functioned sporadically, became a social club, and the second, which renewed its activity in 1923, and also functioned sporadically, maintained a choir and an orchestra, organized instrumental music lessons and even appeared in concerts in Brody and elsewhere.

In 1929, a Yiddish weekly called *"Broder Vochenblatt"* appeared irregularly.

The Jewish Association for Exercise renewed its activity in 1922, stopping in 1928-30, and restarting in 1931; however, it encompassed few sections of the population and had a very small membership.

Even though the Jews of Brody were a decided majority within the city, they were not spared antisemitic incidents. In 1923, there was an attempt to confiscate Jewish dwellings for the church; crucifixes were even brought in. When the Jews objected, many of the local Christians and those from the neighboring villages assembled and broke the windows of the synagogue and of Jewish homes. In the rioting, 12 Jews were hurt. In 1936, antisemitic handbills were distributed in the city. From 1934 and until the outbreak of World War II, there were instances of the arbitrary dismissal of Jews from their jobs in the municipality and its institutions. On the other hand, it should be noted that there were also showings of solidarity with the Jews.

Thus, for example, in 1937, a Jew was chosen to head the Cobblers' Guild (it was accepted practice to rotate the head of the guild – one year a Christian and one year a Jew). Then there were malicious rumors that the Jewish head of the guild had removed the cross from the group's flag. However, the Christian members of the guild stood by him and expressed full faith in him.

[Page 43 - Hebrew]

III. Brody During the Second World War

When the war broke out, Brody was captured by the Red Army on Yom Kippur night, 5700, September 23, 1939. As in all the places ruled by the Soviets, all the private plants, factories and stores in Brody were nationalized. The Jewish owners were allowed to continue working there as managers or as skilled craftsmen. The *Va'ad Ha-Kehillah* and its institutions were disbanded, as were the political parties. Few of the youth volunteered to travel to the Don River Basin to work, and when their work was completed, most of them returned to the city because of the Soviet Union's difficult working and living conditions. In 1939-1940, the Jews of Brody suffered a number of incarcerations of important merchants, manufacturers and community leaders. They were all exiled to the far ends of Russia (January 5, 1940).

When the Russo-German War broke out, the Commissar of the city, a Russian Jew named **Katzman**, publicly called upon the Jews, and especially the youth, to seek to escape into the Soviet Union. A sizable number of Jews were conscripted into the Soviet Army.

The Germans conquered the city on July 1, 1941. The persecutions typical of the Nazi forces occupying Poland began immediately. The wearing of the Star of David became mandatory; a 4:00 p.m. (or 6:00 p.m.) to 4:00 a.m. curfew was instituted; leaving the city was forbidden; the use of public transportation was forbidden; entering public places, walking on the main streets or public squares, even walking on the sidewalks was forbidden. The Jews were ordered to greet all German officials in uniform. They were allowed to shop for food only from 12:00 p.m. to 2:00 p.m., when the shelves were already empty. They were forbidden all business and shop work. Mandatory labor was imposed upon Jewish males aged 14-65 and females aged 18-45. Jews were also forbidden to employ non-Jews.

In the first half of July, the Germans and Ukrainians conducted street hunts. They tortured and brutalized those Jews they caught, and some of them were sent to hard labor in the city. These vicious forays resulted in several hundred wounded and some dead. The most shocking event of those days was the murder of about 250 representatives of the Jewish intelligentsia, public and communally involved personalities. They were invited to the Gestapo headquarters ostensibly to discuss general matters concerning the organization of the Jewish community's life in the city, but it was a trap. They were detained in the Gestapo building for two-three days, debased and tortured, and then conveyed to the lime pits near the old Jewish cemetery and shot to death (July 15-17, 1941). Only the doctors survived the Gestapo: the Germans released them because of the need to supply medical services to the city's population.

That month (July 1941) the authorities ordered lawyer **Abraham Glasberg** to form and head a **Judenrat.** Glasberg had headed the Community *Va'ad* (Council) before the war. A Jewish police force was also established. **Hertz Buchbinder** was appointed to head it (according to others it was **Itche Katz,** a Brody municipal clerk before the war).

[Page 44 - Hebrew]

One of the first tasks of the **Judenrat** was supplying Jewish work forces to the authorities – 150 men a day. The authorities came to the **Judenrat** with never-ending demands to equip and furnish the apartments confiscated from the Jews to supply housing for the German officials. In August 1941 the Germans imposed a very heavy fine upon the **Judenrat** and immediately took a group of hostages. The authorities were now heavy-handedly collecting from the Jews late payments of taxes which had been due even before the war. If the person who owed the money was no longer in Brody, the debt fell upon the **Judenrat,** which activated a special department to handle these demands of the Germans.

Even though for a relatively long time (till the latter part of 1942 and the beginning of 1943) a ghetto was not established in Brody, the Jews lived under difficult, deteriorating conditions. They were plundered regularly by the Germans and Ukrainians, even thrown out of their homes, and therefore became crowded together more and more. They were deprived of their sources of income; their tools, wagons and horses were confiscated, and they were doomed to living on the official starvation rations. People of substance who were able to hide part of their assets maintained themselves by selling off items to non-Jews. There also were Jews who made a living from illegal trade, secretly manufacturing all sorts of products and working in shops. Many tried to work for the Germans, be it in forestry and sawmills, in agriculture (on nearby farms, which passed to the Germans), in the collection of rags and refuse (the companies: *"Alt- und Abfallstoff-Erfassung"* and *"Kaklitski"),* or as administrators for realtors and in factories that produced goods for the German Army. The leather merchant **Mendel Reinhold** and the group of Jews he employed used to buy pelts for the Germans and thus were permitted to roam freely about the area. In Brody a factory was activated that employed about 400 Jews. Working for the Germans was hard and the wage, if paid at all, was minimal, but it entitled one to extra food rations or dismal sustenance at the place of employment; mainly, it allowed illegal trade.

However, not just starvation, cold and crowded housing were the lot of the Jews of Brody. The constant attacks by the German and Ukrainian policemen on dwellings and passersby resulted in many victims injured and killed. The Nazis mainly maltreated those Jews who dressed traditionally. To the delight of the rabble, there were public shearings of their beards and sidelocks. In December 1941 the round-ups began (mainly men were seized, but sometimes women were also taken) for shipment to labor-camps in the region. The transport of young Jews to these camps now became a common sight. In the final count, more than 1,500 Jews from Brody were sent, most of whom succumbed because of the harsh conditions that prevailed in the camps. With the cooperation of the local chapter of the J.S.S. (Jüdische Selbststütze – Jewish Self-Support), whose director was **Leon Blaustein,** the **Judenrat,** to the best of its ability, supplied the Brody camp prisoners with food and clothing, or served as intermediaries for the shipment of packages from family members to the camps. The J.S.S. chapter in Brody dealt with eight camps in the area.

At the end of the spring and in the summer of 1942, the inhabitants of Brody already knew of the liquidation actions in other cities, of the mass murders, and of the transport of Jews to extermination camps in Belzec.

[Page 45 - Hebrew]

Since it was commonly held that working papers protected one from the "actions," the residents began to seek a work card for themselves under any condition, even those who until now had not been constrained to find work to support themselves. The Wehrmacht factories and the operations of the garbage company, *"Todt"*, were considered the most reliable in protecting their workers. The Jewish employment office directed by Holzsaeger (a former vegetable dealer) was now the most sought out institution, for it dealt with finding work. Jews paid huge bribes to German officials and influential Jewish ones for a *"good"* work card. To that end, connections and acquaintances were exploited. In August or September of 1942, the Gestapo ordered all the work cards of the Jews to be brought up to date. In the "Grand Hotel" building there was a special German stamping the documents with a new stamp. At the same time, by order of the authorities, the Judenrat prepared a list of all the unemployed Jews and of those 60 years of age and older.

On Shabbat Shuva (September 19, 1942) the surprise "action" started. German and Ukrainian policemen, aided by Jewish police, drove the Jews from their homes, grabbed them on the streets, and concentrated them in the market square. Many people locked themselves in their homes, hid in cellars, attics, and any hiding place they found, but the German and Ukrainian police fired into the places discovered and at those who attempted to run away. The sick were shot on the spot. In the yard of the Old Age Home, all the residents were slaughtered. The orphanage was destroyed together with its administrator, Nachum Okser. The corpses resulting from the "action" were loaded onto two large trucks and buried in a mass grave in the cemetery. Most of the people who had been caught were transferred from the market square to the train station and loaded onto freight cars, including many who were employed and whose work card provided no protection; even in the morning when the latter, group by group, went out to work, they were led straight to the station. Only a few were released. The "action" ended at six in the evening, and the Germans announced it with a great trumpet blast. That very evening the cars were sent to the death camp at Belzec. The "action's" blood bath resulted in 2,000 to 2,500 driven out and 250-300 dead on the spot.

The next day, Sunday, Yom Kippur Eve, the Jews who had hidden and not been discovered started coming out. Despite the tragic experience and loss of many relatives, the Jews of Brody congregated secretly and held their prayer services, for the authorities had forbade them public prayer.

A few weeks later (November 2, 1942) a second "action" was launched. This one paralleled the first in its form and number of casualties: 2,000-3,000 were transferred to Belzec, and many were murdered on the spot. This time, too, the work cards and plant emblems which workers pasted on their clothes did not provide adequate protection for their bearers. The abandoned Jewish apartments were stripped of all their contents for the German institutions, as had been done in the previous "action."

After this radical reduction in the number of the Jews in Brody, the authorities began to concentrate the Jews of the surrounding towns and villages there. On December 13, 1942, the Jews from Podkamien were transferred to Brody, and on December 22-23, 1942, the Jews from the Dubie work farm were brought in wagons, they and all their possessions. The latter were from the surrounding villages of Ponikwa,

Suchodoly, Jasionow, and Wolochy. After their farms and everything on them had been confiscated, they were brought to work at the aforementioned Dubie farm.

[Page 46 - Hebrew]

Many Jews had come to Brody on their own initiative after escaping the liquidation actions in their own towns, for they knew that Brody did not yet have a ghetto. Thus, for example, many Jews found refuge here in November 1942 from neighboring Radziwillow, even though it was outside the boundaries of Galicia (in Volyn). In the latter part of 1942, many refugees came to Brody from Toporow, Sokolowka, Szczurowice, Podhorce, Lopatyn, Olesko, and Radziechow. The refugees were placed in houses emptied after the "actions." The **Judenrat,** which was now headed by **Rosenfeld (Abraham Glasberg** died in the action of November 2, 1942), called upon all who had come, who were believed to have been property owners, to donate their possessions to the community needs of the Jews of Brody. Those who refused were imprisoned in the jail of the Jewish police or had family members taken as hostages. Many refugees were sent to the labor camps in the manpower quotas frequently demanded by the Germans.

The ghetto in Brody was set up only in December 1942, after the majority of Jews of Brody and the surrounding area had already been exterminated. The German authorities set December 1, 1942 as the last day for transferring all the Jews of Brody to the ghetto, but extended the deadline to January 1, 1943. The bounds of the ghetto, located in the traditional Jewish quarter of the town, encompassed only Szpitalna, Lazienna and Krupnicza streets and the adjoining side streets and alleys. Into this tiny area 5,000-7,000 Jews were packed, including those uprooted from other places. The ghetto was surrounded by a barbed wire fence with only two gates manned by Jewish policemen. From time to time Ukrainian police details would appear. The gates carried signs in three languages: Ukrainian, Polish, and Yiddish. They warned the Jews not to leave the ghetto upon pain of death and threatened the Aryans with heavy fines and imprisonment for entering the ghetto. To approach the fence was dangerous for the Jews because the Ukrainian guards would open fire without warning. Many died beside the fence.

Soon, unbearable conditions reigned in the ghetto. The authorities supplied symbolic food rations; there was a shortage of heating materials, and at the distribution of the meager rations, frightening fights erupted. The poor of the population, the weak and the non-venturesome died in droves. Starving people and starved to death; corpses in the streets became a daily sight. The deaths increased due to a plague of typhus exanthematicus. The **Judenrat** tried to hide the plague from the authorities. Naturally, however, they did not succeed for long. Fearing the plague's spread, the Germans hermetically sealed the ghetto for a time – no one in and no one out. This further aggravated the Jews' already difficult situation. During this time some German institutions housed their workers in the factories outside the ghetto. The tortured Jews also suffered greatly from "visits" of police inside the ghetto and from round-ups of people to be sent to labor camps, which happened again and again. Under these circumstances, underworld forces came to the fore and violence in the ghetto became a common occurrence.

With the setting up of the ghetto in December 1942, the authorities also organized labor camps for men in Brody. The camp's inmates worked in the quarries and in paving roads in the surrounding area. In this camp Jews were constantly killed in various accidents and, among other things, were shot after all the sick and weak had been sorted out.

[Page 47 - Hebrew]

Thus the lives of the surviving Jews in Brody continued to deteriorate, crowded together in the ghetto or imprisoned in the camp, until the spring of 1943.

At the end of March 1943, a number of "actions" and round-ups started which lasted until May, when the Jews of Brody were finally eliminated. We have no clear details of the various "actions." These are the dates mentioned for the "actions": March 31st; May 4th; May 10th and May 13th. These "actions" hit those who lived in the ghetto and the labor camp prisoners. It is possible that in the course of the "actions," a certain number of men and women fit for work were sent to different labor camps, such as Olesko or Lackie. All the exhausted caught in these "actions" were shot on the spot and in the surrounding woods. In order to protect a number of their workers, a number of German factories housed their workers nearby.

Already in the days of the first and second "actions" in Brody (in September and November, 1942), and especially in the frequent "actions" in the spring of 1943 and the abductions for the labor camps, there were some occupants of the ghetto who sought refuge in hiding places. And indeed, the places were set up throughout the ghetto area as best they could be: in camouflaged cells, in cellars, in attics. The poor tried to escape the ghetto if they heard indications of another round-up in time. The escapees hid in the surrounding forests or swamps, or with their employers who indicated a readiness to hide them, and after the round-up returned to the ghetto. Not a few of the Jews of Brody, or refugees from other places, that left the ghetto before the "action," wandered the neighboring forests and fields for weeks and months, singly or in small groups. They found cover in makeshift trenches, hollow tree branches, or farm buildings. They suffered hunger and cold, were pursued by the German and Ukrainian police, as well as by a good part of the local population. After fleeing constantly from place to place, many were forced to return to the ghetto out of lack of choice. Finally, most of them were caught by their pursuers and murdered, with only a few surviving by some fortunate combination of circumstances. The well-to-do built themselves well-hidden underground shelters with emergency exits, stocked with water, food and sanitary facilities. People of means and connections had hideaways even outside the ghetto and were supplied with food by non-Jews either out of friendship or for pay.

Among the Christians who at the risk of their lives hid the Jews of Brody, offered them assistance, fed them, prepared forged papers for them and cared for their children, we will note just a few examples: The Poles **Yazenti Miklashevski,** Tax Department clerk; **Dr. Zawadzki,** the regional doctor; **Kist, Butshkovski** and the local priest. Ukrainians: Burachek; **Mironku Lukanietz; Homeniuk; Timchishin;** farmer **Moroz** from the Radziwillow-Brody Region who was shot for aiding Jews hiding out in the forest; farmer **Karolchuk** from the village of Gaya Sudneskaya who saved two Jewish women and a child by hiding them; **Laya,** administrator of the farm that was transferred to the Germans in the village of Dubie and his wife, who demonstrated great admiration for the Jews working in that camp. He secretly added food to their rations, tried to convince them to flee when they were ordered to move into the ghetto in Brody and gave them food for the journey.

Among those who offered assistance to the Jews there were also lone Germans as, for example, **Hassenstein,** a German from the Reich who was mustered out of the Army and appointed by the authorities in Brody as Head Forester. He dealt fairly with about 1,000 Jews who worked for him in the forest: he supplied them with extra food from his farm, and protected them from the "actions" by keeping them in his house and by hanging signs on the doors of their homes which read: "This house is protected by the Forests Authority – Brody." In the days of the "actions," his wife hid scores of Jews (mostly women and children) in the attic of her house and fed them. She was betrayed to the authorities, stood trial in Lvov for aiding Jews and was sentenced to two years imprisonment at hard labor.

During the period of the "actions," several small groups of Jewish youth had organized in the surrounding forests, and succeeded in obtaining weapons. They resisted their pursuers and raided villages for provisions. According to witnesses, they even entered the ghetto. There were those who raided the warehouse and treasury of the **Judenrat** in order to obtain food and money. There is a story told of two Jewish youths whom the police captured in the forest and imprisoned in the town jail. They killed one of the jailers, fled the jail and entered the ghetto. This served as an excuse for a German reprisal on May 13, 1943. Both in the ghetto, and perhaps in the camp as well, attempts were made to establish an underground organization, to make and maintain contact with the groups in the forest, and organize the escape of the youth to them.

The ghetto in Brody was wiped out on May 21, 1943, the day before *Lag Ba'Omer* 5703. The police surrounded the ghetto at night, set up machine guns, and started the "action."

[Page 48 - Hebrew]

The people were taken from their houses and driven into the market square. All valuables in their possession were taken and they were ordered to kneel with their hands behind their heads. From the market square they were led in groups to the train station and loaded onto freight cars. Even the Jews of the camps who had planned to go work were taken to the train station. In order to drive all the Jews out, the Germans set fire to the buildings of the ghetto. Dreadful sights followed: people engulfed in flames, the weak slaughtered, babies' heads smashed. The walls of the buildings were splattered with blood. The number of those deported for destruction (they were taken to Majdanek in the Lublin district) came to 3,500, and the number killed on the spot – a few hundred. All that remained in the ghetto was a handful of people in hiding.

Among the victims of the extermination “action” were the members of the last **Judenrat: Chairman Itche Katz** (who, as mentioned, had also served for a while as the commander of the Jewish Police), as well as members **Chaim Mordechai Harash** (grain merchant), **Bezalel Meles** (Zionist worker), and **Leon Broczyner** (electrical equipment dealer). It is likely that also among the members of this **Judenrat** were attorney **Bernard Horn, Sigmund Liphschütz** (Zionist worker and mill owner), and **Herz Feiering** (feather exporter). According to one of the versions, the camp remained in existence for another month or two but with a limited number of Jews.

The hunt for hidden Jews continued throughout the city and surrounding area long after the ghetto of Brody had been liquidated. Those caught were herded into barracks and shot to death.

After the liberation of the city by the Soviet Army (July 18, 1944), most of the houses of the Jewish quarter were found destroyed or burned out, and even the cemetery was destroyed. The city itself was damaged to a great extent because the front line passed through it many times. The only remnant that survived was the frame of the old synagogue. Of Brody's pre-war Jewish population about 250 Jews survived, among them a number rescued from the Nazi camps; more than 100 saved in the Soviet Union; and about 100 who were saved in their hiding places with the assistance of local residents. Of the latter, a few resided in Brody for a while after the war before leaving their city.

Author Notes

a. When Eybeschuetz was the Rabbi in Hamburg, he once wrote an amulet for a sick woman during an epidemic. Later on, people said that in that amulet, he wrote a prayer to G-d, to assure the owner of amulet a full recovery by the blessing of the Messiah Shabtai Tzvi [1626 – 1676, a kabbalist, who claimed to be the long-awaited Jewish Messiah]. Rabbi Eybeschuetz denied that he wrote that amulet as he was afraid to admit his inclination to Shabbatism. When Rabbi Yaakov Ben Tzvi Emden (Ya'abetz, 1697 – 1765) found out about that, he came out openly against Rabbi Eybeschuetz and accused him of Shabbatism. A harsh dispute, that lasted six years, ensued, in which all of Europe Rabbi's participated. The Germany's congregations cited with Rabbi Emden while the Polish congregations cited with Rabbi Eybeschuetz. The followers of these two Rabbis called names, cursed and declared a boycott against each other. The dispute subsided only after the advent of the Frankist cult which wanted to exploit the dispute for its own benefits and to create a breach in wall of the traditional Jewish.

[Page 49 - Hebrew]

Bibliography for the article by Natan Michael Gelber: On the Start of the Jewish Settlement in Brody

Archives

Yad Vashem Archive: 01/180; M-1/Q 1858/402; M-1/Q 1342/146; 03/3248; 03/2542; 03/2291; 03/2214; 03/2215; 03/1672; 04/21-1-9

YIVO?: Vilna Archive "Poland" "Brod" file

מ"צ Archive: K.6-1/2; F.3-22; F.3-3; A.214-1

צ"ש Archive: (3) 84.1.2

Books:

"Brody - Ir Va'Em Be'Israel" ["A Jewish Mother City"], no publisher indicated, 1969

N. M. Gelber: "The History of Brody's Jews ("Arim Ve' Imahot Be'Israel)" [Jewish Mother Cities"], Volume 6, Jerusalem 1955.

"Mul Ha'Oyev Ha'Nazi " ["Confronting the Nazi Enemy"], Tel Aviv 1967, Second Volume pp 151-142.

"Sefer Milkhamot Ha'Getao't" ["The Book of the Wars in the Ghetos"], Tel Aviv, 1954, pp 328-331.

Radzivilov - adzivilov: Sefer Zikaron [Memorial Book of Radzivilov] Yizkor Book, Tel Aviv, 1966, pp 237 – 250.

"Sho'at Yehudei Eiropa" ["Europe Jews Holocaust"], 1973, pp 317 – 315.

Journals and Newspapers:

"Idisheh Ilustrirteh Tzeitung" [Yiddish - "Jewish Illustrated Newspaper"], 4/8 1910.

"Der Israelit" [Yiddish - "The Israeli", 2/5 1887 5/28 1867, 8/4/ 1867, 3/31 1871, 4/5 1872, 4/19 1872.

Ha' Boker Or [Hebrew - "The "Morning Light"], Kheshvan 5636 [November 1875].

"Broder Vokhenblat" [Yiddish - "Brody Weekly Newspaper"], 4/12 1929, 4/19 1929.

"Drohibitcher HandlsTzeitung" [Yiddish - "Drohobitch Trade Magazine"], 1/23 1891, 3/13 1891.

"Tag" [Yiddish - "Day"], 7/27 1912, 5/11 1912, 12/12 1912.

"Tagblat" [Yiddish - "Daily Newspaper"], 8/16 1912, 9/18 1912, 5/20 1924, 10/29 1924.

"Der Yudisher Arbeiter" [Yiddish - "The Jewish Worker"], 3/15 1905, 11/15 1905. 9/4 1908, 5/5 1910, 10/25 1912.

"Ladzer Tagblat" [Yiddish - Lodz Daily Newspaper"] 10/21 1929.

"Hamgid" [Hebrew - "The Preacher"], 4/10 1862, 8/21 1872, 2/28 1901, 6/14 1894, 7/26 1894, 9/29 1898." Hamitzpeh" [Hebrew - "The Observatory"], 1904, 1095, 1906, 1907, 1911.

"Ha'Ivri HaTza'ir" [Hebrew - "The Young Jew"], Nisan 5671 [March/April 1911].

"Falksblat" [Yiddish -"People Newspaper"] 1/24/1919, 4/11 1919, 5/2 1919.

"Di Tzionistishe Vakh" ["The Zionist Weeks"], 8/24/ 1934.

"Ha'Tzfira" [Hebrew - "The Siren"] 4/20 1886.

"Shavu'a Ha'Khalutz [Hebrew - "The Pioneer's Week"], 5/31 1924.

"Jüdische Volkszeitug"[German - "Jewish People Newspaper"] – 5/19 1919.

"Hanoar Hacijoni" [Polish – "The Zionist Youth" 4/15 1931.

"Wschod" [Polish - "East"] 9/10 1897, 8/20 1898, 12/20 1898, 2/5/1899. "Przyszłość " [Polish - "Future"], No. 8-9 1937.

"Zew Młodych " [Polish – "Young Voice"], 1902, 1904, 1911, 1912

[Page 50]

Brody, "Jerusalem of Austria"

From the book:
"The History of The Brody Jews", pp 9-11, 325-340

by Nathan Michael Gelber

Translation by Moshe Kutten

Edited by Yocheved Klausner

Brody was such a unique city, that one of the Austrian officials nicknamed it "Jerusalem of Austria" after Austria seized Galicia. Jewish life, economic and cultural, throbbed in it to its fullest.

Even before Austria occupied it, the Jewish community of Brody was known as a community of scholars, Rabbis, and leaders of the Council of Four Lands and of Districts Councils. The families who ruled the community - Babad, Ravits, Rabinovits, Shatzkes and Bik - succeeded to put Brody on the map by establishing Yeshivas and Kloizes [communal houses of learning, praying and gathering[MK]] and by attracting a large number of knowledgeable Rabbis to the city. This way, they managed to establish the city not only as a center of Torah but also of Jewish law - a place where everybody turns to, with tens and hundreds of Rabbis and judges, experts in Jewish law and Halakha.

The prominent families that ruled in the city knew how to improve the community institutions and make Brody an exemplary community in pre-partition Poland. They were also able to defend Brody's reputation, and in time of distress, protect its rights and regulations.

Brody was one of the few cities that the commissars of the Austrian emperor, who came to take over this asset when it fell into their hands, found it necessary to report about in minute details. In this region, which was named Galicia after the partition of Poland, the commissars found for the first time Jews who received secular education, Jewish physicians and merchants, who were familiar with Latin and German languages and culture. Some of these physicians were: Dr. Vishnovitser and the prominent Dr. Yitskhak Ravits, (son of the Rabbi who authored the book Keter Yosef) both studied and graduated in Italy, and Dr. Avraham Uziel who studied at several universities and who welcomed the conquering army of Austria with a beautiful speech, which was also printed in the newspaper **Wiener Diarium.** These people gave the city an aura of splendor and magic and helped it to become the favorite over other cities in the eastern corners of the Habsburg Monarchy.

The greatest development of the city occurred during the Austrian period. Under the Austrian rule, it became the center of the flow of commerce between east and west. The lines of commerce and transportation between Breslau, Leipzig, Manchester, Livorno and Vienna on one side and Berdichev, Kiev as well as the cities of Valachia, Moldavia and Greece and even Istanbul on the other side, all met here. Therefore, it is no wonder that the city experienced a busy life, where many merchants, knowledgeable in many languages settled. It obviously attracted many Jewish teachers who taught Jewish children different foreign languages.

These conditions ensured that the city's Jews would not remain frozen in their spiritual and cultural life, but assimilate, more easily than other Galicia Jews, into the life of the universal civilization. The slogans of the Enlightenment movement found a fertile soil here. The city youths were captured by it and became its pioneers. Dov–Ber Ginzburg, Yaakov–Shmuel Bik, Mendel Lapin, Dr. Yitskhak Erter and R'Nachman Krochmal created a new reputation of the city as a "city of enlightenment" that fought against the Chasidic Judaism on one side and the Mitnagdim movement on the other. It is worthwhile, however, to note that although Brody was known as an Enlightened–city, with a tradition of education and learning, the Chasidic spirit filled its large as well as small Kloizes. The Chasidic movement was the one that continued to spin the yarn of its mystical spirit over the centers of learning for generations, especially over the largest Kloiz (Grand Kloiz) which served as a house of learning for many exceptionally wise and scholarly people – the Brody Sages and Kloiz Sages. Among them were Rabbi Khaim Tsanzer, whom the people of his generation named the "Divine

Kabbalist Chasidic Rabbi", Rabbi Moshe Ostrer, a known *Magid Meisharim* [Jewish preacher [MK]], (who signed, among others, the document of excommunication of Rabbi Jonathan Eybeschutz), Rabbi Naftali Margaliot, Rabbi Efraim Zalman Margaliot and Rabbi Mendel Zolkover. All of these Rabbis were considered "princes," grand rabbis, scholars and holy men of the Jewish community of Brody. These people lived, until the last generation, in the aura of the Chasidic legend. One cannot count the stories we heard in our youth about the Baal–Shem–Tov in Brody and the wars he conducted against his opponents, or about Rabbi Gershon Kitover, and the *Magid* Rabbi Shlomo Kluger and his fights against the innovations of the Enlightenment movement (particularly concerning the transport of the dead on a horse drawn cart).

[Page 51]

We also need to note, that the universal humanitarian principles, adopted by the Galician Enlightenment movement, were not used by the followers as an excuse to abandon the Jewish tradition. For example, one of the movement's scholars, Moshe Stern, published a letter in the newspaper "*Kokhvei Yitskhak*" (Yitskhak's Stars) in which he argued against those who denounce the Jewish particular clothing. Furthermore, there were people who claimed that seeds of the new Jewish national movement came from Brody scholars, as it is easy to identify in this movement a clear self–awareness which is based on the appreciation of our ancestral heritage and historical tradition. Brody was saturated with Jewish folklore and national feelings. Therefore we cannot be surprised by the story of Rabbi Yaakov Shmuel Bik who adopted the Enlightenment and then came back to Chasidism, claiming that he saw in it and in the then spoken national language (Yiddish) the foundations to the Jewish tradition so dear to the soul of the Jewish people. Another story, in which the national tie is more pronounced – is the story of the "Brody Singers," with Berl Broder (Margaliot) as their leader. They were the authors of amusing poems, drenched in humor, in which the satire was aimed against the social conditions of the Jews.

One of the first educated authors, born in Brody, who wrote already in German, was Leo Hertsberg–Frenkel. His stories about the life of the Jews of Galicia were leaning toward the Jews being "half – Asian".

However, one can easily distinguish between them and those of his cousin – Karl Emil Franzus, who also wrote about the life of the Jews of Galicia. The reader of Leo Hertsberg–Frenkel's "Polnische Juden" ["Polish Jews"[MK]], can easily distinguish between them since Leo's stories were inherently imprinted with Jewish folklore.

The gallery of people of the Enlightenment movement in Brody, or from Brody, is large. This movement included people such as: Rabbi Moshe Mordekhai Yuval, Berish Blumenfeld, Yitskhak Blumenfeld and Chaim Gorfunkel. The movement also included Mordekhai Ben–Avigdor Ushpits who was the head of the "Bank of Halbershtam & Nirenshtein" and who studied Jewish Studies in his spare time, as well as Khaim Ginzburg, who was also a Germen poet, Rabbi Yaakov Toporover, Marcus Kalir, Yaakov Levin, Moshe Margaliot. Other people of the movement were Israel Roll (the brilliant translator of classical languages), Rabbi Mordekhai Sterlisker, who lived in Brody until 1851 and who was named the "Lion of the Poets", Hirsh Reitman (initially Yosef Perl's librarian and later the principal of the primary school in Brody), who wrote the outstanding Yiddish parody "Der Kitel" (1863) to Shiller's "Glocke" ["the bell" 1863], and Y. Trakhtenberg and Yehoshua Heshil Schor.

[Page 52]

Ha'Ivri [The Hebrew[MK]] and "Ivri Anokhi" [I am Hebrew[MK]], a newspaper that was published alternately under each name (in order to bypass the newspaper tax), edited by Barukh Verber (during the years 1865 – 1876) and later by his son Yaakov Verber (during the years 1876 – 1890), was loyal to the ideals of the Enlightenment movement as well as to our tradition. At the same time it fought bitterly against the newspaper of the Society of "Religion Keepers" in Lvov, which started its publication in 1873. However, when the national awakening started and the movement toward national independence in our land began to spread, "the Hebrew" did not understand its spirit. It fought against the new trend of emigration to Eretz Israel, and demanded to direct Russian refugees, that passed through the city Brody in droves, toward the United States. He believed that the freedom sun would shine on our nation only in the US.

However, this resistance was not able to prevent the sprouting of the seeds of the Jewish national movement among the city Jewish intelligentsia. People started to comprehend the tragedy imbedded in the situation of the Jews, and recognized the need for a change oriented toward the goals of the Zionist movement. Indeed, the Zionist movement, which penetrated Galicia little by little, with the flow of the pogroms refugees, started to take hold more rapidly, and soon Brody became an important center of the Zionist movement. The Jewish youths who joined the movement enthusiastically, centered their activities on studying Hebrew literature and Hebrew language. Their activities made Brody a model for all other cities and towns of Galicia.

High-school students, who came from the Torah Schools to acquire a general education, taught others in Hebrew classes according to the method of studying "Hebrew in Hebrew". They were guided by the Brody Rabbi's son, Refael Soferman, who intended to become a Hebrew teacher.

Yehuda Leib Landau, Yehuda Pilpel, Braindel Golde Letster, Refael Soferman, Michael Berkowits, Avraham Robinson, M. D. Anderman and Chaim Tartakover, were some of the people who laid the foundations to the organized Zionist movement in Brody. The awareness of Zionism spread naturally throughout all of the Jewish circles in the city as the people mentioned above continued to expand on their initial activity. Newspapers helped to disseminate the news about developments in the national movement. Jewish students who studied in universities in Vienna and Lvov brought with them copies of the newspaper "Selbstemanzipation" [Self- Emancipation[MK]], that was published in Vienna under the editorship of Dr. Natan Birenbaum. Through this newspaper, the news about the establishment of the first Zionist societies became known in Brody.

Initially, the "upper" layers of the Jewish society in Brody did not want to accept the fact that enormous changes of the state of the Jewish nation and its role among other nations are occurring among the Jewish public in Galicia and other countries. However, just a few years later - in 1890 - the first Zionist society - "Zion" was established in Brody. This society had a major impact on the atmosphere among the Jewish youths. The first Maccabee banquet took place in 1891. David Anderman gave a speech in Hebrew about the historical importance of the holiday of the Maccabees. The Hebrew author Reuven Asher Broides, who also spoke in Hebrew, made a very strong impression on his listeners. Many women decided to start learning Hebrew, and many assimilators decided to join the National camp because of his speech. Zigmund Lifshitz and David Hirsh Tiger from Lvov explained, in German and Yiddish, the objectives of the National Jewish movement.

Gradually, the best young people congregated around the "Zion" society. They supplemented their Hebrew knowledge and attended lectures about the problems of the Jewish world. The intelligentsia and the Jewish youths recognized the fact that the world is undergoing major changes, and that the attitude toward Jews among the other nations is not what they expected from the emancipation. Even the assimilators felt that they are not welcomed by the gentiles and that the Poles see in them, at best, allies to their own national–political aspirations. Those who came from the Enlightenment movement were interested in "renewing the pride of the Hebrew language, which was almost forgotten by our youth."

[Page 53]

In 1886/7, a group of young people, under the initiative of Yehuda Leib Pilpel, acted "to encourage the spirit of the nation, and to uproot the assimilation which was becoming more and more popular. We shall celebrate our national holidays, and bring back the Hebrew language literally on the stage – perform a show in Hebrew, spoken as a live language before the audience." As part of their effort, they asked Yehuda Leib Landau, who studied in Brody at the time, "to utilize his talents and his love for his nation to write a play in Hebrew." According to their instructions, "the play was supposed to demonstrate the victory of the nationals over the assimilators". The play, "There is hope", consisted of three acts and was written in simple language for easy acceptance by the audience. It described an episode from the life of a Jewish family, in which the father wished to marry his daughter to a medical student, a Max Blem – an assimilated Polish Jew. The play was performed at a banquet organized in memory of Peretz Smolenskin on 23 February 1893.

The "Zion" Society widened its activities and propaganda for Jewish revival. Many among the Jewish intelligentsia joined the movement despite the strong hype by "The Ivri" against the idea of settlement in Eretz Israel and against the national Jewish movement. The Zionists preached continuously about the national idea among the high-school students. Classes for the Hebrew language, Jewish history and history of Eretz Israel were added during the years 1893 – 1895. Older students were also active in this area and used their free time from their universities to win the hearts of the young people for the idea of the national revival.

When Dr. Theodor Herzl's name started to be known, the enthusiasm for the idea of Zionism was also heightened in Brody. "Zion" Society and Brody youths sent congratulations telegrams to the first Zionist Congress in Basel (27 August 1897). Dr. Herzl was elected honorary president of the "Zion" Society during the gathering that took place on 11 September 1898 in the "Zion" clubhouse.

In 1899, the university students who came home to Brody during the academic vacation, started to organize an academic Zionist society. Chaim Tartakover (1883 – 1944) led all Zionist–cultural activity and succeeded to gather around him a group of male and female students who were devoted to the Zionist idea. He organized the high-school students and youths from all other Jewish population layers. Tartakover also tried, for the first time, to lead them toward pioneering training. Their initial activities involved the organization of national holidays and cultural celebrations. In 1903, Schenkar, Chaim Tartakover, Leon Balaban, Zeev Makh, Zeev Rosenfeld, Barukh Tselnik, Yitshak Hammerman and Anzlem Shtromvasser established the first Zionist society for university students – Techia [Revival[MK]]. The society functioned until 1939 and was active in many Zionist and cultural areas. It employed counselors to guide their members in the spirit of national–Zionism and had a significant influence on the development of the Zionist movement in Brody.

[Page 54]

Intensification of the Zionist education and activity occurred during the years 1904 – 1906. By the initiative and with the assistance of the teacher Yosef Aharonovitz, who later became an author and a labor leader in Eretz Israel, the first pioneering organization in Galicia – *Chalutzei Zion* ["Pioneers of Zion" MK] was established. The organization was formed under the impact of the "Letter from Eretz Israel" sent by Aharon David Gordon, which created an enormous impression on the Brody youth.

In 1908 – 1910, the conference of the central committee for Cultural Activity and the Hebrew Language of the High-school students' movement – *Tse'irei Zion* ["Zion Youths" MK] for the entire province of Galicia was held in Brody.

During the years 1912 – 1914 the Zionist activity concentrated on consolidating its forces, expanding the Hebrew school, enlarging the library and strengthening its loan fund. The fund under the management of Perets Beharav helped small merchants and craft businesses and considerably contributed to their economic success.

In the cultural area, the drama club was active under the management of S. Mirtski, and the Ivriya group concentrated on the dissemination of the Hebrew language and culture. The Hebrew movement thrived in particular among the high-school students and the orthodox youths. The association Hashahar ["Dawn" MK] was established through the initiative of Moshe Rosenblum, Krochmal, Teller, and Yosef Neigebohr. The Hebrew teachers of the movement and older students taught Hebrew to the students of the Beit Hamidrash [Torah School MK], as well as history of the Hebrew literature, Jewish history and general sciences. Fertile cultural work among the working youths was done by the association of Poalei Zion ["Workers of Zion"MK]. Their activities included courses and evening classes that concentrated on the national spirit. Mendel Zinger, Vitlis and Shalom Kupfer headed the association.

During World War II, the fate of the Brody Jewish community was similar to the fate of all other Jewish communities in Poland. Until war broke out between Germany and Russia the Jews in Brody enjoyed a relatively secure life; however, with the German invasion of Poland an extermination camp was established in Brody (in February 1942), under the command of the Nazi Hauptsturmführer Franz Warzok and his assistant Vogel. As many as 364 Jews were murdered immediately. In September 1943, the camp was disbanded and the 600 Jews who were in the camp at the time were murdered in a forest near Brody. The rest of the Brody Jews were sent to the camp on Yanovski Street in Lvov. Their fate was similar to that of the other Jewish communities in the Nazi occupied areas. Very few managed to escape to Russia; the Jewish population was totally annihilated.

Brody, a Jewish city with a brilliant history that existed more than four hundred years died. It was wiped out of the map of the diaspora.

[Page 55]

The Last Fire (May 23, 1867)

by Adela Landau Misis

Translation by John Kallir

Note: *This selection was translated from Adele Landau Misis's original German manuscript by John Kallir, a descendant of the author, rather than from the Hebrew version which appears in* Ner Tamid—Yizkor leBrody

When, in the middle of the last century, a fire alarm sounded in our native town of Brody, panic fear would seize old and young. From past experience they knew: the town is lost! There were no defenses against the raging element. Neither in Brody nor in its environment was there a river, not even a little brook, not a pond, not a spring with sufficient water. Pumps found in a few streets would, after strenuous efforts, send forth a feeble flow of greenish-yellowish water. The wise town fathers had ordered a large barrel (*katjke*) to be placed near each pump, to be filled with water all the way to the top in case of an emergency. The barrels were there but half empty, filled with a thick greenish sludge, more likely to stick in the hose than put out a fire. In the yard of every house there stood a rain barrel, with buckets and fire hooks nearby. But rainwater was used for the laundry and other domestic purposes, while in many houses the buckets had lost their bottoms and the hooks their iron. In addition, the town had a few antediluvian engines of ancient design and, I'd guess, about a dozen firefighters. Now, unless there was absolutely no wind, if a shingle roof in the poor quarter caught fire, it would swiftly spread and the entire town (which was really three-quarters poor) would be reduced to ruins within hours. That happened again and again, every eight or nine years. The most recent fire had occurred in 1859, but I don't remember it because I was only a year old then. The stories of parents and grandparents, however, made it very real and frightening.

One morning in May 1859, Alexander, who slept in our parents' bedroom, woke up crying. He had dreamed the town was on fire, all the *katjkes* were empty, and the fire kept going. Our parents were surprised how a five-year-old could know the connection between "*katjkes*" and "fire." In the afternoon of that day (*Lag B'omer*), there was a wedding feast of people we knew in a *heifel* (villa) in the suburbs. Grandmother Landau loved to attend such occasions. She borrowed the carriage of the Kallir grandparents and took Alexander and me along. Returning in late afternoon, we had reached Lesznow Lane close to our home and grandmother was preparing a tip for the coachman. In those days, small denominations were printed on sheets, like postage stamps, to be cut as needed. Next time you're in Vienna, I'll show you a few. Anyway, grandmother pulled a penny sheet from her bag when a sudden gust of wind tore it from her hands. She was about to shout something to the coachman but, just at the same moment, the storm bell began ringing from the church steeple and desperate cries – Fire! Fire! – arose from all sides. Within two minutes we reached home, where everyone was already frantically preparing for our flight, even though the alarm had rung only a few moments before. The office personnel carried massive ledgers that had to be packed in special bags. In the living room, mother and grandmother had opened the big iron "cash box," where silver candlesticks, dining utensils and jewelry were usually stored. These, too, went into special bags. Also, food, warm clothing and whatever else was needed for our flight. The horses were unharnessed from the carriage and hitched to the dray. Then Uncle Jules raced with the dray to the nearby hospital, loaded up the patients and drove them to safety. I don't know where he took them. Upon his return, women, children and bags were put on the dray and taken away, while the men stayed behind to protect the house. Fanny was only three months old and mother not well. Nurse Libe's baby was brought to us by the woman who usually took care of it. She probably was busy with her own kids. Since no one else was available, they entrusted her baby to me and I watched it all night long. The dray took us far enough away so sparks from the flames couldn't reach us. There we camped on a freshly ploughed field on bundles and bags like emigrants. All around us there were similar groups. Weeping, moaning and children's cries could be heard. There were sick people, as well as pregnant women, and we had to help to the best of our ability since not everyone was as organized and practical as my mother and grandmother. And so we spent a long May night, watching the burning city, trying to guess whose house was going up in flames. Suddenly, little Alexander said, "You see, that's just how it was burning last night!" That reminded us of his dream. When men came up from the city from time to time, their reports were not encouraging, although there were occasional miraculous exceptions with houses remaining untouched in a sea of flames. My dear father came once, reporting that the house of the Landau grandparents had caught fire. Entering the burning house wrapped in wet sheets, grandfather, Uncle Doctor and he were able to salvage some things. Actually, that may not have been necessary for, so far as I remember, only the roof, the entrance gate and a few windows and doors burned, but the interior had remained unscathed. In "modern" fires much that's been saved from the flames is destroyed later by water. That's one problem we didn't have in Brody.

The house of the Kallir grandparents remained untouched, thanks partly to Uncle Jules, who tore down the shingle roof of the adjoining house in back, ignoring the protests of Mrs. Tysmenitzer, its owner. Another guardian angel must have protected the front of their house. Their neighbor's house burned, and so did Nirenstein's in the narrow lane opposite. When the iron shade covering our parents' living room window was pulled up afterwards, they discovered a small burnt hole in the window frame. A spark must have sneaked in but it died from lack of air. Even stranger, the wooden garbage bin in the yard had burned without spreading the fire. The roof of our house was made of iron, whereas that of the Nirensteins was made of zinc, which turned out to be very dangerous. The zinc melted and ran down in hot streams, so no one could come close. Long after the fire, we liked to play with those odd shapes, shining like silver, which we found lying all around. People teased Hirsch Braun that his head was so hard, he didn't mind when the molten metal dropped on his bald spot. One of the undamaged buildings belonged to a certain Mr. Czaczkes, who sent this telegram to his brother in Lemberg:

"BRODY DESTROYED. OUR HOUSE SAVED. CELEBRATE!"

With the dawning day the fire, though less violent, was still burning. We were freezing and exhausted when the cart came to take us and our bundles to Uncle Jules' villa at a safe distance from the fire. We joined a crowd of strangers who had also found refuge there. We stretched out on straw mattresses, brewed tea and relaxed until, finally, we could return to town.

Our townhouse had turned into a campground. People who had suffered merely the loss of their roof or other outside damage to their home returned and adjusted as best they could. But others, who had lost everything in the flames, turned to the lucky few who could offer them a temporary abode. Of course, our house was a popular refuge and we took care of many relatives and friends. The fiery sky had been visible for miles around and people from neighboring villages brought clothing and food (mostly bread). Aunt Libe, a sister of Grandfather Landau (I'll tell you more about her some other time) came to Brody from nearby Witkow and shared a room with Grandmother Kallir and me. She grumbled about the frivolity of "big city people," because grandmother owned a few nightingales which kept singing all through the night.

The terrible news of the disaster spread around the world. Newspapers published extensive reports, as well as appeals, with gratifying results. Contributions arrived from all over. I remember the large sums from Hamburg, which might have once suffered a similar misfortune. Next, it became essential to distribute the collections fairly, to make sure not even the smallest amount was spent wastefully. In this, my dear father played an important role. He had contributed to the public welfare on previous occasions, founding the first orphanage in Galicia in 1859, distributing food and Rumford Soups during times of rising prices. Now he became the head of a "Committee for the Fire Victims," organizing the entire project and leading it to completion. As a consequence, he was awarded Honorary Citizenship although he was only 41 years of age. (Uncle Alexander will show you the handsome diploma, next time you're in Vienna.) All applications, referred to as Bietes (from German Bitten), were addressed to him, to be investigated thoroughly and fairly. Father insisted that the town's reconstruction must receive top priority. Everything else had to wait. All those little houses were rebuilt with better material, better construction and, most important, with iron roofs. Shingle roofs were outlawed. Clearly, that was the right thing, as can be gathered from the fact that no major fires have occurred in Brody since then, i.e. in 62 years! One additional credit is due to the young people who organized a Volunteer Fire Department, with modern equipment and frequent practice sessions.

[Page 59]

Brodyites in Leipzig

by A. Yehuda (Osterzetzer)

Translation by Dr. Nitzan Lebovic

Donated by Dr. Lebovic and Stephen Fein

Not too long after its founding, Brody became an important center of commerce for many countries, from the coasts of the Black Sea to the lands at the North Sea, from Odessa to Hamburg. Merchants from Milan to Hamburg and merchants from Berdyczów, Poltava, Nizhni Novgorod and other towns opened in Brody branches of their businesses. The geographic location of the town enabled it to develop as a trade center between Eastern Europe and Western Europe.

About 15,000 residents settled in the city. Two thirds of them were Jews. Their languages were Yiddish and German, because they had originated in Germany. In 1772, the city was annexed to the Kingdom of Austria. Seven years later, it was declared a free city for trade, which meant that there was no need in Brody to pay customs, not for trade coming in and not for trade going out to any country.

So the importance of Brody grew as a transportation city between east and west. Many trade houses were opened in the town, from many countries. The cultural tendency was pro-Western, with the German language prominent. I remember the street called Kallir, after Alexander Kallir, who came from Germany to Brody in 1785.

Tradesmen from our town used to travel to Lipsia [Leipzig] often, in order to buy textiles, household products, and everything anyone could trade in; and they transferred to Lipsia raw materials such as calf leather and furs. Trains did not exist at the time, so everything was transported in hundreds of wagons carried by horses. The convoy used to leave at the beginning of the fall from Brody to Berdyczów, Kharkov, Poltava and the other urban centers in Poland and Russia, as well as to the west. The wagons always visited the most important fairs. Upon arrival, success was guaranteed.

The wagons transported thousands of tons of goods. When in 1800 a large fire broke out in Brody, the trade fair collapsed in Lipsia. The importance of this trade can be gleaned from the decade between 1770-1780, when our townsmen added to Lipsia gross income of about half a million ducats (gold coins) in cash.

The most important professions of the Brodyites in this town [in Leipzig] were fur and leatherwork, industrialism and trade. For example, in 1800 there were in Lipsia around 50 small business merchants from Brody. They received a temporary license to reside in town, and after a few years received licenses for permanent residency. They were forced to swear on the Bible in a festive celebration, with representatives from the city hall and witnesses (59) from the Jewish community. Only then did they get public positions as city clerks.

Brody was one of the first cities in the world to trade in fur and different professions related to leather cultivation. In 1818, of 35 traders in Lipsia who were sworn in, 28 were Jews, among them 14 from Brody. These posts carried much weight in the eyes of our townspeople, because their occupiers won in time also license for permanent residency in Lipsia. Those Brodyites did not leave their businesses in Brody. They conducted business in both cities simultaneously. At the end of the last century, when emancipation was decided on in Germany, there were already around 1000 fur merchants in Lipsia, about 500 of them Jews. Also, 50% of the 1200 shops were owned by Jews. Those shops traded and sold coats and suits, hats and gloves, shoes, boots, sandals, hand bags, toys etc. The improvement in rights was obvious if we take into consideration that up till the 16th century, Jewish presence in Lipsia was forbidden. Nevertheless, at the same time Jews had the right to visit the town as traders at fairs and to build there storage places and shops. In mid 18th century the traders and visitors started to establish their own little prayer houses, still temporary. The Brodyites also established their own synagogue, which is called the "Brody Synagogue" to our day. Next to their synagogue they opened also a schul. If during the fair someone died, they'd transfer the corpse to be buried in Dessau, till in 1811 Yoel Schlesinger paid to the city of Lipsia hundreds of talers as rent for a cemetery. That was the first and only [Brody] cemetery [in Leipzig].

Other Brodyites who received licenses to stay and work in Lipsia were: Moshe Hischl Yechis, Yaakov David Risberg and Meir Michael Torkotan. Other than these, whose names we know, in 1872 there were other merchants from Brody, including the trade place of the Hermlins. This family is known to have conducted business in Lipsia for five straight generations. One Yeshiva-Bucher with an ability to write, Yosef Ehrlich, who was born in Brody, published at the end of the 18th century a booklet in which he described the history of this family. It is possible to read [information] there about the situation of the Jews of Brody and about the family atmosphere and economy of the Lipsia Jews.

[Page 61]

The Synagogue in Brody

from "The Synagogues in Poland and Their Destruction", Mosad HaRav Kook and "Yad VaShem," Jerusalem, 1943

by David Davidowitz

Translation by Moshe Kutten

Edited by Yocheved Klausner

Like the community itself, even the synagogue in Brod – this old Jewish monument with the impressive classic lines, one of the most beautiful fortress-like synagogues in Poland – was destroyed to its foundations. In his journal-book, S. Ansky writes: "I visited the old synagogue in Brody, which played an important role in the cultural life of the Jews. Here sat the "Wise Men of the Kloiz" [Kloiz was the name given to a house of learning and prayer[MK]], the giants of the Jewish intelligentsia of that time, R'Yekhezkel Landoi, R'Meir Margalyot and others. Here the fight against the Chasidic movement was concentrated. A whole period of Jewish life was connected with Brody and its Kloiz. The synagogue was ancient, and most beautiful inside. The gabay [synagogue administrator,[MK]] showed me old silverware, 'Torah crowns', lamps and lanterns from the sixteenth and the seventeenth centuries, as well as valuable *Parokhot* [curtains covering the front of the Holy Ark in the synagogue[MK]]".

Indeed the synagogue excelled not only from the architectural point of view, but also by its collection of ritual objects, one of the richest and most interesting synagogue collections in Poland. We can mention here, that in the ritual exhibition that took place in Lvov in 1894, a gilded silver platter rich in decoration from the Brody synagogue was displayed. In the center of the platter, inside a small indentation, a box with filigreed doors between four filigreed columns was fixed. The tops of the columns were decorated with birds and deer heads. A crown was placed above the indentation, and a small balcony with five sculpted figures on it, depicting the ceremony of the removal of the Torah from the Holy Ark. Beyond this group, above the balcony the figure of a *shofar* blower was placed. The platter was decorated on its upper part with an eagle crowned with a royal crown, and on its lower part with ornamental wreaths of leaves and animals (a bear in the center). The platter originated in the eighteenth century. Another valuable object from the same synagogue displayed in the exhibition was a Torah Crown, richly decorated with ornaments from the animal kingdom (oryx, eagles, oxen and bears) as well as biblical figures.

Among other ritual objects from the synagogue, it is worthwhile to mention the magnificent Hanukkah Menorah, richly decorated with ornaments from the animal kingdom (including winged lions).

The synagogue itself was decorated with paintings painted by many artists, among them the Russian painter Lokomski, a great admirer of the Brody community. This is the place to mention an interesting historical detail: During the years 1755 – 1739, the city was under the hegemony of the Catholic Bishop of Luchek and Brisk, Franchishek Antony Kubeilski. This priest instituted sermons in the synagogue of Brody that preached conversion to Christianity. He made such sermons himself to the elders of the community and its leaders (such sermons were frequent in western Catholic countries in cities such as Rome and Vienna, but have never been instituted in Poland before).

[Page 62]

We learnt about the fate of Jewish Brody and its famous synagogue from a letter that was sent by Dr. M. Weiss, one of Brody's survivors, to the author Dov Sadan (Schtock) in February 1946: "...I have never imagined... that on the slopes of this mountain (Olesko mountain), in the quarry, our birthplace notables would dig up their graves. After the annihilation of the ghetto, 300 people from our city worked in the death camp located in the Olesko Monastery. They were all shot and murdered on one day in the month of Iyar year 5703 (May 1943). The city of Brody is half in ruins and it is completely deserted. In what used to be the ghetto, between the Hospital Street and the railroad tracks, in the market, in the fish market and their environs, there are mounds and heaps of ruins. Only the walls of the old synagogue are standing in their splendor. The synagogue looks like the Coliseum from afar. From the Jews of Brody, only enough for a *minyan* have survived..."

This is how a whole period of Jewish life which, according to Ansky, was inseparable from its kloiz, was interrupted and ended with the tragic destruction of Jewish life in the city and the destruction of the magnificent synagogue.

[Page 63]

Cantor Prayer Lectern (Amud) near the Torah Ark of the old synagogue

The Torah Ark in the new synagogue

The entrance to the old synagogue

Torah shield (Tas)

Torah Crown (Keter Torah)

Candlesticks and goblet

Hanukkah Menorah

Hanukkah Menorah

Chapter Two: Culture and Society

[Page 67]

The Sages of the Brody Kloiz

by Rabbi I. I. Weissblum

Translated by Yocheved Klausner

Introduction

It has been several years that the former residents of Brody in our beautiful city, headed by my friend and relative R'Moshe Rosenblum, were pleading with me to write an article about the sages of the great *Kloiz* [large house of worship and study] of Brody. I kept postponing this endeavor, because I feared to approach this holy work, and more so after the book about Brody by Prof. N. M. Gelber appeared in print (chapter five, pp. 47–81: The Community and its rabbis – *maggids* – sages of the *Kloiz*– holy people). However, when I understood that there was still a great deal to say on the subject, and that, moreover, my opinion differs from his in many places, and there are some places that need correction and places where I thought there is room for more details – I feared that in time the material that I have will be lost and I shall forget many of the details. Therefore I decided to begin this work, albeit with fear and awe.

I must stress that I was able to write only about some of the Sages of the *Kloiz*, because in Haifa I did not have all the books and sources that I needed to consult. Therefore, my condition was that I shall bring only the details that I found their sources in my own private library or that I obtained from reliable people.[1]

As is well-known, the founder of the Brody *Kloiz*was the great scholar, our teacher Rabbi Chaim son of R'Avraham Segal [SEGA"L] Landa, cousin of the [author of the book] *Noda Biyhuda*. Earlier he served *Av Beit Din*[head of the religious court] in the Podkamin community and then in Brody, the place of residence of his father-in-law, our teacher Rabbi Yakov BABAD, who was great and kindhearted, an honored leader of his people and esteemed head of a respected lineage. He lived under the shield of wisdom as well as money, and founded a *Beit Midrash* [house of learning, synagogue] that was named after him; he supported it with his own money and money that he collected from the well-to-do and charitable people of Brody.

Great scholars of the Torah would sit days and nights in this *Beit Midrash*and study the Torah. They were trusted by all, simple folk and scholars alike: even the *Noda Biyhuda* would not pronounce a verdict or present the solution to a serious problem unless he had "the approbation of the scholars who sit in the *Bet Hamidrash* of the late R' Yakov BABAD z"l [of blessed memory] and the leaders of the *Kloiz*.[2] (*Noda Biyhuda*141, 43). The sages of the *Kloiz* were wise men and great scholars, righteous and holy like angels in Heaven,[3]among them famous Kabbalists. We shall mention some of them:

* R'Eliezer Slipman of Brody, who authored the book Beit Shlomo, a commentary on the Book of Proverbs, with a long introduction on the teachings of the Kabbala (Zholkova, 5540 [1779/80]).
* R'Avraham son of R'Israel of Brody, a famous Kabbalist, author of the book Likutei Amarim, a commentary on poetry according to Kabbala (Zolkov, 5500 [1739/40]), and the book Divrei Hamelech, on the 613 mitzvot (commandments) of the Torah by way of PARDES [esoteric philosophy], as well as pilpul [sharp debate] on the teachings of the RAMBAM [Maimonides], 2 parts (Livorno 5565, [1804/5]).

[Page 68]

* The great scholar and Kabbalist, our teacher Rabbi Menachem-Mendel Zolkover, ABD [head of the religious court] of Stcheritz, son of the rabbi, the Hassid our teacher Efraim Zalman who was the maggid meisharim [righteous preacher] of Zolkov. He was mentioned in the Responsa of R' A. Z. Margaliot: "The member of my family, the famous rabbi, Hassid and Kabbalist, the holy man

our teacher Menachem Mendel Zolkover of Brody." He wrote approbations to the books Margaliot HaTora [Pearls of the Torah] and Toldot Yosef [The history of Yosef] on the book of Shir Hashirim [Song of Songs]. In 5537 [1776/7] his signature was mentioned "signed with other great Kabbalist rabbis, the sages of the great Kloizof the Brody Community." He was among the first ten signatories of 'The Kliva Get[divorce]', together with the great scholar R'Chaim Tzanser. He lived an ascetic life until the age of 70. He devoted all his time to study; he would leave the Beit Hamidrash only to prepare himself for the Holy Sabbath. He served as Dayan [religious judge] and rabbi in Brody, after the great scholar our teacher R'Moshe of Ostraha. The Noda Biyhuda mentions him in his Responsa as "a great and famous rabbi, an excellent Dayan of the holy community of Brody." He was the grandson of the scholar Efraim Zalman Schorr.[4]

Other famous scholars among the Sages of the *Kloiz*:

* The scholar and Kabbalist Efraim son of the great scholar Chacham [wise] Zvi z"l. He was a great Tzadik, as can be seen in his approbation for the book Yesod Ha'emuna Veshoresh Ha'avodaby R'Baruch Kossover, written in 5525 [1764/5] while he was living in Brody.
* His brother, the scholar and Kabbalist Nathan, grandfather of the scholar and Kabbalist R'Yakov of Lissa, died in Brody at an old age on 14 of the month of Shevat 5538 [1778].
* His brother-in-law, the scholar and Kabbalist Moshe Rokach, son of the scholar the rabbi of all those living in Exile [Raban shel kol benei hagola= Exilarch] Elazar, ABD of the communities Brody and Amsterdam.[5]
* The scholar and Kabbalist Yeshayahu Halevi Ish Horowitz, the younger brother of the scholars R'Pinchas son of Zvi Halevi Horowitz, author of Ha'hafla'a and R'Shmuel (Shmelke) ABD of the holy community of Nikolsburg in Moravia, who was born to his father by his second wife at an old age; yet his father had the merit to take him to his Huppa [wedding]. He lived a long life and was the student of the great scholar R'Chaim Tzanser.
* The great scholar and Kabbalist our teacher Naftali Hirtz, ABD in the communities of Kovla and Dubno, son of the scholar our teacher Rabbi Zvi Hirsch ABD in Halberstadt.[6] According to the scholar the tzaddik our teacher Rabbi Israel Segal Landa, RABD [head of the religious court] in the community of Zlotchov, in his

book *Nefesh Chaya*, R'Naftali Hirtz left the rabbinic position in Dubno and relocated to Brody. On the ratification of the "Kliva Divorce" his signature appears as well.

* The scholar and Kabbalist our teacher Zvi Horowitz, author of the book Machane Levi, son of the author of Ha'hafla'a was also one of the sages of the Kloiz. In 5537 [1776/7] he wrote approbation for the book Toldot Yosef, mentioned above, with the other Sages of the Brody Kloiz. His final rest is in Stanislav. My friend, the late Rabbi Fishel Horowitz HY"D [may God avenge his blood] son of the scholar Rabbi David HaLevi Ish Horowitz, ABD Stanislav, showed me his gravestone.

Some of the Sages of the *Kloiz* also spread the BESH"T Hassidism. Apart from those that I shall describe in detail later, I shall mention here:

* The scholar, the holy man our teacher Moshe Leib of Sassov, son of the scholar our teacher Yakov ABD Etinga and the region, was born in Brody, studied in his youth with the *Kloiz* Sages and later studied seven years with the scholar, the holy man

[Page 69]

R'Shmelke ABD of Nikolsburg. After his teacher died he went to holy Rabbi Elimelech of Lizhansk. He became famous as one of the Tzadikim of his generation.

* The holy man R'Zelig of Brody, student of the Maggid of Miedzyrzec and the Maggid of Zlotchov and the holy Rabbi of Zalowi. He was called the Hassid of Brody.
* Our teacher Moshe Aharon of Brody, Hassid and holy man of the lineage of Zvi z"l, a student of our teacher Rabbi Yakov Yitzhak ztz"l [righteous of blessed memory] of Lublin. Toward the end of his life he went to the Holy Land.
* I had written an article about the scholar Rabbi Efraim Zalman Margaliot z"l of Brody, but as I was informed that my friend the scholar Moshe Steinberg, rabbi of Gav-Yam, is preparing an article for the book, I gave up the idea, and I shall convey here a little of the history of the scholar our teacher Shlomo Kluger, the MAHARSHAK, the Maggidof Brody. Although he was not born in Brody and was not one of the Sages of the Kloiz, his scholarship[7] and his righteousness gave him an honored place among them and his name was strongly connected with the name of the town – Brody of his time was remembered by many thanks to him.

* The scholar and Kabbalist our teacher Shlomo son of the Rabbi Aharon Yehuda RABD and Maggid Meisharimin Brody, gained fame in the world by his many books on all subjects of the Torah. It is said that he authored three hundred and seventy five books equal to the gimatria of his name Shlomo. He was born in 5543 [1782/3] in the town Kamerov in Russia–Poland. From the age of 12 years he was educated by the great scholar our teacher Yosef Hochgelehrenter,[8] ABD of the community of Zamosc, author of Mishnat Hachamim. He was ABD in the communities of Kolikov and Yosepov, and Maggid Meisharimin Brody, by the recommendation of the scholar our teacher Rabbi E. Z. Margaliot. Later he was accepted as ABD of Brezhan and was welcomed there splendidly with music and dance. My friend the late Torah scholar our teacher Israel Ilan z"l, born in Brezhan, related that he heard from the elders of the town that the day the MAHARSHAK arrived in Brezhan he became ill and for 12 months he was confined to bed. The townspeople made every effort to restore his health: they spent a great deal of money, the women sold their jewelry, they brought the best doctors from Lvov and Vienna – all to no avail. Until one day, the holy R'Meir of Przemyslany z"l, who was one of the admirers of MAHARSHAK, sent a special envoy with the order that the MAHARSHAK immediately leave Brezhan and he will soon be fully healed. And so it happened. He was indeed healed, returned to Brody and served there over fifty years, taught Torah and issued many Takanot [regulations] in spite of the Maskilim ["enlightened"] of Brody. The regulations were accepted in other towns in Galicia as well. From the Brody elders I heard about his special abstinence and holiness. The people went to him when in need or in trouble and related about the miracles that he performed, although he was not officially part of the Hassidic movement. By the way, I shall mention here something that is not known, but it should be remembered: he wrote a book which he named Regulations for the Ritual Slaughterers [SHUV regulations] which was added to the book Torat Hazevach by the scholar our teacher Rabbi Genzfried z"l (Lwow 5608 [1847/8]) and begins "Thus said Shlomo: I was called to the great city, the holy community of Berdichev to correct the matter of the slaughterers; God helped me and I managed to introduce good regulations and good conduct, and some other communities in Russia adopted those regulations as well." The problem was: in Berdichev there were rumors that one of the slaughterers was not performing the ritual as prescribed in the Halacha and it was decided to invite the

scholar MAHARSHAK to hear the testimonies and the arguments of all sides, and so it was.

[Page 70]

He came, investigated and listened to the arguments of the sides and his decision was against the slaughterer: he was fired from his work. Naturally, the slaughterer and his friends did not accept this verdict quietly. They wrote to the great scholars of the generation and they wrote to our teacher rabbi Yekutiel Asher Enzil Tzuzmir z"l (he served, in his old age, as ABD of the community of Stryj, without compensation, since he was very rich), the best student of the author of Ketzot Hachoshen, and he caused a stir in the entire rabbinic world about the verdict of the MAHARSHAK, stating that it was wrong, etc. etc. In his book of Responsa, which I have in my library, there are many queries on this matter, every reply written at great length, as was his custom. He writes bitterly about the MAHARSHAK and the latter replies, as usual, very modestly and explains the reasons tor firing the slaughterer. In 1935, when I made Aliya with God's help, I heard from a great rabbi the end of the story: After several years, the slaughterer decided to leave Berdichev and make Aliya to Eretz Israel. Here he repented and printed a booklet (which the aforementioned rabbi saw with his own eyes) in which he admits that the MAHARSHAK was right and that he had brought false witnesses. Everybody realized then the greatness of the scholar the MAHARSHAK z"l. He died in Tamuz 5629 [August 1869] in Brody. The scholar our teacher I.S. Nathansohn, rabbi of Lwow, said in his eulogy that the MAHARSHAK had forty thousand pages of Torah commentaries; the MAHARSHAK wrote in 5614 [1853/4] that he had written 136 articles on the Talmud and the Poskim[a scholar who decides on Halacha issues], and every article has some 200 pages, and some eight thousand Responsa. Some 30 books appeared in print and hundreds remained as manuscripts. The first book that was published was Sefer Hachaiym, commentaries on Shulchan Aruch, Orach Chaiym (Zolkov, 5588 [1827/8]). This book had a great impact on the rabbinic world, although the author was quite young. In his approbation to the book, the scholar E. Z. Margaliot of Brody wrote about him: "The rabbi, the sharp scholar - his book is useful to every rabbi and teacher, a good and sensible book of Responsa." The book includes about 6,000 responsa on the four volumes of the codex of law Shulchan Aruch. His son, the scholar our teacher Avraham

Binyamin Kluger z"l served after him as Dayanand Moreh–Tzedek [a Posek– a scholar rabbi who decides on Halcha Issues] in Brody.

Concluding this Introduction, I consider it my duty to mention my brother–in–law (my wife's brother) the scholar and tzaddik Moshe Pinchas z"l, the rabbi of Ruhatin,[9]son of the scholar, the tzaddik our teacher Chaim Halevi Eisen ztz"l ABD of the community of Swiez. He was a great scholar, very erudite, served his Maker with great devotion, his followers and students admired him greatly.

The following Hassidim were famous in Brody as well: the old Hassid R'Moshe Gliener, R'Yehoshua, R'Leibush, R'Meneli the SHUV [slaughterer] and his son R'Shlomo, R'Mendel Parnas. My late friend, his teacher the slaughterer Herman of Swirz, told me that when the rabbi of Ruhatin was nine years old he knew by heart several Tractates. When the rabbis wanted to test him he hid under the bench, so they promised him sweets and asked him references from the Talmud, and he replied: this is on page.... on page.... and gave the first words of the text, etc. etc. They were astounded. He perished in the Holocaust as a young man, with his wife the *Rabbanit* Mrs. Pearl, her sister Mrs. Sara, their son Israel and their daughters Hadassa and Miriam–Rivka.

[Page 71]

Rabbi Moshe of Ostraha (Ostrov)

He was unique, one of the greatest of the early Sages of the *Kloiz*, a famous scholar, a Kabbalist and holy man, of strong opinions.[10] He was called by all R'Moshe of Ostraha, son of the rabbinic scholar our teacher Hillel of Zamozs and grandson of the scholar the Kabbalist our teacher Yakov Temirles (according to R'Moshe of Ostraha in his Introduction to the book *Arugat Habosem*). He wrote the very good book Arugat Habosem [The Fragrant Flowerbed] on *Shir Hashirim* [The Song of Songs] – commentaries by way of Kabbala. The book was first printed in 5585 [1824/5] in Zolkov and the holy Rabbi Sar–Shalom of Belz asked his son to buy it for him. When the book was brought to him he was very happy and joyous. The son asked his father "What brought on this joy? When you want to study and attain the real truth you choose only the books of the old scholars – what made you ask for this book?" The father replied: "Know, my son, that when the fragrance of the book spread over the world, the holy BESHT [Rabbi Israel Ba'al Shem Tov], may his merits protect us, said that when the author wrote the book he was united with the soul of King Shlomo [Salomon] may he rest in peace." And he concluded by saying "Even without this knowledge, which I received from my holy teachers, I knew that Moshe is a very great man, comparable to the old sages.[11] Later, in 5626 [1865/6] his commentaries on the Pentateuch *Heichal Habracha* and *Otzar Chaiym* were printed, as was his book *Darash Moshe*, a precious commentary, by the way of Kabbalah on the Book of Psalms (Lwow 5639 [1878/9]), which was bought by our teacher E. Z. Margaliot of Brody.[12] R'Moshe was a *Maggid Meisharim* [righteous preacher] in Brody and was one of the loyal friends of the BESHT. Every time the BESHT came to Brody, they would spend several hours together. The holy rabbi, the *Maggid* Binyamin of Zlozhitz quotes many of his commentaries on the Torah.[13] He died on 11 Tevet 5545 [24 December 1784] in Brody and there he was put to eternal rest.

Rabbi Chaim Tzanser

A true scholar, the crown of holiness, most famous in his generation, the Kabbalist our teacher Rabbi Chaim of Tzans[14] son of the scholar, the *tzaddik*our teacher Rabbi Menachem Nachum (died 10 Elul 5560 [31 August 1800]). He was one of the most outstanding of the Sages of the Brody *Kloiz*, studied with the famous *Noda Biyhuda* and other great scholars of his time. He was one of the signatories on 10 Tevet 5528 [1768] of the ratification of the *Get of Kliva* [the Kliva Divorce]. Day and night R'Chaim studied the Torah and had special hours dedicated to charity and Free–of–Interest loans. He would say: Why do the Tractates of the Talmud begin with Page 2 and not Page 1? To teach you, that even if you turn nights into days and study the Torah day and night, do not be conceited, since it shows that you have not studied Page 1 yet, and you should start from the beginning. The scholar R'Chaim Tzanser was the head of the speakers on every holy issue, not only in Brody and surroundings but also in the entire Jewish and rabbinic world.[15] It is written on the cover of his book Ne'dar Bakodeshon Pirkei Avot [Wisdom of the Fathers], published in Lwow in 5622 [1861/2], which was in the private library of R'E. Z. Margaliot of Brody "One of the great Elder Scholars, Hassidim of the Old School, who are sitting before God in the Great Kloizof Brody, among the scholars known as the Sages of the Kloiz.[16] Our teacher R'Azriel Levin wrote in the Introduction that the BESHT praised him greatly, saying that his holy soul possessed a spark of the soul of Rabbi Yochanan Ben Zakay. He died on 6 Shevat 5543 [1783]. He left a son who was a genius and a tzaddik, our teacher Rabbi Shmuel Aharon, ABD in Matchov. Of his students we shall mention the scholar R'Elazar Rokach, father of the holy scholar Rabbi Sar–Shalom of Belz and son of the scholar our teacher Shmelke, son of the scholar Rabbi Elazar Rokach ABD Amsterdam and son–in–law of the Kabbalist the scholar Yehuda Zundel Remrezh, who was also one of the students of R'Chaim Tzanser and was a kabbalist and a *tzaddik*.

[Page 72]

Rabbi Yitzhak Halevi Horowitz

The scholar Kabbalist Yitzhak Halevi, son of the scholar Kabbalist Yakov Yukel Horowitz ABD Kharkhov, Gluga, Brody and AHW (Altona, Hamburg, Wandsbek), was one of the greatest of the Sages of the Brody *Kloiz.* He was born in 5475 [1714/5] in the town Bolechov when his father the scholar Yakov Yukel was ABD there. In his later years he was ABD of Kharkhov and the Ludmir district.

After the death of his father, he was appointed ABD of greater Glugau. He served there as ABD six years and in the seventh year he left the position of rabbi and returned to his town, Brody. In 5524 [1763/4], after the death of the scholar Kabbalist Nathan Neta, ABD Brody, he was appointed ABD of Brody, and in 5525 [1764/5] he was again accepted as ABD of AHW, after the death of the scholar Kabbalist Rabbi Yehonatan Eyebeschutz z"l, author of *Kreiti Ufleiti, Urim Vetumim, Ye'arot Devash* and more. While he lived in Brody, before he was appointed ABD, he wrote in 5511 [1750/1] approbation to the Amsterdam Talmud. In 5514 [1753/4] he wrote approbation to the books *Tosefet Shabat* and *Ateret Rosh.* His writings can be found in the book *Hafla'a* and *Hamikne,* in the Responsa of Rabbi Chaim Cohen, in the *Ya'vetz Chaim* queries item 66, in *Noda Biyhuda,* in *Pitchei Teshuva Even Ha'ezer* item 46, etc. etc. Yitzhak died on the 6th of the month of Iyar 5527 [1766/7], in Altona, at the age of 52. He was the son–in–law of R'Yakov BABED of Brody, one of the founders of the Brody *Bet Hamidrash.* The other data and events about our Rabbi Yitzhak Halevi are recorded in the book of the History of the Horowitz Family.

R'Naftali son of R'Levi[17]

The scholar, Kabbalist, our teacher Naftali son of Levi of Brody, author of the books *Ateret Shlema, Bet Beit Levi,* commentaries on the Talmud and RASHI (Zolkov, 5492 [1732]), was one of the Sages of the *Kloiz.* In 5537 [1776/7] he wrote approbation for the book *Toldot Yosef* (A commentary on *Shir Hashirim* by the way of Kabbala by R'Yosef Dov ABD Liskow) with other Sages.[18]The scholar, our teacher Efraim Z. Margaliot, in his Responsa *Beit Efraim,* Tractate Gittin [Divorces], wrote, in the middle of the response "I heard the same commentary on RASHI on the Torah Portion *Vayeshev*[concerning Yosef brothers' conspiracy to kill him] in the name of the late rabbi, our teacher Naftali ben Levi.
[Page 73]

Rabbi Avraham Gershon Kitover

The great scholar, the Kabbalist, the famous Hassid, our teacher Avraham Gershon Kitover, son of the scholar our teacher Efraim, who was judge and moreh tzedek in Kitov, was one of the Sages of the *Kloiz*at the time of the *Noda Biyhuda.* The *Noda Biyhuda* described him as "the darling of my eye and beloved of my heart, a wise man who is superior to a prophet, beloved on earth and desirable in Heaven, the wondrous rabbi, erudite in Torah and Hassidism, wise and perfect, a holy Hassid, a luminary of the children of Israel, a supporting pillar and a strong hammer, our honored teacher Avraham Gershon, may his light shine." The author of *Pri Megadim* [R' Yosef son of Meir Teomim] writes that he has heard from his father z"l that the Hassid R'Gershon Kitover said that he came to Jerusalem[19]and when he saw several nations living there in peace he wept, saying "Now I understand the verse I see every city (Jerusalem on earth) built and living peacefully, while God's city (Jerusalem in Heaven) is humiliated and ruined." In the book *Hibat Yerushalaiym* it is written about him "I heard people tell that when the Rabbi R'Gershon Kitover recited Lamentations in the place where the Temple once stood, he fainted several times, and people could barely revive him. The scholar rabbi Yehonathan Eyebeshutz z"l, when he sent amulets to the Kabbalist our honored teacher Chaim Vilna, quoted the sages of Konstantina, who said about our teacher Rabbi Gershon: "How great is his wisdom in the Science of Kabbala." The holy scholar, author of Toldot Yaakov Yosef quotes his commentaries on the *Ha'azinu* Torah Portion. By the request of the BESHT he met with the holy Rabbi R'Chaim Atar. It is known that the BESHT wanted to meet him, and he reached Istanbul (on his way to Eretz Israel) but, against his will, he had to return. R'Avraham Gershon wrote to the BESHT greetings from the author of *Or Chaiym* [Chayim Atar] and informed him that the letter was received. At the same time he ordered him not to try to set out on the journey again, since "we do it only once" [from the Passover Haggadah].[20] He set up his residence in Hebron, and used to say that living one day in Eretz Israel is valued by the Master of the Universe more than sixty years in the Diaspora. Later he relocated to Jerusalem and died after a few years. He was buried in Jerusalem and next to him his sons R'Chaim Aharon and R'Yakar, who came to Eretz Israel ten years later, and his grandson.

[Page 74]

Rabbi Meir Margaliot

The scholar Kabbalist Rabbi Meir Margaliot, son of the scholar Rabbi Zvi–Hirsh Margaliot (ABD of the community of Yazlowitz and the province of Podolia), was ABD of Lwow and later ABD of Ostraha [Ostrov]. He wrote the book *Meir Netivim*, Part 1 Responsa and Part 2 commentaries on the Talmud and nice interpretations of the Torah Portions (Polnoy, 5551 [1790/1]). He studied with his uncle (his mother's brother), the scholar Arie Leibish Auerbach, ABD Stanislav.

The BESHT used to say about him that he had in him a spark of Abayey [a great Amora a Talmudic sage of the Babilonian Talmud], and the great scholar author of *Noda Biyhuda* refused to sign the release of a "*aguna*" [grant a divorce to a woman of a missing husband without his approval. He was the son of the scholar Mordechai Mordush, ABD of Bamberg and the region, son of the scholar our teacher David, nephew (son of the sister) of the author of *Turei Zahav.* At the end of his book there are new interpretations on the Tractate *Berachot* from the great book *Beer Yitzhak*, written by his elder brother, the sharp scholar our teacher Yitzhak Dov ABD Yazlowitz, as well as some collections written by his father, mentioned above. He wrote also the book *Derech Hatov Vehayashar* [The way of goodness and honesty] (Polnoy 5555, [1794/5]), *Kutonot Or* [coats of light] on the 613 commandments (Berditchev, 5576 [1815/6]) and the book *Sod Yachin Uvoaz* [The secret of Yachin and Boaz (the two columns in the Jerusalem Temple)] (Ostrov 5554 [1793/4]). He was one of the greatest scholars of the *Kloiz* Sages, and one of the loyal followers of the BESHT, as he testifies in his book *Sod Yachin Uvoaz*: "...The way I was taught Torah and Hassidism by my friend the rabbi and Hassid, an example for the entire generation, my teacher Rabbi Israel Baal Shem Tov z"l" and further "from the day I met my teacher my friend the Rav and Hassid Rabbi Israel Baal Shem Tov, may his soul be bound in the bond of the living, I knew with certainty that he was a leader with wisdom and purity, a Hassid and a Tzaddik, who revealed secrets for me, and many wondrous things are being told about him." He wrote in the book *Shemen Tov* Part 2, 106 that the BESHT z"l said that there were three families who are pure generation after generation "as He made the Covenant with Abraham and His pledge to Yitzhak and Yakov": 1. Margaliot, 2. Shapira, 3. Horowitz. He loved the author of *Me'ir Netivim* and the holy Rabbi Pinchas of Koretz and the holy Rabbi Zvi Hirsch Halevi Horowitz ABD Tchortkov, father of the scholars Pinchas Halevi Horowitz, author of *Hafla'a Vehamikne*, ABD Frankfurt am Main and the holy scholar R'Shmelke Halevi Horowitz, ABD Nikolsburg.

His sons were famous scholars – the scholar Shaul ABD Lublin, the scholar Betzalel who took his father's place as ABD and head of the Yeshiva in Ostrov and the scholar Nachman, ABD Polnoy.

Rabbi Yechezkel Landa

The scholar our teacher Yechezkel Landa son of Yehuda Halevi, one of the greatest rabbis of his generation, was of a much honored family of special lineage,[21]famous by the name of his book *Noda Biyhuda*. He was born on 18 Cheshvan 5474 [1714] in Apta [Opatov], to his father R'Yehuda son of Zvi Hirsch, one of the leaders of the town and member of the Council of the Four Lands. Until the age of 13 years he studied Torah with Rabbi Yitzhak Aizik Halevi of Ludmir. When he was 14 he went to the holy community of Brody to study with the Sages of the *Kloiz*, since it was known that this city was full of scholars and writers and that Torah spread from there to the entire Jewish people. He studied with a group of talented and God fearing young people – real lions in the study of the Torah. When he was 18 he married Miss Liba, the daughter of Yakov of Dubno and went to live in the house of his father–in–law [as was the custom]. He persuaded his father–in–law to move to Brody and the latter was accepted as a member of the Sages of the *Kloiz*. In 5494 [1733/4] he was appointed *dayan* [religious judge] without compensation and gained fame. All the scholars of his time would ask his advice – he possessed great knowledge, in the wisdom of the Torah, as well as in research and philosophy and reasoning. In addition to his wisdom and righteousness, he was kind hearted, charitable and always attentive to the needs of the community.

[Page 75]

At the age of thirty he was appointed ABD of Yampol and served there about ten years, and in 5515 [1754/5] he was appointed ABD and head of the Yeshiva in the great city of Prague[22] after Rabbi David Oppenheim. The rooms of the Yeshiva were too small to contain the many students from far and near who came to hear his teachings and they had to hold classes in the courtyard of the synagogue. Study never stopped in his house all his life, even on the Sabbath eve and on fasting days. Contrary to the custom of the heads of the Yeshiva, who began the "semesters" on the first day of the months Cheshvan and Iyar, he would open the study right after the Holidays of Sukkot and Pesach. Every day he would give a lesson on Talmud, and Fridays he would learn with his students the Weekly Portion with RASHI. He loved his students as a father loves his sons and was happy with every success in their study. Among his students were great scholars - R'Avraham Danzig author of *Chayey Adam* and *Chochmat Adam*, R'David Deutch author of Ohel David and R'Eliezer Flekless author of the Responsa *Teshuva Me'ahava*. R'Yechezkel was courageous, stood with pride before kings, spoke wisely and the efforts he made for his people were never rejected. During the Seven–Year–War, when the Austrian Empress Theresa fought against the king of Prussia Frederick II and the city of Prague was under siege, he did not listen to the advice of some of the elders of the community, who left Prague and asked him to join them; he remained in town and made every effort to help his people: he asked the rich to help the poor and forbade the merchants to raise prices. In 5505 [1744/5] the Jews of Prague had been expelled from the city, following a libel that they aided the Prussians in their war on Austria; this time Rabbi Yechezkel was cautious and issued a message to the Jews, stating that any Jew who will help the enemy will be declared traitor and will be excommunicated from the community. He also composed a special prayer for the welfare of the empire and royalty, to be recited in every synagogue at the morning and evening prayers. He ordered to print it in the German language and distributed thousands of copies. The Empress appreciated his activity, and when she visited Prague at the end of the war and the rabbi went to welcome her and praise her for her victory she thanked him, in front of all her ministers, for the loyalty to his country. In 5549 [1788/9], when the emperor Joseph II issued the decree ordering the Jews to recruit to the army, he encouraged the members of his community to obey the order. On 16 Iyar, he spoke to the first 25 soldiers in the presence of many of the residents of the city and army officers. He encouraged the soldiers and hoped that they will keep the Jewish *mitzvoth* [commandments] while in the army. R'Yechezkel died on 17 Iyar 5553 [19 April, 1793] in Prague. He asked not to be overly praised in the eulogies, and not to erect an expensive stone on his grave, only a simple stone costing no more than 18 Gulden and not to engrave on it honorary titles. So it was done, and they engraved on his tombstone only "The famous rabbi our teacher Yechezkel Halevy." It was told that in his room he had a special cabinet that was always locked and he never let the key out of his hand. Even his family did not know what he kept in that cabinet. After he died they opened it and found the *Sefer Hazohar* and the writings of the ARI z"l [the great Kabbalist Rabbi Yitzhak Luria] and some of his own notes and remarks on Kabbala. In several places in his book, he mentions Kabbala subjects.[23] He introduced several regulations, among them regulations against exaggerated luxury, which "provokes envy among the Goyim and causes the raise of taxes." He also reproved the members of his community, not to be like the goyim [gentiles] by going to the theater.

[Page 76]

In the matter of the "Kliva Divorce" R'Yechezkel stood by the scholar R'Israel Lifschitz, who arranged the divorce, contrary to the opinion of the scholar R'Avraham Avish, the Rabbi of Frankfurt. As a result, the leaders of the Frankfurt Community decided, on 9 Cheshvan 5522 [6 November 1761] not to appoint as rabbi of their town neither R'Yechezkel nor any of his descendants, also not to allow them to preach in their synagogue, in case they visited their town. At the time of the great dispute between R'Yakov Emden and R'Yehonatan Eybeschutz, R'Yechezkel published, on 8 Iyar 5512 [22 April, 1752] a letter, asking the rabbis and sages of his generation, to calm down the quarrel. In his opinion, the amulets that R'Yonathan was suspected of using were fake amulets, and he complained that the religious court of justice listened to testimonies in his absence. For the sake of peace, he suggested to conceal the amulets. At the same time, he declared that the honor of R'Yonathan was restored and he can continue to teach Torah (this angered R'Yakov Emden). When he died, he was eulogized and praised (according to the book *Tziyun Lenefesh Chaya*) "As one cannot deny the light of the sun at noontime so one cannot deny his greatness and his good qualities."

His sons that are known to us: 1. The scholar our teacher Rabbi Yakov'ka Landa of Brody; his commentaries were quoted in the first edition of *Noda Biyhuda* and given as an appendix to the second edition. In 5544 (1784) he wrote an approbation to the Pentateuch edition. He died on 13 Av [6 August July] 5583 (1823) in Brody. His son was Rabbi Yehuda Landa of Brody.[24]2. The scholar our teacher Rabbi Shmuel Landa, who inherited the position of his father in Prague. Some of his Responsa are incorporated in *Noda Biyhuda* and his new interpretations in *Ahavat Zion*. He was one of the fighters against the new movements, which aimed to introduce changes in religion and education. 3. Rabbi Israel Landa of Brody, father of the famous scholar our teacher Rabbi Elazar Landa Brod, author of the famous book *Yad Hamelech*, new interpretations on the RAMBAM (Maimonides) (Lwow, 5582 [1821/2]). Brody elders would spoke about his righteousness, his wisdom and his holiness. The scholar MAHARSHAK z"l related that several hours before his death he stood outside in front of his house, which was far from the house of R'Elazar, and yet he could hear him say in a very loud voice his confession [*Viduy*] and *Ani Ma'amin*. He died in 5591 [1830/1] in Brody. His grandson, the righteous scholar R'Israel Landa z"l ABD Zlotchov, had been one of the respected and rich residents of Kiev, but had to flee the town at the time of the Beilis trial, because he was Zeitzov's [a witness in Beilis trial] brother-in-law. In the introduction of his book *Nefesh Chaya*on the Tractate *Beitza* he writes at length about the history of this precious family – the Landa family – and its pedigree.

Rabbi David Tevil

The scholar Kabbalist our teacher David Tevil,[25] born in Brody, was one of the greatest Sages of the *Kloiz*. He was known as a great genius, most brilliant in Talmudic debate. At first he served as ABD in Kharkov and later was accepted as ABD and Head of Yeshiva in Lissa. He studied with all great scholars of his time, as the author of *Noda Biyhuda*, the author of *Beit Meir* and the author of Or Israel. He wrote the book *Michtav LeDavid*. His signature is on the ratification of the Kliva Divorce, with the signatures of R'Chaim Tzanser and others. On 13 Sivan 5505 [13 June 1745] he wrote approbation to the book *Arugat Habosem* by R'Moshe of Ostraha [Ostrov]. He wrote approbation to the book *Divrei Shalom Ve'emet* by R'Naftali Hirtz Wiesel as well, but after he

understood the intentions of the author and the devastating results of the new changes in education, he went openly against them. In his sermon on Shabat before Passover [*Shabat Hagadol*] 5542 [1782] he severely criticized the supporters modifications. Following his sermon, Wiesel wrote his booklet *Rechovot*. He died on 16 Tevet 5552 [11 January, 1792] in Lissa and the scholar R'Eliezer Flekeles eulogized him; the eulogy appears in his book *Olat Chodesh*.
[Page 77]

Rabbi Noach Avraham Halevi Heller

The holy scholar our teacher Noach Avraham Halevi Heller[26] son of the holy scholar Moshe Aharon[27] ABD Sniatyn, son of the scholar our teacher R'Meir[28] ABD Bradshyn, son of the scholar R'Avraham[29] Head of the Yeshiva in the community of Skalia (near Stryj), son of the holy scholar, Head of the Dispora Jews Yom–Tov Lipman Heller. He authored great books: a. on the Talmud, b. Reponsa, c. New interpretations, legends and morals. "He intended to print them, but on Sunday 13 Tamuz 5519 [8 July 1759][30] robbers attacked the town Bolochov, robbed and killed several Jews and burned the town etc. etc., and he was miraculously saved since he hid under the bed." All his books burned down, so he wrote a new book on the Torah Zerizuta DeAvraham (Lwow 5660 [1900]). He was one of the great Sages of the Kloiz, "from the den of lions" and he revealed his secrets to his loyal student the holy Man of God Rabbi Shmuel of Ostrov.[31] R'Noach Avraham was the student of the maggid of Miedzyrzec. At the death of the scholar Moshe Shoham son of R'Dan, he was appointed ABD of the community of Dalina. He died on 18 Elul 5546 [11 September 1786] in Bradschein and was buried there. His sons:

1. Our teacher Rabbi Meir,[32] Maggid Meisharimin Brody, died on 25 Iyar 5540 [30 May 1780].
2. The scholar our teacher Rabbi Avraham Yehuda ABD Toms, is buried in the holy city of Tzfat [Safed].
3. The rabbi and Hassid our teacher Shmuel Zvi, died 3 Nisan 5547 [22 March 1787] and was buried in Brody.[33]

Rabbi Meshulam Igra

The scholar Kabbalist R'Meshulam Igra lived several years in Brody and studied in the Great *Kloiz*. The Sages of the *Kloiz* much appreciated his greatness and wrote about him "all the sages of the generation are not comparable to him." R'Meshulam was born in 5510 [1749/50] in Butchatch, the son of the great rabbi our teacher Shimshon. He was raised and educated by his grandfather, the scholar Kabbalist Efraim Fishel, ABD Kolomea, son of the scholar Meshulam, son of the scholar Yeshayahu, judge and head of the Yeshiva in Lwow, son of the scholar Kabbalist Aharon Meshulam of Lowicz, grandson of the scholar author of *Meginei Shlomo* and the scholar our teacher Meshulam son of Avraham Salzburg ABD Lwow, who died there on 2 Iyar 5405 [18 April 1645] and was laid there to eternal rest. The scholar Rabbi Meshulam Igra was very talented – he was "like a cemented cistern that never loses a drop" [from *Pirkei Avot*– Ethics of the Fathers].

[Page 78]

It was said about him that it was his custom to study Talmud without the commentaries of RASHI and *Tosfot*, and explain the passage according to his own reasoning. Later he would read RASHI, and seeing that his interpretation and the *Tossfot* interpretation were different from his own, he would try to explain why RASHI did not explain as he did, and why the Tosfot differs from RASHI. From all these deliberations he wrote his great book *Igra Rama.*[34] The BESHT, when he once saw him on his father's shoulders, took him in his arms and said to all present in the room: You see, this child's fresh soul emanates directly from Heaven, and it was never in this world in a former incarnation.[35] When he was ten years old, he spoke in the great synagogue in Brody, in front of scholars and sages, in the presence of ABD Brody the famous scholar R'Yitzhak Halevi Ish–Horowitz, also known as R'Itzik'l Hamburger. The child argued with him publicly about a certain issue and won.[36] When he was 13 he married the daughter of the respected rich man, our teacher R'Shmuel Bik of Brody and continued his perpetual study of the Torah at the *Kloiz*. Several years later, his wife asked for a divorce, based on the argument "Can one live with a Torah Scroll?" He accepted, and confessed that he was punished because he did not marry the daughter of one of the great rabbis of the generation. Then he married Miss Rivka Ester, the daughter of the aforementioned scholar R'Itzik'l. When he was seventeen he was appointed ABD of Tisminetz, one of the outstanding and important communities in the world of study. He had many students, who later became famous scholars: the scholar our teacher Rabbi Yakov of Lissa, author of *Chavat Da'at*and *Netivot Hamishpat*, the scholar Kabbalist our teacher Mordechai Banet ABD Nikolsburg, the son of his brother–in–law the scholar Kabbalist Arie Leibush Halevi Ish Horowitz ABD Stanislav, the scholar Arie Leib author of *Ketzot Hachoshen*, the scholar Kabbalist Naftali Hirtz Hakohen of Tisminetz, who was called R'Hertzele Katchiger (his responsum was printed in the Responsa book of Rabbi Meshulam Igra, Choshen Mishpat 24), the scholar Kabbalist Nathan Neta ABD Podhajce, the son of his brother–in–law the holy scholar our teacher Rabbi Naftali Zvi Horowitz, ABD of the community Rufshitz, the scholar Kabbalist Baruch Frenkel ABD Leipnik, author of the book *Baruch Ta'am*, the scholar Kabbalist Moshe Mintz ABD of Old Buda, author of the book *MAHARAM Mintz*, the scholar Kabbalist Shlomo, one of the great sages of Tisminetz, who was appointed in 5554 [1793/4] ABD of Pressburg, died on the second day of *Hol Hamoed* [intermediate days] of the Holiday of Sukkot 5563 [1803] in Pressburg and was laid there to eternal rest.

Rabbi Moshe Mintz

The scholar Kabbalist R'Moshe Mintz, *dayan* and *moreh tzedek* [religious judge and posek] in Brody, was born in Podolia.[37] He was an in–law of the great scholar the KHATAM Sofer and is mentioned in his Responsa Even Ha'ezer 122. He studied with the scholar author of the book *Hemdat Shlomo*. The scholar author of *Noda Biyhuda* mentioned him in his Responsa. *Noda Biyhuda* wrote about him, that he was the exemplary scholar of the entire generation, and according to his recommendation he was appointed in 5550 [1789/90] ABD of Budapest (Old Oboda), after the position of rabbi in that city was not filled for the duration of nine years, from the day of the death of the scholar Kabbalist Nathan Ginsburg, who was so great in Torah and in wisdom that the members of the community could not find a suitable replacement, until they found R'Moshe Mintz. He was respected by all people in town and vicinity, and rabbis from far and near turned to him with questions. As ordained rabbi in the community of Brody, he arranged in 5540 [1779/80] the get [divorce] for the community leader R'Elyakim Getzl of Lebertov.[38] For 41 years he served as ABD in Old Oboda, Budapest and died there in 5591 [1830/1]. He was buried in the old cemetery there, and his gravestone, as well as the gravestone of the rabbi who preceded him, are standing there to this day. Some of his Responsa are printed, titled Responsa of MAHARAM Mintz.

[Page 79]

Rabbi Meir Kristianpoller

He was one of the greatest scholars of his generation, ABD and Head of the Yeshiva in Brody, at the time of the scholar author of the book *Beit Efraim*. Of the many responsa and interpretations in all subjects of the Torah that he has written, only one book was printed, titled *Yad Meir*, about some of the subjects of the Talmud. In the Responsa *Noda Biyhuda* Rabbi Meir was praised, while he was still ABD in Kristianpol (this was the origin of his name Kristianpoller). He was the son of the scholar Kabbalist Zvi Hirsch, ABD Bylkamin, who also left many manuscripts, but only one book was printed, *Meorot Zvi*, on the Talmud. The scholar Kabbalist R'Meir was one of the best students of the holy scholar our teacher R'Shmelke Horowitz ABD Nikolsburg. Rabbi Meir died 15 Nissan 5575 [25 April, 1815]. It was told that Rabbi Meir married his second wife and she bore him every year a son, but, God help us, no one survived. Once, after she had a son again, the Brody Hassidim gave her the advice, that if she wants her son to survive and live a long life, she should invite the holy R'Moshe Leib of Sassov to the Brit [circumcision ceremony]. When her husband R'Meir returned from the synagogue she said that she wished to invite Rabbi Moshe Leib to the Brit, but he refused. She swore that she will not allow the baby to be circumcised unless R'Moshe Leib will be present, and he did not have a choice but to invite R'Moshe Leib. Before the Morning Prayer he went to the river, as was his custom, to perform the ritual immersion [*tevila*]. It was winter and very cold. After immersion he washed his hands and went to the synagogue, where no stove was burning, and prayed, with only his lips moving, as was his custom. When he reached the passage *Vayevarech David*, the people in the synagogue saw drops of sweat bubbling on his shoes. The newborn boy survived and lived a long life; he was the scholar Kabbalist Yechiel Michel Kristianpoller, who became ABD Brody and vicinity.

Notes Introduction

1. The books that I used, besides the books of *Halakha* and *Midrash* mentioned in the detailed sections about the great rabbis, are: *Shem Hagdolim*, A and B, *Ne'dar Bakodesh, History of the Poskim, Toldot Yosef, Or Hayashar* (the Kliva divorce), *Dvar Yom Beyomo, Encyclopedia of the History of Great Jewish Scholars, Writings of the Geonim, Israel Encyclopedia* (*Eshkol*),*Otzar Israel, Arim Ve'Imahot BeIsrael* (Brody) and more. At times I quoted word by word; at times I related the contents, in short.
2. The son-in-law of R'Chaim, the great Kabbalist scholar our teacher R'Shmuel of Brody was one of the greatest sages of the Kloiz. He was the youngest son of the scholar R'Pini Yehoshua, who mentions him as the "head of *Bava Metzi'a* and my wise son, the honored teacher Shmuel Hirtz." He died in Brody in 5521 [1760/1] without offspring.

[Page 80]

3. In the words of the scholar, the *tzadik* Rabbi S. Halberstam ztz"l, ABD of the community of Lwow, in his approbation to the book *Zrizuta DeAvraham.*
4. The father of the scholar Kabbalist our teacher Alexander Sender Schorr, author of *Tevu'at Shor*and *Simla Hadasha* mentions him often in his books, see section 10. He was teacher in Lwow, and because of the war with Sweden he moved to Brody. He became famous among the sages and leaders of the community as a holy man and great scholar. The book *Ma'a lot Hayochasin* relates that "Once a group of Jesuit seminary students who used to rob people spread through the Lwow streets and began a riot, stealing everything and beating all those who were in their way. While he was trying to escape, one of the robbers caught him and saw a golden earring on his ear (as was the custom with a young child). The robber caught the earring and tore it off his ear. The earring was unbroken, and when the robber looked at the ear he saw that it was whole as well. He was terrified and said to him: "you are a holy man, a man of god. Come with me and I'll hide you in my

house". Three days he hid him in his stables and supplied him with only dry bread. When the riots subsided, he went to the holy community of Brody and prayed the *Ne'ila* prayer. Next day he said that he was shown that "the people of Lwow were saved." He died on the 4th of the month of Iyar 5497 [5 May 1737].

5. The scholar Kabbalist our teacher Elazar Rokach, who was called also Margaliot from Krakow, son of the scholar Kabbalist our teacher Shmuel Shmelke Margaliot, ABD of the holy community of Elkish, son of the scholar Kabbalist our teacher Eliezer Margaliot ABD of the holy community of Lovmela (mentioned in the Responsa *Beit Efraim* section *Orach Chaiym* item 23 and section *Sha'arei Tshuva*, item 551), son of the scholar Kabbalist our teacher Menachem Mendel Margaliot Stengen, ABD of the holy community of Przemyslany, son of the scholar Kabbalist our teacher Shmuel Margaliot ABD of the holy community of Pozen (mentioned in the book *Vikuach Maiym Chaiym*), son of the scholar Kabbalist our teacher Moshe Margaliot, leader in the community of Prague, son of the scholar Kabbalist our teacher Yitzhak Aizik Margaliot ABD if the holy community of Nuerenberg, author of *Seder Gitin*, son of the scholar Kabbalist our teacher Moshe Marmonda of the leaders of Livorno; the name of his wife was Margala and their sons called themselves Margaliot in her name (see details in the book *Anaf Etz Avot*, item 202 and following and from 134 and following – about the lives of the scholars of that lineage, described at length). Among his descendants were the sages of the Kloiz of the famed Belz dynasty. The scholar Kabbalist our teacher Elazar Rokach was ABD of the holy community of Brody. In 5474 [1713/4] he wrote an approbation to the book *Zera Baruch*(*Zera Baruch*3, Frankfurt am Oder), in 5481 [1720/1] to the book *Ateret Zvi*on *Choshen Mishpat* and in 5491 [1730/1] to the book *Simla Chadasha* and *Tvuat Shcorr.* He was ABD in several communities in Poland before he was appointed ABD in Brody, and in 5468 [1707/8] he was ABD in Rakov, Lithuaia (as can be seen in his book *Arba'a Turei Even*, item 19). On 27 Elul 5495 [14 September 1735]) he was accepted as Rav of the Ashkenazi holy community in Amsterdam. In honor of his arrival they issued a silver memorial coin, on the obverse was his image and the inscription "Our teacher Rabbi Elazar son of our teacher Rabbi Shmuel ABD of the holy community of Brody" (in Amsterdam, he was called R'Elazar of Brody). On the reverse – "Was welcomed here on Wednesday 27 Elul 5495 for long and good days. Pray for the well-being of the rulers". R'Yakov Emden wrote about this coin in his book *She'ilat Ya'vetz* Part 1 item 170 (Altona 5509 [1749]) "It happened in our time that when the rabbi our teacher Elazar z"l of Brody was appointed as ABD of the holy community of Amsterdam, one person wanted to publicized the Rabbi's name by issuing a silver coin in his honor.

[Page 81]

When the coin was shown to me, I was taken aback and I wondered, and asked myself whether this was done according to the wish of the rabbi and with his approval, since he was known as a great Hassid in his generation. I looked at the coin and I saw the shape of his head and chest with his exact face. In my opinion this is totally and absolutely forbidden, whether he made it for himself or others, made it for him, particularly if they were Jewish. I knew with certainty (and said so) that the rabbi did not know and did not agree since God ensures that no injustice would happen to a righteous man. As I heard, the authorities ordered to conceal it so that "it would not be seen" (my friend and relative, the late R'Naftali Donner z"l, told me that he also has seen the coin). In 5496 [1735/6] in Amsterdam he wrote approbation to the book Zera Israel on the tractates Rosh Hashana and Megila by the scholar Kabbalist our teacher Yakov, author of Rosh Yosef, as well as to the books Reshit Chochma (Amsterdam 5497 [1736/7]) and Ohel Yaakov by our teacher Rabbi I. Sasporto and the book Tashbetz (Amsterdam printing), in 5499 [1738/9] on the books by Maimonides that were printed in Yesnitz and the Responsa book by Rabbi Elazar. In that period he was admitted as Nasi [head of the Sanhedrin] in Eretz Israel and on the 10th of the month of Sivan he left Amsterdam to go to the Holy Land. While passing through Trier, on 24 Sivan he wrote approbation to the book Beit Hillelon the Torah Portions, by Rabbi Hillel son of Rabbi Mordechai from Tisminetz. On Hol Hamoed [intermediate days] Sukkot 5501 [1741] he arrived in Tzefat (Safed), may it be built and renewed soon in our days Amen. When he realized that many of the respected people of Tzefat study the book Hemdat Hayamim attributed by some people to Nathan Ha'azati [a follower of the Massiah pretender – Shabtai Tzvi], he protested fiercely. As a consequence of the dispute, his days were shortened. He planned to go abroad, but before he could realize that he died in 5502 [1742] in Tzefat and was put there to eternal rest (according to the book Tevu'ot Ha'aretzit was on Hol Hamoed Sukkot, but according to the book She'erit Israelit was on Shabat Bereshit [the first Shabat after Sukkot]), although in his will he asked to be buried in Hebron. His books: Sefer Ma'ase Rokeach, a commentary on the Torah with an additional booklet about the Mishkan [Tabernacle] and commentaries on the Mishna; Turei Even in four volumes, which includes 24 responsa and new commentaries on some Tractates and on the RAMBAM [Maimonides]. Added are the teachings of his son in 5499 [1738/9] in Amsterdam and some commentaries by Rabbi Yehuda Leib, son of Rabbi Moshe mentioned above, ABD in the community of Zbarov, published by Rabbi Naftali Hirtz of Brody son of Rabbi Moshe (Lemberg 5549 [1788/9]). He left two sons: 1. The scholar Kabbalist Shalom, ABD Tiktin, who was the son-in-law of his uncle the scholar Kabbalist Yehoshua Horowitz, ABD Horodna (his mother, wife of R'Elazar, was the daughter of the scholar Kabbalist Shmelke HaLevi Horowiitz and the sister of R'Yehoshua). 2. The scholar Kabbalist Moshe ABD Zlotchov (his first wife was the daughter of our teacher Rabbi Naftali Margaliot of Brody and his second wife was the daughter of the Cacham Zvi). In his approbation to the book Birkat Yosef by Rabbi Moshe Teomim, father of the author of Pri Megadim (Zolkov 5507 [1746/7]) he signed: Moshe son of the scholar and Hassid rabbi of Eretz Israel, our teacher Elazar, lived in the communities of Zlotchov and surroundings. The scholar Kabbalist R'Elazar had a brother, a great scholar and a famous Tzadik by the name of R'Aharon Rokach, who was the father-in-law of the holy Tzadik R'Elimelech of Lizhansk. Rabbi Aharon had a son, a scholar and Tzadik who was ABD in the holy community of Bendin; the holy great scholar R'Yitzhak Aizik of Komarno z"l wrote in his book Atzei Eden that he served 30 years in Bendin and in his time there were no questions on unpleasant subjects, and there was never a fire in town, because he protected the town against such events.

[Page 82]

6. His mother was the sister of the scholar Rabbi Chaim Cohen Rappaport, ABD Lwow.
7. The scholar R' Leibush Nathansohn, father of the scholar R'Yosef Shaul, was one of his great admirers. It is told that the scholar R'Tzadok HaKohen said about him that the world could not grasp his greatness.
8. The father-in-law of the scholar Kabbalist R'Moshe (son of the scholar Kabbalist Zvi, ABD of the AHW [Altona, Hamburg, Wandsbek] communities), who was in his youth ABD of Tomashov and later resided in Brody. He died there in 5609 [1848/9] at the age of 84. His commentaries were printed in the booklet *Chut Hameshulash* as an appendix to the book *Mishnat Hassidim*.
9. He filled the place of his father-in-law and uncle the scholar our teacher Israel z"l, the ADMOR of Ruhatin.

Rabbi Moshe of Ostraha

10. [1] Probably refers to the subject of the amulets of R'Eyebeschutz.
11. [2] Publisher's introduction to the book *Darash Moshe* on the book of Psalms.
12. [3] In his introduction to the above.
13. [4] In the book *Torei Zahav*.

Rabbi Chaim Tzanser

14. [1] This is the origin of the name Tzans (beginning with Tz), and not in the days of Rabbi Chaim Halberstam z"l, as was claimed by one author.

On the approbation of the Kliva Divorce in 5528 [1767/8] the signature is Chaim of Tzans.

15. [2] The scholar R'Yakob'ka Landa, son of the scholar author of *Noda Biyhuda* writes about him in the Introduction to that book, saying that his father had a good friend, erudite in Kabbala.

16. [3] His editing notes on the four parts of the *Shulchan Aruch* have been printed by the Publishing House *El Hamekorot.* The notes were written on his own copy of the *Shulchan Aruch* and copied by the scholar E. Z. Margaliot, according to the testimony of the MAHARSHAK of Brody.

R' Naftali son of R'Levi

17. [1] I thought it was worth mentioning, that what Dr. Gelber wrote in his book "The History of the Jews of Brody" about the book Hatzoref according to the testimony of the teachers of the Perl School in Tarnopol – these teachers were known deliberate falsifiers, as was their rabbi Yosef Perl. To defame and insult the Hassidim and Kabbalists every means was justified. Their end, as was the end of the followers of R'Moses Mendelsohn, confirmed their beginning. When bringing a testimony by RAZA"M [Rabbi Efraim Zalman Margaliot] he states that it seems that he was "under the influence of outsiders". Therefore the author and his writings are valid. I wrote about that to Dr. Z. Rabinowitz.

18. [2] The approbation of the scholars R'Mendel Zolkover and R'Zvi Horowitz. In the approbation to the book Toldot Yosefit is written "These three are great rabbis, Hassidim Kabbalists, and Sages of the Great Kloiz of Brody.

[Page 83]

Rabbi Avraham Gershon Kitover

19. [1] Influenced by his brother–in–law the BESHT at the beginning of 5500 [1739/40], since his letter to the BESHT from Tzfat [Safed] is from 5502 [1741/2]. He was the founder of the BESHT Hassidism in Eretz Israel.

20. [2] However, as is known, he came to Eretz Israel only in 5507 [1746/7] and in 5508 [174/7/8] he wrote his famous letter to his brother–in–law the BESHT. According to this missive, he did not meet R'Chaim Atar z"l, the author of *Or Hachaiym.* There are some who doubt the trustworthiness of these letters.

Rabbi Yechezkel Landa

21. [1] He was of the dynasty of RASHI, and wrote "since I am a descendant of RASHI, I tried to resolve correctly his words.

22. [2] According to the "census" held by Rabbi Dr. Pargez of Leipzig, that was published by Prof. David Koifman.

23. [3] The scholar and Kabbalist R'Chaim Tzanzer of Brody asserted that "he had mystic visions".

24. [4] Publisher of *Tziun Lenefesh Chaia*, Tractate *Beitza*, Prague 5556 [1795/6].

Rabbi David Tevil

25. The son of the scholar Kabbalist Nathan Neta, who served as ABD in Brody from 5504 [1743/4] until 5516 1755/6. Under the pressure of the government he was forced to leave his post, because he convened a great assembly of rabbis and scholars in Brody and the assembly announced the excommunication of Yakov Frank and his followers.

Rabbi Noach Avraham Halevi Heller

26. [1] Son–in–law of the famous scholar, our teacher Nachman of Bolokhov, also called Nachman Lisivitcher ztz"l, and brother of the holy scholar our teacher Meshulam Feibish from Zabriza (and not Zbaraz as stated by Dr. Gelber).

27. [2] Son–in–law of the scholar our teacher Israel Moshe Yerushalmi ABD Tisminetz; was nicknamed Yerushalmi because he came to Tisminetz from a Sephardic family in Jerusalem.

28. [3] Son–in–law of the scholar our teacher author of *Yedei Moshe*, commentary on *Midrash Raba*.

29. [4] Son–in–law of the scholar our teacher Yechiel Luria, son of the famous scholar our teacher Shlomo, physician in the holy community of Lublin, grandson of the MAHARSHAL.

30. [5] In the words of his grandson, who published the book *Zerizuta DeAvraham*.

31. [6] Grandson of the holy R'Moshe of Ostraha [Ostrov]. The scholar R'Avraham Binyamin Kluger, RABD Brody, related that the holy scholar our teacher Rabbi Moshe Leib of Sassov once visited his town of birth Brody, and when he walked through the Lemberg Street he said that there was a pleasant fragrance in the air - probably a Tzadik was living in the neighborhood. He asked the people of Brody who accompanied him and they said that there was a God–fearing young man, a great learner and his name was R'Shmuel of Ostrov. They showed him his house, and when the rabbi entered his house, he ran toward the young man and checked his *Tzitzit*, to see whether it was made according to Law, then he said "This is the man who spread the fragrance."

[Page 84]

32. [7] Author of the book *Pri Etz Chaiym*(on the book *Etz Chaiym*) and the book *Divrei Moshe* on the Torah. He was father–in–law of the holy scholar our teacher Yitzhak of Radwil son of the holy scholar our teacher Yechiel Michel, the Maggid of Zlotchov.

33. [8] The members of the Heller family of the holy community of Kolomea, owners of the factory of *Talitot* [Prayer Shawls] were grandchildren of R'Meir mentioned above and perished in the Holocaust together with all townspeople. May God avenge their blood!

Rabbi Meshulam Igra

34. [1] The scholar Kabbalist our teacher Moshe Steinberg, may he live long and good years, ABD Brody, in his Introduction to the book Machaze Avraham, Part 2 by his grandfather the scholar ABD Brody.

35. [2] *Zikaron Larishonim*, Kolomea 1914,

36. [3] His grandson, my in-law and friend, the rabbinic scholar our teacher Rabbi Yeshayahu Halevi Ish-Horowitz, the grandson of the scholar R'Meshulam Horowitz ABD Stanislav, author of the book Bar Levai, son-in-law of the Torah scholar, the respected ancestor of our teacher Zvi Mandelsberg of Kuzmir, told me that he was the son-in-law of the scholar R'Meshulam Igra, and that the following fact was known in the family: When he was ABD in Pressburg, two persons came before him with a very complicated Din Torah [trial according to the Jewish Law]. He listened, then said that he will give the verdict in a month's time, since the required detailed study. The two persons were rich merchants, their business spread over all Galicia. It was a harsh winter, and on their way they stopped for the night in a small town by the name of Zablow. It was late, and only from one house light was seen. They knocked on the door and the local rabbi opened, our teacher Avraham, grandfather of the holy R'Yehuda Zvi of Stretin. He took them in, gave them supper and a place to sleep and he remained awake all night and studied . The two merchants thought that they should pay the rabbi for his hospitality, but since they could not humiliate him by offering money for the food and shelter, they decided to present to him the *Din-Torah* that was pending in the court of the Pressburg's rabbi and they would pay him for that, honorably. So they did. After they put the entire matter before him, he went to the other room and returned after a few minutes with a verdict that was acceptable to both of them. When they returned to R'Meshulam Igra in Pressburg and received his verdict, they were surprised to find that it was exactly the same as they had received from the Zablow rabbi who took only a few minutes to come up with the verdict. Seeing their surprise, R'Meshulam asked "Are you not satisfied with my verdict?" They replied: "Of course, it is a good verdict" and they told him about the rabbi of Zablow who issued the verdict in a very short time. Said R'Meshulam: This is beyond the ability of the regular human mind. Immediately he wrote to the Zablow rabbi saying that since he had some business in the vicinity of the town, he would like to visit him in his house. When he arrived, the rabbi of Zablow asked "What was my merit, that I am privileged to receive such a visit by you, the honorable scholar? R'Meshulam replied: "Last winter you issued a verdict to a complicated *Din Torah* in a very short time, which is very surprising, so I wanted to meet you, the honorable great scholar. The Zablow rabbi replied: "I shall tell you the truth: when I realized that the *Din-Torah* is a very complicated one and I could not find a solution, I went into the other room and prayed and wept, asking not to be

humiliated in front of my guests. Shortly the SHACH [Rabbi Shabtay Cohen, author of Siftei Kohen] appeared before me and enlightened my eyes." Hearing this, R'Meshulam got up and said: "If so, I have nothing more to do here. I thought that you knew how to study

[Page 85]

Rabbi Moshe Mintz

37. [1] Brother–un–law of the scholar Kabbalist R'Moshe Yehoshua Heshl Orenstein ABD Ruhatyin, author of Yam Hatalmud, brother of the scholar author of Yeshuot Yaakov, ABD Lwow.

38. [2] The scholar Kabbalist R'Yosef ABD Snyatin (mentioned in the approbation to the book *Ahavat Dodim*, Sunday 11 Tamuz 5552 [1 July, 1792], signed by Yosef of Zolkov ABD Snyatin) who happened to be in Brody during several days and resided in the house of his father–in–law, was among those who nullified the divorce, against the opinion of the great scholars of the time, as the *Noda Biyhuda*, Meshulam Igra (who was at the time ABD Tisminetz), Sender Margaliot ABD Satanov (uncle and teacher of the scholar E.Z. Margaliot of Brody), Meir Kristianpoller ABD Brody and others – all approved the divorce, as was related by R'Moshe Mintz.

[Page 86]

The Rabbis of Brody of the Past 150 Years

by Meir Wender

Translated by Moshe Kutten

It is almost an impossible task to write about Brody scholars. The city was the center of Torah and Judaism for hundreds of years, and the number of its prominent Torah scholars reached hundreds if not thousands. Not many of them immortalized their names through books that they have published, and details about a few others that have appeared in history books, are extremely sparse. The research of this topic would require much time and an enormous effort, and even then, the unknown would be greater than the known. The *Kloiz*[1] of Brody gained a glorified fame during the eighteenth century. Its people were considered the greatest Jewish scholars of the occult and the revealed[2]. The most prominent leaders were Rabbi Khayim Tzanzer, Rabbi Moshe from Ostrog and Rabbi Khayim Landau from Podkamin. Prominent leader and *Gaon*[3] Rabbi Ephraim-Zalman Margaliot (5521 [1760/1] - 5588 [1827/8]) also studied there, however most of his fame and activity in Brody were in the beginning of the 19thcentury, after the decline of the *Kloiz's* glory. N. B. Gelber[4] laid the foundation for the research about the history of the Brody community and accurately chronicled the scholars of the *Kloiz*; however, his book contains many inaccuracies, so there is room for a deeper and more detailed study. We will restrict ourselves to providing information about Brody's rabbis and *dayanim* [rabbinical judges[MK]] during the period of a hundred and fifty years prior to the Holocaust. However, even within this well-defined period, the hidden and the unknown are considerable.

Rabbis

Kristianpoler Family

Members of the Kristianpoler family, the grandfather, his son and his grandson, held the Brody rabbinate position for three generations, about one hundred years. The patriarch of the dynasty was Rabbi Meir who was born in 5500 [1739/40] to his father R' Tzvi-Hirsh, son of Moshe and grandson of Gavriel, the *A.B.D* [in Hebrew - Av Beit Din or the Head of the Rabbinical Court[MK]] of Bialikomin as well as the *R.A.B.D* [Rabbi and Head of the Rabbinical Court[MK]] in Lvov. Rabbi Meir studied in his own country under Rabbi Shmelke, who later moved to Nikolsburg. He did not join his friends, Rabbi Yosef Stern and Rabbi Mordekhai Mardosh Weinreb to study under Rabbi Yonatan Eybeschutz. Rabbi Meir married the daughter of Rabbi Shekhnish from Brody. He served in the rabbinate of the town of Kristianpol in Eastern Galitsia, and that is where his last name came from. From there he was called to serve in Galina's rabbinate, where he exchanged Halakha questions and answers with the author of "*Noda biYhudah*"[5] who praised him greatly. Rabbi Meir became the first rabbi of the district of Brody in 5545 [1785]. He passed away on 16 Nissan 5575 [April 26, 1815] and was eulogized sullenly by Rabbi Ephraim Zalman Margaliot and Rabbi Tzvi Hirsh Hurwitz, the son of Rabbi Pinkhas, who was the son of Rabbi Tzvi Halevi Hurwitz, author of the book "*Ha'Hafla'ah*"[6]. His teachings and approbations were scattered among various books. Out of all of his writings, only the book "*Yad Ha'Meir*" ["Meir's Memorial"[MK]], was published in Warsaw in the year 5634 [1870/1], containing innovations about the six orders of the *Mishnah*[7]. His son in-law was Rabbi Yehuda Leib, who was the son of the prominent leader R' Yisrael Khaim Daniel of the Wahl family from Iasi.

[Page 87]

His son, Rabbi Yekhiel-Mikhel Ben-ZionKristianpoler who was born in 5553 [1792/3], was not elected to inherit his father's position because of his young age, and the community elected Rabbi Aryeh-Leib

Teomim. Only in the year 5591 [1830/1], Rabbi Yekhiel-Mikhel was elected to serve as the Chief Rabbi of Brody. He served in that tenure for thirty-two years until his death on 9 [Sivan[MK]] 5623, [May 27, 1863]. His wife was Mrs. Khaya-Bluma, the daughter of Rabbi Aharon Padua, *A.B.D*of Brisk, Lithuania, the author of "*Minkhat A'haron*" and the grandson of the minister Rabbi Shaul Wahl. Rabbi Yekhiel Mikhel was one of the most prominent rabbis of his time due to his vast learning, pleasant manners and piety. With all of his religious roots, there was a trace of modernity reflected by his general education and the fact that he was fluent in German and French. This is how he also educated his three daughters, and therefore he was respected by the Poles, as well as by the Austrian officials and the intelligentsia. The Haredi's fought him, at times, and Rabbi Shlomo Kruger nicknamed him "*apikoros*"[8] due to his tolerance toward any person's state of mind. After his death, people from all circles of life mourned and eulogized him. Rabbi Yekhiel-Mikhel Hibner, Chief Rabbi of Nizhnov, wrote many praises about him, such as the fact that he was erudite and knew languages, came from a renowned family, was learnt, modest, benevolent and a man who sanctifies G-d's name among the gentiles. His daughter Sara-Akhsah was the wife of Rabbi Tzvi Hirsh Orenstein, the Rabbi of Lvov. His daughter Breindel married Nathan Riter Von Kalir son of R' Meir. He was the head of the chamber of commerce in Brody and Vienna and was secular, while she kept a Haredi way of life. His son, Rabbi Yisrael was a scholar in Brody. Rabbi Yekhiel's son, Rabbi Meir Kristianpoler, who was born in 5576 (1816), was elected to the Brody's rabbinate after him. He served in his role for twenty years from Shvat [January] 5626 [1866) until his death on 6 Elul 5646 [6 September] (1886). His grandson, Rabbi Alexander Kristianpoler, who was born in 5645 [1884], served as the Rabbi of Lintz in Austria, was deported to the Minsk Ghetto, and perished there in 5702 [1941/2].

Rabbi Arye Yehuda Leibush Te'omim

Rabbi Aryeh Yehuda Leib Te'omim came from a renowned family with lineage tracing back to the Ga'on Rabbi Yona Te'omim Frenkel, author of "Kikayon De'Yona"[9] as well as the renowned Rabbi Shaul Wahl and the Maharshal [10]. He married Mrs. Michal, the daughter of the leader R' Shmuel Bik, one of Brody's honorable people. She was the divorcee of Rabbi Meshulam Igra, who agreed with her father to arrange for her to remarry with a scholar. Indeed, Rabbi Aryeh Leib was known from his youth as a prodigy and was accepted as the Rabbi of the Liznesk community. He was there during the time of Rabbi Elimelekh and was his adversary since he objected to the Hassidic way of life. Rabbi Aryeh Yehuda was accepted to the Brody rabbinate in 5575 (1815) in place of Rabbi Meir Kristianpoler. He became very ill in 5587 (1827) and ceased to function. The heads of the community, accepted, without his knowledge, Rabbi Eliezer Landa to fill the position. However, both of them passed away during the cholera epidemic which spread during the summer of 5591 [1831]. Rabbi Eliezer Landa passed away after Rabbi Te'omim on Saturday 4 Elul [13 August]. Rabbi Teomim's published books were: "Gur Aryeh" ["Lion Cub"MK], "Ayelet A'havim" ["Doe of Loves"MK], and "Ye'elat Hakhen" ["Ibex of Grace"MK].

[Page 88]

Rabbi Elazar Landa

Rabbi Elazar Landa was born in 5538 [1877/8] to his father Rabbi Yisrael Landa son of the famous Rabbi Yekhezkel, the author of "*Noda BiYhuda*" [11] ["Known Among the Jews"MK]. He grew up in his stepfather's home – Rabbi Moshe Khasid, in Rufshitz and later resided in Lvov. He was accepted as the Rabbi of Brody in 5589 (1829), however, he passed away two years later, on 11 Tamuz 5691, from cholera. He was a brilliant scholar and excellent expounder. His Responsa were published in books such as "*Noda BiYhuda*", "*Mey Be'er*" ["Well Water"MK] and "*Zekher Yeshayahu*" ["Memory of Yeshayahu"MK] He became famous by his great book "Yad Hamelech" [literally – the King's Hand but it means "On a Grand Scale"MK] on the *Rambam*[11]. Three parts were printed in Lvov in 5626 [1865/6] and only part D and the rules appendix were left in manuscripts.

Rabbi Yitzkahk Khayut

Rabbi Yitzkhak was the son of the famous Ga'on Rabbi Hirsh Khayut. He was born in Zolkeva on 23 Elul 5602 [4 September 1842]. There are people who claimed that Rabbi Shalom Rokeach[12] of Beltz attended his *Brith* as a relative of the family. Other claimed that when Rabbi Rokeach visited Zholkeva and saw the baby in a crib, he told his father: "It is through this offspring, Yitzkhak, that you will be reckoned" [a phrase taken from Genesis 21:12[MK]], since he would be the one, out of all of his brothers, who would continue the rabbinate dynasty. He studied Torah zealously, from his youth, and excelled due to his sharp mind. At the age of thirteen, he was able to direct the "questions of the unlearned". In his youth, he studied with other students for eighteen hours a day. When his father was accepted to the rabbinate in Kalish, he went there with him. His father showed him the key for opening the treasures of the Torah and hid from him the keys for his other treasures. He was certified to teach by Rabbi Shlomo Kluger. In 5622 [1860/1] he married Mrs. Ethel-Mikhal, the granddaughter of Rabbi Akiva Eger, daughter of the Jewish leader R' Peretz Shapira from Podkamin, a descendant of the author of "*Megaleh Amukut*"[13] ["Discoverer of the Deeps"[MK]], who left twenty thousand guldens to establish a fund for charity institutions.

He was a merchant most of his life, and did not use the rabbinate as a profession to sustain himself by. He rejected three times the pleadings of the heads of Zholkeva's Jewish community, who asked to make him their leader. He kept a Yeshiva on his own account and taught Torah there every day. He edified many students, some of whom became prominent rabbis. He was a public servant, dealing with public needs, was in charge of the Torah schooling, a member of the "*Chovevei Zion*" ["Lovers of Zion"[14][MK]] movement and one of the founders of the "Organization of the Believers" in the city. He possessed noble attributes and was therefore well-liked by people from all circles in town. At his old days he finally acceded to the town people's pleads to accept the burden of the rabbinate position. He was elected with the majority of the votes, in the summer of 5654 [1894], over four other candidates, all of them from Brody: Rabbis Binyamin Kluger, Elazar Landa, Moshe

Reinhold and Nathan Levin. He fell suddenly sick seven years later. All the prayers for him, which lasted three whole days, did not help. He passed away on Wednesday, 24 Shvat, 5661 [13 February 1901]. Rabbis from all over Galicia came to his funeral and relayed praises about him. He left three sons and a daughter. From all of his written essays, only three books have been published: "*Siakh Yitzkhak*" ["Yitzkhak Discourse"MK] about the *Mishnah's* Tractate *Makot,* published in 5660 [1899/1900] in Podgorze [Near KrakowMK], as well as the Responsa book "*Siakh Yitzkhak*" ["Yitzkhak's Dialog"MK], Part A, published in 5670 [1909/10] in Brody. The array of people who presented questions was very diverse and included rabbis from neighboring countries: Russia, Romania, Hungary and Czechoslovakia. The Respona book was published by his student Rabbi Yisrael-Avraham Frenkel from Brody.

[Page 89]

Rabbi Avraham Menakhem Mendel Halevi Steinberg

He was born in Seret, Bukovina in the year 5607 [1846/7] to his father Rabbi Meir, son of R'Shmaia. He studied there with the *Dayan* Rabbi Ben-Tzion Landau. He was a famed Torah scholar from his early childhood, and used to amaze famed adult Torah greats. He was accepted to the rabbinate of Snyatin in 5639 [1878/9] after a fierce fight that took place in town around the election. The rabbi belonged to Sadigura-Chortkov Hassidim who obviously supported him. However, Vizhnitz Hasidim in town objected to him fiercely. When he realized, after several years, that the dispute was not dissipating, he wanted to move to the Zlotshev rabbinate, but he could not achieve that. Over time, people from all circles, who were charmed by his great personality and by his wide fame in the Torah world, reconciled. After the death of his friend "*Maharsham*" (Rabbi Shalom-Mordekhai Hakoehn Schvedron) of Berezhany, he became the stronghold for questions from people from all over, who asked for his opinion. He was accepted to Brody rabbinate in 5664 (1904), thanks to the votes by the Hassidim and their supporters, however, the progressives, due to their influence with the mayor, managed to postpone the formal nomination for several years.

He lived in Brody for six years until World War I broke and he had to escape to Vienna, where he rose above all as one of the most important rabbis among the rabbis in exile. After the war, he returned to Brody and fulfilled the duties of his rabbinical role, as before, until he passed away in 1 Sivan, 5688, [20 May 1928]. Before he went on his exile, he deposited in the bank 29 essays in his handwriting. People succeeded to release the write-ups from Petersburg, only after a tremendous effort. Most of his essays, such as the great commentary about the "*Sefer Yereim*"[15] [The Book of God-Fearing's"MK] written as appendix to an education book, as well as other assays were lost in 5702 [1941/2]. Only three volumes survived from Ghetto Lodz and his grandchildren handled their publishing. During his life the following books were published: "*Kdusha Shvi'it*" ["The Seventh Sanctity"MK] in 5669 [1908/9] and the Responsa book "*Makhaze Avraham*" ["The Vision of Abraham"MK], volume A, in Brody in 5687 [1926/7]. Volume B of the book was published in New York in 5724 [1963/64]. A third volume is also scheduled to be published [Volume C was eventually published in New York in 1988MK]. His sons were all Torah leaders in their own right and occupied important rabbinical positions in several communities in Israel.

Moshe Steinberg, his grandson, inherited his position. He was the son of Rabbi Shmaia A.B.D of Premishlian. He served as the last Rabbi of Brody's Jewish community before its annihilation. He married Mrs. Rakhel, the daughter of Rabbi Yaakov Frenkel-Teomim, the Rabbi of Podgozha. During the German conquest, they were hidden by a Ukrainian farmer in bunkers and hideouts, with a great risk, until the day of the liberation. He was the only Rabbi from before the war who survived in Poland, and was nominated to be the Rabbi of Krakow until 5707 [1947]. He then moved to Prague, and in the beginning of 5708 [1948] he immigrated to the US, where he served as the A.B.D of the Rabbinate Union, the Rabbi of the synagogue "Makhze Avraham" on Broadway, New York, and the rabbi of West Manhattan. He was a remarkable learner from the old generation, and a sermon giver by a divine grace. He prepared his book of answers for publication, which is already in binding, however, he was not fortunate to see the book published. Rabbi Moshe Steinberg passed away on 23 Tammuz, 5747 [20 July 1987].

Dayanim

The first *Dayan* known to us during the period covered here is the rabbi Avraham Hilfor. The Rabbi was listed as subscriber of the book "*Noam Megadim*" in 5564 (1803/4) and signed with the title of *Dometz* [in Hebrew – acronym of "Dayan and Teacher of Righteousness"[16]] in Brody. *[Page 90]*

Rabbi Aryeh-Yehuda Leib author of "Lev Aryeh" ["The Heart of a Lion"MK]

He was born in Brody in the year 5519 [1758/9] as the only son to his mother Zlata and his father Akiva Halevi, the brother of Rabbi Reuven, the rabbi of Bialystok. He was related to the family of the author of "*Turei Zahav*"[17] ["Rows of Gold"MK]. He was orphaned at a very young age and grew up at the home of his uncle, the brother of his mother, Yaakov Segal. In 5538 (1778) he married the daughter of his uncle – Khana-Henia, and after she passed away in 5571 [1810/11] he remarried Ms. Khaya, the daughter of Rabbi Khayim Ettinger of Brody. He studied diligently under the city scholars, and was nominated as a Rabbi and Teacher of Righteousness in 5546 [1785/6]. In the year 5564 [1803/4] he was called to serve as the head of the Yeshiva of Podhaitza, and nine years later came back to Brody to serve as the *A.B.D*and *Maggid* [Jewish preacherMK]. Five years later, he fell sick, and asked the city's honorable people to take care of his wife and children. Rabbi Aryeh-Yehuda Leib passed away on 29 Shvat 5578 [February 5, 1818]. His two-volume book "*Lev Aryeh*" acquired a substantial fame. The book was reprinted many times. Rabbi Shaul Natansohn, attached the proofreading notes that he wrote during his youth on the book's pages. With the author's agreement, he added many warm words about the author's talent. He indicated that the author had a straight way in teaching, the way he was taught by his teachers - the students of Rabbi Yonatan Eybeschutz. He stated that "his teachings of the holy word, were like a spread out dress". His last essays were left, in a written form, with his grandson, Rabbi Ya'akov Levi, "*the Roeh*[the SeerMK] of the Brody community" – the meaning of the title is unfamiliar to me. He published his grandfather's book, in Brody, in 5667 [1905/6], under the name of "*Nakhalei Dvash*" ["Brooks of Honey"MK], about festivals and holidays. Rabbi Steinberg added, with the author's approval, that all of his writings were "based on vast knowledge and consultation". I provided additional details about his history in my book "*Meorei Galicia*" [Galicia's LuminariesMK], Part A, pp 289-291.

Rabbi Shlomo Kluger

The light of Rabbi Shlomo Kluger (acronym Maharshakin Hebrew) shone in the skies of Brody, for about fifty years, and from there, his brilliance glowed throughout the entire Jewish diaspora. He was born in 5546 (1786) in Komarov, Poland to his father, A.B.D Rabbi Yehuda Aharon, a descendant of the Maharal [the acronym is in Hebrew for Rabbi Yehuda Loew Ben Betzalel of PragueMK] and the Maharam [the acronym is in Hebrew for Rabbi Meir Ben Barukh of RothenburgMK] and his mother Gitel, daughter of Rabbi Yosef, A.B.D of Biala, and granddaughter of Rabbi Yaakov, A.B.D of Lutsk, and author of "Kokhvei Yaakov" ["Stars of Yaakov"MK]. He studied under Rabbi Hochgelerenter and Rabbi Yaakov Krantz who was then a Maggidin Zamoshtch. He married Ms. Libah Malia, the daughter of the Jewish leader R' Khayim Weinreb, from Rawa-Ruska and went to study there under his famous Geonim brothers-in-law. His first rabbinate role was in the town of Kulikov, and then from 5575 (1815) as the rabbi in Josefov. In 5580 [1819/20] he was called to serve as a Dometz, Rabbi, A.B.D and a Maggid in the "great Jewish City" of Brody. Rabbi Ephraim Margaliot admired him immensely and spent any free time with him. He stood on guard for any matters related to religion in the city, established proper regulations and taught Torah to students from all layers of the public, because of his humble ways, and hearty attitude towards every person. In matters related to G-d, he stood his ground very firmly, without fear from anybody, and did not shun away from stormy confrontations or piercing arguments with other Geonim. Such an argument erupted about the affairs of the married women from Zhitomyr, the slaughterer from Berdichev, the machine-produced matzah and others. In 5603 (1843) he quarreled with the community leadership concerning the matter of transporting the dead by carts. He won the argument, but asked to be transferred to another location. He accepted Brizhan community's offer to relocate there. However, after his first sermon there, he caught cold, fell sick with the typhus and had to lie down in his bed for many weeks. He saw in it a sign that he must go back to Brody, however, in the meantime, Rabbi Hamburger was nominated to replace him there. Therefore, he just resided in Brody as a private person and was sustained by his admirers, especially the Jewish leader R' Yosef Natansohn. While in Brody, he had a big influence on the community life, and won the trust of the greatest Jewish leaders of his generation. He acquired fame as the greatest teacher of his time, and people from near and far places turned to him for his judgment. He passed away on Wednesday, 1 Tammuz 5629 [10 June 1869]. People from many Jewish settlements mourned and eulogized him.

[Page 91]

His elder son, R' Khayim-Yehuda was the grandfather of Rabbi Avraham Itingah from Dukla. His second son was Rabbi Avraham Binyamin. His oldest daughter Khana married R' Shlomo-Tzvi Halbreich, the head of the community in Sokolovka. Rabbi Shlomo was like a fertile spring - sprouting ideas. Despite being a fast writer, he did not manage to put all of his bountiful thoughts in writing. People said that he authored 345 essays, the same number of essays as the numeric value, in *Gimatria*, of his name – Shlomo, as well as more than 8000 answers. Only thirty of his books, about different subjects of the Torah, were published. Many of his writings are still waiting for somebody to redeem and publish them. Volumes of his essays survived and arrived at the archives of the National Library in Jerusalem. He used to count them by assigning a number to each. The total reached about 160 before he passed away.

Rabbi Kluger's son – Rabbi Avraham Binyamin, who was born in 5601 [1840/1}, served as his right hand man in all halakha matters and public needs. He was not elected to serve in a rabbinate role in Brody and resided there as a private person making a living on his own. He was elected for the rabbinate in Zolkiew, but the election was not realized and he remained in Brody. He had an extensive correspondence with rabbis and authors, and his innovations were imbedded in many books. In addition to all of his innovations, which remained as manuscripts, he published several books including: "Responsa *Sharei Binyamin*" Respona Binyamin's Gates[MK]] "*Ottot Lemoadim*" ["Signs of Holidays"[MK]] and more. When World War I broke, he exiled to Vienna. He passed away, during the war, in 29 Kheshvan, 5676 [November 6, 1915]. He had three children with his wife Pesil - Rabbi Yehuda Aharon, the author of the book "*Toldot Shlomo*" ["The History of Shlomo"[MK]], about his grandfather, R' Sholomo, a wealthy man in Vienna who was childless, and Sara-Leah, the wife of the Jewish leader R' Aharon-Tzvi Weishaus from Stanislav.

Rabbi Yaakov Aryeh Hamburger

He was A.B.D in Zborov, Pshevarsk, Yas, and Rovne, and at the end of his life, the Chief Rabbi, A.B.D, Teacher of Righteousness and Maggid in Brody. This is where, in 5603 (1843), he worked on the book "Torat haRamah "The Teaching of the Ramah [the acronym in Hebrew for Rabbi Meir Abulafia[MK]] and in 5612 (1852), the book "Shoresh Me'Yaakov Hasheni" ["Roots of the Second Yaakov"[MK]].

Rabbi Tzvi-Hirsh Hurvitz

He was the son of Rabbi Yaakov-Yukl from Bolekhov. He studied under his uncle, Rabbi Naftali of Rufshits, the brother of his father. At the age of 18, he married the daughter of the Jewish leader, R' Aleksander-Sender Segal Landa of Brody. He seved as a *Dometz* and *A.B.D* in city of Kashevitz for decades. He passed away on 11 Kheshvan, 5640 [28 October], (1879) and was buried in the nearby town of Zhurovna. He left, in his writings, many innovations but only his will was published: "*Shem Derekh*" ["The Name of the Road"[MK]] 5697 (1937).

[Page 92]

His son, who was born in 5593 (1833), was also a *Dometz*in Brody, under the *Maharshak* [Rabbi Shlomo Kluger, see above[MK]]. Some people claim that he was the son-in-law of R' Aleksander Sender Landa, and not his father. He passed away in Stryj on 22 Elul 5658 [September 9], (1898) according to his son R' Eliyahu from Siget.

Rabbi Yaakov Avigdor

He is a descendant of Rabbi Avigdor Kara of Prague, after whom the family is named. The origin of the family is Istanbul. When they immigrated to Odessa in 5570 (1810) they continued to sign their name with the Hebrew acronym S"T[18] like the Sephardic Jews. The elder daughter, Kheina, married the Jewish leader Osterzetzer and part of the family was named as such. Her brother, Yaakov married her daughter and was her dependent. Rabbi Yaakov moved to Brody in the year 5590 (1829/30) and resided in Brody while serving as the Rabbi of the nearby town of Podkamin. He was named after the town later on. He studied together with Rabbi Shlomo Kluger, and published his first books with indices and editing notes. The Maharshak [Rabbi Shmuel Kluger[MK]] appreciated his knowledge and personality and recommended him as his replacement. He preferred him to his own son – Rabbi Binyamin, and the heads of the community fulfilled his wishes and nominated Rabbi Yaakov as the Rabbi and A.B.D in the city. Many students flocked to town to learn from him and they would remember his radiant image to the days of their old age. He passed away on 27 Nissan 5645 [12 April], (1885) and left a penniless widow and orphans. His book about the six orders of the Mishnah, "Khelek Yaakov" ["Yaakov's Share"[MK]] was never published. A family of rabbis descended from him. His son, Rabbi Avraham Iisaskhar-Ber, A.B.D of Trava-Wloska was the father of Rabbi Yaakov, A.B.Dof Drohobitch and Mexico and Rabbi David, A.B.D of Andrikhov. His second son, Rabbi Shalom was known as one of Brody's sages during the period before First World War. I wrote about him broadly in the beginning of the first volume of my book - "The Encyclopedia of Khakhmei Galicia" ["The Encyclopedia of Galicia's Sages"[MK]].

Rabbi Khayim Yehuda Leib Litvin-Sosnitzer

He was born in 5600 (1839/40), in Bobruisk, to his father R' Yisrael. He was one of the principal avrekhim [Torah Students] who gathered

around the author of "Tzemakh Tzedek" ["The Plant of Justice"MK] from Lubavitch[19]. At the age of fourteen, he married the daughter of the Jewish leader Aba Krasik of Sosnitza in Tsernigov province and was his dependent. This is why he was named Sosnitzer after his location, although his surname was Litvin. When his father-in-law lost his wealth, he moved to Minsk. He fell sick there and went to Germany, Hungary and Galicia to seek a cure. Rabbi Yosef Natansohn from Lvov brought him close to him as he recognized his vast knowledge of the Halakha. Rabbi Natansohn recommended him as the replacement for Rabbi Sholomo Kluger. He served in Brody for seventeen years and did not discriminate against anybody. Due to some family tragedies he took, once again, the wanderer's stick. His wife passed away and he took the daughter of Rabbi Elazar Moshe, A.B.D of Pinsk, for his second wife. His son - the promising prodigy, Rabbi Shimon, the son-in-law of Leibush Hurvitz and *A.B.D* in Stryj, passed away not long after his mother. In the year 5646 (1886) Rabbi Litvin-Sosnitzer was accepted to the rabbinate of Smorgon in the province of Vilna and he served there for seventeen years as well. He passed away on 11 Nissan, 5663 [April 8, 1903]. Out of all of his writings, only the two-volume Responsa "*Sha'arei De'ah*" ["The Gates of Knowledge"MK] was published in 5644 [883/4], in Lemberg-Pshemishl. Additional details about him can be found in the "Encyclopedia of Galicia Sages", Volume 3, pp 464-470.
[Page 93]

Rabbi Yisrael Halevi

He was the grandson of Rabbi Aryeh Leibush, the author of "Lev Aryeh" [Lion's Heart"MK]. He served as a Dometzin Brody at least from the year 5623 (1863). He was the brother-in-law of R' Yosef Elkana, the son of the MaggidRabbi Yosef Moshe of Zlozitz. He published the book of his grandfather "Be'er Mayim" ["Water Well"MK] and wrote an introduction to the book. It is logical to assume that his surname was actually Levi. He was a relative of Rabbi Yaakov "Ha'Roeh" ["The Seer"MK] of Brody community.

Rabbi Menakhem Mendel Schor

He was a Dometzin Brody since 5646 (1886) after the death of Rabbi Yekhiel-Mikhel BenTzion Kristianpoler, while the community did not select a new Rabbi. Perhaps he was Rabbi Manli the Dometzregistered in the Book "Khomer Ba'Kodesh", 5636 [1875/6], together with his son-in-law Rabbi Yosef of Kloiz Sterlisk.

Rabbi Yitzkhak Aizik Schoenfeld

He was a Dayan in Brody after Rabbi Yitzkhak Khayut. He is the author of the books "Ha'Tmuna" ["The Picture"[MK]], published in Lemberg in 5652 [1891/2] and "Imrot Tehorot" ["Pure Phrases"[MK]], 5660 [1899/90]. He passed away at the age of 97 and served as a religious judge even on his last day. His son, Rabbi David-Tzvi, was a Rabbi in Bucharest.

Rabbi Bonim'l

Served as a Dayan in Brody. Dov Sadan recalled about him "that he was like a column that does not move when he prayed, as if there was no such thing as the praying like the Hasidim in this world..." (Dov Sadan: "Mi'mekhoz Ha'Yaldut" [From a Childhood Region[MK]] page 311.
[Page 94]

Rabbi Shlomo Yaakov Kuten

He was born in 5633 [1872/3] to his father Yosef Aharon, the Rabbi of Leshniov. On his mother's side he was related to Rabbi Pinkhas Kurita, Rabbi Gedalia of Linitz, Rabbi Zusha from Anipoli and Rabbi Zeev Volf of Chorny, Ostrov. He married the daughter of Rabbi Monish Halprin, Slaughterer and Kosher Inspector in Brody and edited the book "*Menkahem Meshiv Nefesh*" ["Menakhem the Invigorator"[MK]] of his father-in-law and incorporated his innovations in them. His father passed away in 5653 (1893) when Rabbi Shlomo was twenty years old and he replaced his father as the Rabbi of Leshniov. After the First World War he was elected as the Rabbi and *A.B.D* of Brody. During the last few years before the Holocaust, he moved to become the Rabbi of Vladimiretz, and most likely perished there as a martyr.

Rabbi Yehuda Zundel BABAD[20]

He was born around 5630 (1870) to his father Rabbi Shalom Yaakov son of Avraham, A.B.D in Busk, son of Rabbi Yaakov A.B.Dof Busk and Radzikhov, son of Natan, A.B.D of Yevrov and Busk, brother of Rabbi Yehoshua Heschel, A.B.D of Tarnopol. Rabbi Yehuda served in the rabbinate of Leshniov and Shtervitz. A few years before the break of the Second World War, he was called to serve as the Chief Rabbi and the A.B.D of Brody. The Nazis cut off the thread of his life and he died as a martyr.

Rabbi Yosef Popresh

He was born in Brody to his father, R' Yaakov, one of the community's honorable people, who was the son of Reuven, son of Rabbi Yitzkhak Aizik "*Hagado*l" ["The Great One"MK], who was, on his father's side, the grandson of Rabbi Natan Shapira, the author of "*Megaleh Amukut*" ["Discoverer of the Deep"MK], and on his mother's side, the grandson of the Mekubal[21] Rabbi Meir Hakohen Papirsh. Rabbi Shalom of Belz and Rabbi Yisrael from Ruzhin attested about Rabbi Yosef that he would not take even a walk of more than four cubits without fearing of G-d. His son R' Zeev Wolf moved to Przemysl and gained fame among the Hasidim of the city. R' Zeev Volf was an editor in a printing house and himself an author of two books, by the name of "*Zeved Tov*" ["Good Bestowal"MK]. He died at the age of 73 at the end of the month Shevat 5660 (1900).

Rabbi Yosef was called Poper-BABAD since his mother Hinda was the daughter of the famous *Gaon*Rabbi Yosef BABAD, the rabbi of Tarnopol and the author of the book "*Minkhat Khinukh*" [A Commentary on *Sefer Ha'Khinukh*MK[22]]. He was a wealthy scholar and supported himself through his many assets. When he traveled to Belz for Sabbath, the Rabbi of Belz[23] spent time with him in seclusion and stated later that the youth enlightened him about the *halakha*. Like his ancestors, he served as the president for the fund for the poor of Eretz Yisrael, and contributed much of his own money to charities for the poor, while his daughters baked *khala's* for them. After the death of Rabbi Steinberg in 5688 (1927/8) he presented his candidacy against Rabbi Steinberg's grandson - Rabbi Moshe Steinberg. Since the votes for them were spilt, they casted a lot and he won the rabbinate. However, the authorities invalidated the election under the influence of his opponent's supporters and only in 5694 (1933/4) he was nominated as *A.B.D* alongside with Chief Rabbi Steinberg. He passed away at the end of the summer of 5699 (1939). Three years later, on 8 Tishrei 5702 [29 September 1941], a big massacre took place in Brody, when his wife and six children perished. His wife was the daughter of R' Yisrael Elazar Halevi Kaminer, the brother in law of the Rabbi of Gur (Gora) and his wife Miriam, daughter of R' Yosef Halevi Natanson from Brody. Following his grandfather's book "*Minkhat Khinukh*", he called his books about the Torah commandments "*Minkha Khadasha*" ["New Commentary"[MK]]. Two volumes out of his overall book "*Yabi'a Omer*" [Expressing Views"[MK]] were published during the period between 5694 [1933/4] - 5697 [1937/8]. The third volume was in the process of being printed when the war broke and was lost, like the rest of his writings. His family members republished the two volumes in photo-print in 5728 [1967/8] in Brooklyn, US.

[Page 95]

I did not include **Rabbi Khayim David Monzonin** the list. I wrote about the Monzon Admorim[24] in the third volume of the "Encyclopedia of Galicia Sages" pages 746-750. We also need to mention **Rabbi Rubin** and his wife Eidel nee Belz who was an Admoron her own, whom Prof. Sadan wrote about.

Translator's Notes

1. *Kloiz*– Jewish communal house of learning, praying and gathering.

2. The Jewish Hassidic movement sees reality as having two layers, hidden and revealed. The revealed is the reality based on the traditional Torah and Talmud while the hidden is the mystical interpretation of the Bible.

3. "*Gaon*" was the formal title of the heads of the academies of Sura and Pumbedita in the diaspora of Babylonia. The *geonim* were recognized by the Jews as the highest authority of instruction. It eventually became an honorific title for any rabbi or a scholar who had a great knowledge of Torah.

4. Nathan-Michael Gelber: "*Toldot Yehudei Brody*" (The History of the Jews of Brody) 1548 -1943, Jerusalem, 1955.

5. Rabbi Ezekiel Landa, also known as "*Noda BiYhudah*" [Known among the Jews"] after the title of his major work. *Noda BiYhuda* is a reference to phrase appearing in Psalms 76:2 and also a tribute to his father, whose name was Yehuda (Judah). He was born in Opatow, a small town in Poland, to a wealthy and learned father and became the Chief Rabbi of Prague at a very young age.

6. "Ha'Hafla'ah" ("The Amazing") - Hurvitz's chief work, is an essay about the Mishnah's tractate Ketubot, with an appendix, "Kuntres Aharon." ("Aharon's Booklet"). The second part contains an essay about tractate Kiddushin, also with an appendix that appeared under the title "Sefer Ha'Makneh", "(The Book of the Camp").

7. The Mishnah (from the Hebrew word, which means "study by repetition") was the first major written work of the Jewish oral traditions known as the "Oral Torah". It is also the first major work of rabbinic literature. The rabbis who contributed to the Mishnah were known as the *Tannaim*, of whom approximately 120 are known. The period during which the Mishnah was assembled spanned about 130 years, in the first and second centuries CE. The Mishnah consists of six orders each containing 7–12 tractates. Rabbinic commentaries on the Mishnah from the next four centuries, done in the Land of Israel and in Babylonia, were eventually redacted and compiled as well. In themselves, they are known as *Gemara*. The books, which set out the Mishnah in its original structure, together with the associated *Gemara*, are known as *Talmud*. Two *Talmuds* were compiled, the Babylonian

Talmud (to which the term "*Talmud*" normally refers to) and the Jerusalem *Talmud*. Unlike the Hebrew Mishnah, the *Gemara* is written primarily in Aramaic (from Wikipedia).

8. *Apikoros*- one who negates the rabbinic tradition.

9. Joshua Feivel Te'omim (son of Rabbi Jonah Teomim, who wrote the "*Kikayon De-Yonah*" (Kikayon is a name of a tree. The surname Te'omim means twins in Hebrew).
10. Rabbi Shlomo Luria (his acronym in Hebrew is *Maharshal*) was one of the most prominent Halakha jurists and interpreters of the Talmud in the 16th century.

11. *Rambam*– acronym in Hebrew for Rabbi Moshe Ben Maimon, one of the most prolific and influential Torah scholars of the Middle-Ages in Spain.

12. Rabbi Shalom Rokeakh from Beltz, also known as "*Sar Shalom*" ("Prince of Peace" - "Isaiah 9:6) was the founder of the most prominent Hasidic dynasty - Beltz Hasidic dynasty.

13. Nathan Note Shapira (1585- 1863) – Author of "Megaleh Amukot" (Discoverer of the Deeps") was a prominent Polish rabbi and a Kabbalist.

14. *"Ohavey Tzion"*– ("Lovers of Zion") – a pre Zionism movement which aimed to build *Eretz Yisrael*.

15. "*Sefer Yere'im*"– authored by Rabbi Eliezer son of Shmuel from Metz (1140-1248), in which additions to some of the *Mishna* tractates are detailed.

16. *Dometz*– an acronym in Hebrew which means *Dayan*and Teacher of Righteousness – describes the rabbi who deals with halachic questions brought before him. The term was first mentioned in some of the Dead Sea Scrolls to denote the person who is the leader being the most knowledgeable in the Torah. In the Hassidic communities the *Dometz* is the teacher responsible for all halakhic rulings (as opposed to the chief rabbi, who is responsible for managing the spiritual affairs of the community).

17. David Halevi Segal (1586 – 1667) – the author of: "*Turei Zahav*" (a significant commentary on *Shulkhan Arukh* [literally "Set Table"] which is the most widely consulted work of Jewish law) was as one of the greatest Polish rabbinical authority of his time.

18. Many of the descendants of Sephardic Jews sign their name with the Hebrew acronym of the words "Pure Sephardic" to emphasize the fact that they were descendants of those who did not have to behave as "*anusim*" and remained openly in their Judaism.

19. Rabbi Menachem Mendel Schneerson of Lubavitch (1789-1866), the author of "*Tzemakh Tzedek*" ("The Plant of Justice") was the third *Rebbe* of the Hasidic movement of Khabad.

20. BABAD – a prominent families of Rabbis in Galicia, the name BABAD came from an acronym in Hebrew which means the son of *A.B.D.*

21. Mekubal - a scholar of Kabbalah.

22. *Sefer Hakhinuch*– literally means the Book of Education, was a book published anonymously in 13th century's Spain, which methodically discusses the 613 commandments of the Torah, their biblical source, and philosophical underpinnings. "*Minkhat Khinuch*" serves as a legal commentary through the perspective of the *Talmud* and other sources from the 11-15 centuries.

23. The Belzer Rabbi was the head of the Belzer Hasidic dynasty (also known as *The Rebbe*). At the time of Rabbi Yosef Poprish, the Belzer *Rabbe* was Rabbi Yissachar Dov Rokeach (1894–1926) the grandson of the founder of the dynasty, Rabbi Shalom Rockeah (Also known as "*Sar Shalom*" (which literally means the Minister of Peace).

24. Admor– acronym in Hebrew for the words "Our Master", Teacher and Rabbi a title reserved for a head of a Hasidic family or sect.

[Page 96]

The Brody Singers

by Yosef Parvari (Leiner)

Translated by Yocheved Klausner

The great Folk Poet Itzik Manger said:

The birds are singing for the fields,
The crickets – for the corn,
For the Jews we are the singers –
The singers of the town of Brody.

It can be said that the last century was "the Golden Age" of our town Brody. It was expressed by the fact that several cultural trends developed simultaneously – the enlightenment movement, the revival of the Hebrew language and the Yiddish folk music. The beginning of this music constituted also the pioneer steps of the Yiddish theater. Many of the "Brody Singers," who performed their shows in wine–cellars and restaurants, became actors of Goldfaden's theater.

The founder of the Brody Singers was Berl Margaliot (born in 1815 in Podkamin). He wrote the lyrics and composed the music of many songs, and toured with his band through Galicia, Poland and Rumania. Among the local singers we know about Yakov Dubianski: after his release from the Austrian army in Vienna he organized, together with his friend Berl a band, who first played in "The Red Tavern" which belonged to Berl Stock (grandfather of Dov Sadan) and then in Stari [Old] Brody and in Pinkus' Restaurant, where merchants, agents and clerks would gather to spend a few hours on a glass of wine. Among them were the cantor Efraim Broder who would sing and dance Hassidic dances; Moshe Teich, an actor in Goldfaden's theater; Moshe Weintraub, a jester who joined "The Brody Singers;" R'Naftali Gramenzuger (rhymester, versifier); the jester Yosef Baumhol, who was known as "Yosl Broder";

Yosl Zeshof the *Melamed*; and Alter Kleitnik, who has written many songs for the Brody Singers.

The songs deal mostly with public and social matters, and also "*Amcha*" [simple folk] of all levels. They are joyful and full of jest and good humor, but also mixed with sadness, pain and sorrow, as was life itself in those years. They are a treasure of Jewish folklore, which has not been fully researched yet and was not given the appreciation it deserves.

[Page 97]

Below are three of these poems–songs:

Rest and Joy
[Menucha ve'simcha– from a Shabbat song]

By Shalom Podzamtche

1. God Himself has given us
– To sweeten our lives –
A present, very beautiful:
The good and holy Sabbath.
It gives us rest
And brings us joy,
O, rest, O, joy
Light shall shine for all the Jews!

2. The beautiful times have gone,
Gone far, far away,
The Jew is eternally wandering
But always keeps the Holy
Sabbath.
No rest for him, no joy...
O, rest, O, joy
Light shall shine for all the Jews!

3. Joshua His messenger
With his strong hand
Has taken us to our land.
At home we became a nation,
So there was rest

And there was joy
O, rest, O, joy
Light shall shine for all the Jews!

4. Brothers, believe and hope
Our troubles will end indeed!
Exile will not last forever.
We shall not lose our hope
That rest shall come again
And joy shall come again.
O, rest, O, joy
Light shall shine for all the Jews!

[Page 98]

B. A Jewish Melody

Presented by Yosl Glantz (Pitche), the oldest of the Brody Singers, who lived in Lwow and perished in the ghetto at the age of 85.

1. The Jewish melody
Shines in my heart,
As if a ray of sun
Is bursting from a heavy cloud.
The world is your altar
Where you can always pray
And be the messenger of your people.

2. Through days and nights
On the long road –
Who is wandering
From place to place,
Cold and hungry?
This is the Brody Singer
Who carries with him
All his possessions.
The road is dark and black,
And when he is tired

He sings a song
And feels relieved.

C. The voice of mirth and the voice of gladness [Jeremiah 7:34],
the voice of rejoicing in the tents of the righteous [Psalms 118:15],
the honest and the innocent – may they all be blessed by God,
and Mazel–Tov from the soup–kitchen.

"Open your soul to the hungry, and satisfy the afflicted soul" [Isaiah 58:10]

If a man is blessed by God,
He shall hear the cry of despair of the poor.
His heart and his soul shall hasten to aid his brothers,
Blessed with a good eye he shall add gifts.
Those who are generous of heart shall give with joy,
And shall dedicate their wealth to the poor and needy.

Born to be father to the poor and brother to the troubled,
I founded, from the donations of the charitable,
The "Bread for the Hungry" Association.
Remember me when you are happy and help me,

[Page 99]

Come to me, your righteousness and generosity shall support me,
You are planting a seed that will bear fruit for the poor.
Prepare food, and bring it to my treasure–trove,
Come to the aid of your brethren, make their heart happy,
Help them with a meal and they shall bless you!
A sound of rejoicing they shall together create
Their heart shall thank God and you shall be blessed.

For one silver coin that took their hunger away
  they shall remember you.
Do it for them and live, and they shall pray for
  you,
To bring blessings to you homes.

"The Soup-Kitchen for the People" in the city of Brody.

[Page 100]

The Brody Singers and their Inheritance

by Dov Sadan
From Bimah II (9-10), 1961-1962, pp. 27-33

Translated by Moshe Kutten and Sara Mages

Researchers of the history of the Jewish theater wrote various reference texts about it, and if to place the difference from end to end, here before us are two outstanding examples. Hence, a rather known book, and it is the book of Yitzhak Schiper "*The history of the Jewish Theater and Drama*" with its two volumes; and hence, a book, that is hardly known, and it is the book of Noach Prylucki "*Why the Jewish theater emerged so late.*" The first - his knowledge is extensive and he wove in everything that he accumulated on the subject that is clearly dear to his heart. He unified a long lineage, and even though its links are scattered and even set apart, as required by the fate of an exiled and wandering nation, it does portrait a picture of a prolonged, or prolonged-like, reality. The last, his writing indicates that he had changed his earlier opinion, reduced his review, and values the broad lineage adopted by his predecessor, which was previously his own, with the assumption that its image is realistic. It is obvious, that this disagreement between the adjudicators requires an examination on all sides, and as expected, it can be assumed, that at the end of this investigation the extreme view, which is too wide, will be sentenced to a sizable cut. At the same time, it will undermine the other extreme approach, which grasp a little, and sentence it to a decent completion.

The Jewish theater was born as an institution in 1876, and it was its art since its creation. Here is a declaration, which comes out from the last essay of Noach Prylucki, and there is no need to conduct a thorough investigation in order to say that this assumption needs an expansion, a little or a lot, in several important points. We now settle for one point, namely, the affinity point between the institution, which was created by Avraham Goldfaden and his assistants, and between a band of singers from Brod [Brody in Yiddish[MK]] and their founder, Berl Margaliot[1], who is called Berl Broder after the city in which he lived. The discussion on this point, although a bit late in coming, is also timely - three years ago this small group was a hundred years old. After many appearances in its hometown, the group wandered between the Jewish communities, mainly along the rail line Odessa- Kusta [Constantinople or Istanbul[MK]] and its impact was divided in three different directions. One direction, the simple one, is the singers' students and the students of their students, including those who pretended to be their students, and of them, the imitators and those who imitated the imitators. They took for themselves the well known name which was held as a tested and proven talisman. Hence, the various groups who called themselves by the name Brody singers. They shined and withered, and returned to shine in different places and different times. Those have risen in two different ways, and those descended in two different ways, and so on and so forth, and existed right up to our generation. Their impression emerged hither and thither as the image of the podium of songwriters and their bands. Researcher of miniature art will find their foundation in the format of the repertoire and also in the composition of the actors, and will also be influence by the attempts of the small stage in our country. Another direction, composed of its predecessor, is the theater of Goldfaden and his descendants who had to incorporate songs in plays, initially mechanically and later by organic integration. They used the tradition and conquests of those singers, that through them - the monolog, or better yet, the dialog, was expended to a play with a great plot and a large number of characters. In short, the transition from the podium of Berl Broder's singers to the stage of Avraham Goldfaden's actors, is the transition between the so called, *Bankelsanger* (a street singer), that his performance is swaying between temporary and permanent, in an inn and in a fair, and between an organized and unified troupe of players. The last direction is dialectic, and it is the connecting line between the first and last, kind of a belated repentance to the singing of the first singers, repentance in the presence of genius, meaning, rolling their inheritance and repairing it to a level of art by deepening the program, enriching the tools and polishing them as thin as possible as we have found in Itzik Manger, who redeemed and purified it in the field of lyrics and drama.

[Page 101]

Of course, the centennial was noteworthy, a review of the long and colorful road of the temporary podiums of the first singers up to the end of their triple continuation. However, several reasons caused that the memory of the double anniversary was ignored and passed as if it never existed. We do, however, owe thanks to the decedents of R' Berl – his granddaughter, Mrs. Krasel, and his grandson, Shimshon, who live in New-York. They assisted and encouraged their brother, who was named Berl Marguliot, after his grandfather and protégé, and he who added and wrote a book called: "*Drai Dorot*" [The three generations]. As the name implies, the book is divided into three parts, and indeed, one part, two printed pages, was devoted to their grandfather, the famous singer. Another part was devoted to their father, R' Yitzhak, and it is told, that he was known in his circle for his feuilletons (especially in his nickname *Yam HaZioni*[2]). The last part is devoted to the grandson's songs, the editor himself. Of course, the reader was interested in another proportion of the division of the book, and especially wished to use this window of opportunity to group together all of the singer's songs that aren't to be found, and those, who want to read them, must search in archives where only a few copies remained. He was probably responsible for the two editions that were printed during his life, but, of course, he's not responsible for the late editions. However, the twelve songs, that were given in the book "*Sheloshet HaDorot,*" serve a precious present for the reader.

It is possible, that we wouldn't be mistaken if we assume that the encouragement for that collection came from Dr. Yosef Tannenbaum, who published an important book about his homeland, Galicia, and its introduction testifies it. It says, that in the last three generations "the world rose and the world sank - and in the middle, three tiny shining dots, two or three tiny pearly stars – three generations of the Margaliot family. And if I write about them, it's not only because I compose a personal essay about two of them, but because each of them is a representative of a unique period – three road markers in the great railroad of the last one hundred years.

[Page 102]

Since our attention is devoted to the head of the trio, we will be satisfied with the words of his predecessor, to emphasize the background of his growth he mentions the community of Brody as the center of the *Haskalah* [Enlightenment Movement], and tries to inform us that the *Haskalah* was a movement that its *maskilim* embraced the language of the people [Yiddish,[MK]], wrote in it, and their writing was juicy and good. He counts these *maskilim* by their names - Mendel Lefin, Yaakov Shmuel Byk, Ayzik Ozer Rottenberg, and Yashaya Meir Finkelstein. He especially emphasizes the latter, who contributed a lot for the revival of the Yiddish language as the language of literature. However, in his opinion, the special Galician contribution to poetry and prose in Yiddish, during the *Haskalah* period, is of the comedians, singers and their leader, Berl Broder, who put his mark on that period.

We interpreted the words of the predecessor in order to remark, that if his intention was to explain the background of the group of the singers, and Berl Broder as their leader, he didn't illuminate the overall atmosphere which might explain this unique phenomenon. Mendel Lepin is obviously a household name - the same native of Podolia who went to Berlin, befriended the Mendelson[3] group, returned to his native roots, and wherever he stood, a center of the Haskalah was founded. The impact of his activities was felt a little in Poland and a lot in Belarus and Galicia. His right, for advancing our two national languages is greater than what was attributed to him by his greatest advocates. Of course, his students are also household names - Yaakov Shmuel Byk, who fought for double revision inside the *Haskalah*, alongside the recognition of the value of the Hassidut, and also alongside the recognition of the value of the Yiddish language, and he is almost the firstborn of its ideologues. The same applies for Ayzik Ozer Rottenberg and Yeshayah Meir Finkelshtayn, the guardians of the memory of their rabbi[4] who also published "*Moreh Nevukhim*" ["The guide for the perplexed"]. The first became the patron of Yiddish writers in Romania, and the last became a Yiddish author. Nonetheless, we can't explain how Berl Broder associated with them, and not only that, we cannot prove a real connection between Mendel Lepin's writings and him. On the contrary, from the language of his songs and Berl's language it is obvious that he didn't know the greatness of R' Mendel, and his absorption is from the language spoken at home, in the street and in the city, however, since there is no proof of a line connecting him to a typical educated writer who also wrote tastefully in Yiddish, and the main emphasis is on the "also" - because we cannot include Berl Broder among the few *maskilim* who wrote in the people's spoken language. And not only because of that, his growth isn't their growth, and his education isn't their education, but mostly because that his affinity to Yiddish as the language of his writing, or more precisely: the language of his singing. He had the affinity of a person that the spoken language of the people is the only language that he's able express himself. Out of his biography, which was written by N. M. Gelber who also returned and completed it, we learn about the unique circumstances of his growth, a son of poor family, who was orphaned in his childhood and had to start working as a laborer from a relatively early age. Later, when he became a merchant, he wandered in the cities of Russia for his livelihood. In any case, he was deprived of the time needed for Torah studies and embedded singing talent encouraged him to compose songs during his work. He energized his friends in his journeys and his singing in hostels helped him to seize a good name for himself. Townspeople and artists apprentices gathered around him and thus, the institution-non-institution, which has since gone through many transformations, came about.

[Page 103]

Whoever examines the articles in the biography, both of Gelber and others, finds several differences, either in the matter of the year of his birth date (1815 or 1817), in the matter of the place of birth (Brody or its neighboring Podkamen) or in the matter of the place of his death (Carlsbad or a town in Romania). There are also inconsistencies in several other details, some of which have already been clarified and some that are still vague, hence the words of contradiction or duplication in lexicons or in anthologies. However, there is no vagueness in his poems. The poems are truly his, and they're assembled in the two mentioned collections. Others, which were only preserved orally and given fully or in sections, reveal the unity between the author and his work. The reader would find that the openings of several poems are basically identical. For example, the song about the shepherd starts with: "I am, alas, a poor shepherd," the song about the roofing tile maker starts with "I am, alas, a poor roofing tile maker," the opening of the cantor's song "I am, alas, a poor cantor," the song for the night-guard starts with "I am, alas, a poor night-guard." The same is in the song about the preacher, the wagon owner tec. Even the song about the moneylender starts with the words "I am, alas, a poor moneylender." Their opening is like the opening of the shepherd song, but with the change of the name of the craft. It goes without saying, that this opening is the most typical because its spirit is the spirit of the entire song, the spirit of complete identity between the singer and his subject. This poetic aspect is noticeable and its main aspect is visual, because the common singer was satisfied with the words of the song. However, the singer, Berl Broder himself or his helper, also added an image to the matter- the singer disguise himself as the person he was singing about. In every song the singer appeared in the clothing of the person he was singing about. And if we summarize his songs, between those who begin with that and those who do not begin with that, like the gravedigger song that its opening turns to a man whose origin is dust and his end is dust, and also if we add the various dialogs like the conversation between a tailor and a shoemaker which gave the opening to a couple of singers who portrayed the image of Jewish workers. He was truly a great innovator in all the topics of the literature of the generation, and we cannot find anyone like him, not in his predecessors or among his peers. Moreover, not only his predecessors, but also his most prominent student, Velvel Zbarz'ar, that the world was mostly divided for them according to the division of the Hassidim that all sorts of disgraces bound in them, and all sorts of praises are firmly attached to the *maskilim*. One could not find anywhere a similar wide range of characters, a range that spans the entire topology of the Jewish street. All of that work, incorporating the songs and their presentation, can be considered a primitive art. However, this primitive art encompasses the embryos for souls, and they are the sociological and psychological fabric of the first dramatic theater and its sequel.

[Page 104]

Therefore, the sense of affinity between Berl Broder and Avraham Goldfaden is important, and there are two documents for that. One document is of Goldfaden himself. He regarded the creation of the Brody singers as an important part in the history of the Jewish theater. And these are his words in his autobiography: "Many years before the beginning of the story of our act, kind of "*minnzinger*," who are known by the name "Broder singers"were discovered in the city of Brody in Galicia. In those days, the comedians entertained the audience almost all year round because most of the audience were foreign traders, mainly Jews from Russia, who stopped in Brody on their way to the fair in Lipsia [Leipzig]. At that time, Brody was the starting point for all foreign trade. The singers amused the merry traders and the whole thing became a big business. Later, when the city of Brody fell because of the fierce competition, the singers moved their business to Russia." The other document is of David Yeshayahu Silberbusch, which included memories from his youth. He had heard from Avraham Goldfaden, that when he was fourteen years old, and already fond of writing merrymaking-songs, a new apprentice came to the workshop of his father the watchmaker. He was a native of Brody, he was seventeen, and his name was Nachman. He was a singer-helper to the cantors, and also here, in Old- Constantine, he was a member of the cantor's choir (this community was known to praise for its Cantorial music, and A.B. Gotlober's father served there during that generation). He is the one who brought the cantor's melodies, Berl Broder's jingles and Velel Zbarajer's songs, and also sang the first jingles of the watchmaker's son – Goldfaden himself. The rest of the story is amusing in itself, but it is not of interest for us right now, our case is to establish the connection between the provider and the recipient - between Berl Broder and Avraham Goldfaden.

The line, which is taken into account, is the connection line between him, the young Goldfaden, as the future playwright, and between the former playwright, Shlomo Ettinger, master of comedy and Yiddish fables during the Haskalahperiod. He wasn't awarded to see one printed letter out of his vast work in Yiddish during his lifetime (only one song in Hebrew, which was immaterial, was published during his lifetime). His comedy, "Sarkele," was circulated in hand-written copies, and later, it was printed according to faulty formulas until his savior, Max Weinreichh, rose and published his writings in two volumes. Later, Max Eric, followed suit and published his writings in another edition. However, about three generations have passed between writing and publication, and now, in our discussion, we focus on the days when young Goldfalden left his birthplace, Old Constantine, and traveled to Zhitomir to study at its Rabbinical Beit Midrash [school for Jewish studies[MK]] and the unique quality of his singing, acting and writing helped him to settle there. It was also reinforced in the atmosphere of Lepin's tradition, which was nurtured by his student, the institution's teacher, R' Mordekhai Sukhistover, who was the bridgehead between the life works of Lepin and Mendele [Jewish writer – Mendele Mokher Sfarim[MK]]. It was also strengthened in the atmosphere of affection for the people's spoken language [Yiddish[MK]], which was rooted in the hearts and the pens of other school teachers who were led by Gotlover and Tsvaifel Among his students were Y.Y Lintski and Menashe Margaliot. It's no wonder that in such atmosphere the students, in the manner of students, used this window of opportunity to exercise their desire for flaunting and passion for laughter. When the wife of the head of the school, R' Khaim Zelig Slonimski, brought the hand written manuscript of "Serkele" from Warsaw, she encouraged the students to present it and they accepted the offer enthusiastically. This show was like a turning point in Goldfaden's life, and obviously, in the life of the Jewish theater, because he has done two things for it - he used Berl Broder's oral attempt to revive the writing experience of Shlomo Ettinger, so that we can say that in the short time span, between the foundation of the group of Brody singer, which took place in 1857, and between the presentation of the comedy in 1862, meaning, for only five years a transition took place between the singers' podium and the theater's boards, and it began through the pastoral power that was embodied in that young man – Goldfaden, who carries the living legacy of Berl Broder and expands it.

[Page 105]

Thus, two inclusive family lines were set for us - one wave, which lasted from Shlomo Ettinger, whose writing remained hidden between him and a small group of readers who were able to obtain his writings. It seems that he never imagined that the play would become a real theatrical show. Even if he had known, he wouldn't have seen it as a foundation for a real and permanent theater. Even the author himself couldn't guess that his act of writing would be the foundation for a great and extensive literature. After all, with all of his attachment to the nation's spoken language [Yiddish[MK]], and all of his dedication to knead it in an artistic way, he was bound to the common perception of the *maskilimin* on the need to us the language of the country or the language of the neighbors, and not because the most positive character in the comedy spoke in literary German. The second line is drawn from Berl Broder, whose sayings were greater than his writings, and only few of his songs survived. Most of them were forgotten or imbedded in several folklore songs and songs of various writers. His sayings-signing spread among the crowds, and even he could not have guessed that his amusing jingles are like a sown area its end will come in a hundred years. Even though his stand within the people's spoken language came to him naturally and without the need for ideological justifications, he probably didn't pay attention to its changes and didn't doubt its longevity.

We emphasized this differentiation between the comedian, the perfect artist, the singer and the primitive artist, in order to highlight the differences between them, not only as individuals but also for the fact that they came from different layers inside the *Haskalah*, the first- a descendant of a privilege family, a physician and an author by his craft, the last, from the lower class, a clown not a clown by his craft.

Both lay, from two different ends, the foundations for the Jewish theater. On this end – we find a perspective of theatrical perfection without the prospect for realization, and on that side – dramatic performance without the possibility of achieving perfection. The young man, Avraham Goldfaden, came and connected end to end, and he is, as written, the third, the decisive between them.

And when the two family lines were set, we notice each line and its pedigree. The pedigree of the first line is known, Shlomo Ettinger. Other comedians preceded him, but not necessarily as part of the *Haskalah*in Germany. One should obviously mention the comedies of Wolfson and Eichle. He tells us about the big impression of a comedy that he had read in Lvov, and it is the anonymous *"Di Genarțe velț"* ["The deceived world"]. The unknown author is certainly an important personality, worthy of fame like other famous figures of his generation and region. As a matter fact, there is no other person as important as him is except for Yitzhak Erter with his great personality and achievements. May the God of assumptions forgive me if I add Erter to the group of candidates who might have written this outstanding comedy, or maybe place him at the lead. The pedigree of the second line is unknown - indeed, people say that Berl Broder brought about the transformation between the comedian and the singer in the taverns and in the fairs, as a transformation between somebody who is still somewhat in the realm of religion to somebody who is totally secular. This saying is surprising, in the generation after him we saw Eliakum Tsunzer in Lita and Hirsh Leib Gotlib in Carpathian-Russia and Southern Galicia, who opened as comedians and closed as singers and poets, while he, in the generation before them, opened with what they have closed. However, this popular statement requires a decent examination - because we are talking about the first group of Brody singers and mention Berl Broder and Yosl Broder in one breath, and this breath requires a pause, as there is no comparison between the two. The first, we knew his stage - taverns. We also knew the stage of the last – the court of the Ruzhyn Rabbi and his descendants. To say, a city that placed what it had in order to entertain the visitors from Odessa or Iasi, who were mostly followers of the *Haskalah*or its margins. It also placed what it had to entertain the visitors from Sadagora or Potok-Zolotoy, who were mostly followers of the Hassidut and its center.

[Page 106]

Furthermore, both fell to the edge of the spiritual and intellectual orientation of the generation despite the fact that they were rival each inspection its own camp. They grew from the same background and both preserved the crumbs of Jewish tradition in their work. From them we learn about the existence of a true comical atmosphere - and here are the names of Brody's comedians, from the two brothers Tshornik, to R' Moshe Yampoler and R' Alter Kleitnik, whose jokes nourished the humor of the joyful city. They are few out of many, meaning, kind of ambiance of clowning that was already rooted in the city. It sought an outlet for itself beyond the traditional expressions, such as Purim games, playfulness in a wedding and the like. We discussed one fact or another in order to show the journey of this clowning into the game. One example - the gathering of every resident named Shmuel, from the city and its suburbs, during the big fair. The main goal of the gathering was to publicly and humorously prove the impropriety of the common phrase: "Shmuel is just a fool." The other fact - is the memory of the act that A. Litvin rescued from the mouth of Berl Broder's son. R' Fayvl, one of Belz's Chassid, who was challenged by his brother-in-law, told his wife, Fruma: "today I will make two Fayvls for us" please don't say anything when you see it." On the same day, when R' Fayvl and his wife, Mrs. Kesler, came to visit his brother-in-law, she was called to hurry back home. Upon her arrival she was surprise to find her husband. Only several minutes have passed since her husband told her that they would have to return to Berl's house. When they arrived, they found Fayvl sitting down comfortably and talking to Mrs. Fruma. Before us is an act that was derived from a national folklore joke that gave birth to a comedy act called ,"Qui pro quo," that Berl Broder used in his shows (in our generation, an amusement stage was called by this name in Warsaw). We actually cannot determent which came first, the story or the actual event. In any case, this very act of deceit occupies a tradition in literature - see, from here, Isaac Mayer Dick and his story – "*A Farddreishenish*" [The Mix-Up[MK]], which is entirely built on this theme and develops into an amusing saga, and from here, Shai Agnon – and his story, "*Hakhnasat Kallah*" [The Bridal Canopy], which describes the summons of three men named R' Yudel Natanzon. Of course, it was powered by the magic tricks of Brody's clowns. What matters for us now is this way in Goldfaden's renowned comedy – "*Two Kuni Lemel,*" and in our time the extension of his other comedy about the "*The Three Hotzmachim*" [The Three Misfortunate Jews[MK]] by Itzik Manger.

[Page 107]

And when we mentioned Itzik Manger, we, as defendants, stand on the distance between the beginning and the end, more accurately, between the primitive beginning and the refined end, and this stand requires, first of all, the examination of the legacy of Berl Broder, in terms of collecting his lyrics and their melodies, analysis of his entire subjects and a review of his tools. This is a major issue on itself, and until we reach it, we will return and mention the impact of the writings of this singer on its three directions, and will summarize that he, and his friends, gave birth to a large populace, and conclude with the words of Itzik Manger in the sonata about the Brody Singers in which it says that he jumped onto their wagon and travel with them a good part of the way, through towns and cities, through years of singing, in wandering, in lawlessness and starvation.: and he ends.

"At long wooden tables, sit ordinary Jews and listen.
Here they sigh worried, and here they laugh in tears
Outside the wagon is waiting for us in the rain"

He also describes Berl Broder in a prose chapter in his book *"Close Images"* (Translated by A. Shlonsky, 1941, pg. 56): "He collapses on the bed. Green stars, stars of frost, peeking at him through the window. In his dream, a wagon and a carter, a whip, cities and towns, are admixed endlessly, endlessly".

Translator's footnotes

1. The meaning of the name, Margaliot, in Hebrew is pearls. There is a saying in Hebrew which describes an eloquent person as somebody "who drips pearls (margaliot)." https://www.jewishgen.org/Yizkor/brody/bro096.html - f1r
2. The Hebrew initials form the Hebrew word Yam – sea, so the nickname sounds like the Zionist Sea. https://www.jewishgen.org/Yizkor/brody/bro096.html - f2r
3. The philosopher, Moses Mendelson (1726-1789), is considered the father of the Jewish *Haskalah* (Enlightenment) Movement. He called for secular education and the revival of the Hebrew language and its literature.https://www.jewishgen.org/Yizkor/brody/bro096.html - f3r
4. ERambam's "Moreh Nevochim" was written in 1190 in Judeo-Arabic. https://www.jewishgen.org/Yizkor/brody/bro096.html - f4r

[Page 108]

Brody:
City of Border and Immigrants

by Mendel Zinger

Translated by Moshe Kutten

Edited by Yocheved Klausner

Brody, my hometown, was a border town in Eastern Galicia, bordering with the Czarist Russia, until the First World War. Any disturbance that occurred in the life of the Jewish people in Russia, or in the life of Russian people in general, caused a panic migration, which was felt in this border town. Longtime residents could tell many details about the mass migration from Russia through the city during the 1880's and about the stormy debates and arguments among the Jewish immigrants concerning the fateful question: "America or Eretz Israel?" Old-timers would also tell about famous people, eminent authors and leading Jewish activists, such as Karl Netter[1] and Righteous Among the Nations such as Sir Oliphant[2], who stayed in the city during the mass migration years. Ahad Ha'Am[3] lived in Brody for several months. M. Y. Berdichevski[4] was active in the city for some time, on his way to his studies in Berlin. Interesting impressions from Shalom Aleikhem's[5] visit in Brody are included in his writings.

After the pogroms in Kishinev, and during the war between Russia and Japan (roughly 1904-1905), over one hundred and twenty thousand Jews left Russia. A considerable number of them crossed the borders of Volhyn and Podolia, and arrived in Brody. Many community officials in the city delivered care faithfully to the immigrants, refugees of the war and the pogroms who managed to smuggle through the border; most of them were impoverished - men, women and children, carrying bundles and wretched suitcases, tired and exhausted, without a roof over their heads. There were immigrant families who lay down for days in the corridors of Jewish institutions, or in the entrance porch of the synagogue. An assistance committee was organized, whose members provided advice to the immigrants and helped them find an apartment and work. In one of the city's main streets, a –"tea-kitchen" [soup-kitchen[MK]) was established. It became an important meeting place for all immigrants who were slated to travel together to a port city or for those who wanted first to stop by other major European capitals. Local Jews who wanted to "do business" with the immigrants met in this location, where the assistance committee could keep an eye on them so that they would not swindle the immigrants.

There were quite a few artisans among the immigrants, who easily found work in Brody and could make a living during their stay. Some clung to the city and settled in it permanently. I recall that there were immigrants who made a living in the "tea-kitchen" by authoring couplets and jingles. This "poets" were sitting there and singing their songs for the crowd, often accompanying themselves by strumming on a mandolin. They used to copy their songs by hand and sell them. The topics depicted in these songs were the life in Russia, the pogroms and the life of immigrants. Over time, songs about the life in Brody were authored as well. One popular song was about the war between Russia and Japan. The song begins by mocking Russia for bragging [all poems below are translated to English from the Hebrew versions given.[MK]]:

[Page 109]

Everybody knew,
how big and powerful
the country of Russia was.
It presented itself
in front of the entire world
as the actor with the most
important role on the stage.

..and the last lines of the jingle are:

See now, how she ended up ailing!
She thought she would overcome
easily:
but Japan stood up to her,

and with the world's support beat
the "great hero" - the Russian bear

There were four verses for this jingle. One of them expresses revenge for the pogroms. The verse goes like that:

[Page 110]

We have waited longer and longer,
we have waited for a long time,
Now comes the revenge.
To the battle
with the lion, the fly went,
and the lion is being beaten in this
fight.
This is a revenge for the blood
spilled in Kishinov
Japan is reciprocating,
and he got the punishment he
deserves.
G-od showed him
that everything that happened
was brought upon him because of
the bloody pogroms

In another verse of the jingle, the author mocks Admiral Makarov who suffered an immense defeat in the ocean:

You know Makarov,
this is not Kishinov,
small children are not being
slaughtered here.

Another verse of the jingle settles the account with the reactionary regime and its fight against freedom fighters:

Little Japan is beating the dictator
The little one is killing the big one;
You repressed the people
deported innocent people
They take revenge now from afar

[Page 111]

This big and diversified crowd of women and men were sitting in the large hall of the "tea-house", sipping a cup of tea, listening, and participating in singing these songs. This was reminiscent of the heydays in Brody's from a few decades before, when Berl Broder[6] and his friends used to amuse the city's big merchants and those who were visiting, with their songs and jokes during the evening hours, in the city bars and restaurants. A person by the name of Barukh Kutik (his surname was Shprukh, but he was called Kutik because his wife's – a woman of valor- maiden name), was still alive during my time in the city. He was a tiny old man who was a member of Berl Broder's family. He used to sing for the immigrants, in a weak but sweet voice, the songs of his famous relative, Berl. He was also imitating Berl's gestures, which provoked much laughter. R' Barukh excelled in the singing of the song of the drunk for which these are the verses:

[Page 112]

What is going on outside,
I am standing here bewildered,
the whole city is roaring,
exactly like a grinder.
I won't go home, it is comfortable
for me right here,
the whole city is spinning,
my house would come to me.

While strolling on this trail
walking I could not,
Woe to you, my trail, you are drunk!
not appropriate for you.
Going left, going right,
my house, I could not see:
since, the trail is drunk all right,
it is now clear to me.

...and the city's clock, that's you,
why so slanted stand you?
You changed your stance,
soon you will fall on me.

You need to sound four,
but eight you rung;
if you wanted to follow me
you did well...

The welfare committee was tasked with other roles, guarding the immigrants being the most important of them. Guarding was needed so that they would not become victims of the ships' agents, who were ambushing the immigrants in various places in order to sell them fraudulent train or ship tickets. The committee was helped by young volunteers, who would go around in the streets leading from the border, and would lead any immigrant cart to an agent found reliable by the committee, or direct them to the "tea-house" where the committee members were stationed during most of the day. Repeatedly, the agents or their delegates would assault the youths who came to interrupt their business, and administer them massive beating. When the news about incoming immigrants would reach the city, the agents and the youths would go out to meet them. They would virtually assail the travelers – these to capture them in their deception net, and those to save them from it. At times, fist fights erupted between the two sides. I was privileged to receive a gift in a form of a fist from the agents' representatives and went back home bleeding and with a swollen mouth. It is easy to imagine the impression of this strange reception upon these people who had just experienced the fear and the hardship involved in smuggling the border.

[Page 113]

Among all of these immigrants, refugees of pogroms and war, came a few tens of young people, workers and students, apprentices of all of the various revolutionary ideologies, of which there were many in the Czarist Russia, obviously operating underground there. David Pinski[7], in his theater play "The Tzvi's Family", Shalom Ash[8] in "The Days of the Messiah" and Shalom Aleikhem in several of his stories, described the ideology and political chaos which penetrated all facets of Jewish life. However, when I recall now how abundant were the views and political nuances among them and the resulted stormy and stimulating debates, it seems to me that the literary descriptions were only a hint to the perplexity that was rampant in these circles. This perplexity also spread considerably in the places where the immigrants passed through or stayed for some time.

I recall that among the immigrants were social-revolutionists (on the right and the left), social democrats (Bolsheviks and Mensheviks[9]), and various types of anarchists. Some movements reconciled with Zionism and some were neutral towards it, but most rejected the "Reactionary Zionism"[10] with all of their revolutionary fervor. The main streams were the "Bund"[11], Territorial-Socialists[12], and "Poalei-Tzion"[13]. There were various nuances in each of these streams.

There were many debates between the members of the various streams, which took place in associations gatherings, soup kitchens, and even openly in public locations and streets (the authorities were indifferent about them and did not interfere). In these debates (which often lasted until beyond midnight), members of several streams argued about tens of issues simultaneously. The debates were imbued with Jewish acuteness and Hasidic excitement and drew the hearts of the youths. These political refugees, who had to act underground in Russia, breathed a sigh of relief upon crossing the border. Here they could make a speech, argue and debate at will without interruption. All the dams opened, all the limitations were removed and the freedom of speech was tried to its limits. The youths followed the debates with great interest. They often witnessed brawls that arose at the end of the debates, particularly following the debates between the members of "Poalei Tzion" and the "Bund" – so called Zion haters. More than once, the youths have been dragged into the fights. Then they would have to leave the gathering, along with the adults, not as they came in, through the door, but rather through the window.

There were several Zionist youths among the immigrants. Among those who came to Brody and remained there for a long duration, Yosef Aharonovitz stood out. He did not isolate himself from the rest of the immigrants and took interest in their issues and in the assistance activities aimed to help them. He often participated in the political debates. However, Aharonovitz did all of that only casually. He devoted most of his time and energy to his preparation and the preparation of a group of youths he gathered around him, for making Aliyah to Eretz Israel. His activity was mainly through the "Poalei Tzion" movement and besides the immigrants also among the students of the Gymnasium [High School[MK]]. The plan was that following some learning of the Hebrew language and preparation as workers (later called "Hakhshara" - Hebrew for "preparation"), the group would immigrate to Eretz Israel and establish a settlement together. The settlement was meant to be based on the principle of cooperation at work and life [later called a Kibbutz[MK]]. Yosef Aharonovitz was one of the first immigrants to Eretz Israel. His activities in Brody bore fruit. Numerous members of "Poalei Tzion" clubs and students of the gymnasium made Aliyah during the following years and settled in Eretz Israel.

Translator's footnotes

1. Karl Netter – A Zionist leader (1826-1882) founder of Mikveh Israel, the first modern agricultural settlement in Eretz Israel. https://www.jewishgen.org/Yizkor/brody/bro096.html - f108_1r
2. Probably referring to Sir Laurence Oliphant (1829-1888) – a South African born British author and diplomat. He became an ardent supporter of the Jewish immigration and agricultural settlements in Palestine as he saw these settlements as a means of alleviating Jewish suffering in Eastern Europe. https://www.jewishgen.org/Yizkor/brody/bro096.html - f108_2r
3. Akhad Ha'Am (Literally translated as "one of the common people") – was the pen name of Asher-Zvi Ginzburg (1856 – 1927). He was a Hebrew essayist and one of the most prominent thinkers of the Zionist movement. https://www.jewishgen.org/Yizkor/brody/bro096.html - f108_3r
4. Micha-Yosef Berdichevski – (1865-1921) a Ukrainian born Jewish author (who wrote in Hebrew, Yiddish and German). He was one of the first authors who advocated the freeing of the Jews from the religion, tradition and history way of life. https://www.jewishgen.org/Yizkor/brody/bro096.html - f108_4r
5. Shalom Aleikhem – (literally translates to "Peace be upon you") is the pen name of Solomon Naumovich Rabinovich (1859-1916), the most prominent Yiddish author. Born in Ukraine, he later immigrated to New

York, and lived in Geneva Switzerland and New York. His writings depict the life of the Jews in Eastern Europe. He is also famous for his letters to his wife after immigrating to the US. https://www.jewishgen.org/Yizkor/brody/bro096.html - f108_5r

6. Berl Broder – born Berl Marguliot, was a Ukrainian Jew who became the most famous of the Broder singers (a 19th century comedy and singing group originated in Brody who performed all over Galicia). Berl Broder reputed first to be both a singer and an actor, as well as song writer. His songs are seen as a precursor to the Yiddish theater. https://www.jewishgen.org/Yizkor/brody/bro096.html - f108_6r
7. David Pinski – Yiddish language author and playwright (1872 – 1959). Pinski was the first to introduce to the Yiddish theater a drama about urban Jewish workers, and was also known for writing about human sexuality with a frankness previously unknown in Yiddish literature. https://www.jewishgen.org/Yizkor/brody/bro096.html - f108_7r
8. Shalom Ash - (1880 – 1957) a Jewish Yiddish author, born in Poland and later lived in the US and Israel. Known for controversial books and plays.https://www.jewishgen.org/Yizkor/brody/bro096.html - f108_8r
9. The Mansheviks (derived from Russian for minority) were a nick name given to a faction of Russia's socialistic movement that separated from the Lenin's movement in 1904, initially over a dispute about minor organizational issues). The Mensheviks were known to be more moderate and were more positive towards the liberal opposition movement.https://www.jewishgen.org/Yizkor/brody/bro096.html - f108_9r
10. The Zionism movement headed by Theodore Herzl who represented the Jewish "middle class". This was a rightist political movement. On the Jewish political left were the Socialist-Marxist movements, some of which were not pro Zionism. The left denoted the middle class Zionism – "Reactionary Zionism". https://www.jewishgen.org/Yizkor/brody/bro096.html - f108_10r
11. The Bund (or the Jewish Labor Bund as it was called) was a secular Jewish Socialist-Marxist movement in the Russian Empire who rejected Zionism as a solution for the Jewish problem. https://www.jewishgen.org/Yizkor/brody/bro096.html - f108_11r
12. Territorial-Socialists was a Jewish Socialistic movement who believed that salvation for the Jews would come through territorial

concentration (not necessarily in Palestine) and autonomy. https://www.jewishgen.org/Yizkor/brody/bro096.html - f108_12r

13. Poalei Tzion – meaning "Workers of Zion" was a Zionist Marxist movement founded in Russia and Poland as a contra-measure to the rejection of Zionism by the "Bund". https://www.jewishgen.org/Yizkor/brody/bro096.html - f108_13r

[Page 114]

On the Very Close Connection of the Jews of Brody and of Vohlynia[a]

by Joseph Parvari (Leiner)

Translated by Moshe Kutten

Edited by Rafael Manory

In memory of my exalted friend, Arieh Avatikhi of blessed memory, who devoted his life to serving the public. He would always be my guiding light.

If not for the partition of Poland among Russia, Austria and Prussia at the end of the 18th century, Brody would not have been different from the other towns in the area, such as Radzivilov (Radyvyliv), Dubno, Rovno (Rivne) and others; Podolia and Vohlyn provinces were always considered part of Ukraine, until the Polish Piast Dynasty rulers conquered these areas and annexed them to their kingdom. With the liquidation of Poland as an independent country, Brody was annexed by Habsburg's Austria and the entire land of Vohlyn was annexed by Czarist Russia. Only a small distance of 6 kilometers separated Brody from the border between these two world powers.

Since then and until the First World War, Brody was a Galitsian city, and Vohlyn's towns and settlements became Russian. Even the culture that developed in these places was characteristic to the center of the regime: in Brody—German, and in Vohlyn—Russian. However, the Jews, who were the majority in these places, were influenced only superficially. Deep down, they all remained Jewish with a national identity, faithful to their religion and tradition, and far from assimilation. As far as the bond between Brody's and Vohlyn's Jews—this bond was never severed.

The only road leading from Russia to Austria was the Radzivilov–Brody road. There was a continuous legal and illegal traffic between the two countries, because of the developed commerce relations between the two on one hand, and Jews fleeing Czarist Russia on the other hand. Jews were fleeing Russia because of three main reasons: The desire to avoid military service, the Czarist oppression and the wish to break through to the free world and reach Eretz Israel.

[Page 115]

Indeed, anybody who managed to reach Brody, felt liberated. There was no way back from Brody. This is why a famous phrase was coined [in Yiddish, RM]: "A secret, the entire Brody knows about". This is because every youth in town knew about the border smugglings despite the fact that these were supposed to be shrouded in complete secrecy ...

Many immigrants who reached Brody stayed in it for long durations. Among these immigrants there were many Hebrew language educators and teachers, who dealt in the organizing the youths as part of the pioneering-Zionist movements, such as Yosef Aharonovitz who established the "Pioneers of Zion" association under the "Poalei Zion[2]" movement and others). Thanks to these activities, Brody became a focal point in the Zionist movement.

Between the two World Wars

When the country of Poland was reestablished in 1918, a symbolic signpost was erected at the former border between Brody and Vohlyn, at the 6-km mark on the Brody–Radzivilov road. This signpost read: "Here was the former border between Russia and Austria, two countries that annexed Polish areas to their territory".

While in the Austro-Hungarian Empire, Jewish Brody developed nicely; many Rabbis and famous scholars, as well as the first enlightened people originated from the city, such that the nickname "Yerushalaim of Austria" was affixed to it. However, under the new Polish regime, the city lost its greatness, and the process of social and economic deterioration has begun. Many of its eminent Jews left for larger cities—Lvov, Krakow, Vienna and Rome (Rabbi Peretz Khayut, Dr. Khayim Tartakover, and others), and many immigrated to Eretz Israel

(Asher Barash, Dr. N. M. Gelber, Mendel Zinger, Professors Arieh Tartakover, Dov Sadan, and others). This is when the influence of Vohlyn on Brody began. New Jewish residents, individuals and families, from nearby and from far away arrived. They shaped the cultural image of the city (the highly acclaimed teacher—Naftali Lerner-Naor, the founder of "Beit Haam" (the Community House), the big city library and "Gordonia"[3]; Pnina Gratzberg-Lanski from Berestechko and Yitzkhak Ettinger from Verba, Mordekhai Pursht and others, were all, as mentioned, Vohlyn natives).

During those days, a Hakhshara[4] center, the only one in the city, was established in Brody. This was a branch of the famous Kibbutz-Hakhshara in Klosova. Who were the members, if not the boys and the girls from Vohlyn?. These were young youths of valor, initially consisting of about 50 people. Their life was not easy. Brody was never an industrial town so the pioneers could only obtain a few jobs, in Landgevirtz's flourmill, Parness' linen warehouses and others. During the winter months, they became lumberjacks, and conflicts between them and the gentiles, who were traditionally engaged in this craft, erupted...

Members of the (Socialist) P.P.S. Party [Polish Socialist Party.[MK]] considered the pioneers as competitors of the local workers and took extreme measures against them. The underground communists embittered the lives of the pioneers as well. They even took violent steps: ejection from the market place, beatings and throwing rocks at their windows at night. The pioneers' dwelling stood without windowpanes throughout the entire winter, and the pioneers suffered from the cold in addition to hunger, but they persevered.

[Page 116]

The Partisan Activity during the Holocaust

Similar to youth activities in towns across the rest of Galitsia, Russian and Poland, part of the youth in Brody, organized itself as a defense force. In the ghetto, a new fighters organization, headed by Shmuel Weiler of Beitar[5], and Shlomo Halbershtat and Yaakov Linder from the Socialist youth. The last two fought a heroic battle and were killed in the line of duty. Shmuel Weiler survived and lived to testified in Nazi's trials. He died in 1962 in the diaspora and was brought for burial in Israel.

During that tragic period, there was a strong bond between Brody and Vohlyn. Yekhiel Purkhovnik from Radzivilov, wrote about the youths who organized in the town's ghetto in Radzivilov's Yizkor Book ("Sefer Radzivilov"). When the ghetto was annihilated, those who survived ran away to Brody. Some of them were captured at the old border and were shot on the spot; however, some made it to Brody unscathed, Purkhovnik among them. They built a bunker underneath the house of their friend Henikh Tishker, where 30 people, five of whom were from Radzivilov, found shelter. A Christian woman neighbor provided the food for them.

Half a year later, they went out to the Leshniov forest and joined a mixed partisan group consisting of Russians, Jews and Poles. Purkhovnik was sent to Brody to mobilize the youths to join the partisans. During one of the bloody encounters with the Germans, he managed to transfer 28 youths from the bunker to the forest. In the spring of 1943, just before the annihilation of the ghetto, he managed to take out another 20 people. Other people managed to escape and join the partisans who were about 100-people strong at that time.

The partisans company acted against the Germans and the Ukrainians. In September 1943, a German force of 1500 soldiers surrounded the company. The battle was arduous and bloody and only eleven people survived from the [partisans[RM]] company. In another battle in the village of Punikovicze, four more partisans were killed.

At the end, only three Jewish partisans survived and they returned to Brody. They found a shelter in a bunker under a big house in the center of town, where 40 more Jews were hiding. When the Germans discovered the bunker, everybody ran away to the ghetto. Some returned to Leshniov forest on the next day.

In the summer attack, on 14thJuly 1944, the Red Army's 192nd Tashkent Division, where Purkhovnik served, liberated the city of Brody. He himself excelled in the battle and was awarded the "Red Star" medal. In the face-to-face battle with the Germans to liberate the city of Lvov, Purkhovnik lost his right leg but survived.

Thus, there has always been a tight and effectual bond between the Jews of Brody and of Vohlyn. Indeed, the Jews of Brody remained thankful to the Jews of Vohlyn. I know of two of them who edited Yizkor books for Vohlyn cities—Dr. Yaakov Rotman-Netaneli, a Brody's native from a Dubno Hassidic family, a teacher, poet and author who edited "Sefer Dubno" and Mr. Mendel Zinger (who made Aliyah together with Y. Kh. Brenner[6]), who edited the Kehilah book for Vohlin's Beresteczko and Boremel towns. Brody natives who live in Israel consider these books as a small token payment toward their moral debt to Vohlyn's Jewish community.

Author's Notes

a. Someone from the Brody community might ask—"What does Brody have to do with Vohlyn, given that Brody was located in Galitsia?" However, the author of this article, who is quite familiar with Brody and the tight bond, that existed at the time between its Jews and those of Vohlyn, thinks otherwise. According to his opinion, Brody suckled her culture from Vohlyn's cities and towns, and from there she attained her greatness. Shai Agnon in his book "Bridal Canopy"[1] [p. 468 (in the Hebrew edition[RM])] wrote about her "...that Brod [nickname given to Brody in Yiddish[MK]] was full of Torah students like a garden full of hearty fruits... Where did these many Torah students come from if not from Vohlyn, the students who crossed the border illegally and came to her to be liberated from Czarist Russia?" (as implied by the author of this article). In his letter to SH. Z. Shoken (Chapter Ki Tezeh, page 780), Agnon writes: "...I visited Brod on Sabbath, and was happy to see the city of residence of the Hasid R' Yudel, may his memory be blessed. I felt there like in my own home". Vohlyn Jews who managed to sneak out to Brody felt there, with the help from the city residents, like in their own home.https://www.jewishgen.org/Yizkor/brody/bro096.html - t114_1r

---

Translator's footnotes

1. "The Bridal Canopy" (Hebrew: "Hakhnasat Kallah") by Nobel Prize laureate, Yiddish author Shai Agnon is considered one of the classics of the Yiddish literature. The story tells about the wanderings of a naively pious Hasid—Reb Yudel, in search of a groom and a dowry for his daughter. Some scholars equate the fictional Reb Yudel to a Jewish archetype of Don Quixote.https://www.jewishgen.org/Yizkor/brody/bro096.html - f114_1r
2. "Poalei Zion" (literally "Workers of Israel") was a Socalist–Zionist Jewish workers movement founded in various cities in Poland and Russia at the turn of the 20th century after the Bund rejected Zionism in 1901. The right-wing of the movement headed by Ben Gurion, the first Prime Minister of Israel, formed the Akhdut Ha'Avoda Party, which together with another party formed the "Mapai" Party, the precursor of the Labor Movement in Israel. The left wing of Poalei Zion was later split between the Israel Communist Party ("Maki"), and the other part joined with the "Ha'Shomer Hatzair" (Young Guard) movement to form leftist "Mapam" (The United Workers party). https://www.jewishgen.org/Yizkor/brody/bro096.html - f114_2r
3. "Gordonia" was a Jewish youth movement. Its doctrines were based on the beliefs of Aaron David Gordon, i.e. the salvation of Eretz Israel and the Jewish People through manual labor and the revival of the Hebrew language.https://www.jewishgen.org/Yizkor/brody/bro096.html - f114_3r
4. Hakhshara—Literally, means "preparation", was the name given to preparatory camps in which the Zionist youths learned Hebrew and trained in agricultural and manual labor. The camp was organized as a kibbutz (a commune). The graduates organized themselves into groups pending Aliyah to the Eretz Israel. https://www.jewishgen.org/Yizkor/brody/bro096.html - f114_4r
5. Beitar—Hebrew acronym for the "Jewish Alliance for Joseph Trumpeldor" is a youth movement established in Ukraine by Vladimir Jabotinski, which was associated with the rightist Revisionist movement. After the establishment of Israel the movement became the rightist party of Heruth (later the Likud Party).https://www.jewishgen.org/Yizkor/brody/bro096.html - f114_5r
6. Yosef Khayim Brenner was a Russian-born Hebrew-language author and one of the pioneers of modern Hebrew literature. https://www.jewishgen.org/Yizkor/brody/bro096.html - f114_6r

[Page 117]

The Aliyah of the Halutzim, "Artificial Immigration" and Hakhshara Activities

From his – "With Joseph Chaim Brenner to the Land of Israel Sixty Years Ago", Mo'etzet Po'alei Haifa, 1969, pp. 29-47

by Mendel Zinger

Translated by Moshe Kutten

Yosef Aharonovitz[1], while staying in Brody and being active in the local club of the movement *"Po'alei Zion"*[2] [literally – *"Workers of Zion"*MK], prepared himself to establish the association *"Halutzei Zion"* [literally – *"The Pioneers of Zion"*MK]. He has done so, probably, under the influence of *Menachem Ussishkin's*[3] "Our Plan", published in Russia at the end of 1904, which contained the suggestion of establishing leagues of Jewish workers in the diaspora in preparation for the immigration to *Eretz Israel* [literally - *Land of Israel* – the biblical name for the holy landMK]. The main paragraphs of the by-laws of the association of "the Pioneers of Zion" were: a) The association will only accept into its ranks members who are educated, healthy in their body and soul, Zionists, who know our ancient language, of an age less than thirty and bachelors. b) The duties that the association imposes on its members include learning the skills of working the land by reading books and, as much as possible, by practicing it, studying the Arabic language, getting used to speaking only Hebrew, and continuing studies of it. The topics of studies in the "Pioneers of Zion" club included the socialist and political economy doctrines, the theory of preserving one's health, agronomy, geography of Eretz Israel as well as Hebrew and Arabic.

The atmosphere in Brody provided a unique setting for a national-cultural awakening. The city was saturated with the spirit of the

Haskalah[4] and the knowledge of the Hebrew language. Educational books written in Hebrew could be found in many houses, and booklets of *Yehoshua Heschel Schorr's*[4] "*HeHalutz*" ["*the Pioneer*"MK], published in Brody, were read secretly even by orthodox Jews. Russian language masterpieces, as well as the spirit of the Russian Jewish communities infiltrated into Brody through the nearby border. The city environs were populated by Ukrainians. However, in the city itself, the Jews, about 80 percent of the city's twenty thousand people, were the majority along with a small layer of Polish government employees and scholars. The city had a public high school, in which German was the language of studies. In this rush of the effects of different languages and nations, the Jews, while maintaining such a high majority, could keep their social and spiritual independence. This was also a fertile ground for growing a new national movement.

In the circles of observant Jews, scholars and their students were treated with high respect. Every one of the crafts common among Jews – tailors, carpenters, servants, bakers and cart owners – had their own prayer houses. Every one of them had a sort of a Rabbi, or a scholar, and the members felt obligated to keep several people around him who studied Torah and Talmud with him, day and night. Any Jew, native of the city, kept a high self-esteem and felt proud toward other nationals and his neighbors. He guarded his independent spiritual values and had a great self-confidence. There was, therefore, no wonder that, with the awakening of the political life in Austria under the influence of the Russian Revolution of 1905, and with the broadening of the right to vote to the House of Representatives that induced the awakening of the Jewish national-political movement in Austria, Brody was one of the first cities where the fight for equal national rights for the Jewish people was ignited.

[Page 118]

Before the general election in Austria, a supplementary election to the parliament was held in Brody and the district. The Zionists' candidate was *Adolf Shtand*, who captivated a multitude of voters by storm and later became the nation's darling, exciting the youths and activating them. In this election, the governors tried to hinder the

Zionist candidate using violence and forgeries; however, in the general election of 1907, these tricks were not very useful, and Shtand was elected as the city and district representative to the Austrian parliament. As a result, this national grassroots movement, which thrilled Galicia's Jews in general and Brody's Jews in particular, created the groundwork for the pioneering activity among the youths to prepare them for the immigration to Eretz Israel. One group among these youths – most of whom were members of "Po'alei Zion" – was not satisfied with the preparations of its own members for Aliya [immigration to Israel[MK]]; the members applied to the Zionist youths in Galicia in a leaflet, urging them to join them in the "Workers - Pioneers" movement and follow them to Eretz Israel. The leaflet, published in Yiddish in 1908, (4 of Kheshvan, 1840 years since the destruction of the Temple as was specified in the leaflet), opened with words of admiration about the "wonderful revolution" in Turkey, emphasizing the excitement of the Jewish youth toward freedom fighting and reminding them of their duty to fight for their freedom in our old-new homeland. "For many years" the leaflet stated, "we prayed for our leaders to receive a charter from the Turkish government, and all of a sudden, the regime totally disappeared. Replacing it was a house of representatives, consisting of representatives of all nations in the state of Turkey. It would be illogical that this house of representatives would grant rights to the holy land, to a nation which did not inhabit it, or occupied just a small part of it. Everybody should recognize the fact that we now have to move our activity to Palestine. Let us examine what we have achieved there and what our activity during the last twenty five years brought us" The leaflet proceeded to provide a short description, in a few sentences, about what has been achieved in Eretz Israel. The leaflet authors asked:" Are we satisfied with what has been achieved so far? Are these *Moshavot* [farming communities of private farms with common resources[MK]], whose owners are Jewish, really Hebrew villages? The answer given by the authors was negative – as long as the workers in these farming communities were mostly Arabs. They continued their assessment by claiming that while one cannot totally exonerate the Zionists in Eretz Israel, "we could blame our own Zionists in any town and city even more, because instead of dealing in "diasporic" theories and arguments about how to win the hearts of the nation's masses, they should have known and understood the life, or rather the suffering of our workers and our youths, who live a sorrowful life, which forces them to emigrate. They could then disseminate true information about the life and conditions in Eretz Israel, and who could secure there a job. It would be much more useful to the Zionist movement than ten large assemblies."

[Page 119]

The leaflet's authors tried their best to prove how beneficial the Aliya of healthy people would be, for Eretz Israel and the immigrants themselves. The authors return to examining the situation in Turkey following the revolution - "if previously, when the country was enslaved, the danger was not as substantial, since neither we, nor other nations were doing much there, now many non-Jews would flock to a free Palestine in masses, and we can arrive at a point that when we would be ready to act, the country would be in others' hands! Could we afford to remain silent in such a critical period? No! We, the young Zionists, cannot remain silent. We live in an unprecedented historic hour that we cannot remain silent. In order to correct the mistakes we just mentioned, and in order to move toward our final objective, namely ensuring that Palestine falls into Jewish hands, we gathered and established an association – "*Po'alim – Halutzim*" ["*Workers – Pioneers*"[MK]]. Many members will shortly immigrate to Palestine from Brody and its neighboring towns, but with that, we would not have fulfilled our duty". After outlining the lines of action of "Po'alim – Haluzim", the leaflet ends with the following words: "Comrades, we believe that we are not alone in our thinking that the time to act for the sake of Zionism has come. We are convinced that many of the young Zionists are thinking like us. We therefore call on you not to miss this opportunity, because the time is too critical for us to do so... Only if we all work diligently, our big ideal will come true – to become a free nation living in its ancient land – Palestine!"

The authors of the leaflet were very careful not to insult, with their words, the "realistic" views that dominated in the clubs of "*Po'alei-Zion*"[1] towards Aliya to Eretz Israel, according to which Jewish masses would emigrate to Eretz Israel by a "spontaneous" process only; however, the meetings conducted by these youths and their discussions were filled with the dreams of living and working in Eretz Israel. The "romanticism" of the organization "*HaShomer*" ["*the Guard*"MK], and the willingness to self-sacrifice, attracted the hearts with a massive force; however, when they appealed to the public, or when they needed to voice their ideas and feelings publicly, they encountered resistance. They spent a substantial amount of time carefully wording the leaflet, often erasing words and even whole sentences related to opinions different from the one adopted by most members of "Po'alei-Zion" in Galicia. Only here and there could be found words coming from the depths of the hearts. After completing the formulation of the leaflet, the authors started to look for ways and means to publish it. They certainly did not expect that Zionist newspapers would publish anything that contradicts the thinking and actions of the Zionist establishment. There was a printing-shop in Brody, which belonged to a Jew, but it did not have Hebrew letters needed for printing the leaflet, and none of its workers knew Yiddish very well. A trip to Lvov was not an easy thing to organize; none of the members had a penny in their pockets. After many searches, they found a Jewish worker among the Russian emigrants who opened a lithography shop and worked in it by himself. He agreed to print the leaflet. The price negotiations did not last long, as the subject matter was close to his heart, and he was satisfied with the little the members could afford. They went to work carefully and reverently. The members stood near the worker when he stamped the letters onto the stone, to avoid mistakes, and mainly because they were eager to witness the birth of their spiritual creation.

The creation of the leaflet lasted just a single day. The members started to distribute it among the youths in the city and sent it to members with whom they kept in touch, as well as to newspaper editors. It was a big surprise for them to see their leaflet published in a prominent place in the journal of "Po'alei Zion" – "*Der Yidisher Arbeiter*" ["The Jewish Worker"MK], which was published in Lvov, on 6 of November 1908. The spectacular headline "Workers – Pioneers" astonished the members of the group. They rejoiced because many of their hopes depended on the publication of the leaflet.

[Page 120]

In order to better understand the sequence of events that followed, we need to add that the end of the leaflet contained an address: "Po'alei Zion", attention A". A was the first letter of the member Moshe Arkin, who was the group's initiator and leader (he came back from Eretz Israel and stayed in Brody for a cure).

The "Workers – Pioneers" leaflet was published in the 40th issue of the journal "The Jewish Worker". A week later, immediately following the publication, in the 41st issue, *Katriel* (the political party name of *Leon Khazanovitz*[a]), came out with a harsh attack directed at the members of the group "Workers – Pioneers" and the Journal editors for publishing the leaflet. Using sharp bold style, he attacked the group and its members to the point of a personal insult, by stating that anyone can see that the leaflet members are young, and it is not always a good idea to take advice from them. From the editorial comment, *Katriel* concluded that the "Workers – Pioneers" was established by the members of "Po'alei Zion" in Brody. Based on that assumption he began his questions. His first question was *"Mi Samkha?"*[5] which in Hebrew means *"who nominated you to be leaders"?*, and also who allowed the members of "Po'alei Zion" to establish a group of pioneers, and who gave them the permission to distribute leaflets? *Katriel* continued to elaborate that the questions were asked since the attitude of the party of "Po'alei Zion" toward the issue of groups of pioneers must have been well known to all members. As part of the preparations to the Poalei Zion party's 4th conference, proposals to establish groups of pioneers were published in the newspaper "The Jewish Worker". At the conference, the issue of Eretz Israel was discussed comprehensively, and the proposal was not accepted. The committee for the affairs of Eretz Israel rejected the proposal to establish such groups, submitted by comrade Arkin. So, here come the comrades from Brody, proceed to establish groups of pioneers, and appeal to the public through leaflets. Isn't that a breach of discipline? When individuals are assembled for the purpose of a journey to Eretz Israel, nobody would oppose them. On the contrary, everybody would accompany them with heartfelt wishes. However, the same is not true when it comes to an association, belonging to a political party, who takes upon itself to establish such groups. By doing that, the association assumes a responsibility that it may not be able to carry out, the hope of the pioneers will not be fulfilled, and they will come back, as many before them did, disappointed. Wouldn't that affect negatively our party? How can such an association be allowed to do something like that without obtaining permission from the party leadership? Our friends from Brody appealed to the Zionist youth in general; however, what do these small groups of bourgeois Zionist have in common with the entire Zionist youth? The intentions of our friends from Brody may have been good, but they did not know that the losses caused by an artificial immigration wave to Eretz Israel, exceeded their benefits. Any ten emigrants who were going to Eretz Israel bustling with hope, would not bring as much benefit if weighed against the potential damage caused by one person who comes back disillusioned. They are naive to assume that just by Hebrew studies which they provide to their pioneers, they prepare them for their survival struggle in Eretz Israel. They exaggerate if they think that they are able to help, in advice and action, the youths, "whose situation here is bad" and they are forced to emigrate. I will only raise one more question: have they forgotten that the conference elected a committee to deal with matters related to Eretz Israel, whose location is Krakow and not Brody? Don't they know that appealing to the public in a matter of general interest such as this, without prior approval of the party center, is a violation of its authority? In conclusion, I would like to say that the comrades from Brody, thinking that they were acting for the benefit of the public, may have erred and forgotten about the party leadership. Why would "The Jewish Worker" publish such a leaflet? Wouldn't we find many members of the party, who, relying on the authority of the formal party newspaper, will study Hebrew, which is so close to the hearts of the leaflet's authors, and immigrate to Eretz israel , unprepared, not being suited for the living conditions, and without the need for their working skills? On the eve of the fourth party conference, an article was published in "The Jewish Worker" by comrade *Avner,* who is not a less qualified expert on the issues of Eretz Israel than our comrades from Brody. In his article, comrade Avner mentioned that calling the Zionist youths in the diaspora to immigrate as pioneers to Eretz Israel, as published in the leaflet issued by "*HaPo'el HaTzair*" [literally "*The Young Worker*"MK][7], was an act of recklessness. With the recent publication, "The Jewish Worker" is repeating the same mistake, something that its own correspondent in Eretz Israel has condemned. Katriel ends with a question: "How do we solve this riddle?"

[Page 121]

These words of *L. Khazanovitz* [a] indicated that he was one of the radical followers of the "natural immigration" theory with respect to Eretz Israel, an opinion held by a substantial part of Po'alei Zion in Russia. According to them, any organized action aiding the "artificial immigration" was doomed and therefore forbidden. As a matter of fact, Katriel's words did not hurt us at all. Even his personal insult, presenting himself as the elder, therefore the smarter one, and us, the young ones, who are not as smart as he and people of his age, did not insult us. His words were an echo of the talk of our parents, who opposed our socialistic and Zionist sentiments. His belief and the belief of his co-thinkers, devout followers of the "natural immigration", we considered a belief of people who were weak in character and lacking courage. We were even somewhat proud of the fault of hastiness, that Katriel attributed to us. We were also not very impressed by the threat of an accusation concerning our offense of a breach of discipline. We actually wished wholeheartedly to have such an investigative hearing before a party forum, which would provide us with the greatest publicity. Our adversary was too smart to allow us the opportunity for that; however, during our discussions with friends, the content of which reached his ears, and during his lectures in Brody, people provoked him openly: "do you dare to sue us to an investigative inquiry or a trial by the members?" He never dared to try that.

[Page 122]

Chazanovitz had strong organizational skills, a brain-man who was able to intellectually convince people with a logical rational analysis. Emotional considerations were not valid as far as he was concerned.

Like most of the people of this kind, he was very shrewd and very witty toward the members who opposed him. The opponent of Chazanovitz in the newspaper was *A. L. Schussheim*[b] who had a warm heart and was open to support every pioneering actions and independent thinking. He was a G-d gifted journalist who kept his civilized manners even during an argument with an adversary, especially within the party. He knew how to protect the honor of his opponents, and avoided using harsh words and insulting remarks. This is why his cautious approach vis-a-vis Chazanovitz's sharp attack and his careful words to avoid the sharpening of the quarrel are understandable. *Schussheim* responded on behalf of the editors as follows: "We have to admit that even with the best of our will, we cannot accept this issue as tragically as our comrade *Katriel*. When we published the leaflet, we did not have any intention other than providing information to our readers on the mood and power of the actions taken by a certain part of our members. Concerning the matter of "breaching of discipline" I would like to comment that unfortunately I did not know about our party action during this year. When this issue was debated on the pages of "The Jewish Worker", I was immersed in my own private matters. I did not even read *Avner's* article. One thing I did know from the party tradition though: that we always treated favorably groups of pioneers who organized independently from time to time. . It would be very difficult to consider the action of Brody's group as a breach of discipline. From the fact that the party did not decide to form groups of pioneers, one cannot conclude that this action needs to be condemned. Therefore there is no room here for talking about a breach of discipline. At most, there is a minor violation of authority. We need not be distracted by the fact that the group was formed only for members from Brody and its environs, and this is where the leaflet was directed at. On the matter of artificial immigration, I am, of course, of the same opinion as comrade Katriel. It would be inconceivable to create artificial immigration, not even among the bourgeois Zionists. The leaflet just mentions Palestine as a good country for immigration, and this is not against the party's view"[c]

Without expanding further about the whole dispute, whose time has passed, I wanted to bring some facts proving that it was unreasonable even at the time. "Po'alei Zion" members who were already in Eretz Israel, headed by *Ben Tzvi (Avner),* among them townsmen from my own town, Brody, did not immigrate according to a "*natural immigration*", but through what was named "artificial immigration". Mr. Schussheim was right in his note that "Po'alei Zion" treated all groups of pioneers favorably. This was often clearly reflected in the party's journal. I have already mentioned Yosef Aharonovitz's action in Brody as part of the "Zion Pioneers" association belonging to the "Po'alei – Zion" movement. This action was not performed secretly, and was publicized in the party's journal. In the same year, 1906, an article about the establishment of a group "Workers Pioneers" among the members of "Po'alei Zion" in Lodz, was published in "The Jewish Worker" (no. 14, May 18th). We took the name of our group in Brody from that group. There were things that were previously published about our group in the party's journal. This was also what we told comrade Chazanovitz during a face to face stormy discussion when he came for a visit in Brody. He, of course, was not very convinced.

The management of the "Po'alei Zion" association yielded to Chazanovitz's demand, and published a message in "The Jewish Worker" (no. 43) that it does not have any association with the group "Workers Pioneers" and that they allowed the group, as a curtsey, to publish their note in the party's journal. This message of the association's management sparked a storm among the members in Brody (the dispute spread to other cities by our own initiative. As a result, the membership divided between two opposing camps concerning the issue of pioneering).

[Page 123]

I have an emotional need to mention two meetings that can further describe the life in those days. These meetings were a great source of encouragement to the members of "Workers Pioneers" and to me. They greatly helped us to overcome the difficulties we have encountered. One meeting was with Yosef Aharonovitz who served as the first "Hapo'el Hatzair" delegate from *Eretz Israel* to the eighth Zionist Congress (held in the Hague on 12-14 August 1907) , together with *Israel Shochat*[8], may he live long. (*Yitzhak Ben Tzvi* [Israel second president.[MK]], and

Israel Shochat served together in "Po'alei Zion" in Eretz Israel). I am not sure about the formal arrangement but, if I am not mistaken, the candidacy of Yosef Aharonovitz to the Zionist Congress was short several votes, while in Brody there was an excess which was not used, so they combined Brody's votes in order to gain a second candidate form Eretz Israel. It seems to me that these were votes of the "Po'alei Zion" party, or perhaps it was a mixture of votes of "Po'alei Zion" and the "*General Zionists*" party[9]. In any case, Yosef Aharonovitz came to Brody on September 1st for several days, directly from the Congress, to report to his voters about the Congress. The meeting was held in the offices of the "Po'alei Zion" association in which Aharonovitz was once an active member before immigrating to Eretz Israel (By the way, in this meeting I was nominated to introduce Aharonovitz in front of a big crowd. It was my "maiden speech", I got mixed up, and could hardly finish my introduction...).

From *Yosef Aharonovitz's* speech I recall that he was not impressed by the arguments at the Congress, and they were not aligned according to his taste and spirit. In his speech he incorporated a certain criticism oriented at the labor settlements, namely the groups of the communal settlements. We were somewhat surprised, as we were under the effect of the descriptions of these settlements by Moshe Arkin, who came back from Eretz Israel to Brody for the purpose of curing himself. We also followed the speeches of the leaders of "Po'alei Zion" – *Shlomo Kaplanski* and *Natan Gross* in the Congress. They both demanded recognition of the labor communal settlements as an action of the Zionist movement. Several members of the "Workers Pioneers" group intended to make Aliya and join these groups. However, in his discussions with the members of our group, *Aharonovitz* expressed his satisfaction with our activity, which he saw as a continuation of the pioneering action he helped organizing.

The other meeting was with *Chaia-Bracha Liberman*, who was married in Eretz Israel to *Chaim Tzimerman*, who was a member in the *Um-Juni* group (Kibutz *Degania A*) , and was also among the founders of *Yavniel* [an agricultural settlement in the Lower Galilee established in 1898 on land bought by Baron Rothschild[MK]]. Chaia-Bracha was born in the village of *Strzemilcze,* near Brody, and made Aliya against the will of her parents. On her way to Eretz Israel, she was hosted by her relatives in Brody. At our meeting with her, she told us about her contacts in Eretz Israel, and about the news she received, which were optimistic about her chances to secure a job in the near future. Chaia-Bracha was beautiful, graceful, witty and full of energy. She charmed all of the group's members.

A farewell event was planned when our Aliya day approached. However, my friend Shalom Kupfer and myself, who were two of the party officials among the immigrants, did not agree to an event together with "*Po'alei Tzion*" officials. This is how we settled our account with the party leadership, who ended up being very embarrassed.

The journal "The Jewish Worker" published an article (no. 8, February 19th, 1909) as a result of our request, stating that a farewell party was held jointly by "Po'alei Zion" and "Workers Pioneers".

[Page 124]

The following was stated as a camouflage: "...Following some farewell speeches, Mr. Mendel Zinger added a few kind and warm words which will stay with us for a long time".

I would allow myself to note that the dispute about our leaflet contributed significantly to the pioneering cause, and helped widening the circle of youths who heeded our call.

The resistance to the actions of "Workers Pioneers" that Mr. Chazanoviz wanted to create, did not receive support from any side and was completely forgotten. Even Mr. Chazanovitz himself did not bring it up again. During the following years, many members of "Po'alei Zion" who were "enticed" by the "artificial immigration" continued to make Aliya from Galicia.

Our preparation efforts were quite primitive. Some members prepared themselves, when possible, by working in the vegetable and flower gardens in their parents' home. In most cases, however, the preparation efforts were limited to spiritual preparation toward a life of physical labor and resistance. The spiritual training was done diligently by reading Zionist newspapers, especially news concerning Eretz Israel, by maintaining communication with people who had already immigrated, and mainly by studying the Hebrew language and reading its literature. The more "advanced" people read the magazine *"HaShilo'ach"*[10] to which they had a collective subscription. They read the magazine jointly, including articles on matters of principle, as well as literary articles published in earlier issues. These readings were held jointly with a group of high-school students who studied Hebrew. During the winter, they would meet alternately at the house of one of the students for joint reading, a lecture or just a discussion. During the spring and the summer days, they would mainly meet "on the dikes" (raised embankments, remnants of the city's fortifications from the previous century, a place for a hike among the trees). They had to read Hebrew secretly. As a disguise, the students used to take with them a textbook from school and put it on top just in case one of the professors happened to pass by accidentally, and insisted on checking what his students were doing. Studying Hebrew was considered to be a very suspicious activity by the teachers. Anybody who was caught doing it, particularly by a Polish teacher or an assimilated Jew, would be risking being thoroughly interrogated whether he or she were a member of a Zionist group. This would be particularly harmful, since they would question the student about his or her progress in the school studies in light of the "unproductive" involvement in this "unnecessary" activity.... On Saturday afternoons and on Sundays we went out together to the large and dense pine tree forests near the city. In the forest we felt free, since over there, the inspecting eyes of the teachers of our friends, the high-school students did not reach. In the forest kingdom we could also often unload the burden of the Torah studies, to romp and to wrestle like any youth of our age. Among the works we read during those days, stood out *Y. Ch. Brenner's "Around the Point"*. We argued vigorously and lengthily about the content of the story or the novel (we had arguments even on that definition). Those who read previous writings of Brenner, especially "In the Winter", were comparing *Firman* and *Abramson,* and also finding hints for the fact that optimism is stronger than pessimism. *"Abramson* describes the faith of his nation using pessimistic words such as: "Dark Countries", Large Goyim" [non-Jewish nations[MK]], scattered lambs, scared herd, sheep to the slaughter" – claimed the main speaker – "however, the more dominant were his words in *"The Scroll of Yaakov"*. For example, at the end of that story Abramson writes:

[Page 125]

"....When he woke up and came into the garden on the top of the mountain, the garden that was located as a small dot on the top, he went past this dot to his beloved children, true to his covenant, to spread his seed which would bear fruit – the glow of the blade would turn over him, and would not let him come through the gates. Haters and Amaleks would fight him to bring upon his destruction, but he would endure. Where would he find shelter? He would escape and encircle the garden. Encircle, and encircle, and encircle – the entire day. His would be filled with horror and he would encircle around and around and around". Our members persisted in their reading and found proof to this concept in other sections: "...nevertheless, after all of these problems, understandings and considerations, you are indeed alive, and Mr. So-and-so is alive as well, hardly living – but alive! ...and what is the conclusion? The conclusion is that people are trapped by the same hidden mystery, and their soul finds this hidden sweetness among all this evil. Therefore...? Therefore we cannot look at life as observers only. We must fight, correct, grow and exalt. Hurling complains against the holiness of life is only an observation! Damned are those who are only observers!" When I went back to read *"Around the Point"* years later, I recalled the fantasy worlds in which we floated during those days of our readings. There were some verses and segments in these works that every one of us saw as if they are directed to himself or herself. When *Abramson*, while writing his article: *"The Hebrew Creation at the Beginning of the 20th Century"*, wrote the words: "...he saw himself as one of the first Hebrew young pioneers, the Israelis of tomorrow, one of those individuals where the flame of the sublime visions of the great tragedy was set ablaze in their heart, and who found the path and the way toward the deep desirable outcome", each of us found in them an echo of their own misgivings and hopes.

The members increased their efforts in bringing additional proof to the positive outcome which Brenner arrived at in his "Around the Point" after his own misgivings. However, a most stormy argument erupted around the question of what was this point that the author encircled. We also argued about whether there is only one point, or maybe he meant that there are different points one encounters throughout one's life. In the story itself, hints are actually given to the mysterious point such as:

> "Now is the point: what will happen? Time is passing, the days go on, the person is alive, and life continues as usual. On the other hand – a ship became a wreck at sea, what will happen? What will happen? The point was and then....."

Or,

> "...Since that day in which Chava Blumin visited him, and then just went out and left, the point stood as more sharpened, becoming blurred at times and then returned anew causing unimaginable pain..."

Determining the intentions of the author concerning the point was made even more difficult, by different hints such as:

> "...The fear attacked him again. He had to master the remainder of his strength to pass over the border, the border of the point. His efforts were in vain, there was no passage. The point cut into his heart. The point was unique, small, black, horrible... He tried to bypass it, to circle around it, a magical circle, his lips mumbling: just a little while, just a little while..., and it seemed to him that he jumped over it - and then he realized that he was mistaken: the point was in heaven not on earth – so how can he pass over it? Clearly, I am totally innocent – he was bursting with a revolt – my nose kerchief is totally white! he cried, but his voice was not heard. The point stands undisturbed. All along the way there is one single point. There is no other. All the way to the point and there is no passage. And generations elapse..."

[Page 126]

Since we could not figure out these hints, we came to the conclusion that we should not be satisfied just with theories. A better way would be to turn to the author himself and ask him whether he would be so kind as to uncover the secret for us. In those days a secret conference of the Zionist youth was about to take place in Lvov. Some of our members, who participated in the reading of the book "Around the Point", were among the conference delegates, and they took on themselves to talk to Brenner who lived in Lvov at that time. I do not remember whether or not Brenner provided the solution to this puzzle. I do remember however, that the two youths came back from Lvov full of excitement about the discussion with the author and full of admiration to this "remarkable person". From their description I understood that Brenner was delighted about the fact that youths in Brody, have shown interest in Hebrew literature and in his works, and the fact that they taxed their brains about what exactly did the author mean in this matter or that, or in this statement or that. I decided to look for the right opportunity to meet with Brenner. When I travelled to Lvov from time to time, I was not distracted from this objective. One time I saw him in the company of strangers, and did not dare to interrupt him. However, at another time I saw him surrounded by people with one of my acquaintances among them. I asked my acquaintance and he introduced me to Brenner. Brenner only exchanged a few polite words with me; however the expression on his face was etched in my memory: he seemed to be someone in which heaviness and tenderness were mixed together. As a matter of fact we can use his own words written about Zalman (in his book "Around the Point"): "the expression on this face broadcasted a unique anguish, devotion and willingness to do good. His eyes were the eyes of a poet that are not satisfied with what is out in the open visible to all, but penetrated to the depth of your soul. When you stood in front of his eyes you felt that they penetrate into you, to the point that you would debate whether to disclose everything you had on your heart, or perhaps to cover up somewhat. Brenner's laughter was innocent, coming from the depth of his heart, loud and jubilant, but accompanied by an echo of sad thoughts: Is there a justification for my laughter? A person standing in front of this face once in one's life would never forget it.

These were the words I used to tell my friends about my impression of my "meeting" with Brenner when I returned from Lvov. Meeting with quotation marks, since my words reflected much of my impression from looking at him before our short meeting and after it, and much of what I imagined about him when I read his works.

[Page 127]

Farewell banquet of the Keren Kayemet LeIsrael [JNF] activists, on the occasion of the Aliya of Naftali Lerner-Naor

A group on Achva and Hanoar Hazioni members

[Page 128]

A group of members of "Zionists Socialist Workers" in the Diaspora

A group of members of the Central Aid Organization of the Jews in Germany, EZRA

Notes in the original article

a. Khazanovitz – [A Zionist leader in the "Po'alei Zion" in Galitzia.[MK]] died on September 7th, 1925, in the village of Valkhova in the Russian Carpathia in the midst of his action among the Jewish farmers on behalf of the "Ort" Society. He distanced himself from any association with the "Po'alei Zion" movement.

b. Aharon Leib Schussheim – [A Zionist leader in the "Po'alei Zion" movement in Austria and a noted Journalist and editor.[MK]], born in Radem, Galicia in 1879; died in Buenos Aires in 1955.

c. This point was also raised by D. Schtock (Sadan) in the "HaMizrakh" ["The East"], Shvat, Iyyar, Nisan, 5711 [February, March April, 1951]

Translator's footnotes

1. **Yosef Aharonovitz** – Born in Southren Ukraine and self educated, he made Aliya in 1906, following Yosef Vitkin's "Public Appeal" to Jewish youths in the diaspora. Unlike his mentor, he believed in the need to know how to work the land, before the land is acquired, so he began his career in Israel as a simple agricultural worker. Later on, he became a delegate to two Zionist congresses and the editor of "HaPo'el HaTza'ir" the newspaper of the party. After its unification with the Labor union party to form MAPAI (The Party of Workers in Eretz Israel), he became one of its leaders and thinkers. Before his death in 1937 he served as the head of *Bank Ha-Po'alim* (Israeli largest bank, founded by the labor union *Histadrut).*
2. **Po'alei Zion** – Literally "*Workers of Zion*" - a Socialist-Zionist movement founded in Russia in December 1905. Its most prominent leader was *Ber Borochov.* The movement had expanded to Central and Western Europe and North and South America as well as to Eretz Israel where it established the first kibbutzim. The movement was united by Israel's Ben Gurion with the Ahdut Ha'Avoda movement to form MAPAI party, predecessor of Israel's labor party.
3. **Menachem Usishkin** – A Russian born zionist leader who made Aliya in 1919. In his pamphlet *"Our Program"* he advocated group settlements based on labor Zionism. Under his influence the Zionist movement actively supported the establishment of agricultural settlements, educational and cultural institutions, as well as a Jewish polytechnic which later became the Technion in Haifa, Israel.
4. **Haskalah** – Literally "education" or "enlightenment" often termed the "Jewish Enlightenment" was an extensive intellectual movement among

the Jews of Central and Eastern Europe who advocated emphasis on general secular education and the integration of the Jews as productive members of their local societies. Concurrently, the movement promoted a Jewish cultural revival, manifested mainly in the creation of modern Hebrew-based secular culture.

5. **Mi Samkha?** – the first two Hebrew words of the biblical phrase: "Who nominated you to be our leader, or a judge between us?" thrown at the Jewish Egyptian prince Moshe, when he was trying to intervene between two quarrelling people.
6. **Yehoshua Heschel Schorr** – A Western Galitzian scholar, critic and communal worker native and resident of Brody (1814 – 1895) who was known for his satirical attacks on religious conservatism. He founded and published the HeHalutz magazine which he used to publish and spread his criticism.
7. **HaPoel HaTzair** [Literally "The Young Worker" - a non-Marxist socialist movement formed in 1905 in Palestine by the Jewish immigrants. In 1930, together with *Ahdut HaAvoda* (*Labor Union*) party they form *Mapai* – "The Party of the Workers of Eretz Israel" headed by Israel's first prime minister David Ben Gurion.
8. **Israel Shochat** – A Zionist leader, born in 1886, immigrated to Palestine in 1904. Together with others, he helped found the "*HaShomer*" ("*The Guard*") group, a precursor to Israel Defense Force.
9. **General Zionists Party** - this party, in its many metamorphoses, championed causes such as the encouragement of private initiative and protection of middle-class rights. It was the precursor to the liberal movements and parties formed over the years.
10. **HaShilo'ach** – Jewish monthly magazine, established by Achad Ha'am in 1896 in Odessa. The magazine was published in Berlin and transferred to Jerusalem in 1920. It dealt mainly with issues associated with Zionism, History of the Jewish nation, and Hebrew and Jewish literature.

[Page 129]

The Shomer Branch on Leshniovska Street

by Sonya Katzman-Vinogradov

Translated by Moshe Kutten

Edited by Rafael Manory

It is not easy to describe the sights of a Jewish town in eastern Poland—to tell about the young girls and boys of Brody the way they are etched in the heart and memory of a 70-year old woman, for whom the hardships of six wars have left their marks on the soul and body. However, there is the will to document, to remember and to be remembered, and by doing that, build a memorial for the young lives that were standing at the outset of their road when, all of a sudden, everything was ripped apart by a storm—here it was, and then there is no more. You would never again hear these young voices, singing, debating, raising wishes or weaving dreams. The fluid conversation in Leshniovska Street would never be heard again, the conversation of these noisy youths walking arm in arm, with a youthful joy bursting out from of their being. The youths flowed, marched toward the activities center of Ha'Shomer Ha'tzair"[1] in Brody. A few years before the war broke out, the branch moved to a building that was a former an animal-hair processing factory, owned by the Landau family. Their older daughter, a graduate of "Ha'Shomer Ha'tzair" made Aliya to Eretz Israel, and fulfilled her aspirations in Kibbutz Merkhavia. Her parents agreed to lease the factory buildings, including the big hall and the spacious yard to the local branch of Ha'Shomer Ha'tzair" for a symbolic fee, and by doing that allowed the branch to provide its members the opportunity of enjoying many diversified activities. During the nineteen thirties, most of the Jewish youth was organized with Zionist youth movements. The larger and the most active movement was "Ha'Shomer

Ha'tzair", which I was fortunate to be one of its members. The Shomer branch was teeming with youths, boys and girls, from the young age of ten. The branch graduates, went to a Hakhshara[2] camp . Some made Aliya to Eretz Israel, while the rest looked for every possible way, or a crack in the system, that would allow them to reach Eretz Israel.

During the years 1938–1939 our Shomer battalion – "The Shimshons", which consisted of a boys group and a girls group, took upon itself the principal burden of managing the branch. At the time, there were 12 girls in the "Lahav" group, of which I was a member. Only two survived the war. During the last few years before the war tremendous tensions prevailed in Europe, and especially in Poland. However, even that tension, the rampant antisemitism and the difficult economic conditions of the Jewish community, could not brake the joy of life of the Jewish youths who went on with their day-to-day life. That joy of life was bursting out from the Shomer branch and radiated light and warmth on the entire surroundings.

In the evenings, singing voices, of the distant Eretz Israel's songs, broke through from the windows of the branch. We lived in a harsh and dark reality, but our spirit and thoughts were there, far away ...Our entire being was filled with plans about the world of tomorrow. The dream that we weaved in the Shomer branch filled our heart with faith and hope. It was astonishing as to how we, boys and girls at the age of adolescence, succeeded to form another world in our spirit during those testing days, when the sky was already covered by dark clouds predicting the approaching storm.

[Page 130]

Alongside the singing, the dancing and the vibrant social activities, diverse learning and educational activities, as well as ideological and scouting activities took place at the Shomer branch. We studied the geography of Eretz Israel, "Palestinography" it was called in those days. In our mind, we traveled the length and breadth of Eretz Israel. We climbed the Galilee Mountains, we crossed the Jezreel Valley, we dipped in the See of Galilee and followed the Jordan River through its entire length from its sources to the Dead Sea. We did all of that using books and maps, but the images and landscapes stretched in front of as if they were real. We studied Borokhov's[3] ideology and were convinced that we can turn the Jewish nation's pyramid upside down, with our own hands, so that the Jewish people returning to Eretz Israel will stand on a solid base consisting of a class of workers, farm, industry and construction workers. We studied psychology, sociology, socialist ideologies and more. Important subjects at the top of the world agenda occupied the branch members. We discussed the issues faced by a boy or girl at the beginning of their adolescence. The frank and open teaching by the instructors have eased the discomfort the youths experience at that age. We attributed great importance to the Shomer commandments[4], to their fulfillment in one's life and to faithful adherence to them. They are etched in my memory to this day.

We were taught to adhere to values such or self-fulfillment, preservation of justice in the humane society, faithfulness to one's nation and more. These values were, in our eyes, supreme moral imperatives, and therefore we wanted to live by them and to educate future generations to abide by them.

The Shomer branch was teeming with youths during almost every evening. We came to sing, dance or play even when there were no scheduled battalion or group activities. The Shomer branch played major roles in the life of Brody youths. It served as a shelter from the surrounding world and was a stimulus for the imagination, a source for dreams, faith and love of the nation and its homeland.

In 1939 we, the 17-, 18- and 19-years old boys and girls, served as the counselors and leaders of the younger age groups. We swore to keep allegiance, in Leshniov forest, when we pass from one layer (age group) to another, and the echo of our call was carried out to far away distances – “Shomrim – be strong![5]” The forest served as a field for all sorts of scouting activities – getting around and being able to navigate in the area, initiative, overcoming fear and mutual aid. In that forest, our battalion, the Shimshons, took upon itself the leadership of the branch. The start of the war found us with this responsibility, on 1 September 1939. All the frameworks were shuttered during one single day. Smoke covered our town within one hour. Fire from above and thundering guns from below turned our lives into a huge flame.

According to the Molotov–Ribbentrop agreement, Brody became a Russian city. This is how we earned another two years of living like human beings. The members of the branch turn and spread in many directions. Some wandered to the Soviet Union, but most remained with their parents in Brody.

The Germans invaded the Soviet Union on 22 June 1941. Brody was conquered a week later in one day. Many of the branch members still lived in the city. Only a very few survived and were saved.

Throughout the hell that engulfed us during the German conquest, everybody fought the battle of staying alive on his or her own. There were periods of deep despair, when giving up, surrendering and ending one's life seemed the most suitable solution; however, the survival instinct triumphed. Even when there was no hope at all, when the powers of the body and the soul were exhausted, a flicker remained and this is what kept us alive.

[Page 131]

Today, several decades later, when I try to understand our situation then, it seems to me that we were helped by two sources of power:

a. One source of power was rooted in the belief that it was worthwhile to fight, because we had a goal to fight for. In his book: "A Man's Search for a Meaning", the psychologist Victor Frankl[6], himself a Holocaust survivor, writes that "if one has what to live for—everything is possible".

b. A second source of power were a few good people, humans, whom I found on my arduous road, during critical minutes and situations. These people extended their hands to help me.

I was liberated on 22 July 1944. My physical and emotional situation were very difficult. We were liberated by the Russians. They treated us humanely. Two Russian officers of Jewish descent found us, and they did everything in their power to help us.

The first spark that helped us stand tall and erect again was a group of Jewish children that were on the verge of oblivion when we found them. We gathered them on the streets, we collected those who came out of their hideouts, we took them out of Christian homes, smuggled them out of monasteries and established children homes. The resolve we had to help them recuperate and bring them to Eretz Israel helped us overcome all the difficulties.

The baggage we acquired in our youth at the Shomer branch has directed our steps and actions, knowingly or unknowingly.

After our liberation, I started to search and gather the remnants of the Shomer pioneering youth. What united us was one goal—to leave the land of Poland, a land soaked in blood and go. We had a place to go to. The direction was very clear and unambiguous—Eretz Israel. By helping others, I helped myself.

And now some personal words:

For the hell that surrounded me during the four years of the German conquest, I did find some points of light. One of them was Tadeusz Zak. Tedik arrived in Brody with his father in 1935. His mother passed away a few years earlier and his father married Mrs. Pipel. During the Soviet rule, his father was sent to Siberia.

Tedeusz Zak very actively saved Jews. I was one of the people he saved through self-sacrifice. He spent a lot of effort to save my mother, but to my sorrow, the Ukrainians murdered her and another 35 Jews from Brody on 6 May 1943. May their memory be blessed.

Tedeusz Zak passed away in Warsaw from a heart attack, in 1981. He left a wife, a son and three grandchildren.

He was not recognized officially as a Righteous Among Nations[7] despite the fact that he deserved to be recognized because what he did and because of his personality. It is therefore appropriate to mention him in the Yizkor Book for Brody.

[Page 132]

A group of graduates of "Ha'Shomer Ha'Tzair" youth movement ["Young Guard"[MK]] in Brody
Standing from right to left: Rot, Yosef Fleishman-Bernshtein, Shionyo Tzinker, -, -, Bronshtein, Ovadia Veltman, Zushka Marder, -, Lutvak
Sitting: Natan Reinrat, Reiss, -, -, Leshnober, -, -
Sitting on the floor: Moshe Reinrat, Arie-Leiba'le Hertzberg, Fromer

A group of graduates of "Ha'Somer Ha'Tzair" ["Young Guard"[MK]] in Brody
Standing from right to left: Binyamin-Yuma Hertzberg, Meshulam-Shilek Shtock-Sadan, Michael Lamm, - , Asher Marsh, Doshya Goldshtein, Reissm Zushka Marder, Yona Furman, Yuzyu Katcher, Imanuel Musyo Ettinger, Yisrael Vilner;. Sitting Shmuel Siunyo Katz, Leshnover, Dorka Vengler, Ovadia Veltmen

[Page 133]

A group of members of Ha'Shomer Ha'Tzair"movement [Young Guard"[MK]] in Brody (1935)

Standing from right to left: Vilder, Shiunyo Katz, Rizya Gelman, Yekhiel Liberman, Papka Kreminitzer, Yitzkhak Gelman; Sitting: Hertz-Muki Shmushkin, Meltzya Holtzzagger, Rozhka Mult, Zushka Marder, Zhenia Polishchuk-Dagan, Mota'le Gleikher
Sitting on the floor: Rakhel Katz, Poppah Gelman, Paula Polishchuk Bloishtein, Nushka Fried

A group of members of Ha'Shomer Ha'Tzair"[Young Guard"[MK]] in Brody (1933)

Standing from right to left: Rudeck Aurbakh, Yusyo Mikulintzer, Izyu Raukh, Milek Gemershmidt, -, Fredek Katz
Standing: Greta Geduldig, -, Zhenia Polishchuk-Dagan, Klara Veltman, -
Sitting: -, Lipsker, Dushya Gladshtein, Durka Vengler, Asher Marsh, -
Sitting on the floor: Porter, Hertz-Muki Shmushkin, Yekhiel Lieberman, Mota'le Gleicher

[Page 134]

Members of the branch of "Ha'Shomer Ha'Tzair" movement ["Young Gurad"[MK]] (1929)

A group of of graduates of the "Ha'Shomer Hatzir"
["Young Guard[MK]] movement in Brody (1930)

Standing from right to left: Michael Lamm, -, Zeev VoVa Kurin, Rot, Arie-Leiba'le Hertzberg, Ovadia Veltman, Yehoshua-Hulesh Porter, -

Sitting: Natan Reinart, Shunyo Tzinker, - Lamm, Umek Glantz, Yeruham Hokhberg

Sitting on the floor: Asher Marsh, -, Avraham Tzinker, Yosef Fleishman-Bernshtein

Reclining: Moshe Reinrat

Translator's Notes

1. Ha'Shomer Ha'tzair—Hebrew for "The Young Guard"—a leftist secular Zionist youth movement founded in Galitsia in 1913. It was also the name of a leftist Marxist party during the British Mandate of Palestine, a precursor of the Israeli leftist United Workers Party.
2. Hakhshara – Literally, "preparation" in Hebrew, was the name given to preparatory camps in which the Zionist youths learned Hebrew and trained in agricultural and manual labor. The camp was organized as a Kibbutz (a commune). The graduates organized themselves into groups pending "Aliyah" (emigration to Eretz Israel).
3. Dov Ber Borokhov (1881–1917) was born in Ukraine and was one of the founders of Socialist Labor Zionism. He undertook intensive studies in Yiddish and became a scholar and an author in the language. He settled in New York in 1914 but rushed to visit Ukraine when the Russian Revolution broke, where he contracted pneumonia and died.
4. Ha'Shomer Ha'ttzair movement was based on three pillars (Zionism, Socialism and Judaism) as well as ten Shomer Commandments, which included guidelines for one's life such as the preservation of truth, friendship, freedom and equality, the value of the working person, independent thinking, appreciation of nature, and taking responsibility for one's action.
5. "Shomrim—be strong!" was the traditional call of the Ha'Shomer Ha'tzair movement, usually exclaimed by the leader and the members are supposed to respond with "Strong and courageous!".
6. Victor Emil Frankl (1905–1997) was an Austrian psychiatrist and a Holocaust survivor. In his most famous book:" Man's Search for a Meaning" (Beacon Press, Boston, MA, 2006), previously published in 1946, under the name "From Death-Camp to Existentialism", he describes his experiences as a concentration camp inmate, which led to the development of his theory about finding one's meaning of life as a way to continue leaving.
7. Righteous Among Nations—A honorific used by the State of Israel to describe non-Jews who risked their lives during the Holocaust to save Jews
8. From YadVashem: website - "...They stand in stark contrast to the mainstream of indifference and hostility that prevailed during the Holocaust. Contrary to the general trend, these rescuers regarded the Jews as fellow human beings who came within the bounds of their universe of obligation".

[Page 135]

Jewish Brody in the Last Decade of its Existence, As I Remember It

by Yitzhak Zohar (Izyu Zhorna)

Translated by Moshe Kutten

Edited by Yocheved Klausner

Brody, a main city in Ternopol district, is located on the Podolia-Volhynia border. Since its establishment until the division of Poland in 1772, it was included in the Polish kingdom. Most of the population in this region was Ukrainian (Ruthenian in Polish); however, most of the population in the cities and towns was Jewish with Ukrainian and Polish minorities. The Jews worked mostly as merchants or craftsmen. Most of the physicians, engineers and other free professionals were also Jewish.

Because of its strategic location as a border-town, Brody suffered through all the wars, and was often totally burnt or destroyed. After the division of the kingdom of Poland, the town became part of the Galicia province in the Austrian Empire. As a result of the various wars and conquests, Brody's Jews immigrated to various countries and were replaced by Jewish refugees from Russia. Thanks to these emigration waves, many Jews from our city can be found in different places in the world, mostly in the US, Israel and other places. During the years between the two World Wars, as the Polish regime consolidated in 1920, the Jewish life in the city progressed orderly. The Jews, who constituted a majority of the city population, lived peacefully with their Ukrainian and Polish neighbors. Even the Jews who were scattered in the neighboring towns and villages got along nicely with the gentiles.

There were four elementary schools in the city. Three of them were state schools. The fourth school was Jewish and belonged to the Jewish community. The parents paid tuition for their children who studied in the Jewish school, based on their economic situation. The teaching language in the Jewish school was Polish; however, Hebrew and Jewish studies were also covered. Unlike the Polish state schools, no classes were conducted, in the Jewish school, during the Sabbath or Jewish holidays. Until 1934, the Jewish school consisted of only four grades, after which the students continued their studies in the city's state school. In the Jewish school the classes were separated for boys and girls. In 1934, the classes were unified and a fifth grade was added. This progress continued until the Jewish school grew and became a full-scope elementary school with seven grades. The school's principal – Mr. Mostzisker, who instituted a very strict regimen, organized various clubs such as carpentry, sewing, singing, gymnastics, chess and sports. He also organized a club for a pellet gun shooting, "so that Jewish kids would learn how to use weapons". There was a library in the schools, managed by a teacher (the principal's wife), who was also the sister of General Mond - one of General Pilsudski' associates. Mr. Moustzisker forbade activities by any youth movements to take place in the school.

[Page 136]

In addition to the elementary school, which consisted of seven grades according to the compulsory education law, three high schools operated in Brody. One was a state high-school for boys, which had six grades (four regular high-school grades and two high grades, at the end of which the students passed a test for a matriculation diploma that allowed admission to a university). There was another high-school for girls, which was privately owned by Daodet Levin and another privately own coeducational (boys and girls) business high-school, also owned by Mr. Levin. In all of these schools parents had to pay tuition, a fact that prevented many from continuing their studies because of their economic situation.

Because of these economic constraints, many youths remained idle after graduating from the elementary school. Some found a place in one of the craft shops where they learned a craft. Some immigrated to Palestine after completing the "Hakhshara" ["pioneering training"[MK]]. Others were drafted to the Polish army when they reached the age of 21.

Several Zionist youth movements were active in the city during the last decade of independent Poland: Akiva-Mizrakhi, Hashomer Hatsair, Beitar, and Akhva General Zionists. In addition, the illegal communist party was active in the city. There were several sports clubs active in the city: the Ukrainian "Bohon", the Polish "Gvaizeda", which later on merged with the military sports club, and a Jewish sports club, which operated its own facilities, a football club and a football team. In later years, the Jewish football team merged with the local leftist football team.

A music club by the name "Hazamir" [the "Nightingale" in Hebrew[MK]] under the management of Kalman Harnik from the Jewish school was active in the city. Its activity included an orchestra and various musical courses. Several Jewish clubs with halls for card games, chess, reading and a library were also active in the city. The first club was "Postęp" (=Progress), and later on the club "Vita" (=Life) was established. Postęp consisted mainly of craftsmen, while Vita comprised wealthier mercahnts, industrialists and people of liberal professions (physicians, engineers, pahramacists, attorneys etc.)

There were three large synagouges in the cities, and tens of Batei-Midrash [Jewish study houses,[MK]], Kloizes [communal houses of learning, praying and gathering,[MK]] and Cheders [Torah schools for little children,[MK]], in which children began studies at the ae of 3.

The city, with its Jewish majority, did not experience acts of anti-Semitism in the open. Only toward the latest years, when Polish pilots settled in the new military airport, the city witnessed cases of Jewish beatings in the streets by drunken squadron's soldiers, or soldiers from the artillery unit, from the 43rd infantry brigade, or the 22nd cavalry battalion that were stationed in the city.

When the war broke out on September 1st 1939, panic settled over the city. Many Ukrainians were attracted by the idea of a "free Ukraine" statehood, like its state during the years 1919-1920. The city communists awaited the entry of the Red Army as established by Molotov-Ribbentrop agreement. According to the agreement, the eastern part of Poland was supposed to merge with the Ukraine and Belarus, occupied by Russia. Some of the Polish government ministers or generals, members of the Polish General Staff, stopped in the city in their flight toward Romania, and the city had the "privilege" to receive an aerial bombardment, which claimed many victims. Upon the declaration of "liberation" by Western Ukraine on September 17th, the city communists (most of whom were Jews), organized and seized power, even before the arrival of the Red Army.

[Page 137]

When the Red Army entered the city, the previous Polish officials and police officers were arrested, and the nationalizing of industry, commerce and housing began. Some Jews were jailed and exiled to Russia. Many refugees, mainly Jewish refugees, arrived when the western part of Poland was occupied. Local Jews hosted the Jewish refugees in their homes, but the situation was difficult. At one point, the Russian authorities announced that refugees who wanted to return to the German occupied area could register to do so. Most of the refugees registered; however, instead of returning them to western Poland, they were loaded onto freight boxcars and exiled to Siberia.

Widespread communist propaganda started with the arrival of the Soviets. The city was visited by many bands, orchestras and choruses. The nationalized stores reopened, where the owners now served as sales people or clerks. After the inventories were depleted, the city experienced a severe shortage of consumer goods. Long lines started to stretch at the stores. Some of the merchandise leaked into the black market, which flourished in the city. Many Jews managed to trade their property. Watches generated a strong interest among the newly arrived Soviet soldiers and officers.

Upon the consolidation of the new regime, all the schools, including the high-schools, reopened. The Soviets abolished the customary high tuition. Many hundreds of students, even many who already graduated years ago, surged into the high schools. Instead of a seven grade-elementary school and six grade high-schools the Soviets instituted a combined elementary-high school of ten grades. The schools were filled with students who, previously, could not afford the high-school studies, or did not find any institution where they could acquire a profession. Life in the city continued, more or less, orderly. Jews found all sorts of ways to make a living. Craftsmen worked in newly established cooperatives, former merchants worked as managers in the nationalized stores or as clerks in government and civil offices, positions which were previously forbidden for Jews.

The relative clam was abruptly shattered when Nazi Germany invaded the western areas of the Soviet Union. German airplanes, which appeared over the city as soon as the second day of the invasion, 23rd June 1941, helped to cast a horrific panic over the city. Soviet and local officials started to pack their belongings and flee eastward. The calm never returned despite the mass gathering in the city park, organized by the local military commander, in which he described the "victories" of the Red Army (like – "taking Krakow" and "advancing toward Vienna").

Only a few Jews managed to escape eastward, before the first German soldiers entered the city toward the end of June, despite the fact that the roads eastward remained open and the Russian border was only 70 miles away. Only a few took this opportunity to cross that border and continue eastward into Russia. The Jews did not expect that the situation would develop into something as bad as it eventually became. They knew that they will experience troubles, even just from the local Ukrainian population, but nobody thought that the Nazis, damn them, planned to annihilate the entire Jewish nation.

Much has been written about the Holocaust in Brody. Therefore, I would skip over that period.

[Page 138]

Upon the liberation of Brody, on July 7th 1944, most of the city was in ruins, because the front was nearby for many months. The few who survived the calamity which happened to the Jews, started to return to the ruined city. The deep distress, and the lack of graves of the loved ones, who were murdered in Belzec, forced the few that returned to leave the city by taking advantage of a special permission given by the Soviet Union. This special permission allowed Jews to go to Poland. In July 1945, several tens of Brody's Jews gathered in an abandoned synagogue in Lublin. From there they started to disperse. Most of the survivors from the city itself and its neighboring areas left Poland and settled in camps for displaced people, organized by UNRWA in West

Germany, Austria and Italy. Many went to United States, Israel (Palestine) and other countries when the camps were later dismantled. No Jews were left, except for a few families originally from Brody and a few families from elsewhere, who resettled in the city after the war. There were a few Jews who remained in Poland, adopted Polish names and married gentiles.

An association consisting of former residents of Brody and neighboring areas who immigrated before the Holocaust was active in Israel (Palestine). When the Holocaust survivors arrived in Israel after the war, the association reorganized. About a thousand of former residents of our town participated in the first memorial ceremony to our city martyrs, which took place on May 21st 1951, at the Herzlia high-school in Tel Aviv. A memorial is held annually since then.

To demonstrate the extent of the tragedy that fell upon the Brody Jews (as well as most of the European Jews), I will mention my father's family, the Zhorna family, and my mother's family – Kentshuker family. Like with many other large families, very few survived. I, Yitzhak, the eldest son of Mordechai-Motl Zhorna, was the only survivor from the family of my grandfather Shlomo Zhorna (who was a tavern and restaurant owner from the time of the Austrian rule), as well as from the family of my mother, nee Kentchuker. My paternal grandfather had seven children. Five of them were married and each had two children. Arye-Leib son of Moshe Kentshuker, who passed away in Israel, was the only survivor of the large Kentshuker family from Brody and the neighboring Podkamen. From the 49 members of both our families, we remained only two. The same fate was met by most of the Jewish families of Brody and the neighboring areas. Most of them were decimated without any soul left.

Jewish Brody, that was one of the largest Jewish communities in Europe during its peak in the 18th century, is no more. As early as 1948, a booklet was published by the Soviet Union authorities in honor of the 900th anniversary of the city establishment. It would have been very difficult for the reader to guess that there were ever any Jews in Brody. The city was rebuilt. There are now four high schools, a large industry, eighteen different clubs, a museum, a library and other various institutions. However, there are no Jews left.

[Page 139]

The Tarbut School: A Hebrew evening class
In the center the teachers of the course: Avraham Waltman and Naftali Lernr-Naor

A Hebrew class, Course A of the Tarbut School
In the center the teacher Naftali Lerner-Naor

[Page 140]

The Drama Group of the Jewish Youth in Brody
In the center Mirka Lilian

The Jewish Elementary School

[Page 141]

Fourth Grade students of the Jewish Elementary School (1928)
From left to right:
Standing first row: Grossfeld, Narks, B. Topper, B. Pastas, Unreich, Feuerstein, Fisch, Doner
Second row: Drillich, A. Katcher, Richkin, Furman, I. Friedman, B. Schpruch, Grossman, Ch. Peltz
Third row sitting: S. Gemersmidt (Milk), I. Mikulintzer, W. Hochberg, A. Moshtzisker (the teacher of the class), P. Ashkenazi (the principal of the school), N. Okser (teacher), Abramowitz, I. Recht, M. Hut
Sitting: Zussman, Z. Glanz, I. Katz, W. Singer, I. Shapira

[Page 142]

The Jewish Elementary School: Fourth grade boys 1930
The teachers and the Principal sitting from right to left: Shaul Bernstein, Kalman Harnik, Nachum Okser, Philip Ashkenazi (the principal), Sheinholz and Shkolnik

The Jewish Elementary School: Fourth grade girls
In the center the principal Philip Ashkenazi

[Pages 143-149]

The Sorrow of the Lonely Jewish Homes

by Dov Sadan (Shtock)
From the book "Realm of Childhood" by Dov Sadan

Translated by Moshe Kutten

Edited by Yocheved Klausner

I am praising the poet who established a big memorial to a national hero or to a lonely youth who does not extinguish the candle that illuminates his page of study, when darkness settles over the town and its inhabitants. However, in my opinion, a memorial for "perseverance" and praises should be given, even in a way of a few lines, to another loner, the barkeeper, whose house stood solitarily in a remote village, stuck in the middle of the diaspora and hated by it. He was like a Jewish candle that is flickering but is never extinguished.

If you read the few but colossal lines of the introduction to the poem "My Father", you would be able to envision the head of the barkeeper revealed above the barrels of liquor like the skull of a tortured holy man. His head is rising above a book of yellow parchments, amid the defilement of a tavern, through the hazes of abomination and fumes of repugnance.

I am so sorry that no poet has brought up for us this scene of the lonely man, keeper of the light of Israel, in the times of the night, in the loneliness of the tavern, when darkness is settling in, the darkness of diaspora and the hatred around him. We could see then, how strong is the link between these two lonely figures: the lonely young pupil in his corner, who guards the concealed light in the midst of the darkness of the diaspora and those bearded Jews of the taverns who had to continuously withstand the fear of the tyrant drunks, and who were guarding, with all of their might, the tiny light within themselves. They guarded this light so that it would not vanish in the midst of the ignorance, loathing and scorn that were always surrounding it. My feeling is that the will power of these lonely men was stronger than the will power of the lonely pupil. The learner could amplify his light by studying in isolation and seclusion without interruptions, while the barkeepers were exposed to all four winds of heavens. Their light was very frail to begin with, so much so that their fellow Jews, who were town dwellers, made it a subject for their distasteful jokes. Lo and behold the sense of humor and satire of our own people was nourished by the despair, humiliation, and bewilderment of the tavern owners. Against that, how scanty were the tries in poetry or and otherwise, to portrait the great heroism of these lonely people.

The red inn that my ancestors owned for more than a hundred years was located very close to the custom-house and to the city itself[1]. The Jewish families in the village numbered about a hundred. Proximity to the city and the other Jewish families helped to ease the feeling of isolation during the days. This was not the case at night, particularly during dark and stormy nights, when the scattered Jewish homes in the village felt like they were more scattered. It felt like the gendarmes who rode their horses to the darkest corners, rode their horses even harder.

The fear was magnified during stormy nights when the howls of the wind silenced any cry for help. Even the armed soldier, stationed in front of the inn, seemed to have lost his significance and power. If this was happening in our inn, then it was certainly happening in inns in more remote villages which were located far away from any town or city. In these villages, the inn with the tavern may have been the only Jewish home. A cry for help, vanishing in the darkness of the night, is the picture I visualize when I remember our lonely tavern.

Two figures of gentiles are associated in my mind with this picture. Both figures were idlers, farmers who uprooted themselves from their birthplace, turning from one occupation to another, hanging out between the edge of the village and the beginning of the town. Their outfits were a mixture of clothes – villagers' mantles and city hats. They were the head instigators of anything that has to do with smuggling or stealing. Their hands were in many mischiefs. They were especially great in harassing the Jews of the taverns. They were experts in causing trouble and tormenting people. Their specialty was to create small fears and cause small damages; however, when these small occurrences happened continuously, they had an accumulated effect of a sorrowful affair of immense proportion. The main thing about the pain and contempt was that they were able to inflict suffering and not only getting away with it but also being rewarded for it. They had this power of people of the periphery who were not afraid of the authorities, and even the gendarmes who were called to subdue them, learnt quickly that it is more convenient to ignore them. As a result, these two pests walked around like the kings of the village with nobody daring to resist them.

My grandfather was not the only one that got a taste of Demko's mischiefs. All other tavern owners in the area did as well. Not once did my grandfather wake up in the morning to find the well plugged with dirt while Demko was standing on the side, grinning. Demko knew that that specific day was a market day, and on a market day, an inn without a well is not an inn at all. He knew that Mosh'ko, wanting or not, would tell him in a way of asking: "Dear Demko, there is nobody as swift as you in plugging or unplugging a well. Would you be kind enough to do what you know well, with pay of course? You know that, as far as pay is concerned, I would never lessen your pay or deprive you of it". Demko knew that he had a "monopoly" on this kind of repair jobs, which were always the direct results of his own doing. He knew that Mosh'ko's life and body were dear to him more than his money. He stood there and yawned like a spoiled kid and did not bother to pick up the shovel until some more appeasements and pacifications were thrown at him and until the entire household were encircling him and begging him to start. When Demko completed the job and was paid, he would break away arrogantly and say: "on the next market-day, when the well is plugged again, don't forget to call the specialist, Demko the specialist".

Like Demko, like white Pavlo. His "expertise" involved breaking things. He would swing his cane, as if unintentionally, and drag down, with the bent edge of the cane, a dozen large glasses that were standing on the shelf, or break the window panes.

Breaking the window panes was an event reserved for special nights – such as the meal time of holidays, the joyful time of an Engagement Conditions gathering[2], or a Seven Blessings"[3] gathering. The real problem with all of that were not the damages created by his mischiefs that secured his income, but the fear that he instigated. He would approach my grandfather and say: "you have a license to sell liquors, and I have the license to your glasses". Another expertise of his was creating a significant crack in a liquor barrel, which caused a stream of liquor to be leaking on the floor.

My grandfather used to say that he carried four tyrants on his shoulder: "The first was the Czar, may he live, whom I pay taxes. The second tyrant was the proprietor, whom I pay the lease. He is a parasite, may he die. Then there was this couple - Demko and Pavlo, may they die a sudden death, whom I pay a pension like two old retired clerks. The problem with my retirees is that they would not stop working. I tell them that I would pay their pension without them lifting a finger, but they continue to lift all ten of their fingers to plug my well and break my glasses – I guess they simply like what they are doing".

Demko liked to tell stories about his power and bravery, as taverns with wells in front of them existed not only in our village but also in the neighboring villages of Sokodola, Dobia, Yesinov and others. However, Demko perceived his main achievement and fame to have come from that one evening on Friday night, when he smuggled Hodya, the daughter of a tavern owner along with her sawing machine, and loaded her and her lover – the gentile boy Katolnitski, on his wagon. He then brought them both to Podhorze where Hodya was baptized and later on married her lover. With scorn and mockery, Demko divulged that he heard the tavern owner going out in his white garment to the main road, at the same time on Friday night, and yelling: "My daughter, my daughter, Hodya, Hodya". There was no answer except the echo to his own voice vanishing in the darkness, and the diminishing and receding echo of the wheels of the wagon as it sped away toward Podhorze. Demko boasted that he approached Chaim, the tavern owner, the next day, and asked him: "Chaim, Chaim, why is your face so sad? Isn't it Saturday today? Tell your Hodya to bring you your kugel. You will eat the kugel and your face will be brightened". Chaim gave him a long teary-eyed look, but did not answer. Demko challenged him: "Oy-Vay Tata'le-Mama'le [Oy-Vay Father'le and Mother'le[MK]], Chaim filled up his stomach with okovita [strong alcoholic liquor with a high alcohol content[MK]] and he lost his speech. You talk to him about his daughter Hodya and he does not respond. You talk to him about his kugel and he does not answer".

Demko knew that he could terrify people with this story more than with stories about well plugging or other mischiefs. Most of these lonely tavern owners experienced this fear from tyrants, idlers and drunks. However, the greatest fear of these confused and scorned Jews was the fear that their own offspring's would be tempted by the world around them, by the vacuum of the diaspora that surrounds their weak candle. Only God knows how disturbed the souls of the parents were, how much anxiety and torment-filled sleepless nights these fathers and mothers had to go through, weary after their daily hassle and the non-stop daily uproar of the drunks and their emptiness. They must have been terrified to see the winks thrown over at their daughter by the villagers' sons and her smiles and talk. Like red-hot skewers to their skin was her friendship with the village's boys and the girls.

Nevertheless, what was the use of reprimands and the following reconciliation? Can one simply jail his or her daughter in a room with no door or window to the village? Could they supply her instead with the friendship and companionship of youths from her own people? Is there any matchmaker with whom they have not already consulted? If only they would have a brother or a sister in the city, they could have sent their daughter to stay with them and thus keep her away from the dangers of the remote village. This would eliminate the clouds of suspicion rising in the hearts of the parents and secure the little joy they had in life. On the other hand, how can they send their baby girl away from her own home to be like a lonely finger in a city of strangers? How can they send the bird away from her nest to become a stranger in a faraway place and be like in the phrase: "away from the eyes, away from the heart?" The long and fearful nights continued to come; every night harder than its predecessor. Her father's ears were always directed toward his daughter's bed as if to count the breaths of his sleeping daughter. Her mother's shoeless feet pacing hesitantly on the bare floor and her fingers moving cautiously on the shutters, her eyes watching the gate to see if it is shut. A faint echo of a wagon speeding away on the main road can be heard. An echo that is moving toward the fear of fears: a fear which was always hanging over the house and over the hearts like a mourning garment – the fear of their kids' conversion.

Running after Hodaya, who was named Olga after her conversion, throwing stones and shouting calls of mockery after her in the streets of our town, was one of the most popular engagements of the boys of the Cheder [Jewish Torah School for boys], during the former generation. During our days, she would come to the city, an old farmer woman, walking with her bare feet with her basket on her shoulder and nobody would pay attention to her any longer. The boys of the Cheder became tired of the shouting. The sensation god found them other engagements to get involved in – the conflict between Blokh and Bik, and later on the battle between Shtand and Kulisher. Supporting or opposing these people was not only the business of the parliament voters but also of the Cheder boys. These became involved, class-by-class, supporting one elected candidate or another. This class would be pulling to that direction and the other class to the opposite direction. The Cheder boys also stopped singing the insulting verses that predicted a calamity for the converted woman: "Poor Hodya, she found a bargain. This uncircumcised gentile will thrash her as they thrash crops in the barn. Poor Hodya who converted, this uncircumcised gentile will reap her like they reap the rye in the field". The kids stopped tormenting her because her husband Katulnitski treated her with respect and did not stop loving her during his entire life. Maybe they stopped their harassments because they feared their two sons, who studied to be priests in Lvov. However, her father Chaim carried his shame through his entire life – humiliated and ashamed he passed through the city as if the insults had not ceased, and the stone throwing had not stopped. People looked at him with pity in their eyes, but to him their eyes seemed like eyes of reproach. Even when he was sitting down, either in the synagogue or as a guest in other people's houses, he has always chosen to sit at the edge of the chair or the end of the bench, a sitting of a useless person. My grandfather was always openly showing him affection. Particularly refreshing for him was the custom of accompanying him to the bathhouse before the holidays. During this ritual, Chaim seemed to be like a baby carried on the shoulder of an adult. He would straighten a bit his normal stooped posture. When they returned and sat at the table, tasting tiny bites, one could even hear a bit of openness and looseness in the otherwise curbed and ashamed speech of the gloomy father. However, even during that pleasant time, he would always repeat the question: "aber, R' Moshe, farvos iz es mir gekimen," meaning "but Reb Moshe, why do I deserve this?" My grandfather would keep telling him that most of the unfortunate events that happened in this world have nothing to do with sins. This is just a matter of misfortune or tragedy. My grandfather would point to the newspapers that stood in a mixed pile above the hearth and say: "Chaim, Chaim, if you read all of these newspapers, you will realize how many fathers shed tears over their kids who uprooted themselves and moved to barren lands. He would tell him, in detail, stories involving not only famous and old cases, such as the story about the Mortara child[4], but also about cases closer in time and location. Such was the case that happened during his childhood in the village of Shvidova, near the city of Mariampol. A tavern owner by the name of Aharon Rosenwald resided in that village. The gentiles seduced his son when he reached 18 to join them, and splashed baptism water over him. When the act was done, it was impossible to undo it. The kid converted. Most of the gentiles of that village frequented the tavern and his son was among them. The converted [literally - "destroyed" in Hebrew] son was sitting in his father's tavern eating pork while facing his father. He was not satisfied with his own doing, so he managed to seduce his sister to follow him and she was sent to a monetary. His father ran around in the corridors of lobbyists and offices of VIP's in Lvov, begging them to help release his daughter from her jail at the monastery. These lobbyists launched numerous forays, headed by the renowned attorney Dr. Landsberger, but they all ended up with nothing. The father's tears even softened the heart of the state governor the Baron Poimegarten who was also not able to help. The father returned to his village and to his tavern. His son came to tease him immediately upon his return. He set himself against his father and asked him in the language of the gentiles: “Pania [lord in Polish[MK]] Aharon, are you back from Lvov already? Did you marry your daughter to a Rabbi?

Hearing about these cases, Chaim, the bartender, wondered about how limited the power of the authorities was against the priests and the nuns. My grandfather would also tell him about a case that happened during his youth, not in a remote village like Shvidova, but in the city of Lvov itself. This was a story about a group of Jewish kids who were walking joyfully and cheerily, in the street of Lvov on Sabbath. When their voices were heard at the monastery, two nuns came out angrily and started to yell at the kids. They were angry at the kids's Sabbath festive spirit. They forcibly took one of the kids, Yaakov Faideles, who was already a Bar-Mitzva, inside to their gardens. One of the nuns put a sponge to his forehead, and another nun dipped a small brush in a searing acid, and engraved the word “z³odziej”, meaning thief in Polish. This poor kid with the inscription, that cannot be erased, on his forehead was walking around crying. His widowed mother was whining, and one could not find a Jew in town who was not upset over it.

The renowned Rabbi, Dr. Issachar Ber Levenstein, who was able to melt stones-hearts with his words, became the patron of this orphan. He mobilized the entire gendarmerie to go to the monastery that Shabbat evening. The nuns stood and mocked them all, as the power of the authorities would not extend beyond the entrance to the monastery. My grandfather then added: “We all remember the case of the girl - Mikhalina Aratin who was imprisoned in the monastery of the Felician Nuns. There was no doorstep of a minister or any other important appointed official that her father did not step on. These nuns were also mocking the authorities that tried to secure the girl's release. In those days, there was nobody more high-ranking than Prime Minister Kraber. He issued several decrees trying to help in this matter but to no avail. The community asked him: “You are the head of the government and you do not have the power over these virgins? This is our Jewish fate which is on the short end of the stick”. The Prime Minister answered:

"God forbid, this is not only your fate. What happened to you, happened also to two girls of Mohamed's religion in Bosnia. Dalmatian Christians caught them and imprisoned them in a monastery. Mohamed's community raised hell, so I issued some decrees, but all of them were useless. This is how my grandfather strung one story to another and ended with the greatness of Dr. Yosef Shmuel Blokh, the son of a poor baker from Dukla, who rose to prominence in wisdom and Torah study and served in the parliament in Vienna. He fought the Jew-haters bravely, demonstrated publicly their ignorance and stupidity, and acted vigorously to save the Jewish children who were caught with the help of temptations, swindling and force in the net of conversion.

My grandfather did not prolong his story except to emphasize to Chaim the tavern owner that his misfortune was shared by many. , Chaim, would listen to my father silently, nodding his head with gratitude. However, at the end he would always ask the same question again: "...but Reb Moshe, why do I deserve this?"

Chaim, the bartender with his sighs, my grandfather with his consolations, Demko with his boastings and white Pavlo with his damage causing mischiefs – this was how the world behaved and this is how the wheel turned, that is until the one who commands the wheel, tells it to stop and says that its usefulness has expired and its roll in this world has ended. While the death of a tavern owner was in Heaven's hands, the death of Demko can be attributed to a glass filled to the brim and the death of white Pavlo to a glass filled to the brim and as well as the hands of a human being. This human being was called Chaim Oigenblik. He was a livestock merchant. His short size concealed his great power. He looked like a washed-out creature that gentiles used to discount and insult. One day he was sitting at a table, spread a napkin on it so that he would not have his food placed on a spot where pork meat was previously laid on, and ate whatever he ate. In front of him stood the brilliant comic-artist Pichotzki who told a well-known joke which ended with sting about Jews. This was a story about a person by the name of Rabin who went out on Sabbath and saw a large coin on lying on the ground in the market. He was faced with a dilemma – on one hand, he could not pick it up because of the Sabbath, but on the other hand, he could not leave itthere because of his love of money. He was afraid that other people would take it and so he looked for ways to cover it. However, he did not know what to cover it with. If he covers it with dirt, the wind will blow it off. If he covers it with a stone, people may trip on the stone and find the coin. Then a peasant passed by and Rabin was afraid that he would notice the coin. He proceeded to crouch over it and did whatever he did. On the same day, a committee, responsible for monitoring the cleanliness of the market, visited the town. They came to the market, saw this thing on the ground and started to scream: "Who is doing this in the market?" The peasant testified about what he saw and the committee found Rabin and told him to clean his business off the street. "It is Sabbath today" said Rabin. They angrily asked – "Laying what you laid down is allowed but picking it up is forbidden?" Ignoring their anger, Rabin refused to do it. Hence, they told him to hire somebody to pick it up. He hired the peasant who proceeded to pick up what he picked up and the coin was discovered. The committee shook their hands in disbelief:" What? You did your business on the coin with the face of the Tzar on it?" They took Rabin and put him in jail where he is still sitting. Pichotski completed his joke and all the gentiles in the tavern laughed. He then turned to Chaim Oigenblik and said: "You are sitting here and eating your breakfast and do not even bother about your man Rabin sitting in jail. If I were you, I would lay down my food, go to the Czar and beg him to release Rabin". Pichotski stood in the middle of the tavern, bowed his head towards the floor, and said: "this is how I would have bowed to the Czar.

Oigenblik stood up and said: "this is not how one bows to the Czar. Let me show you how." With these words, Chaim jumped on his feet and quickly threw a punch hitting Pichotski's neck. Pikhotski was swiftly thrown flat on to the floor, with his arms and legs spread. The entire tavern was stunned and astonished. This fall of Pichotski also left a mark on his face - his nose remained flat from that day until the day he died. The same way Chaim repaid Pichotski, he also repaid white Pavlo. One day, Chaim was sitting down and eating his breakfast. Pavlo came and started to provoke him. Chaim asked Pavlo whether he wants one or two logs [a measure of liquid[MK]] of liquor. Pavlo responded: "I want three logs". Thus Chaim went and bought three logs of liquor and said to him: "why should we drink where everybody's eyes are upon us. Moshe will let us use his private room, so that we can drink in private". They went into the private room. While Pavlo drank until the whole world started to dance in front of him, Chaim just pretended to drink. When Pavlo finished, Kahim brought him outside and laid him down in the shade of the wall.

After a while, Chaim entered the tavern steaming and red-faced and said: "dismissed". My grandfather became frightened and asked: what do you mean by dismissed? Chaim answered: his lungs are dismissed. Said my grandfather: Life imprisonment. Chaim asked: Any marks or witnesses? Indeed, when Pavlo was found in his vomit, he was dragged to the hospital and Dr. Soltishik who examined him casually said: "Despicable pig, he got drunk and died, burry the carcass".

From that day on, Chaim Oigenblik saw himself as elevated in status by his bravery, and demanded to be honored and respected. He used to tell the stories about his deeds by not using the first person, as: "I am going, I am doing", but as a second person: "Chaim is going, Chaim is doing". He was especially proud by the praises he received from one of the students, almost a doctor. This student stayed as a guest in his home during school vacations. It was a custom among the sons of wealthy people to spend their free time in the village. This was the world turned upside down – village people were attracted by the city. They said that the city is where the joy and the leisure are, while the city people were drawn by the village life. They said that this is where the joy and the leisure were. While Chaim hosted the student, he told him the story about Pichotski. When he reached the subject matter about lying on the floor with arms and legs spread out and about the flat nose of the gentile, the student became excited and said: "Have you ever heard about Dr. Nordau?" and Chaim answered:" I heard about many doctors. I heard about Dr. Leiblinger, and about Dr. Shorenstein who lived in Brod [Yiddish for Brody[MK]], and about Dr. Rosenzweig who lived in Lemberg [Lvov[MK]] whom the Rabbi from Tsanz [Yiddish for Nowy Sącz] promised to have place in the next world and gave him a sign to support his promise by predicting that that they will die on the same day". The student laughed and said: "Dr. Nordau is not from Brod or Lemberg and not even from Vienna. He lives in Paris. He called the deed like you did with Pichotski "muscle Jewry" meaning "Jews with strong muscles." While talking, the student made his hand into a fist, stretched his arm, and groped his arm's biceps muscle.

Chaim answered: "I understand that your doctor from Paris wanted to say "a Jewish young man who's bones are boney, but what would your doctor say if I told him the story about white Pavlo?" He then proceeded to tell him the details how he made the gentile drunk with three logs, how he brought him to the yard and executed him, and about the fact that Dr. Soltishik found the death to be a result of his excess drinking.

The student heard the story and wrinkled his nose and said: "this is gentile-ness with muscles that are muscular. The deed with Pichotski is a nice deed. However the deed with white Pabvlo is not". Chaim did not answer but in the student's absence he would say: "As far as Pikhotsky is concerned, it is obvious that he is a student, almost a doctor. However when it comes to white Pavlo he is shown to be stupid, almost a gabay [synagogue administrator[MK]]

The term gabay was a joke aimed at my grandfather, who refused to let Chaim be called by the gabay to serve in anything associated with a holy duty since the day he did what he did to white Pavlo.

Translator's footnotes

1. Until WW I, Brody was a border town between the Austro-Hungary empire and Russia
2. Engagement Conditions gathering - an ancient Jewish tradition conducted between the families of an engaged couple where a pre-wedding contract about matters such as the date of the marriage, the amount of the dowry and the details about the financial or other type of support by each side is signed off on.
3. Blessings, recited for a bride and her groom as part of a Jewish wedding
4. Edgardo Levi Mortara was a Jewish child (born 1851, in Bologna, Italy) who was kidnapped by the Vatican police and raised by nuns to become a papal missionary. The affair caused a storm among the European and American Jewish communities at the time.

[Pages 150-151]

Women's Organization in Brody

by Bianca Lilian

Translated by Moshe Kutten

Edited by Rafael Manory

Among other memories from the city of Brody, the activity of the women organization – "Stowarzyszenie Kola Kobiet" (in Polish, "Women Fellowship") is etched deep in my heart. The fellowship was active for many years as an association of volunteers with the objective of providing assistance (actually "secret charity") to the needy population in the city.

The members in this association were the wives of lawyers, physicians, pharmacists and wealthy merchants. Among them, I recall the names* of Mrs. Levin, Mrs. Horn, Mrs. Bilig, Mrs. Halbmilion, Mrs. Sandzer—the pharmacist's wife, Mrs. Shatz and Mrs. Herrnstein. The president of the organization was Mrs. Mirka Lilian, the wife of Mr. Leon Lilian, the deputy commissioner of the internal revenue bureau of Brody. The members of the organization gathered, several times a year, in general assembly meetings. In these meetings, they discussed means for raising funds and ways by which could be delivered to the needy. The assembly meetings were in themselves important social events, in view of the large number of participants and their elevated social status in the city.

The financing of the organization activities came from the monthly membership fee (the fee collector was a Jewish person by the name of Moshe). Another method for fundraising was through art shows, theater shows, dancing balls and more. Participation in these events was voluntary. Among the volunteers one could find the best of the Jewish youths. The names I recall are: Shmuel Lamm, a painter, who now lives in Haifa and who painted the theater sceneries, and Mika Aizenberg, who lives today in Tel Aviv. Others were: Leon Levinshtein(Krokovski), Lunya,

Czermak, Manek Zaltzman, Lola Shpigler, Moretz ShpiglerVeiser, Zigmund Wajsher and others, may their memory be blessed.

In addition, they sold tickets and conducted auctions and lotteries, the entire financing of which was collected from donations by the local wealthy population. Among the donors, I recall the names of the pharmacists Sencher and Kalir, Rutenberg, Kalmus – the owner of the flourmill, Zigmont Lifshitz and others.

Some prominent Poles and Christians participated in these events because the respect they had toward the leaders of the organization.

The assistance provided to the needy included packages of food, clothing, medicines and money for medical treatment. The distribution to the needy took place mainly before the High Holidays, such as Rosh Hashanah and Passover, but there were distributions throughout the entire year as well.

[Page 151]

The driving force behind all that was the person who served as the head of organization, Mrs. Mirka Lilian. She was a person with inexhaustible initiative and energy, and was influential even among Christian circles.

This social activity enhanced the respect for the Jewish population in the city and offered substantial assistance to the needy.

This blessed activity stopped abruptly with the outbreak of the war, in 1939.

The Women Organization in Brody – the leadership
Sitting from left to right: R. Dokht, M. Lillian, Shatz, -, -
Standing from right to left: Frenkel, -, Meles, Freundlich, Feuering, -, -, -

[Page 155]

Chapter Three:

Testimonies to the Holocaust

Correspondence between Shlomo Bardach in the Brody Ghetto and his Sister-in-Law Dora Bardach in Switzerland

Translated by Moshe Kutten

Edited by Rafael Manory

The following are photocopies of two postcards, out of a collection of thirty-five postcards that Shlomo Bardach sent from the Brody Ghetto to his sister-in-law Dora Bardach, who stayed in Switzerland during the war. Although, the responses by the addressee did not survive, the content of the postcards in our hands attests to a relatively active correspondence. The correspondence lasted from 29 April 1941 to 28 December 1943. Three postcards were written in 1941, 18 in 1942 and 14 in 1943.

Among the postcards in the collection there is also a letter, from 24 January 1943, as well as an acknowledgment for receipt of a package sent by "Kajotes," a business for marketing food products in Lisbon.

The content of the postcards is identical and attests to the emotional and physical distress of the sender, which is worsening from day to day. Shlomo Bardach felt the end was imminent, and his cry for help is mixed with a feeling of despair and surrender to his fate.

When the date of the Ghetto annihilation was approaching (21 May 1943), the content of the postcards became even more desperate and depressing. The loss of hope is reflected both explicitly and through hints hidden between the lines. The writer's distress is expressed by the assertion: "My fate is gloomy, I am miserable and wrecked" (a card from 1 April 1943). Four days later, on the fifth of that month, the content of the card is condensed into three sentences only: " I wish to inform you about my presence. May His goodwill be that I would be able to write you again in the future. In the meantime, be happy and healthy. May I remain in your memory forever..."

The way of this collection preserved was unconventional. In the beginning, Issachar Bardach, the husband of the addressee Dora Bardach gave the postcards to Mr. Mendel Zinger, of blessed memory. Because he did not make use of the collection's findings within a reasonable time, the photocopies of the postcards were transferred to Issaschar's cousin, Mr. Avraham Bardach, a member of Kibbutz Kabri in the Galilee. This is the place to express gratitude to Mr. Avraham Bardach, who through deep understanding of the historical value of this unusual primary source that revealed to us a not-insignificant fragment of the suffering of the Jews in the Brody Ghetto between 1941–1943, took care of handing the collection over to the Organization of Former Brody Residents in Israel. This helped in adding an important element to the content and quality of this memorial book.

[Page 156]

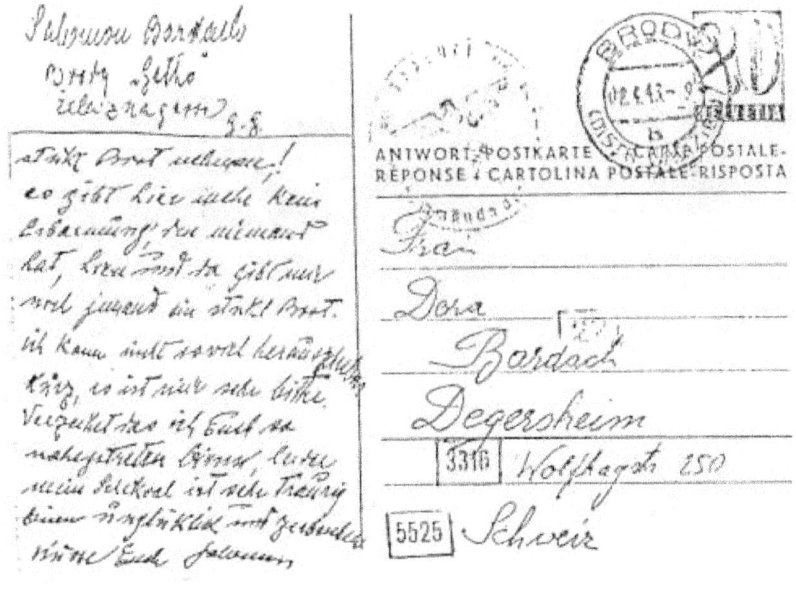

Brody 1. April 1943

Meine Einzige u. teuerste Schwägerin!
Die Karte vom 13.III. habe erhalten, warum
schreibt Ihr mir so wenig, schreibt mir
zwei mal wöchentlich, werde ich auch antworten
denn ich habe kein Geld auf Postkarten zu kaufen.
es ist mir jetzt mit dem Leben recht bitter.
Ich habe nicht kein Groschen Geld mir das Stückl
Brot zu kaufen. Ich gehe abgerissen, keine Schuhe
auf den Füssen, keine Unterhosen, es ist mir
jetzt schlecht. Ich habe gelesen ein Schreiben aus der
Ukraine, schreibt man dort das Ihr einzige eine
Bewilligung bekommen hat ein Paket hieher
zu schicken, also vielleicht wäre es bei
Euch auch möglich, das Ihr mir eine
Bewilligung sicherstellt. Ich bitte viel l. Dora
und l. Frida erbarmt Euch über mich so lange
ich lebe noch, und vergisst nicht an Euer
schwerbetroffenen und bedauerlichen Salomon!
Falls Ihnen möglich ist ein wenig meine Leiden
zu stillen, dann bitte Euch tuts das, aber wie
schneller unterstützt mich! und was nur möglich
Ich erlebe nicht Euch die Nächte vom leichten
nachdenken, wo werde ich auf die Zeit das Trocken

[Page 157]

[Page 158]

"From a Letter to the Editor"

(Received 23 June 1993)

by Shmuel Stoianover and Raphael Shalev

Translated by Moshe Kutten

"We need to emphasize that collaborators participated in all of the actions of the annihilation of the Jewish population in Brody and its environs. Ukrainian collaborators were active in Brody. They played a major role in all the actions. In their enthusiasm to hurt and kill Jews, they were even worse than the Germans. Without their help, The German murderers would not have succeeded to annihilate the masses of the Jewish nation so quickly and so easily".

[Page 159]

"The Last Days of the Community"

by Kalman Harnik
Translated from Yiddish to Hebrew by Yaakov Netaneli-Rotman
Cited from Nathan Michael Gelber's History of the Jews of Brody: "Mother Cities in Israel", Vol. 6, Mosad HaRav Kook, Jerusalem [1955], pp. 397- 406

Translated by Moshe Kutten

Edited by Yocheved Klausner

At Dawn, on the 22 of June 1941, we awakened in panic, to the sound of the horrendous thunders of a bombardment. The war between Germany and the Soviet Union had begun. Eight days later, the city of Brody fell into the hands of the Germans. We spent the eight days in the cellars and hideouts. Whole blocks went up in flames and people were killed in the streets; however, all of that was an innocent children's game compared with the events which would follow.

On the same day, 1st July 1941, the roars by the Ukrainians: "Heil Hitler", in a hurry to festively greet the conquering Germans, arose in our ears. These same people, who just yesterday seemed to be the most enthusiastic supporters of the Bolshevik regime, were the first ones who found a common language with the "Deutsch". They were the ones who offered themselves to the Germans fully, and executed with blind obedience the plans the Germans had in store for the Polish people, with added zealous hatred for the Jews. They turned their back, from the first moment, to their former friends and acquaintances, as proof that they were submissive slaves to the horrible race-theory. They enlisted the most corrupt and wicked among themselves as the public servants, for servicing the conquering Germans. Their service was totally in support of the "Juden Ohne Rechte" [Jews without rights[MK]] plan of stripping away any human rights from the Jews and in full backing of the idea that the "Zum Ausrotten" [the eradication[MK]] of the

Jews must be done in stages of uprooting. These stages should include humiliation, defamation, slander, persecution, looting, and at the end, a complete and final massacre. Two devices were available to these psychopaths: the whip and the gun. The Ukrainians learned this lore in detail from the first day. First, they studied its main idea and then its conclusions. They introduced their own varied destructive versions, which were then executed with evil cruelty and German accuracy.

These crimes were carried out on us for twenty-three months. Twenty three long months lasted this hell. This is how it started: from its first days, the local German commander appointed a municipal administration. The former business-school teacher - Orishchin, was nominated to head it. The lawyer Dudchak was appointed to be the police commissioner (later on somebody by the name of Sokhovich replaced him). A former bank clerk, Boksah, was nominated to be the mayor; allof these nominations belonged to the civil administration. It seemed to us at the time, that the situation would not be intolerable. Jews who served in the independent Ukrainian army during the years 1918 - 1920 pinned hopes on this administration. In particular, Dr. Dolek Lifschitz, the son of Zigmund Lifschitz who was the owner of the flour-mill; Pesakh Husar, the fruit store owner from Goldengass Street, Dr. Feuershtein, the former secretary of the community of Bilitz, Silesia (he handed all of his property for safekeeping to a gentile woman who served as a housemaid in his home; after the ghetto was obliterated, he and his wife asked the maid for shelter, but she threw them out cruelly. Both of them committed suicide. Their seven years old son, Menakhem was helped by some individuals for a short period after their death, but he too perished) and Bertinski, a Jew from Lvov, who served as a judge in Brody. However, the fate of all of these people was similar to the fate of whoever remained in Brody (except Bertinski who survived the Holocaust and currently lives in Poland).

[Page 160]

Tragi-comical was the situation of one Jew named Shprukh. While in captivity in Italy after World War I, he joined the Fascist party, which did not prevent Jews from becoming regular members, at the time. Equipped with the appropriate documents, Shprukh appeared before the German commander Wagner, who was quick to take the whip and teach the Fascist member how to distinguish between Fascism and National Socialism.

Dr. Avraham Glasberg was given the task to assemble the Judenrat [Ghetto's Jewish Council established by the Germans[MK]]. Etel Lemmels' Beit Hamidrash was chosen as its seat. Hertz Buchbinder, the son of a Brody bookbinder, was nominated as the commander of the Ordnungs-Dienst – the Jewish Stewarding Service [or Auxiliary-Police[MK]]. He was an officer in the Ukrainian army after World War I, and acted honorably as the commander of the Jewish Stewarding Service. Initially the Jewish council operated under the authority of the German municipal commander and later under the Gestapo.

The Jewish council was ordered to organize a daily work-force of 150 workers. They were also asked to assemble the furniture for the entire German administration. Starting 5th of July 1941, every Jew between the ages of 12 and 60 was ordered to wear a 10 centimeters wide band with a blue Star of David on it. Jews were forbidden to exit the town or ride the trains during the curfew hours between 4 PM and 6 AM. An exception was made for Mendel Reinhold, a Brody leather merchant, who travelled to Lwow several times to purchase leather for the gendarmes. Shopping for provisions for the Jews was allowed only between 12 PM and 2 PM. At that late time, most of the merchandise has already been sold and the stock in the market has already been depleted. This is the place to mention the horrifying Field-Gendarme Vogel, may he be remembered disgracefully, who abused every Jew he met, women like men. He hit them to prevent them from walking on the sidewalks...

At the same time, Jews were forbidden, under the penalty of death, from engaging in any type of commerce. However, they still had to pay taxes to the last penny. If a taxpayer violated the rule and missed the court hearing, the Jewish Council had to pay his / her debt. The council set up a special fund for this purpose.

The realization of the "Final Solution of the Jewish People" actually started with the education of the Arians – the Polish and the Ukrainians. Besides hitting, looting and rape (rampant despite the race theory of the Führer), the Germans used films, newspapers and advertisement as education material, provided separately for the Germans, and separately for the inferior races in different foreign languages. Jews were depicted in this education material as the cause for plights such as plagues, thefts, fires and well poisonings. The Jews were also accused of being responsible for the results of the World War. The Germans accused the international Jewry of war mongering. Their conclusion was obvious...

[Page 161]

On July 8th 1941, men and women were kidnaped on the city streets indiscriminately. 150 Jews were lined up in rows near Sancher's pharmacy. A German gang gave a "sample lesson" to the "Arian" mob how to treat the Jews. They were attacked with deadly blows. To the amusement of the spectators, they were led "only" for the moment, to the artillery barracks for forced labor. To prevent any illusions (by chance, I was one of the people who were led), one German shot and killed Yankel Shapira (a known mental patient) in our presence. The famous Dr. Kuten was beaten to the pulp, just because he applied directly to the cavalry-captain (Rietmeister). Dr. Kuten held in his pocket, at the time, the key to the clinics in which he worked and he mentioned this to the officer. A day later, on July 9th, the Gesatpo, headed by the infamous hangman Haupt Sturmfuehrer Krieger, appeared at the house of the Treibush family on Shkolna Street, and confiscated it. They placed their flag with the skull depicted on it, symbolizing murder. The flag was displayed on the house for two weeks.

On July 11th, again, 400 Jews are kidnaped in the streets, never to be seen again. At the same time, two teachers from the government high-school, Dr. Michael Friedlander and Henrik Friedlander, as well as Dr. Y. Kuten and Leon Bruchiner, a merchant of electrical products, were arrested. The Jewish Council was ordered to do the following: a) provide a list of all the people who are the city Intelligentsia, b) furnish the Gestapo headquarter and provide clothing to all of its clerks, c) hand over, in a few days, a contribution of 250,000 Zloty!

On the following day, the Jewish intelligentsia was assembled. They were lead to believe that they were supposed to prepare the plans for the establishment of the Ghetto. However, the German had other plans. For three days the executioners humiliated and ridiculed the poor people. At the end, they were led to an unknown location never to be seen again

A list of some of the people who were murdered is presented henceforth according to their profession

Teachers in the Elementary School

OFRICHTIG	A. HARNIK	Dr. FALIK
Mrs. BERMAN	Mrs. LEMELMAN	Mrs. A. KLAR
Sh. BERNSHTAYN	A. MOSTISKER	L. SHENHOLTS

Teachers in the High School

BOGNER	LAURER	H. FRIEDLANDER
D .VERBER	LANDAU	Y. FRIEDLANDER
D. VORM	Mrs. SAPIR	KAPIZA
TENNENBAUM	Dr. FRIEDLANDER	M. SHVEDRON
		SHPILMAN

Engineers

KAPLUSH	ROGOVSKI	STREICHER

Flour Mills Owners

LANDGWIRZ	MARDER	ZWERDLING

[Page 162]

Lawyers

Dr. OPEPPA	Dr. AFROIKH	Dr. HELLER
Dr. AMBUS	Dr. GARFUNKEL	Dr. PERMINGER
		Dr. KANFER

[Page 162]

Pharmacists

BRAVER	Mrs. FINKELSHTAYN	RUTNBERG
Mrs. BRAVER	FISHER (owner of Kalir pharmacy, native of Rava Ruska)	Mrs. RUTNBERG
Sh. KAHANA	Mrs. FISHER	SHVEDRON
FUHRER	Mrs. KREZISYA	Mrs. N. SCHWARZ
Sh. FITSH		SCHTOCK
FITCH		Mrs. SCHTOCK

The people listed above were brought to the cemetery near the lime pit [Wapniarka in Polish) and were murdered there. Physicians were not taken in this "Aktzia" [Nazi German roundup[MK]]. It is worthwhile to add that during the execution of this horrible crime, Gestapo men went around the houses of the victims and looted their property.

But life is going on. Banishment followed banishment. The hope that the nightmare will end somehow was strengthened by all sorts of rumors. Some were even saying that the people who were taken away were alive and continued to work.... Al sorts of blackmailers and con-artists of many kinds were thriving, and they spread encouraging rumors. Civil and military emissaries were sent to the four corners of the world. Notes were sent over to Wiener-Neustadt [a city located south of Vienna[MK]], Leipzig, Munich, Rovno and Hamburg. People were holding on to anything and any person and looking for help everywhere from any acquaintance of an acquaintance and spending the last pennies trying to find out about the fate of the kidnapped... At the same time, the graves of the kidnapped were only one kilometer away... Con-artists exploited again the prevailing confusion and swindled money or articles as if to help the poor prisoners... Jews simply could not believe in the truth... they did not even trust the underground newspapers. In fact, only in these newspapers, the reality was presented as it really was, but Jews were not willing to believe in it and were still waiting for salvation.

Following this Aktzia the calamity of the slave labor camps began. The camps were established in several locations such as Kozaki, Brody, Olesko, Sasov, Zborov, Plukhov, Latski and Yaktorov. Infamous angels of destruction rich in experience headed the camps. Every one of them utilized a unique method of tortures and other atrocities. Every one of them created a unique administration for extermination. Helping them were some Jewish people thirsty for blood-money.

These are the names of these evil butchers (may their name rot in hell): Lambo, Gz'imak, Fuchs, Rog, Hildebrand, Zaltsborn, Silaski, Klaus and Mantel. It is a pity that only one of these people - Gz'imek, was caught and convicted in court for his horrific acts. The rest of them continue their filthy lives somewhere. There is no imagination in existence that could even dream about the psychopathic abominations of these murderers.

[Page 163]

The Jewish Council in Brody made great efforts in order to ease the pain and the suffering of the labor-camps prisoners. They sent them food packages and rescued the sick (such as Dr. Feuerstein). Thousands of people died from the inhuman suffering in these camps.

On 20th of September 1941, the horror of the first Aktzia descended on Brody. A few days earlier the German spread rumors about an Aktzia against non-Jews (Arians). Everything started at 5 o'clock in the morning. Shots were heard at dawn. At the end of the Aktzia, 250 Jews were killed and 2000 were led to their extermination. The Aktzia lasted a day and a half. The miserable victims were initially concentrated in the Ryneck (market) and from there, led in locked cattle cars to Belzec. Only one of them managed to escape just before the stop at Rava Ruska, Tsvengler, a rags merchant.

The second Aktzia raged on October 2nd, a day after Yom Kippur (in a note in the original article the author wrote that it was the evening before Yom Kippur but he was mistaken). The Aktzia claimed 2500 victims. Among the people who were shot to death was the venerable old teacher Nakhum Okser who educated generations of pupils in the elementary school. It is worthwhile to describe how this martyr died. Herman Blokh, Okser's former pupil, who was the acting head of The Jewish Council, hid his former teacher in one of the Judenrat's offices. A Gestapo bloke discovered him there and noted: "What is the number of years of grandpa? Does he still have any teeth?" He shot him directly into his mouth.

I just wanted to note that Mr. Okser told me personally that the silver treasures of the big synagogue were hidden in the cellar of the house for the elderly, which also hosted the city orphanage.

The Ghetto Affair

Everybody enjoyed kind of a "vacation" break due to the preparations for the establishment of the ghetto. The date for completion was set for December 1st 1941, but was postponed to January 1st 1942. The area chosen for the ghetto included the alleys around the Hospital Street, the bathhouse and the Groats Street. The population in these old alleys was always sparse. Now, 15 thousand Jews squeezed into these scanty and narrow streets (before the war, the Jewish population in this area numbered around 7200 people). Besides Jews from the city and its environs, Jews from Sokolovka, Toporov, Radz'ikhov, Olesko, Lupatyn, Podgórze, and Szczurowice, some Jews from the Russian border town of Radzivilov and refugees from Volyn escaped to Brody and settled in the ghetto.

A barbed-wire fence surrounded the ghetto. Two gaps for exit and entrance were left open. The main gate was located near the Trit house. Above the gate, on the side of the ghetto a sign was placed, written in three languages [Yiddish, Polish and German[MK]]: "Halt. This is the Ghetto border. Exit without permission will result in death!" On the city side, the sign was worded differently: "The entrance for Arians is absolutely forbidden! Disobedience can result in imprisonment or a fine of 1000 gold coins". Guards from the Jewish Stewarding Service, and from time to time, a Ukrainian policeman were stationed at the gate.

[Page 164]

Victims fell in the ghetto from its first days. This is the place to raise a tribute to the forgotten figure - Mr. Kohel (he was a merchant and not a Brody native). While standing not far from the barbed-wire fence, the policeman Lozovi shot him to death. There was an old conflict between them, and now the murderer found an opportunity to take revenge. In response to the immediate intervention by the Judenrat, the head of the police said: "This is not a big deal; there is simply one Jew less..."

That Lozovi, a sadist and notorious murderer, spilled the blood of hundreds of Brody Jews. Many Ukrainians were like him: Zarnovits, Simyonuk, Pavlok, Kust and Buiko to name a few. From that point on, complete anarchy prevailed in the ghetto. Murder and massacre were allowed, since it was known that murderers would not be punished. On the contrary, they would probably receive a reward. Food rationing for the Jews in the ghetto was handed over to the official Ukrainian grocery company "Soyuz". It was hardly implemented. It was absolutely impossible to get anything privately. Christians were severely fined for selling food to the Jews. A horrible hunger prevailed. Deaths were becoming more frequent by the day. The streets were filled with hunger-swollen people. Hunger-typhus was rampant. The awful distress and the unhygienic conditions were the direct major causes for it. Everybody tried to hide the severity of the situation from the authorities. In addition, the winter of 1942 was a very harsh winter. The rationing of fire-wood was ridiculously meager. People were forced to dismantle walls and partitions of wooden houses for heating. The horror-scenes that occurred during the distribution of firewood are indescribable. Starving, sick and miserably poor people were scuffling till bleeding, just for a small piece of firewood... The situation got worse and worse. The daily death toll reached 20, then 50. It developed into a normal occurrence. The underworld was floating up to the surface of the public eye in the ghetto, and along with it - horrible atrocities. Carnivorous survival instincts, violence and robbing of the last meager property were rampant in the ghetto and its streets for everybody to see. Wicked people, such as Reuven Meizler (a local thug son of a baker), or Zeinvil (a mentally disabled porter, a strongman native of Brody who was able to kill a person with one hit, who was appointed as a Kapo to the slave laborers in the forced-labor camp in Kozaki, where he was cruel to everybody. He was later deported back to the ghetto), became the executioners of major operations of evil and sadism. Complete anarchy prevailed, in which the weak became the victims of every exploiter and muscleman. The situation became hopeless. The Jewish tendency to explain every natural event as a good sign, or to discover hints of hints of salvation and relief in reality, an optimism that many were hooked on for many days, even intellectuals and academicians, now disappeared completely. In its place, an astounding indifference, and total loss of the ability to face the challenge took over... It was impossible for the situation to worsen and to become more awful than that.

[Page 165]

In this chaos, a cruel and horrible terror took over. The workers in the plants outside the ghetto in the "Arian" side, provided the only "News Service" – the connection to the outside world. They left at dawn and returned at night. Many of them managed to smuggle a piece of bread into the ghetto. These "lucky" workers were safe from any sudden troubles or from various Aktzias. Everybody was willing to pay anything they owned for this certain "piece of paper." An ID card with "a "stamp" on it was becoming the main purpose of one's life. The slogan was "One must get a place of work at any cost!" The firms Tod, Alt und Abfallstoff Eraffsung, workshops that worked for the Wehrmacht [German armed forces[MK]], or Wyklycky, Liegenschaft G. ,a firm that dealt with collecting recyclables and old raw materials and others, enabled its workers to get the ID. The details of the ID included a unique number identifying the holder as working for the army with a stamp: "Able to Work". For that small card and a stamp, people were willing to give up anything: their money, property and even their self-respect. Their perception was that this was the only way for a person to continue one's existence.

When the authorities got hold of the news about the epidemic of typhoid fever in the ghetto, they closed the ghetto for one month and later on for an additional three months. Some of the firms built special housing units for their Jews outside the ghetto. Inside the ghetto, the mood became more and more desperate. There was only one desire - to escape from the ghetto and acquire Arian papers, or at least find a shelter for the children with Christian acquaintances, and thereby perhaps save them.

Up to 10 people crowded every room in the ghetto. Despite the crowding, everybody was so isolated! One was never left alone with his/her thoughts though. There were always many nervous and angry people around you. They all lived as communal tenants; however, everyone has finalized his or her plan and molded it in his thoughts. Everybody had a victim in the family, so everybody knew what to expect. Everybody was trying at least to find a way to save the children. Screams could be heard in the streets, day and night. Shots reverberated outside. There was a rampant SS person here, and the 18 years old murderer Lager-Fuhrer (camp commander) Rug (a Volks-Deutsch - a Polish citizen of German origin) was rampant over there. They forced you to think about salvation, to outwit and act.... At the time of danger, the bunker was one's only salvation. The bunkers were a story of their own. Most have gone through several stages: from a primitive hideout in the attic, or in a hut, to a sophisticated deep pit underground consisting of several rooms and even separate apartments. Some sophisticated bunkers contained food, lighting, radio and water. Some of the people managed to survive in the ghetto and come out alive. Such bunkers were dug out at the families Krsitiampoler, Braun, Katz, Stein and Brandon, all Jewish. A Ukrainian by the name of Borchak, a locksmith who was a communist before World War II, was one of the only Ukrainian righteous who did not stop from helping Jews. He saved many Jews by keeping them in a bunker he dug up in his house, printed fake ID's with false Christian names, and fake stamps that he kept especially for that purpose.

In order to save the children one had to hand them over to stranger gentiles. This is where I feel that it is my duty to mention some of the righteous Christians, those who helped Jews escape, or kept and saved Brody's Jewish children for years. They were undeterred by the dangers and the death penalty they had to face. The following is just a partial list of these people:

Yatsneti Miklashevski (a clerk in the tax office, who frequently did favors and charities), Timchishin, the former deputy governor of Brody, Homnyuk, Professor Buchkovski, Kist, Dr. Zavotski (the regional physician who went from one bunker to another to provide cure to many of the Jewish sick people and smuggled a substantial amount of money from the outside, everything under a life threat), and Mironko Borchak Lukanich (Ukrainian printer who was very truthful in his relations with the Jews, his father was a pig merchant), Kumornik – the executer of the court, and the Polish priest of the Christian community whose name escaped me.

[Page 166]

My three years old daughter was saved by the Mikloshevski family. They hosted her for four and half years. They treated her like their daughter. Unfortunately, many such children were lost to the Jewish nation. I know of Liska Ambus, the daughter of the lawyer Dr. Yosef Ambus who lives today as a Christian in Yelniya (the meaning of the name is - The Hill of the Antelopes). All efforts by Dr. Mordekhai Weiss (a survivor who lives in Haifa), to save her through the Youth Aliyah were unsuccessful. I am sure that there are many of Brody's Jewish children who live as Christians in today's Brody and its environs.

In order to survive, or even just to exist, one had to have a "contact" on the outside. Only then, one could get work outside of the ghetto. Work could only be arranged through the labor bureau for Jews, which was located in Ostereztser's house. Mr. Holtzsetzer (a former vegetable storeowner who was the nephew of the former secretary of the Jewish community) managed the Jewish department of the bureau. Every Job carried a certain fixed price in gold. It was not possible to reduce that price, even by a penny, via bargaining, tears or begging. There was no use in trying. Nothing would have helped! The hearts of the clerks (even the Jewish clerks) were tough and sealed. That was when everything was quiet. During an Aktzia, the job certificate or any other certificate was worthless. The Gestapo did not honor any signature...

At one point, some good news started to arrive from the fronts. A slim hope was awakening. Maybe there is some hope? ... Maybe we would survive and live to see other times... Youth groups met and decided to "break through and escape to the forests". The authority got the wind of it and decided to respond. The government advisor, Dr. Weiss (a German, not to confuse him with the Jewish Dr. Weiss), along with the commander Vartsuk, ordered all Jews who were able to work, to gather on May 4th,

1942, in the barracks courtyard. 1400 Jews came forward for the census. The head of the police – Daum, Hildebrand (the head the Gestapo Jewish department in all of Galicia with a rank of Hauptsturmführer), Rug, German police force, Ukrainian auxiliary police force, the security service headed by the Polish detective Shershen as well as the Jewish Stewarding Service – all were at hand to assist in the administration of the event. Three Jews were shot and killed right there on the spot. One of them was Tsukerman (a student with a Christian looking face and Arian papers. He was actually employed in Tarnopol, but came back to Brody because he was homesick). He was cut down along with the Halpern brothers from Rovno. The authorities organized quarantine camps from which one cannot move away.

Despite all that, there was an increased desire for the establishment of a group for self-defense. Engineer Feuerstein (not a Brody native), even assembled a machine gun at the Lamm machine shop. Several hand guns have been obtained as well. People made preparations for accelerating the establishment of the organization. Borchak and Jack (mentioned above) assisted in the preparations. Engineer Feuerstein served as the leader. Following him was Weiler (he became a partisan in the forests and managed to survive the Holocaust; he lives currently in Paris.

[Page 167]

He wrote a book about the massacre in Brody, which the Jewish Committee in Poland published in Polish). Also following him was Kopel Margolis (a 50 years old tinsmith). Linder, Halbershtadt, Shapira, Scheiner and Reinhold were already in the forest. Altogether, there were about 80 female and male youths, not all Brody natives.

On May 13th, 1945, two of them were arrested in the Leshnow forest and brought to Brody. When they were held in detention in the city hall, they managed to kill one policemen-firefighter and escape towards the ghetto... On the same day, as an immediate response, the ghetto was surrounded from all directions. A band of incited Poles and Ukrainians, headed by German gendarmes along with their infamous leader Vartsuk rioted and stormed into the ghetto. A massacre ensued. The infamous Brody hooligan – Kasianchuk, broke in and made his way into the ghetto holding a sharp ax in his hand, which he used to smash the scalp of anybody he encountered. One of his victims was Kopel Margolis. At the end, eighty people from the community were led to Shnelovka's grove and murdered there. (Kasianchuk was identified in Poland in 1948. He was arrested and brought to trial and was executed for his crimes).

On May 20th 1943 I received a notice that the entire Ukrainian police force went on alert. I penetrated the ghetto immediately and notified the leadership (Harnik was occupied at the time at Miklashevski – who managed a firm for collecting and packaging old garments).

On May 21st, the last remaining Jews were transported to Belzec. Only a few survived. Leon Blaustein (currently lives in Kfar Vitkin, Israel) was born in Brody in 1900 and lived in town until September 14th 1943, four months after the liquidation of the ghetto. He worked in acquiring provisions on behalf of the "Juedische Selbst-Hilfe" [Jewish Self-Help[MK]], with Vartsuk's approval, to eight labor-camps in the area. On the day of the ghetto liquidation, 21st of May 1943, Blaustein was placed on the train destined for Belzec, along with 1670 people. 120 people crowded each train car. During the journey, the SS entertained themselves by shooting into the packed cars... this resulted in wounded and slain people. In Blaustein's car, the passengers broke out through the barbed wire covering the hatches, and started to jump out. One of them crashed on the tracks, another was shot and killed. The voyage continued to gallop toward the darkness of annihilation. Inside, people decided to place two mirrors outside the hatches, so that the jumpers would be able to be warned ahead of time... Blaustein also took out a mirror from his pocket. A phrase was written on the backside of the mirror: "glupi mys'li-madry czyni" ("the fool thinks – the clever acts"). Right there, he made a quick decision: "I must jump!" As if following an order in the gym, with one hand he held the hatch located at the top of the train car, stretched his leg through the hatch and held the outside wall of the car with his second hand. He then bent over and jumped. Upon falling down he crushed his nose on the gravel and stood there breathless, a perfect target for a shot. The warning shouting from the train cars woke him up. He regained his composure and escaped along the tracks back to the deserted ghetto in Brody. There, he found a hideout and this is how he saved himself. Other people who saved themselves include Marash (a philosophy scholar who lives in Australia today) and Mrs. Hochberg, who was 15 at the time. Here and there, some Jews were kidnapped. They were assembled in the barracks and killed by shooting. It was said that the last entire Judenrat, which was headed by Icio (Yitshak) Katz was executed in Krasna. Icio was about 50 years old at the time, a former municipal city clerk. He studied law in Lwow and his father was a merchant. He did not treat properly the miserable people who were his subordinates. He was also cruel to the Jewish partisans who penetrated to the ghetto to acquire food, and sent them to labor-camps, a sure way for annihilation. People who were murdered there included Khaim Mordekhai Kharash, an honest and innocent grain merchant who loved scholars, did good deeds all his life, and always practiced charity. He was 54 years old when he died. It also included Dr. Betsalel Meles, a 54 years old devoted and loyal Zionist who supported the Hebrew language and its culture from his youth. He had a comprehensive general education, and was a member of the Academic Association "Tkhia" ["Revival"[MK]]. Also murdered was Leon Brutsiner. The above mentioned people were all members of the Judenrat, but they proved in their actions that they valued the good of the people as most important. Their major aim was to help, to save and ease the suffering.

[Page 168]

Brody was emptied of its Jews. It became what the Germans called "Judenrein" [Free of Jews[MK]]. Hitler, damn him, achieved his purpose. Only about fifty Jews survived somehow in the bunkers and forests. They got out only in 1944.

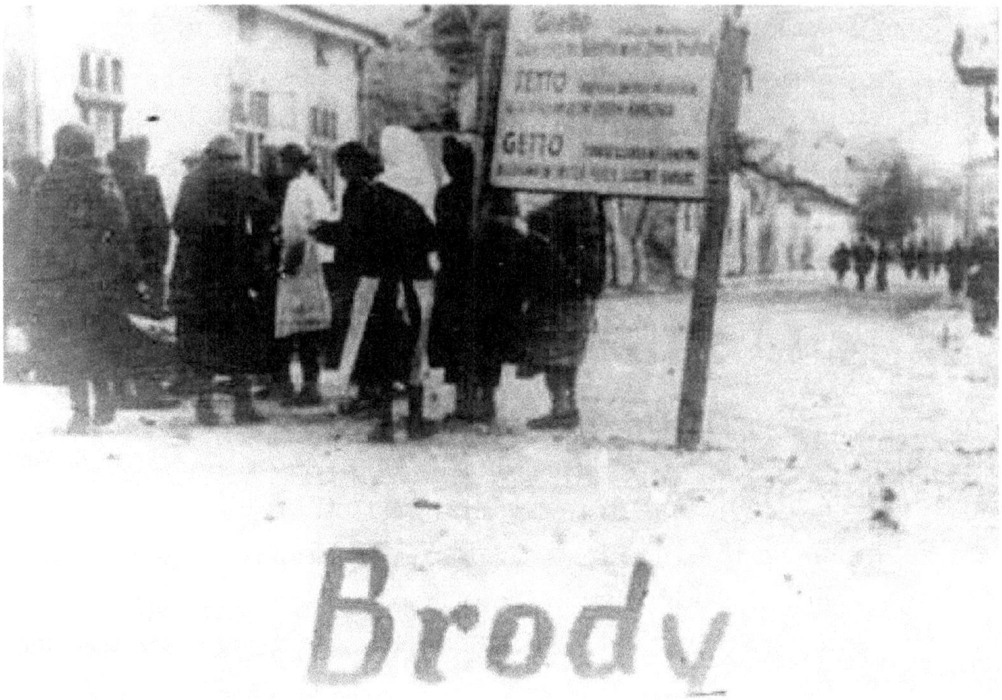

Brody Ghetto, corner of Shpitalka Street

[Page 169]

"I Alone Survived of My Family"

by Gina Lantzeter

Translated by Moshe Kutten

Edited by Yocheved Klausner

My name is Gina Lantzeter. My maiden name was Hochberg. I was born in Brody and lived there before and during the war. My parents Bernard and Diana Hochberg were murdered in the gas chambers in Majdanek, where they were taken during the Aktzia of 21 of May 1943. I was with my parents in the ghetto, and also on the train going to Majdanek. A short time before the train arrived at its destination, my mother threw me out through a small hatch in the boxcar. Fortunately for me, I was not killed, although I was hit by a bullet and was left unconscious. I returned to Brody, a thing that was not very easy to do in May 1943, but this is a story for itself. After spending some time in a forced labor camp, I reached some hiding places in which I stayed until the liberation. These hiding places were full of dangers, but I was lucky and survived. I also had a brother named Zigmond, who was six years older than me. He left Brody on his way to Russia during the early stages of the war, but I never heard from him again.

As far as our very large family – aunts, uncles and cousins – they were all murdered by the Nazis and their collaborators.

My late husband, Henri Lantzeter was also a native of Brody. His father, Arnold, mother Ella and Ella's brother Shmuel all perished in Belzec.

[Page 170]

The Jewish Fighting Organization in Brody

From the collection "Underground Movements in the Ghettoes and the Camps,"
The editor Betty Eisenstein, 1946, published by the War Archives, the Jewish Committee in Cracow (in Polish)

Translated by Moshe Kutten and Sara Mages

In the fall of 1942, it was clear to all of us that the fate of the Jews was decreed to annihilation. In fact, the best of the city's youth was already annihilated in previous *Aktziot* [German round-up of Jews[MK]]. Those who remained decided to take up arms and, at least, die with dignity. A fighting organization was established. The organization had no contact with the outside world, didn't have funds or financial means.

Shmuel Weiler, who brings this testimony, turned to the Pole, Tadeusz Z'ak, and asked him to find out whether the Polish Fighting Organization – or the"Home Army" ("*Armia Krayova*") in Lvov would agree to accept the Jewish fighters into its ranks, or, at least, maintain a contact with the Jewish organization in Brody. Z'ak returned and brought an absolute negative answer. The members of the Polish organization said that they do not want any contact with the Jews.

The Jewish youth didn't give up. It was decided to establish an organization called "The Jewish Fighting Organization" [or ZOB – *Zydowska Organizacja Bojowa*]. In Polish, the name of the organization begins with the word "Jewish," and thus, it was felt that it was a separate organization that didn't receive help from any cause. Based on a suggestion by the teacher, Keller, it was decided to postpone combat operations to the following spring and use the period of fall and winter of 1942 for organization and preparation. A leadership was elected: Shlomo Halbershtadt, Yaakov Linder and Shmuel Weiler. A contact was established with the Ukrainian, Yashek Borchak, a known communist activist. The Organization was based on "trios" (*troika*). Meetings took place every evening. Funds were collected, weapons were acquired and bunkers were prepared. A bulletin, which publicized the news from Radio London, was published. Underground leaflets – "*Gwardzistah*" [Militiamen] "*Neipodelgloshets*" [Freedom] and "*Volnoshets*" [Independence] were brought from Warsaw, and leaflets of the "Polish Workers Party" (PPR) were brought from Lvov.

In December of 1942, Weiler established a contact with a soldier from the German army, a Pole from Pomeran near Poznan (The 452nd German battalion was made up of Polish residents from Poznan and Pomeran). The soldier told Wailer that twenty-two German divisions, under the command of General Paulus, encircled by the Red Army in Stalingrad. The information flowed two-ways. The Jewish organization also provided information, which was carried back t by the German soldier, to the Polish soldiers in the German battalion as well as leaflets.

A branch of the organization was also established in the labor camp where the Germans concentrated the majority of the men from the ghetto who were of working age. Meir Foyershtein, Marian Altura and Mans Klugshlager headed the group in the camp.

In February of 1943, it was decided to open operations in Brody. Two of most devoted members of the organization – Shteiner (aka "Yoshko") and Baumvald (aka "Bunyo"), were sent to the forest to select an appropriate location for digging a shelter for a large company. They were given two handguns, shovels and provisions for the road. Six days later, the two returned and announced that they established in the forest, about 21 kilometers from the narrow-gauge railway, a bunker for twelve men.

[Page 171]

On their return, the young men met two Jews in the forest who were sent by the Jewish Fighting Organization of Krakow to explore potential locations for partisan operations. The Krakow fighters had weapons, Aryan papers, underground literature and also a small military pharmacy. They told that they had another member with them who disappeared without a trace. They walked to Lvov on foot. In the town of

Oleshko they were stopped by a Ukrainian police commander who demanded to see their identity cards. The young men shot the policeman and fled.

After a few days, two young men: Steiner and Baumvald, were sent again to the same location with two others. They were ordered to dig two shelters in the forest, attack the forest guard and take his weapon. Baumvald returned immediately to the ghetto and reported that the order was carried out. Two shelters were dug and camouflaged, the assault on the forest guard was successful, and the group took a rifle as booty.

In March of 1942, members of the organization came in contact with a combat group in Lvov and established a joint headquarter. It was decided to bring underground newspapers from Lvov and distribute them in Brody.

Meanwhile, the Germans ordered all the young men to report for a medical examination and took them to the camp. ZOB members, who had to report, escaped to the forest. Food was brought to them by foot from the city to the narrow-gauge railway, and from there by small wagons to the bunkers. The food shipments were transferred at night. The road passed through meadows and swamps near the villages of Smolana and Zakhodov. One night, the young men who carried the food, encountered a military guard near Smolana. A battle erupted and two Ukrainian guardsmen were killed. The shipment reached its destination intact.

Life got organized in the forest. From time to time reading evenings, in which Moshe Shapira read from his works, took place. At that time they began to purchase weapons. Small groups of fighters conducted attacks on the forest guards. They also purchased weapons with money. The price of a handgun, without bullets, was 1000–1500 Zloty. A special bunker was set up in the forest for hospitalization of patients.

In the ghetto, they trained young women as fighters and medical orderlies. In addition, they collected undergarments and medical supplies. Several members of the Judenrat [Ghetto's Jewish Council established by the German[MK]] supplied food to a military organization. The groups were placed at several locations in the forest: a distance of 17, 18 and 21 kilometers from the narrow-gauge railway in the

Leshniov and Ponikovitsa forests. Liaisons maintained the contact between the groups. They also provided daily reports to the forest headquarters, and reports were sent from there to the headquarters in the city.

On April 28 1943, an hour past midnight, the group's sentries, who stood on guard a distance of 18 kilometers from the railroad, were suddenly attacked by a group of Bandera's men (Ukrainian fascist groups named after the Ukrainian nationalist leader - Bandera). The two sides opened fire. The sentries were wounded and three of Bendrovtzim [members of Bandera's gangs] were killed. Leaflets of the Organization of Ukrainian Nationalists, and also three handguns and bullets were found in the pockets of the slain. The wounded fighters were taken to the ghetto. Dr. Korlandsky, a member of ZOB, bandaged their wounds.

[Page 172]

Since then, the Bendrovtzim never stopped chasing the groups of Jewish fighters who had to guard themselves against two enemies – the Germans on one side and the Bendrovtzim on the other.

The forest detachment grew from day to day. People arrived from Lvov Ghetto. A Jew, who had Aryan papers and "good facial features," led them to Podvortza Station near Lvov inside a group of workers who left for their work. There, they boarded the train and travelled to Ponikovitsa station. A guide waited for them and led them to their destination.

From time to time they changed their route. For a certain period of time, they traveled to Kamionka-Strumilova, and from there they continued by foot. Their excellent guide was a young man who was nicknamed "The little farmer," because he was dressed in farmer's clothing and was amazing in his duty, his manners and movements. The chief liaison, between the headquarters in the forest and the headquarters in the city, was a young woman named "Zusya" (Her real name is unknown. She arrived to Brody with a group of fighters from Lvov). This young woman had Aryan papers and "good facial features."

The headquarters prepared a plan to rob the Judenrat's safe and storage warehouses. A safe was installed in the Judenrat building for storing valuables that were intended for bribing the Germans. The location of the safe was known to ZOB. Ten men carried out the order to confiscate the valuables, that their value was 80,000 Zloty. This act was also intended to strengthen the image of the organization in the ghetto. From here on, all the prisoners in the ghetto knew that there was an active organization of Jewish fighters. The organization also distributed propaganda leaflets in which they encourage the ghetto inhabitants to join the fight. This information shook the entire ghetto because it clarified to the Jews, and to the Judenrat, the fate of the "deportees."

ZOB detachments were organized in Toporov, Zhelechov, and in Lansk, Kozki and Sasov camps. The desertion of youth from these camps to the ghetto, and from the ghetto to the forest, was organized. When the escapes from the camps became frequent, the SS commander, Hauptsturmfuhrer[1] Werzok, arrested the members of the Judenrat, kept them as hostages and sent pursuers after the escapees. Two of the escapees were captured and shot. From now on, a morning search was instituted in all the camps. Weapons weren't found.

In April of 1943, a joint council of the forest headquarters and the city headquarters convened in a hiding place in an attic in the ghetto. The following suggestions were discussed:

To move to the region of Lublin or the Carpathian Mountains where, according to rumors, are strong partisan detachments.

To move to the regions of Wolyn or Podolia where, according to the statement in the underground newspaper "Gwardiazista" ("Gwardia Ludowa" bulletin) [The People's Guard[MK]], large partisan detachments were active there.

The organization sent people to explore the possibility of moving. Three of them were shot and killed by a border patrol near Radzivilov [between the German controlled area of Poland and Ukraine]. Another group informed that strong detachments of Bendrovitzim were stationed near Radzvilov and there is no way to pass through these forests. It was decided to open operations in the vicinity of Brody. A tar factory was blown up near the village Sokolovka. In addition, an attack was organized on the Sasov quarries where the labor camp was located, in order to steal explosives. About fifty

[Page 173]

Kilogram of dynamite was taken. The engineer, Foeirshtein, who worked at the welding workshop, prepared a mine for the explosion of trains. The mine was buried between Krasna Station and Kolkoz, a distance of 40 kilometers from Brody. A locomotive and two cars derailed and several Germans were killed.

The organization's financial resources ran out. Therefore, it was decided to organize an attack on the Government Bank in Brody. On May 13 1943, a group left to execute the task. At noon, it became known that the group encountered a German battalion that was training near the location of our fighters. The group began a battle with the German battalion. Baumwald was slightly wounded in his leg. Izzyo Reinhold was wounded in his hand. The fighters retreated to the forest. Reinhold reached the swamps and hid between the reeds. When one of the Germans, who chased after him, approached his position, he shot and killed him. He lost his handgun in the swamps but he only got out of the reeds after he found his weapon. His got lucky, he arrived to the city and there he was given to a doctor for treatment. Two of the fighters were captured by the Germans, brought to the city and handed to the gendarmes. The gendarmes led them to the prison near City Hall. During the search the fighters managed to pull their sawed-off guns ("Otraz" in the partisans' language) from the folds of their clothing, killed the gendarmes in two shots, ran to the ghetto and there they were hidden.

The gendarmes chased after them in a car and the local residents showed them the direction of their flight. The population resented the Jews for daring to kill a Catholic. The gendarmes surrounded the house in which the fighters hid. They beat the occupants with murderous blows so that they will reveal the hiding place of the young men. Since no one was willing to turn the young men, all of them were placed against the wall. They gave them twenty minutes to reconsider and warn them that they will shot them to death if they don't hand over the young fighters. No one betrayed them. Meanwhile, the gendarmes continued to search for the hideout. One of the gendarmes discovered the entrance, warned the fighters that he would throw a hand grenade inside it and ordered them to get out. In a response, one of the fighters shot at the gendarme but the bullet only hit the gendarme's hat. When he repeated his warning, the young men took their own lives.

All the occupants of the house were shot. With the help of the local firefighters, the gendarmes took the elderly, woman and babies out of the houses and drove them out of town, close to Schnel's estate, and there they shot them to death. The firefighters brutally tortured the unarmed Jews.

Everyone realized that the days of Brody Ghetto are numbered.

The fighting organization published a leaflet calling for self-defense such as the heroic uprising of Warsaw Ghetto (we drew our information from the April issue of "Gwardzista"). In addition, we also encouraged people to leave for the forest. The liaison, Zusya, led a company of young people to the forest. Raids were carried out to obtain food for a large group of people in the forest. At night, we attacked rich Volksdeutsche[2]. We confiscated meat, cattle, flour, etc. We left a confiscation document stamped with of ZOB's seal.

[Page 174]

On May 17 1943, after the denunciation of the forest guard, the forest where the first group was camped was surrounded by two companies of the German army, gendarmes and Ukrainian policemen. The struggle continued all day. Linder, who was bleeding, continued to shot and killed two German soldiers who go closer to him before he ran out of bullets. Another fighter shot all his bullets and then proceeded to hang himself on a tree with his leather belt. Another fighter swallowed his cyanic portion that he kept with him.

Under the cover of the night, the fighters, who remained alive, broke the ring. They arrived to the city torn and tattered, hungry and exhausted, and some of them wounded. They hid outside the ghetto, in the attic of the ruined synagogue. The same day, a storm uprooted the remaining tin sheets over the dilapidated roof. Wet and cold the fighters waited for nightfall. "Gusta" (Stein) informed the headquarters on their arrival. However, before the headquarters had the chance to contact them, one of the firefighters noticed them and notified the gendarmes. Those capture six fighters and led them through the city street to boast about the capture of Jewish partisans.

On 21 May 1943, at dawn, the ghetto was surrounded by SS companies who were sent from Lvov. They were headed by SS Major-General, Katzman, and also by Ukrainian policemen who were summoned from the entire province. The annihilation of the ghetto began. People were taken out of their houses and hiding places and rounded up in the market place. Here stood a big box and everyone had to throw their valuables in it. After all the captured were all robbed, they were forced to sit crouched with their hands clasped behind their backs. When the street filled up, they began to load people into trucks and took them to the train station, a place where they were loaded on freight cars, one to two hundred people in a car. The cars were sealed with lead seals and their locks were wrapped with barbwire. To mislead the members of ZOB, SS commander Wartzog ordered all the camp inhabitants to leave for their day work as usual. Only during work hours he sent armed detachments of Gestapo and they led the camp's youth, who did not suspect anything, to the station.

When they arrived to the station, Wertzog informed them that, at first, he did not intend to harm the camp. However, when he found out that the youth was helping the partisans, he decided to send them from Brody Now, the camp's inhabitants realized that the commander had lied to them and horror seized them. Despite the volley of shots fired by the Gestapo men, they started to run in all directions. Many fell and only a handful survived (many of our friends were killed in this Aktzia, among them the engineer Foyershtein and also Halbershtadt. Izyu Reinhold was seriously injured earlier). About two o'clock, when all those caught, about two thousand five hundred people, were loaded into the cars, a siren announced to the Germans and the Ukrainian policemen about the cessation of work. Later, a lunch was held to all those who participated in the Aktzia. After the meal, the Gestapo boarded the train to accompany the convoy of Jews that was probably sent to Majdanek (one of the escapees testified that the train passed by Belzec) All the way, in which the train passed, was strewn with dead Jews. In several cars people managed to open the doors and jumped outside even though the train was speeding at a speed of 60 kilometer per hour. The men of the Gestapo, who sat on the cars' roof, expected that. They opened fire with machine guns on those who jumped. Only three people managed to survive this train.

Translator's footnotes

1. *Hauptsturmfuhrer* - Nazi Party paramilitary mid-range officer grade level, equivalent of an army's captain.
2. *Volksdeutsche* - a Nazi term to describe “Germans in terms of culture and language or race.” This allowed the German to define people according to their ethnicity rather than citizenship.

[Page 175]

Brody in the Days of the Nazi Conquest

by Amalia Friedman nee Olasker

Translated by Moshe Kutten

Edited by Yocheved Klausner

Brody... only one word – Brody, and in Yiddish Brod, only one syllable, but how deep is the meaning of this syllable; dreams of childhood and youth, home, family, friends and our Jewish street. This is one of the saddest memories of our city that was and it is no more. However, the despair is much deeper when the memory of our city is of the most tragic period – the period of the destruction and annihilation of its Jews.

I will try to recount things chronologically, the way they have been imprinted in my memory, things that one can never forget. I will tell you about a period during which a human being remained lonely in the sea of hatred and blood that flooded the city. Neither a human language nor an author's pen are able to fully express or describe what the eyes saw and ears heard; the awe and fear of one's own heartbeats, and the choking feeling which found a permanent habitation in one's throat. What I had experienced is more than sufficient for one man's life. I will keep my own personal pain to myself. However, for you, my dear townsmen, I will try to tell in concise words, how our city perished, and with it, how all of our dear ones - our grandmothers, grandfathers, fathers, mothers, friends, beloved and acquaintances expired.

The city itself was completely ruined. Only the Prague Bank and the barracks near Roikovka remained standing out of the entire length of Ullanov Krekhowieckich (Zlota) street and its environs. There is a lone charred house standing here and there, everything else is in ruin. Since the war front was near the city and its environs for three months, the entire Polish population was evacuated. This is the main reason for the fact that only a very few survived. Many died in Polish homes, from hunger or by the German oppressors' gunshots that reached them while they sneaked out to forage for food.

Many years passed since then, but to me, it seems like everything happened just yesterday.

Just the fact that the Germans entered Brody City a few days after June 22nd meant an unwritten death verdict for the Jewish community. This was the first sign for the approaching tragic extermination, which was executed in Teutonic punctuality and ended in total annihilation of the Brody Jewry. We did not comprehend the death verdict written on the wall when the sound of the Prussian boots marching on the city soil echoed in the air[11]. At the end of the month, The Gestapo arrived in our city, headed by Commander Kruger. They confiscated a house in the corner of Szkolna and Sloneczna streets (near Kallira street), in which Rabbi Steinberg once lived. The following day, Commander Kruger declared that the Jewish intelligentsia must appear in his office in order to cooperate in establishing organized labor in the city. On the first day, only a small group of people showed up. When Kruger noticed that, he tried to appear in front of the group as a good commander. He served them cigarettes, joked around and complimented the beautiful women in the group. He stonewalled the meeting with his charms until sundown. In the evening, he looked at his watch and stated that it was too late to start the discussion, and asked the group to come back again on the following day. He also asked that nobody from the Jewish Intelligentsia should be absent, so that appropriate arrangements can be started without any loss of time. Everybody left the Gestapo headquarters in an elevated mood, fascinated by the Commander. The news about his open behavior circulated very quickly around the entire city.

[Page 176]

In the following morning, Kruger's satanic plan was fully realized. Nobody from the Jewish Intelligentsia was absent that day. The German showed his true monstrous colors. He ordered everyone to stand up facing the wall and keep their arms up in the air. That lasted the entire day. He spoke to them, using poisonous words. They all got beaten-up. The sighs, moans and cries of these miserable people could be heard in the neighboring streets. I visited my grandfather, who lived on the same street as the Gestapo headquarters, in the evening. The family told me that dreadful screams could be heard since that morning. In the evening, the tortured and beaten up people were loaded onto trucks, and transported to a place near the lime factory. Open pits waited for them. They were all murdered there, and their corpses were covered with lime and then dirt. The Poles who witnessed the massacre said that they saw the earth moving after the bodies were covered. That means that some of the victims were buried alive.

The communists that stayed in town as well as the families of communists who managed to escape before the Nazis came, were among the first victims.

Terror and fear draped our city. Our hearts began to foresee our impending destruction. One evil decree followed another. All Jews had to wear a white band with a blue Star of David on their right hand's sleeve. Disobeying this rule meant one verdict – death; Jews were only allowed to walk the streets until five o'clock in the afternoon. Anybody found outside after five o'clock faced death. More evil decrees followed.

During that time, a Judenrat [German appointed Jewish Council[MK]] was established and Bloch was nominated as its head. A Jewish militia was also established and the young Buchbinder was nominated as its commander. All German decrees, such as a payment of ransom money or arranging for a supply of Jewish men and women for forced labor were executed by the Judenrat. This did not mean the end to the daily kidnapping of Jews in the street and transferring of the kidnapped to labor camps in Jactorow, Latski and others. Nobody ever came back from these camps.

During the first few weeks, the Germans imposed ransom money penalties twice. The amounts of money associated with these ransoms were enormous. Those who were able to raise money brought it to the Judenrat, with the false belief that this money would buy one's life. Valuables such as silverware, carpets and furniture were confiscated by the Germans. When a decree to hand over all jewelry was issued, a long line trailed near the Judenrat. Everybody brought everything they owned, including wedding rings.

All Jewish men and women were forced to report every morning to the area in front of the Judenrat. From there they were taken by Germans or Ukrainians. The work was hard and exhausting. Women worked in a brick factory beyond old Brody. We did not get any wages for our work. We did however "earn" hits by rubber clubs in the face and other parts of the body. We returned in the evening weary, exhausted and hungry to the point of unconsciousness. Especially cruel to us was Wachtmeister (Sargent Major in the Calvary) Vogel. His hobby was to hit people in the face with a rubber club. Especially harsh was the fate of whoever could not choke up the cry of pain and let it get out of his or her mouth, as this was when one's torture has just begun.

[Page 177]

During the fall of 1941, the German declared that the Jews must hand over all the furs they own until a certain date. Subsequently, a search at one family home yielded a fur collar. The entire family was executed by shooting. I do not recall the name of the family.

According to the phrase: "troubles occur in bundles, not one at the time", winter of 1941/42 emerged as a perfect companion to the troubles perpetrated by the Prussian predators. We had to report every morning to clean the snow off the roads and throughways. We cleaned the road all the way to Podgorza and the one toward Leshnow. There were times when the workers did not return from their day's work, because they were shot by a German soldier or a Ukrainian policeman when their frozen arms would not allow them to keep on working.

Upon returning home in the evening, hungry, frozen and exhausted, we had to march in foursome formation carrying the wooden shovels on our shoulders (so that, G-d forbid, we would not be able to lean on them). Upon entering the city, we were forced to sing the songs favored by the murderers. Anybody who did not have the energy to raise his or her voice in singing would be beaten or shot. The Poles and the Ukrainians would gather at on the side of the streets at the entrance to the city, to joke and laugh at our misfortune.

We passed the winter, the spring and the summer doing oppressive work and in fear. Every day seemed to have lasted a hundred days. Awakening every morning, we thought that the day would be the last time we would get to see the sunlight. Lying down to sleep, we asked ourselves whether it would be our last night. Nevertheless, we wanted to live! Despite the horrible cruelty of our daily life, we fought for our life with all of our emotional and mental strength just to gain one more day, one night, one hour or one minute, only to postpone the inevitable death. There was not even a glimmer of hope for us to be able to stay alive, during those dark days. Nevertheless, we preferred the nightmarish life with all of its horrors, over a torturous death by the Nazi thugs and their collaborators.

The total annihilation of our city Jews started on September 9th 1942. This was the day of the first "Aktsia" in Brody, which lasted the whole day from dawn to dark. For us, the whole period seemed to be like one continued long nightmarish darkness. The "Aktsia" was executed by the Gestapo and the Militia by going from one Jewish house to another and murdering their inhabitants.

Most of the Jewish population survived this "Aktisia" by hiding in the forests and the fields. It was made possible by the fact that we have heard, ahead of time, that something unusual was about to happen in the ghetto. When the "Sonderkomando" with its black uniform arrived in the evening before the "Aktsia", we thought that they were coming to kidnap Jews and transfer them to forced labor camps. We did not imagine that they would simply murder the Jews on the spot. However, a more horrific shock hit us on November 2nd, during the second "Aktsia", which lasted three days and three nights without any interruption. The Germans scoured the fields, parks and forests. It was therefore difficult to find a refuge. Gunshots echoed continuously. Every shot meant an end to a human life. Elderly, sick and children were murdered on the spot. All the rest were captured and assembled in the market place near the Kalir pharmacy. The first people to be captured sat on the ground which was wet during the day, and frozen during the night, for more than 70 hours without any food or drink until the end of the "Aktsia". Then they were all marched to the train station, where they were packed into boxcars and transported to Belzec. During the same "Aktsia", the Judenrat and the Jewish Militia were transported to the death camp.

[Page 178]

In order to highlight the meaning of the second Aktsia, I would bring up one episode from my own experience during that period. I and my cousin were the only ones who survived out of my entire big family. After three days of murders, bizarre deaths and evacuation to Belzec, the Aktsia ended. A few lone survivors out of big families, who miraculously survived, started to come out of their hideouts. One needs to harness an inhuman strength just to be able to somewhat provide any description of the "Juden-Rein" [Nazi's term for an area which was "cleaned of Jews"[MK]] city and the lone survivors who were left to live in the Hitler-ish hell, compared to which Dante's Hell is meaningless and insignificant.

I met our neighbor, Sonia Halpern, following the Aktsia. She was also the sole survivor out of her entire family. She said that she has already visited the cemetery, in her search for the bodies of her relatives. She told me that she found her mother's corpse among the infinite piles of corpses that were accumulated there during the Aktsia. She buried her mother in a mass grave. I asked her and she agreed to accompany me to try to find bodies of my own family. Hundreds of corpses were piled on top of each other, one pile after the other, at the edge of the cemetery. It was a shocking sight. The corpses were unrecognizable since the heads were shattered by the "a gunshot into the head". I could only guess who the person was by the clothing. In order to find a particular corpse, it was necessary for me to step on corpses and to move them in order to reach the corpses on the bottom of the pile. I was terrified to the point that I could not comprehend what is happening to me. I was shaking from fear, I cried but I could not identify any of the corpses. One cannot appreciate one's fortune for not experiencing such a horrific spectacle. It would continue to haunt me until the end of my life. The corpses of these miserable people would be buried in mass grave later on. Sonia Halpern would be killed later on in the ghetto. I am the only one that survived from the entire area of old Brody.

It was too dangerous to sleep in the ruins within the city limits. This is why I wandered around the parks and the fields at the outskirts. The winter came early that year and was harsher than usual. During one of these cold nights, the snow began to fall after I fell asleep, and it covered me up with a thick layer. When I woke up, I imagined myself hovering among white clouds. When I finally shook myself out from my sleep, I realized that I am buried alive under a thick layer of snow and had to exert a big effort in order to pull myself out of it.

On December 2nd 1942, 3000 Jews from the city environs were transported to the ghetto. Now the ghetto spread from Kolejowa street starting from the home of Kristianpoler toward the train station, as well as along the Rynek [market in PolishMK] on the side of the Pharmacy of Kalir, through Szpitalna Street to its end. The ghetto was surrounded by barbed wire. It was announced that all Jews must move to the ghetto before the 17th of December 1942. Anybody found outside the ghetto after that date would be shot on the spot. A handful of Jews hid in the villages and with Poles in Brody itself. The farmers usually robbed the hiding Jews and handed them over to the Ukrainian Militia. Hunger, crowding and lack of minimal hygienic conditions caused an accelerated spread of Typhus and Rubella. Shooting directed at Jews at the gate of the ghetto and near its fences became routine. We were taken to work under a heavy guard of the Gestapo and the Ukrainian Militia. The Jewish hospital was full to capacity. There were almost no physicians and no medicines. The ghetto was shrinking by the hour. Jews became sick hour by hour and minute by minute. The total annihilation was proceeding in a lightning speed.

[Page 179]

The year 1943 arrived, and with it the last murderous stage of the annihilation of the ghetto. This stage was known as "Juden-Frei" [Nazi term for designating and area cleansed of JewsMK]. Prior to the final eradication of the ghetto, the Nazis selected young men and women from those who were left, whom they needed for doing forced labor work, and gathered them in the barracks near Roikova. The Germans called the place "a Labor Camp" (ArbeitsLager). The ghetto was subsequently ruined and burnt by the Germans and the Ukrainians. The big synagogue which was located within the ghetto survived. However, even the group of the young Jewish workers claimed daily victims. A Gestapo thug by the name of Fuchs was taking the Jews daily for a roll call. He would choose a random victim, at his will, and ordered him or her to step forward out of the formation. He would then proceed to shoot his victim in the head from behind. Every appearance of this Fuchs meant death. Jews, who used to tell on other people during the early days, shed any residues of human character and became wild animals. They started to steal slices of bread, underwear and even shoelaces from other people. Everybody considered only oneself. Despite the fact that the chances for survival were tiny, or maybe because of that, the will to live was magnified and reached indescribable levels. There were several youths who ran away to the forest when they were taken out of the camp to work.

Munyo Zacks and Wandz'ia Kharash live in America today. Another couple lives in Jerusalem. Achtentuch, Kuperman and others died not long after the war. The refugees of the Nazi hell, who survived, were all broken to their core. The sights of the past are haunting us. Even the nights do not bring us any peace or quiet. Horrific dreams torment us and would not let our wounds heal. I often ask myself in what sense are we better than those who died a martyred death? Words are too pale versus the horrors that we have experienced.

As the time passes, forgetfulness starts being active among the handful that survived and who remained alive out of the six million souls slaughtered, strangled, burnt, tortured, and buried alive[2]. Can an author's pen tell and describe how we felt and experienced, and what we saw?

Immediately after my liberation by the Red Army, I came back to Brody from the forest. This happened in June 1944. The city was no more. All of its inhabitants were dead, only the ruins remained, inanimate and terrifying, causing chills and horror.

May a talented artist rise and succeed in immortalizing the magnificent Jewry of Brody which is no more, the spirit of heroism and holiness that throbbed through its veins while it was breathing its last breath – and thus prevent its memory from descending into the abyss of oblivion.

Translator's footnotes

1. The author uses the Biblical phrase - *MENE, MENE, TEKEL, UFARSIN* - words written by a mysterious hand on the wall of Belshazzar's palace, and interpreted by the Jewish Babylonian scholar Daniel as predicting the doom of the king and his dynasty (Daniel 5:25)..
2. The author uses the term *Sh'erit ha-Pletah,* literally - the surviving remnant, a biblical term (Ezra 9:14) used by Jewish survivors of the Holocaust to refer to themselves.

[Page 180]

Revenge on the Murderer

by Hersh Pollack

Translated by Moshe Kutten

Edited by Yocheved Klausner

I "spent" the period of World War II in the ranks of the Red Army. I was discharged in the spring of 1946 and went back to Poland. I arrived in Krakow during the holiday of Pesach. The first person I met in the street was our townsman, Yosef Leiner. We were very glad to meet. We recalled that we had met shortly on Ukrainian soil, at the beginning of the war, in 1941, during the days of the great withdrawal... A few days following our meeting, Yosef left for Eretz Israel, while I decided to stay in Poland. I went to Silesia and settled in Wroclaw. I met Brody townsmen there as well: Peretz Khudak, Leib Paket and Leib Knetchuker.

At about the same time, I also met Stanisláv Chvartinski, a known athlete from the Polish soccer team of our city. I was very happy to see him. We went to a restaurant and had a meal together. After he had a few drinks, he began to tell me stories from the time of the conquest of our city. Among other things, he disclosed to me that my two sisters, Frida and Regina, were taken out of their hideout in a bunker by one Ukrainian named Jozef Kasianchuk, aka Valenti. I knew Valenti from before the war. We called him Valenti the "Lumpenproletariar [a term originally coined by Karl Marx to describe the lower layer of the working class that is unlikely to be productive or useful to society[MK]]. Chvartinski told me that during the attack by the Red Army on the Germans in Brody, Valenti ran away westward with the Germans. I have decided to find this killer of my sisters and avenge their blood.

I started by collecting addresses of our townsmen. During a period of ten months I traveled to various cities, towns and villages visiting with Polish and Jewish families. In every place I visited, I became aware of additional details about the horrors of the conquest. I visited with the attorney Volnik and Yatzek Miklashevski who saved the daughter of the teacher Kalman Harnik, may his memory be blessed. I also met with Mr. Harnik and Mr. Kahana in Bielsk as well as Blaustein, Yan Strakhora, Menashe Motkhes, Flinter, Hafner, Mamutski, Garstski, Shanitski (Sporza), Vladislav, Mundek Bochek and many others of our townsmen.

I learned gradually that my two sisters, together with Mrs. Halbmilion and Motkhes family – altogether about 30 people – hid in a bunker on Goldhaber Street in the house where a former paper product store of old Mrs. Kanner was located.

The owner of the bunker was Timchishin. Valenty knew about this bunker and about the people hiding in it. He contacted Timchishsin and demanded that he pay him one thousand zloty a month as hash money, otherwise he would inform the authorities.

During the first month, Valenty kept his word; however, in the second month he demanded to double his fee. Since they did not have a choice, they yielded to his demand. However, on 11 of May 1943 after he got paid, Valenty reached an agreement with the German gendarme, according to which he would receive half of the artifacts found in the bunker if he finds one that houses Jews. On May 20th the Gestapo arrived at the bunker and the people hiding in it were taken out. The poor people were transported to the Schnell forest. There, a big grave was prepared ahead of time. The victims were thrown into the grave and were shot by a machine gun. The grave diggers covered the people who were shot with earth. Whoever was not killed already was buried alive.

[Page 181]

As far as I could find out, Kasianchuk lived in Lower Silesia near Marchishov. I reported as such to the defense ministry office in Wroclaw. However, the searches for Valenti did not bear any fruit. I believed therefore that he must be hiding under a false name.

I suggested going and searching after him myself, as I knew him before the war. I was convinced that I would be able to identify him. Equipped with a document issued by the defense ministry and a handgun, I traveled to Wroclaw and its environs. The document stated that the militia, army and all other institutions should help me to arrest the person I identify, with no regard to his name and status. I searched house to house in eight different villages without any result.

I went back to Wroclaw where I asked, in the municipality, to see the list of the residents. At a certain moment I encountered the name Yozef Petski from Podkamen who was born in 1909. I copied the address and went to see him at his home.

When I arrived to the place at dusk, I opened the yard entrance wicket. My eyes saw the wanted Kasianchik coming out of his house, carrying two pails full of silage for the cattle. He recognized me too, placed the pails on the ground and called: "Pollak, thanks G–d you have survived". While saying that, he proceeded to hug and kiss me, but I responded by drawing my handgun and said to him: "I survived in order for you to die, right now!"

The despicable murderer started to beg me not to kill him; I took him to the police station and waited there the whole night until an order was received from Wroclaw to arrest him. He was transferred handcuffed to the Bilnia–Gora jail accompanied by two armed policemen. It happened on 24th of April 1947.

On the 28th of July of the same year I learned that his wife hired a Jewish lawyer, who agreed to defend him on the condition that his wife collect signatures of Jews and Poles testifying that her husband is Polish and not Ukrainian and that he behaved impeccably during the conquest period. Kasianchik's wife went to see Menashe Motkhes to ask him to sign such a testimony. Menashe came to me and told me about it. I contacted the prosecutor who handled war–crimes and notified him about it. The prosecutor told me that the signed testimony would be useless if two witnesses would testify about Kasianchuk's crimes. He told me that Kasianchuk would not be tried under the criminal law, but under the July Manifest [A political manifesto of the Polish Committee of National Liberation, a communist government administration, officially proclaimed in Chelm 22th July 1944MK], according to the War–Crime statute, which stated: "A person who collaborated with the conquering Germans, and acted against persecuted people, because of their race or nationality, and directly or indirectly caused their death – is punishable by death" (the author quoted the law as he recalled it).

When the investigation ended, I hosted two PPR (the Polish Communist Party) experts who followed the case and tried to move the trial to Worclaw. In the meantime, I went to visit with the same people I met during the period of the search for the killer, and thus managed to present eight additional witnesses to the court.

[Page 182]

The trial took place in the court at Worclaw on 18th January 1948. The court hall was packed. The prosecution brought 17 witnesses, 12 of whom were Polish and the other five were Jews, all of them were our townsmen. These were the Jewish witnesses: Kalman Harnik (may his memory be blessed), Hafner, Munyo Shapira (Peretz Shapira's son), Blaustein (may his memory be blessed) and Menashe Motkhes.

All of the horrors and atrocities that our city's Jews experienced during Hitler's conquest were disclosed at the trial. I will mention just a few of the details.

The witness František Kožul who volunteered to testify on his own will, told the court that he saw with his own eyes that during the infamous Aktzia called the "Ukrainian entertainment" ("Ukrainska Poholinka"), Kasianchuk and another man threw a three years old child from the balcony of Kuperman's house (across from Kalmus pharmacy). The poor child was killed instantly.

Another witness testified that he and two of his friends went to see Kasianchuk, who served as the jail commissioner at that time, and asked him to release a Jewish young woman who was previously arrested. They offered a ransom for her. Kasianchuk took out gold coins and a fistful of jewelry and said: I already have enough to last a lifetime. I could eat, drink and enjoy myself as much as I want".

The verdict was given late at night. Jozef Kasianchuk was convicted on five charges. The court also provided the sentence: On four of the charges, Kasianchuk was sentenced to life in prison. On the fifth charge, Kasianchuk was sentenced to death. The final verdict was therefore – death.

Kasianchuk appealed for clemency to the Polish president. His appeal was in vain. The president waived his privilege to issue a clemency. The verdict was executed by hanging on the 5th of March, 1948.

During my searches after the killer "Valenti", I met many of our townsmen. I learned from them an great amount of details about the period of conquest in Brody. I thought that it would be my duty to put them down in writing, so that they can be published in our city's Yizkor–book.

I found out that not everybody was led to the slaughter without resistance. A partisan group was located in the Klektov forest. Another strong partisan group named "Stalingrad" was headed by Yaakov Linder, a communist during the underground days. He was mentioned in the book: "Lokhamei Ha–Getaot" [The Ghetto Fighters'MK] as well as in Professor Bernard Mark's book: "Bleter Far Geshikhte" ["Pages for the History"MK].

Among the fighters against the enemy was Khanokh Tishker from "Ha–Shomer Ha–Tzair" [Literally "The Young Guard" – a Socialist–Zionist, secular Jewish youth movement founded in 1913 in Galicia. It was also the name of the group's political party in pre–1948 Israel–Palestine known later as MAPAMMK], who shot the snitch Ludwig Jantzin and hit him in the shoulder. Yosef Berger, apprentice in the LAMM metal workshop, was captured along with another partisan (whose name I was not able to find), and they were both taken to the Gestapo. At a certain moment when their escort stepped away to report on the capture of the two dangerous Jews, Berger drew his weapon from under his coat, shot the escort and both prisoners ran away. Shlomo Shraga and David Katz (brother–in–law of Yosef Leiner–Parvari) encountered a Ukrainian ambush on their way out of a village, as they were carrying food for the people who were hiding in the bunker, located in Yoel Kristiampoller's house. They were demanded to disclose the location of the bunker they came from. The Ukrainians pulled their nails out and tortured them to death, but they did not talk. They died a martyr's death. Shalom Halbershtadt was also a fighter among the partisans. Dr. Meles committed suicide because he did not want to be a member of the Judenrat. Dr. Horn also died honorably.

[Page 183]

Brave fighters were among Brody townsmen in the ranks of the Red Army as well. Leib Herzberg, Jozef Rogovski and I fought together on the same front. Leib Herzberg was killed during an intense bombardment of the German guns near Dnieperpetrovsk. Yosef Leiner was an officer who fought on all the fronts. The same is true for Natan and Shmuel Reinart. The latter was injured (I think twice) and had the privilege to march with the winners into Berlin.

It is worthwhile to mention that a few of our city's Poles and Ukrainians hid Jews, who survived thanks to these people. Among them was the Ukrainian Timchishin. When he was notified that the Germans discovered the bunker that he kept, he committed suicide by drinking poison.

Yan Borchak hid the Isenbruch family, however, he could not protect them until the liberation day. All the respect and appreciation belongs to the Mamutski family; they hid two Jewish families, the family of the dentist Dr. Berk and another family. Somebody informed the Gestapo and they were executed – the Jews and the Mamutski family including their three small children. All of them were shot and killed in the Schnell forest. Only one son, who was not home at the time, survived. Today, he is an officer in the Polish army.

Michael Schust saved Dr. Berger. Blaustein, Hefner and the teacher Harnik and his daughter were also hidden by Christians and survived. Some of them, like Hefner, Sander, Prachtman and Yitskhak Goldenberg married the women that saved their lives. The first two now live in the USA, the last lives in Herzlia with his wife and adopted son.

The fiend was not satisfied with devil dances in the camps of the human race haters during this horrific period. To our shame and disgrace, he found for himself collaborators in the Jewish community itself: Katz, a former clerk in the Brody municipality, Wechsler, a restaurant owner on Train Street (Kolejowa Street), Benyu Ponikvar – the chairman of the Judenrat, and Reuven (Rubin) Myzels – a fool who sent his own wife to the "Umschlagplatz" [German term to describe the collection point of Jews being sent to a concentration camp[MK]]. During the second Aktzia, he accompanied the Gestapo and the Ukrainian militia men during the house to house search for the poor remaining survivors. After the hangmen searched Shkolnick's house and did not find anything, they were ready to leave. However Myzels said: “I smell the scent of Jewish meat here”. Fortunately for the people who hid in the bunker under the floor and heard it, the Getsapo men did not pay attention to what he said and they left. I was told this story by Khina Schnor, who was hiding among the other people in the bunker.

Following the “Judenrein” [“clean of Jews” – was a Nazi term to designate an area “cleansed” of Jewish presence[MK]] Aktzia, several remaining Jews were taken out of the city and transferred to a camp in Olesko. These people were frail, sick and broken in their soul and body. Rubin Myzels was also on the same truck. He was beaten to death by the other passengers. A woman and her child were handed over to the Gestapo by the woman's Christian husband by the name of Spero.

With great sorrow and burning pain I have to state that only two Jewish families remained in our city, which once had such a vigorous Jewish life: those of Shmuel Stoyanover and Yekhiel (Machek) Gruber. The heart is aching for this Jewish city with a glorious past, which was wiped out from the diaspora's map, and for the times that were and are no more.

[Page 184]

I wrote down these things for the benefit of the future generations of our nation so that they would know and remember, and would never forgive the Nazis and the neo–Hitlerists for their crimes. I wrote these things when the civilized world demanded that West–Germany would not enforce the Statute of Limitation on war–crimes. The arm of justice must capture the last of Hitler's criminals. This would entail the execution of the last will and testament of the six million of our brothers and sisters who were annihilated during World War II.

[Page 185]

In the Days of Wrath

by Vladislava Larissa Choms (Righteous Among the Nations)

Translated by Moshe Kutten

Edited by Yocheved Klausner

This article is dedicated to my dear Brody townswomen

My sympathy to the people of Brody started in 1935, when the Jewish residents of Brody invited me to give a lecture about Palestine. This was an official summary of my five weeks' stay in the ancient land of Israel. My host for the two–days visit was a physician (probably Dr. Cecilie Jawrower), who hosted me at her house that was situated near the market. The big crowd welcomed me enthusiastically. We could not imagine at the time, that our relations and the connections between us would be tightened under complete different circumstances, when the terror would rage, and the injustice and discrimination would take hold over life in Western Europe during the years of 1939 - 1945. In countries with a high–level culture, the animalistic abuse became legal! When the horrific German war–machine crushed the resistance of Poland, which was considered as their most hated enemy, the door has opened for them to achieve their main goal - the destruction and annihilation of the Jewish nation to its foundations. The Jewish population in Poland was the largest in the European countries - about four million people. From the Germans' point of view, this was almost a total fulfillment of their destructive plans. They started with that "cultural" operation a few years earlier, in their own country. This is when Jews started to escape eastward to Poland. Refugee camps were established at the border near Działdowo to absorb the refugees, and the Jewish community organized the aid for them. This "racial cleansing" of the German society, and the superior feeling of being "pure Arians", were steps with dual purpose: On one hand the Germans wiped out the competition from the advanced intellect of the German Jews, and on other hand, they provided a legal authorization for the robbery of the immense property of the exterminated Jews.

According to the 1939 Ribbentrop–Molotov agreement, the two friends divided the lands of Poland between them. The Germans got hold of the western part, and the Russians the eastern part, which included Eastern Little–Poland [Western Galicia[MK]] and the city of Lvov. Without being at war with Russia, we found ourselves, unexpectedly, under a Communist rule, as residents of Lvov. My husband, who served in the 11th Division [of the Polish army[MK]], was stationed in Zolkiew. As a mother and wife of military men, I was candidate for imprisonment or deportation to Asia. To us, at least, the Germans did it without any "racial", national or class classification. Even an advanced age did not have any weight, since all of these people were condemned to die anyway. This is how things lasted for two years. Two and a half million Poles were uprooted from their homes and transported to the Northern or Eastern parts of Russia. The border that was decided upon at the time of the division of Poland between the Soviets and the Germans was rigorously guarded, like all other borders of occupied lands. In spite of that, people managed to escape from Western Poland to us, and vice versa in order to avoid imprisonment. Refugees from the west told us horror stories about the cruel actions of the Germans. They told us about mass murders, violent torturing and extermination of Jews; but, the ordinary brain of a 20th century's person was not able to comprehend and accept murders of women, children and elderly, openly under the sun.... No, it cannot be true!

[Page 186]

This is how the city of Lvov, at the end of 1941, greeted relatively peacefully the change of conquerors, , and especially so in light of the bloody traces left by the Russians in the form of inhumane crimes in Brigdki and in the streets of Lontski, Kazimierzowska and Zmarstinovska.

However, only one day following the entry of the Germans in Lvov, fear descended over the city. According to directive no. 1 of the German city commander, all city employees were to report in the following morning to their places of work. I was employed as a clerk in the petroleum firm "Earth Gasses", so I appeared in my office as directed, in the following morning, in order to hide my real identity. I noticed that two attendance lists were presented for a signature: general and "Jewish". I noticed that the Jewish workers were detained. I was shocked by that. I took the hand of the Jewish clerk Mrs. Klara Lustig (now in Melbourne Australia), who was standing pale and frightened, and pulled her over behind me. As it turned out later, the Jewish workers were arrested, among them, Mrs. Beglaiter–Bogdanovich (today in Haifa). We had to transport Klara Lustig through the entire city (from Meritski square to Gronvaldeska Street), during which time we saw, with a great sense of fear, the Germans with the help of Ukrainians, capturing people suspected of being Jewish, examining documents of passers–by, and guards of Gestapo men already transporting large groups of men and women. Despite the fact that Klara was terrified, we managed to control our nerves and miraculously arrived at her apartment, where her eight-year-old son was waiting for her. This was for me my "fire–test" on the front of the rescuing actions. It was just a coincidence that Klara Lustig, a widow, came from Brody, where she had a large family and many acquaintances.

As early as the following morning, the first blow was landed. While confiscating the apartment of a young lawyer, Dr. Grossman, the Germans killed him and his mother. In the same evening, they arrested and murdered tens of professors from Yan Kazimir University and Lvov Politechion [Polytechnic School[MK]]. On Luntski Street, the Jews, men, women and children, were ordered to dig, with their bare hands, and pull out the corpses of about one hundred Poles, who were murdered by the Bolsheviks and buried in the ground in the square. The panic and fear of the city residents were immense and people talked among themselves by whispering. When I was notified that the Gestapo is looking for a famous Lvov lawyer, after not finding him at home, I organized my first rescue undertaking. The lawyer and his wife were placed in a hideout, and we succeeded in getting most of their important items out of the apartment and transfer them, using a farmer's wagon, to the outskirts and from there, using "good papers", to Krakow. This man died just a short time ago.

Academic youths, whom I supervised before the war, gathered around me. Additional people with good will came as well. People, like me, who could not bear the shame and the trampling of human decency.

[Page 187]

The extortion of "contributions" from the Jewish population started. Following that came the degrading marking of people by an arm band and the forced labor camps for men in Janowski Street [a labor, transit and extermination camp established by the Nazis in the outskirts of Lvov[MK]]. During all of that time, it was impossible to move the Jewish residents from their places. They hoped and believed that "somehow" they will endure. In fact, particularly then, during the first three months, we could still transfer people, send them away, or hide them, as everybody still had some kind of an inventory or valuables [which could be used as payment[MK]]. This strange passiveness, which was very difficult to overcome, took over the Jews, who usually showed resourcefulness and initiative. They became like a bird that froze under the snake's gaze. Many times I had to use all of my will power in order to convince people or simply force them to save themselves!

We need to remember that the state of the Polish society, which was oppressed to the bitter end by two enemies, was very difficult. Middle-aged men in good physical shape were few; most of them were captured by the Germans, crossed the border with the army or were exiled to the USSR. Only women, children, elderly, and some youths remained. The latter were exiled, in groups, to forced labor camps in Germany. Some Polish families, dispossessed of their apartments, lacking the means to sustain themselves, humiliated and persecuted, knew to rise above all of that, and provide help to people in need. This is why the passiveness of the Jews, and in some cases, their loyally toward the Germans, simply paralyzed our operation. Only after the announcement about the transfer of all Jews into the ghetto – and on the same occasion, the Jews were totally robbed during the last inspection – only then, the Jews finally understood their situation, regained their composure, opened their eyes and started to cry for help. However, at that time it was almost impossible to help them, the more so since many people from other cities and towns fled to Lvov and crowded the town. Klara

Lustig had a senseless idea to run away to Brody, where everybody knew her. Following a few attempts to hide, she came back to me and was one of those people whom G–d gave me the possibility to save. She lived for two years with a family of an officer who was a prisoner of war. So through my Klara, a whole line of Brody people came to us for help. At the same time, following a call from Warsaw, a committee whose aim was to help the Jews, was established near the delegation of the Polish government. I was nominated to head this committee. Various political and underground factions helped with people and resources and we received aid grants, which were vital and necessary in light of the shortages and general lack of economical means.

From that moment on, our activity has turned the corner. It was now possible to send envoys to provincial towns. From there, people equipped with appropriate papers were transferred to other places, usually to big cities. Most of the time it was accomplished by women couriers, who were brave and willing to make a sacrifice. Since all the papers were destroyed, the real names of these women were never disclosed. Only the names in the new documents were available. It is therefore very difficult for me to mention any of them or provide any details, though I did provide names and details to "Yad Vashem" for those from Lvov whom I knew.

As I mentioned above, our rescue actions started to evolve and expand, but at the same time, we had to continue our relentless fight with the Germans, who were very well aware of our efforts. This was, for us, like a "dance over the edge of the abyss", a term that was well known by the people active in the Polish underground. Every one of us who was involved in the operation of rescuing and aiding Jews, was first of all an active member in "*Armia Krajowa*" ["Home Army" - the largest Polish underground resistance organization[MK]], and would not have been allowed to put in jeopardy our main vision, namely - preparing the country for an armed fight with the conqueror. Every one of us was liable to be abused, tortured, or killed by the Germans. Just curiosity, or needless chatter of people, without any bad intentions, was very dangerous to us. We were afraid of the "Volksdeutsche" [a term used by the Nazis to describe people of German decent who lived in other countries[MK]], who were able to point at Jewish houses with their eyes closed. Besides, they knew very well who, in Poland of the days before the war, was an active adversary of racial discrimination.

[Page 188]

In the meantime, the German insanity and rampage intensified with no restraints (year 1943). Transports of naked people were continuously taken out from the ghetto toward "*Piaskowa–Gora*" [literally *Sandy–Hill*, name of a district and a forest near Lvov where executions of Jews took place[MK]]. The underground command issued a declaration condemning the mass slaughtering of fellow citizens just for being Jewish: "Murder and slaughter that are unprecedented in the world's history! Infants, children, women, elderly and handicapped people are being murdered mercilessly. They are poisoned or dying slowly while being buried alive. They live in a hell of humiliation, indescribable misery and cruelty. We call all citizens to help in rescuing the victims. The responsibility for the spilled blood of the Polish and Jewish victims falls on the German hangmen and their collaborators".

Now when I am looking back at all of that, I cannot understand how these few people could stand against the German might with bare hands, exposed and forsaken? It appears that saving a human being gave them an ultimate fulfillment.

We rescued people, who were destined to annihilation, from the ghetto and Janow camps. A few individual even managed to escape from the pits near "Piaskowa–Gora" and to arrive in the darkness of the night to our houses in the outskirts of the town. Our liaisons furnished them with documents, clothes and money and directed them toward border crossings in the mountains and even toward the inner circles of the German organization "Todt"[a] that was advancing into the Ukraine. Women were directed toward Austria or Germany as work volunteers. This rescue operation was directed at anybody whom it was possible the rescue; regretfully, it was very difficult, or even impossible to save the elderly.

Also regretfully, in many cases we failed, despite all the efforts. Memories of cases where we had to abandon the rescue attempt are haunting and depressing me to this day!

Book Editor's Notes

a. An organization with an economic orientation. It was named after the German initiator who established a network of workshops that became available for use by the German army fighting in the east. Todt recruited Jewish craftsmen (tailors, shoemakers, carpenters, furriers, underwear seamstresses, etc....). Their employment was like a temporary guarantee for securing their life. The "*Todt*" organization spread with the advancement of the German army (the Editor).

[Page 189]

Testimony

by Genya Rosenfeld-Berger

Translated by Moshe Kutten

Edited by Simon Godfrey

Upon the Germans' entry into Brody, I was left alone with our three years old son, after my husband was taken away on Pesach, together with other Brody townsmen, to build airports in Bessarabia. I sold everything we owned in the house in order to survive, I sensed the approaching disaster and started to prepare my child for living among the gentiles. I only spoke to him in Polish. I changed the names of all of our relatives to Christian names, and eventually, a Christian woman in Podkamen agreed to keep him for what remained of our money. I missed my son very much and went to see him from a distance. I climbed on the fence of the house just to hear his voice. After several weeks, when I finally dared to visit, he had already forgotten the names of his relatives. After the ghetto was sealed off I sent money to that Christian woman.

Four weeks before the ghetto was liquidated, a Jewish boy was discovered at a Christian women house. In order to frighten the Christians who held Jewish children, and to deter us, the Germans lead the captured boy, and the Christian women who hid him, around the ghetto and finally killed them both.

Afterwards, the Christian woman brought my boy back to me because she was scared of the Germans. During the night before the liquidation of the ghetto I hid in the cellar of the Yudenrat together with my son, my mother and several other Jews. After I helped in organizing the cellar, I went up to the attic of the neighboring house, where, for the previous four weeks, I had saved some food scraps from the deserted houses of the ghetto. The suffering of the children in the cellar was indescribable. They were hungry, lived in awful filth, and were shivering from the cold.

After four weeks, when I left to look for Christian acquaintances, our bunker was discovered, and everyone was killed. In desperation, I went to the assembly place for Jews in the old Polish army's barracks. When I arrived, I heard that a roundup would take place there the next day. I ran away at night and hid in an open field. The following day, all the people in the old Polish army barracks were eliminated.

In September 1943, I went to see my Polish neighbor Valchak, the chimney sweeper in the city and he gave me some clothes. I cleaned myself up and stayed over in his attic. After a few days, he found me another hiding place in his firewood shed. During very cold days, he would bring me into his house, despite the fact that a Ukrainian policeman Lozovoi, an infamous murderer, lived across the street. Until the beginning of 1944 I remained with him but when the battle front approached, the population was forced to leave the city. Valchak moved me to another location together with his family and hid me. When the order to abandon the city was issued, he told me to leave without him as he could not help me any longer. The city was heavily bombarded by the Russians.

[Page 190]

I left wearing Christian clothes that the Gentile had prepared for me. I met two Jewish acquaintances and together we approached the front. The Germans captured us but mistook us for Christians and forced us to work in their kitchen. After several weeks, they transferred us together with the rest of the Polish women to the Yanov camp in Lvov. I escaped from there and hid as a Pole until the liberation

[Page 191]

The Hand of Fate

by Pessya Loewy

Translated by Moshe Kutten

Edited by Simon Godfrey

When the Second World War broke out I was in Warsaw with my husband, daughter and two sons. In November 1939, I decided to travel back to Brody to check on my house and the house of my father in law, Yaakov Loewy, who was nicknamed "Yaakov the Observer" as he was the supervisor of the ritual slaughter.

I took my daughter with me, and with great difficulty, while risking our lives we managed to cross the border between the Germans and the Russians near Pshemishl. Brody was controlled by the Russians at the time. I found everybody at the house, however, the militia warned us that we would need to leave Brody and go to Russia, since only the locals were allowed to live in the city. It was possible for me to receive a local ID certificate, as I was born here, and married and had my children. My husband and his family had also been in Brody for many generations.

I walked around the city park the whole night, but I could not make my mind as to what I should do. If I decide to get a local ID, I would not be able to go back and see my husband and my sons again, as they lived across the border. While still debating with myself, I received a letter from my husband, telling me that he was involved in commerce, and asked me to cross the border if it was possible and come back to him with our daughter. I cried the whole night. I felt that I was breaking apart, without the ability to make any decision.

The next day I did try to go back across the border near Pshemishl, but everybody who came with me to the border had to go back. The Germans simply did not allow anybody to cross.

In Brody, they began to expel the “foreigners” in the middle of the night. In the meantime, my younger son arrived form Warsaw with a neighbor of my husband. After a while, my second son came by himself. I arranged for the children to sleep at a village with an acquaintance and I slept away from the house to avoid deportation. The one night that I stayed in my father in law's house, they woke me up in the middle of the night to deport me. I was astounded. Fear got hold of me, and without knowing what I was saying, I told them that my children were sleeping in the village. After a short while, they brought the children and the four of us were deported to Siberia, to the end of the world. We were convinced that our life would end over there on the prairies and in the jungles, while in Warsaw the war would end and my husband would survive alone without the family he loved so much. The bitter truth was completely different. The deportation from by my birth-place, Brody, was also our salvation. Despite the suffering, hunger and humiliation that were part of our life in different places in Russia, we survived. However, my husband who stayed behind in Warsaw did not escape from the Germans. He tried to escape from the Germans on three occasions, but they caught him each time. Perhaps he saw it as the hand of G-d's in whome he believed so much. He perished along with millions of Jews at the hands of the murderers.

[Page 192]

In the Days of the Conquest

(Excerpts from a Diary)

by Fanya Zorne Laufer

Translated by Moshe Kutten

Edited by Yocheved Klausner

(Fanya was born on May 9th, 1928 in the village of Dubya near Brody. When the war between Germany and Russia broke out on June 1941, she was 13 years old. She has just completed the seventh grade in Brody's elementary school. From that point on, her life became a long saga of suffering and torture by the Nazis and their collaborators, the Ukrainian fascists. This talented and pretty girl grew up among these people. She survived miraculously.

As it turned out, Brody had its own Anna Frank. We bring here the first part of Fanya's diary, which describes the period until her escape to the forest, where she lived under inhumane conditions before she was liberated by the Red Army in the summer of 1944).

The End of June 1941

Joyful and full of bright hopes, I completed the academic year at the school in Brody with very good grades in my report card. I went home to my parents in the village of Dubya in order to spend the summer vacation with them. My parents owned a beautiful and well-organized farm. My father was an able farmer with a lot of knowledge. He loved his work and worked hard in the fields. He raised beautiful animals, and my mother took care of the flower garden and the orchards. Our trees bore plenty of fruit: apples, pears, plums and cherries.

During the summer months we used to invite various guests to our farm. This time, my parents allowed me to invite my best friend, Miryam

Halbmilion, from Brody. However, it was not to be. My joy did not last long. The war descended on us like a thunder from the sky. The Germans invaded Russia.

Beginning of July 1941

I was engulfed by fear. The Germans reached us. There was no place to escape. Father was comforting us, saying that the devil may not be as bad as people described it. "After all, I'm just a farmer and an agriculturalist" he said. The German army entered our village. The Ukrainians, jubilant and overjoyed, welcomed the German army with bread and salt. The priest marched at the head of the parade, the rest of the villagers following him. They were holding national flags. It looked like a religious parade of the church. They were convinced that the Germans would give them a country of their own – a fascist Ukrainian country.

I stood behind the fence, with my father, and looked at them. Mother did not come out of the house. My heart shrank from pain. I was not scared though. I was never scared when I was with Father.

[Page 193]

The young and healthy looking German soldiers were riding their military cars, full of Nazi pride and they were singing. For now, they did not know who we were, but they will know in no time. We were only five families in this small village. We were all farmers. What was awaiting us? Our village was mostly populated by Ukrainians. They were nationalists, radical and anti-Semitic. They threatened us, not once, that they would slaughter all the Jews when the time comes. We would be the first ones to be killed. This would be their victory.

The First Night with the Germans

Evening descended. Singing was heard in the streets. The German soldiers were drinking and dancing with the Ukrainians. There was a dark and eerie silence in our home. All of a sudden, German soldiers broke into our house, accompanied by local Ukrainians. The collaborators pointed at us and yelled – "Jude". They have already managed to learn the word.

"Ah, das sind verfluchte Juden. Gold! Brilianten!" ("Ah, these are damn Jews. Gold! Diamonds!" They searched the whole house, turned everything upside down and took whatever they liked, even the rice stock. They looked at me as if I was an animal in the circus. "Hey Hans, shau, hier hast du eine kleine Jüdin – sie sieht doch aus wie eine Aryen, eine hell blonde Jüdin" (Hey, Hans, look, we have here a little Jew girl who looks like an Arian with bright blond hair!"). He pulled me by force by the hair, to the middle of the room. I burst into tears. Mother and Father came to my help. "Gut Gott, jezt haben wir keine Zeit zu euch, wir müssten nach Osten. Ihr Juden seid shuldig das wir Krieg haben" (Good G-d. We do not have time for you now. We must continue eastward. You Jews are to blame for the fact that we are at war). They left our house slamming the door. We breathed a sigh of relief. It looked like the longest night of our life. We did not put on the light. We lay down to rest in one room, just in case they would come back. We wanted to be together.

Independent Ukrainian State

The German army advanced eastward. There were no Germans left in our villages. The conquest authorities allowed the Ukrainians complete independence. The yellow-blue flag was displayed on every house. The Ukrainians were sharpening their knives. Horrible rumors spread. A pogrom against the Jews took place in Lvov. Thousands of Jews were killed there on July 1st-2nd. Thousands were slaughtered and murdered in Zhelechov. Our brethren were being killed mercilessly everywhere.

The Ukrainian peasants entered the towns, robbed whatever they could put their hands on and returned to their villages with carts loaded with Jewish property: bedding, carpets and even a piano which I saw loaded on a cart in our own village. The Ukrainian fascists were going around in the streets with Jewish blood on their hands. They murdered any Jew they captured. Good Ukrainians did not exist anymore. Where were the decent people?

My father was very sad. He had believed in his good neighbors. However, Mother kept repeating "I always knew it would end up like that. I told you to throw out everything and leave". Every night we expected that they would come to slaughter us. My Ukrainian friends consoled me: "When they come, we would not let them kill you. You are like one of us. You do no look like a Jew". I asked Marinka when that would be, and she told me that the village council has not made a decision yet, but it would certainly come. According to her "there isn't any mercy for the Jews, because you are sucking our blood".

[Page 194]

Yesterday night they slaughtered all the Jews in the neighboring Podhorza. Nobody survived except one baby girl who was crying in her crib, but not for long. One of the murderers came back, took her out of the crib, and smashed her little head on the wall. He boasted about his heroic act himself.

We waited for our turn. We did not sleep at night. We walked around dazed. This continued day after day, night after night. During the day, other people came to talk about the situation. Everybody was desperate. The young people went out to sleep in the field. One of them tied himself to a tree. Father did not want to go out of the house. "I am not afraid to die" he claimed. So we were just sitting down idly and waiting.

The end of independent Ukraine arrived one bright day. The Germans reconsidered and took back the control of the government from the Ukrainians, who held it for three weeks. The Jews breathed a sigh of relief.

A company of German military gendarmes arrived in Brody. Its commander forbade murdering Jews. Our Ukrainians regretted the fact that they have not seized the opportunity to eliminate us earlier.

Beginning of 1942

The Germans spread all over like locusts. They visited us and took everything. They also stole cattle and wheat from the Ukrainians. We stole some of the wheat that grew in our own field to grind at home for a loaf of bread.

An order to wear a white band on one's sleeve was issued. One could not get out of the house without it. A gentile girl passed me a note from my best friend, Miryam Halbmilion in Brody, asking me to come visit her and perhaps bring some food, as she is dying from hunger in the city. Mother gave me two young hens, the last ones we had left, a bit of flour and peas. I went to Brody dressed like a Ukrainian Shiksa - [A disparaging Yiddish term given by the Jews to a non-Jewish woman or girl, derived from the Hebrew word Sheketz – meaning "an object of loathing"[MK]] going barefoot, with a long skirt and black head kerchief.

Visiting the City

I did not recognize the city. Ruins were everywhere. Broken window-panes, and the windows covered with pieces of wood. Brody, which was previously a bustling city, was now full of German soldiers. Here and there one could find a Jew wearing the yellow band, passing by. The faces were hungry and frightened. I found Miryam at her home. The food I brought was priceless these days. Miryam was now mature and somber. When we completed our academic year, we were joyful and mischievous. We both changed so quickly. A person does not recognize his/her friends anymore. Miryam's parents asked if there were some decent people left in our village, whether it would be possible to live with them for a fee, since they are talking about establishing a ghetto in the city. My response to them was negative.

[Page 195]

I came back home, more broken than before. I found out that in Lvov, a ghetto has already been established in Janovski Street, and a forced labor camp was operating in the Latski Village. Thousands of Jews were killed there day by day. They beat, mainly the young ones, and they murdered everyone. Whoever managed to get out of the camp was either a cripple or sick with typhus. In most cases these people died shortly thereafter.

Fall 1942

At the end of the summer, they took me and my entire family for hard labor duty in Polvork. This place used to be a farm of a rich Pole by the name of Pilatovski. Upon the arrival of the Red Army, in September 1939, the authorities nationalized the farm and converted it to a

Sobkhoz (a Soviet farm), and now it served as "a labor camp". We and several other Jews from the surrounding areas worked in the camp. They added our own farm land to the camp. We were working in the camp without any wages or food. The Germans did not care how we lived and how we survived. The Ukrainians' task was to guard us.

My father worked with the animals and the horses and my mother worked in the field. I had some luck, due to my young age. They assigned me to work in the chicken coop and the pig sty, and when needed, also in the kitchen of the German who managed the camp on behalf of the Nazi conquest authorities. The work was above my ability, but it had a positive aspect. I would steal potatoes from the pigs' food and some produce from the kitchen and bring them to my family. By stealing the food, I saved them from dying of hunger.

The German manager's wife caught me once, holding a pail of spoiled pears. She told me: "You are lucky. If my husband would have seen it, you would have been eliminated".

They have already intended to kill me. I was saved by a miracle. One old horse died. I was ordered to cut its meat and cook it for the pigs. I was desperate, as I did not know how to do it. I felt nauseated. My cousin, Khanokh Zorna, who also worked in the camp, noticed and came to my help. I cooked the meat and gave it to the pigs. The following day, the two largest pigs died. What a disaster! The Oberleiter [supervisor[MK]] came over and yelled: "Du verfluchtes Schwein, das ist ein Sabotage, du wirst bei mir krapieren, ich mus dich töten!" (You damn pig, this is sabotage. You will now breathe your last breath. I must kill you!"). He had already drawn his gun. Fortunately for me, a Polish manager, August Liya, appeared at the same moment and told the German that I was not at fault. He told him that the horse was probably sick before it has expired and it had not been a good idea to feed its meat to the pigs. He managed to convince the German who let me go.

I did not find it necessary to tell my parents. I did not want to frighten them. They were happy to hear that I was fine and that I have enough food to eat.

December 1942

People were saying that the ghetto was ready to receive people from the city's environs. Brody's Jews already resided in it. They were suffering and dying there from hunger and illnesses. Now it was the turn of the people from the city's environs. We thought that since we may be considered needed workers, the Germans would leave us in the farm. But no: they did not need us. They wanted to annihilate us.

[Page 196]

The order to move us to the ghetto has arrived. The righteous Pole, Maria Liya, offered my mother to hide me, despite the fact that she could face a death penalty for saving the life of a Jew. She found for me a hiding place in a nearby Polish village. It was clear to all of us that anybody who would not find a similar hiding place would perish. The Ukrainians were joyful and told us: “Now you would join the Himmelskomando” (The “heavens department” in sarcasm).

I said good-bye to my father in the middle of the night. I had the feeling that I would not see him again. He caressed my hair and said: “You go Fani. At least, maybe you would be the one to survive”. Mother gave me a small package.

The righteous Pole woman told me that all the Jews would be moved to the ghetto in a few days. I cried and asked to be brought back there, to my parents. I wanted to be together with them. I wanted to face our common fate together. But they would not allow me to go.

[Page 197]

Brody Happenings during the Years 1941-1943

by Malvina (Mishka) Lillian-Dembinsky

Translated by Moshe Kutten

Edited by Yocheved Klausner

When the Germans entered Brody, nobody imagined what kind of dangers we were facing. Despite the rumors that reached us about the Nazis' horrors, nobody believed. Refugees that passed by or friendly Poles told us about the terror in the neighboring towns, but we, the Brody people, could not believe them. There were plenty of opportunities to retreat with the Red Army before the arrival of the Germans, but only a few did that. Most of the people remained in Brody, believing that Brody does not face any danger. The city elders claimed that the righteous of so many generations that were buried in the old Okopisko cemetery, would certainly protect Brody. People thought that life would return to normal under the Germans, who promised complete freedom and re-establishment of cultural life, after the fall of the communist regime.

The Germans knew how to entice the intellectuals "to organize the cultural life in the city". This is how they managed to gather the best spiritual intellects in Brody and annihilate them. The first Jews to be taken were the ones who worked in the Russian offices, among them, Lipa Halpern, the son of Leizer Halpern. There were only a few individuals who did not believe the Germans and proceeded to commit suicide. One of them was the pharmacist who worked in Kalir's pharmacy.

Among the victims who did believe the Germans were: David Worm, religion teacher, the sister of Dr. Bogner, a physician who now lives in Australia, the wife of Kuba Schwartz, a pharmacist, engineer Streicher and his son, Professor Shvedron and his wife, Dr. Shmider, Spillman, Dr. Lifschitz, Dr. Mendel-Leib Chachkes, a religion teacher in the State High-School, Dr. Blig and Dr. Dolek Lifschitz.

There were those who did not believe the Germans and did not report to the meeting as ordered by the Germans; among them were the finance consultant Lilian Leon, Professor Dr. Bernhaut, the lawyer Horn and more. Although the intellectuals were taken to an unknown location, nobody believed that they were annihilated, until the Poles, who saw the event with their own eyes, gave a description of how the victims were murdered in the forests of Brody.

During the same time, Brody Jewish community was ordered to organize a Judenrat so that the Germans could accomplish, through it, anything they wanted from the Jewish residents. Lawyer Horn, whose brother is now in Israel, Ponikver and others joined the Judenrat. At the same time Jews were ordered to wear a band with the Star of David on their sleeve. A Jewish police force was also organized in the city following an order issued by the Germans.

[Page 198]

Phase B

The second phase began by confiscating Jewish property, especially furs, jewelry and other valuables. Sadly, there were cowards among us, who showed the Germans where to go and who to take from. The order was: "whoever does not surrender their valuables faces death. This was when people still resided in their homes.

Three Aktzia's took place during the years 1941 – 1945. There is no need to explain the meaning of this word here. When the call: "Jews, run away! Aktzia!" came, one day [20th of September 1941[MK]] early at dawn, everybody knew what to expect. Anybody who was captured during the Aktzia by an S.S. person disappeared forever. Whoever succeeded to escape and hide was temporarily safe and free to move about again. Among those who were caught during the first Aktzia were the members of the Rogovski family. The Nazis and collaborators robbed and ruined whatever they could put their hands on.

The second Aktzia occurred just a short time after the first one [October 2nd 1941[MK]]. It was not very different from the first Aktzia. Many people were taken away, and those who remained were happy they were still alive. We lived on Okrenzhna Street in Mrs. Streicher's house. This was after her husband was taken away from her. The lawyer, Dr. Horn, lived downstairs. When the cry – "Aktzia" was heard, everybody ran away from the house to hide. I managed to find a place to hide in the attic of the house of a Polish woman just across from our house. Through a narrow crack, I saw the Nazis taking Dr. Horn and his wife, Hefner's wife with her children and several other Jews who lived in our street. They were all beaten brutally and were taken to the market. In the evening they were loaded on the train cars destined for the death camp. After a day of shooting, screaming and fearing death, we went back home. Amidst widespread grief, we were happy to see that none of our family was missing. We were given the authorization to continue "living".

Some despicable acts were done by the Ukrainians, who offered to help but ended up deceivingly squeezing out the last pennies from the Jews. Then the third Aktzia took place. When I heard, a day in advance, about the preparations for a third Aktzia I decided to run away from Brody and hide in Ponikva's forests. I walked around the forest, alone with a baby and just a bit of food in my back bag. In the forest we felt "good". Peace and quiet descended over the entire forest. I did some thinking during my time in the forest. What would I do if I would not find my mother and father alive when I am back? If they are dead, what do I need to live for? I decided to go back. On the way, I found out that the Aktzia ended. Once again I was lucky to see my parents and the rest of the family alive.

During every Aktzia, the Nazis selected the young people and sent them to forced labor camps. Leon Blaushtayn (may his memory be blessed) took on himself the difficult and dangerous task of establishing communication between the laborers and their families. He also passed food and clothes packages to the camps.

[Page 199]

On December 1942, the Nazi oppressor declared its intention to transfer to the ghetto the Jewish population from Brody and the towns and villages - Vlokhi, Ponykva, Podkamen, Hotsisko, Brodskaya, Ponykovytsya, and other places. The area around the big synagogue was declared as the ghetto area. Most of the Jews, my parents included, were transferred to the ghetto. I decided to hide in the Polish village of Hotsisko In Rodeskaya. I assumed that I would be safer among the Poles. However, two weeks later, thugs descended upon the village and pulled out the hiding Jews from their beds. During the previous two weeks I was convinced that I was the only Jewish person in the village. They brought us all to the police station. During the investigation we were all brutally beaten. Later on they loaded us onto horse drawn carts and proceeded towards the place where they intended to execute us. However the murderers changed their minds on the way to that place, and decided to hand us over to the Brody police, which was then controlled by the Ukrainians. The police contacted the Judenrat and asked for a collective ransom for our release. Since my parents did not have enough money to pay for everyone, we faced the danger that they would execute us all. Among the arrested people were Preminger and his wife. After tedious negotiations, the Judenrat succeeded in securing the ransom and its representative, Ponikver, came to the jail house. The police released us and transported us to the ghetto. This is how I met with my parents once again.

Fear prevailed in the ghetto. People slept in their clothes. Thugs would enter the ghetto daily but unexpectedly, and started shooting with no provocation. Hunger also took a terrible toll. I saw my father suffering from hunger. I heard his groans at night. The crowding was horrible. Twenty people lived in one room. In our room, we also had Lazar and his wife, Halpern and his wife Lilian, as well as Mrs. Streicher. Crowding, lack of minimal hygienic conditions and lice resulted in total deterioration of the morale. Quarrels erupted everywhere for insignificant reasons. A typhus epidemic was eminent. People got involved in all sorts of dubious dealings just to get some food in their mouth. Mrs. Beskes tried to earn a living by baking cakes, often made of moldy flour.

Some people managed to escape from the ghetto. There were some who built underground bunkers in the ghetto for the purpose of hiding in them when the time of "Juden Frei" [Nazi term for making an area free of Jews[MK]] would come. We knew that the end was coming. The sword of Democles was hovering above our heads. Rumors spread in the ghetto that a partisan group is being organized. Only a few managed to join them though. There were some who secured hiding places under the floor with Polish families. These Poles put themselves in great danger for protecting Jews. Gunshots and murders became a daily routine. I recall a funeral of a person by the name of Goldstein, who died of natural causes (just upon moving into the ghetto). They organized for the funeral to take place outside the ghetto, with a permit from the authorities. I remember saying to myself, "how human this death is. At least people know where he was buried". I recall another horrible story about an Aktzia of infants. The Germans loaded three trucks with infants in order to murder them. There was a huge thrill in the ghetto when one of the trucks came back. We found out that the order was to execute just a certain number of children, and return the rest back to the ghetto. This was a demonstration of the infamous "German order".

In the area of the Polish former military barracks, across from Royekovka Park, a forced labor camp was established for young people who were able to work hard physical labor. People who succeeded to join this camp were very happy! There was some freedom of movement in there. Through these people we got all sorts of news from the outside, and from the front, and sometimes even some material aid. They provided the only communication with the outside world. One time, a few youths managed to escape from the camp. They were captured by the S.S and were brought back to the camp for execution. Yona Tsukerman was among them. When his mother heard about it, she arrived at the camp accompanied by a representative of the Judenrat, and started to kiss the feet of the murderers. However, nothing helped.

They killed him in front of her eyes. There was no room for any pity in the heart of these predators.

[Page 200]

After some time, we found out that a new Aktzia was imminent. Panic ensued. People started to hide in all sorts of hiding places, inside the ghetto and outside. Myself, my son and my father escaped to a place outside the city, which I knew to have had a hideout under the floor. It was an empty house near Vali. We barely got into the pit and placed the cover on the opening, crowding inside with the feeling that we have managed to evade the danger, when we heard people running, screaming and the noises of gunshots. After about three hours, we started to suffocate because of a deficiency in oxygen. It was an awful feeling – the feeling of death by suffocation. It was clear to me that we would need to leave the hideout at any price; otherwise we were destined to die a slow and torturous death. My father tried to carve a crack with a knife, but got injured and failed. I decided that it was better to die from gunshots and started to yell for help. Several people, who heard me, rushed to open the cover and pulled us out half dead. These were Polish acquaintances of my father. They explained that the Aktzia was not oriented toward the Jews this time, but toward young Poles. The Germans intended to capture them for forced labor. The Poles took me and my child and hid us in the near-by deserted synagogue. I saw all the destruction and the torn Torah scrolls which were thrown on the floor. I stayed at the synagogue until the evening hours and went back to the ghetto.

Things were about the same until spring 1943, the day which was declared as the ghetto elimination day. From time to time, we heard about a neighboring town becoming "Juden-frei", but we just continued to live with the hope that disaster would not reach us. This was, of course, a false hope. It did reach us. When the news arrived, people started to react in all sorts of ways. Some remained apathetic and did not even try to find a place to hide. However, most of the people scattered around in various "holes" which they had prepared in advance for emergencies. Most of the prepared hideouts were sufficient for hardly two or three people. But more people occupied these hideouts. In most cases, food and water was sufficient only for about 24 hours, so people knew that they would not last long. There was also the problem of small children. People refused to accept them for the fear that their crying would put everybody else in danger.

A hideout was prepared for the residents in the yard of the house we lived in. I went in with my son. Other people were - Pepa Frenkel with her son, Sonya Frenkel with her parents, the wife of Hesyu Memot - Sofiya nee Halpern and her son and some others. We heard dogs barking, gunshots and yelling. Early in the morning, we started to suffocate from lack of oxygen. I knew that I would have to leave the hideout. We sneaked out and managed to reach our house and went down to the cellar. We waited in the cellar for a few hours when I heard someone calling us. My husband arrived at the house. He had been in the labor camp of Royekova the whole time. He told me about the extermination of the ghetto. S.S. people and the Ukrainian Police participated in the operation. They were going around and pulled out the people discovered by their dogs. They proceeded to shoot the people in groups and burn their bodies. While this was going on, Jewish members of the labor camps were sent into the ghetto with carts, and ordered to take out from the ghetto anything of value, including food, coal and clothing.

I left my son with my parents with the hope that if I save myself, I would be able to save him and them as well. I joined a forced labor-group pretending to be one of them, and managed to leave the burning ghetto.

[Page 201]

Poles were standing on the two sides of the road watching with pity in their eyes. On the way to the camp, somebody told me that they found the people who stayed with me in the bunker.

I remained in the camp for three days. The situation in the camp was horrible. They beat-up people daily. In order to scare us, they would also kill two or three people daily and hang them. In spite of all that, I managed to escape from the camp on the third day. I arrived at the house that I used to live in and entered the adjacent house where a Polish family by the name of Lokashchkevich lived. They knew my father, and despite of the danger involved, they accepted me under their protection. They kept me for more than a year until the end of 1943. During all of that time, about twenty Jews, among them the daughter of Professor Shvedron, were hiding in a hiding place in the adjacent house.

At that same time, rumors about the final elimination of the ghetto and the execution of people who were captured, reached me. I also found out about the extermination of the Bezhezhin Jews, among them Dr. Izidor Lilian, his wife and son. Later on I also heard about the annihilation of the Royovka's labor camp. Some of the people were executed on the spot, and some were sent to a concentration camp.

One day, S.S people arrived at a house of a Polish woman who hid Jews. They executed the Jews together with the rescuer woman and her daughter.

The city of Brody became "Juden-frei".

Among other stories, I heard about a little girl going around in the street holding a sign with the words "I am Jewish" written on it. This is how a Polish Judge who hid her for a while sent her out. She was Lela Lifshits, the daughter of Dolek and Hela Lifshits.

In the fall of 1943, when the front approached Radzivilov, an "evacuation" or deportation order for the entire population of Brody was issued. This is when I saw Brody for the last time. Disguised as a Christian, my saviors and I managed to leave Brody ruined, bombed-out and bleeding.

[Page 202]

Testimony (in third person)

by Raphael Shalev (Fulu Shlinger)

Translated by Moshe Kutten

Rafael (Fulu) is the third son of Yaakov Shlinger, the eldest son of Elazar and Malka (Mala). Yaakov was born in 1895 in the village of Berlin near Brody where his parents moved from Brody to manage a store and an Inn.

Yaakov had a brother named Yarom and three sisters - Golda, Khanna and Leah. In 1905, the family returned to Brody and joined the grandmother Mala, who lived on Leshnover Street, near Lendgevirts' flour mill. Elazar, the grandfather, was killed during one of the invasions by foreign armies during the First World War. Yaakov Shlinger studied in a Kheder [a religious school for Jewish boys common until the end of the 19th century[MK]], and later on was a pupil in the Jewish elementary school in Brody. During the First World War he served in the Austrian army and was discharged at the age of 23. He and his brother, Yarom, worked in flour mills: Yarom at Lendgevirts' and Yaakov at Lifshits' (which was located on the other side of the city on Lemberg – Lvov Street). As his first wife, Yaakov married a wealthy farmers' daughter from Ponykva, whose father used to bring agricultural produce from his farm to the market in Brody. Yaakov's eldest son Elazar was born in 1924. Unfortunately, Yaakov's first wife passed away in 1927 immediately following the birth of their second son – Yitshak. In 1928, Yaakov married, for the second time, a wife by the name of Sima (Fulu's mother). Sima who was born in 1901, was the eldest daughter of Menakhem Krem who lived in Valla–Mala and was a painter, specializing in painting and decorating of synagogues. He and his brother were professional painters, but they also served as the Gabai's [synagogue's administrators[MK]] at the synagogue of the tailors on Krupna Street. Sima became on orphan at the age 16 after her mother's death, and she was tasked with raising her younger siblings, her brother David and sister Sheindel. Her father, Menakhem Krem who was a soldier in the Austrian army, moved to Vienna with his family when the First World War broke. They returned to Brody at the end of the war. David joined the Russian Red Army forces on their retreat, and later resided in Kiev. The family lost communication with him. Sheindel married at a young age a person by the name of Knark who served as a travelling agent in Lamberg (Lvov), representing a business firm. They lived with the grandfather Menakhem Krem. Shandel's son, Genik, was born in 1930. Sheindel worked as a seamstress and embroiderer of needlepoints, tablecloths and napkins. At a certain time she separated from her husband, and since then, Genik was raised alternately by his grandfather and his aunt Sima. Sima's eldest son, Fulu, was born in 1930. Meir (1933) and Ira (1937) were born after him. Yaakov (Yekah) and Sima Shlinger lived on Ogrodova Street (in a suburb of Brody close to village of Polvarki –Mala). The family of Barukh Hokhberg, who produced and sold milk products, was their neighbor. The family of Barukh's eldest daughter, Adela (who was married to Yarom Shlinger), and the family of Golda (the sister of Yarom and Yaakov) were also living in the same house. Fulu spent long hours playing in Hokhberg family's yard, especially with Rivka, the daughter of Adela and Yarom, who was his own age. In 1937, after Arye was born, the family of Yaakov Shlinger moved to a bigger apartment on 11 Kalir Street, in the building owned by the metalworker Fogel, who also lived in the building along with three other families and the family of the gate-keeper. He and his laundrywoman wife lived in the backyard.

[Page 203]

At the age of 14, Leizer, the oldest son of Yaakov Shlinger, began serving as an apprentice with the shoemaker Munyo Kahana. Fulu and his brother were also students in the Jewish school as well as at the Kheder on the Shul Street (a street named after the large Synagogue [shul means synagogue in Yiddish[MK]). Yaakov was working very hard and managed, just barely, to provide for the needs of his family. A laundry–woman, Zushya, who arrived once a week from the village near Smolno, used to bring fresh farm produce – milk, eggs and cheeses. The family went to the Turkish bathhouse, once a week, near the large synagogue. The family used to go on vacation, once a year, to the village of Kolpin near Ponykva. Yaakov used to purchase jewelry for Sima to cheer her up. Before the holidays they bought clothing for the entire family. During the year they used to fit various items of clothing and pass them up from the big to the small children. Before the winter, they would buy firewood and coals and stored them in the storage located in the yard. The "Water–drawer" would bring the water from the well in the street, located across from the house. They used to visit Grandmother Mala often. She owned a small single story house on Leshnover Street, with a sparkling wooden floor, fancy and shiny furniture, with many embroidery pictures that were hanging on the wall. She earned a living from a small pension provided to her after her husband was killed. Her two daughters, Kahana and Leah, lived with her. Yaakov and Yarom helped her with the chore of buying necessities and various other chores. They used to go on walks on Saturday mornings to visit Grandfather Menakhem Krem and to slide down the walkway in Mala–Valy.

The Shlinger family's routine was interrupted abruptly by the heavy bombardment of the city at the outbreak of the Second World War in 1939. Many people got hurt and countless houses were destroyed. The tenants in the house where the family lived, barely managed to clear the building's cellar (which served as a feathers' warehouse) when the war started, but did not have the time to stock food and other supplies. The Soviet Union's forces invaded the city a few days later.

1939 – 1941:

Under the communist regime, the privately owned flour mills became cooperatives. So did all other businesses and workshops. The Polish language and studies of bible and religion were banned in the schools. Studies were held in Russian and Ukrainian. The young children were taught to be pioneers and the big children - Komsomol's [The Communist youth league[MK]]. Life in the community was conducted under a strict discipline. The religious life ceased and most of the synagogues were closed. Food supply was severely curtailed, and acquiring any food involved spending long hours of standing in numerous lines, which family members actually took turns to do. Many products could not be procured at all. The city was congested by the many refugees from areas conquered by the Germans and people who were deported from Germany and Austria. Over time, The Russians deported some of them to the Soviet Union and drafted many people to the Soviet army. The sons of Yaakov Shlinger from his first wife were among the drafted youths. Neither was seen after the war. On the top of this chaos, a major inter–city highway was being constructed through the city at the time. The traffic on this road was horrendous, particularly because of numerous military transports. Grandmother Mala was ran over by a vehicle and killed on this road.

The war between Germany and Russia started in 1941. The German air force bombed the city heavily. The Shlinger family found shelter in the cellar of the building. Again, many houses on the street were burnt or destroyed. Following the entry of the Germans into the city, Yaakov and his two eldest sons were ordered to report for a forced labor duty (laying underground telephone and power cables). The studies at the Jewish school were terminated. Severe economic distress found its way into the house. Food was rationed. Yaakov suffered from severe edemas in his legs due to the work hardship combined with undernourishment. There was no other choice but to barter clothes, shoes and other items with gentiles from the neighboring villager for food.

[Page 204]

In order to ease somewhat the family economic distress, Fulu (who was below the recruiting age for forced labor) was sent to work with Yaakov's friend, Mr. Kut, who was the grains supplier to the flour mills where Yaakov and Yarom worked before the German conquest. At the beginning, Fulu just worked a few hours per day on the farm. Later on, he stayed overnight with the Kut's, fed the animals, cleaned the stables and the cowshed, accompanied the cows to the pasture, and helped in all other field work – plowing, seeding, watering and harvesting of grains. Despite of his young age (just 11–12) he was quick and diligent and Mr. Kut was extremely pleased with him. Fulu would go back to Brody in the evenings when he completed his work early. However, when he finished late, he had to stay in the village for the night due to the night curfew imposed on the Jews. When he would arrive home, he had to witness the economic distress of the family, gradually deteriorating to a lower and lower level without the ability to be more helpful.

During the first aktzia (on September 1941), Yaakov, Elazar and Yitskhak were sent to Belzec on the first transport of Brody's Jews. Yaakov's brother – Yarom, was also in this transport. Sima Shlinger with her two youngest sons – Meir and Arye escaped. At the time of the aktzia she was visiting the house of her sisters in law on Ogrodova Street. After the husbands were taken, she moved to live with her sister in law Adela.

The women of the family along with their children were captured during the second aktzia (October 1941), because somebody informed on them. They were all sent to Belzec in a transport. Only Mrs. Hochberg, Adela's mother, escaped. During the search of the house she hid in a shelter she found in the yard. She was left all alone.

During the two akzias, Fulu stayed in village of Polvarki Mala, hiding among the beet bushes in the field. A thorough search was conducted in the village itself during which all other Jews were found and sent on the transport to Belzec. Fulu received help from Mr. Kut and his family. By helping him they put themselves in great danger as villagers used to inform the authorities about violations. When Fulu sneaked back into the city after the second aktzia, he only found Mrs. Hochberg. She gave him a package with the family pictures and some mementoes (all of which were burnt later at the end of the war when the Kut family's house was damaged in one of the bombardments).

During the period that followed the second aktzia, it became more risky for Fulu to stay in the village. All the Jews were now concentrated in the ghetto which was surrounded by a barbed wire fence. Mrs. Hochberg also moved to the ghetto. Fulu, who arrived at her house on Ogrodova Street, found it deserted and broken into, with all of the content robbed. Fulu continued to sneak into the ghetto and back to the Kut's to get some necessities and food. These helped a bit in light of the shortages and hunger that were widespread in the ghetto. At one point Fulu contracted typhus, which was rampant in the ghetto. His recovery from the disease was attributed to a special dessert, made by

Mrs. Hochberg, from Hungarian plums she managed to procure through an obscured method. The drink succeeded miraculously to reduce Fulu's fever, by accelerating the operation of the Intestines and clearing the digestive tract. Fulu continued stealth movements between the village and the ghetto.

[Page 205]

During the spring of 1943, the city of Brody was declared "Juden – Rein [a term coined by the Nazis for a place "free" of Jews[MK]]. Most of the Jews who remained in the ghetto were loaded onto cattle cars on trains leaving for Belzec. The rest were executed at the edge of the ghetto, near the cattle slaughterhouse on Shul Street. Ukrainian policemen searched zealously after a handful of Jews who still remained in ghetto, in the city or its environs. The Jews were considered sub–humans who were condemned to die a cruel and tortured death...

Small groups of Jewish children managed to escape the ghetto and hide in the area of the village of Polvarki Mala. All of these groups were subsequently captured by the Ukrainian policemen with the help of the Ukrainian collaborators. Fulu also managed to escape the ghetto along with a group of five children. He was lucky again when his group was captured. At the time of the raid he was at Kut's house, waiting for Mr. Kut to come back home, at night as he usually did. But Mr. Kut did not come back until the first light of dawn. Fulu hid in the attic above the cowshed. He drank from the milk that he took from the cows, and ate the food leftovers off the plates of the dogs who knew him well. When he returned to his group's hideout he only found their scattered possessions.

He turned to a new hideout – in Spitalka (a junkyard containing junk and leftover refuse dumped there after the main road construction). He found a shelter in a ditch along with some of his friends, Nunek, and Israel who escaped with his sisters – his twin Chana and the elder sister, Rivka, who served as the group's leader and its spokesperson. The five orphans suffered from a prolonged starvation. Their bodies were reduced to bones and skin. Their scanty and tattered clothes were infested with Itchy lice, which they could not get rid of. They lay down around refuse of rusty tins and garbage. They labored in their breathing because of the dump's stinky smell. They experienced simultaneously despair and hope. They lived for the next minute and just wished to survive the day...

From their hideout, they could view the road leading from the village to the city. In the case of danger, they could retreat and escape to the fields and from there to Leshnov's forest. The escape routes were on trails which they knew well from the school's social and nature studies. At night they would go, one at a time, to forage for food. They risked being discovered during their travel and when they went in and out of the hideout. Being discovered meant a certain death to them and any villagers that would have helped them. Fulu used to sneak behind the back yard of Kut's house and wait there patiently, examining the surroundings and verifying that there are no strangers in and around the house. The housewife, Maria Kutova would usually go out to check for the reason of the dogs' barking. A swishing noise sounded by Fulu served as a sign. She would bring him something to eat but warned him that this should be the last time he would be allowed to bother them as he put them all in a great danger. When he felt that she would inform the authorities, he stopped to bother her family. He would wait until the dogs were released in the inner court. Mrs. Kut would bring the dogs their food and disappear behind the closed door. Fulu would then rush forward and grab some of the dogs' food. Luckily for him, the dogs knew him well and did not object sharing their food with him. He would only take a small portion of their food, and they would just friendly wiggle their tails... Hungry and shivering from the cold he would then hurry back to the hideout before sunrise to avoid being discovered. He would try his luck again the next day.

[Page 206]

The children thought that none of the villagers discovered their hideout and continued to hide at the dump. At night, they lay on the cold ground waiting for sunrise, so that its dawning rays would warm their bodies a bit. The rays gifted by G–d, that nobody can rob them of – penetrating, warming and reviving the frail and frosty body parts.... One morning, a loud voice woke them up and ordered them to get out of their hideout. They found themselves being led toward the ghetto, hurried up by the rifle–bayonets of the two Ukrainian gendarmes. They passed through the village, near Ogrodova and Polna Streets, and entered Kalir Street. They passed Fulu's house and approached the ghetto's fence. As they continued to walk along the streets of the ghetto – they witnessed the destruction, broken windows and doors and thrown–out belongings everywhere. When they passed along Shull Street, to the edge of the ghetto near the slaughterhouse, Fulu recalled his mother's words who promised him that he would survive this hell and his duty would then be to tell the world about what really happened. He would be the one to continue the family... So, he contacted his mother in his thoughts, requesting, in his imagination, that she fulfill her promise... The children understood that they are being led to their death; The stabbing by the bayonets hurrying them up, the awful smell of burning bodies, the screams, the begging and prayers of Jews pleading for their lives, mixed with the urging by Germans and their Ukrainian collaborators, did not leave any room for doubts...

As a routine procedure for the execution, the executioners would force a group of Jews into a house with a forced–in opening. They would then gun down the people inside. They would proceed to lead another group into the house to shoot them such that the bodies of the latest group would just fall on the top of the bodies of the previous group and so on. When the house was filled up, they would pour kerosene and set the pile and the house ablaze. They would then move to the next house and the process repeated itself... The five children went through the same process. However, two of the children, Fulu and Nunek were extremely lucky. The gunshot failed to kill them; they rose above the pile of bodies before the pile was set ablaze, and they managed to escape towards the swamps. Smoke rising to heaven and the last cries of “Shma Israel” accompanied them as they escaped – two remnants that were taxed with the duty to preserve what they saw and eventually testify about these horrific acts.

Through winding and treacherous roads, with the blessed aid of the goddess of luck and the help of Providence, as well as by resourcefulness and survival aptitudes which were learnt and enhanced over time – Nunek and Fulu succeeded in surviving the war unscathed...

After they were saved, they parted ways. Nunek was hidden by friends of his family in Polvarski Mala. He later met Fulu in a British confinement camp in Cyprus after their separate failed attempts to immigrate to Eretz Israel illegally [illegally because of the British refusal to allow Jewish immigration to Eretz Israel before, during and after World War II[MK]]. They both arrived in Eretz Israel (legally) on December 1947. Nunek was recruited to the Palmach [an elite fighting underground unit of the Jewish labor movement force – "Hagana"– during the British mandate occupation of Palestine.[MK]] and was killed during the battles in the Jerusalem Corridor trying to secure the passage to the besieged city . With his death, another bud of Brody Jews was severed. After leaving Brody, Fulu joined an association of Jewish orphans "La–Matara" [On the Target[MK]] in Krakow, Poland. They crossed the border to Czechoslovakia as Greek refugees. They stayed in Prague for some time, and then crossed over to the area controlled by the Americans where they lodged for about a year. They crossed the Alps to Austria and arrived in Italy where they boarded the ship "Moledet" [Homeland[MK]], which tried to "illegaly" break the British blockade. The ship sailed to Palestine but had to broadcast a distress signal prior to sinking. British destroyers towed the disabled ship to the Haifa's harbor. Fulu and his friends were transported on deportation ships to Cyprus. Eight months later, they immigrated to independent Israel.

[Page 207]

The group was absorbed into kibbutz Tel Yitshak. They were all recruited and served in the "Haganah". They fought in the battles of the Triangle [an area shaped like a triangle on Israel's eastern border with the West Bank mostly populated by Israeli Arabs[MK]]. When the Hagana became part of the Israeli Defense Force, many of the group members joined the Israeli air force and were among its founders. Fulu served in the Israeli air force for many years as an airplane engines mechanic and inspector of the advanced jet engines. He served in the air force as a soldier and later on as a civilian until he retired in 1990.

In 1953, Fulu married Paula (Poli) nee Weiss, who immigrated to Israel from Galatz, Romania. She passed away in 1887 after a long and arduous illness. Their old daughter, Sima, was born in 1954, served in the IDFAir Force as a draftswoman. Their son, Yaakov, who was born in 1955, served (and continue to serve) as the IDF paratroopers' senior combat medic. He is an agronomist who specialized in the economy and business software of agriculture. He married Dina, nee Reuveni (came from Teheran, Iran). They have a son named Ehud (born in 1983), and a daughter named Shani (born 1986). Fulu's third son, Shlomo (born 1960), served and continue to serve in the professional arm of IDF, as an electric and electronic engineer dealing with electronic systems. He married Chana, nee Nahum (from Iraq). They have a son named Or (born 1991), and expecting another baby shortly.

One survivor allowed for the continuation of the dynasty to be secured and woven into the fulfilment of the prophesy of the ingathering of the exiles in the land of our ancestors...

[Page 208]

Memories from Brody

by Berta Landgeuertz Miasnik

Translated by Moshe Kutten

Edited by Rafael Manory

My name is Berta Miasnik née Landgeuertz. I was born in Brody to my parents Eliyahu and Erna Langeuertz. Our family was distinguished and respected in our city. We owned a flourishing mill for grinding flour, buckwheat and groats. We employed many workers and clerks until the 1939 conquest of the city by the Soviet army. We used to sell our products, particularly the buckwheat, to many countries in Europe. We shipped our products through the ports of Danzig, and Gdinia [Gdansk[MK]]. An "hakhshara kibbutz"[1] called Kolsova was established in Brody. My father, of blessed memory, employed fifty of the kibbutz pioneers, who could not find employment anywhere else, in our mill. Brody was part of the Austrian empire prior to the First World War. During the war with the Russians, my father was drafted into the Austrian army. He was captured as prisoner of war and was sent to Siberia for several years. When the war ended, my father returned to Brody and married my mother, Erna, the daughter of Moshe and Brakha Levin. My parents had two children, my brother Yulek, of blessed memory, and I, Berta. Our family had a nice, cultural life. My father, Eliyahu, managed the flourishing farm and mill, and my mother ran the house and educated the children. My brother and I studied in the gymnasium until the Soviet conquest. My mother was active in many areas of charity. She also served as the chairperson of the school committee, was active in the orphanage committee and aided needy children and adults in several institutions.

When the Soviets came, they first nationalized all the mills, confiscated our entire property and evicted us from our house. We moved to live with Grandfather Moshe Levin. My father managed to run away from Brody just before the agents of the N.K.V.D[2], came to our house to arrest and send him to Siberia. After that, we continued to live peacefully with Grandfather Levin until the cursed Germans came in all of a sudden and conquered the city. As it turned out, our troubles have just begun.

During the first few days, the Germans requested that my father, along with several tens of community leaders, public servants, physicians, and businessmen, report to the Gestapo office. The Germans told them that they are planning to establish a separate Jewish district in Brody, and demanded that the prominent people prepare a plan for supplying food and necessities to the district. They called them to report in every morning and released them in the evenings. On the third day, none of them came back. They have never returned. Despite all our efforts and the fortune we invested in trying to learn about their fate, we have never succeeded in finding out where they have been taken to and what happened to them. When we realized the seriousness of the situation, we managed to procure a labor certificate for my brother Yulek, after paying a substantial amount of money, to work in a German firm that operated a vital factory for the Germans (Damn them). We thought that this employment would save him and us from extermination. However, even that did not provide any salvation. My brother was murdered during the first aktzia. Following the aktzia, when only I and my mother were left, we started to look for a shelter with villagers, acquaintances of my father, may his name be blessed. For a fortune-worth of cash, gold jewelry and furs, we found a hiding place with the families of Kravchuk, Shonvits, and Yemnik, who kept and sustained us in their cowsheds, pit or even in the forest. We were driven out several times, often in pouring rain and when it was extremely cold. We did not know who else to turn to. We were frightened, filthy and sick without shoes or clothing. We wandered around in unfamiliar and foreign environs and knocked on doors of people we did not know. We were very fortunate not to be handed over to the Gestapo. This is, thanks G-d, how we survived. After the war, we helped the people who helped us. We sent those people packages and money. When the diplomatic relations between Israel and the Soviet

Union were cut off, we continued to send them packages through Canada, England and the US. After the war, we found out the villagers who kept us, also kept Rabbi Shteinberg and his wife, as well as the Braun family.

[Page 209]

After the war ended, we could not stay in Brody where my father, my brother, and other family members were murdered. We left Russia and crossed over to Poland. This is where I met my husband, Asher Miasnik. We got married in Vienna, and immediately moved to Israel where we established a home and a family. We have two sons, and now, thanks G-d, we are blessed with eight grandchildren. In the US, we have my mother's brother, Freddie and his sister Frida.

Translator's footnotes

1. A "kibbutz hachsharah" was a camp simulating kibbutz life. Such camps were established throughout Eastern Europe to prepare pioneers for their life in a kibbutz in Eretz Israel
2. N.K.V.D. was Stalin's secret police

[Page 210]

My Mother—Pela Pepernik-Poliner

by Rivka Flumin (daughter of Rivka and Yitskhak Poliner, and the granddaughter of Khaya and Shmuel Pepernik)

Translated by Moshe Kutten

Edited by Rafael Manory

We were five children in our house, three brothers and two sisters. My parents were wealthy as they received a large inheritance that included fields and forests, from their parents. My parents owned a general store. Our apartment was rather specious. We had two servants, a man and a woman who worked at my mother's parents and continued to serve my parents in their house and fields. They were gentile Poles, but spoke Yiddish fluently.

My mother was the eldest of the five children, and thus was taxed with the burden of assisting in raising the other children. The Rabbi, who had taught my grandfather lived in my parents' house and was also teaching Torah to my mother's siblings. My grandparents' house was quite large and they allocated one of the rooms to be a synagogue. People from all over the city came to pray there.

The Russians invaded Poland in 1939 and the whole situation in city deteriorated. The Russians confiscated our lands and established Kolkhozes [Russian commune farms[MK]] on them. Everything was run as a collective. This unpleasant situation did not last long. In 1941, the Germans entered the city and things got to be a lot worse for the Jews.

The Germans took all the youths to forced labor camps far away from home and have not returned them as of yet. There was a rumor that they have been burnt in Belzec, which was like Auschwitz on a small scale.

One day, the Germans took all the Jews in the city to Auschwitz. People stood in a wide square, and had to throw their gold and valuables into wooden boxes. My grandmother held a two years old baby in her arms. At one point one German came close to her and saw her earrings, hit her until she shed blood, and ripped the earrings forcefully from her ears along with the flesh. My grandmother fainted and the baby fell off her arms. My mother, who witnessed this shocking and horrific event, suffered a nervous breakdown and started to run away from the formation. She managed to find shelter in an abandoned warehouse and hide there. The Germans passed through the warehouse but did not search it thoroughly.

The rest of the people were taken on trains to the death camps and the crematories.

Four days later, the Germans proceeded to rob the homes of the Jews.

A few days later, my mother ran away to the village where our family still owned much property. The gentiles drove her away from the village yelling at her that she faces great danger. My mother ran away to the forests. She was only 15 at the time. She thought of turning herself in to the Mayor. The Mayor was an acquaintance of my grandparents and my mother thought that because of that they would just kill her without torturing her like they used to.

[Page 211]

On her way (to the Town Hall [RM]), she encountered a gentile woman who carried pales with water from the well and was walking on the trail in the opposite direction. My mother wanted to hide, but it was too late. The gentile woman saw and recognized her. She asked my mother, how she succeeded to stay alive and escape the ghetto unscathed. The woman's husband used to work for my grandparents' forests and fields. The woman was poor but she spoke to my mother and convinced her not to turn herself in to the police but come with her and perhaps she would be reunited with her family. She hid my mother in a barn, and provided her with food and water.

However, a few days later my mother had to leave her hiding place with that gentile woman, because the other gentiles in the village found out about her and wanted to turn her in to the police. The gentile woman was frightened because of the villagers' threats on her and her family members' life.

My mother hid in the forest. She was there by herself. The gentile woman came once every two weeks with some bread and potatoes. My mother ate just a little portion every day so that the food would last for several days. In the winter my mother found shelter in a bunker that was previously occupied by Jews who have been captured and executed. The bunker, which was also located in the forest, was very tight and small; one could only sit or lay in it. A tree was growing around the cover to the bunker and hid the entrance. My mother stayed in the bunker the whole winter. She only came out to meet with the gentile woman who gave her food. These meetings were held in the forest during snow storms. The gentile woman thought that the war would end in a short while and she hoped that my mother would reward her with a portion of the land and fields owned by my grandparents. However, as the war lingered on, the husband of the gentile woman's started to object his wife's continuing support of my mother with food. However, the gentile woman persisted in bring my mother food. She and her children had mercy on my mother.

Before the end of the war gangs of Banderovits Ukrainians[1], started to attack the Poles and they were forced to leave their villages and escape. Only then, my mother dared to get out of her hideout and meet Jewish acquaintances, who also came out of hideouts arranged and supported by Polish villagers.

In 1944, the Soviets returned to the area, and my mother left the forest, thin and frail, covered with frost bites. The Russians took care of her and healed her up. The Red Army took my mother all the way to Kremenets where she regained her strength. Over time she started to do business and even study.

At the end of the war, my mother met my father. They met in Brody in the market, after Father returned from the hospital in Tula, Russia, where his arm was amputated. They remained in Brody and started a business. They resettled and established a flourishing and successful life. Over time, they started to think about Eretz Israel. They traveled from Brody to Poland and registered there for immigration. They crossed the border to Czechoslovakia illegally, and in 1947 they went to Germany. They had to abandon their entire property on the way. During the period from 1947 to 1949 they stayed in Hofgeismar near the city of Kassel in Germany. [They made their way to Israel in 1949[MK]]

Translator's footnote

1. Gangs of Ukrainian nationalists who followed their leader Stepan Bandera. While the main goal of their movement was to establish an independent Ukraine, they were known for their collaboration with the Nazis and their cruelty towards what they considered "foreigners" such as Poles and Jews.

[Page 212]

My Father, My Mother, and My Sister

by Bronia Roth

Translated by Moshe Kutten

Edited by Rafael Manory

I would like to sketch the portraits of three people, my father, my mother and my sister.

My Father, Yones Rot, lived in Shvabim (in Brody suburbs) and perished along with a group of Jewish workers who worked in the Engineer Lustman & Co. sawmill.

On May 21st 1943, the final extermination of Brody's Jews took place. The plant manager got an order from the Gestapo that in preparation for the Gestapo men visit to the sawmill the Jewish workers should dress festively and wait, in formation, holding their work certificate in their hand. The Jews did not really understand what was in store for them and reported to the plant yard according to the order. Suddenly, a Gestapo car appeared. The Gestapo men led the Jews like a cattle herd with sticks to a train boxcar that was already standing on the rail tracks and was already overflowing with Jews from the ghetto. The train was going to Belzec's gas chambers. A detailed description of this last journey was given to us by an eye witness, Mr. Marash (who now resides in Australia). He succeeded to jump off the moving train and this is how he survived.

My Mother, Sharlotta Roth perished about one month after the annihilation of the ghetto. When the ghetto was annihilated, she managed to hide in a half-ruined cellar, full of feathers, for seven days and nights. When the dust settled and quiet descended on the ghetto, she came out of her hiding. Since she did not have anywhere to go, she just trudged her way to the city and gave herself in to the Germans. They put her in the barracks of the Polish army's 43rd battalion (near

Roykuvka) where other Jews, who were captured and brought up from other hideouts, were already jailed. She managed to escape through the back gate. However, she was spotted, by chance, by a young volkdeutsch [A Nazi term for a Pole with a German ethnic background[MK]]. He brought her back from her escape route and jailed her, for several days, in a storage shed without food or water, along with another woman (a porter's wife) with a child. One morning, he shot the two women and the child in their head, in the middle of the yard, as a warning and punishment to anybody who tried to escape. The killings were witnessed by all other Jews who were ordered to stand around and sing. Nevertheless, some of these Jews managed miraculously to survive and they now live in Israel.

My Sister, Regina Roth, even before the Second World War, as a young girl she was active in Zionist organizations. In 1937 she went to an Hakhshara camp [training for agricultural work in Eretz Israel– RM] in Beilsko–Biala to prepare herself for immigration to Eretz Israel. Unfortunately, World War II broke before she got her "certificate" (immigration permit issued by the British Mandate Authorities– RM). She returned to Brody with her husband, whom she met in the camp. In 1940 a baby girl was born to them, and together they went into the ghetto. Her husband was recruited for forced labor at the train station. This is where he and his friends were murdered.

[Page 213]

May 21st, 1943, was a bright and beautiful spring day, but a cruel and tragic day for the Jews of Brody. This was the day of the ghetto's annihilation. All the Jews were captured and were gathered in the Brody market square. There were many young women with children and babies in their arms, kneeling on their knees, surrounded by rows of Ukrainian and German policemen, and waiting, the entire day, for their transport to the death camp. Suddenly, my sister saw a drape–covered window that led to a cellar (in the house of the pharmacist Klemus). She told some men who happened to stand around her and they tore the fabric and enlarged the hole in the drape, so that several mothers with their babies could sneak into the cellar. Crammed into a very small room of the cellar, they endured pain and sorrow for several days and nights, feeding their babies with just a few sugar cubes. One night, having no choice, when the hunger and the cold became unbearable, they came out of the cellar. After getting out, my sister and her baby endured horrific and nerve–racking experiences: They wandered around from a stable to a cowshed, hiding in pits and doghouses, until they managed to find a shelter with a lonely farmer family. A Polish woman, by the name of Matilda Galinovska, took care of them for several days. She moved the baby to the city of Lvov, under the care of Mrs. Vladislava Khoms(?), a known Polish public activist, who saved many Jews. My sister was afraid to follow her baby girl to Lvov. In 1944, when the Russians approached Brody, the Polish civilian population was evacuated, and my sister was identified as a Jew. The Germans shot her to death against the walls of the houses.

[Page 214]

Testimony

by Abraham (ben Khaim Noah) Shapira

Translated by Moshe Kutten

Edited by Rafael Manory

The invasion of the German army on the 22nd of June, 1941, without of a declaration of war, surprised Brody's residents, the same way it surprised the Soviet army. The announcements on the German radio about the progress of the Nazi army, the broadcasts by the Soviet radio about the containment of the Germans and the roars of the airplanes foretold the future. Before the actual arrival of the Germans, German airplanes flew low above the city and bombarded its streets. Many Jews were killed then.

Upon the entrance of the Nazi army into the city, the German soldiers started looting Jewish homes. A few days later, they established a Ukrainian militia. The Germans and the Ukrainians began capturing Jews on the streets. Some of those captured disappeared, their fate is unknown to this day. A Judenrat was organized under German orders. Also established were forced labor camps in Kozaky, Pluhiv, Jaktorov, Olesko and Latski[1]. The main type of work was in construction and widening of roads. The work in Kozaki was in a coal-mine and the regime was slightly looser. All the camps were surrounded by barbwires and kept under the watch of Ukrainian guards. In Latski near Zolochiv, the Germans established two separate camps: one for Jews wearing yellow patches in front and also in the back and the other for gentiles who were sentenced to hard labor; they wore a red triangular patch. Jews and gentiles worked together, but the gentiles were receiving much better treatment.

We started very early in the morning, at five o'clock, regardless of the weather, carrying tools on our back and under torrents of beatings by the Ukrainians. They often shot people and killed many. During the noon-break they would bring us "soup". At the end of the work day, we returned to the camp and lied down exhausted, with our wet clothes, on our berths which were arranged in five stories.

Many people got sick with pneumonia and typhus, which were rampant in the Latski camp. They buried the dead on the hill. The Judenrat made sure to fulfill the quota for the camp by bringing in more Jews to replace those who died.

The commander of the camp, S.S. Obersturmführer Vartzug, often showed up during the night to review the feet of the workers. Whoever had dirty feet received twenty five floggings. We obviously did not have any means for washing ourselves. This was just one of drunken Vartzug's amusements.

One day, the Germans brought an old Jew and his wife to the camp. The drunken Ukrainians ordered them to dance. I do not know what their fate turned out to be.

If somebody managed to escape, his relatives would have been brought over to the camp to replace him regardless of their age. If an escapee was captured, he would be shot on the spot. Sometimes, they would hang the "guilty one" upside-down until he expired.

At night, one could only go to the restroom in a group and under the watch of the Ukrainian guards, who took that opportunity to abuse the Jews.

Every morning before going to work they would arrange us in a formation, and the Jewish commander of the camp read the names aloud, according to the list, in order to verify that all were present.

The Judenrat organized shipment of packages from the relatives in the city to the camp prisoners. The wagon owner, Moshe der Criemer (from Crimea), a WWI handicapped veteran who had a prosthetic leg, used to come with his wagon and distribute the packages.

We did not work on Sunday. However, from time to time, they would gather and take the professionals to work in various other places outside of the camp. Some people were transferred to the infamous Yanovski camp. On day, they were looking for metalsmiths and carpenters. The Jewish policeman Mr. Mas, who knew me from home, hinted to me to declare myself a carpenter. I followed his suggestion. As a result, I arrived at Latski on Passover evening 1942. From there, a few of us, all professionals, were transferred to work for a German firm by the name of "Hoch und Tiefbau" whose manager was a German by the name of Vitelitski. Our job was to take apart homes of Jews after the aktzias. We loaded the collected the materials from the dismantled houses onto boxcars which were sent to unknown destinations. The conditions there were much better than in Latski's camp. After work, we lodged with local Jewish families who received us warmly. The carpenters, whom I worked with, knew that I was not a professional carpenter and assigned me to work on all sorts of tasks that did not require carpentry know-how. If the Germans would have discovered that I am not really a carpenter as I claimed, they would have shot me on the spot.

After the ghetto of Zolochiv, was established, we were housed in the old Polish army barracks and we continue our work from there. A short time before the final extermination of the Zlochov ghetto, the Germans encircled our camp. They proceeded to shoot and kill most of the Jews. A few professionals were transferred to the Yanovsky camp in Lvov. I managed to escape, avoiding a barrage of bullets, together with two other young men. We wandered around in the forests, bunkers, sewer pipes and the ruins of the houses in the city.

As the Red Army advanced, the front approached Zlochov. The Russians have failed to conquer the city for half a year, and many of the Jews who hid in the forests were killed. In 1944, I was freed by the Russians. After the end of the war, I moved to Poland and from there, with the help of the 'Ha-Brikha'[2] movement, through Czechoslovakia, Austria, and Cyprus to Israel.

Translator's footnotes

1. See reference to Latski labor camp in an article from Yad Vashem Collection: http://www.jewishgen.org/yizkor/pinkas_poland/pol2_00217.html
2. The 'Ha-Brikhah' movement (translated literally as "The Escape") was a Zionist movement responsible for the "illegal" immigration of more than 300,000 Jews to Eretz Israel at the end of World War II and beyond, until the establishment of Israel.

[Page 216]

Two Testimonies

by Clara–Khaya Zhorna

Translated by Moshe Kutten

Edited by Rafael Manory

First Testimony

Until the outbreak of the war in 1941, we lived in the village of Dubya near Brody. We owned a farm there. Following the arrival of the Germans to the village, we were ordered to report for forced labor in the agricultural ranch of Polvork, where the Germans transferred everything we owned–horses, cows, vegetables, potatoes, and agricultural tools. Jews from various places worked in the farm including from Ponikva, Sukhodola, Yasyunov, Lokkhi (?), as well as a few people from Brody, who thought that they would be saved from being sent to the camps if they worked in the farm. The farm was organized as a forced labor camp, but the conditions in it were much better than in Latski camp or the coal mining camps.

In November 1941, The German S.S people ordered all the Jews to move to Brody. They established a ghetto in the city. Until then we struggled through very grueling work in the farm. One S.S person, Peshkin, was particularly cruel and we did not have anything to eat, since the German took everything we owned. My husband, my daughter Fanya, who was still a student at school, and myself worked very hard. Fanya worked with the hogs, and cooked food for them in large pots. One day, they brought a horse carcass for her to cook. After the pigs ate the meat, some of the pigs died. The S.S guard hit my daughter, blaming her for the death of the pigs. He hit my husband and me too. He hit my sister Ester Faier(?) so hard, that poor her could not go to work. They took her husband and her two children to the death camp in

Belzec. They also took my older sister with her children and grandchildren. In December 1941, the Germans told us to move to the Brody's ghetto and take all of our remaining belongings with us, but what have we got left to take after the Germans have already taken our possessions? They told us that they established the ghetto as a Jewish city and that we would be able to live there. However, we knew what is waiting for us in the ghetto. There was one gentile guy at the farm, who told us to flee and not go to the ghetto as the Germans do not intend to keep us alive. His wife also helped us tremendously by bringing us food. She became friendly with my daughter Fanya and told her to go to an acquaintance of hers in the village of Yasyunov who was very poor but kind. She told my daughter that she would be able to stay with her. She said she was afraid to keep my daughter herself, but would send food to that woman to sustain my daughter. Other people told my daughter that she looked like a gentile, as she was blond with two braids, however, her parents would have to move to the ghetto. We loaded everything we owned on horse–drawn carts, said a tearing goodbye and went on our way to the ghetto. Our daughter went to Yasyunov.

The head of the ghetto's Judenrat, Katz, told us to settle in a house that belonged to Trit on Shpiltalna Street. The Jews who previously resided in that house were captured and sent to camps. The former residents built double walls and hid in the attic, but they were all found and transferred to some place, only G–d knows where.

We moved to that house. We knew that they would take us to the camps sooner or later, but there was nothing we could do about it. During the aktzia we ran away to Ostrovchik. When Trit returned to the house, we returned as well. Some people in the ghetto hid in the attics or in the bathrooms with their kids.

[Page 217]

The Germans forced several people to dig pits in the Schnell forest. When they came to take my husband for the digging work, he was very sick so they did not take him. The Germans later threw Jews into the pits and buried them alive. Several people, who managed to escape, told us about what happened in the forest. Following every aktzia, rivers of bloods could be seen flowing in the streets. I was on Kalir Street the day after the aktzia. I saw blood on the walls, blood of murdered Jews.

Following the extermination of the ghetto, the Judenrat ordered all the people who survived to gather in one place under the watch of the Jewish policemen. The Germans selected some and positioned them on the right side and the others on the left side. They sent all the young ones to an unknown place. The husband of my younger sister, Shimon Foyerstein also disappeared. My sister and her children remained in the ghetto for now.

The Jewish policemen searched the attics all over the ghetto. They transferred the people they found to an unknown location.

The ghetto was exterminated on Friday, May 22nd, 1943. We did not sleep during the previous night between Thursday and Friday. People tried to flee from the ghetto. Anyone who had a bunker, did hide in it. I asked my husband to his view, on whether to flee or to stay. My husband said that we should not run away because the Germans would be looking for us after we leave the house. Only the Rubinstein family decided to flee and started to pack a few things because Rubinstein's sister had a bunker on Shkolna Street. I had the strong will to live. I also wanted to know the fate of my daughter, Fanya. I decided to try to run away from this hell at any price, even if they kill me in the street. My husband did not want to follow me. My sisters, who stayed with us with their children, had to remain behind because of their children. I went out and followed the Rubinstein family. When they lay down on the ground so did I. I followed them to Shkolna Street. There were no shootings on that street. The bunker we arrived at was more of a pit then a bunker and it contained some firewood and garbage. I entered the pit with them. Sixteen people were sitting on the shelter floor, all trembling with fear. When I entered, they started to yell at me that I entered a hideout that was not mine. However, the Rubinsteins acknowledged that they have lived with me together, so they allowed me to stay. It was very crowded in the pit, and very hard to breathe. There were little children, sick with typhoid fever, who cried all the time. When they cried, the adults yelled that the children must be strangled to death. However, the parents answered that the children would die with them. They said that they did not have the heart to choke their children, and thus the children stayed. The ghetto was in flames the whole night. We heard hand–grenades being thrown into neighboring houses as well as shouts and cries. It was a horrible experience. I regretted leaving my husband and others, but I wanted so badly to stay alive.

Second Testimony

I vividly recall the day of Brody's ghetto annihilation. The spring day of May 22nd, 1943 began with a grey dawn. The ghetto was wrapped in morning's mists. Silence descended on the ghetto–the silence before a disaster. The fear that was hanging in the air, penetrated everybody's nerve cords. Nobody managed to sleep. Even the children stayed awake. They sighed and wailed. Most certainly, in their small heads theyre–visited the experiences during the days of fear and hunger. The fear did not let go of anybody. It lived among us and inside us. Five families, about twenty people, stayed in a small single room. Everyone was immersed in his or her own silence awaiting for something horrible to happen. Then again, everybody hoped for this nightmare to end. A silent moan or a heart–tearing sigh could be heard once in a while. I dared to leave my bed and take a peak into the street. The entire ghetto could be viewed from our window, as we lived on the upper floor. A few groups of people gathered around the barbed wire fence. I knew who they were: The Ukrainian police. I could see two cars and shadows of lines of cars circling the ghetto. They waited for the morning mists to clear, in order to start their last "feast" in the town called Brody.

[Page 218]

Excited, I began waking everybody up. They all slept, one beside the other, on the floor: "Dress–up! Quickly! Faster!" Perhaps we would be able to escape this hell; perhaps somebody could save her or his soul. Everybody dressed–up silently. Even the children who woke–up did not cry. They felt the tense atmosphere and just pressed harder against their mothers' bosom.

The mist started to dissipate slowly and the light strengthened. I could hear the first shootings through the window. They came closer and closer.

I hurried everybody up. Faster! Faster! Let us leave the apartment–to the attic! We had an attic with a double wall in our house. It was discovered in one of the small aktzias, but... there wasn't any better alternative. Slowly we started to move toward the staircase, and began to climb, holding small bundles. Then, I had a thought–this is not a shelter. It was previously discovered too easily. I searched for my husband's hand–please come with me, maybe they will let us enter some other shelter. One thought kept bothering me–I want to live, to survive. I need to find a real shelter and to squeeze into it, even by force. I converted my thoughts into deeds and found myself in the street. I noticed people running across the street and joined them. In the adjacent alley a dilapidated house was standing. Its entrance was almost entirely ruined and was blocked by rags and garbage. People stood in–line in front of the entrance to the cellar, entering one after the other, slowly and quietly. I took a step toward the entrance, and I felt a hand pushing me aside. An angry voice sounded: "Stranger, what are you doing here? there is no room for you!". But my will to live was so strong, that words could not discourage or frighten me. I pushed myself into the musty cellar forcibly. The cellar was filled with people and duvets. When I was finally in, I breathed a sigh of relief. A storm was raving outside. Shots were heard as well as loud orders, sighs, moans and cries and explosions of hand–grenades thrown into cellars.

We wait. "Shma Israel!" - our lips are mumbling fearfully. What happens if they would discover us? Or perhaps they would not find us? Why would anybody search in such a ruin...? I wished that the main beam above would not fail us...". I began to notice the people who were sitting around me. All of a sudden, I heard a whispering sound calling me: "Khai'che". This was the voice of a close acquaintance of mine, Henya, my neighbor's daughter–in–law. Hence, we did have some of "our" people here. I breathed another sigh of relief. Up above, the operation continued: echoes of shots, explosions of hand–grenades and shouts of the Germans and Ukrainians, filled with mad anger. The smell of gunpowder penetrated my nostrils and cries filtered into my ears. The screams of horror penetrated even here below ground.

[Page 219]

A whole day passed, and the noises and voices did not subside. There were three little children in our shelter. The suffocating atmosphere and lack of air began to affect them. They began to scream. The adults cover their mouths, initially tenderly out of worry, and then forcibly and violently, out of desperation, just to force them to be quiet, "even if it means forever", just to ensure that their cries would not be heard on the street level, so that they would not able to find us. The long–awaited night arrived. I could not stop my thoughts. The entire time, I was thinking about how to sneak out of there, to escape from this hell through the open fields to the forest.

Up on the street level, things have quieted down. I approached Henya and offered to try sneak out carefully together and escape the ghetto under the cover of the night towards the fields and the forests. Since the barbwire fences have been removed, I hoped that we would be able, somehow, to pass out of the ghetto and then through the fields to the nearby village. I told Henya, that my heart tells me that the shelter will be discovered the next day, and this is why I am not willing to continue to stay in. For a moment, Henya was deeply in thought. "Good, I will accompany you, but I need to tell my mother in–law right away, since tomorrow, it may be too late". Her family tried to convince her not do it. They claimed that escaping the following night would better and that they would go with her then. I tried to hasten her decision–making process: "Henya are you coming?". She decided: "Yes, I am coming with you". She took a small bundle with her and said: "Let's go". We started to squeeze between people and make our way toward the entrance. We began to hear people yelling behind us that if the Germans would catch us, we will be forced to tell our captors about the shelter. People yelled: "Stop them! Don't let them leave!" Henya, with a decisive movement, pushed the person who was standing in front of her, out of her way and said: "You would not dare to stop us. Everyone is responsible for their own fate". We squeezed ourselves through the narrow opening with great difficulty. Henya whispered in my ear: "Wait here for a moment". She grabbed a small pail, filled it up with water and went down again. I understood that she brought the water to the people in the shelter. After receiving the water, nobody dared to go out anymore.

We got out. The moon illuminated the whole ghetto with a melancholic light. The ghetto was burning. The smell of burnt bodies hanged in the air and filled the space. I could hardly keep myself from fainting. I kept saying to myself: "Onward, quicker, onward beyond the ghetto's walls, move forward as far as possible toward the fields and the forests, away from the piles of bodies that we encountered on our way". It seemed that our escape from the ghetto was miraculous. We progressed slowly in a field of wheat, which was not very tall as of yet. It was time to consider our next steps and decide how and where to progress. The roads were very well guarded, to ensure that nobody escapes from the ghetto.

We left the burning ghetto behind us. Everything that was dear to our hearts remained there: our husbands, sisters, children and relatives. We knew that there was no force in the world that could save them now. We knew that we would never see them again. But what would happen to us?

Our actions were fed by a single thought: to live, to survive at any price.

[Page 220]

"What We Ourselves Experienced"

by Khayim and Bina Gasthalter
Translated to Hebrew from Yiddish Rivka Kviatkovski – a partisan and a Yiddish author.

Translated by Moshe Kutten

Edited by Rafael Manory

On 22 June 1941, at five o'clock in the morning while most of the city residents where asleep, a few loud bomb-like blasts were heard, immediately followed by the humming of airplanes. I jumped off my bed. That night I slept at my sister's, who lived in Furman's house. The house was located in the center of the market square, so I immediately noticed Russian ambulances transporting wounded soldiers. I asked a friend of mine, commander Kuznetzov, what has just happened. He answered that these were training exercises, as he really did not know the truth at that time. A short while later, I happened to meet an army captain whom I knew, and he said that the loud noises were German airplanes that dropped bombs on the airport that was located near the city. A big commotion commenced, as soldiers, cars and tanks begun to swarm around the city. A general mobilization, from young to old, was announced. Some Jews begun to bundle up their belongings, and ran away eastward, toward the Soviet Union. I got a recruitment order to the Red Army, under the signature of the city commander, Navlichenko, who was later exposed as a traitor, working for the Germans during their conquest period and was rewarded by them with an important position in the city of Lvov[6].

All the new recruits were ordered to gather in the castle-square (Schloss-Platz), which was located in the center of the city, where the road to the village of Smolno[6] began. Several hundred Jews, a few Ukrainians and some Poles gathered in the square. They held us there until very late at night. They gave us some canned meat and some bread rusks to eat, but we were ordered not to eat the food until we got an order to do so. And indeed, we did not touch the food, as no order was ever given.

The order to leave the castle was received at midnight, June 23rd. They arranged us in a formation consisting of several lines. They did not tell us where we were going, only that we needed to be ready to leave. All of a sudden, a gunshot was heard from beyond the wall of the castle. As a result, the Ukrainian recruits started to riot because they were waiting impatiently for the arrival of the Germans. The young commander ordered us to leave the castle ground, so we started to march. As I was familiar with the surroundings, I realized that we were marching toward the town of Radzikhov[6]. A break was announced in the middle of our march. We stopped at a small forest. Our commander tried to call somebody but did not get through because all the lines were already disconnected. We lay there until the next morning. We saw the helmets of Ukrainian soldiers who were escaping from the front. At approximately eight o'clock in the morning, our commander ordered us to retreat quickly. At this point, we started running rather than walking. We soon found ourselves back on the grounds of our city's castle, where we started. We were held in the castle until three o'clock in the afternoon, when we were ordered to march again, this time toward the town of Leshniov[6].

[Page 221]

Very near the town there is the forest of Leshniov, and that's where we were ordered to stop and rest. We then continued our march toward Leshniov. On the way, a few men's legs gave way. Suddenly, the commander Navlichenko approached one of them, my friend Mamut, who owned a tobacco store on Gold Street (Gold Gas), drew his revolver and asked him why he was limping. My friend told him that his legs could not carry him any longer. The commander asked him to take off his shoes. When he did, his feet were bleeding. The commander had pity on him and did not shoot him.

At about half pass four in the afternoon we reached the vicinity of Leshniov. We were told to lie down on the ground. That was where I got my assignment to join the artillery corps. We waited there for additional orders. At around five o'clock in the afternoon, a German plane was seen flying above us. Our commander ordered us to shoot at the plane with our rifles, which we did, and the plane disappeared. A few minutes later, we heard the rambling of a large number of bombers approaching. They proceeded to bomb the entire forest where we stayed. Forty bombers came, dropped their bombs and disappeared. Forty more bombers came and continued the bombing. Alternating squadrons of bombers continued to bomb the forest for three and a half hours. I really do not know how I managed to get out of that hell alive. A splinter of wood was peeled off the butt of my rifle, probably because of shrapnel hit. At around seven thirty, when the evening fell, the bombardment ceased; however, Messerschmitt planes, with machine guns, continued to shoot from their machine guns once and a while. They apparently were looking for anybody who got out alive from the bombardment. They flew over the pine treetops and showered the forest with hails of bullets. At around eight o'clock, silence descended on the forest. I got out from behind the bushes and crawled in the dark. I noticed that somebody else was crawling in the forest and asked in Russian: "Kto idiat" (who is walking?). When I approached, I saw that it was my friend Schwartz, who lived in our city on Leshniov Street. We walked together in the dark, stepping on bodies of slain soldiers. We even met some Russian soldiers who told us that they want to wait in the forest until dawn. I told my friend that my brothers live in the village of Boldury[6] near Leshniov, and that we would better go to see them because there was no point in waiting in the forest for the Germans. I was also afraid of the Ukrainian gangs, about whom we heard that were trying to make the German takeover easier for them. We also did not know what direction the Germans were coming from and realized that we cannot rely on the Red Army, which seemed to be dazed and stunned.

We walked through the forest until we found the road that crossed it. We turned right and arrived at a village. A farmer, whom we happened to meet, told us that we arrived at Vyrov[6], a village adjacent to Boldury, our intended destination. A few Ukrainians were already roaming the area and one of them suggested that we hand him over our weapons. Since I spoke fluent Ukrainian, I told him that we needed our weapons for the same purpose he needed his. At that point, I wanted to reach a shelter as soon as possible, as I did not want to fall into the hands of the Germans as a war prisoner and as a Jew. We arrived at Boldury and found my two brothers, Hermann and Benyamin, at their homes. Hermann told me that the Russians did not recruit him but said that Benyamin was recruited. Benyamin's group of recruits was brought to the village of Gaya Satrobrodskaya[6] and was told to wait there until a certain date. They were told that they could return home if nobody would come for them. My brothers were very happy to see me. They gave me civilian clothes and told me that the Germans may show up at any moment. However, as the village was already surrounded, there was no sense in escaping. We went to sleep with one of my brothers who lived in the village. My other brother lived in a flourmill, and he said that various people visit the mill, so it would be better for us not to stay there.

[Page 222]

During the following day, on Friday, we saw only village residents in the village. On Saturday morning, Simkha Schwartz and myself woke up went to the camp where my brothers now stayed. Along the way, we spotted a company of the Red Army, about twenty people, dragging a wheeled canon. I suggested to my friend that we avoid passing by them, take a shortcut around, and exit by the bridge near the mill. That's what we did. However, we did not notice the two Russian officers who were standing on the bridge, holding a map. They told us to wait, and then started to question where we were coming from. We told them that we were Brody residents and showed them our papers. They asked us if we were from Brody why did we come to that area. I told the officers that I have two brothers residing in the village and that we came to be with them since Brody was bombarded the previous day. One of the officers acknowledged the fact that Brody was bombarded, but questioned our traveling going westward from Brody, toward the Germans, rather than eastward. They also suspected our short army-style haircuts. My brother Benyamin showed up during this discussion and confirmed the fact that he was my brother, and that we came from Brody. The officer told him, that if he was my brother he should go and stand with us. He called a soldier and ordered him to hand us over to the officer located in the forest. He did not mention any names but added in Russian the words: "nyemedlyeno rastrelat" (Shoot them immediately). It was not difficult to see why we became frightened. The soldier brought us to a higher ranked officer and told him the words, which I will never forget: "Komandir Nikolai prikazal nyemedlyeno rastrelat" ("Commander Nikolai ordered to shoot them immediately"). That officer was bearded, and his cloths were sullied. He sent the "red soldier" who brought us back to his unit, looked at me and asked: "How did you end up here?" I have to mention here, that I worked as the manager of a restaurant in Brody, which was located where the known Klapper restaurant once was. This particular officer visited the restaurant daily. Our staff, under my supervision, always treated him nicely. He kept saying that the restaurant deserved to be highly praised. Since he recognized me, he released us immediately, and provided us with certificates forbidding Russian military personnel from detaining us. He also stated that they need to detain Ukrainians rather than Jews. This is how we were saved from a sudden death. We returned joyfully to my brothers, who have already given up on seeing us alive again. Our joy was short-lived though, since during the following day, the first Germans entered the village of Boldury. This was when all the troubles started–rapes, aktzias, murders, typhus epidemics and many other horrors beyond the comprehension of a regular person.

It was Sunday, when a guard of German soldiers riding on their horses entered the village. Two of the soldiers arrived at my brother's yard and one of them asked:" Are you Jewish?" When my brother acknowledged that he is, the soldiers ordered him to hand over two chickens, which were strolling around in the yard and, then continued on their way.

Later, we talked to the village farmers who had already made it to Brody and back. They said the Germans conquered the city two or three days before. In the meantime, the Ukrainians have already established their own police force in the villages, in order to enforce their regime. The farmers told us that, in the suburbs of the city, Ukrainian policemen and German soldiers have forced Jews to work in variety of jobs. I feared to go back to my apartment, which was located on 7 Kalir

Street, where my wife and her family remained, because I was told that they were asking for papers from people on the roads. I was told that Jews were not allowed to stay away from where they resided. My brother knew a young gentile who served with the Ukrainian police, and he agreed to travel to Brody and tell my family that I was alive and well, staying in my brothers' village. The gentile went to Brody but found my apartment locked, because my family, when they saw a Ukrainian policeman knocking on the door, refused to open the door for him. They simply did not believe his story. I found out about it when my brother asked the same policeman to bring me back to my home in Brody.

[Page 223]

The Germans have been only a few days in Brody, but the city did not look like its former self. One could not see joyful Jewish faces anymore. Only a few Jewish women, whose husbands were taken to forced labor camps in various places, could be seen passing and going in the streets. Anybody who was not taken to work hid in their home and did not go out to the street. A few days later, the entire intelligentsia – engineers, lawyers, high school and elementary school teachers, was ordered to register with the Gestapo, which was located in Shkolna Street, in Derbitz's house. The order stated that the Gestapo needs the intelligentsia's cooperation in establishing the new city leadership and regulations. The Germans claimed to have designated intelligentsia to be the representatives of the Jews and therefore they had to report to the Gestapo. People did not understand the meaning of the order and started to congregate toward the Gestapo's building, not guessing that it would be their last trek. I passed through the corridor of the house, where my apartment was located, when I happened to meet my brother's friend Hirsh Tritt. He told me that he received the invitation by the Gestapo but I advised him not to go. He listened to my advice and went back home. I am not sure about his fate after that. We found out that none of the intelligentsia people, who reported to the Gestapo, returned home. Their fate was unknown. Some people claimed that they were sent to forced labor camps in Germany. Some other people claimed to have seen them being loaded onto train cars to an unknown destination. A few people even said that some of these people wrote home, and they were alive and well, working somewhere. Only after the liberation by the Red Army, their mass grave was found located not too far from The Jewish cemetery, near the Leshniov Forest. The damned Germans murdered and buried all the Jewish intelligentsia during the same night they have gathered in the Gestapo. They simply transferred them all to that location and shot them all.

A short time later, the Germans established the Judenrat (Jewish Council), which was alleged to be the Jewish leadership for the city. In reality, this was a body, which conveyed and executed the Germans' orders and instructions. The Judenrat was initially located in Shkolna Street, and its first president was the former bank owner, Hermann Blokh (the son of the community leader and the commerce and rail advisor, Eliezer Blokh). His presidency lasted only a short period because he was a too decent man. After he told them that he could not execute their orders, the Germans hit him in his face until he bled. After his resignation, he was replaced by a person called Itzi Katz, who seemed to enjoy executing the murderers' orders. Prior to the war, Katz was a municipal clerk. One could learn about this person's character, from the fact that the city Jews wanted to contribute candles for the synagogue when he left the municipality, still during the Polish regime. The manager of the Judenrat's department of labor was a Jew by the name of Holtszeger. We did not derive any pleasure from him either, nor did we from his replacement–Benyu Ponykover. We actually did not derive any gratification from any of the people who assisted the Germans. A Jewish police force, which was attached to the Judenrat, was also established. The policemen were equipped with rubber batons, wore blue uniforms, and a Star–of– David made of tin was pinned on their coats. They did not usually cause any troubles for us, except their commander Rubin, who was previously a baker who was cruel to his victims. People said that he ended up being shot by Jewish partisans who encountered him in the forest.

[Page 224]

The Germans published new decrees often. Every Jews was required to wear a band with a blue Start of David on her or his arm. Initially, it was made of cloth. Later on, the Jews were ordered to wear a white band made of plastic-like material with a blue Star of David and a red number on it. This was actually a half-band and was worn on one's arm. Whoever removed the band was condemned to death. Later on, the Jews were ordered to hand over all of their furs. Whoever was found to own one after that was executed. This was the reason why they executed Dr. Chachkes. He did not hand over a fur, which was later found in his house. Jews were forbidden from walking on the sidewalks. Every action that contradicted the language of that decree carried with it a brutal beating. Most of the time, the city central command's deputy officer - by the name of Fogell, participated in these beatings. These orders were issued by the national headquarters, which was located in the city and headed by an officer by the name of Weiss. The head of the German gendarme was an officer by the name of Daun. He was an infamous murderer who wore red boots. Only a very few people in the German gendarme, were decent. As we later found out, some of them alerted people about future events ahead of time, such as when would be an attack on the ghetto or when we would need to be particularly careful. Especially cruel were the people of the Ukrainian police, who beat and robbed the Jews, even when they have not received any order to do so. Among the Ukrainian policemen was a fellow by the name of Lazovyou who murdered Jews whenever he had a chance. Two more fellows by the names of Stoliar and Pendzyuk were as cruel as he was. These were the worst among the Ukrainian policemen during the German regime. People searched for them after the war, but could not find them. Perhaps they ran away with the Germans to Germany.

A sizeable portion of the Jewish population consisted of youths who could endure hard work. The Germans announced that they need workers to send to the Latzki forced labor camp near Zolochov[6] to dig for coal, which was discovered there. However, in the notice, it was announced that the workforce would be replaced every two weeks. I too received such a notice, but decided not to report for work and to escape to the village of Holoskovytza[6], located just eight kilometers from Brody, where my parents lived. I hid there in a barn's attic enveloped in hay for several days, until I was notified that it was safe to return to Brody when calm returned to the city. I heard repeatedly that the people who were sent to the Latski Camp worked extremely hard. Jewish workers were also sent to the Poluchov Camp near Zolochov[6], some of whom were released and replaced by others. However, the returnees were so worn out from their hard labor that they could not walk back to Brody. Our neighbor, Michael Gotlieb, told me horrible stories about the labor camps. In Latski the Ukrainian policemen, who guarded the camp, cruelly beat people who worked in hard labor. For their subsistence, they only received a small piece of bread and water. Nobody ever came back to Brody alive from Latski.

[Page 225]

I would, from time to time, remove my armband, and go to the village of Holoskovytza, to bring some food from the village for us and our neighbors. These included Meir Hart and his father in-law R' Yankele Hurwitz, as well as Mordekhai Roth, the Gotlieb family, the painter Skald, Moti Schwartzwald and Selka Friedfeld nee Wachs. All these people lived at 7 Kalir Street. Before the first aktzia took place in the ghetto, an old Christian woman, who previously served at the Neumann family on 3rd of May Street (Neumann had a tool shop there), advised me to run away from the city. She knew that my parents lived in Holoskovytza as she was herself from that village. She heard from other Christians, who had connections with German officials, that a pogrom was imminent. I rather believed her but did have some doubts too, although I knew that with these murderers, any rumor might have some truth in it. I told the story to all of my acquaintances. Some laughed at me, others said that it was possible. In any case, I decided to leave town with my wife. It is worth noting that initially, when a rumor about an aktzia began to spread, we did not really understand the meaning of that word, however, we did assume that they would capture Jews and send them to camps, and would possibly shoot some on the spot. I did not ponder about it much. My wife Bina nee Ordover and I left the city. We removed our armbands and walked toward Holoskovytza. This was on Thursday. A Ukrainian acquaintance from the village came to us on Saturday and congratulated me for being lucky. He told me about a pogrom that was taking place in Brody, where they shoot Jews in the streets. He told us about the wife of our acquaintance, the photographer Boksdorf who was seen lying dead on Kolejowa Street. All the Christians in the city knew her as they all came to have their photographs taken by her husband at their shop. The Ukrainian acquaintance also told me that some of the Jews were taken to the train station, possibly for sending them somewhere. He advised me to hide somewhere, since nobody knew what would happen in the villages. We went to a Christian acquaintance that allowed us to hide in the hay in the attic of his barn. We laid down there during the whole day and went back to my parents at night where we stayed until the following morning. The Christian acquaintance told us later on, that quiet returned to Brody and that it was safe to return to the city.

Upon our return, we heard that shots were fired in the streets. Many Jews were killed on the spot and many have been transported to Belzec. The quiet lasted a while, however more Jews were taken for forced labor. Some of these people worked in growing lanugo. I always tried to avoid going to work, as I did not want to be under the supervision of the oppressors. However, this was not easy, since it was forbidden for men to wander around outside. The Germans did not have accurate information, but one had to be very careful. As mentioned above, we lived on Kalir Street, in a house owned by my wife's grandfather Bitaticher. This was a single-story house, with many apartments on the first floor. I tried to find a place where a hiding shelter could be established. I noticed that under the floor, in the corridor, there was a round dome-like protrusion. I pulled two planks off the floor and saw that there were no bricks underneath, just sand. I cannot express my joy at this discovery. With a stick I checked and found that the thickness of the sand layer was 80 centimeters and sometimes even less. I thought that by removing the sand, we could build a hiding shelter for several people. It would not be a tiny achievement if we could arrange for a shelter under the floor. I took the idea from thought to reality. I waited until the evening, told my secret to Moti Schwartzwald, and decided to work on it together. I removed the sand and he carried it out to the yard and deposited it in the storage shed. We obviously needed to be very careful, as the shelter was only big enough for five or six people. We had to be very wary of children and even youths. The

Germans and the Ukrainians often threatened children with their revolvers trying to force them to tell where Jews were hiding. They often succeeded to extract the secret out of them.

We worked until midnight and completed the hideout. We went back and fastened the floor planks. I created a cover made of a box filled with sand. This was to make sure that if somebody stood on the cover, it would not sound like an empty container. The cover rotated with the help of a screwdriver positioned diagonally.

[Page 226]

It was therefore very difficult, or almost impossible to discover it. I positioned a table on top of the two planks. One would enter the hideaway by opening the cover. The table would remain as it stood. Later on, we realized that it was practically impossible to discover this deception.

The entrance to the hideout was through our kitchen. However, in our apartment we had two rooms. I camouflaged the entrance to the small room with a large buffet cabinet. When the Germans would search the house, they would move the cabinet and yell: "These damn Jews have already gotten out". They would not bother to search any further. I hid in the hideout below the floor and placed the cabinet in its place when the Germans came to take men for forced labor. Moti Schwartzwald also hid under the floor. As mentioned above, I had two brothers that resided in Boldury, a village near Leshniov. They leased the mill and pools there. The estate owner was a man by the name of Rudolf. My wife suggested that, with the help of my Christian acquaintance, she could travel to Boldury to find out how they were doing. Since any travel by Jewish men was dangerous, I agreed and she went on her way the following morning. At noon of the same day, shots were heard in the street. Through the windows, we saw Jews being led by German soldiers with helmets on their heads, loaded with ammunition and hand grenades on their belts, as if they were going into a battle. Ukrainian policemen holding rifles accompanied them. With one leap, we all jumped into the hideout – Moti Schwartzwald, his wife, their sister in law Sela Friedfeld and my wife's grandmother, Mrs. Bitaticher, and I. However, after getting in I realized that I left a crowbar at the door blocking the entrance door to the house. That would tell the searches that somebody was in the house. I jumped out and told Moti to close the cover behind me. I wanted to remove the crowbar so that the searchers would not be sure whether there were people in the house or not. I was at the door in one leap but heard the Germans at the adjacent house, the house of Schutlender, and some heavy footsteps approaching our house. I was afraid to enter the hideout again for the fear that it would be discovered. I noticed a small opening in the wall through which the chimney cleaners swept out the soot. I entered the chimney and listened weather there was anybody in the corridor. Since there was a total silence, I continued to climb. I was pleased that I could crawl from one chimney to the other, as the chimneys for all the apartments were connected via one main channel built to conduct the smoke. I was certain that even if somebody would look into the chimney, he would not be able to see me. However, my self–confidence evaporated and fear grew when, while moving my arm, I touched another human being who preceded me in hiding in the chimney. I soon found out that this was one of our house's tenants, whose full name escaped me. I only recalled his nickname–Leib the Tregger (Porter in Yiddish). He became frightened of me initially, but after we recognized each other, we just sat down quietly and even smoked cigarettes together. We heard shouts and shots coming from the street and discussions in German and Ukrainian coming from our apartment.

Later on, we found that they did not take anybody from our apartment and the quiet returned in the evening. Whoever stayed in the hideout came out. The house tenants gathered and we closed the main gate. My chimney–friend and I were black all over. We boiled some water and showered. We ate and told each other what happened to us during the last few hours. It turned out later that the event of the last few hours constituted what was later be known to be the second aktzia. We were told that the captured Jews were taken to the train station and transported to an unknown location. The rumors said that they were taken to Belzec.

There were no more kidnappings or shootings. However, a decree was announced that a ghetto would be established in Brody and that all the remaining Jews would have to reside within its limits. The Rynek (market place in Polish) was excluded from the ghetto; however, the ghetto included all the streets behind it to Podzmecha Street (under the castle of the Potoski's). Kalir Street (to just after the pharmacy of Leon Kalir, and to the slaughterhouse on the Railroad Street) was included in the ghetto.

[Page 227]

People started to sell all of their belongings to the Christians in the city and its environs in an effort to bring some food to the ghetto. A sale meant getting nothing or close to nothing. Valuables sold for insignificantly low prices. A suit or golden watch brought hardly five to ten kilos of flour or several dozens of eggs. When the sellers tried to bargain, the Christian buyers would say: "The Germans would shoot all of you soon, and we would get anything you own for nothing". However, the Germans did not allow Christians to steal Jewish property. There were even some cases when the Germans shot to death dishonest merchants.

The flurry of activity associated with the establishment of the ghetto was extensive. They planned to house in the ghetto, not only the remaining Jews of the city, but also the Jews from all the nearby settlements and villages. All Jews from the city environs were ordered to leave their localities and come to the city. The Germans allocated Kalir Street for them, and the residents on Kalir Street were forced to relocate to other streets. They packed 12–15 people in one room. We were ordered to settle in Brafer's(?) house on Shpitalna (Hospital) Street. The Kandel family, Katz, the family of the leather merchant and Avraham Parles (a Russian Jew) already lived in that house. Beside them and us, the Sklar family, Yosef Schwartzwald and his family, as well as the Donner family (Berish Donner's son), the cutter's wife, son, and my wife's grandmother Sheva Bitaticher, were also ordered to settle there.

In locations marked as the entrances to the ghetto, the authorities stuck poles and posted on them large–letters signs in Polish and Ukrainians: "Stop! This is the Ghetto Boundary!" From the Christian side of the sign, a warning was that entering the ghetto was punishable by death was posted. The warning on the Jewish side stated that leaving the ghetto was punishable by death. Despite of the warnings, as I would describe below, many people left and entered the ghetto daily. They have done so not because the penalty was reduced or because they did not feel that it was real, but because of the hopelessness and the apathy it caused, and because life was considered worthless despite the fact that everybody wanted to live.

My wife and I decided to sneak out of the ghetto as soon as possible. I could not get used to the fact that I would have to live in confinement and wait for orders by the Germans and the Ukrainians. Indeed, it was not difficult to guess the purpose of the ghetto, where most of the remaining Jews were to be concentrated. We could not think about fighting our enemies. This was impossible especially because of the fact that the intelligentsia fell into the trap of deceit and was completely annihilated. Also, the Jewish power diminished as a result of the two aktzias that took place unexpectedly by the armed Germans and Ukrainians police forces, assisted by auxiliary guards, firemen, and alike, thus eliminating the possibility of an uprising.

I began to contact Christian acquaintances, residents of the village of Holoskovytza. I found a Christian Pole, Mikolai Magratich who told me that he discussed our matter with his mother-in-law Hanka Kaval, who knew us as honest people. She resided outside of the village and was willing to hide us even without payment. When I had some money, I gave it to her so that she can prepare firewood for the winter, the height of which was expected to arrive sometimes between December 1942 and January 1943. I told her that we would move to Holoskovytza shortly thereafter. Upon hearing of our plan, my friend Moti Schwartzwald asked if he could accompany us. His wife refused to leave the ghetto as she wanted to stay with her sister and placed her fate in the hands of God. I contacted the Christian women and she agreed to have Schwartzwald join us. We decided to leave Brody on Saturday evening so that we could reach the village on the same night. On the planned day, we left the city and walked toward the Gayuvka (guard's hut) in the forest near Kosachyzna[6]. I was very familiar with the road and we arrived at Holoskovytza in no time. When we reached the Christian woman's house, it was already dark outside. I peeked through the window and observed that she was home alone. She was happy to see us and made the table for us. She then proceeded to bring us to a small compartment she prepared for us. Its size was about two and a half meter long and about one meter wide. She placed a wooden stove in the corner with firewood ready to be burnt. My wife liked the place. However, Moti Schwartzwald murmured disappointedly: "so be it; we'll see what will our fate be". The Christian woman placed two straw mattresses for us on the floor. We got used to our situation there. It was, from all points of view, better than in the ghetto, since we had the feeling that we had more freedom despite being confined to a small room. We stayed there for a few days. Our Christian woman told us that she heard other Christians saying that the barbwire fence around the ghetto has not been opened yet. However, she heard that they would open it in a short while.

[Page 228]

Ten days after we entered our hideout, Schwartzwald began to regret his decision to join us and he told me: "Khayim, if you would bring me back to the ghetto, I would move back there". He stated his reasons for his decision. First, he was not used to the peasants' food. Secondly, in the ghetto, Jews were still sleeping on regular bed sheets, while he could not get used to sleeping on the straw mattresses. I brought him back to Brody one evening. This was a very difficult thing to do. I did not know exactly how they arranged the ghetto and its guards. I was also afraid of encountering patrols that would be looking for victims for the Germans. We arrived all the way to Smolno[6], and observed a floodlight illuminating the railroad trucks leading from Brody to Lvov. Floodlights were used, because somebody blew up the tracks between Zabolottze[6] and Ponykovytza[6]. The floodlight moved back and forth. When it started to move right, we ran following its beam. When it stopped to switch direction to the left, we fell on the ground. We repeated this process three times until we got out of danger. At that point, we had to get into the ghetto. When we approached the ghetto, we saw that a Jewish policeman standing at every entrance, however, the ghetto itself was not illuminated. The Jewish auxiliary policeman asked in German: "Wer dort?" ("Who is there?"). I answered in Polish:"Czo

Chcesz" ("What do you want?"). My main fear was that I would be arrested and then I would not be able to get back to my hideout in the village where my wife remained, as she was not very familiar with the area. After we got into the ghetto, our acquaintances in the ghetto were happy to see us. I did not find any significant change compared to what the conditions were when we last left. We parted ways and I went on my way back to the village. The previous scene with the auxiliary policeman repeated itself. He asked me in German, I answered in Polish, and I got out of the ghetto. The same scene with the floodlight repeated itself near Smolno[6] as well. The floodlight illuminated and I avoided it. My way back from there was easier, since I was only responsible for myself. I was back in my hideout after a short time.

[Page 229]

From that time onwards, only my wife and I were sitting in the shelter. Daily, at noontime, the Christian woman would allow us to leave the hideout and enter her house. As I mentioned above, her house was located about six hundred meters away from the village wall. When she saw anybody approaching the house, she would warn us and we would just enter the hideout. Our luck did not last long. About a month later, our woman landlord came back from the village, where her children lived. She told some of them about us (not all of them, as some were scared of us). She proceeded to say that, in her opinion, we should leave her house for a while because of that. She also told us that the mail carrier, whom she met on her way back from the village, told her that a search would be conducted in her house a short while later. There was a reason for the intended search. The landlord's cousin was sent to Germany to work and he escaped without permission. The Germans requested the Ukrainian police to search the houses of all of his relatives. The mail carrier was in contact with the village authorities, and this was how he learned about that. This was not good news. It was in the middle of winter, the fields were covered with snow and the time was eleven o'clock in the morning. We could not leave during the day, as all sorts of people were roaming around, including the Bandroviches who ruled the countryside and were known to kill Jews. I planned to stay until the evening and then try to enter the city. We knew that the barbwire fence was already in place but we did not have any other choice. Nobody showed up in the house that day, so we left the warm hideout compartment in the evening, anguished and fearful, and walked back toward our city. When we arrived at the hut of the forest guard, we decided to turn to the guard, whose name was Prishchevski. I knew him very well from before the war, and decided to ask him to let us stay in his hut until the morning. I only found his wife in the hut. She stated that she could not take the risk of hiding Jews on her own, a crime punishable by death. She suggested that we wait outside until her husband comes back, as he was expected to arrive back shortly thereafter. It was as she said. When he arrived, we proceeded to greet him. He greeted us back, but was not very happy to hear our request. He claimed that the Germans frequented the forest to search for Jews. He said that for that reason, hiding inside his hut was out of the question. I understood that he allowed us to get into a closet that was standing in the yard. I thanked him for that and we got into the closet quickly. There was severe frost and snow outside. The closet was loose and fractured, and the wind penetrated and pushed in a great deal of snow through the cracks between the planks. I collected some hay and created a pit–like depression and we laid in it to sleep. We covered ourselves with a blanket, given to us for the road, by our woman landlord. We soon felt warm but could not fall asleep because we were worried about how to enter the ghetto.

As we observed the first light of dawn, and could hear the clatter of the farmers' wagons travelling to the city, we started our progress toward the city. We were careful to lower our faces to avoid recognition by the Christians and we arrived at the Railroad Street. We have already seen the barbwire fence of the ghetto when we arrived at the slaughterhouse. I noticed that the fence consisted only of three loose wires. I stepped on the lower wire and lifted the other two, so both my wife and I could enter the ghetto. We found unbelievable hunger and distress in the ghetto this time around. There was no food distribution at all, and the food was meager even before that. Prior to the establishment of the ghetto, one hundred grams of bread per person was distributed. The people were standing in lines to get it. One line was designated for the Jews and another for the Christians. They would often serve two Christians before they serve a Jew. Deputy Officer Vogel, from the city headquarters would often appear at these lines and hit everybody on their heads, claiming that the line people were forming was not sufficiently straight.

[Page 230]

We had to go back to the same house we lived in previously because we did not have any other choice. We received orders and decrees, through the Judenrat, daily. On one day, the Judenrat person came in and begged: "Have a pity on us. The Gestapo demanded that we give them ten kilogram of gold, otherwise they would exterminate the entire ghetto". Everybody gave whatever they had–rings, watches and such. The following day, a decree was issued that the Jews should give the S.S. so many kilos of leather, otherwise they would kill one hundred Jews. Orders were piling up, one order on the top of the other, often in a form of an enticement. For example, they would offer, that Jews who would secure a permit to wear the letter W (short for Wermacht, meaning–"in the service of the German military") could leave the ghetto and work outside. The person overseeing the work for the Jews was the former delicatessen's owner by the name of Holtszeger. Everybody tried to get the letter W, and they all were willing to pay for it with the last remnant of their property. This was how a whole enterprise called Altstofferfassung, "collection and packing of old rags," was formed. The manager of this enterprise was a Pole by the name Miklaszewski. One would need a lot of luck to be accepted to work there. Most of the workers were occupied with the collection of scrap iron and rags. Whoever succeeded in being accepted there, his work would have been much easier than any other type of work. A person, who worked in collection, received a can from Miklaszewski, with the name of the enterprise and the name of the authority (Genneralgubernement – General Government[1]) printed on it. I have succeeded, thanks to a large sum on money, to get a can for myself from Miklaszewski, and like any other can owners, managed to avoid being kidnapped to do other type works. I was also allowed to get out of the ghetto, which offered me the opportunities to get some food from the outside and bring it into the ghetto. As I mentioned, the can owners were tasked with the job of collecting scrap metal and old rags. Whoever managed to collect 400 kilos of scrap metal and 100 kilos of rags was allowed to move freely for the rest of the month. The collection point was at the former scrap metal warehouse owned by Katz, on Wesola Street (behind the town hall). Katz was also employed by Miklaszewski and was provided with that auspicious can. The Jews who were employed in this enterprise, managed somehow to collect the required quantity. If they were not successful, they would have had pay a penalty at the collection point, so somebody else would be able to complete the quota. Miklaszewski himself behaved honestly. He often warned us when we should be careful, as he was dealing with the Germans. His best friend was the teacher Harnik whom he hid along with his family. The rumor said that he also hid the rabbi of the city, R' Moshe Shteinberg, who now lives in New York. The Rabbi himself also owned such a can. Altogether, about forty to fifty Jews were employed by this enterprise.

I did not trust the Germans, despite the fact that I owned a can, and tried not to wander around too much in the streets. In the meantime, a typhus epidemic began to spread in the ghetto, and this was the worst of all calamities. People fell like flies in the streets. My mother, may she rest in peace, became ill with that disease. Only a physician who resided in the ghetto was allowed to treat the ghetto residents. A young physician, by the name of Dr. Korlandski, resided in the ghetto. However, his diagnosis was useless without a medicine. He would write a prescription, but to get the prescription filled, one had to go to the pharmacy, which was located outside of the ghetto in the Christian side. In order to get there, a special permission had to be obtained from the Judenrat. The Judenrat would simply accumulate a large number of prescriptions, as a walk to the pharmacy was only allowed for a small number of times. I decided to fetch the medicine for my mother quickly by myself. I had done it many times before, when I sneaked out of the ghetto by stripping off any sign of being a Jew, which the Germans imposed on us. I went to the pharmacy and received the required medicine. The pharmacy was located in the market square used to be owned by Leon Kalir (who was the head of the Jewish community in

Brody). A Christian pharmacist, who treated the Jews decently, owned it after the ghetto was established. People said that he was a Pole from Krakow. He was tall and blond and so was his wife. The pharmacy closed one day and the couple disappeared. They have been exposed as being Jews who had Aryan papers. People said that a day before they disappeared, a Christian customer who recognized them entered the pharmacy and asked them what they were doing in Brody. This guest did not report them to the German authorities, but the couple did not reopen the pharmacy in the afternoon, and left Brody in a hurry. The customer, most likely, came from around the city where the couple resided before moving to Brody.

[Page 231]

My mother recovered from her illness and was already out of bed, but the typhus epidemic continued to cause havoc. I became sick as well, and lay down feverish in my bed. I recall, through the fogs of a dream, that my wife and her grandmother, pulled me out of the bed, dressed me up, and while holding me near the window, explained to me that German officers, accompanied by Ukrainian policemen, were breaking into houses and shooting anybody they found lying in bed. They claimed that by doing so, they prevented the disease from spreading to areas outside of the ghetto. Indeed, a short while later, two German officers barged into our house, with drawn handguns in their hands, however, when they realized that all the beds were made, they left. Several tens of Jews were shot to death in the ghetto that day. The murderers provided the ghetto with a cart, which we called "Kechet'ke" (A small coach in Yiddish), with which the bodies of the dead were taken out daily to the cemetery. It is difficult to portray this repulsive event to anybody who did not experience it. I certainly do not have the energy and the ability to describe that atrocious sight, nor can I describe well other horrific events.

Since rumors began to spread that the Germans were planning to exterminate the ghetto in a short while, we decided to build a hideout for ourselves, similar to other hideouts in all other houses. The Barter house, where we lived, had a tinsmith workshop with scraps of sheet metals and tools scattered around. There was a large cellar located beneath the workshop where we arranged the hideout. The cellar, which was to be accessed through a tall ladder, could house about 25 people. Some people had to remain above to camouflage the hideout's entrance, and I looked for a smaller hideout where people who stayed behind could escape and hide. The house had a small yard, where a small storage shed, with long wooden planks, stood. The planks were the same length as the planks of the first floor storage. I arranged a hideout by placing a floor stretching between the storages, at a height of about 80 cm. This was big enough to hold about five to six people. We could close the small hideout by placing two planks, which were very difficult to spot from the outside. The small hideout could be accessed through a small ladder. Two guards stayed awake from among us at night at all times, in order to allow all others to sleep and avoid having our foes surprise us with a sudden assault. These were the conditions under which we had to live in the ghetto. In the evenings, we gathered and discussed politics and other matters. During these discussions, a person by the name of Mr. Olzker (I forgot his first name) was adamant in his claim that Hitler's defeat was near, and with it, our freedom. Some people joked, particularly during the battles around Stalingrad, that there were rumors about Hitler renting a two–room apartment with a kitchen, so that he could return to his previous craft [casual laborer[MK]]. Despite the later denials of people who were involved, I saw with my own eyes, that some of the people hiding were busy doing other things.

[Page 232]

I sneaked out of the ghetto from time to time. I had a Christian acquaintance, who worked, before the war, at Neumann's tool shop on 3rd of May Street[2]. The Neumann family did not remain in the city, and the Christian woman lived in their house. She was an old woman, about seventy years old, very observant in her religion. She was a native of the village of Holoskovytza6], where her married children, were still residing. We called the old woman “Babchu” (grandmother). She told me that if I ever needed to hide for several days, I could stay with her. I visited her weekly and would bring her gifts, some clothing or something else, and thanked her for willing to help me in time of need. One time, when I came to visit her, she advised me not to stay in the ghetto, because she heard that the Ukrainians were in town, headed by a person by the name of Lufatinski and his son–in–law, the priest Demchinski. These two appealed to the German authorities from time to time, requesting to rid them from the Jews. Since she heard about them from several people, she warned me to leave the ghetto. There was another story associated with that woman. In one of my excursions outside the ghetto, I walked on Kosciolna Street (near their church), when I happened to meet a Christian by the name of Barachek who told me to get off the streets, because a pogrom has begun in the ghetto. Without any hesitations, I went into the old woman's house on 3rd of May Street and asked her to hide me. I also asked her to go out to the street and find out what was going on in the ghetto. She agreed and put me in one of the former stores located in the house under her apartment, and went out to the street. When she came back, she told me that there were horrible shootings on Kalir Street. Jews were being transported on trucks toward Stary–Brody (old Brody) which was a western suburb of the city, on the main road from Brody to Lvov. She did not know exactly where they were being transported from there. A short while later, my wife, who miraculously survived and escaped from the ghetto, came to my hideout. She told me that two Jewish youths, one by the name of Lerner from Leshniovska Street and another by the name of Mikolintzer, escaped from the ghetto to the Leshniov forest located just outside of the city. They were hoping to hide there, or to organize a group of other ghetto's escapees. Germans who were in the forest captured them, brought them to the city and delivered them to the Ukrainian police, located on Kosciolna Street, in the former magistrate building (town hall). The Germans who brought the youths did not check in their pockets. One of them had a handgun. Just as they were handing them over to the jail guard, whose name was Timchishin, as he was about to close the jail gate, the owner of the handgun shot the guard and killed him. The two youths escaped from the jailhouse, and because the hour was eleven o'clock in the morning, they realized that they would not be able to run away from the city. Therefore, they escaped into the ghetto, to its main street of Kalir, entered house no. 7, which was our former house, and asked the residents to hide them. The Jews who lived in this house were the ones who were deported from the village of Ponykovytza, while my parents lived in the adjacent house. The residents of the house allowed the youths to hide in the hideout, which I built under the floor of the first floor. Soon enough, German and Ukrainians encircled that house and the houses around it. They shot every Jews they encountered, and demanded that the residents hand over the youth to them. However, no one responded to this demand. At the end, the commander of the German gendarme, whose name was Daun, entered our former kitchen. The youths, who were hiding underneath, most likely recognized his voice. They lifted the planks covering the hideout and one of them shot at the commander, but missed. The commander threw a hand grenade into the hideout and the two youths, the heroes of our city, were killed.

During the commotion, my wife managed to escape, and crossed the barbwires to the other side of Podzamche Street and reached me. At two o'clock in the afternoon, the Christian woman told us that quiet returned to the ghetto, and that some Jews were seen walking around. My wife stayed with the old woman, and I returned to the ghetto to check on my parents and my wife's grandmother. Our neighbor, Michael Gottlieb, whom I met on my way, told me that my father was alive. I took that as being told that my mother did not survive.

[Page 233]

It turned out to be true. When I returned to the ghetto, I went directly to Kalir Street, where the calamity happened. My father was alone, and he was crying his heart out. It was difficult to calm him down. I was also crying. Our former house was soaked with blood, including its staircase, all the way from top to bottom. The few that have miraculously survived, as they hid in various hideouts located in the yard and in other houses of the ward, told us the details of the pogrom: The Germans encircled the ward where the house into which the youths escaped was located, and shot everyone who came out of house no. 7. Then they entered the house and shot everybody they encountered in the house and near it. Even the firefighters took part in the murders alongside the Germans. The firemen pounded anyone they encountered with their axes, and killed them.

My father told me how my mother was killed and how he happened to survive. After the pogrom in the house, which lasted about 40 or 45 minutes, the Germans ordered anyone who was found in the street or at home to climb onto trucks. Anybody who responded was taken outside of the city. My mother was loaded onto one truck, and my father on another. One truck had already left, however, the last truck with my father on it, did not go, as an order was received from the Sturmführer (Assault leader– RM) Vartzug, who was located in Zolochov[6], to stop the pogrom and called off all actions associated with it. This was how my father survived. I could not feel any joy in that.

Deep grief descended on the ghetto following the pogrom. About seven hundred people were killed that day. They were all buried in a mass grave in the forest of the estate owner Schnell, a few kilometers outside of the city. The Christians told us that the trucks brought the captured Jews to kill them where the graves were ready prepared ahead of time. They pulled out two people at the time, and the German policemen shot and murdered them. The Christians told us that the ground on the top of the mass grave moved since some of the people were only injured when the fell into the graves. These Christians were the people who covered the two mass graves.

This is the place to recall a story about four people who were injured during the time we still lived at 7 Kalir Street. Two Hasidic Jews brought over to our house the Rabbi of Yavrov, Rabbi Faivishi Rubin, the grandson of the Rabbanit Idilya (the daughter of R' Shalom Rokakh, the founder of the Beltz dynasty). The Rabbi wanted to live in this specific house, as it contained a Beit–Midrash {House of learning for Jewish studies [RM]] that used to belong to my wife's grandfather, Rabbi Leibish Bitaticher. We welcomed him very warmly, and he stayed with us the entire time. Jews came to see him all the time, handing over small pieces of papers with notes (Kvit'lach in Yiddish), but he did not accept just everybody. He loved us very much and he kept telling us that nothing would happen to us, even during the most difficult times. Before the establishment of the ghetto, however, he said that he wanted to move with Rabbi Pini–Pinkhas Shapira. On the day of the pogrom, they led them both to the Schnell forest and killed them along with the rest of the Jews. This was on the 14th of May 1943.

[Page 234]

Those who survived had to continue to endure the life in the ghetto. The families living in our house continued with the guard duty at night. I wanted my father to move with us, but he did not want to move from Shotlender's house that was allocated to him. He lived there with his good friend, so we were meeting and parting ways continuously. On 20th May, 1943, Avraham Parles (who was nicknamed Avram “the Rusisher”(Avram “the Russian” in Yiddish), was standing guard. At three o'clock at night, we heard Avraham yelling in his husky voice: “Wake up children, wake up, we are doomed!” I, and several other men, arrived at the corridor in one leap. We peeked through the windows and saw several people running here and there and yelling that German army units surrounded the ghetto. People tried to run away and hide. Everybody thought that other hideouts were better than their own. Some people ran away to their relatives or acquaintances, and there were those who hoped to be able to run away from the ghetto. People looked like fish caught in a net. We quickly led all the people of the house and Pini Korsower's relatives to the big hideout below the tinsmith workshop. I decided to stay up, camouflage the hideout, and then go to the small hideout in the yard. My wife accompanied me. Yosl Schwartzwald, his wife and his daughter Edzi who initially went to the big hideouts, decided to come with me to the small hideout as Yosl and I always stayed together. He took his cousin's wife and her three years old son with him, as her husband Fishel Schwartzwald (the tailor), was recruited to the Red Army before the Germans arrived, and was away from Brody. The issue with the child was not easy, as the small hideout was but a small chamber made of planks. However, we could not deny him access and managed to let everybody in. Schwartzwald and I remained at the gate of the house, and observed that fewer and fewer Jews were on the street, just like on Yom Kippur[3] eve, when the congregation would gather in the synagogues for the prayer of “Kol Nidrei”[4]. At the end, we saw a frightened woman running and yelling: “They are already marching into the ghetto!” We through a peek at the big hideout, which was covered with scarp metals, where forty souls were hiding, and jumped like cats into the small hideout. We lowered the cover down, warned the child to be quiet and listened to the activities outside. Initially we heard the footsteps of the soldiers and the orders yelled by their commanders. From time to time, we heard cries of people whose hideout was found and the ensued gunshots. We could also hear people talking in German in the lower floor of our house. Surprisingly the child, Shlomka, did not make any crying noise. Perhaps he understood what his cry would cause. We heard the Germans trampling the floors of the rooms, turning over furniture. They even reached the storage–shed, which was the continuation of the room where we were hiding. One German yelled: "Kamm, oben ist noch etwas da" ("come, there is something else up here"). They went up to the upper floor, which was the extension of the storage shed. We were then under their feet. Through the cracks between the planks, I could see their boots and their green uniforms. We heard a gunshot. They did this on purpose, to frighten babies, who would cry when they heard it. The child Shlomka did not utter a word. Although his mother held her hand over his mouth, he was remarkably quiet. A few minutes later, the Germans left the house. Later on, I saw that they marked the house with chalk, as a sign that they had already searched it.

[Page 235]

We sat in the hideout until noon. We heard the sound of a trumpet, similar to what we used to hear from the army barracks. A few minutes later, we heard some orders being barked and the resulting soldiers' footsteps. Silence descended. We could not hear any signs of life coming from the ghetto. We continued to sit down in the hideout until nightfall without knowing what to do, since we did not know whether there were any guards still stationed around the ghetto. At the end, we decided to stay in the hideout until the morning. We ate some food that we managed to bring with us to the hideout. Ukrainian policemen and their families rummaged around the house in the dark. They were looking for the remnants of any properties left by the victims. Shortly thereafter, we heard noises of horses and carts, but they were blurry. We could not determine the language of the discussions. When the silence returned, I decided to come out from the hideout and investigate what happened. I also wanted to search the rooms for any leftover food. Etli Schwartzwald told me that she left five or six loafs of bread in their apartment. She baked bread in the oven for her family and other people. We were sure that we would find the bread, as neither the Germans, nor the Ukrainians were short of bread. Their hands were busy stealing more valuable things. The problem was that I did not know how to climb up to the top floor without being detected by our foes. I had another task of getting rid of our and the child's waste (we took special tools for that). I did not hesitate much. I raised the cover, jumped up, closed the cover and listened. There was a dead silence around. I then had to enter the corridor and climb up to the upper floor. However, the staircase was near the gate leading out to the street. I risked my life and hurried up the staircase. At the same moment, the wind rolled a piece of paper toward me. Its rustling gave me a shiver, as I suspected that somebody was following me. I climbed up to the upper floor and was happy to find the pillow cover with the six loafs of bread in it. I threw them out above the rail to the yard below, took some water in a container and several other necessities and returned to the hideout. I did not know what to do then. Approximately around four o'clock in the afternoon, we heard the rattling of carts and conversing voices. This time the exchange was in Yiddish. Despite of that, we decided not to come out until we knew for sure, what was going around us. At seven o'clock at night, quiet descended again, and it continued overnight. We sat down and ate. We tried to always, have somebody among us remain awake to guard and try to quiet down the snoring noises of the sleeping people, so that they would not be heard outside. The morning arrived again. At eight o'clock in the morning, we heard a noise of a commotion coming from the ghetto. We could also hear people taking in Yiddish in our own yard. I peeked through s crack in the floor and saw two acquaintances, honest owners of houses. One was Uri Leshnover who was a rug merchant in the city, and the name of the other was Landau. I opened the cover of the hideout, jumped into the storage shed and called: “Landau!” However, when they saw me they yelled at me: “Hide. You are bringing disaster on us!" I hurried up and returned to the hideout. I did not know at the time what the reason for their warning was.

Soon after that, I heard the sound of footsteps in the yard, and heard somebody calling my name: "Gasthalter! Gasthalter!" The person who called me was Landau. I jumped out from the storage shed, and my acquaintances disclosed the enormity of the tragedy. The latest extermination action by the Germans resulted in the sending of the last transport to Belzec. Following that action, the Germans declared Brody as being free of Jews. That meant that Jews were not allowed to stay in the city any longer. Some men survived the aktzia. They and the people, who came out of their hiding, have been assigned to a single Jewish auxiliary policeman for every five people. They were provided with a horse and a cart, handled by a peasant, and were tasked with collecting anything that was abandoned by the families who were taken away. Leshnover and Landau were willing to take me with them. They gave me a yellow piece of cloth to saw a yellow Star–of–David on my chest. I joined them in collecting the remnants of the Jews' properties and bringing them to the building, which was the former barracks of the 43rd Polish army battalion, across from the city park. I asked them to come back the following day, as I had to discuss this with the people who have been hiding with me in the hideout. They told me that women could not be seen in the street. If spotted, they would be killed on the spot. They apologized about hesitating to talk to me previously. They told me that they had to report to the Jewish auxiliary police about finding people who were hiding. The Jewish police people told them that we were allowed to come out of the hideout, and said they would try to help us as much as possible. We parted ways and I returned to the house, climbed up to the hideout and proceeded to describe the situation we found ourselves in to the people, who were hiding there with me. The question was, what would we do about the people who were staying in our main hideout. We could not have them join us. To do so we would have to walk in street. Even if we would have succeeded to do so, the Ukrainian policemen, whom Leshnover and Landau told us about, were roaming the ghetto and shooting anybody they were encountering. They could have caught us in our attempt to remove the scrap metals above cover. We knew that an inventory of food for several days containing rusks and canned food was prepared in the main hideout. As we were discussing the matter, we heard shouts and cries of children. We knew immediately that the main hideout was found. We were told later that Ukrainian policemen, who raided the houses and burrowed after gold, discovered the hideout with all of the residents in it. They transported them to the nearby fish market (Fishplatz) and killed them all on the spot.

[Page 236]

The following people, who were hiding in the large hideout were murdered: Avraham Parles and his wife, the painter, Sklar, his wife and their daughter – Eva, the leather merchant – Katz and his two daughters, Pini Korsower, my wife's grandmother – Sheva Bitaticher, the two children of Yosl Schwartzwald, Israel Doner's wife and children. There were several other people whose name I did not know or I have forgotten.

The following day, we heard again the hustle of carts and the chatter in the street. I jumped out of the hideout and ventured very carefully out to the street. I saw the opened cover of the large hideout. I returned to our small hideout and went out to the street together with Yosl Schwartzwald, after we attached the yellow patches on our chest. We then accompanied the carts to collect the remnants of the murdered residents' belongings. My wife and the wife of Yosl Schwartzwald remained in the hideout, because the Ukrainian policemen were shooting women and children when they saw them. As we mentioned we were tasked with collecting the remaining belongings and bring them at noon to the barracks. We also had to sleep at the barracks at night.

The person who was responsible for the warehouse and the collected belongings was a young Pole native of Poznan, by the name of Roog. I was not enthusiastic about going to the barracks, as I despised detention and was willing to risk a great deal to avoid confinement. I also had to call on the hideout where our wives were staying, in order to care for them and bring them food. Schwartzwald and I decided to sneak out before the carts stopped by the barracks at noon, and to forage for food in the emptied apartments. We did find some food to bring to our wives and the child. We found bread and canned food and brought the food to the hideout. We stayed there until we heard the carts returning. The Germans in the warehouse were not strict in their inspection and examination. The Jewish inspectors pretended not to see, and thus we managed to slip out for several days. One day, we went to the hideout to visit our wives and came out again as usual when the carts came back. However, many carts and their former ghetto residents' owners did not show up in the afternoon. We knew that they did not hide anywhere, as there was no place to hide. That meant that, going back to warehouse could mean sudden death. I had to do something to escape this trap. I got out of the ghetto, went to old Christian woman and asked her to take my wife into her house. Despite her great fear, she agreed. I went back to the ghetto, and took a pillowcase and wrapped my wife's head with it. I walked her to the barbwires of the former ghetto and told her to go to the old woman. I wished her that she would not encounter anybody on her way and arrive safely at her destination. When she went on her way, I returned to the collection work.

[Page 237]

When the evening arrived, I did not have anything to do in the former ghetto, but I was worried about the people who remained in the hideout. Schwartzwald told me that he had a Christian acquaintance in the village of Ponykovytza[6] and that he and his wife would take his cousin and her son there. Thus, I went in the barracks that night while Schwartzwald went back to the hideout to his wife and cousin. We never met again, and I do not know their fate.

There were three hundreds Jews in the barracks. Ukrainian policemen, holding automatic weapon, or a guard of German gendarmes stood at the gate at all times. The commander, Roog, was a ravenous murderer. He killed two or three Jews every morning with his small pistol. He used to get drunk and shoot at anybody he wanted to. In the meantime, I got a message that my wife arrived safely at the old Christian woman's house. However, the woman warned me not to join her because of her fear of being caught. She told me that it was much easier to hide a woman and told me to stay at the barracks as long as possible. I accepted my fate and was content with the fact that my wife was safe. I spent the following several days in the horrible barracks where victims were claimed daily. That continued until the arrival of Sturmführer Vartzug who came from Zolochov[6] accompanied by another SS officer. They ordered us to get out of our rooms and take with us our money and any belongings we had. The Sturmführer spread a blanket on the ground in the middle of the barracks' yard and ordered us to throw on it everything we owned. I complied with his order. Commander Roog and the German officer went back to our rooms to check whether anything was hidden. A few minutes later, they called out a name of a person, I do not recall. A Yeshiva student, whom I did not know, stepped forward immediately. A few dollars and a certificate were found in his bed. The officer drew his pistol and killed him on the spot. He said that this was how they would treat any Jew, who would dare to cheat the German Reich.

They ordered us to return to our rooms, however, it was clear that our situation had worsened. The guards at the gate would allow us until that day to step out to the kiosk to buy cigarettes. They forbade us from doing so at that point. There were only men at the barracks, and some hoped that they would employ us for some time. Some were indeed sent, under guard, to work in various places, cutting firewood for the gendarmes on Jurydyka Street and similar other jobs. However, when we saw that they brought Jewish women and children to the barracks we understood what they intended to do with us. The guard at the gate was reinforced and both the German and Ukrainian guards began carrying automatic weapons. They should not have had to worry about any resistance by the Jews, not only in the barracks, which were located in the middle of the city, but also from outside of the city, since the city and its environs were emptied of the last of its Jews. In general, there was also no chance for any successful resistance by the Jews in the periphery towns and the cities, especially armed resistance, and in anywhere else in the Western Ukraine. The main reason for this was the collaboration of the Ukrainian population with the German conquerors. They acted hand in hand. The Ukrainians were eager to murder their Jewish neighbors, as the Jewish property would fall into their hands.

Even the Poles, who hated the Ukrainians and even more so, the Germans, helped in the prosecution of the Jews. Here is one example, which happened during of the extermination actions in our city: a Yeshiva student by the name of Shraga, wanted to get out of the city, which was surrounded by Ukrainian police. A Ukrainian policeman, stopped him. What did Shraga do? With a quick motion, he managed to grab the policeman's rifle. A Pole jumped out of his apartment, at the same moment, hit Shraga on his head with a hoe and killed him. The Polish population assisted the Germans and the Ukrainians in battering the Jews every step of the way. In places where the Poles did stand with the Jews, the Germans failed in their prosecution. An illustration for that could be found in the village of Hochiska Brodska[6], where the Poles acted together with the Jews. The Germans did not dare to venture into the village, especially at night. The Germans were great heroes against an unarmed nation in its exile, particularly when they tricked it as they did in our city when they first killed the entire intelligentsia. In real battles, even in an uneven fight such as the Warsaw Ghetto uprising, Jews were much more heroic, and managed to claim many victims among their enemies and to destroy war machines.

[Page 238]

Indeed, Brody Jews fought in defensive and offensive battles in various places, in the forests and the fields, in groups and sometimes in couples. However, everything was finished after the extermination of the ghetto due to the assistance that the Ukrainians provided to the Germans. The brothers Drilikh, two youths with guts, collected around them a group of other youths. They dug a bunker in the forest where they had a machinegun. The Ukrainians, who were afraid to go to the forest by themselves, discovered them and reported them to the German authorities. The Germans surrounded the forest from all directions, and after a fierce battle, which lasted several hours, the Germans blew up the bunker and destroyed it. It was not easy to fight the Germans, the same way it was difficult to hide with the Christian population. First, anybody who hid a Jew risked being killed. Secondly, even if there were Christians who were willing to hide Jews, they would demand a small fortune for it. Many of them took the money, and after several days, they delivered the Jews to the Ukrainian gangs or police, or even killed them with their own hands.

This was how my brother Benyamin was murdered. A Christian who promised to hide him, took all the money from him, and later burnt my brother and his wife alive in a cowshed he hid them in. Christian villagers reported on my other brother, Yehuda-Tsvi, who was also called Hermann. They told the Germans that he was a politician who hated the Germans. He was arrested immediately and was brought over to the Gestapo headquarters on Lantski Street. I was told that no prisoner came back alive from there. My sister, Leah, and her three-year old son, Yehuda, lived in Ternopol. They had Aryan papers that a Christian acquaintance arranged for them. They stayed in the city during almost the entire war until one day when she encountered a Christian acquaintance from Brody who recognized her. Unfortunately for her, a Ukrainian policeman was just coming towards them. When he found out that they were Jewish, he killed them on the spot, first the child, and then the mother. Christian residents of Ternopol, who helped my sister without knowing that she was Jewish, told me the story after the war.

We now return to the barracks in our city, where the last of the city Jews stayed. One morning, the manager Roog, who did not have an apartment in the barracks, entered the barracks accompanied by the head of the police Daun, whom I have already described. Daun looked like Hitler, damn him, particularly because of his mustache. He said: "We will now witness what would be done with people who do not obey our orders". He then opened a small cell and ordered the people who occupied it to come out. A woman and a child came out. I did not know the woman, but saw her working in the barracks' kitchen. Following her, Gringraz and other Jews whom I did not know came out. A woman by the name of Zeidwarm, who used to live on Gnesia? Street, and her ten years old son, was among them. Her father was in the barracks with us. The manager started to list all of the offences of these men and women - this person wanted to sell a ring near the gate, that person tried to escape, that women hid her son and more. They placed them at the wall and shot them all. The gendarmes, with automatic guns, stood at the gate, ready to shoot the rest of us for any sign of resistance. The shots were executed in a certain order. First, the children were shot and then the mothers. Daun ordered to load the bodies (thirteen altogether) on a cart, which was transported to the former ghetto, where they put the cart and its content ablaze. That happened on a Saturday. The following day we realized, based on the behavior of the administration, that we all were facing extermination.

[Page 239]

We laid down to sleep at night, but sleeping was the farthest away from my mind. I came out to the yard, in which people were allowed to walk around until late at night. The gate was locked, and the guard was situated outside. I wandered around aimlessly. I reached the cellars of the barracks, and walked from one cellar to another. Brody people would certainly recall that when the war between Poland and Germany erupted, the Germans threw bombs at the city from their airplanes. One bomb hit the general hospital, one hit the house of Tsvi–Hersh Goldinshtein on Gold Street, one hit the house of Rabbi Davdili Manzon and another bomb hit the barracks. A U–bomb hit the other side of the barrack rather than the front, opposite the city park. The ruins of the bomb were still there and I noticed an opening through which I could see a streetlight that illuminated the alley. When I peeked, I noticed that I could stick my head through it. I stepped forward carefully, approached the opening, and listened to check whether there was anybody wandering around in the alley. Down the ally, it was less dangerous, first, because I was hidden by the ruins and secondly nobody would be walking around in a dead–end alley near empty cellars at night. I peeked again beyond the opening and realized that I could slip easily through it. I did not see anybody. I knew that the alley was leading to Dr. Horn's house. I did not hesitate much longer, took off the yellow patch off and slipped out without any problem. I went directly toward 3rd of May Street, where the old woman house was, and where my wife was staying. On my way, I encountered several German and Ukrainian policemen. I lighted a cigarette and thus hid my face as if to protect the lighted match from the wind, so that they could not see me eye to eye,. I used this trick several times until I arrived at the house. I hesitated to enter the Christian woman's house, since she hosted a student who ate at her table. I also knew that my wife does not stay in any of the rooms of the house but in one of the empty stores. The house had several entrances, which led to the stores. I stood near every entrance and whispered her name – “Bina!” How happy I was when I heard my wife's voice, opening the door. We closed the door behind us and exchanged our experiences during the previous few days. She told me that the old Christian woman treated her like a daughter. When she was alone, she closed the gate, called my wife up to her room, and fed her with anything she had. My wife called her “Babchu” and the old woman called my wife “my child”. We could not fall asleep after we told each other what happened. We thought about our fate. We also thought about how we would be able to overcome the difficulties that were lying ahead of us. I told myself, repeatedly, that we would survive the war and be fortunate to witness the fall of Hitler, damn him, something that every surviving Jew prayed for. We finally fell asleep. In the morning, the old woman came in and was happy to see me. She told me that I was fortunate to escape the barracks because she heard that the end of the camp was near.

[Page 240]

She brought us some food. We could see through the cracks of the old stores everything that was occurring in the street. We saw marching German soldiers and heard their singing – “hei–li, hei–li, hei–la, he–la”, and their anti–Semitic songs. The most frightening was the song “When Jewish blood is dripping over the sharp tip of the knife”. We had to hide and to listen to these songs quietly and helplessly. There was no shortage of scares. Searches were held, once and a while, with the excuse that Jews, ghetto escapees and refugees were hiding in homes of Christians. A Christian by the name of Shvalyuk, an owner of a sausage store, was murdered because he hid Jews in his house.

We stayed ten weeks with the Christian woman. However, a new problem developed–the trouble of the Banderovich Ukrainians. They got their name from their leader, Stephan Bandera, who murdered the Polish Minister of Interior, Pieracki and robbed a bank in Horodenka. He escaped to Germany before the war and hid there. (Editor's note: The author confuses Bandera's story here with that of his accomplice, Mykola Lebed. Bandera was in prison in Poland until the war started and was released by the Germans when they entered Poland. RM). When the war erupted, as Hitler armies advanced into Poland, Bandera organized all the Ukrainian criminals who stayed in Germany as a private militia. After the Germans promised him that they would declare Ukraine as an independent country, with him as its head when they conquer Western Ukraine, he organized Ukrainians not only in Germany, but outside as well, particularly in Western Ukraine, and urged them to resist and strike the Poles. Even before the Germans arrived, Bandera's voice could be heard daily on the German radio: "Beat the Jews and free Ukraine!" Indeed, the Banderovich gangs would attack Jews in the villages and Polish farmers in settlements built before the parceling of the nobles' estates. This was the situation in Western Ukraine even before the war, during the Polish regime, and definitely much more so during the war under the German occupation. That triggered a huge Polish flight from Western Ukraine.

The Banderoviches came to the old Polish woman who hid us, after they have inquired how many rooms she owned, and announced that some Poles would come to live with her. We were therefore happy to hear from the old woman, that she talked already with her daughter who lived in the village of Holoskovytza[6], who said that she was willing to hide us and had already started to prepare for it. We decided to move there, although it was not a simple matter. These were summer days and according to the war regulations, citizens could only be in the streets until six in the evening, meaning only when there was plenty of light outside. Many Christians knew us in the city, but we did not have any choice. One day, the old woman dressed my wife as a Christian with a kerchief on her head, and went with her outside of the city. From there, my wife walked alone to the village, to the house of the old woman's daughter. My wife knew where the daughter lived, as we visited her before. I stayed with the old woman for several more days, and was almost discovered. They came to look for hiding Jews, but I miraculously hid under in the attic under the roof shingles, and the searchers did not notice me. Because these were the harvest days, I told the woman to buy me a new sickle and this was what she did. I left Brody and went to the village where my wife was, camouflaged by my wild–growing facial hair and with the sickle, which I carried on my back the way farmers did when they were walking home from the city. Deep troubles began immediately upon my arrival, troubles that continued all the way to the liberation.

[Page 241]

I made my way to the village at night. I came to the house of the young Christian woman, and she brought me to the closet where my wife was and where she prepared the hideout for us. She placed a crate by the wooden wall of a closet, about eighty centimeters high and fifty centimeters wide. On the crate, there was a barrel, above which, she piled up hay, several meter high and wide. Inside the hay, she created a three–meter crawl tunnel, which we had to crawl through to reach the barrel, and the crate in which we stayed. If one of sat in the crate, the other would have had to lie down in the barrel. The crawl–tunnel was plugged with a hay sheaf so air could only penetrate through the cracks in the wall near us. It was not easy to find the wall, as we were surrounded by several meters of hay. During the nights, we were able to get out of our hole and lay down on the hay. The Christian woman handed us food after she removed the hay sheaf. According to an agreed–upon sign, “pss,” I would crawl out of the hideout and take the food that she wrapped with a kerchief. To say that these were difficult conditions was an understatement. However, we were content with staying like that to the end of the war. However, this was not to be. The Christian women sustained us for about two and half months. She kept saying that her husband does not know about us, but we knew that he knew very well. Until one day, when she told us, that we would need to look for another place to hide, because she was scared of her husband, and because she needed the hay to feed the animals. I begged her to allow us to stay a few more days so that I could try to find another shelter. I knew that this would not be an easy job, since only Ukrainians lived in the village. The few Poles who lived there were afraid to behave differently than their neighbors, and at the end of the day, they were not “lovers of the people of Israel” either.

The few days passed quickly before we were forced to leave this hideout. Fall's chill was already in the air, especially at night. We went to the fields and hid in a canvas field. The farmers made canvas out of this crop. This was a dangerous place, since the gentiles who were working in the fields could have discover us. We also had to endure the rain and the cold. Before we left, the Christian woman offered us to come to her house once every two days. We would come in the evening, and she served us food, and gave us some cooked potatoes and bread to take with us. We dared to go to her at night, even when she did not know about it. We were wandering around in the fields until the harvest. When the canvas, millet and corn were harvested and the clean–up completed, we did not have a place to hide. The fall began to turn into winter, and our worries about our fate, depressed us tremendously.

In the meantime, the Christian woman, who hid us in her barn, told us that her mother visited her and told her to warn us not to return to Brody, since all the Jews who stayed in the barracks were all taken to the cemetery and were murdered there. She said that eyewitnesses told her that some of the Jews who were led to the cemetery still had some money, which they kept illegally. When they realized that their end was near, they took out the money bills, tore them up and threw the pieces in the faces of the Ukrainian policemen. One woman, the wife of Hertz Bukhbinder (the owner of the shoe store), stood up and yelled in a loud voice that was heard throughout the city streets: "You murderers, the world will take revenge of you, Hitlerian animals and Ukrainian slaughterers. The Russians will take revenge of our blood that you have spilled for no reason". The policemen remained silent and did not respond.

[Page 242]

We knew then, that we could not go back to the city. We decided to find a hideout in the village, no matter what happened. We decided to contact a young Christian, about twenty–five years old, whom I knew as somebody who hated the Germans and the Banderoviches because he was a Communist. He was the cousin of the Christian woman's husband who hid us previously. His name was Harycz Mowczan. I waited for him, one night, in his the yard. He greeted me cordially and said: "Khayim, you did well by contacting me. I heard from my (female) cousin that you were somewhere in the village, and now that you have contacted me I would help you as much as I could." The first thing I asked him to do was to secure a gun and a hundred rounds of ammunition for me. He did it during the same night. He told me to bring my wife immediately. When we arrived, he brought us to his hay attic above the cowshed. He did this without the knowledge of his mother. He was orphaned from his father and had a fifteen years old brother by the name of Alexander, and even a younger sister by the name of Olga. Harycz told us that we do not need to be warry about his brother, and his sister was too young to understand, but he was afraid of his mother, who was very frightened. Therefore, we stayed in the cowshed attic. Harycz brought us some food, although very little, because he himself was poor, and his family had hardly anything to eat. He would take me, in the evenings, to various places to forage for food. We searched and found some food in stables of other farmers. Sometimes we would find some flour and even chickens, which he would cook and bring to us. His younger brother would burn woods in the field to make charcoals and would bring them to us for our use. We could then cook in the attic, so that we would not need to contact other farmers to get food. Doing so would have meant an immediate danger from the hands of the Bandroviches who were ambushing Jews and shooting them.

We were told that there were two million Ukrainians, armed with all sorts of weapons, which they prepared for themselves upon Poland's defeat, before the Russians invaded Western Ukraine. Indeed, we saw tens of carts and horses being loaded from boxcars with all sort weapons. Harycz told us that the Banderoviches used to appear at night by the farms and take horses and carts as they pleased. In some cases, the farmers themselves were forced to go wherever there were ordered to. Sometimes, a trip would last three or four days. We also heard how they have bombed transports with German soldiers or their arms. They smeared the rail tracks between Brody and Zabolottze[6] with soap and shot at the cargo train loaded with German soldiers traveling to the front. The Banderoviches did that because the Germans broke their promise to help them establish an independent state when they invaded Western Ukraine. After the invasion, they told Bandera that there was no use in establishing the independent state as long as the war was still going on. They told him that Hitler would establish it only after the war. Stephan Bandera did not like that, so he and his followers went underground. Their moto became: "We hit the Germans, annihilate the Jews, prevent the Red army from invading and establish an independent Ukraine". Indeed, they killed not only Jews, but also Germans and Russian partisans whom they encountered in the forests.

In the meantime, another Ukrainian nationalist by the name of Bulba agreed to collaborate with the Germans. He agreed to wait until the end of the war to establish an independent Ukraine. Bulba was a native of Volhyn, and his followers–the Bulbaches joined the ranks of the German army and fought shoulder to shoulder with the German soldiers them against the army of the Soviet Union.

[Page 243]

Their unit was named the S.S. Halichina. It included many Ukrainians, natives of Galitzia, not only from Vohlyn. Among the German soldiers, many other Russian soldiers deserted to fight against the Soviet Union. They were named Vlasoviches after their commander, Vlasov. These soldiers included former Don Kazakhs, as well some Georgians, who probably ran away from the Red Army. There were also Soviet soldiers who were taken prisoners of war, but did not want to die from hunger, like the rest of the Russian prisoners of war. I saw this with my own eyes when such a Russian soldier, who served in the German army, helped me, knowing well that I was Jewish. This was proof that not all of these soldiers were loyal to the Germans. However, the Vlasoviches were worse than the Germans.

More and more rumors began to spread about defeats by the Germans, but we were still far away from salvation. In the meantime, we stayed with Harycz, who treated me like his own father. He had consoled us that we would live to see the end of the war and that our life would improve. When we asked him how we would pay back for his dedication and effort, he would answer that his reward would be seeing us alive and well with these horrific days behind us. We stayed with him for eight months. Nobody besides his brother and sister knew about us. However, the peaceful stay did not last much longer. Harycz himself was very poor, and had hardly enough for his family, especially before the harvest. We, therefore, were going to nearby villages to look for food. At one time, we went to the village of Hlushyn[6] and entered the barn of a "Volk-Deutsch" (Christians whose ethnic background and name were German. These people enjoyed some privileges, despite the fact that they spoke Polish or Ukrainian. They "proved" their Germanism by prosecuting the Jews). I stood on guard outside, with the pistol in my hand, and Harycz began to bring out things from the barn. At first, he brought a fur and told me that I would be able to cover myself with that fur in the winter. Then, he carried out a sack of flour, and later on, a few other minor items. We then realized that the objects would be too heavy to carry, since we had three kilometers to go back to Harycz's village. Harycz did not hesitate for long. He asked me to wait a minute for him, went into the barn and brought a horse out. We placed the items we took on the horse's back. Harycz also found a hunting rifle, which he also took, the kind one use to hunt in the fields. We blocked the gate to the yard of the farmer's house, so that we would be able to know if anybody would hear us. We went on our way back toward Holoskovytza[6] village. When we approach the village, we heard some gunshots from the direction we came from. We unloaded the horse, freed it and spurred it to go back to his barn. We left all the objects on the ground, and started to hurry. Nobody noticed us, so Harycz suggested that we bring the objects to a neighboring farm and hide them in the barn, and come the following day to fetch them. We covered the objects with hay, however we took with us the fur and one chicken. Since we could not get hold of a kosher butcher, we ate from Harycz butchered chicken. We went up to the Hirka (attic), talked a bit and fell asleep. The following day, their Sabbath, Harycz went out to the street and came back to say that we should calm down, because he did not hear anybody talking about this matter. We fetched the objects, brought them over, and camouflaged them with hay, so that Harycz's mom would not find them. Among the items, we had a pack of fine tobacco leaves (Virginia). We untied the drying tobacco leaves bunch from the strings tied by "Volk–Deutch". They were dry enough. We covered them with hay as well.

[Page 244]

On Monday morning, Harycz went out to the village and all of a sudden, I heard Germans shouting in the yard. I peeked through a small crack in the hay roof and saw the head of the German police from Brody accompanied by a farmer, whom I understood to be the "Volk–Deutch" whose farm we visited two days ago, and a German soldier. The head of the police had an automatic rifle with him. The other two were equipped with regular rifles. Harycz's mother was very frightful. She came down running with her two younger children. The "Volk–Deutch" yelled at her: "Where is my tobacco and all other things, that you son stole from me", and slapped her in the face. When I realized how big of a trouble this was, I did not hesitate for long. I enlarged the hole in the other side of the roof and jumped to Harycz neighbor's garden. I told my wife to hold on to the wooden frame of the roof, and held her so that she would be able to come down too. We ran into the gardens that were stretched behind the farmers' houses. Our luck was that the policemen were too busy with the tobacco leaves they found hidden under the hay and the fact that we were not seen by any other farmer (according to what Harycz had told me later). We ran into the fields and saw that several tens of farmers run after us. We even heard somebody calling me by my first name: "Khayim, Khayim". I got scared and started to run even faster, until I lost my wife behind me. When I got tired of running in the wet fields and the swamps, I saw myself near the village of Ponykovytsya. I was afraid to return and farmers who went by me looked at me puzzled and asked where I came from. I told them that I ran away from Germany, where I was send under Germans' order. As many Ukrainians used to run away from there, and because I spoke fluent Ukrainian, they believed me, welcomed me in and fed me. I could not stay long there as there were people who knew me to be Jewish in that neighborhood. I remembered that, in that village, there was a Christian by the name of Miro Omluk, native of Holoskovytza[6], who married a woman from Ponykovytsya and I knew him as a decent guy. I went to him in the evening and told him my story. He welcomed my nicely. I asked him to go to Holoskovytza[6], and let me know what happened to my wife. He promised to do so the following day, as he was busy until very late at night. In the meantime, he brought me up to his hay attic and gave me a loaf of bread. The following day he went to the other village. When he came back, at eight o'clock at night, he told me what happened during the last thirty–six hours since I separated from my wife.

He found Harycz, who told him that he entered his yard innocently unaware of the fact that the Germans were looking for the stolen objects. A German saw him and pulled him into the house under his gun. The German began to question him whether he was the owner of the house. When he acknowledged, the German proceeded to arrest him, because traces of flour were found in his house and because the village farmers testified that all the evidence was pointing to Harycz. In addition, they found the tobacco in his house, and therefore found no reason to continue with their investigation. Harycz resigned to his fate and agreed with the investigator, however he asked to be fed, before they transferred him to the gendarmerie in Brody. The German sat with him in the yard, while the other two were busy with folding the tobacco, which was like a fortune to them and its being missing was strongly felt.

[Page 245]

Harycz took the food, jumped like a cat, and began to run with full speed away from the yard. When the villagers asked him why he was running so fast, he told them that the Germans were in the village and that they were kidnapping anybody they encountered for force labor in Germany. The villagers began to run into the fields. This was probably when I saw them, heard Harycz calling my name being called, and thought that they were running after me to capture me.

As he was running, Harycz met my wife, just as the villagers tried to rob her of her watch. Harycz stopped them from doing so by saying that when it comes to this watch, he should be the one to get it. Since he gave up on it, they should do the same. Harycz did not go back to the village that night, because of his fear of the Germans. However, he did protect my wife so that she would not get hurt. People ridiculed him as a friend of the Jews and even wanted to beat him because of that, but he was not a coward. He kept a long stick under his coat and warned everybody to stay away from him if they did not want to be shot to death. He fought with these villagers until the evening. He then brought my wife to Mirko's brother and told him everything. They brought her up to the hay attic and provided her with some food. They locked the door with a chain from outside. Harycz feared going back to his own farm, either to stay or the fetch anything. His main fear was that the Germans would capture and jail him because he ran away from them under their noses.

Based on Mirko Omluk's report, I went back to Holoskovytza to meet with my wife. Mirko could not transport me because he had some family business to attend. I had to walk back to the village through the fields. This was not an easy thing to do, since, at night, the Banderovich gangs were moving around on the roads and transporting weapons from village to village. Because the Germans did not wander around in the countryside, the Ukrainians could move easily. They had connections in every village and were also sending spies to investigate whether the road was available to transport weapons. That was the reason why I could not use the paved roads, and had to move stealthily through the fields until I got close to the village. I leaped over the stream, and found myself quickly behind Harycz's house. He happened to be to be in his yard at the time. When he saw me, he walked me to the yard where he hid my wife and opened the cowshed's locked door. My wife came down from the hay attic upon hearing the agreed upon sign, "pss". When they saw me, she and Harycz started to probe me where I was and what happened to me. However, I was weak and exhausted from my last few days' adventures and my hunger, to the point that I got confused and lost consciousness. I fainted and fell on the floor. When I came around, I thought that somebody just hit me on the head and was proceeding to obstruct my mouth and choke me. I was sure that the Bandoroviches captured me. I quickly put my hand in my pocket and drew the pistol in order to protect myself. At that moment, I heard the voice of Harycz, who pulled the pistol forcefully from my hand as if to say: "This is very nice of you. We were trying our best to rescue you, and you want to kill us". Only then, I saw that Harycz and my wife were standing over me, she was holding a bottle and he a spoon. He stuck the spoon in my mouth to allow some air into it and my breath recovered. They told me that they had to open my mouth forcibly when I fainted, and pour some of the vinegar that the farmer had around, to cause me to regain consciousness. We asked the farmer who hosted my wife for the last four days to house us both for another night so that we could find another hideout and he agreed to our request.

[Page 246]

German policemen came to Harycz's house to arrest him. However, he slept in his friend's house, rather than his house. When he heard about the search, he decided to hide in the city of Brody. The villagers did not like him and he feared that they would extradite him to his pursuers. His fear was justified because the villagers did not consider him a Ukrainian nationalist, and because he kept claiming that the Red army would retaliate against all of the German collaborators when it would take over. People said about him that he was a communist, and they hated communists as much as they hated Jews. Therefore, Harycz ran away to his relatives in Brody, and was coming once in a while to the village to inquire about his family and about my wife and me. He told us that we could stay in his house, because he was hiding in Brody, and therefore the Germans would not look for him in his house. He asked his mother to support us, to the best of her ability. We accepted his offer and stayed in his house. He would come, from time to time at night to visit us, and then went back to the city. The Ukrainians, who followed him, reported about his hideout in Brody to the Germans who went there at night and arrested him. The Germans made him an offer. They told him that he committed several offenses punishable by death or life sentence. However, if he would agree to travel to France as a German soldier and fight against the English, they would dismiss all charges. He agreed and left for France from Brody's train station.

The Germans' elation did not last long, because Harycz came back to see me three days later. He told me that when they transported him through Lvov[6], he jumped from the moving train and arrived home from there. He advised us to leave his house, as the Germans would now look for him. However, he planned to leave his home and go to his friends in the village. He stated that he would be more careful that time and would not wander around during the day any longer to avoid being seen by the villagers. We, on the other hand, did not have anybody to ask for a shelter. I decided to hide in the haystacks of other farmers without their knowledge. I had to secure food though, by any means possible. Some farmers agreed to provide us with food willingly, as long as we would leave their house immediately, as they were scared of the Germans as well as of the organized gangs of the Ukrainian nationalists.

We settled in a hay attic in a cowshed owned by a farmer named Josef Gilvuch, a Pole, not a bad man, whom I knew well. I did not want to tell him that we stay in his attic, as he would probably be scared to keep us on his farm. However, it was clear to me that if he would find us, he would tell us to leave his place, at the most, but would not cause us any harm. At nights, when the work at the cowshed ended, I would make sure that nobody was in the yard, and then jumped out of the attic and go to other farms to look for food. It was the winter of 1944, and we stayed in this attic for ten whole weeks without anybody knowing. Our lack was that the farmer did not need to use the hay from where we stayed, as he used hay from another barn, so that we could just stay without being disturbed. However, one morning, we saw soldiers with German uniforms in the farmer's yard. These were Vlasov soldiers. As mentioned above, these soldiers deserted the Soviet army to serve with Hitler's army. They brought their horses to the farmer, who was a blacksmith, for re–shoeing. Some of the Vlasov soldiers settled in the farmer's home, and held their horses in the cowshed. We listened to all of their conversations, as we understood both Russian and Ukrainian. We heard them cursing the Jews. We realized that we would need to leave this worthy hideout, for the fear that one of these guests would come up to the attic to fetch hay for his horses, and thus would find that and us would be our end. We waited until the evening, as it was impossible to get out during the day without risking our lives.

[Page 247]

We sneaked out at dark, and went down from the attic, without knowing what to do. I recalled the Christian woman who told me once that I could seek her help again, when in trouble. We came to her house and entered the cowshed. I saw several Germans walking around in the yard, and therefore waited for her outside. When she came out of her house and saw me, she was horrified and told me that German soldiers were staying in her house permanently. I calmed her down by saying that my Jewishness was not engraved on my forehead and it was doubtful that a German would expect to find Jews wandering around in that village anyway. I asked her to allow us to stay for one night only and we would continue on our way the next day. She agreed because her heart would not let her throw us out in such a cold night that it was. She ordered us to climb up to the hay attic, and promised to bring us some food shortly. She only requested us not to show ourselves to her husband and children. Shortly thereafter, she brought us a hot apple bowl and a bottle of milk. After we revived our soul with the food, we fell asleep immediately. We woke up at dawn by thunderous sounds of firing cannons. These were the cannons of the advancing Red Army. All the farmers hid in their cellars, but our farmer was sitting in the cowshed on a wooden box. He was old and deaf. I peeked at him and saw him sitting and dowsing off. He would wake up a bit after every round, but would dowse off again afterwards.

At eleven o'clock in the morning, the cannons fell silent. We became hungry again, and the Christian woman brought us a kettle full of buckwheat and meat. She told her son–in–law, named Simko Kshonertztik about us. He knew us from before the war and he sent us the food. He scooped a kettle–full from a big pot of the kitchen of the German soldiers staying in his home and sent it to us. She also told us that at that point of time, as the German defeat was nearing, and the Red Army arriving soon, we would be able to stay by her for a few more days. We obviously agreed and settled down. However, the roar of the cannons stopped completely, and we understood that the German army advanced again. The Christian woman came and told us that she feared that the Germans would find us when they would come up to fetch hay for their horses. Her son–in–law came and brought us food. He also gave me another clean white shirt when he saw my torn one. We parted ways, thanking him for his kindness. I was clueless as to where we can go as there was nobody left whom I could ask for a refuge. I thought about going with another solution. I thought that we would go to other villages, and pretend to be Ukrainians. Since I spoke their language fluently, perhaps we would be successful. I hoped that, in the meantime, the end of the war would come and we would be freed. We knew that the Red Army was near, stationed somewhere between Kiev and Brody, but we were not sure exactly where things stand.

[Page 248]

We left the village, just after waking up. We moved through a field and a meadow, passed the village of Vysotzky[6], and arrived at a settlement, which was formally inhabited by Poles who abandoned it. Ukrainians who came from the area of Vyshnivchyk[6] settled in it in their place. This was attractive to us. Vyshnivchyk was near Lvov, far enough from Brody, so I was sure that none of the settlers knew me, something we lack in villages near Brody, where many of the villagers knew me. We decided to stop by one of these settlers' home. I asked my wife to cover her head and her mouth with a kerchief, and not to speak a word, since her Ukrainian was not fluent, and any Ukrainian listener would identify her immediately. I entered the house and told the farmer that my wife had a toothache and that she was very weak. I told him that we would just like to rest for a while. The farmer accepted us warmly and asked where we were from. We responded that we were from the village of Holoskovytza, into which the Russians penetrated and burnt my house and farm. I told him that we had relatives in the Czech village of Zabolottze and added that we intend to celebrate the coming Easter with them. The farmer offered to host us for the night and we immediately agreed. My wife did not talk, only held her hand on her mouth as a sign for her severe aching. As my hair grew wild, the farmer offered me to cut my hair, as it was customary among the peasants to cut each other's hair. I agreed for him to cut my beard but not my mustache, which I wore to camouflage my look as a peasant. I hoped that none of my acquaintances from the before the war would recognize me with my mustache. When we arrived near the Czech village (called by that name after the Czech farmers who settled there during the days of Maria Theresa and Josef the 2nd, and were assimilated among the Ukrainians). We did not want to enter the village during the day and set down to rest on the side of the road. All of a sudden, we saw two horse riders. When they approached, we realized that they were German soldiers (field gendarmes). Their badges consisted of a silvery moon– shaped badge hanged via a metal chain. When they passed, they saw us sitting down, but did not show any interest in us. However, after they passed by us, one of them turned his head back toward us. I told my wife that if they would come back to inquire, it would be the end of us, because they had automatic rifles. I knew I could not defend myself, particularly when my wife was there as well. Luckily, they continued on their way, and we breathed a sigh of relief.

We decided to enter the village in the evening, but feared the return of the gendarmes, perhaps we would encounter them again and they would ask us who we are. Besides, a German soldier was standing guard at the entrance to the Czech village. He held a rifle on his shoulder and stood by a specially built guard booth. I asked my wife to walk in front of me without stopping. I did not wait for the guard to stop me but approached him first and asked him, in broken German imitating the talk of the local Ukrainians, for a cigarette. He gave me a few cigarettes and said: "Gai veiter, du Schwein" meaning "continue ahead, you pig". This was how they nicknamed the Ukrainians. That was how my wife and I entered the Czech village. I realized that it was too early to enter a Christian home, especially on a Sunday. We passed through the village and arrived at another small village called Chishky. We felt more comfortable there. I asked one peasant, wether we may be able to stay there at night and he advised me to see the Soltis, or the village chief (The Jews used to call him judge). At first, we really did not want to take his advice. We knew that the Soltis maintained contact with the Germans, who actually nominated all the Soltises during their conquest. The previous ones, who served under the Russians, were usually gotten rid of by the local population. However, we did go to the Soltis on the account that I pretended to be a Ukrainian and hoped that my Ukrainian would not give me in. I left my wife in the yard, went in and found the Soltis at home and told him the same story I used before. I told him that we were running away from the Russians, who burnt my house and my property and added that we do not have a roof above our heads. I reminded the Soltis that we were entitled to receive sleeping arrangements for several days as refugees. He agreed with me, however he claimed that, according to the law he must see our identification papers. I told him that that would be impossible because all of our papers were destroyed in the same fire. He insisted that would be not be possible for him to help us because he claimed that all sorts of Poles, and even Jews were wandering around asking to be sheltered. He claimed that there were still many of them around despite the fact that they have been prosecuted during the entire duration of the war. He claimed that he must report any Jew he encountered with to the German headquarters. He claimed that it does not mean that we could not find arrangement for sleeping in the village, but he himself did not have the authority to help anybody who does not have papers. He suggested that we contact the German headquarters, which was near his house, and they would be able, after an investigation, to order one of the peasants to let us sleep at this house. I thanked him for the advice and told him that I would do that immediately. We went out of his house to try our luck, obviously not in the German headquarters. At the edge of the village, we went into a farmer's yard. It was already getting dark when we entered the house. At the house, we found a Christian woman, about sixty years old, whom we told the same story. She took a pity on us and asked us to sit down and she served us some food. She said that her daughter and son–in–law were visiting with neighbors and should come back soon. She said she was convinced that they would certainly not banish us and would accept her offer to allow poor people to stay with them. We asked if we could sleep in the barn, as the cold was not that harsh and that we were very tired from the road. I told her that our underwear's were already filthy, so that we would not be able to sleep on clean beds. My reason for that was of course different. I always tried to avoid sleeping in an enclosed room and preferred to sleep outside, for security reason and to keep an eye on any visiting Germans.

[Page 249]

The old woman obliged and got us to the barn, we laid down, but before we fell asleep, I heard somebody opening the barn and calling: "Diadku, Diadku" (Uncle, uncle). This was how the locals called a stranger (same as in Yiddish, Fetter). I responded that we have already eaten, while holding the pistol in my pocket, as I did not who was calling. He identified himself and insisted that his mother-in-law told him that we had hardly had anything to eat, and therefore he prepared dinner for us. I thanked him and tried to tell him that whatever we had was enough, but he did not give up. I asked his permission to eat in the barn because my wife did not feel very well. I went with him and he gave me a bowl full of dumplings, which was considered one of the best meals, and some other food. I brought it over to the barn and we ate some of it. We left the rest for the morning. We stayed with them for two days when we decided to return to Holoskovytza, where I knew almost every farmer and every corner.

As we went on our way, we saw, from a distance, horse riding German guards passing by and had to hide repeatedly to avoid being detected. We arrived again at Vysotzky, and stopped by the farmer who hosted us previously for a few days. It was Easter evening, and he was surprised to see us as we told him that we were travelling to an aunt for Easter. We told him that we did not find the aunt at home, because she left for the holiday, to stay with her children who resided in Krasna[6] near Lvov. We had therefore to return. He gave us some provisions for the road and some of the baked goods that his wife made for the holiday. At the edge of the village, we entered another villager's house, and again told him about the fire etc... He offered us to stay with him for the night and we accepted the offer. As we realized that this was a very poor farmer, we gave him the baked food that we got and he enjoyed them tremendously. He told us that the Germans took, among other things, the crops that he harvested from his fields, and he and his family were always hungry. He was not able to feed us but agreed to host us at his house. We stayed only two days with him, because sleeping arrangements without a little bit of food, imposed hardship on us, especially in a village where we did not have any acquaintances and where it would have been difficult to get food by other means.

[Page 250]

We arrived back at Holoskovytza when it was still daylight. I found a haystack in the field, which I really did not know why it was left there. Perhaps, the owner was no longer alive. We rested inside the haystack only for a short while, as walking later at night was restricted because of the state of war. We entered the village where an army headquarters was newly established, and as we were told that, it was located in the house of the priest, Penchinski. The name sounded Polish, but the priest was a Ukrainian and an infamous Jew hater. He preached on their Sabbaths from the church pulpit, even before the war, that the Jews were communists and that they murdered the Christians' god. We not only had to pass near the priest's house where the army headquarters was staged, but all the villagers knew me. My luck was that my mustache was a good camouflage, as were my mixed clothing, and my fur bonnet with its brown hair pointing outside. Even my mother, who gave birth to me, would not have recognized me. We decided that my wife would bend down as if she was tying her shoelaces if I happened to greet one of the farmers whom I knew with the words – "Slava Bohu!" (Glory to God!) and by taking off my bonnet allowing me to hide my face. We did that until we arrived at a pre-agreed place. It worked as we planned. We entered the village and I saw a cart moving toward us, carrying a villager who was nationalist and a known Jews hater. I greeted him as we agreed and he did not even turn his head and continued on his way. We made our way on the side of the backyard gardens bypassing the main road, until we arrived at the house of a Christian woman whom I knew belonged to an evangelistic denomination. I decided to tell her who I am and ask her for help. She told me that she does not live in her own house anymore, and I should better contact her cousin whom we do not need to fear. I knew where his house was. It was destroyed during the recent shooting exchange between the Germans and the Red Army. However, the barn was still standing. It contained a cellar full of straw and hay. I understood that we would be able to hide there peacefully. We went in and indeed found the cellar. We prepared a hard surface and lay down to sleep. The cellar was covered with two wooden planks, which preserved the heat. Food was something else, as it was not possible to get out at night. The Germans stood guard everywhere because the front was advancing closer and closer. We moved to Harycz's hay attic for two nights. He himself was not sleeping in his own house. I remembered about the evangelist women at the edge of the village and went to her house, one evening. When she saw me, she asked me what our needs are. I asked her if we could stay with her for several days. She responded that she was willing to share the best of the best of food with us. However, she could not allow us to sleep or stay by her because she lived at the edge of the village and the Banderoviches were visiting her often. She said that they would kill us all if they saw us. I thought that her reasoning was logical and I thanked her. She even offered me to let her know where I am staying, and she would bring me the food there. I told her that I did not stay more than two days in one location and do not usually make orders for food. I told her that I would manage my food supply myself.

[Page 251]

We left and went back to where we came from. During the night, I heard several gunshots and then quiet returned. I really did not understand the meaning of the gunshots at the time. However, Harycz came to me in the morning and asked whether I heard what happened with Henke Khileve (this was the name of the Christian woman I asked the night before to sleep by her). He told me that she hosted several Jewish families in her house, since the extermination of the ghetto, among them, Dr. Preminger's family, the Lishner family, and several other families whom I did not know. She took all of their property, and when she realized that the war was not ending, she reported them to one of the Ukrainian gangs and its people murdered them all. When I told him that I visited her just the night before, he held his head with amazement and told me: “You need to be very careful not to lose your life by such twisted acts”. He reminded me and added that not all people were named Harycz.

We knew that two other Jews were hiding in the village, the cousin of my wife, Benyamin Margrovitz, and his son. On those summer evenings, I walked around in the fields, my pistol in my hand – this was what I was instructed by Harycz to do. He would say: "Be ready with your finger on the trigger. If anybody asked you who you were, you should shoot him immediately and you would be the winner. If they would find the body later, they would be convinced that the Germans killed him. If you would allow a Ukrainian to approach you, you would be the looser". When I was walking in the rye and wheat field, I saw a person leaving the trail and going down into the wheat field. I saw that this was not a figure of an adult, but of a youth, and I thought that he might have been Jewish. I started to talk in Ukrainian, and the boy stood up. I asked him if he was Benyamin's son and he acknowledged, all shook–up with fear: "Yes" he said. "I am Benyamin's son, Michael". The boy must have been about ten or eleven years old. I calmed him down and asked him to bring me to his father. He brought me to his father who was lying down in the rye field nearby. The father asked me to find him some food. I went back and called Harycz and together we went to a farmer's orchard that was bursting with apples and pears. However, when we arrived, we found the farmer. We told him to lay down with his face toward the ground. In order not to offend him too much, Harycz climbed on a tree in the orchard of the farmer's neighbor. He put most of the fruits in a sack and we left the place. However, Harycz insisted that he had another sack. He suggested to leave the filled–up sack where we were and go back to fill the second one. He told me to take one sack for myself and one sack for Margrovitz. By the time we came back, the farmer woke his neighbor up and they stood there together in their white outfits. We did not want to fight with them, two on two, just for a few apples. However when we stood up, they thought that we were part of a gang of robbers and they started to run towards us. We allowed them to approach up to about ten meters from us. I saw that they do not intend to stop and shot above their heads. We then took the sack of apples and brought them to the Magrovitzs. We ordered them to run in the opposite direction from the one we came from. I went to my wife and Harycz went to his friend. My frightened wife asked me what happened and I told her that I really did not know. She told me that she thought that somebody was shooting at me. When things calmed down the next day, I told her the real story. Harycz told her that the villagers claimed that real robbers, apple thieves, robbed them and that they were idiots to run after them as they almost lost their own life for just a few apples. Since that day, I used to meet the Margarovizs, often, and help them as much as I could.

[Page 252]

We went back to the barn in which we stayed most of the time, as we were afraid to stay by Harycz's . One morning, a truck with two Germans entered the barn. They started to fix the broken truck. The tires had no air in them, and other parts were broken. They worked on the truck almost the entire day. We could not move, or even cough. We were afraid that someone would step on the plank that served as the cellar's cover. The Germans left with the truck in the evening, but came back the next day. This time they did not work for long. The night finally arrived and we heard gunshots more intense than we ever heard during the entire length of the war. We also saw streaks of rounds on the horizon, but did not know what kind of a machine gun created such streaks. During the following day, we heard that these were rounds of katyusha. The shells also hit Holoskovytza and the village of Boratyn (about three kilometers away) and burned rows of houses. We also heard some shots and hand grenades, and realized that the fighting was in the village itself. We were very surprised and frightened when we heard a rustling sound above us and saw that somebody was lifting the cover of the cellar. We saw a soldier with the uniform of the Red Army (wearing the sickle and the hammer badge) sticking his head through the opening. He asked who we were and we responded that we were Jews. He stroked out head and stated the village has been conquered. I did notice some nervousness in his voice and asked him about the size of the conquering force that entered the village. He said that the force included a military battalion and two tanks. I understood that this might not be sufficient and asked him to leave us where we were and not tell the villagers, as our life would not be safe if they would find about our stay in the village. He went and camouflaged the cellar cover like it was before. A few minutes later, he came back and brought us smoking tobacco and bread, and promised to come back in the evening.

At eleven o'clock in the morning, we heard the rumpling of gunshots, shouts and explosions. We even heard the Red soldier, who saw us two hours ago, yelling: “Fani, ya vash”, meaning, “Sirs, I am yours”, which meant that he was surrendering to the Germans. However, they shot and killed him. Perhaps he attempted to escape to our hideout and did not have the time to do so. He died about two hundred meters from our hideout. Later on, we heard that a Red Army company with two tanks, with that soldier among them penetrated the village. However, Brody city itself was not taken. The Russians intended to bypass the city and first conquest all the villages surrounding it. However, the Germans reinforced their forces and took back the village of Holoskovytza. In the ensuing battle, almost the entire Red Army company of soldiers was killed. Only a few survived in the nearby village of Ponykovytsya and managed to escape through the forests and join their headquarters, which was located just a few kilometers east of Brody.

The following night, The Red soldiers came back and attacked the village where we stayed. The Russians shot katyushas onto our village of Holoskovytza from the village of Vlakhy,[6] which was located thirteen kilometers away. We listened to the shootings until we fell asleep. We only left a small crack in the cover above the cellar to allow for some air, and to know what part of the day it was. During the night, I saw light and thought that it was already morning. However, when I lifted the cover, I realized that the whole barn was burning and it was about to collapse. I yelled at my wife to get out, and we jumped into the yard. We entered the house, which was already in ruins and thought about staying in it for a while to allow us the time to think what do. I saw a bucket and thought it contained water we could drink. However, it was full of old peals of potatoes instead.

[Page 253]

A truck was burning in the yard with bullets bursting out it. We left the yard immediately for the fear that cannon shells could hit us. While we were walking in the village in the dark, we entered the yard of a farmer I knew. A German soldier stood there holding a rifle. He hinted to us to be quiet. He probably thought that we were local villagers. He pointed at the house and ordered us to get in. The house was empty. I was not sure what he hinted to be quiet about, but I guessed that the Red Army soldiers were already in the village fighting the Germans. This turned out to be true.

The night approached and we had to think about a place to hide. At night, it was difficult to recognize two poor Jews walking around amid so many Ukrainians. It was not the case during the day. The Ukrainians were eager to get rid of any Jews among them, when they realized that the Russian were getting closer and closer. Remaining Jews among them could testify against them and verify the stories about their numerous gruesome crimes. However, we did not know what direction we should go and decided to go in the direction where I knew some farmers. That was a mistake. If we would have gone the other way, we might have broken ourselves a path through the front to the Red Army line, but since we went the other way, we encountered a German guard and heard him call: “Wer ist?” (Who is it?). I responded: “Tzivil” (A civilian), and we were allowed to continue in our way. Dawn was nearing. I entered the farm of another acquaintance from before the war, a person by the name of Dimitriu Savitzki, without knowing, what would be his response. When he arrived a few minutes later, I whispered his name and asked his permission to hide in his farm until the shooting stops. He agreed, but told me to block the door, because Banderoviches were staying by him, hiding from the cannon shells. If they would see me, they would kill me. We did what he suggested as the dawn was already breaking. We blocked the door with a rod that he fetched and settled in the corner of the stable. Around ten o'clock in the morning, we heard knocking on the wall. We did not open. We heard somebody opening the door to the adjacent stable. There was just a person–tall partition between the two stables. We saw two figures dressed with officer ranked German uniforms on the other side of the partition. They were actually Vlasoviches . When they saw me, they gave me an order in Russian: “Otkroy” (Open). I opened the partition and they said to me, again in Russian: “Davai loshadi” (give us the horses). I responded: “Biri” (take). At that moment, Savitzki arrived. When he saw me standing with these two soldiers he panicked, not so much because of the horses, but because of us. He knew that if they find out, who we were, they would not only kill us but him too. However, to calm things down, I told him in Ukrainian (and I used a low voice): “These officers just want to take the horses”. He breathed a sigh of relief, however, he tried to convince them not to take his horses. They responded that they must have the horses, however, if he wanted, he could go with them, and they would give him two of their exhausted horses, which was the reason they had to replace them. Dimitriu understood that this would be better option than not having anything and he went with them. A short while later, he came back home with two other horses.

That brought new troubles. We blocked again the stable door and sat down, cuddled in the corner without asking Dimitriu's permission. The neighbors began to enter the stable to check on the type of horses the Germans gave Savitzki. When they saw us, we covered ourselves above our heads and pretended to sleep. They asked Dimitriu who he was sheltering in his stable. We heard him responding that we were poor people, residents of the neighboring village, whose house was burnt from all the shooting.

[Page 254]

He said that his family were good Christians and that they could not refuse to such a request. He repeated this response for the difficult questions neighbors kept asking him, until the night fell. At night, he brought us something to eat and told me: “Khayim, you would need to vacate the place. My brother is an enthusiastic Banderovich. He would kill you if he found you. There was no doubt that the Germans would do the same”. He was right, of course. I promised him to leave his farm at night. At nine o'clock at night, we left his farm to look for another hideout. We went to Savitzki's sister, whom I also knew. She welcomed us warmly but said that she was willing to feed us, but not to host us for the night. “Khayim”, she said, “I have children. They would kill us all because of you”. We had to continue to wander around grudgingly. In the meantime, a rumor was spreading among the villagers in Holoskovytza that my wife and I were burnt alive. The owner of the barn, Krawczuk spread the rumor. He saw his barn being burnt to the ground, when he left his farm, and he knew that we were hiding in it. This rumor spread among the people who knew us, and among people who were looking for us to kill us. As we found out later, that rumor actually acted in our favor, as people were not preoccupied with our fate after that.

When I realized that there was nobody else who would dare the hide us, I decided to go again to an elderly and God-fearing Christian woman, whose name was Palaishka, who lived alone. I wanted to get into her cowshed without her knowledge and hide there. We passed through several alleys, and arrived at her small yard in no time. I went to the cowshed and wanted to open its wooden door. However, I found it locked and thought that the old woman slept there. I pushed the door forcibly, took it off its hinges and fell, full length, down o the cowshed floor. When I stood up and returned the door onto its hinges, I heard somebody whispering. I approached and asked who was there. Mishka Margovitz , the son of my mother's cousin, whom I brought the apples to, responded. We were happy to see him. He was happy too, although he was very frightened initially. He stated that the old woman, Palaishka, was hosting and sustaining him. He also told me that when I moved from one side of the village to another, while we were staying with Stavtzki, the Russians conquered the quarter, he climbed over a truck left by the Germans and took several military blankets, shoes and other items and gave some of them to the old woman. However, when the Germans attacked again, Mishka abandoned the truck and instead of running away with the Russians, he stayed in the German controlled area. I asked him why he did that, and he responded that the Russians would return soon. The Russians indeed had eventually returned, however we met death, face-to-face, several times before they came. I asked Mishka about his father, Benyamin. He told me that a farmer once promised them a chicken so they went to the other side of the village to get it. They did that despite my warning to them not to do so, because the area was infested with the Banderoviches. The area was located near a small stream, which flowed through a meadow where the animals used to graze. The Banderoviches have been using the area to meet and communicate with other villages, and they held their underground meetings there. When the father and son where already on their way back from the farmer, holding the chicken in a sack, Mishka went ahead and his father followed him. They encountered several Banderoviches coming across from them. They passed the little boy and did not stop him because they thought that he was a small gentile boy. However, when they saw his father, with a sack on his back, they stopped him and started to talk to him. Based on his accent they understood that he was Jewish and that the boy walking ahead of him was Jewish as well. They went and brought the boy back and arrested both of them. They ordered them to sit down on the ground, with their face down, and with one leg attached to the other so that they could not talk to each other. They walked around with their pistols in their hands and one of them went to their commander to ask him what to do with the two. The messenger came back quickly holding two hoes in his hand and ordered them both to stand to walk, Mishka first, followed by his father. When they came to a small stream, they had to cross it over a plank. Mishka crossed the stream first. As soon as we was on the other side of the stream, he started to run away with all his might, through the grazing meadow. One murderer ran after him and managed to hold on to his coat. However, Mishka managed to jump into the stream. The Ukrainian murderer shot after him, but the boy stayed in the water without moving. His hand was only slightly hit by a round. The murderer thought that the boy was killed and did not want to get into the water to check. The boy heard his father's shouts when they killed him by hitting his head with a hoe. When the calm returned around him, he went back to the village and went into the house of a young Christian, by the name of Michael Yetzishin. The young Christian changed his clothes and hid him behind the stove. The elderly woman came in after two days and she put him in her cowshed, where all three of us got together. The elderly woman was very fond of the boy, because she had a goat that only ate from a Mishka's hand.

[Page 255]

Mishka feared that if the elderly woman would see my wife and me, she would refuse to host any of us. As the size of the cellar was no more than 1 meter by 1.2 meter, we decided to sit down there only during the days and enter the cowshed at night. As far as food was concerned, we managed by me going out on my own to find it. I received food from some Christians, and my wife visited other Christian acquaintances. Mishka continued to receive food from the old woman. We spent several weeks that way.

A couple of Catholic Greeks, also adopted by the old woman, were staying in her yard. We were acquaintances from before the war and they saw us. The man was about forty–five years old and his wife was younger than him. The wife kept telling the old woman that Jews were wandering around in her yard and that it was not a healthy situation. I did not have any other choice but discuss this with them. I decided to pay them a visit in the evening. I wanted to ask them what damage we were causing them by us putting down our poor heads at night when all other doors had been shut off for us. I wanted to tell them that the situation would be worsening as the day of liberation was approaching. Movement of citizens would become more difficult. If that would be the case for citizens who were gentiles, it would be more so for us. Although Mishka advised me not to see the Greek farmer, whose name was Vasil Pozir, because he was known to be a very difficult man. Despite Harycz's advice I put the pistol in my pocket and went to see the Greek farmer at eight o'clock that evening. I greeted him with the greeting – "Dobri vecher" ("good evening"), as he was my acquaintance from before the war. I thanked him for inviting me in and asked him whether I caused him any harm to him or his wife. He responded fearfully that he does not know from anything. I told him to make sure that it stayed that way. I told him that I do not want them to mention us to the old woman. I reminded him that we did not have much to lose. However, he did. He had kids and owned a farm and some wheat fields. All of these could easily go up in flames overnight. When he heard me saying these things he started to tremble as if he was struck by high fever. He asked me if we needed anything, and I answered that we really did not need anything. I told him that we have everything we need, and we were part of a huge network of partisans with tremendous power. The only thing we need was for people not to talk about us. His wife asked to be excused and I told her to wait until after I left and to enforce it, I held my hand in my pocket. She understood the hint and obeyed. I greeted them a friendly good night and left their room. Mishka and my wife waited for me impatiently, because they feared that the farmer would hurt me. When I told them that everything was fine, they calmed down.

[Page 256]

The situation worsened day by day. It was difficult to get out, because the movement of citizens after six o'clock in the evening was forbidden according to the war regulations. Horses and German tanks were stationed in every yard. Field kitchens were established in the yards to prepare food for the front line. The Red Army was positioned east of Brody, in the sundew fields. Every travel and movement was made difficult by the German guards. There was no choice but to wait. Mishka decided to tell the elderly woman that we were also staying with her, and that she would need to feed us as well. She agreed, particularly after we explained to her that the arrival of the Russians was imminent. However, the danger was still real. Germans and their horses were stationed in the other part of the cowshed. We saw them through the cracks in the wall planks. At times, when I saw that they were away, and only the horses were there, I crossed the partition and took some of the bread loafs they used to feed the horses with. These were square loafs, sometimes nice and fresh to eat, and sometimes moldy. Four horses were housed behind the wall. Among the Germans, wearing German uniforms was a Russian–speaking soldier. I heard him saying once, that the time for the end of the war had come. He continued to say that it the end would be the defeat of Hitler and his gangs. I understood that he was not really one of the Vlasov people, but rather a war prisoner who signed a declaration that he would be willing to serve in the German army. I understood from his talk that he was not loyal to the Germans and I decided to reveal myself, because we were close to death from hunger, with no salvation in sight. Mishka and my wife objected and claimed that he may report us to the Germans. However, I acted the same way I always did, I took a chance. One morning, I told Mishka and my wife to hide in the cellar and I went up by myself to the hay attic above the cowshed where I could view the cowshed and the German horses. Vanya, the Russian, was there by himself. I greeted him in Russian and asked him unexpectedly, who he was. In the beginning, I did not want to tell him that I am a Jew. I just told him that I am hiding from the Germans. I told him that he looks like an honest man and I was therefore asking him for help. He asked me what kind of help I needed. I told him that I only need one thing – food. He promised to bring me some food right away. He told me not to reveal myself to any other Russian speaking soldiers because nighty-nine percent of them where Vlasoviches. He told me that he happened not to be one, and I just found him by chance. The Russian went out and I returned to the hideout in the cellar. I told Mishka and my wife about the conversation with that soldier. They questioned me as to whether he may have gone out to call the Germans to kill me. I was certain that Vanya would not do that. Only a few minutes passed when we heard knocks on the wooden planks from the other side of the wall. I jumped out and he gave me a pale full of water and several loaves of bread, as well as some chocolate and German cigarettes. I wanted to hug and kiss him. At that point, I told him that we were Jewish, but I did not see any change in his face. He promised to help us as much as he could, and we did not suffer from hunger since then. He visited us every evening and spent hours with us. He told us that he was a Saratov native, and that he was captured as prisoner of war. The conditions in the prisoners' camp were so horrible that many prisoners died from hunger and their guards killed some more. As the Germans had already retreated and continued in their retreat, German officers came to them with an offer. Anybody who was willing to fight against the Red Army would be getting the same pay and rights of other German soldiers, and that they would not lack anything. Many prisoners, including Vanya himself, agreed to join the German army. Their job was to provide supplies to the front lines. He would go out every day for several hours, with two horses harnessed to a cart, bring the supplies and came back to the village. He would then clean the horses and feed them and was generally content with his situation. He told us that we just have to wait a short while longer for the Russians to liberate us.

[Page 257]

One day, Vanya stopped by to say goodbye. He told us to hide well as the Germans were retreating, and the Russians were expected to arrive, perhaps on the same day. We asked him why he would not stay with us to wait for the Russians and he responded that the Russians considered him a traitor. He feared that he would be would be sentenced to death after his case would be investigated and found to have served in the German army. He thought that it would be easier for him, after the war, the escape the entanglement he was in if he would go with the Germans. He said a hearty goodbye.

The whole day after that was quiet. No movement of any army could be seen or heard. However, the tumult returned in the evening, along with Vanya and his horses. He came to let us know, that the Germans succeeded in pushing the Russians back a few tens of kilometers, and they returned to their previous positions. Vanya was transporting supplies to the front lines again. The front was located near Brody. According to his information, the front line starched from the villages of Olvaki[6], Lypky[6], Vlakhy[6], Shchurovitza[6], Boratyn[6], Ponykva[6] and Sukhodoly[6], all of which were villages located between ten to fifteen kilometers away from Holoskovytza where we were hiding.

A short while later, Vanya came back to say goodbye. He said: “Bivaite zdaravai, mi odstogaim!” (meaning “Be healthy, we are leaving!”). The Russians initiated a major counterattack. Based on what he heard, they were not going to stop until they reach Berlin. Indeed, after the Germans left the village, we heard loud blasts of cannons, mortars and katyushas. Silence descended around one o'clock in the afternoon. We peeked through the cracks between the wooden planks and saw a group of about three hundreds disoriented Germans, walking slowly aimlessly, with their head down. They walked back and forth until they disappeared. Dead silence followed. Around three o'clock in the afternoon, we saw four Russian telephone experts, stretching telephone wires. I ran towards them and asked them whether the city of Brody has been conquered. One of them told me that it was, the night before.

I immediately called my wife and Mishka Margovitz. We said goodbye to the elderly woman and started to walk toward the city through the fields. The Russian soldiers, who passed us, yelled at us not to go through the fields because they might be mined. They said that we could step on a mine and get ourselves killed. They suggested that we had better walk on trails that passed through the fields, which somebody had already stepped on. We took the advice and walked on trails from Holoskovytza to Hlushin[6]. From there, there was a better road – an actual paved road leading to Brody, Zolochov[6] and Lvov. While we were on that road, the Germans began a new counterattack from their position in Zvelotcha[6]. Bombs rained down like a torrent. We, as well as the Russian soldiers, had to hide in ditches, which were abundant in the fields, during the entire length of the war. When we finally arrived to the Brody–Lvov[6] main road, the danger subsided. The road was packed with Russian soldiers. Some officers stopped and asked us why we were so pale and looking like walking dead. We told them that we were Jews. They advised us to stop by the headquarters in Brody and they would take care of us. When we entered the city, we could still not believe that we were finally liberated. The Russians fed us at the headquarters and then the N.K.V.D[5] interrogated us for several hours. They asked where we hid, and what happened to us during the German conquest.

[Page 258]

At the end of the day, they told us to return to the headquarters the next day. We worked there for several days. Tens of German war prisoners, as well as Russians in German uniforms were jailed there. Several days later, we were told that we were free to go and could start looking for an apartment.

We stayed in Brody for another year and a half. From Brody we moved to Poland, Germany and from there to Eretz Israel. This was a long but safe road. This was the fulfillment of a dream.

May these memories serve as a memorial to the Jews of Brody and their fate during the years 1941–1944. As all other Jews, they stretched their hands, during the villain murderous regime, asking for help from the world and they did not get it. They fell by the evil killers. Some tried to help themselves, as did the partisans. May our memories serve as a proof to the power of life and the love of life, which burnt in these victims until their last breath was choked. Because of them, we won the right to build a home in our homeland – the State of Israel.

Tzfat (Safed), 12 April, 1966.

Translator's Notes

1. The General Government, sometimes also called General was a territory in Poland (which included what is now Western Ukraine) carved out by the Nazis after they invaded, Poland. According to the agreement between Nazi Germany and the Soviet Union, Occupied Poland was split into three zones: the General Government in its center, Polish land annexed by the Nazis and Polish areas annexed by the Soviet Union.
2. The Third of May is a Polish National holiday to commemorate the establishment of the Constitution of May 3rd 1791, declaring Poland as a Constitutional Monarchy. Despite the fact that the constitution the official law of the land only for one year (until the Russian–Polish war of 1792), historians consider the Polish 1791 constitution as an important milestone in history of the Polish nation and of the world.
3. Yom Kippur – The Jewish Day of Atonement.
4. A declaration recited (written and read in Aramaic) before the services on the evening of Yom Kippur. The name of the declaration comes from its opening words – Kol Nidrei ("All my vows"). It states that all vows one undertakes on his own volition (not to others) are annulled, relinquished and abandoned.
5. N.K.V.D. – In Russian – Narodnyi Komissariat Vnutrennikh Del – People's Commissariat for Internal Affairs. The Soviet Union's ministry level law enforcement agency (predecessor of the KGB), which was responsible for the execution of the will of the ruling Communist Party. While it contains a regular police force of the Soviet Union, it was notorious for its activities in the Gulags, including mass execution, forced labors, mass deportations of entire nations and ethnic groups and other atrocities.
6. Current names and coordinates for villages and towns mentioned in the article:
   Boldury–possibly Bovdury 50°11' N 25°05' E
   Boratyn–49.995 N, 25.175 E
   Gaya Satrobrodskaya – Hai, 50°02' N 25°12' E
   Holoskovytza, Holoskovychi, 50.02 N, 25.08 E
   Hochiska Brodska, Gutsisko–Brodzke, 49°57' N 25°11' E (found using the JewishGen.org Gazetteer radius search)
   Hlushyn–50.033 N, 25.114 E
   Kosachyzna, Kosarshchyna, 50.05 N, 25.09 E
   Krasna, Krasne, 50°32' N 25°21' E

Lvov, Lviv, 49°50' N 24°00' E
Leshniov, Leshniv, 50°14' N 25°05' E
Lypky?
Radzikhov, Radekhiv, 50°17' N 24°39' E
Olvaky?
Ponykovitza, Ponykovytsya, 50.053 N, 25.049 E
Ponykva–49.980 N, 25.133 E
Shchurovitza, Shchurovichi, 50°16' N 25°02' E
Smolno, Smilne–50.08 N, 25.11 E
Sukhodoly–50.006 N, 25.108 E
Vlakhy?
Vyshnivchyk – 49°14' N 25°22' E
Vysotzky, Vysots'ko, 50.032 N, 25.031 E
Vyrov–a village by that name is relatively far from Boldury
Zabolottze, Zabolottzi, 50.04 N, 24.98 E
Zolochov, Zolochiv 49.82 N, 24.90 E

[Page 261]

Chapter Four:

Remembrances

A String of Memories

by Joseph Parvari (Leiner)

Translated by Moshe Kutten

Edited by Yocheved Klausner

I can visualize the city in which I was born and grew up. I was one and a half years old when World War I broke. My first memories are associated with the different armies that passed through the city: The Austro–Hungarian army, attacking Russia and then panicky retreating, the Cossacks, who were chasing after it, passing through the city like a storm, riding on their horses (this is also mentioned by Michael Sholokhov in his book "Quietly Flows the Don"). Austria returned, and then a year later, The Czar came back and later on, the Red Army. The Russian soldiers wore those red ribbons on their chests and they stuck red flowers in the barrels of their rifles. I can visualize the leaders of the Red Army standing on the terrace of the "Europa Hotel", in the corner of Lvov Street (Lemberger Gasse) giving speeches. Austria returned, and then left to make room for the Ukrainians. Then, a year and a half later, the Polish legions of General Joseph Haller came and attacked the Jews. There were soldiers who simply beat the Jews and robbed their property, and others who ripped the peahs (side locks) and beards of Jews with the flesh. People, whose hair and flesh were ripped–off, tied a white kerchief around their faces and looked as if they had a toothache. These soldiers took people who prayed on Sabbaths and holidays out of the synagogues, transported them outside of the city, and forced them to dig communication bunkers... As time passed, the Polish regime and its institutions stabilized, and their rule lasted about seventeen years.

In the meantime, I started to attend a "cheder" [Jewish Torah school for preschoolers[MK]]. At the beginning I studied with R' Uri Anstendig at the Shtibel [A Hasidic small praying and meeting house[MK]], which was part of the old synagogue in Brody. Later on, I attended the cheder of R' Noah Shapira (who was nicknamed "The Red") in the Beit Hamidrash [Jewish house of prayer and bible studies[MK]] of R' Yehuda Nathason on Shpitalna Street. The Rabbi's assistant used to bring us back home from the cheder. The "Shkutzim" [derogatory nickname given to the gentile children[MK]] would throw stones at us and attack us on the way home, and we would just run away from them.

When I was six years old, my father and mentor, may his memory be blessed, passed away. I stopped going to the cheder and enrolled in the Jewish elementary school. The language of studies in the school was Polish. The principal, the teachers and the students were all Jewish. The attractive two-story building was located on Korzeniowskiego Street. Boys and girls studied in separate classes. During my time, the school principal was Philip Ashkenazi, a nice old person sporting a white mustache. My first teacher was Mr. Arnold Moshtzisker, who initially continued to wear his Austrian army uniform. He instituted a strict military discipline with us. His pedagogic policy was based on punishment and beating (his two sons and my friends, Yolek and Tadzo, currently live in England, please forgive me).

[Page 262]

Among the other teachers, I remember our German teacher Mr. Yitzkahk Shpatz (we still studied German at that time), who sported a pointed beard and the students nicknamed him – "Shpitzberdchen" [pointed beard in Yiddish[MK]]. I also remember the old men Mr. Vogel, Mr. Faibin (Tovim), Mrs. Lemelman, Mr. Yitzhak Shkolnik with his hoarse voice, who was the music teacher and Mr. Nakhum Okser, the Bible teacher, who deserves a separate discussion as he was a unique figure. He was the head of the orphanage for many years. He also lived in the orphanage, which was located on 21 Goldhaber Street (also called

Leshnever Street). He taught in the elementary school in the morning hours, and dedicated the afternoon and evening hours to educating the orphans. Despite of his advanced age, he used to sit down with his students and teach them the Five Books of Moses personally. He began his day by reciting the prayer "Modeh–Ani"[1] with his pupils and then continued with the morning prayer (Shaharit), always allowing one of his pupils to serve as cantor. After a very modest breakfast (a piece of bread with jelly and a cup of tea), he would arrange the orphans in pairs and marched together with them to the elementary school. Upon their return, they would eat a meager lunch and sit down to work on their homework and to study the Torah with him. In the evenings, they prayed the afternoon and evening prayers (Minha and Maariv), ate a meager meal similar to the morning and lunch meals, recited the bedtime prayer Shma[2] and went to sleep.

In time, other teachers arrived – Shoenholtz, Klar, Harnik, Bernstein and Grinberg. All of them, like the former ones from before the war, were natives of the city of Zaleszczyki [Zaliztsi]. In time, three additional classes were added totaling seven grades. The Jewish community of the city maintained the school, the orphanage and the senior citizen house. I am not aware of any support by the Polish authorities of these institutions. They were all sustained by the contributions of the members of the Jewish community through the monthly membership fees.

I loved Mr. Okser and was happy to have been educated in the orphanage under his mentorship and management. I considered it to have been privileged to be among the pupils of this noble old man. I learned a great deal from him. He was not only a teacher but an excellent educator as well. He was an intelligent philosopher, with deep knowledge of Hebrew and universal literature. When I grew up and left the city, I corresponded with him in Hebrew, and was very proud to receive his letters with the heading "Ben Porat Yosef"[3].

I cried my heart out, after the war, when I heard about the bitter fate my teacher had encountered. Immediately upon arriving in Brody, The Nazis, damn them, went to Mr. Okser's house at the orphanage and found him sitting, as usual, with the orphans teaching them Torah. The Nazis, damn them, took the children outside of the city. Mr. Okser joined his pupils. They asked the teacher how old he was. He did not answer. They proceeded to ask him: "Do you have any teeth left, you old fool?" He smiled and they ordered him to open his mouth to show them. When he opened his mouth, they shot him in his face and stomach. He fell bleeding on the ground and died as a martyr.

I remember hearing about the Balfour Declaration and the rumors circulating concerning the British Mandate of Eretz Yisrael. I remembered the young Jewish men and women, who marched through the city streets with pride and joy. These were the first pioneers who organized themselves to immigrate to our old land. They were different from the simple city Jews, who were standing in their shops, six days a week, selling products not available in the village, to the neighboring villagers. They were also different from the Jewish craftsmen who were busy in their daily craft. They all looked young, erect and proud and they danced and sang.

[Page 263]

During that time, I have just completed four grades at the Jewish elementary school and transferred to the Polish school that had seven grades. That was where I encountered, for the first time, Polish and Ukrainian children. They and their teachers were Jew-haters. As an example, I could mention Mr. Vitvitzki, our arts, crafts and music teacher, who called us all "Yoyneh" [making fun of the Yiddish pronunciation of the biblical name Jonah[MK]]. Most of the students went to study a craft after the seventh grade. Some went to study carpentry, some printing, and the rest studied other crafts. I prepared myself for high school and was elated when I passed the tests and was accepted at the city's Gymnasium [High-School]. I have encountered the hatred of Jews, even there, by the students and professors, Poles and Ukrainians alike. Most of the Jewish youths were members of the Zionist youth organizations, like "Hashomer Hatzair", "Akhva" and "Brit Trumpeldor"[4]. The rules at the school forbade participation in such organizations, and students who joined them were harassed in school and some were expelled. The organizations conducted their activities at the community center on Goldhaber Street. This was where Jewish kids congregated and spent their evenings and Sabbaths. This was where they heard about Eretz Yisrael and where they studied Hebrew. This was also, where Hebrew songs were learned and sung aloud. This was where the pioneers left for their Hakhshara camps [preparation camps for pioneers immigrating to Eretz Yisrael[MK]], and where they left to immigrate to Eretz Yisarel from, starting from the Second Immigration [1904–1914[MK]] and on.

The Jewish organizations of "Hehalutz"[5], the "Union of Poalei Zion"[6], the management of "Keren Kayemet Le'Israel"[7], and "Ezra"[8] were all stationed in that house. The community house was the Zionist and cultural center of the city. The "Lector" library, which the teacher Naftali Lerner–Naor transferred upon his arrival to Brody from Boromel, Vohlyn, added another facet to the house. Lerner–Naor, who was accepted as a teacher in the Jewish elementary school, brought with him his vigor and eagerness to serve the public, but was not content with just that. He initiated Hebrew courses and established a cultural club, its circle of students growing continuously. He was also an active member of the Union of Poalei Zion and together with Dr. Mordekhai Weiss, Dr. Meles, Yitzkhak Shorr, the Singer brothers, David Hamermen, Shoshana Weizer and others helped in organizing "Eretz Israel Ha'Ovedet"[9] activities. Mr. Lerner immigrated to Eretz Israel and became the principle of a school in Safed where he was buried.

Anti–Semitism at school and in the streets pushed me to become a frequent visitor in that house. The union people mobilized me, my friend Yitzhak Etinger (who lives today in Rekhovot, Israel) and Pnina Hertzberg–Lanski (today a member of Kibutz Afikim, Israel) to organize a local chapter of "Gordonia"[10] organization, a pioneers youth union. Tens of youths joined us in no time and we have integrated our activity with other Zionist organizations. Initially, I wrote articles to the youth section of the "Khvila" newspaper[11] until we decided to issue a printed newspaper by the name of "the "Young Gordonian" in Polish. I was forced to publish my articles under a pseudonym to avoid being thrown out of high-school. I got in trouble anyway, because as part of a written test given by our literature teacher, Mrs. Klebosovna , I compared the life of the Jews in the diaspora to a ship in a cold and stormy sea, and related my wish to run away from it and immigrate to the land of the sun and freedom. The entire teaching staff, headed by the principal Kzhiznovski attacked me. Even the Jewish professors, Dr. Edmond Bernhaut and Dr. Mendel-Leib Chachkes joined them in threatening me. I was barely allowed to continue my studies. There was another incident at school. The sixth and seventh grades students of the school were required to perform, twice a week, exercises as part of Poland's military preparedness.

[Page 264]

The Polish corporals and officers used this opportunity to abuse the Jewish students. I would never forget the maneuver ordered by General Anders who was infamous in his hatred of Jews (He was initially captured by the Russians. When the German–Russian war broke, the Russians gave him the command of the free Polish army, but he left Russia during the battle of Stalingrad, and arrived in our old land through Iran. From there, he went to fight the Germans in Italy. Many of the Jews, who were recruited into his army after many obstacles, did not follow him and remained in Eretz Israel).

Well, one hot morning, we went out for a whole day exercise. The pretense was that the enemy was attacking our city, which lacked any army force to defend it. We were, presumably, the only force tasked with stopping the attackers until enforcements would arrive. The attacking force in this maneuver was the Polish Cavalry Battalion no. 22, which was also called Yazlobeichikh. After a long march, we took positions in in the swamps near the neighboring village of Berlin. The cavalry battalion that attacked us was aided by fire from the infantry. Our defeat was certain. At the end of the maneuver, General Anders appeared before us to analyze the whole operation. In his speech he emphasized that we could have stopped the enemy if not the “zhids”[12] among us who were the first to run away from the battlefield. At that moment I felt dizzy and fainted.

I left the high-school when I realized how desperate the situation in our city was, particularly in terms of employment. The gates to our old land were closed and one had to struggle in order to secure an immigration certificate. The boredom and despair raised havoc among the youth cadres, though one has to give them credit for their curiosity about the world events, literature, art and politics as well as for being devoted to sports. There were four soccer teams in the city: one team was Polish and was called – "Goiazde", another team was a Ukrainian called "Bohon", yet another one was Jewish and its name was – "Maccabi". The last one was an international team, which was called "Nafshod" (Forward), and was made of workers. I played in that team. In the 1930's, when the communist propaganda was very strong, the news and the literature about the new idyllic life in Russia, the socialistic build–up and the immense happiness of the people, lured many of us to join a front which was anti–Zionist . During those days, the communist party and the Komsomol[13] operated underground. However, a new radical–leftist Jewish party, "AYAP" (Algemeine Yiddish Arbeiter Partei – The General Jewish Workers Party) was established. Many members joined it from the ranks of Zionist movements of "Hehalutz" and "Hashomer Hatzair". These organizations were formally affiliated with the Zionist movement, however in actuality, they operated as part of the Communist underground. Many of the youths were caught and brought to trial, and there were some who were jailed and sent to a detention camp in Bereza Kartuska[14].

Our city seemed to be in a deep sleep. The Poles and the Ukrainians harassed the Jews and boycotted them economically and socially. The crises in all facets of life deepened gradually. Many of the Jews could not secure a job, the youths remained without employment and everything just deteriorated.

My own status in my house became unbearable. After the passing of my father, my mother, Rivka nee Weintraub (the sister of R' Benyamin Weintraub, a honest and God fearing Jew, who was an administrator–manager (called gabai in Hebrew) in Beit Midrash, was left with five daughters and me, the youngest child. My dear sisters worked to support the family and to allow me to continue my studies. My eldest sisters, Rakhel and Pnina, married and moved out of the house. They lived in the city of Lvov. The other three sisters, Sara, Tzila and Etka, were all members of the Zionist organization "Hehalutz" and dreamed about immigrating to Eretz Yisrael. Their aspiration was not fulfilled. Sara moved to Lvov to work in a kindergarten, Tzila worked in a store of a jewelry merchant, Mr. Izidor Ostrecher, and Etka was a seamstress. Tzila married David Katz and Etka married Shunyo Blaustein (Benzak).

[Page 265]

Since I was not able to continue with my studies, I became a private tutor for straggling students. I felt choked under this town's atmosphere, so I went to Krakow to study bookkeeping and even found a suitable job. I did not sever my connection with my native city and the following story is a testimony to that. The police searched the house of one of my girlfriends, Bela Adler, in Stary Brody and found my "revolutionary" letter. In this letter, I described the anger of the workers who in the summer of 1936 demonstrated against the Polish authorities in Lvov and Krakow. During that demonstration, the police opened fire and killed some of the demonstrators, among them our friend Reuven Petzsek. Following the search and the finding of my letters, my friends Bela Adler, Anshel Glass and Metzik Gruber were arrested, brought to trial and sentenced to long jail terms.

In Krakow, I participated in the editorial work of a Jewish children bi-weekly magazine, published in Polish – "Eshnav La'Olam" – "A Window to the World". I dedicated my first articles that appeared on "Mother's Day" to my mother and to my life in the orphanage of Brody, with an emphasis on the values of the educator Nakhum Okser, who was, in many aspects, likened to Janusz Korczak.

The German army invaded Poland on September 1st, 1939 and brought an end to my tranquil life in Krakow. The flame of war took hold throughout Poland. As the cruel enemy advanced, tens of thousands of Polish citizens, me included, began to escape eastward. I bought a bicycle in Tarnow and rode it all the way back to our town.

On the first day of the Jewish New Year, the sun shone like in any other nice summer day. Hundreds of residents walked down the street named after Ulanov Krykhivtzi[15], which was also called Zlota Street, and before that Goldgass (meaning – Golden Street). Polish Ministers, officers and generals who escaped Poland on the way to Romania, were sitting in cafes along the streets. The Germans got hold of this (as they had many spies), and a squadron of Messerschmitt airplanes showed up suddenly and bombed the entire length of the street from its western end all the way up to the Christian hospital near the embankments (Vali). The whole street became a stream of blood instantaneously. About two hundred people were killed in that aerial attack; most of them were Jewish youths and Poles. The officers jumped for their lives through the windows directly onto their waiting cars parked in the street.

A similar attack occurred during the following day – Shabbat Shuva[16]. The Germans hit ammunition boxcars that were parked in the train station. As a result, bullets and shells started to fly whistling in all directions. A firebomb, directed at the old synagogue hit Mr. Benyamin Kling's flourmill and it went up in flames. Many other houses, which were also bombed, burned and collapsed. The number of victims kept rising by the hour. The Jews were sitting fearfully and recited Psalms. The following day, Sunday 17th of September, after the last of the Polish soldiers escaped on their way to Romania, a deadly silence descended upon the city, accompanied by shooting sounds from the German guns approaching the city. A rumor was suddenly spread about the Red army coming to the help of Poland. The truth was known only later. The Soviet Russia did not come to save Poland, but to invade and divide it with the Germans according the Ribbentrop–Molotov agreement, which was signed a month earlier. According to that agreement, The Soviet Union seized the eastern part of Poland, until the rivers of Bug and San and the Hitler Germany took the western part. Poland disappeared from the European map on that day. After twenty years of an independent Polish regime, Brody, together with the entire Western Ukraine, became an inseparable part of the Soviet–Union.

[Page 266]

When the news about the imminent arrival of the Red Army became known, The Jews breathed a sigh of relief, not so – the Ukrainians. When the Red army delayed its arrival into the city, the Ukrainians tried to use the opportunity to inflict a holocaust upon the Jews. Anarchy was rampant in the city. The poor Poles, who lost their statehood, were depressed and apathetic. Only the Ukrainians raised their heads. However, a Jewish self–defense force was quickly established. The Jewish youths captured the police building and army barracks, took out most of the weapons and together with some communists established a temporary revolutionary committee. They rose to keep the order and guard the life of the city population.

A week later, on Sukkoth evening, the first units of the Red Army entered the city. They entered not necessarily through the victory gates prepared in their honor. In fact, by the time the Red Army entered the city, the fall rain had ruined most of the decorations, including the pictures of Stalin and Molotov. A new regime was established upon the arrival of the Red Army. The first announcements were posted in Russian, Ukrainian and Yiddish. They announced an emergency state in the city and a curfew, according to which it was forbidden to get out on the streets from the evening hours until the morning.

Silence descended upon the city. Everyone understood that the situation changed to such an extent that there was no force that could change it back. All the organizations and national parties dispersed or went underground. Hundreds of signs containing Polish or Jewish symbols disappeared. The shopkeepers sold whatever they have left of their merchandise, and closed their shops. Replacing these shops were the government–run shops, containing inferior merchandise. Long lines, tens of meters long, were stretched at their doors. By the time a customer reached the shop itself, there was nothing left in it. The shopkeepers knew how to deal in different ways, and the prices climbed up from one day to another.

During the fall of 1939, the first Soviet election to the national assembly in Lvov took place. The assembly decided to ask comrade Stalin to agree for Ukraine and western Belarus, which had just won their freedom from the cruel Polish imperialism, to join the Soviet Union. A short time later, Stalin was kind enough to offer his generous acceptance of this proposal.

Life, somehow, began to return to its normal routine. Many Jews occupied various positions in trade, economic and public institutions. Craftsmen organized under cooperative formats. Everything was nationalized – residential buildings, businesses, factories, banks, hotels and theaters. The farms of the landowners, all of whom managed to run away abroad, were divided among the peasants, who organized themselves in kolkhozes. All schools became governmental, and the languages of study became Ukrainian and Russian. The Jews continued to participate in public prayers at the synagogues, despite the fact that the Soviet law treated a gathering of more than three people as unlawful and counter-revolutionist. Wealthy Jews and Jews who were known to be unsympathetic and nationalistic were jailed or sent over to Siberia in the middle of the night.

[Page 267]

Brody became a typical Soviet city. Red flags were hoisted in its streets and pictures of Stalin, wearing a red uniform, were posted in most places. The citizens were sad, but the Jews rejoiced about the fact that the hand of the Nazi oppressor could not reach them.

Like many others, I began to work for the Soviets in constructing the highway between Kiev and Lvov. Later on, I worked as a comptroller in their governmental bank. In July 1940, I transferred to Lvov and from there to Tarnopol to serve as the head accountant of a trade business. In Pesach of 1941, I managed to come back to Brody to celebrate the Passover Seder with my family. It turned out to be the last time I managed to visit the city, as Hitler, damn him, attacked Russia on June 22nd and I could see in front of my eyes the tragedy from September 1939 – returning. German armored vehicles crossed the border and German airplanes bombed all of Ukraine and Belarus's cities. I was recruited into the Red Army on the same day, and spent an extremely long and torturous way with it, from the Russian border to Stalingrad and from there, through Romania, Hungary, and Czecho-slovakia all the way to Austria where I was lucky to see the end of the war on 9 May 1945.

During the big retreat in the summer of 1941, I met town people from Brody twice. One time I met with Natan Reinart (now in Poland), Asher (Dzonek) Richter (now lives in Petach Tiqva, Israel) and Professor Rosenstein (who died in Russia). The other time I met Arye (Leib) Hertzberg, Tzvi (Hersh) Polak (who now lives in Beer–Sheva, Israel) and Yosef Rogovski (who now lives in Poland). They told me about the horrible bombardments that took place in our city at the beginning of the war and the fierce battles in the city between the Germans and the Russians. I learned that the city, which changed hands several times, suffered tremendously and was mostly ruined. The Red Army liberated the city in July 1944, after it was on the front line for several months. I was in Romania then. Upon hearing about the liberation, I immediately sent a letter to the city government to ask whether anybody from my family survived. I received a response, a month later, which said that nobody from my family was known to survive.

After the war ended, I stayed in Hungary for several months, until my unit (I served as an officer in the Engineering Corps) returned to Russia. I was discharged from the army in Chernovitz. As a former Polish subject, I was allowed to return to Poland; however, I first wanted to see our city, Brody. I came for a few days visit in September. The following is what I wrote down in my journal about my findings.

Brody 13 September 1945

My hometown has been destroyed.....

My notes are dedicated to the memory of my relatives and all my beloved, who died as martyrs.

I left Tarnopol in the morning, on my way to Brody. In Krasny–Busk [Krasnosil'tzi[MK]] I changed the train to one going toward Moscow. The train speeds through small towns (Zkomazha, Ozhdov, Konty, Zablotze) without stopping. All of a sudden, the train stopped in Brody, but I did not know where I should get out. The station itself disappeared. I got off the train and watched the deserted and empty streets of the city as if on a map drawn on the palm of my hand. The streets looked like they have shrunk, or as if they were dying.

[Page 268]

Kolejowa Street (The Train Street) – I passed through it in five minutes. I perceived the street as being very long once. Here is the market (Rynek) – it is in ruins. I walk toward the street of my residence – Lvov Street (Lembergergas, called Mitzkevitz Street by the Poles) – ruins and empty lots covered by green weeds are everywhere. It is difficult for me to find our alley – Zameknita. My heart is crying: “Where is the street? Where is the house?” I do find the house based on some external marks. This is where it once stood, and it disappeared. Helpless, I leave the place.

I meet some farmers in the market, but the Jewish stores and stalls are all gone. I walk in the streets where my sisters once lived. Their apartments, like many others that survived, are empty. The farmers tell me that the Germans killed all the residents and their children during the aktzia's. This is the end. Only I survived. I am the only person in my family who is alive.

Goldhaber Street still exists, but the orphanage is gone. Old Mr. Okser was murdered like his pupils. When they took them, he went with them and was killed with them, exactly as he always used to say: "When the herd is lost, the shepherd would die too".

Brody became a cemetery, a ruined city. Like a remnant of a fort, the mighty walls of the old synagogue are still standing, surrounded by rubbish piles and bricks. These were once residential houses. Underneath these houses there were bunkers, which the Jews built and hid like mice. A barbed wire fence surrounded the area, with Ukrainian policemen who stood on guard. Along with the Gestapo men, they shot anybody who dared to show up. There was also the Judenrat, and corrupt Jewish–militia men, who were not that much better than the Germans. The people died in the streets from fear, typhus, Germans bullets and in the gas chambers of Belzec. There isn't any living soul left. A desolate desert was left behind. Oh my G–d in Heaven, alas, my eyes who have to see all that!

The city is dead. Its soul is gone, like the souls of the Jewish children, whom the Germans caught by their legs and smashed their heads with deadly force onto the telephone pole.

I want to run away from these ruins and from this cemetery, but I stay a while longer. Dr. Bogner, who survived along with his mother thanks to a good–hearted gentile who hid them both, hosts me. I hear some additional details from them. In our conversation, we mention known names of teachers, professors and others. They took Dr. Bernhaut along with his wife. Professor Chachkes came home and did not find his wife. They took her and her little daughter to the train station. He hurried up there, penetrated through the guard wall and broke into the death boxcar of his wife. The Ukrainians killed the physicians Shmider and Bilig in a neighboring village. They smashed their skulls with an ax.

They murdered. They murdered everyone. They captured my brother–in–law, David Katz (the husband of my sister Tzila), together with the painter Shlomo Shraga , when they returned from the village carrying a sack full of food for their wives and children who hid in the bunker under Christiampoler's house (the one of R' Yualchis Hoiz in the market). The murderers interrogated them cruelly, trying to find out who gave them the food and where their families were hiding. They tortured them for three days, but they remained silent. At the end, they just shot them. They also killed my friends. The Banderovich'es captured my school–friend Dr. Yosef Shtikler. They kept him alive as he was needed for them as a physician. He was lucky and managed to escape from them (we met in Israel in 1950, and he now lives in Canada).

[Page 269]

My friend Munyo Kacher, was a militia man. He was lucky to stay alive. At the completion of the "Judenfrei" operation (The annihilation of the ghetto and the forced labor camps), they killed all the Jewish militia policemen and all the members of the Judenrat including the leader – banker Herman Blokh.

Brody, Friday 14 September 1945

The fate of my dear mother...

I woke up after a nightmarish night. I took a glance at my writing from yesterday. Can one put down everything on paper? Can I count all the places where my poor brothers were killed and slaughtered? Every step is soaked with Jewish blood. There are thousands of people in the pits in "Vapniarka". Thousands of murdered bodies were buried in the yard of the Graf Schnell's estate in Stary Brody. Thousands of people were taken to Belzec. The brave among them, like Marash (who now lives in Australia) saved their life by jumping off the speeding train through a hatch.

I found out today, that they captured my mother along with many others, during the first aktzia and transported her to Belzec. Who knows in what shape she arrived there, and what was she thinking during her last moments?

Yes, this is Brody. This is the city in where I was born, grew up, and went to school. The city where I played, worked and loved. The house of Adela Petzyuk is still standing at the market. Where is she today? (She left Brody before the war and immigrated to Belgium. About a year later, I found out that she survived, and we met in Israel).

I went to visit Marusya, a Ukrainian girl who learned how to sew with my sister Etka. She gave me a picture of my sister. This is the only memento I have of her now. This is it.

As the evening fell, I came to the apartment of Sender Prekhtman. A Christian woman hid him during the war. She converted and he married her. She lit Sabbath candles, and a minyan gathered at her house including the Vonsh brothers, Yitzkahk Goldberg and others. We prayed together and said Kadish.

After the service, I was invited by Vonsh for dinner. After dinner, I returned to Dr. Bogner.

Brody Saturday, 15 September 1945

There is nobody left from my family...

In the morning, I went to pray again at Prekhtman's (he now lives in the USA). Brody, which was once an ebullient city, now looks like a cemetery. There are several thousand residents, some of which are the former Ukrainians. Most of the Poles left for Western Poland, and settled on new lands which Poland received from Germany (Shlonsk). The rest are new faces – Russians who came from the Soviet Union, most of whom – officers. Silence rules in the city, as if everyone died. I walk around among the ruined streets and my heart cries. I mourn everybody.

[Page 270]

An Ukrainian woman tells me how the German forced Jewish mothers to dig graves for their children. This is what my sisters Tzila and Etka and all other mothers had to do. They shot the children in front of their mothers and then they ordered them to undress and enter the same graves and lie down on top of their children. Only then, the hail of bullets came that put an end to their inhumane misery.

I am trying to envision these mothers, the horror in their eyes that had to witness what they saw, and the pain they experienced.

This is how the Jewish city died....

Brody, Sunday, 16 September 1945

Farewell to Brody...

I accompanied my acquaintance, Yitzkhak Goldberg (who now lives in Hertzlia, Israel) to the cemetery, to say goodbye to the dead and the murdered. I did it since I was skeptical whether I would ever return to this place. It was the day before Yom Kipur. The cemetery was deserted and in ruins. I could not find the stone of my father, may his memory be blessed. My friend, Yitzkhak, suggested that we should not spend too much time at that place. There was still a life–threatening danger from the Banderovich murderers who have not disappeared, and were still active in the area. They continued to attack and kill Jews, particularly Russian Jews (and I was still wearing my Red Army uniform).

I wanted to visit the old cemetery, at the corner of Chicha Street, but the Soviets started to take it apart even before the war and convert it into a sport stadium. Whatever they have not completed, the Germans finished. The old cemetery does not exist anymore.

The only thing left for me to do was to peek at the tall wall of a ruined house on Zlota Street where a sign written in Ukrainian, in large letters says: "Let us not forget, that in this city, 17 thousands Soviet citizens were killed and annihilated by the German fascist murderers. Their blood demands that we avenge their fate!"

I read and reread that sign.

I managed to get a seat in an officer's car that was going to Lvov. I arrived at the big city in the evening. I went to the only synagogue that survived in it.

I saw again the destruction in front of my eyes, and the words: "Never forget".

I will certainly not forget!!!

Translator's Notes

1. Modeh Ani prayer – recited by observant Jews upon waking up, thanking G–d for being alive: "I thank you, living and enduring King, for You have graciously returned my soul within me. Great is your faithfulness".
2. The Shmah prayer serves as a centerpiece of the morning and evening Jewish services. The first verse encapsulates the monotheistic essence of Judaism: "Hear, O' Israel: the Lord is our God, the Lord is one". The Talmud says that when one goes to sleep at night, his soul goes up to heaven for a daily accounting. That leaves the body "unprotected," so to speak. Jews say the Shema and add the blessing "Hamapil" to counter-act that.
3. Ben Porat Yosef – (literally translated, as "A charming son is Yosef"). This phrase is part of the blessing that Jacob gave to Yosef before he died (found in the book of Genesis). Jewish people use this phrase for protection against the evil eye since Yosef symbolizes a person unharmed by others.
4. Youth organizations were affiliated with Zionist parties and movements. "Hashomer Hatzair" was affiliated with the leftist worker party by that name (later named MAPAM which was the acronym for "the Worker Party in Eretz Yisrael"). "Achva" was affiliated with the centrist Zionists movement. "Brit Trumpledor" (or "Beitar") was affiliated with the rightist revisionist Herut party.
5. Hehalutz – literally meaning "The Pioneer", was a Zionist pioneer movement, part of "Poalei Zion" or "Workers of Zion" – a Marxist Zionist Party founded in Poland.
6. Poalei Tzion – literally meaning "Workers of Zion", was a movement of Marxist–Zionist Jewish workers founded in various cities of Poland, Europe and the Russian Empire at about the turn of the 20th century.
7. Keren Kayement Le'Israel – An non–profit organization which was originally founded in 1901 to buy and develop land in Ottoman Palestine (Later the British Mandate for Palestine, and subsequently Israel and the Palestinian territories) for Jewish settlement. Since its inception, the organization planted over 240 million trees in Israel, built 180 dams and reservoirs, developed 250,000 acres of land and established more than 1,000 parks.
8. Ezra – a religious Zionist movement originally affiliated with the religious Agudat Yisrael party in Israel. The organization founded many kibbutzim and moshavim and now works among potential new immigrants in USA, Canada, Russia, Belarus, Ukraine, England and Germany.
9. Ertez Yisrael Ha'Ovedet– a term used to describe all the economic, social and cultural enterprises associated with the labor movement.

10. Gordonia – the movement's doctrines were based on the beliefs of Aharon David Gordon, i.e. – the salvation of Eretz Yisrael and the Jewish People would come through manual labor and the revival of the Hebrew language.
11. Khvila – Literally "Today" in Polish. A Daily Hebrew Zionist newspaper published in Warsaw between 1925 and the period before World War II.
12. Zhids – Insulting form of the word Jew.
13. Komsomol – the Communist youth organization.
14. The Bereza Kartuska prison was a Detention Camp in the Second Polish Republic, based in Bereza Kartuska, Polesie Voivodeship (today Biaroza in Belarus). Created on June 17, 1934 by an order of President Ignacy Moscicki, the camp was established to detain people who were viewed by the Polish state as a "threat to security, peace and social order".
15. Ulanov Krechowieckich – a street named after Krykhivtzi – a village near the town of Ulanov in the Stanislawow district (now called Iwano–Frankiwsk) where a Polish cavalry regiment defeated the attacking Germans in May 1918.
16. Shabbat Shuva – refers to the Shabbat that occurs during the Ten Days of Repentance between Rosh Hashanah and Yom Kippur. Only one Shabbat can occur between these dates. This Shabbat is named after the first word –"Shuva" (or) of the Haftarah (a section from the Book of Prophets read in public at the Shabbat service).

[Page 271]

In Memory of the City of Brody
– a "Mother City" in Israel

by Miriam Lieberbaum (Dishel)

Translated by Moshe Kutten

Twenty years have passed since the somber news stated arriving in Eretz Yisrael: "Jewish Galicia is no more". Our Jewish city is in ruins. Our "Mother City" among the cities of the people of Israel was wiped off the map. Its synagogues, and its "Batei Midrash" [houses of pray and study.[MK]] were destroyed. Foreigners occupy Mom and Dad's house. Jewish Brody was extinguished, blown away like smoke, and wiped out of its existence. Embers saved from the big fire can be found here and there, most of whom came to build their homes in our reborn land.

My native city rises in front of my eyes, every so often, during night dreams and hallucinations, while sleeping or awake. Its narrow streets paved with cobblestones, particularly the street I used to live on, Galina Street, where scanty wooden houses stood on both sides. However, the Brody I remember is the one we found in ruins in 1918, when we came back from Bohemia after World War I. This was when we started to build our life anew.

Most of the Jewish people in the city were very poor. Making a living was hard like the biblical parting of the Red Sea. We, the children, were dressed in rags, and carefully guarded our only pair of shoes. We mainly tried to help in bringing food home. I will never forget the following incident: It happened in 1919. Hunger was rampant in the city. A rumor was spread that plenty of potatoes could be found at the train station. A few children, me among them, went to the station with the hope to collect some of them. We indeed succeeded. Everyone gathered a few potatoes in a small bag, despite the guard. We began to return home with our bags. On our way, Ukrainians thugs attacked us.

They took the potatoes and beat us. We stood there crying. Suddenly, my friend, the late Yona Furman stood beside me and told me: "Don't cry, I managed to hide a few potatoes and I will readily share them with you". We took the remaining potatoes and divided amongst ourselves. Everybody went home with two poatatoes.

The life in the city was poor from a financial point of view, but it was full of inner beauty and brotherly love. That same human warmth rises and fills my heart with tender and pleasant memories, even now, after more than half a century.

My family consisted of simple, working people. People like us surrounded us: painters, carpenters and haulers, who were also the people who were there for us. I recall the attack by the Ukrainians on the Jewish city residents. Our Jewish self–defense force consisted of these same people, who came forward and stood–up in defense of the life and the property of their fellow citizens.

An "organization of professional trades people" existed in Brody. The organization included the members of one family, all of which were painters. We called every one of them Shraga, and nicknamed them as a group – Shraga'lach ['lach – Yiddish ending signifying plural.[MK]]. They became the symbol for the organized Jewish laborer. They appeared anywhere when wrong and injustice occurred. They helped when a worker did not get paid on time, when the wage was too low or where a proprietor mistreated his workers.

[Page 272]

I recall one case where the "Shraga'lach" were involved. This was sometimes in 1920 or 1921. A very poor family resided in one of a landlord's houses. They could not afford paying the rent for a long time, so the landlord had them evicted. He threw them out onto the street without the means to secure another roof above their heads. When the Shraga'lach brothers heard about it, they covered the walls in the entire neighborhood with death notices about the passing of that landlord. They even had a funeral organized for this evil man. The story spread throughout the whole city and people were shocked. When the news reached that landlord, he did not respond angrily because he understood that his act of throwing the miserable family onto the street was evil. He found the family, brought them back to the apartment and asked for their forgiveness for the wrong he caused them.

And there is another picture, which differs completely from the previous one. In recalling this story, I see myself standing on Train Street in front of a large, tall and attractive house, painted white all over. In the center of the house there is a large hall and long tables were arranged in the middle with long benches stretching from the adjacent kitchen to all sides. The kitchen is large and clean, and the smell of hot soup is rising from it. This was the soup kitchen. All the poor, impoverished, homeless and lonely people were coming there to receive their only hot meal of the day. The meal was meager, perhaps several potatoes or groats in a hot soup, but it was provided with warm hearts from everybody's generous contribution, namely from public funds.

While dealing with the subject of "helping others", how can I forget my own father, Zalman, who was our city's animal disease "expert". People would come to call on my father to provide relief to "the sick" and salvation when a horse ailed or a cow fell in the cow shed. I remember well that always, when we set down to celebrate our holidays, particularly during the Passover Seder, our neighbor Motl would show up shouting: "Zalman, my horse is sick!", and my father would rise up from the Seder table, sigh and go to save the sick horse. As a response to my mother's complains he would mumble:" How can we allow the horse to die on this holiday evening? This would constitute cruelty to animals. And how would Motl make a living without his horse?" Mother would sigh and ask him with a broken heart: "Tell me Zalman, why does Motl's horse became sick only during the evening before Sabbaths and holidays?" Father would answer her: "When else would do you want a horse of a tradesman to get sick?"

The memories are numerous. I just wanted to highlight some of that spirit of "helping others" that existed among us. Other people would probably bring up other more important things, but to me, that spirit was close to my heart, and these memories are still the freshest on my mind.

[Page 273]

In Memoriam

by Yitzhak Zorne-Zohar

Translated by Moshe Kutten

Edited by Rafael Manory

When Brody was liberated on 7 July 1944, it was a city mostly in ruins, as the front has been close to it for many months. The few who survived the Holocaust, started to return to the ruined city. The heavy distress and the non-existence of graves, even for family members, who were annihilated in the Belzec extermination camp, forced the few who returned to leave the city. They took advantage of the permits that allowed the Jews to leave the Soviet Union and move to Poland. In July 1945, a few tens of Brody's Jews gathered in a deserted synagogue in Lublin, and scattered from there. Most of "She'erit Ha'Pleta"[1] of the city and its environs left Poland and moved to the camps for displaced people and refugees that were managed by UNRRA[2] in West Germany, Austria and Italy. When the camps were liquidated, part of them immigrated to the US, Israel and other countries. No Jews were left in Brody itself, except several families of Brody's Jews and several families who settled in Brody for the first time after the war. A few Jews remained in Poland, some of them have adopted Polish names and married gentile partners.

In Israel, there was an organization of people from Brody and its environ who arrived in Israel before the Holocaust. When the people from the She'erit Ha'Pleta arrived, the organization reorganized itself as the Organization of Former Residents of Brody and its Environ. The first memorial ceremony for our city's martyrs took place on 21 May, 1951, at the "Hertzliya" gymnasium in Tel Aviv. About a thousand people participated in the ceremony. Since then a ceremony was held every year to this day.

To demonstrate the magnitude of the tragedy that came upon Brody's Jewish population (and most of the Jewish population in Europe), where there was no survivor out of large families, I would mention my family. My father's family—Zorne, and my mother's family - Kenchoker. I am the sole survivor of the family of my grandfather Shlomo Zorne (he owned a restaurant and a bar since the time of the Austrian regime) who had seven children, five of whom were married, and each had two children. Aryeh Leib, son of Moshe Kenchoker who passed away in Israel, was the sole survivor of my mother's broad Kenchoker family from Brody and Podkamin near Brody.

Like my family, most of the Jewish families of Brody and its environs were exterminated.

Translator's Notes

1. She'erit Ha'Pleta—in Hebrew, "the surviving remnants," a biblical term (Ezra 9:14 and I Chronicles 4:43) used today to describe the few Jews who survived the Holocaust.
2. UNRRA – The United Nations Relief and Rehabilitation Administration.

[Page 274]

Brody

by David Altman

Translated by Moshe Kutten

Edited by Yocheved Klausner

Brody had everything that the Jewish cities in Galicia were characterized by.

The long time that the city was under the Austro–Hungarian rule made its mark on its architecture. The city contained beautiful houses, built along straight paved streets with sidewalks. Its center was especially beautiful, with parks and trees. This is in contrary to towns closer to the Russian border, which were similar to the towns depicted in the classical literature...such as Katrielovka of Shalom Aleichem.

There was a general high school in the city for boys and girls as well as a four–grade Jewish school.

As a district city, located in the heart of a rural region, Brody was a city of commerce with many workshops. Thousands of villagers visited the city every Monday, bringing their produce to the market and buying their provisions in the shops and workshops. The city also contained sawmills, as this was a region of forests, as well as flourmills.

Most of the workers in the city's workshops and factories were Jewish. Under the Polish regime, the city management and all the official institutions were in Polish hands, despite the fact that most of the population consisted of Ukrainians and Jews. This was the method of "Poland–ization" that the Poles instituted and implemented along all levels of government. There were only very few, if any, Jewish civil servants...

As far as professions were concerned, it is worthwhile to note that most of the physicians and lawyers were Jewish. The Jews were also the teachers in the high school.

The Attitude of the Non–Jewish Population towards the Jews

We heard about anti–Semitism and pogroms against the Jews from information received from other places and in the newspapers. In our city, there was no contact between the Jews and the non–Jews. The Jews lived in the center of the city and the non–Jews around the city center. The Poles owned small farms and were the civil servants. The treatment of the Jews by the authorities was fair, since they were dependent on the Jewish population. The Poles were the governing minority and both the Ukrainians and the Jews accepted that.

The Attitude of the Ukrainians towards the Jews

The relationship between the Ukrainians and the Jews, before the Holocaust, was good. For example, my father worked as a porter at the train station, where going goods were loaded and coming goods were unloaded. My father worked with the Ukrainians. Workers from the two nationalities also worked side by side on the train itself. They even established a common cooperative.

[Page 275]

During the last ten years, the cooperative contained equal numbers of Jewish and Ukrainians workers. They worked together and divided the pay. My uncle was the cooperative's treasurer. The Ukrainians, who were the depressed majority, maintained good relations with the Jews.

The city experienced religious tolerance. It had Polish, Ukrainian and Russian churches as well as synagogues. I do not recall any case of somebody harming a church nor a synagogue.

The attitude of the Ukrainians towards the Jews changed completely during the war. Thousands of Jews could have been saved if the Ukrainians' attitude would have been at least sympathetic. There were many forests in Ukraine. However, no one could survive in the forests alone. The Germans did not enter the forests. Those who searched the forests were the Ukrainians. They received payment for their effort. The Germans rewarded them with the property of the Jews: the property of the entire city, with the entire content of thousands of houses Obviously, the Germans took cream of the crop at the beginning.

Jewish Self–Rule

The Jews organized themselves as a self–ruled community with a community board. They fulfilled all the roles of the civil servants within the community, such as philanthropic assistance, education, religious services and more.

The heads of the community were honorable people recognized as such by the entire Jewish population. This leadership tried to maintain proper relations with the authorities, and it was also the entity that every needy Jew turned to. The community established charity institutions, such as an old age house, an orphanage and a soup kitchen. Brody was a border town, and as such was host to many soldiers as well as three military barracks with thousands of Polish soldiers.

During our major holidays – Pesach [Passover[MK]], Rosh Ha'Shanah [Jewish New Year[MK]] and Yom Kippur [Day of Atonement[MK]], people from the city management and the Polish high command were hosted by us. We kept special seats for them and they participated in the prayers. I worked at repairs in officers' houses. They respected us and we maintained good relations with them.

Secular and Religious People

The leader of the religious people was the city's Rabbi. However, the religious people were not the majority in the city. The religion did not affect our day-to-day life. Two large synagogues and many more small ones existed and many Jews did go to pray in them. However, this was it. My father was a Cohen, but he worked on Saturdays during the season and he did not hide it. Yet he was invited to make the first Aliyah [Torah reading[MK]] in the synagogue during the holidays, with the honor reserved for a Cohen.

We did keep Kosher at home. Movies and theater shows were conducted on Friday evenings. There were those who went to the synagogue on Saturdays, and there were those who went to the coffee shops.

I worked three years as a barber. There was only one barbershop which was closed on Saturday – the one of the city's Rabbi. However there was no pressure whatsoever by the religious people.

The Zionist Activity

The Zionist activity was very substantial. There was a community house, where the activities of the youth movements took place, all of them around the same yard. Every movement was allocated its own room where meetings took place.

[Page 276]

I remember the elections to the Zionist Congress in 1935. The political map of the city can be described, based on the numbers of votes. The Tzionim Klaliyim - General Zionists[1], received 256 votes, Ha'Mmizrakhi[2] - 286, Eretz Israel Ha'Ovedet[3] - 508 and the State Party - 126[4]. The Revisionists[5] did not participate in the election because they received only 37 votes in the previous election. This distribution reflects the general direction of the community - the progressive labor direction.

In our club of Ha'Shomer Ha'Tzair - the Young Guard[6], the authorities discovered and confiscated Marxist books. They took away our license to assemble legally and we operated underground for almost three years. We rented a house and placed guards during our meetings. We held many meetings in the nearby forest, an ideal location for summer activities.

During the years of 1936–1938 we were more than 200 members strong. This was a large club with several age groups– Kfirim (Young Lions), Scouts, Older Scouts, Adolescent Scouts and Adolescents. Many of the members of that club are scattered throughout Israel - they immigrated to Israel before 1940 and are members of Kibbutzim.

Cultural Life and Sports

A musical club existed in the city as well as sports clubs. One was a Zionist sports club and the other a workers' club. Large theater troupes performed in our clubs. There were also soccer clubs. Ha'Shomer Ha'Tzair occupied always a high standing in the table tennis league.

The cultural life was carried out freely. The only limitations were the capabilities and resources, since the city was poor and many families lived in poverty.

My Home

My family lived in Brody for many years. Our economic situation was very difficult. My father was a porter and the owner of a cart. He worked with his brothers. Our ten-person family lived in the poor part of the city and occupied a room and a half in a rickety house. I was the elder child. In the wintertime, we used to put buckets on the floor since the roof leaked. From time to time we had to seal the holes in the roof.

We were not the only ones in that situation. Numerous other families with many children, experienced that same situation. They were very poor, and received just a meager support.

This is why I had to go to work at the age of twelve, in order to help supporting the family.

I recall myself as a small child, going around, carrying an ax and a saw to the yards of Jews who traded in firewood. They would buy large logs of wood, from which I used to chop small pieces for firewood. I along with other boys like myself used also to work in the production of ropes and paper bags. We always looked for ways to make a living. I studied seven grades. My brothers – only four grades. There was no way by which we could continue our studies.

I was one of the best students when I graduated from the seventh grade, without any books. The school principal (a non–Jew) came to my father's house and tried to convince my father to let me continue my studies in the high school. He said that he would arrange a scholarship for me. My father refused.

I sympathize with my father. He did not have any other choice. I had to help him in supporting the family. I never knew what was to own one's own money. I gave everything I earned to my mother. The money was safer with her... My father, depressed by all the troubles and hardships would sometimes spend money on alcohol or a game of cards.

[Page 277]

Despite the fact that our life was a life of distress, holidays were real holidays, and the Saturday was celebrated with a Khallah. People were not driven to hopelessness. I had friends who owned a carpentry shop, and they offered me a job. This is how I became and remained a carpenter.

I was an avid reader. Books accompanied me throughout the day, and especially late at night. I borrowed books in the library, free. I loved reading, even when walking. People used to laugh at me, as I would often encounter a tree. I used to read at the table. I also looked for ways to escape in sports. I played soccer and volleyball.

Ha'Shomer Ha'Tzair

We were all members of the Ha'Shomer Ha'Tzair movement. Our parents did not give us their blessing for joining the movement, as they saw it as a distraction from the daily routine. Neither my father nor my mother comprehended its meaning, as they were not educated people. We participated in the movement because of the drive to be among kids of our age group. We felt the protection offered by this togetherness.

All Zionist youth movements were active in Brody. The movements comprised clubs as well as Hakhsharot[7]. Pioneering was the essence of the activity. The extent of the activity was considerably large in proportion to the size of the population.

I participated in the Ha'shomer Ha'Tzair from the age of ten until 1940 – almost ten years. It could be said that the club was my home. Everything I did not have at home, I had at the movement. It was an uplifting of knowledge, since we studied in the club, as well as of friendship. The movement gave me the ability of looking forward. It allowed me to think about what I wished for myself and to see what could be anticipated in the future. The movement filled my life with content since I hardly had a home... Maybe I did not describe it properly. I did have a home. However, there were ten souls occupying an apartment the size of 6 by 4 meters (a room and a tiny kitchen). That is how we lived in crammed conditions. In the movement, I felt free. I felt that I live my own life. During the last two years, my age group friends started to go to the Hakhshara camps. I did not have the chance to do it. The war interrupted everything

The Arrival of the Russians

When the Russians arrived in Brody in 1939, all the members of the movement found themselves suddenly without perspective and aimless. The Russian regime was not an oppressive regime, however, the daily routine changed completely. Activities of all parties and youth movements were forbidden. There was some economic improvement; however, life became hollow. All the energy was directed toward the daily routine and toward developing the sense of adaptability to ensure survival.

Public and cultural life dwindled until it ceased entirely. Everything that happened before ceased following the arrival of the Russians.

There were Jews who helped the commissars. It was not very difficult to find people who did. However, we lived our life with a feeling of emptiness. Since we could not be active, we followed the call to improve our life by moving eastward and work in our profession. We saw that as the only opportunity to improve our life, and we went for it. Only later, we found out that the reality was different from the propaganda.

[Page 278]

The Exodus to the East

When advertisements appeared in the city calling for everyone who is interested to work in their profession under good conditions, to leave for an industrial region in the east for a duration of one year, a group of about twenty people was organized. Among the people in the group were members and leaders of our youth movement's club and myself. We registered and left.

We registered for one year of work in Magnitogorsk in the Ural Mountains with the promise that we would be able to return home at the end of the period. Our goal was to return home since we only wanted to expand our horizons.

We have not reached Magnitogorsk. We reached only as far as Tula. Most of the members left that place due to the harsh work conditions. Only five members, all of whom the leaders of the youth movement club, stayed.

A month before the end of the period, we were all arrested by the N.K.V.D[8] under the false accusation that we were a group of counter-revolutionists sent by the Polish authorities to cause a counter-revolution in the Soviet Union. The people arrested were David Altman [the author[MK]], Yitzkhak Veltman, Misko Gringrass, Shmuel Zaltz and Heinech Jung.

Imprisonment and Camps

The investigation lasted five months. At the end, we were all sentenced to five years in prison and three years of revocation of citizenship. The leader of our group, who was also the head of the club, Yitzkhak Veltman, was sentenced to seven years. This was the beginning of our life in the Soviet Union's camps and jails.

The Camps' Population

The prisoners in the camps represented the entire range of the general population of the Soviet Union: workers, soldiers, civil servants, members of the Communist Party, officials and academicians. The common general indictment was subversion against the regime.

I heard from people who were previously in the center of things, that the authorities notified them one bright day that they are under arrest. There were accused of things they did not do and were sentenced to long imprisonment periods. They had no way to ask for justice. Whoever was inside, stayed inside. The period was during the war in Finland, at the beginning of World War II.

The most popular slogan during those days was: "There are three types of people in the Soviet Union – those who were jailed, those who are now in jail and those who will be jailed".

A Day in the Life of a Prisoner

The conditions in the camp were very hard. The wakeup call sounded at 5 AM when there was still darkness. You put on clothes unsuitable for the Russian winter. We would arrange ourselves in brigades in the big courtyard. We underwent an inspection and started to leave through the gates for a march to the workplace. Our luck was that the quarries were located only a kilometer and a half away from the camp. The walk was not that long.

[Page 279]

It was forbidden to turn left or right during the march, as they would shoot at you without warning. We had to walk with our arms crossed behind our backs.

Upon arriving to the workplace, we separated into groups. A quota was imposed on each group – a certain numbers of filled up trollies.

The food was rationed. There was almost no food provided in the morning, only some hot tea. At noon, when we came back from work, the ration included soup with no content and 600 grams of black bread. That was the entire food ration. If you were "stachanovitz", meaning, if your brigade succeeded to fulfill the quota – you would have gotten more bread.

The camp consisted of wooden huts with bunks along their entire length. This is where we slept. It is obvious that thefts were rampant among the prisoners. It was difficult to keep the same pair of shoes from one day to another.

The Carpenters' Brigade

The work at the quarry was exceptionally hard. During one of the morning roll calls, I gathered enough courage to tell the camp commander that my friend Shmuel Zaltz and I were carpenters and that we could bring much more benefit in carpentry work than in the quarry. He took down our request and approved our transfer. We were transferred to the carpenters' brigade.

It became much easier for us, in terms of the work itself and in terms of the attitude toward us. We worked on fixing trollies and trucks. We also went to the forests to cut down trees and make boards out of them. This was a much harder type of work. However, as I was knowledgeable about using the ax and the saw, we managed to meet the quota.

The March: The Walking Camp

The winter of 1941 was approaching. The Germans invaded the Soviet Union and started to approach the region where our camp was located. Bombs and shells fell around our camp, although nothing hit us directly. The Germans knew that the camp housed political anticommunist prisoners and they avoided hitting us.

The front was approaching, so the Russians decided to move the camp. However, they did not have transportation resources. On one of the evenings, we received the order to leave on foot the following day. Everybody took whatever was possible to carry out of the personal belongings. There were 1700 prisoners in the camp. We walked from dark to dark during the entire day. During a difficult march like that, no one counts the days, or keeps track of the date. We did have a public radio, so we received information on what was going on. This is how we found out that all Polish prisoners were given amnesty and that the Anders Army was being organized. We submitted a petition to the camp commander to be included among the freed Polish prisoners. However, since the five of us were the only Poles, they simply did not know what to do with us. He promised to find out at the district and that he would let us know when he received an answer to his inquiry... We were not freed.

We walked kilometers after kilometers. Whoever looked backward saw a line of people stretching to infinity. People started to throw things they took from the camp since it was difficult to carry them.

[Page 280]

We started in October. We went between the lines of the German and Russian armies. We went through the forests since German or Russian armor units occupied the roads. Nobody knew where everyone else was. We walked for a month along the Russian roads, in a muddy region during the rainy season and the bitter cold. During the night, they would scatter us on the weeds to sleep. There were no organized meals. Everybody ate whatever he managed to collect while walking – potatoes, cabbage or carrots. This border area was almost empty of people, except convoys of refugees.

Whoever lagged behind, during the march, was shot. After a month, only about five hundred survived. We arrived at the city of Ryazan near the Oka River. This is where we washed ourselves for the first time. We took a haircut and shaved. They sprayed our lice infested clothes. They kept us in jail for some time. At the end of that period, they loaded us on boats heading for the river Volga.

We did not know at the time where were we being transported. It was during the month of November and the river froze. The boats stopped and could not move. We tried unsuccessfully to break our way through but failed. They kept us inside these boats for a month. We received very little food. The dead were thrown under the ice. One could only leave the boat for toileting. The rest of the time, we lay down on the bunks.

After a month, when they took us out of there, we could not recognize each other. We were all utterly yellow. They lead us through snowy forests to the nearest train station. I think that there was no guiding hand for this journey. There were no leaders. The same N.K.V.D people who stayed with us dragged themselves with us.

On the Train

Upon our arrival to the train station, they loaded us on freight cars. Following a few days of travelling, they built bunks. Every car carried a hundred people. We began to travel form one station to another. We encountered convoys of the Red army all the time. During the winter of 1941, grueling battles took place near Moscow. Our destination was the coalmines in Kazakhstan. Many died during the month–long ride.

In the morning we received a cup of cold water, utterly frozen with a frozen piece of bread. Many people who were so hungry that they ate the frozen bread with the cold water became sick with typhus. We were four friends who supported each other. We watched each other and did not eat the food as it was served. We waited in line until we could use the small iron stove that was installed in each car. We used the stove to boil the water and warm up the bread. That is how we managed to survive.

The Camp Located on the Gate between Europe and Asia

We arrived at a camp in Orsk at the end of December. Orsk is located south of the Ural Mountains in a place where the Ural Mountains end and the prairies of Kazakhstan begin. This place is infamous for its dust storms in the summer and snowstorms in the winter. The temperatures are extremely high in the summer and extremely cold in the winter.

[Page 281]

We arrived at Orsk 190 men. Following a medical examination, only twenty men were found fit for work. All the rest were taken to hospitals. Only a few survived.

My leg froze and I wandered around limping for several days. At the end they took me to the camp's central hospital along with my friend Shmuel Zaltz.

The camp itself was huge. It housed about 8000 people who were scattered among eight sub-camps.

In the Hospital

My friend, Shmuel Zaltz, and I spent half a year in the hospital. We suffered from a disease common among the prisoners: the stomach could not digest food. This is how people die a slow death without even noticing. My luck was that the camp physician used to work in the previous camp. From our discussions she found out that I was a barber. She arranged for me to cut the prisoners' hair. I used to go around from one bed to another, shave, and give haircuts. I started to get a bit of porridge, a bit of soup and a piece of bread. My condition improved and I started to recuperate. My friend recovered as well. However, at a certain stage he started to swell. He told me that he wanted to die. He took salt water and died.

When I started to work as a barber, and was able to move around, they made me a hospital orderly. I was also put in charge of transporting the dead to the cemetery. A cart equipped with a large box was there. There was also a cellar, where they put the dead from all the sub–camps. In the morning, the cart driver and I would load the bodies onto the large box. I would sign the receipts and so we went. The cemetery was located about five or six kilometers away, on the prairie. Large graves were dug out, where we laid down the bodies. Other workers would come and cover the graves. I worked in this job for two years. I buried 8000 people during these two years.

There were people from different places in the camp: soldiers from the front, Georgians, Bukharian's. Every sub–camp was assigned a different type of work. One camp handled the copper factory, another one the train cars etc.

In this Russian camp, our treatment was different from the treatment in a German concentration camp. They did not yell "Jew" at me, maybe because there were not as many Jews in the camp... However, the life regimen was such that people reached total exhaustion after several months. This is when they were taken to the hospital, and most of them did not make it alive from there.

Among all the transports that arrived at the camp, one transport depressed me the most. The transport consisted of people from Georgia who were transported through the prairie in the winter and they all arrived frozen. I remember that we filled bags with arms and legs that we cut from them. In a short while, there was no trace of them left.

The soldiers, who were brought to us from the Stalingrad area, brought the typhus disease with them. I became sick as well. There was one difference: I lived in relative good conditions, under physicians care. This is how I survived the war. Most of the others did not.

At that time, I managed to transfer my friend Yitzkhak Veltman to us from another sub–camp. He was transferred to us a sick man, and stayed in my camp as a resident and worked with me at the hospital. Until today, I am not really sure whether I served him well by transferring him to my camp or not.

[Page 282]

I did improve his situation, as he recovered and gained strength. However, subsequently a medical committee examined him found him fit to work and he was sent to the Far East to work on building the Trans–Siberian railroad.

Another friend, Misko Gringrass, was transferred to my camp. He was a tailor. He worked as such back home and in the camps. His camp was assigned to work for the camp commander. Thugs who were in charge in that camp, asked him to do work for them but he refused.

Thieves and robbers, who were also responsible for the distribution of the bread, the kitchen work and every other powerful position, ruled his camp. Prisoners who did not accept their authority were informed about to the camp command. They informed about my friend that he was heard saying that he was waiting for the Germans to win the war and similar other accusations. As a result of this defamation, he was transferred to jail with all those who were waiting for trial. He was taken to court and was sentenced to another ten years. Finally he was brought back to our camp and worked as a tailor.

The Liberation

The last thing that happened to me before my release was that I was called to the commander of the department who dealt with the records and he gave me a souvenir: the file with all of my documents and papers since my initial imprisonment.

I took the file and hid it deep inside my luggage that I took with me. I knew that if they catch me again with this file in Russia, I would be back inside...When I entered the last train to Poland, they told me that they check all the passengers thoroughly. I ripped the file then, since I did not want to risk my freedom. Everything about my past was lost.

My Friend Yitzkhak

I found out later that my friend, Yitzkhak Veltman survived. I would like to tell about him a bit.

He was released in 1947 after seven years of imprisonment. He got a ticket for a train that was going to a central city. He was arrested there, as he did not have the right to stay there. He could only stay in a border district. He was given another ticket to a remote town in Kazakhstan.

When the infamous Jewish Doctors Trials[9] started, they arrested him again. They interrogated him about me and my whereabouts, and about what happened to me. They knew that we continued to be in touch. After I was released, I sent him a detailed letter about the way I managed to get the certificates. He never received that letter.

He was held for two more years, until Stalin's death. Only then, he was permitted to move to another city. He worked and studied in the evenings until he graduated from a technical university and got a civil engineer diploma. He married his wife who helped him and stood by him during extremely difficult times.

A year later, when the Jewish exodus from USSR started, he submitted a request to leave and immigrate to Israel. They rejected his requests year after year. He did manage to immigrate only about five years ago [The book was published in 1994[MK]]. He is very ill today, but we keep in close touch.

[Page 283]

Returning to my City

I did not meet any Nazis during the war. When we stayed in a camp, which was near the Moscow region, the Germans approached, so they transferred us deeper into Russia.

During the last year of the war, when the Red Army freed our native region, I wrote a letter to the mayor and asked him to check whether any of family members – parents or siblings, survived. A short while later I got a response that my entire family was murdered along with the entire Jewish population of the city. The German exterminated my family in the ghetto.

So even before leaving Russia, I knew that I should not expect to find anybody alive... In spite of that certainty, I knew in my heart that I would have to go back there and search...otherwise I would always have thoughts and doubts about the fact that I could have checked and had not done so.

Upon receiving the certificates, I traveled to and visited the city. Our Ukrainian neighbors, who worked with my father as porters, told me what happened. They showed me the place where my family was murdered when the ghetto was exterminated. The entire family was murdered. Nobody survived.

Two days later, I felt that I do not have any reason to stay in that cemetery. I went back to Lvov and waited for a train to take me away from there. I left two or three weeks later. When I arrived in Poland, I found out that remnants of our movement are organizing Aliyah[10] groups [kibbutzim]. I knew at once that my road ahead was very clear. I knew what I was going to do with my life from then on.

After the War – The Organization of the Kibbutz

The train I was riding on stopped at the Krakow's station. Somebody told me that a kibbutz of our movement – Ha'Shomer Ha'Tzair was being organized in Lodz. I knew immediately that this was my destiny. There was no other.

I went to Lodz and joined the Kibbutz which consisted of people with the same background as me: concentration camps' survivors, forest partisans, and "alumni" of Russian labor–camps.

Our group – five hundred people strong, was scheduled to travel from Austria to Marseille. From there our group was slated to board a ship that would bring us to Eretz Israel. We were arrested in Austria, as our papers were forged.

This is when we began to be transferred from one camp to another until we reached the last camp in the region of Nuerenberg. We spent one year in that camp. Overall our wandering around from camp to camp lasted about two years, before we received the news about our impending Aliyah. This is how we ended up on the ship "Exodus".

The Exodus story – the events on the beaches of Eretz Israel and the battle with the English military under the command of a kibbutz member, Mordekhai Rozman, is very well known. At the end of the battle, we were sent back to Marseilles and from there to Hamburg. From there we were again transferred from one camp to another.

During those days of wandering, we managed to organize a full daily routine. The schedule included studies and part or full time work. We had all sorts of undertakings just that we would not degenerate and sink into depression. We organized Friday night gatherings, and many

other cultural activities. We tried our best and succeeded to be an example, both culturally and socially, for other kibbutzim in the area.
[Page 284]

The period we spent on Exodus, brought us very closer together. Our stay on the ship – three months at sea, from our deportation, through the La Manche channel to Hamburg in northern Germany, lasted a very long period.

Later on, we were jailed in a camp surrounded by barbed wire fences, guarded by the British military units equipped with tanks. We continued to live in a camp regime. The British tried to break our spirit but they never succeeded. Exodus immigrants totaled 4700 people, most of who were organized as kibbutzim and youth movement groups. We therefore managed to keep our cultural and social activities under the Exodus framework. These activities created a life frame, which enabled us to overcome the hard conditions.

Aliyah to Ertez Israel and the Period in Kibbutz Ma'anit; The War of Independence.

When we got off the ship in Haifa, for the second time, we were sent as a group slated for Kibbutz Ma'anit[11]. We arrived at the kibbutz, which was surrounded by Arab villages, on January 1948.

The attacks on the Kibbutz started in April 1948. We were under siege until the end of 1948. We just moved from one war to another. This was like a natural continuation to what we experienced before...

We were a very unified group. We lived our life within the group. The Ma'anit Kibbutz members were older than us, so we merely maintained working relations with them. They did not manage to create deeper relations with us.

The country itself was like the Garden of Eden for us. We were very emotional to see a Jewish farmer, a Jewish wagoner, or a Jewish driver. We were excited to see the surroundings, the landscape... that was the eve of the outbreak of the War of Independence. We really did not know what hardships were waiting for us. We enjoyed the encounter with our land, although we really did not know it very well. There were no opportunities for trips or treks. Hostile events were frequent throughout the country. Our area was surrounded. In order for anybody to leave, even for a single day, one would have to get a special permission from the district commander. This situation lasted for about a year. Even when a cease–fire was declared in the country, in the middle of the war, there was no cease–fire in Ma'anit.

Gal–On

Mordekhai Rozman, the commander of Exodus, continued to be in contact with us. His Kibbutz was looking for hashlamah[12]. Mordekhai came to us in Ma'anit to try to convince us to move to Gal–On. We agreed.

The transfer to Ga–On hurt us tremendously". The Gal–On kibbutz itself experienced a crisis at that time. Many members did not move to live at the new location and stayed behind in Nes–Tziona.

I stayed in Gal–On from 1949 until 1952 when I moved to Kibbutz Gazit.

Gazit

I established a good relationship with the members of an Argentinian group during their stay in Gal–On. I found common language with many of their members. When I transferred to Gazit, I knew that I would find my place in it.

I worked in the woodshop from the beginning, and therefore I felt that I am contributing in an essential field. This was the period where the kibbutz experienced a thrust in construction. The pace of the work required all one's power and energy. Social life was lively and I felt good from the first moment.

I saw in the Argentinian group in Gazit, the continuation of our club from the old days. Such passion! It was as if I was still with my club. It was the continuation of what was, and what had been interrupted. Despite the fact that I lived in a pitiable hut, as compared to a building in Gal–On, I did not feel that I dropped in rank. I finally had an organized life with a suitable social circle of friends.

I have experienced poverty during my childhood, during my stay in the Russian camps and during the years of the illegal immigration. I always had an unorganized life. This is the reason why I was not after material things. I was content with what I had and went along with the rest of the members through the same road – from a hut to a Swedish Hut, to a building and from there to veterans housing.

Taking Care of Seniors

I have been taking care of the elderly parents of the kibbutz members for quite some time now. It started from the fact that I felt close to the first parents, the Romanians and the Yiddish speaking people. I receive a lot of satisfaction from this activity.

My Family in the Kibbutz

As far as establishing a family for myself is concerned: The main thing that I wanted was to create a continuance. Many years ago, I took a vow that I would not be the last of my family to carry our name. I wanted to ensure the preservation of our name. That meant building a family. I succeeded to do so. I met my wife in 1952. We married, and she is my partner since. My sons are well versed in my past, although not in all the details. We have three sons: Tzvi'ka, Tamir and Ronen. Tzvi'ka was joined by a cute and loyal Swiss girl and they have two sons: Danny and Michael. A girl from Haifa – Smadar, joined Tamir and they have a cute daughter – Inbar. Ronen is still a bachelor, planning his college studies. They all live with us, something that brings us a lot of happiness.

May this situation remain the same for many years.

Moreshet[13] Club

I am a member of the Moreshet club from the day it was established. Abba Kovner said, in one of our first meetings, that if we would not tell about what we have experienced, if our generation would not perpetuate our past, the next generation would not do it either...

[Page 286]

In the beginning, I did not tell anybody all of the details of my past. There were only a few people who could put down their past in writing. However, in the last few years, when the distance in time grew, people started to reach the age when things could not be postponed any longer... There is plenty of material, substantially more that can be published. The first action of Moreshet club was to take personal testimonies, and through the personal stories, we tried to weave the story of the period. There is a substantial amount of material lying around in the Center for the Holocaust Studies and Research located in kibbutz Giv'at Khaviva which waits for proper handling.

The generation that experienced the Holocaust, is now thinking about the past more than in previous years. I also have the feeling that we need to tell the story, since many souls walked that road, but only a few survived to tell about it. This is something that is both a burden and a duty, because you are the spokesman of all these people who passed.

Translator's Notes

1. General Zionists Party – centrist liberal party who later joined to form the center right Likud party.
2. Eretz Israel Ha'Ovedet (The Working Eretz Israel) – The labor movement's party.
3. Ha'Mizrahi party – the precursor to the centrist National Religious Party.
4. Medinah Ivrit – the Jewish State party – was a Zionist party who separated from The Revisionist party (see below) because of it secession from the Zionist Union who rejected the idea of a Jewish state at the time. It existed as a separate party until 1946 when the Revisionist Party rejoined the Jewish Union when the horrible scale of the Holocaust became known.
5. Revisionist Zionists – the fraction of the Zionist movement which was the founding ideology of the non–religious right in Israel. It advocated the establishment of a Jewish state in whole of Palestine from the start even during the period when it was not supported by the Jewish Union and the Zionist Congress.
6. Ha'Sshomer Ha'Tzair (the Young Guards) – a leftist socialist Zionist youth movement.
7. Hakhsharot – Pioneers preparation camps.

8. N.K.V.D – the Soviet Union's secret police, the predecessor of the KGB responsible for mass deportations and executions of millions of people.
9. The Doctor Trials were an anti–Semitic act initiated by Stalin. On January 1953, a group of prominent physicians (mostly Jewish) were charged of being members in a Jewish organization associated with a plot to kill the leaders of the Soviet Union by medical poisoning. This followed by anti–Semitic propaganda, condemnation and additional trials of many Jewish academicians. A few weeks after the death of Stalin in April 1953, the new Soviet leadership cited a lack of evidence and the cases were dropped.
10. Aliyah – ("ascent" in Hebrew) is the term used to define immigration of Jews from the diaspora to the Land of Israel (Eretz Israel in Hebrew). Also defined as "the act of going up"–that is, towards Jerusalem– "making Aliyah" by moving to the Land of Israel is one of the most basic tenets of Zionism.
11. Kibbutz Ma'anit is settled on the entrance of "Wadi Ara"– one of the main roads to the north of the country – in the neighborhood of three other Kibbutzim and near the main ideological center of of Givat Haviva. Wadi Ara, located northwest of the green line in Haifa district, in an area in Israel populated mainly by Arab citizens of Israel. The meaning of the name Ma'anit is "furrow", which symbolizes the agricultural attitude and goal of the kibbutz.
12. Hash'lama (completion in Hebrew) – a group of pioneers who joins an established kibbutz in order to fulfill the members' quota.
13. Moreshet was founded by a group of Jewish partisans and ghetto fighters, who arrived in Israel after World War II. This group, headed by Abba Kovner – one of the leaders of the Vilnius Ghetto underground and commander of the Jewish battalion in the Naroch forests in Lithuania – took upon itself a historic mission: to give a real expression to the last wishes and requests of hundreds of Holocaust survivors by presenting their testimonies and artifacts for future generations [cited from Moreshet website– www.moreshet.org].

[Page 287]

How My Family and Rabbi Steinberg's Family Were Saved

by Ya'akov Braun

Translated by Moshe Kutten

Edited by Yocheved Klausner

I wish to write a few lines about our family and the family of Rabbi Steinberg, may his memory be blessed, the Rabbi of the city of Brody. During the Holocaust, a common fate of struggle and faith lead to the salvation and survival of these two families – Braun and Shteinberg.

My father, Mordekhai (Markus) Braun and my mother Leah, nee Katz, were the heads of the Braun family. We were five children. Our eldest, Israel (Sonyu), survived but he died in Israel from a malignant disease. Pnina (Pepeh), may she live a long life, is married to Arnold and she has a daughter named Ronit (also married). Pnina and her daughter live in Kiryat Ono. I, Ya'akov, am married to Margalit and we have three children. Our daughter Enat, is married and she has two children. Her son Dror is a captain in the air force, is married and lives in Tel-Aviv. The youngest is Eran. He is also an officer, in the Intelligence corps. He lives with us in Kiryat Ono. My little brother and sister perished in the aktzia held by the Gestapo in Brody on Yom Kipur of 1942. They were only four and two years old respectively. May their memory be blessed.

We had not recovered from the loss of my little and pure brother and sister, when we had to leave the city and find a shelter in the forests and villages surrounding the city. After our failure to find the Ukrainian family who previously agreed to hide us, acquaintances of my father recommended a Ukrainian by the name of Kravchuk from the village of Ponikva. Kravchuk was a devoted Christian, married with no children. The turmoil in the city was tremendous and everybody looked for ways to save themselves.

When my mother, Leah, may her memory be blessed, realized that the city's Rabbi, Moshe Steinberg and his wife did not have anywhere to run away to, she urged my father Mordekhai to take the Rabbi and his wife with us. She wanted to take them to that same gentile, despite the fact that he agreed only to hide us, and even that was in exchange to large sums of money in gold and jewelry. Steinberg family did not have any financial means. However, my father agreed with my mother's request and he fulfilled it. Throughout the entire period of 18 months until the day of the liberation, we were together, the five members of the Braun family, the Rabbi and his wife, altogether seven people. As mentioned above, my father paid Kravchuk a considerable amount of money every month, for us and for the Rabbi's family.

During the 18 months, we experienced horrific events. From the start, we realized that the hideout prepared by the gentile was only suitable for a short period. Fear overtook his will to hide us, and this is how we found ourselves wandering aimlessly around in the infinite forests without food or water. This is when the Rabbi's spirit and faith were very helpful to us. He and my father always believed that we, all seven of us, will survive at the end. However our situation became worse and worse. Locals found out about us, and were looking for us in the forests. To Kravchuk's credit, it can be said that he did not abandon us even after he sent us to the forests. He and several other gentile acquaintances of my father found a natural bunker with a depth of about 10 meters for us to hide in. We were lowered to the bunker via a ladder. The gentiles told us that we would only be able to hide there for 24 hours. However we stayed in that bunker in inhuman conditions for six months. We lay on cold rocks the entire time, in almost complete darkness. It was a "solitary confinement," which we could not get out off without help from the outside. Once again, to his credit, Kravchuk did not abandon us. He walked several kilometers at night, back and forth, to bring us water and bread. He was not able to bring us the food every night, but we survived in this accursed location only thanks to his persistence. After several months of wandering in the forests and half a year in the bunker, the gentile brought us back to the original hideout, where we stayed until the liberation in April 1944.

[Page 288]

Rabbi Steinberg and his wife went to the US and settled in New York where they both died a few years back.

Our eldest brother, Israel, went to England and from there to Canada. He immigrated to Israel in the late sixties, but as mentioned before, a malignant disease overpowered him, and he passed away shortly thereafter. My parents and my sister Pnina immigrated to Israel in 1950. My father passed away in 1981 and my mother in 1985. May their memory be blessed.

Rabbi Shteinberg greatly appreciated my father's help. He published a book in New York, in which he described the events of those days and the part that my father took in saving his and his wife's life.

During my trips to the US, I visited the Steinbergs several times and we reminisced together. My parents corresponded continuously with the Steinbergs during their life. Both families kept in touch and corresponded continuously with the gentile Kravchuk.

[Page 289]

A group of members of the socialist Zionist workers – "Hitakhdut" ["Union"[MK]]

Members of the popular group “Akhva” [“brotherhood”MK]

[Page 290]

Members of the group: “He'Khalutz” [“the Pioneer”MK] in Brody

Members of the group: "He'Khalutz" ["the Pioneer"[MK]] in Brody

[Page 291]

A group of member of the "Gordonia" in Brody

A group of the youth movement "Bnei Akiva"

[Page 292]

The Last "Oleh" from Brody

by Issac (Yitzchak) Weltman

Donated by David Polen

When I recall what happened to me in the 40 years I spent in the Soviet Union – long dark years, replete with atrocities and cruelty in the gulags of the far East, the plains of Kazakhstan and the deserts of Turkmenistan in central Asia, the degrading and cruel interrogations, forced labour in temperatures of –60 degrees and constant hunger in the first 10 years, I ask myself where I had the strength to overcome all this, and the answer is educations and faith.

The education I soaked up from childhood in Hashomer Hatzair[1], a warm, but poor Ken[2] in Brody seeded foundations–values in me that accompanied me in my youth, adulthood and into old age. I knew deep down that only in Eretz Yisrael[3], our historical homeland, can the Jewish people realize renewed and productive lives without "Diaspora–ism", go back to the land; the movement instilled one clear goal in us: Aliya to Israel and kibbutz.

I was born in 1921 in the city of Brody to a traditional Jewish family that celebrated the Shabbat and all the holidays. On Shabbat we went to the synagogue to pray. My father Avraham Ben Ovadia zl'[4] was a Hebrew teacher, who also taught literature and Tanach (bible). He was a Russian refugee. Born in Uman not far from Kiev in Tzarist Russia from whence he ran away during the 1903 pogroms he settled in Brody, married my mother Hannah Reif zl' from Lupatin, a town close to Brody. My older sister Rivka zl' was born in 1909, married Pinchas Garfunkel of Brody and lived on Kolyova St. My second sister Chaya (Klara) zl' was born in 1916 and was active in Hashomer Hatzair. My youngest sister Frieda zl' was born in 1927. My parents and sisters perished in the Holocaust, and to this day I do not know how, or where. I have 3 more brothers in Israel: Ovadia born 1911, made Aliya[5] in 1935 and lives in kibbutz Gat; Shaul–Ezra, born 1913, made Aliya in 1939, fought in the (Jewish) Brigade 1944–1945 and in the War of Independence, lives in Petach Tikva; and Pinchas born 1919, made Aliya in 1948, lives in Moshav Ta'ashur in the Negev. We lived on 7 Vasola St., behind the Jewish school. Later we moved to 4 Krupniche St.

At home we spoke Hebrew - a rarity in Brody. Thus writes the renowned Brodian Professor Dov Sadan in his book "From the Circle of Youth": "Even in those days, there were those that kept the embers glowing. The last Hebrew teacher in our city Mr. Weltman, a Russian refugee that settled here, preserved the Hebrew language in his home, and when he strolled through the streets with two of his sons he spoke our language (Hebrew) with them. They were always followed by astounded youngsters who envied them. I happened to stroll with them one day and was lucky to stop outside the closed train station and listen in to their conversation spoken in fluent Hebrew, while I could do nothing but listen".

In the 1930's my father and Mr. Lerner, the Hebrew teacher established the "Tarbut" (culture) Hebrew school where they taught the Hebrew language, literature, Jewish culture and bible studies. My father was an ardent Zionist. A blue and white JNF box always hung on the wall in the house and we also had Hebrew books and biblical texts. I did not go to "cheder". Abba taught us chumash and prayers at home. For a period I sang in the Great Synagogue choir.

In 1932 I joined Hashomer Hatzair. The ken (nest) was located in the community center opposite the Ukrainian church on Leshnyovski St.; later it moved to Landau's factory on the same street. I was a group leader (madrich), a large squad leader and from 1938 served as a member of the leadership committee (mazkirut).

Ken activity was teeming: scouting, sports, debates and discussion evenings. I loved the hikes to Leshniyovski Forest. All Shabbat and holiday activities were held at the forest. We would light bon fires, sing songs about kibbutz, the Jezreel valley, the Galilee, the Kinneret (sea of Galilee), Jerusalem, working the land. We danced the Hora had 'mifkadim' (flagship ceremonies). We delved into auto-didactic study of science and knowledge: world history, Jewish history from ancient times to the modern period, philosophy, psychology, astronomy, Zionist history, labour movements in the Diaspora and Eretz Yisrael. The Ken had a large library; we also borrowed books from other libraries. We read late into the night by candlelight broadening our horizons. We also had journals, materials and newsletters sent to us by the central Hashomer office.

Stormy arguments erupted in the Ken when a group began wondering whether the Zionist solution was an answer to the problems of the suffering Jewish community. They believed that redemption would come from the Russian revolution. We would then argue into the small hours of the night, trying to change their minds, resorting to arguments from Borochov's theories and the doctrines of the Hebrew labour movement in Israel; fighting over every person who wanted to defect to the anti-Zionist underground.

The following members of the 1939 Hashomer graduate group managed to make Aliya after much suffering: David Altman, Kibbutz Gazit; Shmuel Zilberschits, Afula; Sonia Katzman, kibbutz Beit Zera; Rachel Katz, Haifa; Nunia Rausch, Kfar Saba; Lucia Auerbach, Haifa; and a few older ones - Isaac Rauch, Tel-Aviv; Shiko (Joshua) Mendel, Be'er Sheva, and others.

Suddenly, the war was upon us. At the beginning of September 1939 Nazi planes bombed the train station. Most of Poland was run over in the blitzkrieg that shattered all resistance. In the middle of September long columns of the Polish army marched through Brody on the way to Romania.

On September 17 the Red Army conquered western Ukraine and Belarus and we found ourselves under the new regime. Initially, the population of Brody was sympathetic toward the Soviet government. Members of the Ukrainian communist party organized a very friendly reception with flowers, red flags and slogans. In the first few months many of these communists secured positions with the local government that had been previously closed to them; young Jews got positions in the post-office, militia, banks and co-operatives; Jews were placed in all levels of government, economic and cultural institutions. The Soviets also created many opportunities for study and training.

However, the first days of naïve belief quickly faded. The new Soviet regime leaves[6] no room for doubt: it will not tolerate "foreign" ideas and organizations. The traditional (intolerant) approach of the regime to Zionism now determines its attitudes towards Zionist organizations. Yet, we (Hashomer) continue to meet, sing, study - albeit with extreme caution... until a day in 1939 when the N.K.V.D. enter the Ken (meeting place), execute a search and confiscate our flag and stamp. We were put on the "black list".

I travelled to Lvov to the Hashomer office at 6 Slovetsky St. for consultation. They sent me to the Hashomer Hatzair Hachshara[7] in Djikov, a few km from Lvov that was still in operation at the time.

The economic situation in our town was dire, especially in our home. We were on the threshold of poverty. My father was sick and couldn't work. I began working at 14 as an assistant in Hollander's shoe shop and later at a saw-mill next to the train station. Eventually this job also ended. There were many unemployed in town. So, along with some friends, I decided to volunteer to work for a year in Russia. We thought that there far from home, where no one knew us, the N.K.V.D. wouldn't harass us. We received an advance on our salary and a free train ticket. We left Brody at the end of 1940 - myself, David Altman, Michael Greengrass, Shmuel Katz, Mundek Gadoldig and Heinrich Teshker. On February 4 we arrived at Kosia-Gora, not far from the capital city Tula where we were taken to a large factory for the manufacture of cement and molding iron. I worked as an assembler of mechanical implements. When the year was up we intended to return to Brody.

We were arrested one by one on the night of February 3 and taken to a special internment center for political prisoners of the N.K.V.D. located in the basement of the splendid N.K.V.D. building in Tula. Even the local population was ignorant of its existence.

I was held in solitary confinement from day one. Life in prison was very difficult and cruel. I never saw daylight. During the day I was not allowed to sleep and interrogations were held at night. This continued for two months. Much pressure and torture were exerted to get me to sign a confession. I had a particularly hard time as I knew no Russian. Thus, I did not understand what they said and could not read their protocols.

I was hungry all the time as the food I got was never sufficient. At times, I received no food for a whole day when the interrogator was dissatisfied with my answers. On April 15, 1941 the whole group was found guilty of Zionist activism and belonging to Hashomer Hatzair. Following articles 10–58 and 11–58 we were sentenced to five years in a 'closed' camp. I, as leader of the group, was sentenced to 7 years hard labour at the camps and 5 years of exile. We were transferred to a quarry not far from Keluga, a city in the vicinity of Tula. The work was very hard: smashing large boulders into small stones by hand.

When the Russo–German war began our situation went from bad to worse; there was little food, the work was very hard and we also had to work Saturdays.

At the end of September 1941 the German army was approaching Moscow. The Russians decided to move the camp farther east. It was a terrible transfer. We walked hundreds of kilometers in the cold and rainy fall weather along muddy side–roads. The guards rode on horses accompanied by dogs on the sides to prevent escape. Our clothes and shoes were torn and wet and we had nowhere to dry them. We received no food. Once a day the guards allowed us to dig up potatoes and collect cabbages that had been left behind in the fields alongside the road. We never washed and everyone was infected with lice. We kept going for three months. Anyone lagging in the last few rows, ill or tired to death, was shot on the spot. We were scared to death of finding ourselves in the last row. At night we were corralled into an empty barn left by the kolchozniks[8] who were also fleeing east for fear of the Nazis. We finally arrived at Riazan, a city in the east on the Oka River. There we were loaded into the bottom of a boat. It was terribly cold. We were all wet and hungry. We sailed for 7 days until the river froze over. Many died on the boat and the piles of bodies accompanied us until we got to the railroad station in Morom. There we were loaded like cattle onto railroad cars in the month of December. To this day I do not understand how we survived under those conditions.

On January 1, 1942 we arrived at a camp in Oresk – 150 people, all sick... 10% of the total that began the journey. After a few days of rest I was sent to dig foundations for factory buildings. The ground at minus 40 was frozen.

During 1942 our dear friend Shumuel Katz gave up unable to endure the difficult conditions at the camp any longer. He drank profuse quantities of water with salt, swelled up and died... may he rest in peace.

In the summer of 1943 I parted from my dear friend David Altman, as I was sent from Orsk on a long journey to the fareast to the camps in the city of Komsomolsk on the shores of the Amoor River where we began laying the infrastructure for a railway to the port of Sovietskaya on the Pacific Ocean. It was to be a 500 km track in the taiga forest. Not a soul lived there, only the army guarding us ensuring we did not escape. Every 10 km there was a camp. All the work was hard labour: sawing, cutting down trees with a hand saw and pulling a tack'cha (wheelbarrow) filled with soil and rocks. Conditions were very difficult. We worked in extreme cold temperatures without fitting clothing, always hungry. Many died of malnutrition, scurvy and other diseases.

In 1946 I was sent to a camp in Outer Mongolia in the Nasohki train station on the border with Mongolia. I worked there building the railroad from Ulan Ude to Ulan Bator. During this time from 1942 until I was released in 1948 I was registered, along with many of the prisoners, as part of Ander's Polish army and the army organized by Wanda Vasilevskaya. When the lists were sent to Moscow my name was always deleted. Even at the end of 1945 when a large contingent of prisoners was released they did not let me go. I was considered very dangerous. Thus, months and years passed with no hope... only despair. By then I knew that my family – parents and sisters, in Brody was no longer alive. New prisoners arriving at the camp told us that the Nazis had killed them all.

I was left with a single ray of hope – that I might get lucky and manage to make contact with my brothers in Israel and perhaps a miracle would occur and we would be united.

February 4 1948 – after 7 years as a prisoner I was released from the camp to spend the next 5 years banished in exile. I received 2 loaves of bread, a herring and B= kilo of sugar – 10 day provisions for the train journey, along with a ticket to my destination in Turkmenistan. I had no clothes, not even underwear, no shirts and not a penny in my pocket. I arrived in Tashkent with no clue how to begin my new life.

I sat for 2 days in the train station, desperate, weak and hungry. I couldn't leave the station due to the cold and wet weather. On the third day, a local man approached and asked if I wanted to work. "Gladly" I responded. He explained the work would be done in the Para–Kum desert with a group of topographers preparing maps for digging a canal from Amu–Daria to the Caspian Sea. The man also told me conditions would be difficult – a very hot summer, no water, living in tents and moving daily by camel and donkey back from place to place, with payment being rendered at the end of the season; I would only receive clothes and food from the first day. I had little choice and agreed. On February 28 we travelled by camel convoy to the work place. At the end of the season I got paid and quit. In 1949 I received a temporary identity card for 3 months and went to work in a new city – Navit–Dag, which they began building in Turkmenistan. They had found oil there and needed workers. I began working as a porter carrying logs and later designing platforms. There I met my wife Polina who helped me greatly and went along with me no matter what fate brought.

From Navit–Dag I wrote my first letter to Israel and through the Histadrut[9] I got addresses for my brother Ovadia and my friend David Altman.

On 6.9.50 I was arrested for a second time. My house was searched and all the letters and photographs I had received from Israel were confiscated, along with Yiddish books. I was taken to the internal N.K.V.D. prison in the Turkmeni capital – Esh Kabad. This was the period when Jewish persecution was organized by a special decree from the dictator Stalin and Zionists were arrested and murdered.

My interrogation lasted 6 months. I was charged with pursuing my Zionist activities after I had been released from the camp in 1948 and had conspired with the enemies of the Soviet State to topple the government. The letters I had written to Israel were presented as the incriminating evidence.

On March 10 1952, without trial, I was sentenced to exile for life in Kazakhstan charged with Zionist activity. On March 20th I was taken under heavy guard to the remote village of Ak–Tau in Kazakhstan. I was to report to the N.K.V.D. office twice a month. My wife followed promptly. We began a new life in the new location rife with political prisoners. After Stalin's death (Sept. 20, 1954) I was released from exile, but stayed put as I was not given identity papers for lack of a birth certificate. I told them that all my documents from Brody were in my file with the N.K.V.D. to no avail. Only in 1955 was I permitted to travel to Brody to bring them a copy of my birth certificate, or a certificate indicating the archives did not have the document.

And so, after 15 years I am travelling to Brody. I was very excited. The whole way I thought I might find traces of my family, that there would be someone who could tell me what happened to them. I arrived in Brody in the morning to find the rail station in ruins. I walked to town. I encountered strangers speaking Ukrainian; half the 'rink' (market) was gone, replaced by green grass. I walked toward the synagogue and saw a roofless structure, no windows or doors, as after a big fire. The entire area behind the synagogue, where the ghetto had been, was empty with only remnants of houses left behind. It was very quiet and sad. After this I went through Zloty St. to the magistrate building that houses the government offices. I presented my request to several officials. They looked at me as though I was a creature from another planet and sent me from one to another, until I got to an N.K.V.D. officer. He explained that the Brody archives were now housed in the central city of Lvov and that is where I needed to go. There were a few hours until the train to Lvov was to depart so I walked about town. The central park was deserted; few trees remained. The statute of author Kuznievski had been removed. The municipal clock wasn't working. The 'kushari' (military canteen) was overrun by an army of N.K.V.D. officials. The Grand Prager bank and the rest of Zloty street hadn't changed; only of the Jews there was no sign.

I walked to Leshnyovski St. toward the 5th house where my family had lived. I saw the green gate of the community center and walked to the well. Our alley – Krupniche, was on the left and the house – no. 4. I went in. Ukrainians from the Krakow area, 1000 km from Brody, were living there. They don't know what happened here during the Nazi era. They live here since 1946. The local Ukrainians were removed from Brody from 1945–1947. The Poles left for Poland. The entire city suddenly seemed strange and hostile.

I travelled to Lvov and there I received the required certificate in lieu of the birth certificate that was not found in the central archives.

Finally, at the end of 1957 I received a document from both the High Court and the Attorney General's office that my conviction from 1941 had been overturned and the investigation into my file was terminated for lack of evidence[10]. After all the bitter events that I lived I had only one goal in life – to make Aliya at all costs. I knew that the only way it was going to happen was through Poland.

I travelled to the Polish embassy in Moscow and there I was told that while there was a Polish–Soviet agreement to return Polish citizens to Poland as long as the N.K.V.D. objected they could not assist me and I needed to make the request to the appropriate Soviet body.

I wrote many such requests. On March 4 1959 I got an answer – "the matter will not be discussed as there are no documents certifying past Polish citizenship"[11]. After that I moved around to many places in Siberia. All the while I kept in touch with my brothers and friends in Israel. In Krasnoyarsk, Siberia, where I lived for 17 years I studied at the Technion (technical Institute) graduating as a certified technician. I got a good job with a company assembling heavy equipment and my economic situation improved. Where ever there were Jews interested in learning Hebrew I taught the aleph–bet to children and adults. With the aid of Israeli stamps I told them about our holidays, the history of Zionism and the kibbutz movement. At night I listened to "kol Yisrael"[12]. I travelled to Moscow to attend every event where Israel was represented. In 1963 an international film festival in Moscow featured Israeli films. In 1966 I went to see the Israeli booth at the international exhibition showing agricultural implements.

Many Jews in Siberia knew my brothers and asked what was happening in Israel. Beginning in 1965 I submitted requests to make Aliya, but was refused. My brother Shaul from Israel wrote letters to

Gromyko – the Soviet foreign–affairs minister and to President Voroshilov but never received an answer.

In 1975, one of the KGB agents, out of the goodness of his heart, told me that if I wanted to make Aliya I was wasting my time in Krasnoyarsk as it was a closed city. He suggested I move to the western sector of the Soviet Union where I had a better chance of getting an exit visa. Following my requests I was transferred in 1976 to the city of Smolensk where I submitted a request for a visa. Only in 1979 after being refused for 14 years I got a visa to emigrate to Israel. Finally, on June 3 1979 my wife and I took our first steps on Israeli soil. I hadn't seen my brothers in over 40 years. In 1980 I was inducted into the organization of the “Prisoners of Zion from the Soviet Union”.

Document # 1

Translated from Russian

Certificate
20 September 1954
No. 1/15–87

This certificate is given to the settler Ignatz Ben Avraham Weltman, born 1921 in Brody – the region of Lvov, a Jew sentenced in compliance with articles 58–10 and 58–11 to seven years in prison and released for re–settlement.

The certificate is to be presented to the Passport Division of the Interior Department of the settlement.

Director of the Interior Ministry

Document # 3

Translated from Russian

The office of the Attorney General of the Russian Federation of Soviet States
16.9. 1957
No. 9/8–8371–56

City of Iskitim region of Novosibirsk
The Iskitim Railroad Directorate

We are informing you that following the decision of the Presidency of the Supreme Court of the Federation of Soviet States of July 30 1957 the sentence of the Regional Court of the 15–16 of April 1941, as well as the Supreme Court's sentence of the Russian Republic from 1.5.54 have been rescinded, and the case against you terminated for lack of evidence.

The attorney in charge
Of the Department for monitoring
National Security Investigations

Document # 4
Translated from Russian

Russian Federation of Soviet States
Supreme Court
August 1957
No. 7 article–959

Certificate

I hereby certify that the sentence of the Regional Court from the 15–16 of April convicting Ignatz Ben Avraham Weltman born in 1921 that worked as an assembler in the meteorological factory in Kosogorsk following article 10–58 and 11–58 of the criminal code of the Soviet Republic, as well as the Supreme Court's sentence of the Russian Republic from 1.5.54 have been rescinded based on the decision of the Presidency of the Supreme Soviet Court from July 30 1957 and the case terminated for lack of evidence.

Secretary to the President of the Supreme Court
Citizen Ignatz Ben Avraham Weltman
The city of Krasnoyarsk Teckstilezh'ki St. 16 apt. 9

In response to your application from 11.11.59 I am informing you that your request will not be discussed as you have no documents certifying your past Polish citizenship.

Director of the Interior Ministry of Novosibirsk

Organization of Brody area émigrés

Tel Aviv August 15 1979

Certificate

I hereby certify that Mr. Yitzchak (aka Ignatz) Ben Avraham Weltman was born in Brody, a town known as Jerusalem D'Austria (Galicia), later of Poland and now the Soviet Union.

The above mentioned was born in 1921 and from early childhood – like the rest of his family – an ardent Zionist, who in his youth joined Hashomer Hatzair and was a member of its leadership. Following the onset of war between Germany and Russia in September 1939 (WW II) and the invasion of the Red army in Eastern Poland he was prevented from going to the Hachshara and making Aliya. He remained in Brody and continued his Zionist activities underground for which he paid a high price: he was arrested and sentenced to prison and hard labour in the 'gulags' and later exiled to the hinterlands. He was finally released and allowed to reach a safe haven in our country.

His time working in the Soviet Union and his suffering for our homeland will be recorded as part of his service to this country.

Sincerely, chairman of the organization

Translator's footnotes

1. Hashomer Hatzair – Young Guard, Zionist youth movement.
2. Ken = nest, the abode of the youth movement.
3. Eretz Yisrael – The land of Israel.
4. Zl' – zichrnono li'bracha – of blessed memory
5. Aliya = to go up; return to the land of Israel.
6. I mostly preserved the tenses as presented by the author, in spite of the lack of consistency (GS).
7. Hachshara = agricultural training center.
8. Russian peasants.
9. Histadrut = National Labour Union of Israel.
10. See appended documents/certificates.
11. IBID
12. The "voice of Israel" radio program.

[Page 302]

Members of the popular group "Akhva" (1938) ["brotherhood"[MK]]

Members of the popular group "Akhva" (1934) ["brotherhood"[MK]]

[Page 303]

The branch of the popular group "Akhva" ["brotherhood"[MK]] (1938)

Group of members of "Ha'Shomer Ha'Tzair" [Young Guard"[MK]] (the first group)

Standing from right to left: Binyamin-Yuma Hertzberg, Zeev Vove Kurin, Zushka Merder, Asher Marsh, Imanuel-Musyo Ettinger, Shiunyo Katz, - Reiss;
Standing in the front row: Michael Lamm, Dorka Vengler, Leshnover, -;
Sitting: Yona Furman, Dushya Gladshtein, Meshulem-Shilk Shtok-Sadan, -, Ovadia Veltman

[Page 304]

A group of members of "He'Khalutz" ["the Pioneer"[MK]]
Brody company, Kibbutz Klosova

A group of Members of the academic Zionist movement "Akhva" ["brotherhood"[MK]]

Standing from right to left: -, -, Misyu Rofshtein, Ra'aya Katz, Hokhberg, Yulek Frenkel, Pepke Frenkel, Dr. Izidor-Izyu Lillian (Physician), Lupati, Misha Brandwein, -, -, Fitch (the young one) Kantor, Dorot, Dr. France, Irke Freifeld, -, -, -

Sitting: Tartakover, Manya Lamm, David Worm, Lusya Ofefa, Dr. Milek Halprin (Physician), Musia Lillian, Milek Tzitron, Khava-Eva Golan nee Gemershmidt, Shimon-Shimek Fitch

[Page 305]

My Family in Brody before World War I

by Shmuel Lamm

Translated by Moshe Kutten

Edited by Yocheved Klausner

The two residential buildings and my father's factory were located in one of the most beautiful corners of Brody. This corner bordered with the Jewish Hospital, on Pyekreska-Szpitalna Street. These places were my favorites for outings and painting.

The factory and the residential buildings were situated around a big courtyard with flowers, all sorts of fruit trees, a vegetable garden, all sorts of poultry birds and even a peacock. A horse and a cart, which my father used on his trips to places outside the city, were also positioned there. My father, Ya'akov Lamm, loved people and was loved by people. He was a modest man, a workingman who was also employed by the city of Brody as an assessor. Many of his inventions, in the field of mechanics, were registered in the Polish Patent Bureau. He received orders from Brody and from far-away cities such as Bialystok and Lvov. My mother, Gitla Lamm, was a modest, soft-spoken woman and a house wife extraordinaire. Despite the fact that we were nine children at home, my mother always found time to read a book. Our maternal grandmother lived with us after our grandfather passed away at the age of 104.

The children's names were Avraham, Simha, Moshe, Chana, Ester, Shmuel (myself), Yitzhak, Manya and Matilda.

At the outbreak of First World War in 1914, our family ran away to Zlotchov on a cart. The Russians arrived there a short while later and we returned to Brody with the Russians. Our factory was mobilized to work for the Red Army. We fixed all sorts weapons as well as cars. Upon the retreat of the Austrian army from Brody in 1916, we ran away to Lvov and stayed there until the end of the war. During the war, two of my brothers, Avraham and Simha served in the Austrian army as professionals specialized in fixing cars and weapons. My father and my brother Moshe got jobs in fixing agricultural machines in a plant in Lvov. Since my father was an exceptional professional, he remained on that job until the end of the war. We were fortunate to see the procession of Lvov Jews, celebrating the Balfour Declaration in 1917. A short while later, at the end of the war, we experienced firsthand the war between the Poles and the Ukrainians, a war won by the Poles. The Polish soldiers were allowed 24 hours to rob the Jews: they burnt synagogues with the people trapped inside, robbed and murdered many Jews in Lvov. At the end of the riots, a funeral for the murdered took place. Tens of thousands of Jews participated in it.

We returned to Brody in 1921. We did not recognize the place we used to live in. Everything was ruined. The two residential buildings and the factory were destroyed. In their place, we found an empty plot. They even uprooted the fruit trees. My father and the boys started to build everything from scratch. First, they rebuilt the factory, and then the residential building. Orders started to flow in from all over Poland. The business flourished. Later on, we built an iron casting factory.

[Page 306]

Two of my brothers got married. Avraham married Berta Tzernetz. A boy and a girl were born to them - Enosh and Ditah. Simha (Simon) married Shenka Bialitzka. They had a son named Shonyo. Moshe (Morris) married Rosa Poliner and they immigrated to the US. Chana married Frank Levin and they had a son named Willy. Ester, Shmuel and Yitzhak immigrated to Eretz Israel during a very short period of time (1933-1934). Manya arrived in 1937 but could not get accustomed to the life in Eretz Israel and she went back to Poland. She managed to marry Pink and she bore him a son. She became a teacher in one of Brody's schools. When the Russians entered Brody with the outbreak of World War II, they confiscated the factory, put a commissar in charge of it and sent my father with two of my brothers to work somewhere else. That was the reason why they did not run away, when the time came, with the Russians. My brother Moshe wrote to them from the US to run away with the Russians, and they managed to reply that they would remain the owners of the property with the Germans. This was the extent of their ignorance about what was in store for them. Their fate was sealed, together with the fate of the rest of the Jewish city residents. They served the Germans until the last moment. My father was sent to the death camps three times but was brought back since he was needed at the factory.

I do not know how everybody perished in the Holocaust. My father, mother, brothers, sisters, uncle and aunt and the rest of the relatives were all murdered at the hands of the German oppressor, every one of them in a different way. May their memory blessed.

Morris and Rose passed away in the US. Ronya and her husband Yitzhak, as well as Ester passed away in Israel.

As opposed to my own parents, Yehudit Cohen from Mikhalova, the mother of my wife Pnina knew in her heart, even as early as 1934, that no Jews would remain alive in Poland. She would say in Yiddish, every time she managed to send another child away from Poland: - "another child is safe". This is how Pnina, her sisters Leah and Rina, her brother Mendel, may his memory be blessed, who immigrated to the US but passed away there at an early age, managed to get out and survive. Her father, Yitzkhak Cohen passed away before the Germans entry. Her mother Pnina along with her married sons Moshe, Gutka and their children were all sent to the Trebilnka incinerators and murdered by the Nazi oppressor. May their memory be blessed.

[Page 307]

How Fortunate was I

by Hinda Wahl (Hela Tuch-Tuviel)

Translated by Moshe Kutten

Edited by Yocheved Klausner

I was born in a very Haredi house in Mikolayev (Drohobitz district). My father, the Hassid Yitzkhak Wahl, married my mother to be, Vincha Minitzer who came from a very rich house and we owned many fields as well as businesses. We were raised by the Torah and religion. Our house served as a meeting place for the entire village. The Torah was studied in it. My father was the most honorable person in the village. Even the non-religious villagers dared not enter the house without a Kippah on their heads.

Despite the fact that we were devout people, our family was progressive. My father did not oppose Zionism and education. He even agreed to have a donation box for the K"KL-JNF[1] in our house. My brother collected donations for the JNF and was active in the movement. Some of the children in our family studied in Brody and the rest in Radzikhov. We had a Torah scroll in our house, bequeathed to my father by my grandfather, who was convinced that my father deserved to live his life in a house suitable for accommodating a scroll. We assembled a minyan, and conducted organized religious life.

The dominant theme in our house was the longing for Eretz Israel. We would receive a calendar from Eretz Israel annually. We would review it reverently and caress the pages so dear to us, with love. The calendar would be hung in a place of honor. I remember myself standing in front of the calendar looking at the picture of the Wailing Wall drawn on it. Sad thoughts would flood my head, mixed with a glimmer of hope. I wished, with all my being, that the words printed on the calendar: "Next Year in Jerusalem[2]", would become a reality. I would be standing and looking at the calendar, with my heart filled with a strong will and hope that I would, some day, reach Eretz Israel.

We were nine children in the house. Miryam, the oldest sister, married Shulem Wahl and they owned a leather business as well as a small wholesale and retail store. My second sister – Ester, married Hersh Zomer. They owned a small wholesale beer shop. My brother Shaul Wahl was an owner of a grain shop. He was named after the famed Shaul Wahl who was, according to the Jewish tradition, a king for six hours[i]. All of these relatives lived in Brody. We also moved to Brody in 1934. Malka and Charna lived near Radzikhov. Krina married Herman Doner. I was told that she worked at a clothes warehouse in Dubno when the Red Army approached Lvov in 1944. Details about her whereabouts vanished after that. My brother Yosef studied in a business school and later on served in the Polish army. He organized an escape from the Nazis' captivity but was caught. He never returned to us. Our youngest sister, Henia, was in the Brody ghetto. I found out that, she too, was taken away from us too soon.

[Page 308]

World War II broke in 1939. I found out that my brother was in Lublin. I went there to look for him, but was caught and sent to Auschwitz. We were employed at forced labor in harsh conditions and I suffered tremendously. However, even when I was subjected to endless tortures, I kept the hope that I would, someday arrive in Israel and would be fortunate to see the Promised Land with my own eyes. At the same time, I made a vow that, when I would be lucky to be saved, I would devote all of my energy and time to take care of the children who suffered so much.

Indeed, after being tortured for so long that I began to think that the end would never come, the US army liberated us in 1945. Along with many other refugees, I went through Czechoslovakia to Vienna and from Vienna through Semmering to Kapfenberg where I met my husband to be, Tzvi Tuch. We arrived in Rome under the "Illegal Immigration[4]" organization. This is where I married my husband and where we started both to work voluntarily in a sanatorium leased by the Joint[5].We did all the menial jobs for no pay, despite the fact that everybody laughed at us and asked us why we do the work without getting paid. We gradually made progress in our work until I was appointed headmistress. I worked for the youths who were on the way to Eretz Israel as illegal immigrants. I devoted myself to this work with all my heart, as this was a way for me to fulfil my vow. We kept in touch with all of these youths, who are now grown adults, up to the present time.

In the meantime, a cousin of my husband, who lived in France, heard about our survival, and sent us tickets to go to France. We only stayed there for half a year despite the fact that my husband was offered an appealing job. I did not accept my husband cousin's pleas to stay in France. I told him that I want to have my kids born in Israel.

I was able, at last, to realize my life ambition and to make Aliyah[6]. We had the right to receive a free apartment, but we did not accept it. We worked and paid for the apartment. I was continuously crying and asking myself why I was so much luckier than many others to reach Israel and to give birth to two cute daughters.

In Israel, I looked for a job in children institutions. I worked at Armon House, Kiryat Ya'arim, Zionist Youth House and the Mizrahi Girls Youths institution.

Tears come to my eyes, even today, when I think about this childhood prayer of getting to Israel and its fulfillment.

Notes by the Book Editor

i. Shaul Wahl (1541 – 1617) was the financial broker of the Polish king Sigismund the 3rd (1566-1632). He was also the lobbyist in behalf of all Polish and Lithuanian Jews. His lobbying efforts lead to the establishment of the autonomous institution of the Polish Jews “The Council of the Four Lands”[3] (1580). A folktale was widespread among the Jews that Shaul Wahl served as the unofficial king for one day after the death of the king Bathory (1586) and before the coronation of the new king. The folktale claims that Shaul Wahl enacted laws favoring the Jews during that day. Many Polish Jewish families and some English Jewish families claim to be related to him

Translator's footnotes

1. K"KL – Keren Kyayemet Le'Israel – or the Jewish National Fund (JNF) was established in 1901, by the first Zionist Congress. The KKL-JNF's objectives were purchasing and developing the land of Israel as well as strengthening the bond between the Jewish people and its homeland. Worldwide contributions were collected in a Blue Box and by sale of the fund's stamps and book inscriptions.
2. The words - "Next Year in Jerusalem" appear at the end of the Passover Seder, as well as the conclusion of the last prayers on Yom Kipur.
3. The Council of the Four Lands, established in 1580, was the body that conducted the spiritual and political affairs of Polish Jewry and represented them with the authorities. This committee had a number of important regulations, some of which are also common nowadays. It was named after the name of four countries that made up the great kingdom of Poland - Poland, Small Poland, Vohlin and Western Galicia. The Council also directed part of Lithuanian's Jewry, in a subsequent period.
4. Illegal Immigration – following the Arab revolt in Palestine (1936-1939), the British government issued a "white paper" which imposed severe limits on the Jewish immigration to Palestine. This was seen by the Jewish population as a betrayal of the mandatory terms and the terms of the Balfour declaration from 1919, especially in light of the increasing persecution of Jews in Europe. In response, the Jewish Zionists organized Aliyah Bet, a program of illegal immigration into Palestine.
5. The Joint – short for the American Jewish Joint Distribution Committee (JDC) is the world's leading Jewish humanitarian assistance organization. Established after World War I to help displaced Jews, JDC has demonstrated that all Jews are responsible for one another and for improving the well-being of vulnerable people around the world.
6. Aliyah - the immigration of Jews from the diaspora to the Land of Israel (Eretz Israel in Hebrew) is defined as "the act of going up" or ascending towards Jerusalem. "Making Aliyah" is one of the most basic tenets of Zionism.

[Page 309]

From My Father's House

by Naftali Harash

Translated by Moshe Kutten

Translated by Rafael Manory

My father returned with his seven-members family to Brody in 1927 from Hungary, where they immigrated to during World War I. My father was a soldier of the Russian Czar then. Following hardships and wandering around in exile, lasting many years, we decided to return to Brody and unite with our family who stayed there. When we returned to Brody we were known as the "Madiars" [the Magyars, i.e., "The Hungarians"[MK]].

In Brody, my father had to start everything from scratch. It was not easy to settle down and to support a family in a new place. My father was a religious man, and he made sure that his children learn Torah in a "Kheder"[1]. Our family was an exemplary traditional family. My mother, of blessed memory, was a "Yidishe Mameh" [Jewish Mother[MK]], in the full sense of the word. My father, of blessed memory, was an honest, good natured and loved by all his acquaintances and anybody who knew him. He was a symbol of purity and gentleness, always looking for ways to do favors for others. He sat down to studies for many days, and at the same time dealing in business to support his family with dignity. When we, the children, grew up, we helped with support of the family, in modesty and respectably, as parents like ours deserved.

When I reached the age of 17 I joined a Zionistic youth movement, and was sent to a Hakhshara[2], in preparation of making "Aliyah" (immigration to Eretz Israel-RM). My parents objected to it, but gave up when they realized that I was determined in my decision. After completing the Hakhshara I started preparing to make Aliyah immediately. The long awaited day was not late in coming. I was fortunate to have my request to immigrate approved and I immigrated to Israel. From the day my feet touched the Israel's soil, I had only one thought: to bring the rest of the family to Israel. I worked hard in a citrus grove earning 15 grush[3] a day. I saved one mil after the other, until I had enough money to pay for a certificate of immigration issued by the English Mandatory Immigration Department, for my family. I received the long-awaited certificate for my parents and two of my brothers who were below the age of 18. I could not add the other two sisters to the certificate, as they were older than 18.

In the meantime, a third sister made Aliyah as a pioneer. Only that sister and I survived from our entire big family. My parents did not use the certificate because my dear mother, of blessed memory, did not want to leave the two sisters alone in a foreign land, as it was impossible to add them to the certificate. In the meantime, the war broke in 1939 and the Nazis, may their memory be forgotten, murdered them all. I never saw anyone of my family members again. The only thing left as a memory from them is the unused certificate.

While talking about exceptional people, it is impossible not to mention my uncle, Khayim Mordekhai Kharash, who was known in Brody not just as regular person but as a "Lamed Vav'nik".[4] This man did more than his ability for the community's neediest. There was not a Sabbath when he did not host one or two of the town's needy' s guests.

[Page 310]

When a needy bride had to get married, and did not have the means to buy her wedding dress, she would find a shelter in Khayim Mordekhai Kharash's house. A lavish wedding would be arranged with tables set sumptuously. All of that was paid by Khayim Mordekhai Kharash, and it wasn't a rare occurrence by him. Everybody in town remembers these events. Khayim Mordekhai did not live for himself. He lived to serve the public. Charities and benevolence were an integral part of the day-to-day life. He really observed the Jewish phrase:[5] "Let anyone who is hungry sit down and eat."

His entire family perished, except one daughter who lives in the USA.

Translator's footnotes

1. Kheder—a traditional religious school for small kids.
2. Hakhshara—a Zionist preparation camp for pioneers immigrating to Israel.
3. Grush—Until 1948, the Palestinian Lira was equivalent to the English pound. It was divided into 100 Grush (or one thousand mils).
4. Lamed Vavnik—someone considered to be one of the 36 righteous individuals whose righteousness upholds the world, according to a mystic Jewish belief. It is said that at all times there are 36 special people in the world, and that were it not for them, all of them, if even one of them was missing, the world would come to an end. The two Hebrew letters for 36 are Lamed (30) and Vav (6).

Editor's note

5. This sentence is taken from the Passover Haggadah (the story traditionally read at the table on the first (and outside Israel, also the second) night of Passover.

[Page 311]

My family of Blessed Memory

by Joseph Kahana

Translated by Moshe Kutten

My late father was born in the town of Stanislavtchik, near Brody, to his father Moshe-Zelig HaKohen. He was orphaned at a young age when his mother passed away, and was sent to study agriculture at a relatively young age. As time passed, he progressed with his studies to the point that he achieved the rank of a farm manager. My mother Etya, may her memory be blessed, was the daughter of David Hersh Patchnik, who was known in Brody and its environs as a Torah scholar and as a devout observant. My mother had four sisters and one brother, all settled in Brody and its surroundings. The youngest of my mother's sisters, Khana (Khan'che), married Betzalel Wilder. They lived in the town of Stanislavtchik and raised one son and six daughters. One of them, Sara, and her husband Yekhiel Shpilka now live in Afula, Israel. They lost their only daughter during the Holocaust and came to Israel with their son who was born in a camp in Germany. The brother of my mother, Mordekhai (Moti) Patchnik, lived the entire time with his family in Brody. He was a man of letters and served as a Gabai [synagogue administrator[MK]] in Beit Midrash[1] "Betzalel". His youngest daughter made Aliya in 1934 and married Yitzkhak Lamm, a Brody native.

In 1913 my father took the management of the Dembina farm, owned by the famed Graff Chertoriski. The farm was adjacent to the city of Trembowla in the Podolia province, where the whole family moved to, except of my older brother, Khayim Leibish, who stayed behind with my grandfather in Brody, where he continued with his studies. We experienced hard life during the First World War and immediately after it, as the only Jewish family at the big palace of the Graff and its surroundings. In 1919, my father decided, under the persuasion of my mother, to leave the farm and move back to Brody to live near

Grandfather. We left on our way back to Brody in March of that year, but regrettably did not find Grandfather alive. He passed away just four days before we arrived. For us, this was a very gloomy beginning. My father bought a house using some of his savings, and the rest of the savings were used by him to deal in trade (in which he did not succeed due to his lack of business sense). The house was located in Ostrovchik Street no. 11, where my parents lived until their last days. My father's spiritual world widened significantly in the city. In the Beit Ha'Midrash (Di Mitelsteh Kloiz" - "The Middle Kloiz[2]") where he prayed, he found the meaning of his life. He was one of the first people to arrive in the morning and among the last people to leave in the evening. He was observant, truthful, diligent and good-hearted. Those were the reasons why people loved him, may his memory be blessed! My mother was also humble and diligent, composed and limitlessly devoted to the family. May her soul live in memory forever!

[Page 312]

We were four brothers in our family. One brother, whose name was Mordekhai, passed away in 1920, when he was only 18 years old. Everybody in Brody called my oldest brother, Khaim Leibish, by his nickname - the "Broder-Kind" – "the Child of Brody". Starting in 1919, he owned a textile store called "Brink" adjacent to the store of Mita Frenkel. In 1932, he closed the store and started to work at the city hall. He continued with this work until his last years. He lived on Kolejowa Street in a nice house where my sister in-law, Sara, managed a restaurant. They had two children: a beautiful girl by the name of Nuna, whose life was cut short abruptly at the age of 15, and a son named Yosef, also a very cute child. My sister in-law and her two children were taken to Auschwitz and never came back. A few months later, my brother committed suicide. My second brother, Avraham, was a very talented man. He married Hinda Klein (Sapir) from Staro-Brody, where they owned a beautiful house with a wonderful fruit tree grove around it. Avraham worked with the firm of Lustman-Koren, who owned a sawmill in Brody, near the railroad. In 1934, my brother was sent to the Carpathian forests as a wood-expert and he worked there until the Nazi invasion into Poland. My brother, my sister in-law and their three children were subsequently murdered by the Nazis. My wife's sister, Ester (Azhya) married David Khodek from Brestechko. Starting in 1935, they lived in Brody, in the house owned by Holtzager Brink. My brother in-law's brother, Peretz Khodek and his wife Rivka, nee Aperman survived the Holocaust and they live today in Ashkelon, Israel. My wife also had an uncle who lived in Brody. He was the elder Rabbi Avraham Levin who completed the book of Rabbi Steinberg.

The Nazis murdered more than 60 people from my closer family, who lived in Brody and its environs. May their memory be blessed!

Translator's footnotes

1. Beit Midrash – Literally means "A house of learning" was a study hall or a school for religious studies, usually in or adjacent to a synagogue or a Yeshiva. It is also a word used to describe the level of studies below the academic level of a yeshiva.
2. Kloiz – Jewish communal house of learning, praying and gathering.

[Page 313]

Members of My Family and Images of Brody Preserved in My Heart

by Joseph Ettinger

Translated by Moshe Kutten

Edited by Yocheved Klausner

I am always able to see the image of my mother, Miryam Ettinger nee Goldring, in front of my eyes, short built and full of radiant love for her two children. Her husband, my father R' Shmuel Ettinger, may his memory be blessed, passed away and was taken away from her prematurely. My mother wished to bestow on my sister Liza and I the best material and spiritual values. She had always mentioned her eminent educator, Dr. Herzl, who was a teacher in the local Jewish school and who always aroused in her the love for the Jewish nation. We inherited the love for the Jewish people, the Jewish way of life and the nice and warm attitude toward other people.

My grandfather, R' Shlomo Shmaryahu Goldring, may his memory be blessed, my mother's father, was a man of Torah and good manners. He lived by the phrase: "The world is built around three things: Torah, work and charity". Anonymous charity was his main trait. He took care of the city orphans for years. My grandfather raised eleven sons and two daughters, and endowed them with the guidelines for an exemplary self-discipline. Along with that endowment, he always remained a loving and loved father. He is engraved in my memory as a person with his long white beard who maintained a puritan way of life. He would often urge me to accompany him on his way to the great synagogue, where he served as one of the Gabais [synagogue administrator[MK]]. He was very proud of his wide branching family. Dressed in his white robe against the lighted candles, his Yom Kippur's blessing of his grandchildren is still ringing in my ears: "Always be proud and be a righteous Jew!"

My uncle, my father's brother, R' Khayim Ettinger, may his memory be blessed, moved in 1926 with his family from the town of Berestechko to Brody. He was a scholar. He knew his way around the Jewish Talmud like R' Shmuel knew his way around the Babylonian city of Naharde'a[1]. Moral and honest was my uncle, R' Khayim. He contributed significantly to my education and to the shaping of my personality. He won me over with his pleasant manners and his scolding, always directing me to doing good deeds. In 1943, my uncle Khayim was murdered by the Nazis. May his memory be blessed.

Dear people, whose images are etched in my memory, taught me the Torah. I experienced the heavy hand of my teacher, R' Avraham Der Roiter's (red-hair) since the age of three. Fear and horror would get hold of me every time he would approach me with the intention of punishing me with his thumb. Yaakov, the son of the famous butcher in town, R' Melekh Unreich, studied with me in the "Kheder[2]". The butcher sported a large belly, which saved him when a bullet lodged in his stomach. Among my prominent teachers, was Nakhum Okser, the father of the city orphans and a dedicated educator. I still keep in my memory his amazing stories drawn from the bible. I would also mention Mr. Arnold Mustzisker, who let me have the honor of feeling the wrath of his strong arm, for which I am actually thankful. There were also my teacher and educator in the elementary school, Mr. Kalman Henrik, my teacher Shaul Bernshtein, teacher Arye-Leon Sheinholtz who guided me through the mysteries of our religion and Jewish identity, as well as Mr. Keller, my elementary school teacher, an historian who published research articles on the subject of "Pan-Europa[3]". I would also mention the principal of the elementary school, Philip Ashkenazi, who was active in the movement for the assimilation of the city Jews and the school treasurer, Mr. Wildholtz, who did not comprehend the meaning of the regime change when the Austrian government was replaced by the Polish one. There was also professor Tchatchkes, who was the religion and Jewish history teacher in the local high-school. He was not fluid in the Polish language and therefore his lectures about historical affairs of our national history drew thunders of laughter among the students.

[Page 314]

As far as acquiring a profession, blacksmithing and turnery, is concerned, I need to favorably mention R' Yaakov Lamm who helped me tremendously and with dedication. His sons Avraham and Simkha helped him. I would also mention R' Chone Zinger, the brother of the journalist Mendel Zinger, who taught us English. Thanks to him, my absorption in the British army during World War II was relatively easy.

A whole line of our town people is "passing" in front of my eyes. I would have wished, if I could, to write a few words for each one of them. Operatives of the Ha'Shomer Hatzair youth movement, and people of ZTG (the Jewish sports organization), with whom I spent most of my free time, are in this procession of images. Those were the days! I loved the walkway of the main street – Zlota (Gold Street!). I used to stroll worriless in this street along with other teenagers, feeling healthy in both my body and my soul.

I asked the beautiful, innocent and virtuous Nushka Freed, a member of Ha'Shomer Hatzair movement, to join me on my way eastward, but she preferred to stay with her parents. Like many others, she did not want to believe in the horror stories, which circulated around the town about the cruelty of the Germans. The Nazis and their collaborators the Ukrainians murdered her, her parents, her grandmother and her aunts.

I shall mention many others, only by their names:

Eli Moshe Lehrer the shoemaker and his sons
Yosef Katcher, locksmith, gym teacher and soccer player
Mundek Khutiner, gym teacher
Moshe Reinart, counselor in the Hashomer Hatzair youth movement
Ibah Frider, soccer player
Munyo Frider, soccer player
Khayim-Noakh Shapira, dedicated Melamed [Jewish Torah teacher[MK]]
The Schwarzman family, carpenters.
Members of the Perels family, wheat merchants
My friend, Tzadok Gruber, who was killed as a soldier in Ukraine
Khayim Khazan, Mohel
David Sapir, caretaker at the Big Synagogue
R' Aleksander, caretaker at the Big Synagogue
R' Moshe Gliner from the Khevra Kadsiha [the Jewish burial society[MK]]
R' Zauber, Talmud teacher and synagogue preacher

Yuma and Leib Hertzberg and their parents

Gershon Eisenberg, mason

[Page 315]

Kalmus, pharmacist

Rabbi Yosa'le Popper

Dr. Adolf Yung, physician

Diamant - according to Kalman Hernik, Dr. Diamant told the Gestapo people who came to arrest him: “Let go of me and salute! You are standing in front of a captain in army of King Wilhelm the 2nd. The Germans' response was: “nevertheless - a Jew”.

Schleifer – he was nearsighted and threatened to sue anybody who would blow into his ear.

Mendel Parnes – his nickname was “trenzak” (sacks opener), sacks merchant.

“Black” Papka (Di Shvatze Papka), owner of a prestigious coffee house.

Hozer, owner of a candy store.

Arye Zigelboim, his son Yitzkhak, his brother Eli and their families.

Rabbi Heshel Doner.

Pinkhas Doner, baker

Holtzzager, the registrar of the Brody congregation

Perl Pestes (Perl di langeh – 'long” Perl) - owner of a popular restaurant

Max Rismak and sons, industrialists

Fox and sons, books.

Waltman, Hebrew teacher

Brestling, calligraphy teacher

Klaper, restaurant owner

Kristiampoler, electrical engineer

Dr. Horn, lawyer

Moshe Zabber (Moshe “der krimmer”), owner of a horse drawn cart and a poet of rhymes

Chone Kachkeh, owner of a horse drawn cart

Yosef Kahana, water drawer

Minka Fush, sold kosher milk

Polga, sheet metal worker

Dr. Oprecht – physician

Lipah Halprin, wealthy affluent merchant, was considered the town's ”rich man”

Shlomo Dishel – butcher

Artzi Shorr – municipal auxiliary policeman

Dr. Maximilian Hirt, lawyer
Dr. Bernard Lustig, lawyer
Tzimels, orthopedic physician
Nunek Rogovski, violinist
Redziviller, barber and accordion player
Yosef Misit, butcher
Mutzik Bernstein

[Page 316]

Lupateh, bakery owner
Ordentlich (Stochek!)Weiss brothers, butchers
Uri Anshtendig, *Melamed*
Moshe Shorr, merchant
Khaim Rofeh, paramedic and physician's assistant
Golda Kopika, member of the women Chevra Kadisha (burial society)
Tzoler, paramedic and physician's assistant
Moshe Tantzer, exceptional swimmer who saved me from drowning
Levenshtein, the conductor of the Big Synagogue chorus
Boikhes, merchant
Vilner brothers, porters
Gavriel Seidenworm
Naftali Seidenboim, murdered by a Ukrainian
Shvedron, merchant, alcoholic beverages
Ostersetzer, who prayed with a mournful voice at the Big Synagogue
Feuershtein, tailor
Margarovitz, sheet metal worker
Zilberg, owner of a bicycle repair shop
Masser, sign painter
Noakh Schtok, painter and promoter
Shmuel Kokosh, tailor (last resort)
Melech, locksmith
Mrs. Kanner, seller of stationery
Chinyo Eisenbruch, printing-shop worker
Andziya Bruchner
Maness Sapir and his wife Charllota
Akselrod, gravestone engraver
Fitch-Veinschtok, printer and stationery merchant
Turchyo Kaplush

Dr. Kaplush, municipal physician

Feuerstein, goldsmith

Dr. Ambus, lawyer

Avraham Kantor – owner of an agricultural machinery shop

Max Kantor, student and painter

Yisrael-Yulek Shvabish, student and soccer player

Tzverdling – merchant who would remove his hat when talking to the mayor on the phone

Rubinshtein, producer of ropes

[Page 317]

Leib'ele, sheet metal worker

At the end of this multi-colored procession, I would like to turn the attention to Parnes' restaurant on 1 Kalir Street. People from a different world were meeting there, who were not very careful about the integrity of their manners. Many of them had character traits similar to that of Robin Hood.

We had in our town some shady creatures as well, which were dear to my heart and I would like to mention their names:

Motl Shtreicher

Michael Mintzer

Itzi Boiko and his son Khaskel

Moshe Katolik who converted but returned to his roots a short while later

Ber'ale Gritzman

Yehuda Bloi

Meir Printz

Dr. Kohen – who lost his mind while working on his second doctor degree thesis. He was held in a mental hospital in Lemberg, and when he was released he did not know about World War I.

Yonas Berri

Itzik Meshko with his dogs

Okah Shilda, who gave birth to a baby boy from the gentile Vasilly

All of these people integrated into the Jewish street in Brody, my beloved city, and remained in my memory.

Translator's footnotes

1. Naharde'a – a major city in Babylon located on a major canal connecting the rivers Tigris and Euphrates. This Babylonian city was the principal seat of the leadership of the exiled Jews and the center of Jewish learning and scholarship during the period started with the conquest of Jerusalem by the Babylonian king Nebuchadnezzar II, in 586 BCE and the place where the Jewish Babylonian Talmud was developed. Rabbi Shmuel was a scholar of the first generation of the scholar dynasty of the Amoraim.
2. Kheder – Jewish religious school for preschoolers.
3. Pan-Europa - is the oldest European unification movement. It began with the publishing, in 1923 of the manifesto of "PanEuropa" by Count Richard Nikolaus von Coudenhove-Kalergi's. The manifesto presented the idea of a unified European State. In its original form, the movement was independent of all political parties, but had a set of principles by which it appraised politicians, parties, and institutions. The movement had four main basic principles: liberalism, Christianity, social responsibility, and pro-Europeanism. At the same time, it openly welcomed and acknowledged the contributions of Judaism and Islam whose heritages they share.

[Page 318]

There Was a Pious Man

by Ya'akov Lieberman

Translated by Moshe Kutten

Edited by Yocheved Klausner

My father, may his memory be blessed, R' Eliezer Yosef Lieberman, was a Husiatyn Hassid[1]. A righteous man, loved by people and loving people, learned, scholar and observant of every commandment, minor or major. He devoted every available time to the Torah and to studying religious books.

Following World War I, any time the Husiatyn Rabbi would come from Vienna to visit his Hasidim in Galicia, my father would abandon all of his business affairs and would travel to see the Rabbi, usually to the city of Lvov. He would also put a lot of effort in convincing his older sons to accompany him. His sorrow was enormous when he succeeded to put in only one son, our brother Meir under the care of the Rabbi. My father and brother's trust in the Rabbi was absolute. It did not lessen even a bit, when the Rabbi's advice failed short of solving a problem, and there is a story about that and this is how it goes: When my brother Meir came of age, he was obliged to report for a medical check-up by the army. My father asked the Rabbi for a good advice about how to save his son from eating non-Kosher food, desecrating the Sabbath and other sins, unavoidable while serving in the army. The Rabbi hinted that Meir should steal the border and arrive in Vienna, where he would study in a Yeshiva until the danger would pass. However, my brother was captured at the Czech-Polish border, and after some jail time he was brought over to Brody and was released on bail until the scheduled medical checks held in Kamionka Strumilowa [a city in Lvov province[MK]]. My father exchanged letters with the Rabbi again, but following the new advice and bribery extended to the members of the committee and its physicians, my brother was found fit to serve in the army. The postponement of his enlistment was due to the bribe paid annually, an event that lasted a few years. However, the trust of my father and brothers in the Rabbi did not wane.

My father's first priority was raising his sons according to the ways of the Torah, to keep the commandments, carry out good deeds, be honest and tell the truth. Nothing angered him more than hearing a lie. In addition to the secular education bestowed on his children as part of the compulsory elementary school education, my father made sure to supplement our secular knowledge by private teaching. In educating his sons, the emphasis was mainly placed on the religious education. He would wake up his older sons who helped him in his business, to go to the Kloiz[2] and study Gemara[3] for several hours in the morning. The same duty was imposed upon them in the evening. We were taught by R' Avraham-Menakhem-Mendel-Halevi-Shteinberg. My father would hold weekly exams for his sons about their studies in the Kloiz and the studies with the Rabbi during the week. My father was not fortunate to enjoy this privilege later in life, because the two younger sons separated from his pious ways before they reached the age in which they could study in the "Kloiz". My father was tired of his effort to ensure that his sons would follow his ways, due to the examples set by his older sons and due to the diffusion of the new ways into almost every Hasidic house in the city.

[Page 319]

My father was totally against high school. His sons had to acquire general education secretly if they wished to do so, and compliment their education after they left his home. The same was true about learning Hebrew[4] to be able to converse and read its literature. The fact that his descendants strayed away from the road he sketched for them was a source of deep indescribable sorrow for him. Except for our brother Meir, he resented the way of life his other sons carved for themselves.

I recall his answer to one of his sons, who tried to calm him down after he became aware of the fact that my sister Miriam was caught by the Zionist bug. He responded: "The Rabbi says that in a wedding the "shkotzim"[5] run ahead of the procession (paraphrasing the Zionists who wish immigrate to Eretz Israel before the arrival of the Messiah).

When he was notified that one of his sons speaks Hebrew in public and was active in a Zionist youth movement he remarked -" It would be better if he would convert rather than follow Jeroboam ben Nevat"[6].

I recall the events of one Thursday night when I came back home following a lesson with the city's Rabbi. I was surprised to see my mother baking, and my father wrapping and packaging of challahs in papers and piling them up on the table. When I asked for the meaning of this busy activity, my mother, may her memory be blessed, whispered in my ear, sighting: "You do not know how deep the distress among our people, and how many are the needy these arduous days". A few minutes later, my father asked me to help him in his charity duty. He loaded a sack on my shoulder, shouldered a sack himself, twice as big, and we went out. After a short distance, he unloaded the sack off my shoulder, took out several packages and ordered me to stay put and guard the two sacks until he would come back. He disappeared in the darkness of an alley and came back empty-handed, a short while later. We shouldered the sacks again and continued to walk. These stops repeated until my sack was emptied out. This is when my father ordered me to return home and he continued on his way. Before parting ways, he asked me if I want to wake up later than usual to go to the "Kloiz". I did not answer him, and he apparently decided to try me and wait until I woke up by myself. As I was always an enthusiastic morning-sleeper, I woke up quite late, almost late for the regular Morning Prayer. My father left a message for me with Mother, that I should not be in a hurry to come to help him after the prayer that day if the prayer would end late, and use the time to buy myself some cakes from the caretaker and stay at the Kloiz to finish the daily Talmud page.

When I came back home the day after our night strollig, I thought that my mother would be more open-hearted when my father was out, and reveal who were the needy people we visited. I was wrong. She replied - "There are only a few grown-ups who know how to keep their mouth shut, and more so – the teens. If one does not know – he is not obligated to be tried not to reveal the secret".

My mother passed away in year 5686 (1925/6) when she was only forty-five years old. She was a very gentle woman, modest, charitable and good-hearted. She was an exemplary housewife and mother. A person from the town who hid with my father, in the same house, for a short while told me that my father was murdered on Yom Kippur [Day of Atonement[MK]] in Toporov. During that holy day, it was impossible to stop my pious father from going out to synagogue and pray in public.

Just prior to the Holocaust, after the Husiatyn Rabbi settled in Eretz Israel, signs of his willingness to emigrate began to emerge in his letters, but the Holocaust put an end to his wishes.

Translator's footnotes

1. Husiatyn Hasidic dynasty originated from the Ruzhin Hasidic family in the city Husiatyn, Ukraine. The dynasty moved to Vienna in Austria at the beginning of the First World War, and from 1937 was located in Tel Aviv, Israel. Following the death of the fourth Rebbe without descendants in 1968, it ceased to operate as a Hasidic dynasty.
2. A place of praying, studying and meeting for the Jews in Eastern Europe
3. The Jewish Talmud, is what is called “oral Torah” the central text of the Rabbinical Judaism consists of two parts: The Mishnah – contains the core text and the Gemara embodies the analysis and interpretation of the Mishnah and the holy Bible.
4. In the diaspora, Jews generally refrained from using Hebrew, the “holy tongue,” for common, non-holy, everyday speech and used other languages, some specifically created by combining local dialects with Hebrew lettering and words.
5. The plural form of “sheigetz”, the Yiddish word for non-Jewish boy often used disparagingly and literally means "detestable," "abomination", "loathed", "blemish" and actually translates as "rascal", "scoundrel" or "varmint".
6. Jeroboam ben Nevat (Jeroboam son of Nevat) – King of the northern Kingdom of Israel was an officer in King Salomon court who fled to Egypt following the statement by the profit Elijah that he would inherit the Kingdom of Salomon. He lead the revolt against Salomon's son and successor, Rehoboam which led to the secession of the ten northern tribes of Israel to form the separate Kingdom of Israel.

[Page 320]

Friday at Home

by Berta Kalenberg (Margulies)

Translated by Moshe Kutten

Edited by Yocheved Klausner

Strange and weird things occur during one's life. However, most of these occurrences are being forgotten quickly and they disappear from one's memory as if they never happened. On the other hand, there are things, which are etched in one's memory forever. Here I am in Brody at home, many years ago and the day is Friday. As usual, that was a day packed and filled with work and a hard day for me.

My mother went to the store and the burden was left on my shoulders. My father went to the synagogue and has not returned as of yet. I had to arrange everything in the house, dress up the little children and watch over the baking in the oven until he returned. The wonderful smell coming from the oven is indescribable. Here comes the time for taking the round and brown challahs and the black bread out of the oven. The taste of the bread is like the taste of heaven! After that, I had to store all of these foods in the cabinets, before my little students arrive. Only then, time has come to take care of myself, as I am a human too. After all of the running around and these activities, I deserved a little bit of care for myself. I had to wash my long hair in a large bowl. Even there, there was a waiting line, as eight heads were also waiting to be taken care of, one after the other...and we had to hurry up before the Sabbath.

And then, the clock rang twelve and my students arrived – Shimon, Frida, Yehoshua Leshnover, Khana Meizelsh and some other children from the first, second and third grades of the elementary school. They are glad and happy to come to my house, firstly because the warm and tasty cakes were delicious to their palate. Secondly, they come to me to learn how to read and write, so that they would be prepared for Sunday.

I could not possibly visit them at their homes on Friday as the day was so short and the task was great.

The house is bursting with action. One student learns a song by heart; the other is having trouble with a solution to an arithmetic problem. I am running from one child to another and helping everybody. These were all good students and their grades were good and even excellent. However, their parents insisted that their grades should be all "exceptional"... and this is why I had to invest a lot of effort in helping them. My monthly wage was between eight to ten "golden" coins per child [Zloty is golden in polish and also a unit of money[MK]]. I did not actually receive real money, but every child's family helped in supporting my large family. My mother received meat for the Sabbath from the butcher, who was the father of one student. In another store, she received shoes, and yet in another store she received fabrics for the holidays. We received every commodity our family needed in lieu of money.

After the students have left, the house is quieter. My parents and my sisters are preparing to welcome the Holy Sabbath. My mother spreads a pure white tablecloth over the table, lights the candles, and recites the blessing. She looks at each child to make sure that every detail of him or her clothing is in order.

[Page 321]

I request to hurry up and finish the food, as I must hurry to the "Gordonia" youth movement in which I am member. However, here comes the opposition. My father, may his memory be blessed, opposed my way of life. He was pious and God-fearing and decided to protect me with all his might.

With the help of my brother, I managed to sneak out of the house and arrive at the club. However, when I arrived at the community house, my father caught me, and in front of everybody, hit me, and demanded that I come back home. My situation was very sorrowful.

I would never forget that night. I did not go to sleep at home. I went to sleep at my friend's Pnina Teketch. My mother was looking for me among my friends. In her hands, she held a small jug full of cocoa for me. She found me in the yard.

Tears streamed down of both of our eyes. However, I was confident of my feeling and the goal I had chosen. I did not return home. I decided to make Aliya to Eretz Israel. This was thirty years ago. That Friday would never be wiped out of my memory.

[Page 322]

My Family's Fate

by Eliezer Tolmetz

Translated by Moshe Kutten

Edited by Yocheved Klausner

I arrived in Eretz Israel in 1935 and reside today in Tel-Aviv with my wife Rachel. My daughter Edith, her husband Eli and children Asaf, Yuval and Gali reside in Haifa. My son Rami resides in Jerusalem.

My father, Avraham Landau, perished in Brody during the Holocaust. My mother Gitl, nee Tenenbaum, passed away in Brody before the war. My brothers Yanka'le and Zinda'le perished in the Holocaust.

My paternal grandfather, Yisrael Landau, passed away in Brody during the Russian rule.

My paternal grandmother Sheinda'le passed away before the war.

My maternal grandfather, Shalom Tenenbaum perished in the Holocaust.

My maternal grandmother, Reiza'le Tenenbaum passed away before the war.

My mother Gita'le passed away before the war

My maternal uncle, Avraham Tenenbaum and his wife perished in Brody during the Holocaust. My other maternal uncle Nakhman Tenenbaum arrived in Eretz Israel as a pioneer in 1925, passed away in Haifa in 1958. His wife Dora, their daughter Ra'aya Ilan and their son Yaakov Tene reside today in Jerusalem.

Additional relatives whom I recall:

The children of my grandfather Shalom Tenenbaum's sister:

Munyo Pelver, arrived in Eretz Israel from Shanghai, after the World War, and passed away in Tel-Aviv. Khana Rot made Aliya to Eretz Israel in the 1920's and passed away in Tel-Aviv. Rozya Knopf, her husband and their children Milek, Gita'le and Kobush perished in the Holocaust. Liza Grinfeld, her husband and their children Dzhonek and Lusya perished in the Holocaust.

[Page 323]

My Family's Fate

by Leah Shduel

Translated by Moshe Kutten

Edited by Rafael Manory

We were four generations of Brody natives in the Landau family: Grandmother, Father, us the children and the grandchildren. We were eight children in the house.

Grandmother Khaya Landau was the sister of Reiza'le Weintraub of Brody. She passed away many years ago.

My father passed away from grief during the Russian rule in our city.

My mother Sheinda'le passed away many years ago from a disease.

My eldest brother, Avraham Landau, his wife, nee Friedman from Busk, and their sons Yanka'le and Zinda'le were annihilated by the Germans.

Avraham's eldest son, Leizer Landau, from Avraham's first wife Gitla Tenenbaum, lives in Israel since 1935. His name today is Eliezer Tolmetz.

My brother Leib Landau, his wife Rachel, daughter of Undik Kamionka Strumiłowa, and their two children—Yosa'le and Sheinda'le were annihilated by the Germans.

My sister Keila, her husband Natan Katz and their daughter Sheinda'le became Hitler's victims.

My sister Pearl, her husband Leib Raht and their daughter Sheinda'le were murdered by the Germans.

My sister Ester passed away before the war.

My brother Milek Landau, his wife and their two daughters were murdered by the Germans.

My sister, Tzviya Landau, who was single, was annihilated by the Germans.

I, Lei'che Landau, the youngest daughter—ran away from home, against my entire family's will. I arrived in Eretz Israel, as a pioneer and a member of the youth movement "Bnei Akiva". I was initially a member of Kvutzat Avraham[1], and later on a member of Kibbutz "Kfar Etzion" until 1948. I returned to Gush Etzion when it was liberated by our soldiers in the Six-Day War.

After the end of Second World War, when the war refugees started to show up in Eretz Israel, I was told by one of the family friends that my family were still alive, hidden in a bunker owned by a Christian family. A day or two before the end of the war, a Jewish youth from Brody showed the German Gestapo their hideout. This was their end.

I never found out who was that Jewish traitor.

Editor's note

1. "Kvutzat Avraham" (named after Rabbi Avraham Yitzhack HaCohen Kook, who was still alive at the time) was a youth group from the religious "Bnei Akiva" youth movement. Established in 1935, the group was involved in "Hakhshara", i.e., preparation for life in an agricultural settlement in Eretz Israel. The group established the Kibbutz Kfar Etzion in 1943.

[Page 324]

My Family

by Lola Rotenberg-Buchan

Translated by Moshe Kutten

Edited by Rafael Manory

To evoke the memory of our city Brody, my relatives and my dear ones, of whom I dream about endlessly, I have to go back to the roots of our family, a modest and ill-fated family that was also noble and cultural.

Firstly, I recall my father, Zigmond [Zygmunt in Polish[MK]], son of Yekhezkel Rotenberg, who was born in Kolomea (today Kolomyia, Ukraine-RM) in 1869. His mother Betty, was the daughter of Khayim Khayut, the son of a famed family in Brody who were the descendants of the Provence Hassids[1] (Rabbi Tzvi Peretz[2] the son of Shlomo Khayut, 1876–1926, came from the same family). My father's mother became a widow one year after the birth of her son, my father Zigmond. Despite the fact that she was still a young and beautiful woman, she did not remarry, because she wanted to devote her entire life to raising and educating her only son. With great difficulty, she sent her son to the Jewish school and to the high school in Brody, from which my father graduated in 1886 at the age of 17. He then began to work at the pharmacy owned by Mr. Kulak. From then on, my father specialized in pharmaceutical science. In 1889, he enrolled at Lvov University, and obtained his diploma in pharmaceutical science in 1892.

In 1893, he returned to Brody and worked in a pharmacy. Later on, he completed a year of compulsory service in the Austrian military while working at the same time, in pharmacies in the cities of Burshtyn (or Bursztyn-RM) and Ternopol [today Ternopil, Ukraine.[MK]]

In 1896, my father bought himself a pharmacy in the adjacent town of Olesko, and this was where he started his Jewish public service. He established a school named after Baron Hirsch,[3] and took care of its growth. In 1911, he left Olesko, returned to Brody and opened his own pharmacy named "Under G-d's Care". Initially the pharmacy was located on ground floor of "Hotel Europa", in the corner of Lvov Street ("Lemberger Gas," also called Mickiewicz St. during the Polish rule). Later on, he moved the pharmacy to the corner of Third of May and Farna (or Koscielna) streets, across from the "Roikovka" municipal park. The place on the lower floor of "Hotel Europa" was acquired by the restaurant of Mr. Zorne, a member of a famed family in Brody, from which only one Brody native survived–Yitzkahk Zohar (Zorne) who now lives in Ramat Gan, Israel.

And so, there were four pharmacies in Brody: the one of Zigmond Rotenberg, the one owned by Mr. Sentcher, another one owned by Mr. Kalmus on Rynek B St. [Rynek means city square in Polish[MK]] and the one owned by Leon Kalir on Rynek D St.

According to government regulations, Father had to leave the pharmacy open on holidays and Sabbaths (except during the "Days of Awe"[4] of Rosh Hashanah and Yom Kippur). He did keep the Jewish tradition, but nevertheless he was an intellectual and a progressive man and married a woman who was worthy of him and he of her. His wife—Sidonia, was the daughter of Stefanie (Fannie), the niece of the famed R' Yehoshua Schorr[6] and great-granddaughter of R' Yekhezkel Landau (1714–1793) who was Av Beit Din[5] in Brody, one of the scholars of Brody, Chief Rabbi of Prague and author of the renowned book "Noda B'Yehuda" ["Known among the Jews"[MK]]. Sidonia's father was

[Page 325]

Dr. Henrik Leiblinger, Brody's municipal physician, who died at the age of 51 after contracting typhus from a patient under his care.

My mother, Sidonia, received Jewish, as well as general-secular education at her parents' home and was highly educated. She played the piano beautifully and participated as a concert pianist in concerts held at the "Music Association". She wrote beautiful stories and poems in the languages she was proficient in — mainly Polish and German. In addition, she translated the book "Quo Vadis' by Henryk Sienkiewicz, laureate of the Nobel Prize in literature, from Polish to German, and also started to translate the book "Pharaoh" by the Polish writer

Bolesław Prus. However, her premature death cut her work short. She passed away at the age of 32.

My parents, who were both single children in their respective families, wanted to establish a large family, and indeed, they had five children: Paula, the wife of Henryk Muschisker, me, Henyu, Stefan and Zigfrid, who carried the name of his mother. She died just two weeks after he was born. His name Zigfrid comes from her name Sidonya-Zisya.

Father, who had to take care of five children, married again with Ernestina Rozwald (who worked in the pharmacy). A daughter was born to them. She is my little sister Mira (Lusya). His second wife did not live long either and passed away prematurely (she was 49 when she died). Mira sacrificed her life for Father; she could have been saved with her relatives, who survived the war. However, she chose to stay with Father.

Translator's footnotes

1. Provence Hassids–Provence, in Southern France was the birthplace of the Kabala–the Jewish mystical interpretation of the Holy Scriptures. This is also one of the birthplaces of the Askkenazi Hassidic movement.
2. Rabbi Tzvi Peretz Khayut – born in Brody in 1876. He was the grandson of Zvi Hirsch Khayut – one of the reknown Jewish Galitsian Talmudic scholars. Khayut was ordained as a rabbi but he also studied at a university and attained a PhD in Philosophy. He served as the rabbi of the Jewish community in Florence, Italy from 1901 and headed the rabbinical school in Florence. Subsequently and until 1918, Khayut served as a rabbi in the city of Trieste. From 1918 to his death, Khayut served as the chief rabbi of the Jewish community of Vienna. In addition, he was also the Chairman of the Zionist General Council from 1921 to 1925. Khayut died in Vienna in 1927. His remains were later taken to Israel and he was reburied in Tel Aviv.
3. Baron Moritz von Hirsch–(1831–1896), was a German Jewish financier and philanthropist who set up charitable foundations to promote Jewish education and improve the life of oppressed European Jewry. He is also known as the founder of the Jewish Colonization Association, which sponsored large-scale Jewish immigration to Argentina.

4, Days of Awe–[From http://www.jewfaq.org/holiday3.htm] "The ten days starting with Rosh Hashanah and ending with Yom Kippur are commonly known as the Days of Awe (Yamim Noraim) or the Days of Repentance. This is a time for serious introspection, a time to consider the sins of the previous year and repent before Yom Kippur". Here however, the pharmacy was closed only on the actual High Holydays, Rosh Hashana and Yom Kippur.

4. Av Beit Din (or ABD) – an honorific title for the presiding rabbi of a rabbinical court.

[Page 326]

About My Family That Is No More

by Pnina Hertzberg Lansky

Translated by Moshe Kutten

Edited by Rafael Manory

My parents, David and Tova and my brothers and sisters, of blessed memory, were born in Berestetchko near Brody. We lived and grew up in Berestetchko, until my father decided in 1922, because of his businesses, to move to Brody. In Brody, we resided on Kalir Street. At that time, my father was a crops trader and our situation was good. My parents were Zionists from their early youth years. The Hebrew language was close to their hearts, and they educated us according to that tradition. We attended the "Tarbut" ["Culture"MK] school and talked Hebrew amongst ourselves. Already in our childhood we belonged to Zionist organizations. My brothers Arie and Benyamin were members of "Ha'Shomer Ha'Tzair"[1], my sister Khana was a member of "Ha'Khalutz"[2] ["The Pioneer"MK]. My younger sister Brandil was a student at the Jewish school in Brody and I was a member on "Gordonia"[3]. We were all devoted to public service and worked for the "Keren Kayemet Le'Israel (KKL)"[4], acted in "Ezra"[5] ["Help"MK] and helped pioneers to make Aliya to Eretz Israel. We also participated in all sorts of activities for the organization "Eretz Israel Ha'Ovedet"[6].

Our house was always filled with friends who came to consult and organize the work among the youth. A Zionist and pioneering atmosphere reigned in the house. I also recall pictures of Herzl, A. D. Gordon and Trumpeldor, as well as the blue money-box[7], decorating the walls of our house. My brother Arie was one of the first youths to attend "Ha'Shomer Ha'Tzair" and I was one of the founders of "Gordonia's" branch in Brody. We built an exemplary branch together with my friend Yitzkhak Ettinger and Yosef Leiner. We gathered tens of the city's youths and taught them Zionism, Hebrew and scouting, and prepared them towards being the builders of Eretz Israel in the future.

Our center was in the hall of the famed community center on Goldhaber Street, where the library was located. This is where most of the Zionist youth branches, such as "Ha'Shomer Hatzir", Ha'Khalutz" and "Akhva"[8] were concentrated. Also concentrated there were the centers of the "Ha'Hitakhdut"[9] party and the Zionist institutions like "Ertez Israel Ha'Ovedet" , "Ezra" and KKL.

My family members contributed significantly to the activities of these organizations. We were all among the leaders of the Jewish youth, and we all had one single aspiration. At the same time, I participated in a "Hakhshara"[10] camp and made Aliya to Ertez Israel. I was a member of a kibbutz from the first day. The other members of my family prepared to make Aliya to Eretz Israel as well. However, the gates at Palestine were locked and they did not manage to immigrate. That is when the bitter fate came and put an end to everything. Second World War broke, the Nazi oppressor captured Poland and the western part of the Soviet Union, which included our city of Brody. All the members of my family were transferred to the ghetto, and when the day came, they were all murdered among the six million of our people. Since then, I remained alone, and my heart weeps bitterly about the terrible loss.

May their memory be forever bound in the bundle of the living.

Translator's notes

1. Ha'Shomer Ha'Tzair—"The Young Guardian"—a leftist secular Zionist youth movement founded in Galitsia in 1913. It was also the name of a leftist Marxist party during the British Mandate of Palestine, a precursor for the Israeli leftist United Workers Party ("Mapam").
2. Ha'Khalutz—literally meaning "The Pioneer", was a Zionist pioneer movement, part of "Poalei Zion" or "Workers of Zion"—a Socialist Zionist Party founded in Poland.
3. Gordonia - the movement's doctrines were based on the beliefs of Aharon David Gordon, i.e. , that the salvation of Eretz Yisrael and the Jewish People would come through manual labor and the revival of the Hebrew language.
4. Keren Kayemet Le' Israel (KKL)—or the Jewish National Fund (JDF) was established in 1901, by the first Zionist Congress. The KKL-JNF's

objectives were the purchasing and developing the land of Israel as well as strengthening the bond between the Jewish people and its homeland. Worldwide contributions were accumulated in a blue money-box and sale of the fund's stamps and book inscriptions.

5. "Ezra"—a religious Zionist movement originally affiliated with the Haredi Agudat Yisrael party. The organization founded many kibbutzim and moshavim and now works among potential new immigrants in USA, Canada, Russia, Belarus, Ukraine, England and Germany.
6. Eretz Israel Ha'Ovedet (The Working Eretz Israel)—The labor movement's party.
7. The Blue Money-Box was used to collect small contributions for the KKL.
8. Achva"—"Brotherhood" was a youth movement that was affiliated with the centrist Zionists movement"
9. "Ha'Hitakhdut"—"the Union" was a party founded in 1920 as a union between two moderate factions of the Zionist labor movement, Poalei Tzion" ("Workers of Zion") and the Palestinian Labor Party. Two youth organizations, Gardenia and Nocham were associated with the party.
10. Hakhshara—was a camp simulating kibbutz life. Such camps were established throughout Eastern Europe to prepare pioneers for their life in a kibbutz in Eretz Israel.

[Page 327]

Memories from my Father's Home

by Hadassah Esther Nathan (Weiss)

Translated by Moshe Kutten

My memories reach my childhood days. My home will always be engraved in my memory as a Zionist home, in which the love for the Jewish people bordered with zealotry. I do not recall the age when I started to speak Hebrew, but I found a picture of me at the age of two years in my grandmother's house in Haifa with the following words written on its back side: "Hadassah, is two years old, speaking Hebrew and knows already many words, such as bread, home, dog, mosquito etc. ..."

My school's first Hebrew writing teacher was Mr. Lerner, who, at that time, managed the public library in the "Community House". My knowledge of Hebrew was farther enriched at home by Mrs. Shoshana Weiser. Mr. Likhtman who came from Berstechko replaced her, after she made Aliya to Eretz Israel. He was a self-taught, shy bachelor and a brilliant scholar of the Hebrew language. I studied in the Jewish school, in which the teaching language was Polish, until the fifth grade. However, there were some scheduled lessons taught in Hebrew. From the first grade, I was taught by some of the senior teachers, among them Mr. Nakhum Okser, who later on managed a Jewish orphanage until his death. The orphanage was destroyed during the Holocaust, his head and all of his students were slaughtered. The image of the dedicated teacher Okser reminds me the image of Janusz Korczak.

The first principal of the Jewish school was Mr. Ashkenazi, an assimilated Jew who did not have a strong connection to Jews or Judaism. Mr. Muschisker, who portrayed a much more ethnic and Jewish image, replaced him later on. As a teacher, he was an exceptional educator, but also strict. His wife was my home-room teacher for five years. Not many Jewish children were fortunate to have such a famed educator as a teacher. She was a very enlightened woman who bestowed a broad life foundation onto her students - rich and poor alike. She taught us to understand not only what is written in books, but also everything around us. I would never forget the pleasant craft lessons during which, while we worked she read us stories from the children magazine “Plomik”. She would later lend us the magazine to take home, with clear instructions to strictly guard and preserve the shape of the booklet.

I was also taught Hebrew in school by a young teacher by the name of Kahana. She made Aliya to Eretz Israel a short while later. Her emigration affected me greatly. I recall the day of her departure when I sang the “Ha'Tikva' so enthusiastically, that several teachers made an observation about that to me.

One of the delightful things in our school was the children chorus under the conduction of teacher Harnik, who also managed a symphony orchestra in Brody called “Ha'Zamir” [The Nightingale”], which was the only one of its kind in our city. At the sounds of another orchestra, a military one of wind instruments, we used to march in parades celebrating the national holidays of Poland. The Jewish school gave us the ability to sense the social Jewish autonomy, taught a little Hebrew and religion, but educated us to be loyal citizens of the Polish government.

[Page 328]

One of the events that were important to me at school at that time, was the visit of an author from Eretz Israel by the name of Moshe Stavsky who wrote children stories. Our school would organize celebrations and parties, such as a Hannukah party, but these did not leave any special memories. On the other hand, I actively participated in similar celebrations in the “Community House”, organized and executed under the guidance of my father. I will never forget how I recited the poem “Ken Latzipor” [The Bird's Nest”[MK]] by the poet Khayim Nakhman Bialik[1], in the yard of the “Community House”. I was only seven years old at the time.

Another lively image in that house was Mrs. Weiler, whose endless vigor had a major effect and contributed to the success of the parties.

Since I remember myself, my father always served as the “chairman” of something. He was the chairman of the Keren Kayemet Le'Israel”[2],

"Hit'akhdut Poalei Tzion"[3] or the "Community House" (which was used by all Zionist movements, and where all Zionist activities were concentrated).

A big Zionist event in our city, where my father almost always played a major role, was the 21 of Tammuz – the memorial day for Herzl and Bialik. On that day, almost every year, my father would give a speech in the Big Synagogue, during a festive gathering, in their honor and memory. Jewish youths would go around the city holding the Blue Money-Box of the Keren Kayemet Le'Israel.

A great joy always swept the city on Purim. The needy people were especially joyful. They would dress up in costumes, sing and dance and collect pocket money. Activists of the Keren Kayemet Le'Israel took advantage of that day to collect contributions.

Mr. David Hamerman and Mrs. Adela Weiler assisted Father in all Zionist activities. My father often neglected his business and professional occupation for these activities.

There was a pioneering Hakhshara[4] in our city, whose members lived a life of poverty, because they did not have adequate employment (they cut trees in the winter and worked in small industries in the summer). My father used to look for work and employment for them and served as their patron. I recall that sadly most of the rich industrialists employed them unwillingly.

The local radical religious people exhibited strong resistance to Zionism, but the youths among them were slowly waking up to Zionism and some joined the "Mizrakhi"[5] ranks.

The inability of finding employment pushed the Jewish youth toward the Zionist movement, as they found in it solutions for their problems. Many of those who eventually perished in the Holocaust, waited for their turn of making Aliya to Eretz Israel, and progressing on that waiting line was not very easy. These were wonderful young people, who came mostly from low income homes. Intelligent, mostly self-educated, they conducted a cultural life in the evenings at the branches of the Zionist movements, often on an empty stomach. The youths who attended high schools participated less in this activity, but the counselors in the Zionist groups came from among their ranks. I recall the movements of "Ha'Shomer Ha'Tzair"[6] and "Gordonia"[7] as centers of vibrant youth with a strong ideological foundation.

Academic youth concentrated around the movement of "Academian Akhva" [Academic Brotherhood"MK] called later "Young Akhva" ["Young Brotherhood"MK] whose objective was to attract Jewish college students and bring them to closer to the Zionist movement.

[Page 329]

One of the important events in our city, which left its mark on the entire area, were the elections to the Polish "Sejm"[8]. The Zionist movement was interested in the success of a Zionist candidate, such as Dr. Heller from Lvov. The Zionist conducted a vigorous campaign in our city, and they even banded with the Ukrainian minority in order to achieve majority. Our house hummed like a hive during the day of the election.

My father, who was a physician, dealt also with linguistics and wrote poems. He knew many languages including Arabic. I remember the impression and amazement of Mr. Naftali Ziegel, a famed publisher from Lvov, who visited our city as a delegate of the Zionist movement, when he noticed my father's scholarship.

My father was a warm-hearted Jew, "crazy" about Zionism, a bit nervous but good-hearted. He would often take me, during the Sabbath morning round, to visit the sick among the poor. We would distribute all sorts of pastries and sweets among them. He also forced me to bring one of my poor Jewish school classmate friends home for lunch daily.

The holiday of Hanukkah was a big celebration in our house. I always had a big Hanukkah menorah, which my father weaved with his own hands from willow branches. I used to invite my girlfriends, even Christian ones to the lighting of the candles. Under the lights of the candles, my father told everybody stories about the Israelites' heroism. Father authored a specially decorated booklet for each of the Jewish holidays (I kept one of the booklets - the one about Hanukkah, with me until today as a memorial). In all of these booklets, my father emphasized the connection between religion and nationality.

Another important holiday in our house was the holiday of Passover - the holiday of the liberation from slavery. We obviously also celebrated the holidays of Lag Ba'Omer[9] and TU Bi'Shvat[10] according to tradition. I also remember feeding the birds on Shabbat Shirah[11].

Besides Zionism, my father loved nature. He would take me to walks in the forests around our city, trips that lasted an entire day and sometimes in the mornings before the start of the schooldays. On the way, he would buy me raisins and almonds, and tell me about vineyards and citrus orchards so that "I would not forget" Eretz Israel during these trips.

I do not remember the details, but I recall that every pioneer had to undergo a medical check-up by my father before making Aliyah to Eretz Israel and my father gave them a medical certificate. Many people in Israel possess such a certificate. It goes without saying that he never charged money for the check-up.

Only a few people of Brody's working intellectuals were Zionist activists. I recall two of them – Dr. Meles and Dr. Glasberg. Both were lawyers, learned and honest people. Only a very few Jews in our city were fully assimilated.

My father always educated and prepared me towards our Aliya to Eretz Israel. Besides Hebrew, he also taught me Arabic in my youth, since he believed in peace with the Arabs and cooperation with them in the future. He developed in me a strong national pride, which often helped me during the Nazi conquest, when I was among the gentiles.

The period I have described here was full of light and hope compared to the horrible days that followed it.

Those are the Jews I remember: the porters who worked in the market, those with the "Feyertopim" ("fire-caldrons hats") and their "burkes" ["cloaks"MK], the Hasidim with their white socks

[Page 330]

and the shtreimels [round fur hatsMK]; I remember all the female and male beggars, all the insane and the mentally ill people who wandered around the streets of our city, also the esteemed home owners, the merchants – rich and poor, and the paunchy pharmacy owners as well as the thin ones. I remember the shoemakers, tinsmiths, plumbers, tailors and patch fixers, poultry sellers and butchers, ice-cream sellers with their carts, sellers of Kvasnitza (pickled apples) who carried the ware in their buckets, Jewish cart owners with their carriages, bakers and beigel peddlers.

I remember the houses of the poor, whose windows reached the floor, on Shilgass, Labetgase, Leshniovska Lvovska, Shpitalna and Zlota streets and also in Roikuvka (the municipal park) with the statue of Koz'niovsky[12] and the clock tower. I remember Vali, Leswhniovska and Zamek forest, Stara-Brody with its "Maccabi" team who played soccer with the gentiles, the train station where people used to ride a carriage to reach it although it was not too far away.

I remember the Jewish physicians, the lawyers and their flaunting dressed up wives, the school children in their uniforms, the "Palass" ["Palace"MK] movie house and my beloved alleys.

When I reminisce about all that good and bad, everything seems like a dream that evaporated and disappeared.

Brody was a Jewish town with all of its plights, but it was a happy town that was destroyed. When I write these words, tears streaming down from my eyes, a sharp pain nips my heart, my lips are trembling, and I ask: should all of that have had to happen?

...And here I recall a horrendous scene – a religious man - Moishe'le Gliner, standing in our yard after the killing (the Aktsia), lifting his arms toward Heavens and crying: "Ribbono Shel Olam [Master of the UniverseMK] you are a robber and a murderer...why did you allow all of this to happen?...

...and nothing happened after that...the sky shone, the birds flew freely, the trees stood erect, and only Moishe'le stood there, straddle-legged, with a hoarse throat, tears streaming down his cheeks, his beard covered by a kerchief[13], and his arms raised towards heaven...

Translator's Notes

1. Khayim Nakhman Bialik (1873-1934) – born in Volhyn, Ukraine, was a poet who wrote mainly in Hebrew (and in Yiddish). One of the pioneers of Modern Hebrew poetry, he stablished himself as the National Poet of Israel. He made Aliya in 1924 and lived in Tel-Aviv. He did not live to

see the establishment of the independent Jewish state. He died in Vienna in 1934, following an operation.

2. Keren Kayemet Le' Israel (KKL) – The Jewish National Fund (JDF) – was established in 1901, by the first Zionist Congress. The KKL-JNF's objectives were purchasing and developing the land of Eretz Israel as well as strengthening the bond between the Jewish people and its homeland. Worldwide contributions were accumulated in a Blue Money-Box and sale of the fund's stamps and book inscriptions.
3. "Hitakhdut" – "the Union", was a party founded in 1920 as a union between two moderate factions of the Zionist labor movement - Poalei Tzion" ("Workers of Zion") and the Palestinian Labor Party.
4. Hakhshara – literally means, "preparation", was the name given to preparatory camps in which the Zionist youths learned Hebrew and trained in agricultural and manual labor. The camp was organized as a Kibbutz (a commune). The graduates organized themselves into groups waiting for Aliyah to the Eretz Israel.
5. Mizrakhi - a religious Zionist movement, precursor of the centrist National Religious Party.
6. Ha'Shomer Ha'Tzair – Hebrew for "The Young Guard" – a leftist Marxist Zionist youth movement founded in Galitsia in 1913. It was also the name of a leftist Marxist party during the British Mandate of Palestine, a precursor of the Israeli leftist United Workers Party.
7. Gordonia – a Zionist youth movement whose doctrines were based on the beliefs of Aharon David Gordon, i.e. - The salvation of Eretz Israel and the Jewish People would come through manual labor and the revival of the Hebrew language.
8. The Polish Sejm – is the lower house of the Polish parliament.
9. Lag Ba'Omer – Jewish holiday celebrated on the 33rd day of the Counting of the Omer (counting the days from Passover – when the Omer – wheat and barley offering took place at the Temple in Jerusalem – to Shavuot, the day of the wheat harvest and the day when the Torah was given to the Jews by G-d). The holiday is a festive day marking the death of the great and mystic Rabbi Shimon Bar Yokhai, the disciple of Rabbi Akiva. It is celebrated with outings (on which the children traditionally play with bows and arrows and light bonfires). Many visit the resting place (in Meron, northern Israel) of Rabbi Shimon Bar Yokhai.
10. TU Bi'Shvat - a holiday, on the 15th of the Hebrew Month of Shvat. This holiday is celebrated to honor the trees and is also known as the New Year of the trees.
11. Shabbat Shirah literally means the Sabbath of the Song, is the Sabbath when the Torah portion Beshalakh in the Book of Exodus is read. This portion tells the story about the Israelites' Exodus from Egypt, the parting

of the sea by Moses, the drowning of Pharaoh's army and the reality of the wandering in the desert. This Torah portion contains Moses's Song of the Sea (Exodus 15:1-19). The Ashkenazi custom is to feed the birds on that day, in recognition for their help to Moshe in the desert.

12. Koz'niovsky – a Polish author and poet.
13. Nazis and their collaborators used to pull the Jews' beards along with the facial flesh. Jews, who were abused in such a way, covered their beards with kerchiefs.

[Page 331]

A Visit to Brody, 47 Years Later...

by Tziporah Rom

Translated by Moshe Kutten

Edited by Rafael Manory

My name is Tziporah Rom. I was reborn at the age of eighteen when I made Aliya to Eretz Israel, but my real birthplace was the city of Brody. I was then called Nionia Spodek—the only daughter of Yehuda Spodek and Khana née Steiner.

In 1991, my work brought me to the city of Lvov, and from there, I looked for a way to visit my birthplace of Brody, which I left after the murder of my parents in March 1944.

Anatoly, whom I used to drive me around during the day came at 9 o'clock in the morning. It was raining outside, but the rain stopped when we left Lvov and turned east. The road was in fine condition with no potholes, as this is the main road leading to Kiev. This is the major highway between two large cities, Kiev, the capital East Ukraine and Lvov, the capital of Western Ukraine.

In the beginning of our journey, I do not recognize the names, but things start slowly to become familiar, as if they are being pulled from the depths of a forgotten past. First, a town by the name of Busk and then Olesko, with its large mansion on the top of the hill, which is called, even today, the "palace" of Olesko. On the opposite hill, the Soviets built a frightening statue depicting galloping horses that seem to jump over the road, in honor of Soviet General Budoni and his soldiers who reached that spot during the First World War.

I remembered the area as very flat, but it turned out to be hilly. We also encountered forests, gloomy colorless villages and crowds of people at every intersection going to Easter Masses.

We approach the intersection of the road leading to Zlochov [Zlochiv[MK]] and arrive at the entrance to the city of Brody. A station of the road-traffic police is located at the wide grass-covered intersection at the entrance. There is also a very tall pole containing a sign, which says "Brody". At the top of the pole, the year 1084 is indicated as the year when the city was first established. Indeed—I was born in a very old city.

We enter the city through Lvovska St. Small one-story houses surrounded by gardens are lining the beginning of the street. This is the neighborhood of Satro-Brody [Old-Brody[MK]]. One of the major city streets led from here to the center of town. We continue on Lvovska St. and cross the railroad tracks, the main track that runs from Lvov eastward. There was a relatively large train station in Brody at the time. On the left side, I see an open lot through which the Sokhobolka stream used to cross, but now, there is no stream. Instead, there is sewer canal full of trash. Beyond this open lot, there is a small mound with railroad tracks on it. This is where waiting trains or waiting train cars used to stop. Train cars, full of people who were fleeing Germany, stopped here in June 1940 and were captured by the Soviets and were taken to forced-labor camps in Russia. When these cars stood here in June 1940, we, the kids, ran to bring the people in the train-cars food and drinks. On the right side of the street, stood the Jewish cemetery, which was very old. Nothing remained of it, and in its place, and in place of the local power station that was adjacent to the cemetery, there is now a wide and spacious soccer field. Here the street should have turned right, but there is no entry for vehicles in that direction and we had to continue straight. We enter through Zyblikiewicz St.; we cross Kolejowa St., i.e., the Train Road, which led to a relatively large and beautiful station that was restored to its original form—and here we are, next to the old synagogue of the city. This synagogue was the place of prayer of Rabbi Yisrael Ba'al Shem Tov[1]. The local Ukrainians and the intellectuals of the area consider Ba'al Shem Tov as part of their heritage, and this is the reason they have an interest, at least a declared one, to care for the restoration of this synagogue. The walls of the synagogue are partly ruined, although some of the large Hebrew inscriptions were preserved. There are struts around the building, as if repair works are taking place, but by talking to people I found out that the place looks like that for years and that nobody has been working here for several years. The place attracts foreigners and casual Jewish tourists who come to the city, albite very rarely.

[Page 332]

The road ahead should have lead us, through Shpiltana St. to where the ghetto was located, however, we turn right and stop at the center of town — at the “Rynek” (the market), opposite the building of the Central Post Office. A large building called “Soukyenitsa” (“The Shops”) once stood on this square, until the Germans' invasion in June 1941. This building was constructed to serve as a mall. It had four sides and the shops were located on the inner side, with a covered walkway between the shops and the street and with beautiful arched openings. This allowed convenient access to the shops on market days even when it rained or snowed outside. Most of the shops were owned by the city Jews who traded in textiles, ready-made clothes and shoes, as well as all sorts of artisans. The fabric store of Moshe Merder's family was there and so was Ira Lessniovera's shop and the shop of my aunt Shulamit née Steiner, whose two daughters Tzila and Dozya now reside in Florida, US. There was also the store of my uncle, Shmil Steiner who perished along with his entire family—his wife Dinah and his daughters Vitah and Rinya, when one of the Ukrainians handed them over to the Gestapo in order to take over their house and property.

During the invasion, the Germans bombed the city and the Soukyenitsa building suffered a direct hit and burned completely. Frightened and curious we watched the fire, from the house of Zuzya Shekhter that was located across the road from the building. We were children then, and for us, this was more of a peculiar and thrilling type of an event rather than a frightening one. The fear and anxiety developed only later on during the Nazi conquest. Stalls were placed in the open lot following the destruction of the building. After the liberation, the Soviets built a shabby one-story building that was used as a local grocery shop. Several concrete cubes that were meant to serve as pots for plants and flowers, were now full of mud, and only here and there, patches of a fresh spring grass managed to sprout despite the neglect. Several elderly men, who were sitting in one of the corners smoking watched us for a minute, but quickly returned to attend to their own matters, because neither Anatoly's car nor us did not seem to be interesting enough for them.

[Page 333]

The Post Office building, is still standing, and like it, the alley and the house behind it, which was once owned by the Merder family and where I played with their younger daughter Rozya. Their entire family perished, except for the oldest daughter Zushka who now lives in Paris, and her cousins Frida and Regina Lesshiover, who made Aliya as students and settled in Haifa, where they have lived until their death. The next house was owned by the Rotenbergs—the tea sellers. This is the family home of Tushka Latchki, now in Haifa. The two-story house had an inner yard into which I escaped from my piano lessons. My mother thought that a girl from a good home should play the piano, and sent me to a teacher by the name of Lutka Sapir who lived in this house. The lessons were supposed to be held at a certain time but sometimes, the previous lessons would last a bit longer and I won a few minutes of a ball game, instead of piano practice.

We parked the car and started to walk. By now I was very familiar with my surroundings. Everything came back to me, and I could easily find my way around in any direction. We continued to walk toward the corner of what used to be Rynek D St., near the house where my cousin, Shmilek Mikolintzer, worked at a fur shop. Across from us is Zlota St., now called Lenin St., (a name that will probably be changed again). This was a major street, and the most popular destination of anybody who had free time during weekdays. During the Sabbaths, this street was the place for families who wished to walk around, leisurely. All the beautiful stores, with the most modern kinds of merchandise were once located on Zlota St. I recall the store for men's shirts with replaceable collars and Goldinstein's store for women's underwear. Up on the street parallel to Zlota, a street named after Kozheniowski [a Polish author and poet[MK]] (Farna St. by the people), there was the large shoe store of the Metches family, from which only one daughter survived the Holocaust. She married a man from Radzivilov and they now live in Sao Paulo, Brazil. The second shoe store was owned by the Bukhbinder family. My aunt Frida, the widow of my uncle Kalman, was managing it. Her elderly father used to sit down at the entrance and watch the people passing by.

Tzukra St. crosses Zlota St. exactly in the middle. Tzukra St. leads to Czerkiewna St., where Bertzia Landgewirtz and my cousins Vita and Rernia Steiner once resided. Hotel Bristol, the only hotel in the city, is still standing here in the corner of Zlota St. Its strange shape is entirely unlike any other buildings in the center of the city even though other two-story buildings already stood here, even those, which were built with terraces. My family leased Hotel Bristol when the Soviet arrived in 1939, in order to be able to declare that they are working people rather than merchants. At that time, a merchant could have assumed, with high degree of probability, that he or she would be deported to Siberia. Opposite Hotel Bristol stood the ice-cream store of "Black Papka", a place we were always yearning for. When we behaved "as we should", our parents, mine and the parents of my friend, Zozia, would invite us to eat Ice cream at Papka's. We would then eat the ice cream elegantly at a table, served on beautiful dishes and spoons and not just like by licking it off a cone that one buys from a mobile stand. There are no such stores in that street now. Instead of Papka's, a residential apartment is standing.

We approach the "Roikovka"—the central city park. During our childhood, we used to play around its walkways and trees. The "Roikovka" is where we established friendship bonds that we would remember better than any other social ties that we would tie later throughout our lives. I approach the corner of the park and expect to see the clock tower appearing in front of me, but it is not there anymore. It was probably destroyed. The garden itself seems to have been shrunken and converted into a small garden, with neither form nor comeliness. Even the statue of Yozef Kuzhniowski — a Polish author and poet and Brody native—is missing. I was told that the Ukrainians took it down and gave it as a gift to the Poles who were expelled from the city. Indeed, the city is now Ukrainian, not Polish, and, G-d forbid, not Jewish like it was until 1939. It is worthwhile to note that there were 22,000 people in Brody then, 18,000 of whom were Jewish and the rest Poles and Ukrainians.

[Page 334]

On the left side of the park, stands the “Brigade” building; this was once one of the most beautiful houses in the city. Built in French style, covered entirely by green marble, the house had a slanted greenish roof, decorated with plaster ornamental moldings and statues positioned above the window ledges. The building still stands, but it lost its grandeur—the roof is rusted, the walls are dirty and the window ledges are broken. Beyond the park stands the “Koszary”—the Barracks—where the Germans gathered the last of the Jews before they left the city in the spring of 1944. At the end, the corner house is standing with its front still somewhat protruding into the street. Shevlok's store, where non-Kosher sausages were sold, occupied this house. For us, children, the store was the embodiment of “treif” [non-Kosher[MK]], which was forbidden for us as Jews, as well as repulsive. The house is still there and this store was also converted into an apartment.

I turn right from Zlota St. at the end of the park. Nothing changed in this part of the street. The same houses are standing as they were once, only the people have changed. Greta Shvadron lived in the second house, along with her mother, her little brother, and her grandfather, who was rich once. Her mother used to always sit by the window, move the curtain, lean on a pillow that covered the windowsill and look outside. I look curiously at that window; there are white curtains in the window, the same as then, but there is another family living there now. The Shvadrons were murdered by the Germans. Only Greta survived and she now lives in New York. Adjacent to the Shvadrons' house, a refugees' family from Germany with two sons, Max and Nathan, lived. The boys used to also sit down by the window and look outside at the children who play in the park. We, the girls, used to sneak some glances towards them, because we were intrigued by their language, clothing and behavior. That family was deported to Russia in 1940.

The next house was once a club of the city's merchants intended for prominent and wealthy men, something like a local “Rotary” club. The club was called the "Municipal Union–Vita" and my father was a member of that club. As women were not allowed inside, our mothers used to walk with us around the park and along Zlota St., until they were fed up with it, and then they would send us inside to call our fathers out from the club to go home. We were very curious to know what they are doing in there, since even we could only reach as far as the checkroom door. This went on until one day, when the "Cerberus" (the "dog" that watched the entrance; by "dog" I mean the gatekeeper who was guarding "the gate to hell") was not standing by the door and we managed to get in. We then discover the big secret—the men were sitting around small tables playing cards or playing pool around a large pool table. Some sat down at a bar and chatted—what a big deal! Now I walked into the yard to look around and find that the place is now an apartment and the yard is filthy. In the house before the near corner lived my friend, Milah Hirt, whose father was a dentist and it was rumored that he had a piece of platinum in his skull. The second floor served as a dental laboratory and we loved to stay there and create figurines from plaster. A big house stands in the corner. This was the public elementary school. The building now serves as a municipal library. This is the corner of Kochanowskigo St.—called after the same author whose statue was removed from the park, along with all other signs of Polish culture. And in the Polish church that stood in the same street, the Ukrainians established a municipal warehouse. The municipal administration—"The Magistrat"—is now occupying a new building, since the old one was destroyed in the war, along with all the documents related to the censuses, and ownership of assets.

[Page 335]

Opposite the Polish church, a house stands near the Jewish school, in which the stationary shop of Kutzian was located. It is now a grocery shop almost empty of merchandise. At this Jewish school we learned to think, read and write. We acquired our learning practices and also buds of our worldview. This is where I studied since the first grade, and so did my best friends and cousins. This school was considered the best and the most disciplined school in the city. The best teachers were employed by the school. The principal, during my time was Mr.

Muschisker. Here, in the in the yard of this building, whose arched entrance was preserved as I remember it, I spent my most meaningful childhood years. Here I learned how to read. Here I tied social connections, which are still intact today, such as the one with Tushka Klatchki. Here I learned a chapter in the structure of society and its motives through observing the behavior of our teachers and disciplinarian principal, whose treatment of children of low income parents was very stringent. The school building remained the same as it was, however, but it is now divided into individual apartments, and laundry hanged on cloth-lines in the yard. The two-story Shekhters' house with its terrace stills stands in the right corner of the street, but without the wild vine bushes, which climbed on it and covered it with green-reddish leaves.

After circling around the city center, we arrive again at the Rynek. Here we turn right onto what used to be called the Goldhaber St. and is now Ivan Franko St., after a Ukrainian writer. On this street, my grandmother, Mirka-Leah Steiner, lived in a little house at no. 43, and my grandmother Dvora Spudek, my father Yehuda, whose name in Polish was Yulius, but his friends called him Yidle, my mother Khan'tche (Anna in Polish) née Steiner and I lived in the house at no. 74. I was born in that house, and remained the only child to my parents. In summer of 1941, it was very clear that all of the Jews would have to move to the ghetto. This was a horrible threat, and anyone who could tried to escape from that fate. Everybody tried to find a place to hide, to avoid being caged in that frightening and sealed ghetto. My parents looked for such a place for us as well; we had a good chance to find one due to our large circle of acquaintances, and due to the small size of our family, just three souls. Indeed, in the beginning of the fall, a Ukrainian family, who lived in Folwarki Maleh [a village near the Jewish cemetery[MK]], was found, who agreed to take us in. The head of that family, Vladek Sidorchuk, and my father designed the hideout together, so that it could stand the foreseen hardships waiting for us. First, it had to hold three people comfortably for an unspecified duration, since the victory over the Germans was not even on the horizon. Second, the place had to be secure and hidden from any curious eyes, particularly those of hostile and envious neighbors, as well as from searches by the local militia and the Germans. Sidorchuk dug a large pit in one of the corners of the wheat barn and converted it into a small compartment. He reinforced it with wood logs, opened a vent and covered it from above with strong and compacted timbers. He spread straw and stubble above the entire structure. The place was quite shallow and enabled us only to lie down or sit down. There was room for three sleeping pads, on which we slept, and on which we sat during the day. One would enter this small compartment only by squeezing through an opening below the rabbit cage that was attached to the barn.

[Page 336]

The Ukrainian family took care of handing us water, food and even newspapers. We took a more thorough wash at the family's residence up at their house, every few weeks, after a careful logistic planning and strict security arrangements. "Yad VaShem" (the central authority for Holocaust commemoration in Israel[RM]) recognized the Sidorchuk family members as "Righteous among the Nations" because of their actions.

My parents were killed during the German retreat in spring of 1944, after spending 16 months in the bunker, when there was already hope that the liberation would arrive. I am staring at the places where our house and the house of my grandmother stood. Instead of houses, there are now two-story apartment buildings, drab and repulsive. I am obviously biased. Was our house more attractive? I cannot remember, and it really does not matter, as so many memories of happiness are associated in my mind with that house.

During my time, Goldhaber St. was lined on both sides with luffa trees; on the right, the trees were all the way to the house of the Mushtzinski, the Pole who owned an excellent bakery and also the first private car in the city. Just in before his house was the turn toward "Vali", an artificial mound that was erected as part of the city defenses in past centuries. Trees grew up during the years and the place became a pleasant promenade avenue, and a meeting place for young couples. I see the hill's curves curling from afar, but the trees, most of which were chestnut trees with their elegant white flowers just about ready to bloom, were still standing bare without their leaves. On the left side of

Goldhaber St., the linden trees are still standing, beautify trimmed, waiting for the spring and the summer.

In place of the "Pompa" (the public water pump) and the surrounding houses, there is now a small public park with a statue commemorating the war's fallen. There is not even one Jewish name among the engraved names on the statue. We proceed down the street and discover part of the Kharash familiy's house. When I was a child, I considered it to be big and impressive, but now it looks low and shriveled, as if it has aged and sunk into the ground. We arrive at the "Rugatka"[2], the Y-shape intersection of the roads leading to villages around Brody—Radzivlon [Radyvyliv[MK]], Leszniov [Leshniv[MK]] , and Boldory [Bovdory[MK]]. These villages were known to have one or two Jewish families each. We continue to go straight ahead though. On the right side of the road lies what was once the Polish cemetery of the city. The statue of Holy Jan that once stood at the turn to the cemetery is not there now. The walkway and the fence are neglected, and so is the cemetery itself, which was once very well looked after. We are approaching the Jewish Cemetery, which lies on the left side of the road, just at the entrance to Leszniovski Forest. I see the gray gravestones from afar. Large stones crowded together. There are some, which stand upright, and there are those who lean on each other, as if they draw strength from the one another. The stones are impressive in their splendor and even in their neglect. They are crammed together and their rows seem like guarding the past. Most of the gravestones that were made of a simple local stone remained standing, whereas the luxurious ones made of marble, were all stolen from the cemetery. Most of the inscriptions on the gravestones are eroded, however, one can still decipher, here and there, a portion of a name or the year of death. There are quite a few gravestones, standing there for tens and hundreds of years, like soldiers who guard the secret of the greatness of the Jewish community that once thrived in this place, and a community from which nothing was left except this cemetery.

We drove to see the ravine of death, the place that marked the end of the road for many of Brody's Jews who were murdered here. At the beginning of 1941, when the Jews were still unaware of the methods used by the Nazis, and came to the gathering of the respected people of the community at the invitation of the Germans. It turned out that the gathering was planned so that they would become an easy prey for the Nazis. They were all shot here, in this ravine of death. This is how the Jewish community lost its leaders at once, early in the beginning of the Nazi conquest.

[Page 337]

The ravine of death was used again in May 1943 when the ghetto was annihilated. We, my parents and I, sat in the bunker of Sidorchuk family in Plwarky Maleh, at that time, and could clearly hear the roar of the engines of the vehicles that were carrying the victims on their last journey, and then the horrible rattle of the machine guns.

There is no memorial for the victims here. There isn't even a remnant or trace to what happened here, and there are not many witnesses who could testify about these horrors. There are also no people left who would be interested in preserving the memory of this cursed place.

We return to the city through a street that leads back from the east, from the direction of the villages Yazlovtchik [Yazlivchyk[MK]], Konyushkov [Konyushkyv[MK]], Berlyn and Boldury [Bovdury[MK]]. The road leads back towards the place where the flourmill of the Landgvirtz family was located. We pass near the the "tartak"—the largest lumber mill, within the boundaries of which my father had the warehouses of wheat and beans he traded with. The most beautiful chestnut trees were located there. Located near the "tartak" was once also a Jewish nursing home. It is obviously not there anymore, however, the house with the veranda—the glass-covered terrace, where the local priest used to live, is still standing in the corner of Ogrodnitza St. Even a portion of Landau's big house, in the yard of which the branch of the Ha'Somer Ha'Tzair youth movement used to be, is still standing.

We arrive at the corner of Sloneczna St., turn right onto Kalir St. to get back at the Rynek. New houses were built along Sloneczna St., but Kalir St.remained the same as it once was. It is just sparser as no new houses were built to replace the ones that were destroyed.

It is time to say goodbye to the city and the past. We drove along Lvovska St., going west this time. Down the road, we encounter a religious procession celebrating the end of the Easter holiday. We bypass the procession by going over to the main road. From there over a high hill, I can see the entire city stretching below. I do not fill any longing, sadness, or any other feeling toward this place.

I was born here, and this is where I spent my childhood years. However, this is the place where I lost my parents, my family and my friends. I could not find any emotional tie to this place in myself any longer.

[Page 338]

Tombstones from the old cemetery in Brody

The grave of R' Dudale in the new cemetery in Brody

Translator's Notes

1. Rabbi Yisrael Ba'al Shem Tov (circa 1700–1760) –Name meaning "Owner of the Good Name", a famed Rabbi considered to be the founder of the mystic Hassidic movement.
2. "Rugatka" is the Russian word for the slingshot, which has the shape of the letter Y with the short arms for tying the sling and the bottom arm for holding.

[Page 341]

Chapter Five:
Images and Eulogies

Our Teacher Nachum Okser, Brody's Janusz Korczak

By Joseph Parvari (Leiner)

Translated by Dov Biran

We all remember him, our dear teacher Nahum Okser. We met him in the twenties, at the Jewish Community School on Koznowski Street (opposite the Catholic Church). The Austrian Monarchy had fallen apart, and our town Brody, in the north of Galicia on the previous Russian border, had become a Polish city after 150 years of subjugation. But the city atmosphere was from the old days, and we felt this at school. Our first teachers, Wildholz and Okser, still clung to German culture, and their lessons were in that language.

Other teachers, such as Arnold Moscisker and his wife, and the school Headmaster, Philip Ashkenazi, already preferred Polish and even forbade [us] quite firmly to speak Yiddish.

The first to captivate our hearts was Mr. Nahum Okser--an elderly person, short, fattish, but with a beautiful face, pink cheeks with a little white pointed beard. Behind his gold-rimmed spectacles were his good, merry, smiling eyes. Such was our teacher for Scriptures and Hebrew (*Loshen Kodesh*). He used to start his lesson with a literal translation (from Hebrew to German) from Genesis: "In the beginning God – *Elohim* – created – *bara'* – heaven – *ha'shamaim* – and earth – *ha'aretz–"* and we, his little pupils, repeated after him word for word. In teaching Hebrew he also had a special method, with questions and answers, such as: "I am standing. What am I doing?" "You are standing." This was followed by exercises in grammar, such as: "My book, your book," etc. And indeed, the two basic subjects we learned from Mr. Okser were the Pentateuch and the Hebrew language.

Among the city's public institutions such as the Jewish community school, the people's kitchen, the old-age home, and the hospital, the Orphan Home was the most prominent. This was due to the management of its Director, Mr. Nahum Okser. For Mr. Okser was not only a teacher at the local school. His main activity was the Orphan Home at 25 Goldhaber Street. At noon, when school lessons ended, Okser would assemble his pupils and, just as he had brought them to school in the morning, he would take them back to the Orphan Home, at which he was both Director and educator.

I remember the Yiddishes Weisenhaus [Jewish Orphan Home] of Brody: A large building with a kitchen, a spacious dining-hall, two separate sleeping halls--one for the boys and one for the girls--the management office, and the living quarters of Mrs. Okser and the lovely Ms. Sarah Ehrenkranz. Sarah had grown up in that very same Home and remained as economic manager. Eventually, she married Mr. Okser when his first wife passed away. Although there was a great difference in age between them, they managed an exemplary family life and together were dedicated to their common goal, namely the education of the orphans, for whom they cared with much love just like the love parents give their own children.

[Page 343]

A Letter from Brody

by Heinrich Adler

Translated by Moshe Kutten

Edited by Rafael Manory

*Brody, August 20 1927**

The number of Jewish members elected to the municipal council exceeded significantly the number of their non-Jewish colleagues (30 vs. 18) and provided the elected Jewish members an upper hand in the voting. That's how they managed, during one of the first meetings of the council, to change the names of all the streets in the city. If the thirty representatives of more than three quarters of the city's population would have really wanted to exploit their numerical advantage over their 18 non-Jewish colleagues, according to the above-mentioned vote, I would have advised them to change the names of the streets—Slonchna ("Sunny" Str. in Polish, and how rare is the sun there!), Muzichna ("Music" Str. in Polish, what a ridicule of reality was in this name...) and others. I would have advised the use of such names as Dr. L. Artes Str., Rabbi Sh. Kluger Str., Dr. H. Schor Str., Nachman Kromchel Str. and many other names that would have connected to the history of the city and who played such a major role at the beginnings of the Jewish spiritual revival. Perhaps these prominent names would have reminded the local Jewish officials of the dissonant disharmony with the glorious past that deserved so much recognition. This is because it seems that in this city, where a handful seeds for the language revival and the initial literacy in Modern Hebrew were seeded, the sea of the cultural assimilation is swelling.

Let us Begin with the School

There is a school here, a so-called "Jewish Elementary School." It is supported 50% by the state and the rest is financed by the Jewish community. This school could have been an exemplary institution, where the national Judaism of the children of the "almost fully Jewish" city is nourished. In reality this institution is a very strange creation where one teacher is translating the holy scriptures into a German-Yiddish mix, another teacher translates them into Polish, and the third—the only true educator in the teaching-house—teaches "Hebrew in Hebrew" ... One cannot place the blame on the school principal, Mr. Ashkenazi, who, despite of his own views (he is an extreme assimilationist) values the educational work of the above-mentioned Hebrew teacher, who is a member of his teaching staff. The responsibility for this situation is placed at the Jewish community, which does not properly utilize its right to select the proper teachers whose salary they are financing—meaning selecting national Jews. In a city that lacks ideological assimilation, it is absurd to hand over the education of the young Jewish generation to "Poles of Jewish descent", who are brought over for this purpose from all over Poland!

[Page 344]

This situation is amazing in light of the fact that the head of the Jewish community is a prominent figure such as Leon Kalir—formerly the leader of the local assimilated Jewry, who is devoted to the Jewish-national ideology for years now (The son-in-law of Mr. Kalir is Dr. Kutin, who made Aliya to Eretz Israel, and who, while currently staying in Brody, gave an enthusiastic speech about Eretz Israel). The only true vehicle for the national education of the Jewish youth are the Hebrew courses, which are organized by the local branch of "Tarbut"[1] and are developing nicely thanks to the vigorous management of Mr. Naftali Lerner, Brody's enthusiastic pioneer of the Jewish culture and its language.

The courses are divided into five groups that attract 160 Hebrew learners taught by two teachers. Attached to the courses, there is an exemplary Jewish kindergarten. The thought of establishing a Jewish high school is not realistic in the current situation, although here is the place where one of the first Jewish high schools should have been established. Along with the only state high school in town, there is also a private high school, currently starting to grow, where 90% of the students are Jewish, and its principal is a Jewish teacher. However, one could not find any single inspiring teacher among the Jewish teaching staff (six altogether) who would dare to assume the task of heading a Jewish public high school. Therefore, it would be desirable that the central Jewish institutions in Lvov handle this matter. I strongly hope that the proposal of establishing a Jewish high school in Brody could be easily realized.

Our order of discussion now moves to the world of the adults. As I mentioned earlier, the organized life suffers of apathy. Names like "Beit HaAm" ("Community House"), "Tikvat Zion" ("Hope of Zion") and "Hatkhyia" ("The Revival"[MK]) and alike only arouse pleasant past memories. This state of apathy left its mark on the results of the elections to the Zionist Congress. In Brody, a city with about 10,000 of "subconscious" Zionists (almost the entire Jewish population), there were only 320 "shoklim" (electors)[2], of whom only 170 have casted their votes. They divided their votes among the "Tzionim Klaliyim,"[3] which received 35 votes, "Ha'Mizrakhi"[4]—53 votes and "Poalei Tzion"[5]—14 votes. Within the general atmosphere of inaction, the local branch of the "Hitakhdut"[6] shows the bulk of the action. Its members take an active role in the committees of the "Keren Ha'Yesod"[7], "Keren Kayemet"[8], and "Tarbut". Thanks to the blessed initiative of Mr. Naftali Lerner, as well as his financial contribution, a library named after Ekhad Ha'Am[9] was established (replacing the wonderful library of the Community House that was destroyed). His library contains already, after only a short period of operation, 1200 volumes, 400 of which are Hebrew books, and has attracted sixty permanent readers. The library constitutes a cultural oasis in the city. The musical club nourishes the musical tradition of Brody under the conductor baton of Mr. Shkolnik, while the sport club "Ha'Koakh" ("The Force"[RM]), looks after the physical health of the Jewish youth.

In the area of economic rehabilitation and recovery of the economic life among the Jewish population, the fiscal basis of which was destroyed during the First World War, the "Popular Jewish Bank" is making history. This is thanks to the blessed cooperation of the management team, headed by D. Y. Heller, and the efforts of the chair of the audit committee, Mr. Bloch and the head of the institution, Mr. Y. Goldwarm. The bank was established in the year 1900, by the JCA (Jewish Colonization Association), as a limited partnership, but changed to a cooperative in 1922. Despite going through a difficult crisis, the bank still exists today. It consists of 1032 members, most of whom, come from the layer of small businesses and craftsmen (meaning basically 60% of the Jewish population). The operating capital of the bank consists of 30,000 guldens from membership fees and reserves, 15,000 guldens from a loan by the PKO (Polska Kasa Oszczdnosi, i.e., Polish Universal Savings Bank), and 56,000 guldens of credit from the Zionist center. Its campaign for encouraging savings among the Jews, along with the 10% loan provision, increased its capital by 60,000 guldens coming from savings accounts. By providing loans to the impoverished Jewish society, the bank managed to curb the rampage of exorbitant interest rates. During the last few months, the bank extended 787 loans totaling 243,381 guldens. The vitality and popularity of the bank's commercial deals are evident by the financial turnover during the last seven months, totaling more than 3,000,000 guldens. The national character of the bank is symbolized by the continuous allocation of its excess income to Zionist and general Jewish funds.

[Page 345]

The first task faced by the new municipal council is to cure some of the "wounds of war," which are still causing pain in the city. Public opinion tends to support the election of Dr. Rittel as the mayor of the city. He can be credited with the development of the city while serving as a mayor before the war broke out. Let us hope that Dr. Rittel, formerly an assimilated Jew, would know how to treat the Jewish population based on its needs.

One of the first worries of the city officials should be the act of providing electricity to the city. The smoky kerosene lamps amplify the gloominess of the residents. A new light, light powered by electricity, which would illuminate Brody, would also have a symbolic value.

Translator's Notes

1. "Tarbut"— (literally means "culture" in Hebrew) was a secular Zionist organization established in 1922 in Warsaw. It operated a network of Hebrew language schools in the Pale of Settlement. Most of its activities were during the period between the World Wars but some schools still operate today.
2. Shokel—electorate or a member of the election committee was any person (18 years and older) who bought his/her membership by acquiring "Zionist Shekels" (used by the Zionist movement to calculate the annual membership tax). A member older than 24 years was entitled to present his/her own candidacy. The numbers of Shekels purchased at a certain region determined the number of delegates that the region was entitled to send to the Zionist Congress.
3. Tzionim Klaliyim—General Zionists or the General Zionists Party—was a centrist secular liberal party that later joined the Revisionist party (Herut, "Freedom") to form the center-right Likud party of today.
4. Ha'Mizrakhi—acronym for Merkaz Ruḥani ("Spiritual Center"), which combines to mean "The Eastern" was a religious movement within the World Zionist Organization—the precursor to the National Religious Party of today.
5. Poalei Tzion—literally meaning "Workers of Zion", was a movement of leftist-Zionist Jewish workers founded in various cities of Poland, Europe and the Russian Empire at about the turn of the 20th century.
6. Hitahdut—Union, was a Zionist Labor party founded in 1920, merging HaPoel HaTzair (the Young Worker) party and Tzeirei Tzion (the "Youth of Zion") party.
7. Keren Ha'Yesod—literally "The Foundation Fund", founded in 1920 as the official fundraising organization of the Zionist movement and Israel (after 1948).
8. Keren Kayement Le'Israel—KKL- A nonprofit fund and organization originally founded in 1901 to buy and develop land in Ottoman Palestine (Later the British Mandate for Palestine, and subsequently Israel and the Palestinian territories) for Jewish settlement. Since its inception, the organization planted over 240 million trees in Israel, built 180 dams and reservoirs, developed 250,000 acres of land and established more than 1,000 parks.
9. Ekhad Ha'Am—literally "One of the Common People"—was the pen name of Asher-Zvi Ginzburg (1856–1927), who was a Russian-born Hebrew essayist and one of the most prominent thinkers of the Zionist movement.

Editor's Note

* This is the date of the actual letter that is reproduced here.

[Page 346]

Through the Window

by Hadassah Esther Nathan (Weiss)

Translated from the Hebrew by Beverly Shulster

My small window
Is my whole world here
Through the window I will look
and see the cherry blossom.

The world is bright with color.
Flowers fall from the tree
Becoming white. Green
the small blackberry bush.

In the morning the nightingale will
sing
And towards my window he will cry
Oh, I'm sad, sad am I
About your sad and painful life.

The locust, the musician of May
On the glass will burst into song
Oh, my child, it will buzz,
The time of your youth has passed.

[Page 347]

Samuel Weiler

From Publications of the Partisan Fighters Museum, Tel–Aviv, Tevet 5732 – December 1971

By Joseph Parvari (Leiner)

Translated by Moshe Kutten

Edited by Rafael Manory

One of the last commanders of the Beitar organization (In Hebrew the acronym for "The covenant of Yosef Trumpeldor"[1]) in Brody was Shmuel Weiler, of blessed memory, great–grandson and grandson to a Rabbinic dynasty, a graduate of the Polish Gymnasium, a handsome youth, brave and fearless, and limitlessly dedicated to the national movement.

In 1941 he was a resident of the ghetto. Here, in Brody, despite all of the suffering and the horrible conditions in the ghetto he dreamt about rescuing his nations' honor and about raising the flag of the struggle against the invader and the oppressor of the Jews.

He was one of the few who survived the war. Based on his written testimony[2] that he provided to the Jewish Historical Institute in Krakow, one can assemble a short review of the fight of the local youth against the Nazi regime.

Shmuel Weiler, the commander of Beitar, together with several friends, including Shlomo Halbershtadt, a former member of the "Hashomer Hatzair"[3] movement, Yaakov Linder, a member of the "Komsomol" (The Communist Youth Movement) and the teacher Adolf Klar, established a fighting organization in the ghetto by the name of ZOB (Zydowska Bojowa Organizacja = The Jewish Fighting (or Combat) Organization), headed by Shmuel Weiler, which was the nucleus of the local partisan movement. The Jewish fighters contacted the Polish fighters in Lvov and asked for their help; however, the Poles refused to accept them in their ranks, and to provide any weapons. Thus, the organization, which was isolated from the outside world, decided to secure the needed financial means on its own, and to acquire the necessary weapons by purchasing it or by force. Among the few who were willing to assist the organization, was the Ukrainian Communist activist, Yashko Buraczek, a friend of the Jews, who has meanwhile passed away. The organization received the first handgun from him.

Weiler managed to contact an ethnic Pole, a soldier who served in the 45th battalion of the German army infantry (there were Poles from Pomerania, Silesia and Poznan who served in the Wehrmacht). This Pole told Weiler about the huge defeat suffered by the German forces headed by von Paulus, during the winter of 1942/43 in Stalingrad. The organization published and disseminated this and other news via leaflets. The news helped in raising the morale among the Jews and in forging their will to survive. However, the organization was not satisfied with only this type of actions. It decided to start open struggle, get out of the ghetto, and run away to the surrounding forests. They planned to join the partisans and fight against the Germans.

The organization continued its activities by performing sabotage actions. Near the village of Sukolovka, its members blew up a tar factory. Tar was a needed raw material for producing ammunition. The forced labor camp at the Sasov quarry was attacked too in order to get hold of dynamite for the production of mines. An underground member, the engineer Fauerstein, invented a mine for blowing up railroad tracks. The mine was placed about 40 kilometers from Brody between Krasna and Kolkosh stations and caused the derailment of a train locomotive, the destruction of two boxcars full of weapons and ammunition, and the death of tens of German soldiers.

[Page 348]

Despite the harsh conditions and the never–ending lurking dangers, at every moment the fighters were also keen at preserving their cultural life even while in the forest. They organized meetings on Saturdays and evenings, in which they gave lectures on current events. Moishe'le Shapira stood out in these meetings in which he read from his poems about the Jewish people, its enemy and the fight against it.

At about the same time, it was announced that the organization was accepted into the ranks of the GL–Gwardia Ludowa–organization, the "Elite People's Guard," the Polish underground leftist resistance organization in Lvov. The GL organization promised to provide commanders, as well as non–Jewish partisans and weapons.

When its funds had dwindled, the organization decided to rob the national bank branch in Brody. Twelve people set off to carry out this undertaking on 13th of May 1943. At noontime, the members heard that the force encountered a German army unit. A battle ensued, in which two of the group members - Bunyo and Izyu Reinhold, were slightly wounded. The group was forced to retreat toward the forest. The German succeeded in capturing two of the fighters in the swamps and they handed them over to the city gendarmerie. While their clothing were being searched, the fighters managed to draw their guns, kill a policeman and run away to the ghetto. The house in which they were hiding, was surrounded by the police force and its residents were taken out and shot to death. When the fighters saw that they do not have any hope of escape, they committed suicide.

At that point, it was clear that the time had come for an uprising. The organization called for active resistance against the oppressor. They encouraged the Jews to follow the example of Ghetto Warsaw, which fought heroically against the Germans. They appealed the people to escape to the forest and join the partisans. Many abided by the appeal. In order to sustain themselves, groups of members attacked the farms of rich "volkdeutsches" and confiscated meat and flour. They left a note in every place they raided, acknowledging the confiscation of the produce, stamped by the organization logo.

On 17th May 1943, a force consisting of two German army companies, Ukrainian police and the gendarmerie attacked a group of the organization members. The ensued battle lasted the whole day. Unfortunately, the attackers had the upper hand. Thirty Jewish warriors died a heroic death. The survivors returned to the city and hid in the attic of the ruined synagogue. The police discovered their hiding place and they were captured. After that incident, the head of the Judenrat demanded that Shmuel Weiler sign a declaration that he would not incite the youths to fight against the Germans. Weiler refused. The Judenrat then demanded that Weiler's mother sign in his name and she refused as well.

During the night of May 20/21, 1943, the ghetto was surrounded by S.S. units that arrived from Lvov, headed by Major–General Katzman, may his name be damned, and Ukrainian police forces that were mobilized from throughout the environs joined them. They entered the ghetto and forced out people from their homes and hideouts. After robbing them of everything they owned, they loaded them up on trucks and transferred them to the train station. From there they transported them in crowded and sealed boxcars to the death camp of Majdanek (one of the survivors testified later that the train bypassed the Belzac camp). Many tried to jump off the moving train, but only three managed to survive.

Miraculously, Shmuel Weiler himself survived. After the liberation by the Red Army, he and his mother moved to Poland and from there to France. In France, he continued his work in the movement and became the secretary general of the right–wing Herut–Hatzohar Union party[4]. He served as a journalist for the party's newspaper, “Herut”, in Israel and acted on behalf of and for the benefit of the state of Israel. He played a major role in organizing the weapon shipment via the ship Altalena. He served as a delegate in the Zionist congresses and visited Israel.

[Page 349]

The author would like to mention that a group of Jewish partisans from the neighboring city of Radzivilov, was also active in the area of Brody during the conquest years (see article by Yekhiel Porochovnik in the Yizkor book for the city of Radzivilov–Sefer Radzivilov, pp. 232–250[5]. Shmuel Weiler did not mention the group in his testimony since most of their activities occurred after the extermination of the ghetto. Most of the members of this group later joined Russian units and fought in the ranks of the Red Army.

Shmuel Weiler passed away in Paris in 1962, at the age of 48, after suffering from a malignant disease. His mother, Adela Weiler transferred his body in December 1962 to Israel, and he was buried in Kiryat Shaul cemetery [near Tel Aviv[MK]]. Adela Weiler passed away in October 1971.

She was a public figure and an industrious Zionist leader in Brody. She was buried near her son.

Her memory and the memory of her son would be forever bound in the bundle of the living among all of Israel heroes.

Translator's Notes

1. Beitar–A Revisionist Zionist youth organization founded in Riga, Latvia, by Zeev Jabotinski (the leader of the Revisionist Movement, linked to the right wing Herut Party. The organization was named after the leader of Jewish settlers in Tel–Hai, Yosef Trumpeldor, who was killed in defense of the settlement.
2. Shmuel Weiler's testimony was taken from the collection "Underground Movements in the Ghettoes and the Camps," edited by Betty Eisenstein, 1946, published by the War Archives, the Jewish Committee in Krakow (in Polish). The testimony also appears in Brody Yizkor Book, pp. 170–174: (http://www.jewishgen.org/Yizkor/brody/bro170.html)
3. Hashomer Hatzair–Translated literally as "The Young Guard" is a leftist Marxist Zionist youth movement affiliated with a party by the name of Hashomer Hatzair–Workers Party of Palestine (later unified with other movements to form the leftist Mapam and Meretz parties). The organization was established in Galitzia in 1913. The movement is active today in Israel and internationally.
4. Likud Party – Literally translated as "consolidation", is a union of center–right wing parties formed by Menahem Begin. The senior party in the Likud is Herut (translated literally as "Freedom") which was formed in 1948 as a successor to the Revisionist Irgun militant underground organization. The first union was formed in 1965 between Herut and the centrist Liberals party. Several other small parties joined in 1988.
5. Radzivilov's Yizkor book: http://www.jewishgen.org/Yizkor/Radzivilov/rad251.html

[Page 350]

Fanya Zorne:

The Polish woman with whom I hid told me about an “Aktsia” (Action) against children aged 3-5 in Radziwilov (near Brody). All the children were thrown in sacks and the Germans shot into the sacks, after which they were buried in the ground. The ground continued to move for a while thereafter

Alas, German Mothers

by Fanya Zorne

Translated from Polish to Hebrew by Zvi Natan

Translated from the Hebrew by Beverly Shulster

Alas, German Mothers
Who so love their children
They give not a sword
But bread with butter.
They fill their bellies
While our children die--
Not even a slice of bread
Like cats sick with hunger,
In ditches, in ghettos of death
to fill quotas.
With no excitement
You hear this news,
No twinge in your heart.

If were taken from you
Your beloved children
Your blonde-headed children . . .

Apparently, here have returned

The days of the Tartars!
If you could hear the screams go up
And then see the piles of bodies;
If you could feel the pain of the mothers
Torn from their babies--
Would that in strange lands,
In camps, in ghettos
Burning with longing
You'd die at forced labor
In poverty, misery.

Alas, German mothers,
You cannot feel.
Your hearts are stone.

April, 1943

[Page 352]

The Brody "Klezmers"

By Samuel Lamm

Translated by Moshe Kutten

Edited by Rafael Manory

In the middle of the last century, there was a family of klezmers[1] headed by Rabbi Shmuel Weintraub, may his memory be blessed, who were nicknamed "the Chortkover"[2]. They were famed artists and their reputation reached the most remote corners of Galicia. The granddaughter of R' Shmuel was my mother, may her memory be blessed. She told me that R' Shmuel, whom I am named after, was a fountain of music. The band was also famous through the fact that R' Shmuel played notes that sounded, in one instance, like a nightingale, and in another like a lion's roar. R' Shmuel was able to play a "deer hunt", including how deer is being shot and how they fall down.

One could not decide upon a date for a wedding without consulting first with the Chertkover.

R' Shmuel came from a very pious family. My mother told me that he and his brother played once at a ball where boys and girls danced together. When the news about that ball reached their parents, they excommunicated the two boys and sat Shiva as if they were dead.

In the band of R' Shmuel two of his sons, R' Yoshe Vev (Yosef Zeev) and Moshe, stood out. R' Shmuel's grandchildren scattered about in Austria and Germany. One of them played at the court of the emperor Franz Joseph the First.

During the 1930's my brother visited a remote place in Galicia by the name of Mendenice—larger than a village but also not quite a town, and stopped by the synagogue. An elderly Jewish person approached him and asked who he was and where did he come from? He answered in Yiddish "I am the Chortkover's grandson". The old man got a satisfactory answer to his question.

Translator's Notes

1. Klezmer—literally "musical instrument" in Hebrew, is a Yiddish term that originated in Eastern Europe for professional musicians who played Jewish folk music (usually on violin).
2. Chortkov—a city in Galicia, about 38 miles SSE of Ternopil (Tarnopol). At the end of the 19th century the Jewish population in the city was more than 2000 people.

[Page 353]

In Memory of My Parents Simcha and Yasse Weiser

by Shoshana Weiser

Translated by Shmuel Herold

Donated by Brian Blitz

A picture of the new synagogue in which my parents had worshipped all their lives, and where my late father had served as beadle, provoked in me a strange reaction.

In front of me, I saw this sanctuary in 1918 after the First World War. It stood out as a tombstone, a sort of monument, surrounded by its four walls, its broken windows looking out to the horizon, without a roof, thistles growing between its walls, pasture for the goats.

The [fortress] synagogue had served as a stable for the horses of an enemy at a time when the war raged on both sides of the town, and invasions of two enemies had turned it into a desolate wilderness. Desolate too was the "new synagogue" [a study house], and just a few Torah scrolls survived and remained in the Jewish district.

As soon as we returned to the town, before we had a roof over our heads, my late father decided to restore the former glory of the [fortress] synagogue. Repair of the roof and the removal of weeds were his first actions. Despite the poverty of the population, the donors did not disappoint and contributed generously. The synagogue was rebuilt, the restoration of the holy ark and the eastern wall were carried out by a renowned craftsman without payment, and the Polish government dispatched a special group of people from Warsaw to see the wonderful work of his hands.

Shortly before the High Holy days, when the synagogue had already been completed, a wrinkled lady arrived dressed in tatters with a donation. She [was a woman who] used to sell candy at the entrance of a building in the street by the station. Her name was Rosa. She had just one request – that her 14-year-old son should act as cantor on Simchat Torah. “He sings beautifully,” said the woman. “He is very talented.”

The mother hadn't exaggerated. This wonder-boy was Jonah Furman of blessed memory. This was his first public appearance. He continued to be the cantor there for many years.

[Page 354]

Two Episodes

by Shoshana Weiser

Translated by Moshe Kutten

Edited by Rafael Manory

A "The Rope that did not follow the bucket"[1]

The porters of Brody were not as rude and vulgar like porters in other cities. Their curses were not as dangerous. They were simpletons who would not be the cause of any world calamity. They loved scholarly students and appreciated anybody who studied anything.

One of the porters in the city had a son, and the father decided that his son would not be a porter... He sent him to high school and after the matriculation exams, that son went to Vienna to study medicine. He excelled in his studies, received a doctor degree and was accepted as a lecturer in the faculty he studied in.

One day, the docent arrived at his parents for a visit. The porter invited all of Brody's porters to his house to welcome the professor, the porter son. My attempt to sneak in and see how the professor reacts to the reception of the porters has failed—entry was only allowed for porters.

B. Small talk of scholarly students

The House of the Music Society in Brody served as a club for the Jewish intelligentsia, as well as a venue for art shows such as concerts and theater shows.

In the evenings before the shows, we—the youth, gathered in the corridor waiting for the opportunity to gain a free or discounted ticket, as in "fix yourself in the corridor before entering the lounge."[2] Among the people who walked the corridor was a small man, a man in miniature. The only thing that was big by him were his glasses. He amazed people with his stories and jokes, and the more he talked, the bigger his circle of listeners became. He was not nicely clothed, and the books, which I never saw him without, were not bound by garnished covers but were mostly pamphlets and notebooks that were worn-out from use.

To this day, fifty years later, the memory of these evenings was not erased from my heart, although I do not remember even one word from these stories.

Who would imagine that this person, so small (in body) would be so big (in spirit). Today he is well known in the Hebrew and general literature worlds. The number of prizes that were distributed based on his recommendation and judgement is greater than the number of years he has lived. He is, of course, the tenured professor of the Hebrew University in Jerusalem, Dov Sadan.

Translator's Notes

1. "The rope followed the bucket" (Genesis 44:19), as in the rope following the bucket that drops into the well. A phrase used to describe a situation when a result follows the cause or one thing follows another (son follows his father, one problem follows the other, etc...)
2. A phrase originating from the *Mishna,* which basically means "behave yourself in this world if you want to enter paradise in the next world", or a person needs to prove oneself first in order to receive a recognition or a benefit.

[Page 355]

In Memory of Our Father Yaakov Unreich of blessed memory

by Rivka Matsuhewicz née Unreich

Translated by Moshe Kutten

Edited by Rafael Manory

Two years ago [two years before the book was published in 1994[MK]] we lost a dear man, two years ago, a native of Brody, a proud Jew, who foresaw the Holocaust approaching and imminent even before the breakout of the Second World War.

At the age of 20 he enlisted in the Polish army and served in the army for three years. One day during his service, he saw gentiles burning a doll in the image of a Jewish person. At that moment, he understood the meaning of antisemitism and decided to immigrate to Eretz Yisrael.

After his military service he became a member of "Brit Ha'Khayal"[1], bought a ticket for a ship and departed for Warsaw.

He said good-bye to his family that was very wealthy, to his father, a good-hearted man by the name of Elimelekh, who was a famous philanthropist in his city, to his mother Sara and his brothers. He took a pillow, and hit the road on his own to Eretz Yisrael.

He boarded the ship "Parita,"[2] which was built to carry cattle. After long weeks of wandering under hard physical conditions, the ship ran aground on the beach of Tel Aviv in [August of] 1939. The British were waiting for them. They arrested them and jailed them in a detention camp for some time.

My father was a merchant in Israel. He was a very smart man, full of stories about Brody and Galitzia. His entire family perished in the Holocaust.

He married Ahuva, née Fishkin, from Rubizhevitch and they established a glorious family with many grandchildren.

Translator's Notes

1. "Brit Ha'khyal" ("The Soldier Alliance") was a rightist-Revisionist Zionist association of Jewish adult reservists in the Polish Army formed in December 1932 in Radom, Poland by Zeev Jabotinski. Its principles included militarism, discipline, ceremony, ritual, honor and loyalty The goal was prepare a cadre of loyalists in preparation for the establishment of a Jewish state on the two banks of the Jordan River.
2. Parita was an "illegal immigrant" ship acquired by the Revisionist movement, which set sail from Constantza, Romania, on the Black Sea on July 12, 1939, carrying 857 Beitar youth movement and Brith Hakhayal members from Germany, Austria, Poland and Romania who had fled Europe. The ship ran aground on the beach of Tel Aviv on 22 August 1939 after a 42-day sail filled with hardships and struggles. The immigrants were arrested by the British Army but were released shortly thereafter and allowed to stay in Eretz Yisrael.

[Page 356]

My Father's House (a poem)

by Fanya Zorne

Translated from Polish into Hebrew by Moshe Shlomi

Translated from Hebrew by Moshe Kutten Edited by Rafael Manory

On a lowly hill in a not-so-big a village
a deserted house stands, with a railing in front of it,
adorned with a scarf made of vine—intertwining,
ascending up and up to the edge of the roof
of the gloomy house.
A veteran of storms,
It is the only one who is fearless -
why would it care?
Surrounding the house, rose bushes,
planted by an amateur
are rising up to the sun above
as if waiting for someone miraculous.
Neglect is everywhere—in the garden, the house
and the orchard.
Who deserted it and for whom they were left?
Sunrays had once pushed through the window
and from there a reply came swiftly
youthful girls' laughter—
with a hoe and a mattock
they hurried, running to bring order
in the flowerbeds.
Today nobody casts a glance at them.

From the soiled windows
Naked walls are seen,
Only one thing is watching –
a flower standing on the windowsill.
It survived and saw everything,

[Page 357]

one mute witness,
but only it knows the gloomy history–
the parents' farewell to their nurtured girl
the last in the line.
It saw and shared their pain
In its flowery brotherly heart,
It saw how, when the girl left,
Her mother fainted collapsing at the door,
and the father looking with a tearing eye, not knowing
whether to care for the mother, or run after the other as long as his legs can carry him.

About a week later,
villains came and ordered them to go
to the ghetto, to the wanderings.
It saw how, with tearing eyes,
they said farewell to their daughter
leaving toward their cruel fate of misery and hardships
it saw the last glance
from the train car

Here, at the garden and house and the orchard...
Oh My G-d, how mysterious are your judgements!

Would they perish, or perhaps their world would emerge and return?
The silent house remains—
It has passed through the winter,
and today, spring is here
and the buds are sharing their fragrance,
But only inside the house
there is no clue or sign of life.
You—the fiery daffodils
are calling in vain.
You—rose bush—are rising up in vain
to face the expanding world.

[Page 358]

There is nobody—they are not at home—
an evil and cruel world took them from here.
Would they come back? You would certainly ask me.
I wouldn't know.

I would only know this—before the sun would rise
The dew would sting the eyes.
Lonely, the house is standing,
on a hill, in a not-so-big a village.
Why are you so silent?
Why is it that you are reflecting
so much worry,
grief and sorrow?

Are you longing for me?
Is it so bad for you without me?
Know that I am sending you my soul
and all of my thoughts,
regardless of whether we would come back to you
or would never return.

[Page 359]

Profiles from Brody

by Joseph Kahana

Translated by Moshe Kutten

Edited by Rafael Manory

Every city has its own character(s).

A. Who in Brody didn't know Dr. Oifrecht? He was the physician of the Sick Fund organization (Kupat Holim). He was an older bachelor whose hair was gray and his beard was black. When he was asked "How come you have gray hair but a black beard?" he would answer simply: "When my beard started to grow I was already eighteen years old, therefore my beard is eighteen years younger than my hair".

B. I remember the Messer family who used to live in a single house built on the "Valles" (the dirt embankments). Mr. Messer was a sign painter who spoke German. One night his wife left the house without him sensing it. He locked the door as a habit and went to sleep. When the wife came back, the door was locked and she had to wait at the door for a long time until her husband woke up from her knockings on the door. From that day on, Mr. Messer would ask his wife every evening: 'Regina, are you home?". After he getting a positive answer, he would go and take a peek at the mirror and ask seriously: "Am I here?" and he would answer: "yes". He would then go and lock the door.

C. There was a carriage driver in Brody and his name was Moshe the "Krumer" because of his wooden leg. He was a big joker and liked jokes and singing. He owned a cart with rubber wheels and a splendid pair of horses. One day, he carried in his cart a woman who went to invite her deceased husband to the wedding of their daughter. He waited for her at the gate of the cemetery until she came back. When he saw her, her face seemed very worried. He asked her: “What happened?” She answered: “I forgot to mention to my husband that Passover is approaching, and that I do not have any money left.” (It was forbidden for her to reenter the cemetery according to the Jewish law”). Moshe had pity on her and asked her to point out for him the location of her husband's grave from afar, so that he could go to him and tell him about her wish. When he came back Moshe told her: “I told your deceased husband everything; however, he said, he was very sorry that her wish came too late, and that there was nothing he could do about it, except that he invites you to spend Passover with him”.

D. There were many water drawers in Brody, and Moshe “Wasser Tregger” [Yiddish for “the water carrier”] was one of them. He was a young man and not necessarily too smart. In addition to drawing and carrying water, he worked as a night-guard at Mr. Sapir's shop in the market. When he was asked how is it to be working as a night guard for Mr. Sapir he would answer: “Sapir thinks that he is smart, and in exchange for dinner, he wants me to sleep in his shop. However, what do I do? I enter the shop every night and do not close my eyes until morning. Of course, Mr. Sapir thinks that I slept the whole night.”

[Page 360]

Our Father Joseph Parvari, of blessed memory

by Uri and Elazar Parvari

Translated by Moshe Kutten

Edited by Rafael Manory

When we were small children, our father used to tell us about his native city. He told us about how he started, at the age of four, to study in a "*Kheder*"[1]. He told us about the students' newspaper in school and the soccer games with the Poles. His father, Uri, spent his time in *Beit Ha'Midrash*[2], studying *Kabbalah*[3] and his mother Rivka was the breadwinner for eight souls working at her grocery store. When our father was six years old, his father died at the age of 72 from a typhus epidemic, which raged in the city. His mother was left with her five daughters and him, the youngest child born to older parents. After graduating from high school, he left the city and worked as a book-keeper in Krakow and was an activist in the "Gordonia"[4] pioneering youth organization.

When he was 26 years old, the World War broke out. The Germans invaded Poland and advanced eastward. As he was an athlete he decided to escape on a bicycle. He travelled long distances between villages and rundown roads, procuring food and fixing many flat tires, until he reached the Soviets. He managed to convince them that he is sympathizer of the Communist regime and that is how he was accepted into the Red Army.

The following five years passed by him getting involved in blood-shedding battles, including the battle of Stalingrad, until he was fortunate to rejoice over the victory over the German army and participate in the liberation of Poland, Romania and Hungary. However, when he was discharged from the army and returned to Brody, everything was already lost. His 67 years old mother, his five sisters Rachel, Pepka, Sara, Tzila, and Etka, along with their six children and their husbands were gone. They were all taken to Treblinka and murdered.

Our father did not stay quiet since. He devoted most of his efforts to the perpetuation of the memory of his city's Jewish people. The people of Brody became for him a substitute for the family that perished. Those who came to Israel after its establishment, he took care of finding them a job. If someone was unskilled in any profession, he would ask his place of work to hire that person on a temporary basis as a helper. He would employ that person and teach him basic accounting (he would compete any overflow at home himself), and then he would find the person a permanent place of work.

During Sabbaths and holidays, it would have been difficult to find Father during a moment of leisure. He would sit at his desk, copy the material for the Brody Yizkor book and correspond with ex-Brody residents all over the world. We carefully preserve copies of all this correspondence, a good part of which is written in Yiddish and Polish. They fill many thick folders. The destroyed world of Brody continued to live in his heart. He remembered, phenomenally, almost every Jewish person in Brody, their address and their occupation. He remembered every street and every house. During the years, he collected so much information about the city, in order to be able to embed any missing part into this world that lived in his imagination, while continuously coping with the ever-increasing time distance and the fear of oblivion. His life dream was to immortalize that world that was gone and only existed in his memory in a "Brody Yizkor Book".

To our sorrow, he was not fortunate to see the book published. He collapsed while continuously laboring over the work and died after several weeks of terrible suffering. The world of Brody as it was imaged in his memory disappeared with him.

We see the publication of this book as the fulfillment of his life dream.

May his memory be blessed.

Translator's Notes

1. *Kheder* – a traditional religious school for small kids.
2. Beit Midrash – literally means "A house of learning" was a study hall or a school for religious studies, usually in or adjacent to a synagogue or a Yeshiva. It is also a word used to describe the level of studies below the academic level of a yeshiva.
3. *Kabbalah* - originally developed within the realm of Jewish tradition in the seventeenth century French region of Provence, France, *Kabbalah* is a set of esoteric teachings meant to explain the relationship between an unchanging, eternal, and mysterious infinity and the mortal and finite universe (God's creation).
4. Gordonia - the movement's doctrines were based on the beliefs of Aharon David Gordon, i.e. - the salvation of Eretz Yisrael and the Jewish People would come through manual labor and the revival of the Hebrew language.

[Page 362]

Our City Brody

His Speech during the celebration of his 70th birthday

by Shaul Perlmutter

Translated by Moshe Kutten

I see here new faces. I do not know you, the owners of the new faces, and you do not know me, however, "Ask your father and he will tell you" [Deuteronomy 32:7[MK]]. I knew your parents and they knew me, they may have been my students, I am one of the last Mohicans that remained from the survivors of the Holocaust from Brody.

I would like to talk to you a bit. Let us talk about the past. Recall the forgotten old memories. We can then talk some about the present and later peek a little into the future. Perhaps the things that I would tell you, would not be pleasant and it would be difficult to incorporate them into this celebration of ours. This is because I am not going to talk to you in a routine way, but as a brother to brother or a brother to sister. I will tell you what I really feel. I will only tell you about things that my heart will put in my mouth.

The truth can be said that I am really "Ger Vetoshav"[1] among you. I came to you in Brody, about fifty years ago, lonely and alone, with neither a relative nor an acquaintance, and you have accepted me with open arms, and, in a short while, I have acquired loyal friends among you.

By Brody, my Brody, I do not mean the city itself. Cursed is its land, which opened her mouth to swallow the blood of our holy and pure brothers and sisters. By Brody, I mean our people, Brody's people. They are" Talit She'Kula Tkhelet"[2], a Talit without a flaw. I see them now, in my mind, they are here in this hall. Here is Mr. Idel Prives, an honest man, devoted to Zionism and Jewish holy values. I taught his two sons. He was a good friend, dedicated ally and devoted brother throughout my entire stay in Brody. His wife, who is the only one that survived from the entire family, lives today in our land. I met my wife, may her memory be blessed, in their house. Here are the Tartakover brothers, who raised the flag of our nation's revival. I especially remember Dr. Khayim Tartakover, may his memory be blessed, with admiration and a tremor of holiness. An innocent man, that every bit of his being was devoted to our national and cultural idea. Dr. Tartakover possessed many more traits and exalted virtues that not everybody is fortunate to own. This platform would be too short to describe them all, and therefore, I will instead just make use the short phrase - "Silence is his praise" [Psalms 65[MK]]. The descendants of these families live among us in our land. Many of them are my students. Now I see Dr. Anderman, may his memory be blessed, a humble man. He was one of the firsts who dreamt the dream of the return to Zion. Although he did not give speeches, and was not conspicuous, he was also not like this Jew who would go around with a hammer in his hand to wake up the crowd to chant the psalms, while he himself would go to sleep. The love for our people, our land and our language filled his life until his last day. His descendants are with us in our land, and I taught some of them.

[Page 363]

Now I stroll a little in the streets of Brody and its alleys. I am entering a narrow alley, I hear a humming noise and see a shining light. I approach ... this is the Beit Hamidrash[3], the workshop of the soul of our nation. Jews of all ages are sitting here, bent over and leaning, immersing themselves in the old and worn-out pages of the Gemara[4]. They weave a tractate, the tractate of the survival of our nation. I have often gone in to be with them and "sat amid the dust of their feet" [to study.[MK]].

Saturday in Brody - holiness is engulfing the city. I can see them in my imagination, I see the Jews of Brody with their black velvet long coats with silk sashes, shtreimels[5], on their heads, Tallith's under their arms, flocking to the Beit Ha'Midrash, to worship G-d. Every one of them looks to me like the high priest. Sometimes they look to me like soldiers – soldiers of G-d of Israel. A mysterious and enormous force attracts me to them and I join them instantly. I am already with them in

Bet Ha'Midrash, I pray with them and together we build G-d's destroyed and deserted temple.

It would be an unatoned crime not to mention here the high-school students. These delightful youths would come to the "Community House" in the afternoon, or at dusk, to "quench their thirst" and find a mend for their soul, which was detained in the mornings by the gentiles at the high school. It is difficult for me to break-up from Brody's people, so I retrieve some of them from the deep well of my memory and pass them here in front of you.

It is a summer noon. The Holy One, Blessed Be He took the sun out of its holster. There is no air and it is difficult to breath. People look for a shade to hide from the sweltering rays of the sun. All of us go outside of the city at dusk to rest in the bosom of nature and breath fresh air, celebrating an insignificant event, which is not considered important during any other time of the year, perhaps a recess day or Gnosya[6] day. We are going to Gedalia's "Yuridika". We called him "Tevye the Dairyman"[7]. Our joy was endless. The walls separating between the various ages fall instantly, broken and destroyed. We, the youths, together with the adults, dance like young goats, roll on the soft grass, frolic and go wild. Who would tell us what to do? We were young, full of energy and life, hidden inside us during the day, and here, under nature's open spaces, under the bright sky, they found an outlet and broke out. We were happy. We feel like we all members of the same family. We feel that we are children, children of nature, which does not discriminate between one child and another.

This is how we spent several hours outdoors and then went back home at a late hour. On our way back, we would pass near the "Kornveg" [corn way[MK]]. In my imagination, I am pausing there a bit. Brody youths are promenading there, joined together, walking arm in arm in the narrow trail of the "Kornveg". This is where the first threads, the threads of love are spun and woven. They enter the small forest. I hear their joyful laughter, and the forest's echo in response. They continue to stroll. I hear the secretive discourse of the leaves. The trees are swaying, as if they are praying for the wellbeing of the children. The moon above and the stars in their paths, accompany them on their way and I hear their blessing: "may your luck shine on you like the sun at mid-day".

[Page 364]

I now recall "Amkha" [ordinary folks[MK]] - porters, tailors, shoemakers, carpenters, and waggoneers. I remember this waggoneer, sitting on his cart seat, humming and chanting a popular folk song "Hoy Khava", or "Yosle, daineh shvartze oigen" ["Yosle – your black eyes"[MK]]. Where are you now? Would you know how much my soul is longing for you?

All layers of Brody's people, including all its kinds and forms, are passing in front of me now. Everything is gone, but not forgotten.

Deceased Brody's people are dear to me. You, the ones who are in this hall, are dear to me. You are my kith and kin, may you be blessed with a good life. Now we move from the imaginary world of the past, to the world of reality, to the present. Despite this move, experiences and memories from Brody are coming up and springing in my head, a whole depth of memories. How can I move on?... Never mind...I build a bridge through which we would pass from the past to the present. I am on the bridge... come and follow me.

In the twilight of my years, when my life is approaching its end, when I go through self-examination and summarize everything, I realize that most of my life I spent with and among you. A thread runs through all of those years. I am still standing on the bridge. I see Brody from afar. Brody people are waiving their hands to me. It is probably difficult, for them too, to say goodbye to me, and therefore please excuse me if I pause here on the bridge for another minute and talk just a little more about Brody.

We were a cohesive unit in Brody. We felt the feeling expressed by the Psalms song "For brethren to dwell together in unity". We danced together on Simkhat Torah and the holiday of Passover, and went together to the old cemetery on the Ninth of Av. We laughed, were happy, sighed and cried together. When the First World War broke out and I found myself in Vienna, even there the chain was not cut off. We met often, and visited each other. In our land, now, I am with and among you.

Here in our land, due to the passing time and due to the difficult conditions that I was always under, I did not see all of you, but I always tried to find out about you. I was happy in your joyous occasions, and felt pain when you did. I often met with some of my close friends (Moshe Okin and Netanel Rotman), at times even daily. We spilled our bitterness brother to brother and opened our sealed hearts, man to his friends. We received our relief by doing that, and it made it easier to carry out our life's load and distress. The cities of Brody, Vienna and Tel-Aviv, are our milestones, steps in our joint life that we shared together, and every step was an entire period. We have common experiences and memories, which are hard to forget, even when we do not talk about them.

Friends! Brothers and sisters! It would not be bragging for me to say that I did not seek prominence. However, I did not know the meanings of jealousy and envy. I did not chase after money, nor did I pursue honor. G-d is my witness that I did not initiate this celebration. The committee members are my witnesses that I tried, in vain and applied all the efforts, to dodge this commotion and honor. Hence, you would understand how I feel now when I see all the devoted and sincere friendship that is pouring onto me from every one of you. I don't know how to explain these feelings.

[Page 365]

I have lost the appropriate key with which I can open my heart and show you what is happening inside now, but believe me that I am always with you. "I cry out like the jackals when I think of your grief, I am like a violin for your songs[8]" .I am happy to celebrate your joy, Believe me, all of me is yours, and in these moments, my soul is simply going out to you.

I did not quench my thirst from the cup of life. I was content with one small single sip. Even that small sip was often forbidden. The sky of my life has been foggy and cloudy for the last few years. My entire narrow world is squeezed into my small space, like the Ninth of Av. You have now inserted a ray of light into my heart, to light the darkness of my constricted world. This light would shine and illuminate the rest of my years that remain for me on this earth. Together with you and among you, my narrow world has just widened and expanded, and everything seems like songs. I am happy to be with you on the same train, the train of life. That train passes from one stop to another. Several people get off in each stop, and some board to replace them. I have already done several full circles, but I am still on the train. However, the tribulations on the way have weakened me, my energy diminished, but I am happy to be with you. My heart is wounded and bleeding about the fact that my beloved wife is not here with me now. My heart breaks over my students (boys and girls), and my absent beloved friends. ...there were people and they are all gone... Please forgive me! I am leaving you for tiny moment - leaving this world. I am now among all of those I mentioned previously. I am immersing myself with their memory... All my dear ones are passing in front me like sheep being counted.

Please forgive my poetic effusion; please believe me that my words come out by themselves. A lot has been accumulated in my heart lately - a sea of great bitterness and torments of the soul. My heart is overflowing and cannot contain everything. It is bursting out, flooding and encountering things it did not mean to encounter. When one's heart is full, his mouth talks. Whom should I talk to if not in front of you?

I beg you – please have pity on me and do not judge me in the scale of demerit, because there is G-d in heavens. This G-d is kind and merciful, but sometimes He is zealot and vengeful. He has been castigating me severely, like I was his step-son... Please do not find any extraneous intent in my words... I know that G-d is a just judge, and there is no evil in His ruling. He pays evil with evil, and righteousness with righteousness, so if I was punished severely, my sins have been unbearable. However, my G-d! I pray to You together with the rest of Your children – "Avinu Malkeinu[9] ["Our Father, Our King"MK]. I ask you to have a pity on me: "As a Father who pities his children" [Psalm 103:13-14MK]. Why didn't You show your compassion with me - Your son, and why didn't You stand by me in my sorrow? Maybe I sinned, but who am I and what am I? A weak and worthless creature. But You, the great G-d, the heroic and horrific, You are almighty. Why did You let my evil urge overcome the good urge. I, Shaul your servant, a child of

Your servants, accept Your mastery. I yield before You, I bow before You, and "lick the dust of Your feet" [Isiah 49:23MK]. However, I do like the sun and ask for a bit of light, as it says[10]: "G-d wrapped himself in a white Talit and his bright glory shone from one edge of the world to another". You are the light. I would like to be able to stand from afar and enjoy Your light. Would anybody's share diminish by that? I know that there is G-d in Heaven. I know that there is an after-life and that everything is determined by heavenly justice[11]. In Heaven everything is considered, weighted, and recorded... I am sure that they would forgive me for my words here, since they know over there that I am not the one who is talking now. It is not I who is talking. The sorrow and pain are talking now from my throat. Had You known, and perhaps it is good that You do not know, about the dark grief, which oppresses and presses my heart day and night, like an iron forceps for the last eight years... until it seems to me that my head would explode to pieces. It is very hard for me to concentrate even now. I am collapsing... I have entered into a difficult maze and it is difficult for me to get out of it. Who knows? Perhaps I lost my mind, or I am possessed... My friends and students, land, heaven, towns and fields, please have mercy on me!
[Page 366]

I am finishing, however, I would like to add a few more words at the end of my talk, and then I would cease. Life is beautiful. It is worthwhile to live! The world is so big and beautiful! All the good and the beauty that exists in the world, was created for the benefit of humankind. Even our sages, bless their memory, said: "grab and eat, grab and drink, as the world we are leaving is a tavern" [compared to the next worldMK]. Live life to the fullest, because "we will all die like the water spilled on the ground that could not be recollected" {Shmuel II 14:14MK]. This is why every moment counts.

When I began my talk, I said that I would try to look ahead to the future. I will fulfill my promise now. I sneak into the future through the time wormholes. I squeeze through the hidden and unknown and talk to you from the other side of the screen, which separates between the present and the future; you will hear the voice calling you - Brody people. You would recognize the voice. Please listen carefully.

My Brody brothers and sisters! Consolidate your sparse lines, as long as you are still riding on the train of life. Carry the flag of Brody with honor and pride. A prominent Historian would, one day, write about the people of Brody and about their actions. He will write about the city, about its leaders, heroes and scholars. He would have enough to write about. One generation must tell the next generation about Brody, so that whatever was not written down would not sink into oblivion. That is how we would be able to preserve our past for the benefit of our decendants, natives of our land, and children of future generations. They would not go through the steps we had to go through. They would not talk about their Brody's past or their Vienna's past. A new generation would rise, a generation who would not experience and would never know about the bitter life in the diaspora. They will be free people, wholesome in their soul and body without any complications. They will be rooted in the ground of our homeland. They would grow and flourish "like trees in the field" [Deuteronomy 20:19[MK]]. "They shall still bring forth fruit in old age; they shall be full of sap and richness" [Psalms 92:15). Past, present and future will be unified. They will walk with their heads held high, with a powerful stride. They will know that the land under their feet and our land's blue sky above their heads are theirs. Any outsiders who will harbor an intent to harm us would know that they put their life on the line. They will add bright pages to the history of our nation, in our land and the diaspora, history that will be studied in our schools.

Should the children of Brody natives really want to know about the history of their ancestors, they would be able to read the Brody Yizkor Book that would be published shortly. I would like to record a few words for this book, and these would be my final words:

"Remember that I and my nation, and all of those who came before me, bequest life to those who would come after me. Live and enjoy life!"

Translator's Notes

1. Ger Vetoshav – literally means "alien resident" in Hebrew. In Judaism it means a gentile living in Eretz Israel who accepts on oneself (and observes) the Noahide Laws (the minimum set of imperatives which in

Jewish tradition that are said to be applicable to non-Jews, consisting of seven out of the 613 commandments in Judaism). The term was coined after the statement made by Abraham when he came to the sons of Chet and asked for a burial place for his wife Sara: "I am a stranger and a resident with you; give me a possession of a burial place with you that I could bury my dead from before me." (Genesis 23:4)

2. Talit She'Kula Tekehlet – literally means "a Talit – prayer shawl that it is entirely azure This is an expression in Hebrew, which means that anything or anybody is without any fault (particularly from moral point of view). The phrase is based the Torah portion of Korakh (Book of Numbers) in which Korakh asked Moshe after Israel was commanded with the azure tzitzit, weather a Talit which is entirely azure provides a a relief from the commandment.
3. Beit Ha'Midrash - literally means "A house of learning", was a study hall or a school for religious studies, usually in or adjacent to a synagogue or a Yeshiva. It is also a word used to describe the level of studies below the academic level of a yeshiva.
4. The Jewish Talmud, is what is called "oral Torah" the central text of the Rabbinical Judaism consists of two parts: The Mishnah – contains the core text and the Gemara embodies the analysis and interpretation of the Mishnah and the holy Bible.
5. Shtreimel – Black fur hat warn by married Haredi and Hasidic Jews.
6. Gnosya day - Birthday or a day of a coronation (of a king)
7. Tevya the Dairyman – Fictional character portrayed by Shalom Aleikhem in a series of short stories about the life of Jews in Russia at the turn of the nineteen century. The stories were adapted for audio recordings and the Broadway musical and the film "Fiddler on the Roof".
8. Adapted from Yehuda Halevi poem (also used as a lament for Ninth of Av)– "Zion, do you ask if your captives are at peace?"
9. Avinu Malkeinu – "Our Father, Our King" is a Jewish prayer originated in the "Talmud" and is chanted during the "Ten Days of Repentance" between Rosh Hashanah and Yom Kippur. The prayer asks for forgiveness and contains about forty wishes and pleas.
10. According to Bereshit Rabah book (83:4) – Rabbi Shimon Bar Yehotzedek asked Rabbi Shmuel Bar Nakhmani:"How did G-d create light?", and Rabbi Yehotzedek responded: "G-d wrapped himself in a white Tallit and his bright glory shone from one edge of the world to another".
11. According to Jewish Halakha, "Death by Heavenly Justice" is a punishment imposed on somebody for committing about fifteen sins deliberately. Since this punishment is imposed by G-d (who knows all secrets of the heart) rather than by man, there is no need for testimonies nor warnings.

[Page 367]

"Kaddish" for the Lost

The story of the Szmuszkin Family, which I heard from my father and Mother Chaim and Zehava (Hertz) Szmuszkin and from My father's sister Selka Hensel

by Avshalom Sion-Szmuszkin

Translated by Moshe Kutten

Edited by Yocheved Klausner

a. Menakhem Szmuszkin Smuggles his Son Avraham-Aba from Berdichev to Brody

The youth Avraham-Aba, son of Menakhem Szmuszkin, was twenty-three years old in 1905, toward the end of the Japan-Russia war. At this age, Avraham was required to enlist. He was slated to be sent to Vladivostok, a city on the border with Japan, as a soldier of the Russian military. His family lived in Berdichev and he was the eldest son of his father's second wife. His father, Menakhem, son of Eliezer who was the son of Moshe, was a handsome man, modernly dressed, with a very dignified appearance. He was the descendant of R' Levi Yitzkhak of Berdichev and was very wealthy. Like all other Szmuszkin's in Russia, he was a merchant of coral beads and a Jewelry designer. His trade relations reached the ends of the world and his agents reached very distant places.

Menakhem Szmuszkin managed to smuggle his son, Avraham-Aba, from Berdichev to his agents who were waiting in Radzivilov at the Russian border and from there to Brody. The Galician city Brody was located just eight kilometers away from Radzivilov across the Austrian border. At that time it was part of the Austro-Hungarian Empire. The border between Russia and the Austrian empire stretched between the two cities.

From 1779 until 1879, Brody was a "tax-free" city ("Freistadt"), and its residents were prosperous. Whoever managed to enter its limits would not be expelled and was not obligated to pay taxes. Brody people used the phrase in Yiddish: "ferfalen vi in Brodi" (lost like in Brody). The Russian Jews in Galicia were nicknamed "Fonye", while the Galician Jews with whom they came to mix were nicknamed "Kiry". When its status as a "free tax" zone was terminated, [after WW I[MK]] Brody started to deteriorate. In the beginning, traces of her splendor lingered, but its transit trade was replaced, in many cases, by the smuggling trade.

Grandfather Menakhem opened an agency of coral beads for his son Avraham-Aba in Brody, since one needs a business to make a living in addition to studying Torah. He rented an apartment for him and also a store, or a warehouse where he sent the corals. When Avraham-Aba established the warehouse, he needed locks to secure it, so he went to look for locks in the store adjacent to his agency – a wholesaler store for iron and construction supplies owned by the Epstein family.

b. The Family of Rakhel and Ephraim Epstein

R' Ephraim Epstein was one of Brody's most honorable people. He helped build the Husiatyn Hassidic[1] synagogue, as a member of the Husiatyn Hasidic dynasty. He was a righteous person, pious, noble, liberal and sociable. His wife, Grandmother Rakhel was short built, really tiny, but active and full of inexhaustible energy. She always dressed with great care. She commanded in all matters and everybody respected her opinion. The family of Rakhel and Ephraim Epstein consisted of two daughters and two sons - the older daughter Matilda (Mattel), the second daughter Gitya and the two brothers - pleasant manners' Manes, and the young Khaim Epstein.

[Page 368]

The Epstein family was very wealthy. Their house, on Zelazna Street, was a spacious one story private house, surrounded by a sizeable yard. The people who prayed in the synagogue and the Kloiz [house of learning and praying[MK]] were frequently invited for a Kiddush on Sabbaths and holidays. Preparations for a Kiddush would last two or even three days. The guests would leave such a Kiddush satiated like after a hearty meal. During Sabbaths and holidays, the house was exceptionally beautiful. The house shone brightly such that the white tablecloths in that house seemed whiter than in any other house. One could feel the presence of the Shekhinna [Devine Presence[MK]] in the house.

The holiday of Simkhat Torah[2], was a true celebration in Grandfather Ephraim's house. A custom was established in town that the entire congregation of the synagogue and kloiz would go to Ephraim Epstein's house. A large Sukkah was erected in the yard filled with an abundance of special types of foods – all sorts of meats and fish, stuffed doughs, and baked food items. They would also provide beer, honey cakes, and nuts for the holiday of Simkhat Torah. Grandmother would prepare a special type of a desert and the food included noodles kugel as well as sweet and salty rice kugel. People used to say: "we are going to Ephraim Epstein's – good cooking would be there".

c. How Avraham-Aba Fell in Love with Matilda

Mother Matilda and Father Avraham-Aba used to tell the story of their courting that occurred during the time Menakhem, son of Elazar, did not want his son to be recruited to go to the Russian-Japan war. They would tell the story on Sabbaths, after the afternoon nap, at tea time when the kids were still too young to go to the youth movements or other places. Mother Mattel would first tell the story about how Avraham-Aba went out to find a store where he can buy a lock to lock the warehouse and entered R' Efrayim's store. Mattel happened to be there, she had come to the store to look for her mother. Perhaps she needed some money, or wanted to tell her mother something. She was a little older than fifteen years, but not yet sixteen, still a student in school. When the youth Avraham saw the young girl standing and talking to her mother, his heart became excited and he was captivated by her.

Father would continue the story: "in my heart I knew that she is the one, but I did not know what to do next and how". He started to inquire about the girl's family background. He knew that the girl's parents had a store, but he needed to find out more information and inquire further. He asked around, and when all the conditions turned out to be to be proper, including the girl's appearance, Father sent a matchmaker. Additional mutual investigations, inquiries, common in the days, commenced. A year later, Avraham-Aba Szmuszkin and Matilde Epstein got married. At the wedding wine was spilled like water, delicacies were served abundantly in exquisite food vessels, and the joy was immense. The groom's father Menachem and his third wife came from Russia with their children.

[Page 369]

d. Avraham-Aba and Matilda Szmuszkin's Home

Avraham-Aba and Matilda formed a happy and loving couple. They complimented each other's qualities, and helped each other. Hansome Avraham had bright eyes. He showered each morning with cold water, and people used to say that he possessed a "good pigment". His manners commanded respect. His good nature radiated from his face. He spoke politely and softly, and respected everybody. Matilda was smart, practical, agile and talented. She provided a firm support for Father. They lived in Rynek D Street [Rynek means market in Polish. Ryneck D was one of the streets that surrounded the market[MK]], in the center of town, near the Kalir pharmacy. They lived on the second floor above the store. The entrance to their apartment was through a staircase leading from the street. A large baking stove, heated by firewood, replaced by coal a few years later, was situated in the big kitchen. A large dinner table filled the large room with a closet and a bed positioned on the side. There were also two bedrooms, one for the parents, one for the children. The bathroom was in the corner of the balcony. The store was not far: it was a big and flourishing store of building materials, tools and agricultural machines, on Kolyova Street on the way to the train station.

Matilda and Avraham's home was very religious, but not Haredi[3]. Sabbaths and holidays were celebrated in splendor and grace, according to the Jewish tradition. Avraham Szmuszkin was not a Hasidic Jew and thus prayed in the synagogue named after Shaul Kharif, where very orthodox Jews prayed. On holidays, religious festivals and Sabbaths he would sing Shabbat songs between and after the meals: "Lord, Master of the Universe, you are the king, the king of kings..."[4]. His pleasant voice resonates in my ears even today. How pleasurable was it to sit down at the table on which a "samovar" was placed (made of silver on Sabbath and copper during week days), and also sweet and salty cakes and sorts of confections, splendidly made by the exemplary housewife – Mattel, whose delicacies and recipes made a name for her, and her reputation was wide-spread.

The children were members of Zionist youth movements such as "Ha'Shomer Ha'Tzair" (the "Young Guard") or the "Zionist Youth". They studied in the public school in the morning and Hebrew in the afternoon. Avraham-Aba contributed tremendously to the establishment of Hebrew courses. The objective was the eventual immigration to Erez Israel, and therefore, Avraham-Aba placed great importance to the study of the language, as a means for a faster assimilation in the new land. A good, progressive and relaxed atmosphere prevailed in the house. The house was open to friends as well as family members and friends of the children, who were frequently helped by Avraham-Aba

e. "Your Children are like Olive Plants around your Table..." [Psalm 128, verse 3[MK]]

A special and hearty chapter was the relationship with Grandfather R' Epstein's family. His house was a meeting place for the entire family: His elder daughter - Matilda, and her husband, Avraham-Aba Szmuszkin with their children, Khayim, Selka, Hertz, Manya and Efraim. The second daughter - Gitya and her spouse - Elimelekh Eisenthal from Krakow and their daughter Khaya'le. There were two sons – big Manes, a modest and pleasant mannered who was the most God-fearing person of all, and his wife, Pesia, daughter to a well-known Rabbis dynasty - Shvedron, along with their daughter Leah. The youngest sibling in the family was Khayim Epstein, his wife – Etya, nee Hertz, and their son Ephraim and daughter Leah.

Gitya and her husband Elimelekh along with their daughter Leah continued to live in Grandfather and Grandmother's house on Zelazna Street. Mattel, Manes and Khayim left the house after they were married and lived close by with their families. The two sons, Manes and Khayim, continued to work with their father Ephraim in the store. The Eisenthal family worked in the leather industry and Matilda assisted Avraham in his business.

Every Sabbath night (Friday evening) and the evening before holidays the entire family would gather at the home of Grandfather and Grandmother Epstein, even when everybody established their own families and lived in their own houses.

[Page 370]

Prior to lighting of the candles, everybody would gather to wait for the blessings and the good wishes expressed by their beloved grandfather. At the conclusion of Yom Kippur, [Day of Atonement[MK]] everybody would come together with mutual love and friendship. When the whole family gathered, there was an enormous joy, coming from the heart. These moments roused and made a mark of feelings of happiness and love on everybody in family and became part of the Jewish folklore in town.

f. My Heart is in the East, and I am at the edge of the West.

During the time when the economic conditions were good, life was nice and comfortable. Only one thought bothered Avarahm-Aba: the thought of not being able to fulfil his dream of immigrating to Eretz Israel. Before World War I broke out, the family of Menakhem Szmuszkin, Avraham's father, left their city of Berdichev and emigrated to Eretz Israel. They were members of the so called "Second Aliyah[5] " and lived in Segera [today Moshav Ilaniya[MK]]. Grandfather Menakhem became ill. He could not endure the hunger, rampant in Eretz Israel, the extremely harsh conditions, and the cruel Ottoman regime, whose attitude toward the small Jewish settlements was very hostile. In order to avoid deportation by the Ottomans, like all other foreigners, he destroyed all the family passports. He succumbed to his illness in 1915, when he was only 56 years old. He left a wife and seven children. Their life became unbearable. The death of Grandfather Menakhem was a hard blow to Avraham's plan. His childhood dream and life aspiration could not be fulfilled. He did not reach the land that he so desired, and had to stay in Brody with his expanding family.

g. Ups, Downs and Crises

World War I destroyed the economic basis of the family. That period was abounding with anguish and suffering. When the Russians came to town, they hunted after Avraham Szmuszkin as a deserter from the army, seemingly based on a pre-defined list. The Austrians took him captive along with other foreign subjects. The captured subjects were concentrated in a camp near Vienna, the capital of the empire. Mother Matilda along with her three little children stayed behind in the city. Their suffering was considerable. When the war broke, Khayim was six years old, Selka was two, and Hertz was just born. After the war, the wounds started to heal. Life returned to normal and the economic conditions improved steadily. Sadly, anther blow hit the family during the early part of the 1930's when deterioration began again. The reason for it was the policy of harsh decrees by the Polish government. Most of the Jews lost their fortune. There was another reason for the Szmuszkin's deterioration: a partnership with an unreliable and dishonest person.

In the beginning, Avraham-Aba Szmuszkin was secure in his business. He received a dowry, owned a big store, and did well in his business. He sold many farmers plows and scythes on credit. When they were late in their payments due to the horrific economic crisis in Poland, he lost his fortune. The story goes as follows: the Polish finance minister, Vladislav Grabski, enacted a Moratorium Law, allowing postponement of paying the debts. The farmers never paid off their debts and that affected the economic situation of the family. From a position of wealth, they became impoverished. Their store could no longer provide their needs as abundantly as before.

[Page 371]

"Grabski Aliyah" became part of Israel's history. Many Jews immigrated to Eretz Israel, due to the extremely brutal economic crisis in Poland. Avraham-Aba Szmuszkin tried to find out about the possibility of making Aliyah as well. However, the discouraging responses he received from his family in Sejera, dissuaded him from this plan. His spirit sank. He kept to himself, engulfed with sadness and despair. The process of the family deterioration continued all the way until the Holocaust, which eradicated the foundations of the glorious and rooted Judaism and caused the death of most of our family members, men, women and children, along with the six million of our people, G-d avenge their blood.

h. The Story of the Daring Ha'apala[6] of Khaym Szmuszkin

Khayim, the elder son of Avraham-Aba and Matilda Szmuszkin immigrated to Eretz Israel illegally in 1935 along roads which were not really roads, stealing borders, and becoming a stow-away passenger on a ship bound to Jaffa. He did not have entry permit to any of the European countries he crossed, nor did he have one for entering Palestine, which was under the British mandate at the time.

Khayim Szmuszkin arrived at Eretz Israel in June 1935 on the evening before Shavuoth[7]. He took advantage of the fact that he (and his family) lacked citizenship of any country and the fact that he owned a “Nansen's Passport”[1]. Knowing that he did not have any chance of securing an entry certificate to Palestine, he took the risk and succeeded. His brother Hertz tried to follow him in a similar way but was unfortunate. He was captured, beaten, and sent back to Brody.

i. World War II and the German Occupation in Brody

There were eight thousand Jews in Brody before the war, about two thirds of the entire population. Most of the residents were Poles and Ukrainians, some Slovaks and even Germans. German was taught as a compulsory language in school due to the proximity to Austria, although not the conversational German. Grandfather Epstein was not alive then. He passed away following surgery at the young age of 56. Grandmother Rakhel passed away at a ripe old age of 90 about half a year before the war.

The Red Army entered Brody in September 1939. When the war broke, people assumed, based on what was known until that time that the war situation was temporary, and that people would be able to continue living after that. Avraham-Aba Szmuszkin, Khayim, and Manes Epstein and

Elimelekh Eisenthal gathered all the valuables, the silver and gold they were able to amass, and put them in in large boxes. They dug out a big pit of a depth of three meters under the floor of Grandfather Epstein's house and hid the boxes in it. There was a tendency in these families to crowd together at a time of distress. Avraham and Matilda along with Manya, Hertz and Froim'cho relocated at Grandmother Epstein's house. Gitah, her husband and daughter already lived in the house while Manes and Khayim's families moved in separate rooms. Unfortunately, the crisis did not pass as they have hoped.

[Page 372]

The Germans invaded Brody from all directions in July 1941. Chaos descended. People did not know what was going on. Unexpectedly, all the intellectuals were ordered to gather, as if to discuss issues associated with the organization of the community's day-to-day life. When they all gathered, they were beaten, humiliated and were loaded onto trucks. The police [the Ukrainian police[MK]] and the Gestapo transported them to the local forest, positioned them near dug-out lime pits and shot them all. One of them managed to escape. He told people what he saw with his own eyes. All the families realized that they would need to hide and that they were facing a difficult period ahead. People were being captured in the street, forced into staircases and searched in their pockets, other were murdered. Normal life ceased to exist. The Germans and the Ukrainians robbed the Jews and drove them out of their houses. Work tools, carts and horses were confiscated. The official hunger rations heralded a miserable existence. Shops stayed closed; children did not go to school; people did not go to work. War was upon them. Leaving the city was forbidden, and so were the use of public transportation, entrance into public places, walking in the main streets and plazas and even walking on sidewalks.

People did not know what to think, how to plan, and what to do next: should they join their parents or go to their children, should they go to work or turn anywhere else. Later on, curfew was imposed, and a real panic ensued. People remained without work or property, or anything else. A Jewish militia and Judenrat, which served the Germans, were established. These people knew all the addresses and where everybody was. They knew which Jewish family would yield a larger property. The poor people were taken first. They opened forced-labor camps, not in Brody itself, but close by in Zlotchov. German and Ukrainian policemen patrolled the streets at night and conducted raids nightly. They identified Jews in the streets and captured them like dogs. They took Jews out of their beds. Those who managed to escape dug bunkers in the forest. Some managed to arrange and camouflage hideouts in their homes behind bookshelves or in cellars, where they hid during searches.

In an attempt to escape the city, several people convinced a Christian foreman to take them to work in the forest. Khayim and Manes Epstein, Elimelekh Eisenthal, Shmuel Henzel and several other people from Brody and Radzivilov went to the forest and stayed there. Fortunately for them, the Germans did not think to look in the forest. Men were hiding in the forest while the women and the children hid in the city. However, there was no food in the city. There was no place to buy food. Everything was acquired by bartering or on the black market. Women went to the villages to barter valuables for food. The situation in the city worsened.

j. The End

On Rosh Hashanah 5702 (22 September 1941), the family still managed to gather in Grandfather's house for Minyan and prayer. Rumors circulated during the Ten Days of Repentance[8], that the Germans were planning a large operation in Yom Kippur. Selka came home on the evening before Shabbath Shuva[9] [Friday evening[MK]] and urged Aba-Avraham and the rest of the family to spend the night in the forest. Father did not want to go there: "What will be, will be. G-d is everywhere". Avraham-Aba was a true believer. Mother Matilda said: "You see that Father does not want to go. I cannot argue with him. He may know what he is doing." Everyone quieted. Mother did not say anything. Even Manya did not talk. She was already twenty years old by then. The little Froim'cho was silent. He was already fourteen years old by then. Everybody stayed (Hertz was already out of the house). Father had to push Selka out. "Go, go, it is already late. It would be dark soon. How would you walk in the dark?" Selka said later on: "I lighted the candles for Mother. This was Friday. I do not recall if that was also the evening before Yom Kippur, but it was Friday for sure [Yom Kippur was Sunday September 21 1942[MK]]. Mother accompanied me out. We went further and further away from home....and then she started to go back...I looked at her...she looked at me...and that was it..."

[Page 373]

The first Aktzia started the following day on Shabbat Shuva, 19 September, nineteen hundred forty-two. The Jews were driven out of their houses, kidnapped in the streets, and were concentrated in the market plaza by German, Ukrainian and Jewish policeman. The people who were discovered hiding, the sick and the old were shot on the spot.

"During the night, - who could sleep after such a day – we sat there and listened. We heard loud shots and a commotion. It was not very far, and at night one can hear better....I did not want to believe that this was happening. The following day I found an opened house, empty, overturned and ruined. There was nobody in the house. Everybody disappeared as if they were never there..."

Hetshu (Hertz), who was about twenty six years old by then, stayed in the labor camp, where he worked, during that night. One day, sometime later, he was walking with a friend and was captured. That happened during the second Akztia on 2 November, nineteen hundred forty-two. Somebody said that he jumped from the train bound for Belzec. However, not every jump was successful.

We heard it everywhere: "That uncle is gone, this uncle is dead, that aunt is murdered...there are no longer people here and there are no longer people there". However life went on. Selka said: "Until then, I really did not know how much power a person has, and how much a person can endure".

The situation became intolerable. It was impossible to breath. Selka and her husband remained practically alone. They decided to leave Brody to a place where they were not recognized. They ran away from place to place, through the fields. They hid among the wheat spikes when they heard the roar of airplanes. They bribed policemen and ordinary gentiles. They were captured once by the Gestapo but managed to sneak out. They ran away from Brody to Vyshnevets. and from there to Lvov and back. Sometimes they used a vehicle and relied on dubious people who could easily betray them despite the money they received. It must be said though that there were some gentiles who helped them despite the fact they risked themselves by doing so.

At the end of the war, Selka and her husband trundled their way to Italy and from there to Israel.

k. Over but Not Done With

From our family, only Khayim Szmuszkin and his sister Selka Henzel, the children of Avraham-Aba and Matilda Szmuszkin survived. Khayim – my father, left before the hell started. Selka survived it. They have both fulfilled their father's dream, which he could not fulfill himself. They both live in Israel with their families.

The rest of the family members were not as fortunate. Let this story serve as a dedication to their beloved memory, and also as a memorial that sanctifies their pure souls.

Editor's Notes

1. Nansen - the Norwegian representative at the League of Nations, who initiated the international convention, which grants the status of "International Subject" to refugees who lack citizenship. With a Nansen passport, it was possible to go anywhere and stay there if the owner of the passport was not detained from entering that country.

Translator's Notes

2. Husiatyn Hasidic dynasty originated from the Ruzhin Hasidic family in the city Husiatyn, Ukraine. The dynasty moved to Vienna in Austria at the beginning of the First World War, and from 1937 was located in Tel Aviv, Israel. Following the death of the fourth Rebbe without descendants in 1968, it ceased to operate as a Hasidic dynasty.
3. Simkhat Torah - a Jewish holiday, celebrated at the conclusion of the eight days fall holiday of Sukkot. It marks the conclusion of the annual cycle of public Torah readings, and the beginning of a new cycle.
4. Haredi – the word means "to tremble" or "to fear." Haredi Jewish is the most orthodox stream of Judaism (also referred to as "Ultra-Orthodox"), of which Hasidic Judaism is part.

5. "Yah Ribbon Alam", Piyyut (poem) written in Aramaic and authored by Israel Najara (1555-1625) is part of the Jewish Shabbat songs and is chanted at the onset of the Sabbath (Friday evening).
6. "Second Aliya" – was a wave of immigration (mainly from Russia and the Pale of Settlement], to the Ottoman Empire's controlled Palestine. It took place between 1904 and 1914. Most of the immigrants were idealists, inspired by the revolutionary ideals then sweeping the Russian Empire who sought to create a communal agricultural settlement system in Palestine. They thus founded the kibbutz movement.
7. Ha'apala is the Hebrew word [which literally means ascending] for the "illegal immigration" to Eretz Israel during the British rule of Palestine before and just right after WW II. People who participated in this endeavor boarded dilapidated ships bought by the Jewish Agency, which attempted to break the blockade imposed by the British military. Many of the illegal immigrants were caught and sent back or kept in camps in Cyprus and elsewhere.
8. Shavuoth – is a Jewish holiday that commemorates the Giving of the Torah by G-d to the Jewish people and the time of the wheat harvest in the historic land of Israel.
9. The ten first days of the Jewish new Year starting with Rosh Hashana and culminating in Yom Kippur are called the Days of Awe or the Ten Days of Repentance. This is the time to consider the sins of the previous year, time for a serious introspection and the opportunity for asking forgiveness from one another before one's fate is sealed on Yom Kippur.
10. Shabbath Shuva – the Saturday between Rosh Hashana and Yom Kippur. The name Shuva [literally means] is taken from the chapter in the Bible (Hosea 14:2-10) read on that Shabbath. The chapter begins with the words: ", O' Israel, to the L-rd your G-d...".

[Page 374]

My Friend Nunek

Words expressed on 29 June 1993 in a Eulogy at the mass grave for Latrun defenders who were killed and buried as unknown soldiers

by Raphael (Fulu) Shalev-Shlinger

Translated by Moshe Kutten

Fifty years passed from the day of the murder of the last Jews in Brody Ghetto. You - Nunek-Nakum, son of Miriam (nee Shwartz) and Yosef Hurwitz, was the only remnant left of these two families - your mother's side and your father's side. You were thirteen years old when you, I, and several other peers from our age group, found a place to hide in Folwarki Maleh village. The city of Brody and its surroundings was declared "Juden Frei" – a region clear of Jews. Informing [about hiding Jews[MK]] was rampant in the area and the Ukrainian policemen continued to transport their orphaned victims to the location at the barb-wired fence across which one could see the village Smolno. There, in that place, right at the edge of the ghetto, all the remaining Jews were shot and killed. Both of us, you - Nunek and I - your friend, managed, miraculously, to escape that hell. There is no logical explanation for miracles and wonders, yet, we may have survived to be able to provide a live testimony to the brutality and cruelty of the Nazi oppressors and the Ukrainian collaborators, may their names and memory be wiped out.

Nunek arrived at the British internment camps in Cyprus following twisted roads and soul. He trained there as a warrior with the "Hagana"[1] units , together with other Ma'apilim[2]. When he arrived in Israel, he volunteered to serve in the Harel Brigade[3] of the Palmakh[[4]. During the War of Independence, Nunek fought in Jerusalem area. He was wounded in one of the battles, and before he had completely recuperated from his wounds, he joined the warriors in Latrun[5]. He fell in the battle to liberate the road to Jerusalem on July 17, 1948 when he was seventeen years old. His body was transferred on February 28, 1950 from a temporary burial location together with the bodies of nineteen other warriors to Mount Herzl[6] and was buried in a mass grave with a full state ceremony. Those fighters fell before they had a chance to taste life.

I managed to find out about the place of burial of these defenders of the homeland only recently after long years of searching. So at almost the fiftieth anniversary, we have gathered here to honor these warriors, and to preserve the memory of their sacrifice, made in order to ensure our survival. We are uniting ourselves with the memory of Nunek and his nineteen comrades who were buried here in the mass grave. Your name – Nunek is going to be mentioned in a Yizkor Book, the Yizkor book for the city of Brody, your native city that is going to be published shortly. Fate probably caused the delay of the publication of the book, so that your name could be included along with other Brody youths who fell during Israel's battles.

May their memory be blessed!
May your soul be bound in the bond of the living!

Translator's Notes

1. Haganah - The underground military organization of the Jewish population in Eretz Yisrael during the period of 1929-1948.
2. Ma'apilim - Jews who immigrated illegally to Palestine during British control in the 1930s and 1940s. Over 100,000 people attempted to illegally enter Palestine. Over half were stopped by British patrols, and more than 50,000 people were placed in internment camps in Atlit (Palestine) and the islands of Cyprus and Mauritius.
3. Har'el Brigade – The Palmakh brigade formed in 1948 to fight in the defense of Jerusalem and Jerusalem Corridor. The name Har'el means “Mountain of G-d” in Hebrew referring to Mount Zion in Jerusalem. Its first commander was Yitzkhak Rabin, later the IDF Chief of Staff and Israel's prime minister.
4. Palmakh – the elite fighting force of the Haganah.
5. Latrun – named after a monastery located on the major highway between Tel-Aviv and Jerusalem. The British built a Tegart fort over-looking the highway in that location and made it into a police station for the British forces. When they left, they handed it to the Jordanian Arab

Legion. During the War of Independence, Latrun saw a series of military engagements between the Israel Defense Forces and the Jordanian Arab Legion between 25 May and 18 July 1948 as it commanded the only road linking the centers of Jewish population and Jerusalem, giving Latrun strategic importance in the battle for Jerusalem.

6. Mount Herzl – the national cemetery in Jerusalem.

[Page 375]

List of the "Righteous of the Nations of the World" Who Saved a Few of Brody's Jews

Translated by Moshe Kutten

Names of the Saviors	Names of the Saved	Comments
Buraczek Jan	izenbrukh family	The savior could not protect the family all the way to the liberation
Glasda Iwan	Melah Halpern	
Golik Wladek	Mendel Furman (Brick)	
Zak Tadeuusz	Sonia Katzman-Vinograd	Zak Tadeusz passed away in Warsaw and left a wife and three grandchildren
Choms Larisa Wladyslawa (fake name - Dionizy)	Klara Lustig and her daughter	During the years of the occupation Larisa Choms was active in Lvov and its environs for the sake of the local Jews. After the fall of 1943 she headed the RPZ council (A council for providing help to the Jews). Her agent, Vladek Yokalo acted to save the Jews of Brody and its environs. She passed away in Israel and was buried in Haifa
Jukalo Wlasyslaw and Walter Wladek	Bianca and Herman Lilian and many other Jews in Lvov	
Lukaniec Powdyk	Anni Mist	
Lukaszczekiewicz Genia	Malvina Friedman nee Lillian Bianca and Herman Lilian and child	

Mamucki family	Zigmond Berk (Dentist) and family	The family was discovered as somebody informed on them. The two families, the savior and the saved were murdered
Mowczan Harycz	Khayim and Bina Gasthalter	
Miklaszewski Maria and Jacenty and their daughter Wladzia	Kalman Henrik and his daughter Israela	
Sydorczuk Wlodymir, his wife Sofia (Zonka) and their son Josef	Tzipora Rom nee Spodek	
Pawluk Boczko	Erna Landgeuertz and her daughter Berta	
Kut Iwan (Iasko), his wife Maria, and their sons Jaroslaw and Szczepan (Stefan)	Refael (Polo) Shalev (Shlinger)	
Kut Anton	Tonia Berger	
Krawczuk Lukian and Panko	Rabbi Moshe Halevi Shteinberg, Yaakov Braun and family	
Rot Dola	Shust Michael	Rut was a fearless woman, the wife of Jukalo Wladek, a righteous of the Nations of the World". She helped the Jewish people of Brody to survive. She was active in actions risking death.
Szust Michal	Dr. Bogner	

[Page 377]

Ukrainians who saved Brody's Jews with the people they saved
From left to right: Yasku Bortchak, Irena Shayer, Matchik Gruber, Ivan-Ilia Shchuk, Guzyuk, Tzibrok, Paulib, Iliashtchok (Bodyonivitz, Chobit, Romanyetz, Shmulik Stoianover

[Page 378]

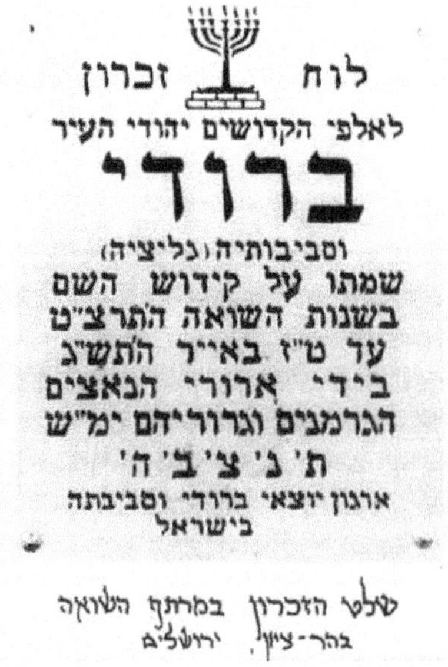

Memorial plaque for Brody martyrs in the Holocaust Museum cellar

[Page 381]

Chapter Six:
Memorial Pages

יזכור

יִזְכֹּר אֱלֹהִים אֶת כָּל הַנְּשָׁמוֹת שֶׁל קְהִלַּת בְּרוֹדִי בֵּין שְׁאָר קְהִלּוֹת בֵּית יִשְׂרָאֵל בְּגוֹלַת אֵירוֹפָּה שֶׁהֶעֱלוּ עַל מוֹקֵד בִּשְׁנוֹת הַשּׁוֹאָה תַּ"שׁ-תַּשַׁ"ה. שִׁשָּׁה מִילְיוֹן אֲנָשִׁים וְנָשִׁים, יְלָדִים וִילָדוֹת, בַּחוּרִים וּבְתוּלוֹת, זָקֵן וָטַף, שֶׁנֶּהֶרְגוּ וְשֶׁנִּטְבְּחוּ בְּאַכְזָרִיּוּת אֲיֻמָּה וְנִרְצְחוּ בְּרֶצַח הֲמוֹנִים בִּמְקוֹמוֹת מְגוּרֵיהֶם בֶּעָרִים, בָּעֲיָרוֹת וּבַכְּפָרִים, וְיִתְרָם הוּבְלוּ כַּצֹּאן לַטֶּבַח לְמַחֲנוֹת־הָרִכּוּז וְנִסְפּוּ בְּמִיתוֹת מְשֻׁנּוֹת וְנוֹרָאוֹת, וְנִשְׂרְפוּ לְאֵפֶר בְּכִבְשְׁנֵי־הָאֵשׁ שֶׁל מַחֲנוֹת־הַהַשְׁמָדָה הָאֲיֻמִּים בְּגֶרְמַנְיָה, בְּפוֹלִין וּבִשְׁאָר אֲרָצוֹת בִּידֵי עַם־הַמְרַצְּחִים הַגֶּרְמָנִי עִם עוֹזְרָיו הָרוֹצְחִים מִשְּׁאָר הָעַמִּים, שֶׁהָיוּ בְּעֵצָה אַחַת לְהַשְׁמִיד וְלַהֲרֹג וּלְאַבֵּד אֶת הָעָם הַיְּהוּדִי וְלִמְחוֹת אֶת זֵכֶר הַיַּהֲדוּת וּלְכַלּוֹת כָּל אֲשֶׁר בְּשֵׁם יִשְׂרָאֵל יִקָּרֵא.

אֵל נְקָמוֹת, שׁוֹפֵט הָאָרֶץ, זְכֹר נָא אֶת נַחֲלֵי הַדָּם שֶׁנִּשְׁפַּךְ כַּמַּיִם, דְּמֵי אָבוֹת וּבָנִים, אִמָּהוֹת וְעוֹלְלֵיהֶן, רַבָּנָן וְתַלְמִידֵיהֶם, וְהָשֵׁב גְּמוּל שִׁבְעָתַיִם לְצוֹרְרֵי עַמֶּךָ. שַׁוְעַת "שְׁמַע יִשְׂרָאֵל" שֶׁזָּעֲקוּ הַלְּקוּחִים לַמָּוֶת אַל תִּדֹּם, וְאֶנְקַת הַמְעֻנִּים תַּעֲלֶה לִפְנֵי כִּסֵּא כְבוֹדֶךָ, לִנְקֹם, בִּמְהֵרָה בְּיָמֵינוּ לְעֵינֵינוּ, אֶת נִקְמַת דַּם בָּנֶיךָ וּבְנוֹתֶיךָ הַקְּדוֹשִׁים וְהַטְּהוֹרִים, שֶׁלֹּא זָכוּ לָבוֹא לְקֶבֶר יִשְׂרָאֵל, כַּכָּתוּב: כִּי דַם עֲבָדָיו יִקּוֹם וְנָקָם יָשִׁיב לְצָרָיו, וְכִפֶּר אַדְמָתוֹ עַמּוֹ: אָמֵן סֶלָה.

[Page 382]

The list of Brody martyrs who perished in the Holocaust, is the fruit of the work by four of the community natives: David Altman, Shmuel Stoyanover, Zehava and Khaim Shmushkin. They are all now residing in Israel. They worked, for many months, gathered and registered the names of the Brody people, victims of the Holocaust. Brody's natives added a significant number of victims as well.

However, despite their strictness and diligence in performing this whole mission, we fear that a significant number of our martyrs were omitted. It is also possible that errors were made. We ask for forgiveness by the relatives and acquaintances for these errors and omissions.

[Pages 383-419]

List of the Martyrs of Brody and its Environs

Transliterated by Moshe Kutten

Notes: Due to the fact that Hebrew lacks vowels, names may have been spelled inaccurately.

An effort was made to verify the spelling by comparing it to the spelling on an entry on the YAD VASHEM database for the same family or individuals.

If an entry could not be found, the name was spelled according to the most frequent spelling found in the YAD VASHEM or Jewishgen.org databases.

The Hebrew Transliteration ANSI Standard (Z39.25-1975) used by Jewishgen.org was used when possible

Surname	Father's first name(s)	Mother's first name(s)	Children	Additional names and remarks
א Alef				
AVNER	Yaakov	Yides née SHRAYBSHTAYN	Khana'le & another son	
EGBOR	Mendel			
ADLER	Avraham			
ADLER				entire family
AURBAKH	Aryeh (Leiba'le)			entire family
AUERBAKH	Mendel	Sabina-Sima	Victor, Yaakov, Yerakhmiel-Rudolf &	

			Rakhel	
OLSKER	Dolek			
OLSKER	Yaakov	Rivka	David	
UNREICH	Itamar			
UNREIKH	Elimelekh			entire family
UNREIKH	Leibish	Roz'a née MOTKES		
UNREIKH	Melekh	Sara	Tontsiya, Motl, Mindel & Moshe	
UNREIKH	Simkha			
UNREIKH		Shifra née BEINISH		
OSTERZETSER				Jeweler. entire family
OFEFA		Ernestina née VAYNRAT		
OFEFA	Dr. Henrikh		Stela	Stela - Attorney, born in Brody
OFEFA				
OPRAYKH	Dr. Mark	Dr. Vanda née OFEFA	Alfred	
OKNER Leib	Leib	Khaya		
OKNER	Mortis			entire family
OKS		Tsila née DISHEL		
OKS				
OKSENNHAUT	Yosef	wife	children	entire family
OKSENHAUT	Tsvi (Hersh)	wife	son	
OKSER	Nakhum	wife		Nakhum was nicknamed "Janusz Korczak of Brody" - Father of the Orphans
AURBACH	Leiba'le			entire family
ORDOVER	Volf			
ORDOVER Rivka		Rivka	Anshel, Yudl & Bronia	
ORDOVER		Shoshana		
ORDOVER				entire family

ORDENTLIKH	Aba			
ORDENTLIKH	Bernard	Pela	Ginya & Zisha	
ORDENTLIKH	David	Khava		
ORDENTLIKH	Zigmond	Khaya	son	
ORDENTLIKH	Khaim-Yisrael			
ORDENTLIKH	Yaakov	Shifra	Yona-Yosef & another son	
ORDENTLIKH	Shmuel	Shprintsa		
ETTINGER		Berta		
ETTINGER	Khaim			
ETTINGER		Miryam		
ETTINGER		Sonya		
ETTINGER		Rebeka née FRENKEL	Sonya	
ETTINGER		Rakhel		
ETTINGER	Shmuel			
AYBER				entire family
AYZENBEG	Gershon			
AYZENBEG	Luba	Katya née KATSMAN		
AYZENBRUKH		Khana		
AYZENBRUKH				entire family
AYZENTAL	Elimelekh	Gisya née EPSHTAYN	Khaya (Khitsya)	
IMBAR	Yitskhak	Leah		
AKHTENTUKH	Moshe			entire family
AKHTENTUKH	Tsvi	Lusya		
AKHTENTUKH		Reiziya née GELMAN		
ALTURA	Avraham			entire family
ALTURA		Lorkah		
ALTMAN Hersh-Volf	Hersh-Volf	Dora née FELDER	Gizela, Klara, Yosef, Zelig, Bronya, Anshel & Yehuda	
ALTER/ LANDAU	Morah			entire family
ALTERMAN	Lulas			entire family

AMPER		Niusya		entire family
ANSHTENDIG	Yitskhak (Itsik)			
ANSHTENDIG		Adiella		
ANSHTENDIG	Ira			
APELBAUM	Mordekhai			
APELBAUM				entire family
EPSHTAYN	Khaim	Etil (Etl)	Efraim, Leah (Dontsiya) & Khaya (Khitsya)	
AKSLER				entire family
AKSELROD	Zeev-Volf	Beila	Breina, Tauba, three more daughters, Avraham, Faivel, Mikhael & Berl	entire family perished in Slovakia
AKSELROD	Yisrael	Rakhel-Rukhtsiya	Malka, Breina & Sara	From Podkamin
AKSELROD	Yisrael	Onni née MAS	Mikhael Motl'le	
AKSELROD	Leib-Hirsh	Pesa	Breina, Sheva & Tova	Leib-Hirsh from Sokolovka
ARENDER				entire family
ASHKENAZI	Hersh-Volf	Popa née BURSHTYN		
ASHKENAZI		Rakhel		
ASHKENAZI		Sara	Aharon Yitskhak	
ב Bet				
BAUMVALD	Herman			entire family
BAUMVALD	Yaakov-Natan	Hinda	Velvish & Yisrael	
BALASH	Motl'le			entire family
BABCHUK		Batya née HALBMILION	children	
BOIKHES				entire family
BOIMVALD	Yitskhak			
BUKHBINDER	Herts			entire family
BUKHBINDER	Shmuel (Milek)			entire family

BUKHBINDER				The young BUKHBINDER
BUKHBINDER				entire family
BUKHMAN	Lazer			entire family
BULKHOVER	Buzio			entire family
BOMSE				entire family
BONHARD	Zalman			entire family
BONHARD	Yitskhak	Zelda		
BONHARD-LOFELSHTIL	Hedvik			
BONHARD-LOFELSHTIL		Gusta		
BONHARD-LOFELSHTIL	Moshe			
BOSKOBOINIK	Asher	Lina née KATS		
BOKSDORF				entire family
BOKSER				entire family
BURSHTAYN	Yaakov	Tsila née KUPPERBEG		
BURSHTAYN	Pinkhas	Feiga	Lemel, Mikhael, Serka & Sara	
BEZMAN				entire family
BITATICHER		Bat-Sheva		Grandmother of Bina GESTHALTER
BEICHER	Yosef			entire family
BILET	Hilel	Yeta née GLAZER		
BIK				entire family
BLAUER	Leibish			entire family
BLAUSHTAYN	Dr. Karol	Hermina née SHTIPEL	Yidviga & Gusta	Gusta - 4 years old
BLAUSHTAYN				entire family
BLABEN	Kunyo			entire family
BLABEN				carpenter
BLOIR	Tsvi	Malka née MAYZELS		
BLOISHTAYN		Etil née LAYINER	children	
BLOKH	Herman			

BLOKH	Shifra		Yaakov, Leah & Mikahel	
BLAYER				entire family
BLER			Nina & another daughter	entire family
BASEKHES	Zusia			
BER	Getsel			
BRAUN	Gershon-Efraim		Dvora	Dvora married to ROZENGARTEN
BRAUN		Khana		entire family
BRAUN	Yosef			entire family
BRAUN	Yehsyahu	Tsipa	Velvel'le, Yetka & two more children	
BRAUN	Leib	Feiga née LEVINSKI		
BRAUN	Leib	Malka née STOIYANOVER		
BRAUN	Lipa	wife	Manya	
BRAUN	Meir	Felitsya	Ester, Khaim, Yetka, Lipa, Leib & Mezya	
BRAUN		Pesya		
BRAUN				entire family
BRAUNA	Yeshayahu	Khasya		
BRAUNER	Yeshayahu	Khana		
BRATER				
BRAFER				entire family
BERGMAN		Perl née LEINER	Children	
BERGER	Yosef			entire family
BERGER	Moshe		Bilha & Amikhai	
BARDUKH		Batya		
BERDA	Shlomo			entire family
BARUKH				entire family
BRUCHINER	Aryeh (Leon)	Etka	Sitka & Bulek	
BREI	Khaneh			entire family
BRAYTMAN	Eduard	Khana		

BRIL		Batya		entire family
BRINER	Yeshayahu	Khasya		
BARLES	Dr. Daniel			
BREMLER	Beniu			entire family
BRENDON				entire family
BERNHAUT	Dr. Edmond	wife		
BERNSHTAYN	Avraham	Shoshana		
BERNSHTAYN	Mendel	Frida née ROT		
BERNSHTAYN	Shaul	wife		
BRESLING	Tsvi		Zalman & Beila	
BRESLER				entire family
BARAK	Zigmond	Bela née AKER	Dz'onek & two more children	Dentist. Wife's name from Yad Vashem testimony by his nephew
ג Gimmel				
GABES				entire family
GALTSER	Rabbi Khaneh			entire family
GASENBAUER				entire family
GARFUNKEL				entire family
GOTLIB		Ester née LANTSTER		
GOTLIB	Ben-Tsion	Sara née VASERMAN	two children	
GOTLIB	Mikhael	Sara	Mali	
GUTMAN				entire family
GOTFRID		Khana		
GOTFRID	Kheskel			
GULD		Sara'le		entire family
GULD	husband	wife née LANDGEVIRTS		
GOLDHABER	Moshe			
GOLDZAYGER				entire family
GLODINSHTAYN	Eliyahu (Elu)	wife née GALTSER	son	
GLODINSHTAYN	Yaakov (Kuba)			
GLODINSHTAYN	Mikhael			

	(Makhtsia)			
GOLDINSHTAYN	Tsvi (Hersh)	Malka née SHTSINSKI		
GOLDMAN				Paramedic. Entire family
GOLDENBERG	Aharon			
GOLDENBERG		Gisha		
GOLDENBERG	Yitskhak			
GOLDENBERG		Leah		
GOLDENBERG	Moshe-Yitskak	Gita née KHARASH	Sheindel, Sharlota, Liza, Ahraon & Shimon	
GOLDENBERG		Feiga		
GOLDENBERG	Pesakh	Khana née VEXLER	Khanukkah'le	
GOLDENBERG		Sheina		
GOLDENBERG	Shimon			
GOLDGINGER	Aryeh			entire family
GOLDRING	Vili	Manya née ETTINGER	Bobi & Henrieta	
GOLDRING		Reiza		
GOLDRING	Shmaryahu			
GOLDRING		Sara		
GOLDSHTAYN		Ester	Liza & Yaakov	
GOLDSHTAYN	Aryeh (Leon)	Leah (Leika)	Iziu, Dolek & Genk	
GOLDSHTAYN	Barukh (Bertsia)	Tontsya	Manek	
GUREVIT	Mikhael			
GINZBURG	Aba	wife	Moshe	
GEER	Barukh	Khuma	Dozya & another son	
GLAZER		Manya		
GELMAN		wife née MAGID	Yitskhak, Reizya, Poppa, Rivka & Zisiu	
GLANTS	Moshe	Tonya		
GELTSER	Nakhum	Manda	Lunek (11 Yrs.	

			Old) & Eliezer	
GAMPLING	Leiba'le			entire family
GEMERSHMIDT		Miryam née SHAYN Leibush & Perl		
GASTHALTER	Benyamin			Khaim's brother
GASTHALTER	Yaakov		Ahuva, Ester & Tsvi	
GASTHALTER		Leah	Yehuda	
GASTHALTER	Yehuda-Tsvi (Herman)			
GASTHALTER			Yona Shoshana Miryam-Ronit	
GASTHALTER			Benyamin, Yehuda & Leah	
GRUBER	Matetyahu	wife née ZELTS	Dolka & Zdezislav	
GROSS	Benyamin			
GROSS	Shlomo	Riva née PESTES		
GROSSMAN	Efraim (Froike)			entire family
GROSSMAN	Moshe			entire family
GROSSMAN	Dr.			Dr. Grossman's mother
GROSSKOPF				entire family
GRINBERG	Lezer			entire family
GRINBERG	Leibush	Yenti	children	
GRINBERG	Shaul	Rivka		
GRINBERG	Shmuel	Peppi	children	
GRINGRASS	Shepsel	Sheindel	David, Shimon & Gusta	
GRINFELD	Dz'onek			
GRINFELD	Yekhezkel (Kheskel)			
GRINFELD		Lusya		
GRINFELD	husband	Liza	Dz'onek & Lusya	
GRINER	Benyamin			entire family
GRINSHPAN				entire family

GARFUNKEL		Yeta		
GARFUNKEL	Yisrael			entire family
GARFUNKEL	Pinkhas	Rivka née VELTMAN		
GARFUNKEL	Shmuel			
ד Dalet				
DODEL	Hersh-Leib		Rivka, Feiga & Yehuda	
DUKHT		Rozya née GOLDBERG		
DONER	Pinkhas	Bilha	Retsa, Moshe & Mordekhai	
DONER				entire family
DIAMENT	Musyo			
DINIVITS		Berta	Rozya & Hersh'ele	
DISHEL	Zalman	Elka	Shlomo	
DEMB		Rozya		entire family
DRIZNER	Yatsek			entire family
DRILIKH	Betsalel (Tsali)			entire family
DRILIKH	Pinkhas			entire family
ה Hey				
HOZENBAND	Daniel		David	
HOZENBAND	Naftali		David	
HOZER				entire family
HOKHBERG		Bela		
HOKHBERG	Barukh	Fradel née SHLINGER	Victor	
HOKHBERG	Berl (Bernard)			
HOKHBERG	Dina			
HOKHBERG	Zigmond			
HOKHBERG	Moshe (Mozes)	wife	2 children	entire family
HOKHBERG		Selka		entire family
HOKHBERG		Klara		
HOKHBERG	Shlomo (Salo)			
HOKHBERG	Shmuel			

	(Samuel)			
HOLENDER		Sara née SHVARTS		
HOLENDER				entire family
HOLTSZEGER		Malka		
HOLTSZEGER				entire family
HOMBERGER		Bina née BEN-TSION Leizer		
HURVITS	Yaakov	Sara		
HURVITS				entire family
HORN	Dr. Bernard			
HORENSHTAYN	Nakhum			entire family
HORENSHTAYN				entire family
HIBNOVER		Khana		
HAYBER	Benyamin			
HAYBER	Yitskhak			
HAYMAN	David			
HIRT				entire family
HIRSHTRIT				entire family
HAKOHEN	Avraham	Hinda née KLAYN (SAPIR)	Three children	
HAKOHEN	Khaim-Leibish	wife	two children	
HALBERTAL		Ester		
HALBERTAL		Khaya		
HALBERTAL		Rakhel		
HALBERSHTAD	Shlomo			
HALBERSHTAD				entire family
HALPERIN		Leah		
HALPERIN	Lipa			
HALPERIN	Shalom			
HALPEREN	Yosef (Yuzyu)			son of Binka and Herman LILIAN
HALPEREN	Lazer	Fanya née FRIDMAN	Leopold, Arna, Sofya & Shiyunyu	
HALPEREN	Dr. Milek			
HALPEREN		Sonya		
HALPEREN			five children	entire family

HALPEREN				entire family from Yurovska street
HELLER		Miryam née ZINGER	Motl	
HELLER	Shlomo			
HEMPELING	Uri			
HEMPELING	Moshe			
HEMPELING	Sara			
HAMERMAN	Mordekhai	Hinda née DIAMENT		
HAMERMAN	Mordekhai	Adela		
HAMERMAN	Nakhman			entire family
HAMERMAN	Pinkhas			
HAMERMAN	Shmuel		Khava & Rivka	
HAMERMAN				entire family
HENDELSMAN	Lezel			
HENDELSMAN	Tsvi			
HENDELSMAN				
HENZEL	Moshe	Batya	Yosef, Yoni, Tsvi & Sonya	
HENZEL				entire family
HART	Meir	Leah		
HART	Shimon			
HERMELIN	Aryeh	Tsipora	Miryam	
HERMELIN	Berl	Manya		
HERMELIN	Leib	Feiga née HAYNEMAN		
HERNIK		Elza née KAHANA		
HERTSBERG	David	Tova	Khana, Aryeh & Benyamin	
HERTSMAN	Dr. Salo	Tonka née GARFUNKEL		
ו Vav				
VAHL		Bilha		
VAHL		Dvora	daughter	
VAHL	Hersh	Hinda née ZOMER		

VAHL		Khana		
VAHL		Khashya		
VAHL	Yosef		son	
VAHL	Yitskhak	Minka		
VAHL	Yisrael			
VAHL	Yisrael-Natan			
VAHL	Menakhem-Volf	Peshi née ZOMER	son & daughter	
VAHL		Miryam		
VAHL	Moshe	wife née ZOMER	son	
VAHL	Azriel			
VAHL		Feiga		
VAHL	Shalom			
VAHL-LOKERMAN	Avraham		son	
VAHL-LOKERMAN	Ben-Tsion		son	
VAHL-LOKERMAN		Bashya		
VAHL-LOKERMAN	Dov (Berish)			
VAHL-LOKERMAN		Hinda		
VAHL-LOKERMAN		Henya-Rakhel		
VAHL-LOKERMAN	Yosef (Yozef)			
VAHL-LOKERMAN	Yakov (Kuba)		son	
VAHL-LOKERMAN	Meir-Yaakov		son	
VAHL-LOKERMAN		Malka		
VAHL-LOKERMAN		Meta-Tova		
VAHL-LOKERMAN		Nekha-Rivka	daugther	
VAHL-LOKERMAN	Cherni			
VAHL-LOKERMAN	Kehat		son	
VAHL-LOKERMAN		Krina		
VAHL-LOKERMAN		Rakhel	daughter	
VAHL-LOKERMAN		Rakhel		
VAHL-LOKERMAN	Shimel		son	
VAHL-LOKERMAN	Shalom			
VAHL-LOKERMAN			son	Forest- guard
VAHL-LOKERMAN	Shimshon		son	
VALMAN				entire family
VASSERMAN	Yehoshua-Heshel			

VASSERMAN	Yitskhak-Aizik			
VASSERMAN				entire family
VAKS	Shunyo			entire family
VAKS				entire family
VAKSMAN	Itsyu			
VAKSMAN	Hodel			
VAKSMAN	Zisha			
VAKSMAN		Leah		
VAKSMAN	Meir			
VAKSMAN	Pinkhas			entire family
VARSHBER				entire family
VOLMAN	husband	wife	Manya, Selka & Mina	
VOLFSON				entire family
VOLFTSON				entire family
VORM-SEGAL	Yehuda	Cherna née HENZEL	Yakir	
VITEL	Moshe	Feigeh née RUBINSHTAYN		
VAYZER	Ben-Tsion			VAYZER Ben-Tsion's brother
VAYLER	Volf			entire family
VAYLER	Yaakov	Genya née GINTSBURG	daugther	
VAYLER	Moshe			entire family
VAYLER	Kuni	Mirel		
VAYLER	Shalom			
VAYLER				entire family
VAYNTROIB	Barukh	Khana	Sara, Yehoshua, Leah, Basha & Beila	
VAYNTROIB	David	wife née CHACHKES	two children	
VAYNTROIB	Vik			
VAYNTROIB	Zeev			
VAYNTROIB	Leon	Amalya née KNIGEL	Beni	
VAYNTROIB	Moshe			

VAYNTROIB		Frida née HENDELSMAN	Duzya & Izyu	
VAYNTROIB	Klara			
VAYNTROIB	Rakhel			
VAYNTROIB	husband	wife née LEVIN	children	
VAYNTROIB	Simkha			entire family
VAYNSHTOK	Yehuda			entire family
VAYNSHTOK		Rozya		entire family
VAYNSHELBOIM	Eliyahu (Elu)	Tsipora née MAYZELS		
VAYS				entire family
VAYS	Izyu			entire family
VAYCHER				entire family
VILDER	Betsalel	Khana	Rivka, Miryam, Leah & Yosef	
VILDER		Dvora		
VILDER	Yosef			
VILDER	Nakhum	Tsila	Ester & Malka	
VILDER		Rivka	Miryam, Leah & Dvora	
VILNER				entire family. Father - a tailor
VILNER	Izyu			entire family
VILNER	Yosef	Khana née ZILBERG	Mans	
VILNER	Moshe	Yeta née TSVERLING	Feigeh, Menashe & Rim	
VIROBLIASKI	Misha			
VISHNIVITSER				entire family
VELTMAN	Avraham	Khana née RAYF	Rivaka, Khaya (Klara) & Frida	
VESTLER	Avraham	wife		
VESTLER	Itsyu	Golda	Kheskel	
VESTLER		Ester-Khaya	Dina & Khay'ke	
VESTLER	Herts		Khana'le & two more children	
VESTLER	Kheskel	Perl née BRAUN	Hershel'e & Yaakov	

VESTLER	Yaakov	wife	Ester & Khaya	
VESTLER	Akiva	Rozya	Shmuel & Matka	
VERBER	David	Manya	Moshe, Yaakov & another son	
ז Zayin				
ZAUBER	Motl			entire family
ZAUBER	Moshe	wife	Onni & Mikahel	
ZAUBER	Shmuel (Shmul)			
ZAUBER	Simkha			
ZALTS	Melekh			entire family
ZALTS	Shmuel (Shmulik)			entire family
ZAKS	Munyo			
ZUKHMAN	Yehoshua			entire family
ZUKHMAN	Yaakov			
ZUKHMAN		Rakhel		
ZOMER	Hersh	Hinda	Peshi, Menakhem, Volf, Moshe, Ester & Malka	
ZOMER		Ester-Malka née VAHL		
ZOMER		Regina		entire family
ZIGELBOIM	Izyu	Mala	Miryam	
ZAYDENVURM	Gavriel	Beila	Naftali, Eliezer & Hersh'le	
ZAYDENVURM	father		daughter	
ZILBERG	Avraham	wife	Mina, Berta & Slima	Avraham's father
ZILBERBERG				entire family
ZILBERSHTAYN	Noakh	Rivka		Berta LANDAU, Noakh's sister
ZILBERSHITS	Zelig	Khasya-Libah née BURINGER	Sender, Salo & Hersh	
ZINGER		Adela		
ZINGER	Elazar	Feiga	Reuven & Shmuel	

ZINGER		Ester	Mindel	
ZINGER		Beila		
ZINGER	Volf	Khaya	Khana, Avraham & Rivka	
ZINGER	Yosef			
ZINGER	Yaakov			
ZINGER				entire family
ZISMAN		Adela	Shoshana	
ZISMAN	Yekhezkel		Moshe	
ZISMAN	Yekutiel			
ZALTSMAN	husband	wife	Gina	
ZESLER	Dolek			
ZESLER				entire family
ט Tet				
TARLOVSKI	Elu			entire family
TEHAT	Zushia			
TEHAT	Kahnokh			
TEHAT	Maks			
TOLMATS	Yaakov (Yanke'le)			
TOMASHOVER	Berta			
TOMASHOVER	Klara			
TOMASHOVER	Shmuel			
TOPAS	Kalman			entire family
TOPER	Munyo			entire family
TOPER				entire family
TOPERMAN	Yosef (Yosa'le)			entire family
TURK				entire family
TAYKH	Ervin			
TAYKH		Gitel		
TAYKH	Mula-Moshe			
TIMITS			Brendel'le Leah Roiza	entire family
TISMINITSER	Ester			entire family (five people)

TIKKES				entire family
TISH	Ovadia			
TISH		Sara		
TISHKER	Khanokh (Hainekh)	Yatka	two children	
TLIMAK	Adolf	Henya née KHAMTSNIK	Yosef (Yosi), Aryeh (Leon) & Yitskhak (Frits)	
TENEN	Hinik			from Podkamin
TENEN		Lena		from Podkamin
TENNENBAUM	Avraham	wife		
TENNENBAUM	Adolf			
TENNENBAUM		Golda		
TENNENBAUM		Dvora		
TENNENBAUM	Zeev-Volf	Siril	Yehoshua, Khay'ke, Moshe & Sheindel	
TENNENBAUM	Shalom			
TENTSER	Yaakov	Khana	Brakha, Henya, Khaya, Yitskhak, Leib & Moshe	
TENTSER	Yitskhak-Leib			entire family
TENTSER	Moshe			entire family
TESSLER	David			entire family
TKACH				entire family
TREGER				entire family
TRATKOVER	Zeev-Volf	Peppi	Benyamin & Khasya	
TRATKOVER	Khasya			
TRATKOVER				entire family
TRAYGER				entire family
י Yod				
JORNA	Efraim	Regina née HALPREN	son daughter	
JORNA	Berl (Bernard)	Genya née CHERMAK	Dzonyu & daughter	

JORNA	Khaim			
JORNA	Yosef	Genya		
JORNA	Yaakov	wife	Nusya & Rozya	
JORNA	Yitskhak			
JORNA	Yitskhak	wife	Elza, Velvel & another baby son	
JORNA	Yisrael (Siunyu)			
JORNA	Maks	Zilta		
JORNA	Mordekhai (Motl)	Dina née KANCHUKER	Khaim-Munyo	
JORNA		Fanya née KANER		
JORNA		Klara		
JORNA	Shlomo	Breindel née SHTERNBERG		
JORNA	Shmuel	Fanya	Yosef & Tsesya	
JORNA		Sara- Sherl	Rakhel	
YAVROVER		Dr. Tsetsilya		a physician
YAVROVER				entire family
YASER				entire family
YAR	Khaim	Miryam née KUPERBERG	Munyo & Klartsiya	
YOLLES				entire family
YUNG	Khanokh (Hainekh)			
YUNGER		Roza		
YUNGER		Sara		
	R' Yose'le			entire family. R' Yosel'e - Melamed in "Talmud Torah"
	R' Yitskhak-David			entire family. R' Yitskhak-David - Melamed in "Talmud Torah"
YEKELS		Tony née HORENSHTAYN		
YEKELS		Nunya née HORENSHTAYN		

	Yerukham			The telephonist
YARITS	Avraham	Dvora-Tuiba		
YISRAELOVITS				entire family
כ Kaf				
KHODAK	David	Ester		
KHODAK	Nakhman			
KHUTINER				entire family
	R' Khaim			entire family. R' Khaim - Melamed in "Talmud Torah"
KHALFON		Feiga née LUTS		
KHARAK	Sender			
KHARAK		Shen'ka		
KHARASH	Khaim-Mordekhai	Sheindel née MARGOLIS	Naftali, Yaakov, Frida & Natka	
KHARASH	Moshe-Yitskhak		Sheindel, Leah, Aharon & Shimon	
KHARASH	Nunyo	Sheindel	Netanel	
KOHEN		Yehudit née LAMM		
KOHEN	Moshe	wife	children	
	husband	Gutka née KOHEN	children	
	husband	Gitel née KOHEN	children	
KAHANA	Avraham	Hinda	Betsalel Shmuel Sara	
KAHANA	Bruno			
KHANA	Gershon			
KAHANA	Khain Leibish	Khaya-Sara	Mitah, Nunah, Yosef & Izyu	
KAHANA		Yeti		
KAHANA	Yisrael	Hinda née VILDER	children	
KAHANA	Shulik	Sharlota		
KAHANA				entire family
KHOMET	Henyu			entire family
KATS	Itsyu			
KATS		Irma		

KATS	Benyamin			
KATS	David			entire family
KATS	Khaim	Khaya	David, Malka, Perl & Sheindel	
KATS	Yitskhak	Dorah	Edek	
KATS	Yisrael	Khava	Aryeh, Moshe, Paltiel & Sara	
KATS	Yisrael		Aryeh-Leibel	
KATS	Malka		children	
KATS	Natan	Kilah née LANDAU	Sheinda'le	
KATS	husband	Tisla née LAYNER	children	
KATS	Shiyonyu			
KATS		Sheina		entire family
KATS			two daughters	entire family
KATS			Avraham Ester Gitel	entire family
KTSMAN	Yaakov	Ra'aya-Ratza née PESEK	Munya & Misha	
KATSMAN	Yitskahk	Etil	two children	
KATSMAN	Mikahel	Leah	Dozya & Munya	
KARY	David			entire family
ל Lamed				
LAUFER		Fanya née JORNA		
LAU	Yisrael	wife née TSIN		
LUTVAK	Avraham			
LEVIN	Rabbi Avraham			
LEVIN		Khana		
LEVIN	Dr. Yitskhak	Idah née FROIND	Moshe-Mauritsi	
LEVIN	Moshe-Simkha	Brakha-Peppa	Victor, Paulina & relatives	
LEVIN	Frank	Khana LAMM	Vili, Manya & Matilda	
LEVIN				entire family
LEVINSKA		Liza		
LEVINSKI	Yaakov (Kuba)			
LEVINSKI	Shmuel			

LUPATIN				entire family
LUTS		Khana née ROZENFELD		
LETUSHER				entire family
LIBERMAN	Eliezer-Yosef		Khaim Lena	
LIBERMAN	Khaim			entire family
LIBERMAN	Meir	Dvora		
LIBERMAN	Tsvi			
LIBERMAN		Reina-Golda		
LIDMAN	Yitskhak (Itsik)			entire family. Itsik - paramedic
	Leiba'le			the tinsmith
LAYNER		Rivka	Sara	Rivka the mother
LAYNER		Rivka	Rakhel & Sara	
LILIAN	Dr. Izidor (izyu)	Zusya née SARER	Risyu	
LILIAN	Leon	Marya (Mirka)		
LINDER	Yaakov			
LINZEN			Gitl'le, Vaikel & Yisrael	entire family
LIPSKER	Itsyu			
LIPSKER	Khaim-Yitskhak		Leah, Asher & Rakhel	
LIFSHITS	Dr. Dolek		Lela	
LISHNER				entire family
LAMM	Avraham	Berta née CHERNITS		
LAMM	Yaakov	Gitel		
LAMM	Yaakov			entire family
LAMM	Simkha-Simon	Shenka née BIALITSKI	two sons	
LENGOVER		Tsila née LANDGEVIRTS		
LANDAU	Avraham	Ester née FRIDMAN	Zinda'le & Yankel'le	
LANDAU		Berta née ZILBERSHTAYN		
LANDAU		Gusta		
LANDAU	Yehoshua	wife née KAHANA		

		Bruno		
LANDAU	Leib	Rakhel née INDIK	Yosel'le & Sheindel'le	
LANDAU	Motl			entire family
LANDAU	Melekh	wife	two daughters	
LANDAU	Maks			
LANDAU		Tsviya		
LANDAU		Sara		
LANDGEVIRTS	Eliyahu	Erna		
LANDGEVIRTS	Herman	Sabiina	Yisrael (Yulek)	
LANDGEVIRTS	Yolyus			Eli's son
LANDGEVIRTS	Yulyus			Herman's son
LANDGEVIRTS	Yosef	Selka	Tinka, Doz'ya & Gutya	
LANDGEVIRTS	Yitskhak	Simkha		
LANDGEVIRTS	Mordekhai		Mondek & Henyu	
LANDGEVIRTS		Simah		
LANDGEVIRTS		Regina		
LANSBAUM	Vilu	Khaya née PECHNIK		
LANDSBAUM			Elza & Dora	
LENTS	Mordekhai			
LENTSUT	Leizer	wife née VAYNTRAUB	Munyo, Yeshayahu & Freidel	
LANTSTER		Eva		
LANTSTER	Arnold			
LANTSTER	Henri			
LAMTSTER	Shmuel			
LETSTER	Shmuel	Ester née GRINBERG	two children	
LERNER	Avraham		children	
LERNER	Asher		Tsvi & Gershon	
LERNER	Khaim	Ester	Margoli	
LERNER	Moshe	Etel		
LESHNOVER	Uri			

LESHNOVER	Khaim-Tsvi	Perl née BRAUN	Sara, Ruiza'le, Munyo & Tsila	
LESHNOVER				entire family
מ Mem				
MEIR	Naftali-Herts	Dvora	Menashe & Klara	
MEIR				entire family
MANALA				entire family
MAS	Isar	Manya née FINKELSHTAYN		
MARSH				entire family
MAGID				entire family
MOTKES	Itsyu	wife née VAYNTRAUB	Rozya & Munyo	
MOTKES	Yaakov		Brendel'le, Motl'le & Pinkhas	
MOLET		Shoshana		
MOLET				entire family
MONDSHAYN	Maks			entire family
MONDSHAYN	Shmuel	Sharlota-Anni	Anni & Vilhelm	
MIEZES	Yaakov (Yentsyu)	Manya née HAMERMAN	Batka & Lusya	
MIEZES		Rstza née RUTENBERG		
MEIBLUM	Yaakov	Malka née ROTHAU	Tuvia & Leah	
MEIBLUM		Edela		
MEIBLUM				entire family
MEIZELS	Yaakov			
MEIZELS	Natan			
MEIZLER	Avraham			
MEIZLER		Gitl		
MEIZLER	Yisrael	Hinda		Grandmother Khana
MEIZLER	Shlomo	Matilda	Regina & Sara	
MEIZLER				entire family

MEIZLER				newspapers' distributer
MILER	Aryeh-Leib	Khana née SHTERNBERG	Yitskhak (Izyu) & Shulamit (Slimka)	
MILER	Ira (Yeria)			
MILER				watchmaker. Entire family
MINTSER	Yosef			
MINTSER	Yisrael			
MINTSER	Moti			
MINTSER	Menashe			
MINTSER	Sheindel			
MIST				entire family
MIKOLINTSER		Linka		
MIKOLINTSER		Fanya		
MIKOLINTSER	Shmuel (Shmil)	wife	baby	
MAKH-KRAMPF				entire family
MELMAN	Makhtsi		Shepsel Yitskhak	
MELES	Dr. Betsalel	Sofya née OPEPA		
MAMUT	Yisrael	Ester née LIBERMAN	Mina & Ada	
MAMUT	Tsvi (Hesyu)	Sofya née HALPERN	son	
MAMUT		Sara (Sara'le) née MENDEL		
MENDEL	Gershon	Sheina née GOLDINSHTAYN	Brakha (Bronka)	
MENDEL	Lezer			entire family
MENDEL	Ira			entire family
MENDEL	Shmuel (Milek)	Malka née TSIMEND	Moshe	
MAENSON	Dov-Ber (Bernyu)	Zisel	Barukh (Buszyo) & Khaim-David	Elder son of Admor of Brody - Khaim David (Dudale) Manson (died in 1931)
MANSON	Shalom			Youngest son of

				Admor of Brody - Khaim David (Dudale) Manson (died in 1931)
MENKES	Munyo			
MENKES				entire family
MATZAS				entire family
MAKLER				entire family
MARGOLIS	Hersh			entire family
MARGOLIS	Zelig			entire family
MARGOLIS		Khana		
MARGOLIS	Yisrael		Khana, Yehoshua, Mendel & Tsvi	
MARGOLIS		Leah		
MARGOLIS	Meir	Rakhel née STOIYANOVER	Mintsiya	
MARGOLIS	Natan	Rivka	Nakhum, Gusta, Gershon & Henya	
MARGOLIS	Pesakh			entire family
MARGOLIS		Pesya	Leah	
MARGOLIS	Kopel	wife	Mordekhai (Motek) & Salka	
MARGOLIS	Shmuel (Milek)	Ester née SHNOR		
MARGROVITS	Benyamin	Khana	Izyu, Genya, Leah & Peskhya	
MARGROVITS			Mishka	
MARDER		Gusta		
MARDER		Dozya		
MARDER	Henyu			
MARDER	Victor	Paulina née LANDGEVIRTS	Andziya	
MARDER	Zeinvol	wife	baby girl	
MARDER		Tina		
MARDER	Yosef			
MARDER	Munia			
MARDER	Moshe	Zisl née	Herts'ka &	

		LESHNOVER	Rozya	
MARDER	Nisan	Khantsiya née RAYS	baby boy	
MARDER		Selka		
	Moshe			
נ Nun				
NEBELKOPF	Eliezer		Ester, Hersh, Khana, Tema, Leah & Shlomo	
NEBELKOPF	Aryeh (Leiba'le)			entire family
NEBELKOPF	Volf			entire family
NEBELKOPF	Meir			entire family
NOIMAN		Golda		
NOIMAN		Fanya		
NOIMAN				entire family
NELKEN				entire family
NEKER		Zelda née KANCZUKER		
NARKES		Adela		entire family
NARKES	Aharon	Feiga née KHOMET		entire family
NARKES	Buzyo			entire family
NARKES	Yekhezkel (Kheskel)			entire family
NARKES	Melekh			entire family
NARKES	Shlomo			entire family
ס Samech				
SAM	Nakhum			entire family
SEGAL	Dov			
SEGAL	Yeshayahu			
SEGAL	Shlomo	Zuzi née LAVIR (or LAUYER)		
SEGAL		Sara née VAYNTROB		
SEGAL			baby	entire family
SOBOL		Berta		entire family

STOYONOVER	Izidor	Sara'le née MARGOLIS		
STOYONOVER	Itsyu			entire family
STOYONOVER	Dudik			
STOYONOVER		Zisl	Khaim, Magid, Avraham & Rusha	
STOYONOVER	Khaim	Manya née CHULIK	2 children	
STOYONOVER	Yosef-Aryeh		Khana, Meir & Rivka	
STOYONOVER	Yaakov	Leah SHKLAVER	Zisl'le & Khana'le	
STOYONOVER	Leah			
STOYONOVER	Leib			
STOYONOVER	Moshe	Roz'a née SHVARTS		
STOYONOVER	Moshe-Reuven	Batya née SHKLAVER	Tsvi (Hersh)	
STOYONOVER		Rivka		
STOYONOVER	Shmuel	Zusya-Dvora née LAZAR	Rakhel	
SIROTA	David			entire family
SMOLANIK				entire family
SPODEK		Dvora née KHUTINER		
SPODEK	Yehuda (Yidl)	Khana (Khanche) née SHTAYNER		
SPODEK	Simkha	Dvora née KHUTINER		
SPIVAK	Khaim			entire family
SPIVAK	Munyo			entire family
SAPIR	Efraim			
SAPIR		Khaya née HEFTER (or HFTER)	Itsyu, Brendel'le, Polo, Roiza'le & Reiza'le	
SAPIR	Yona			entire family
SAPIR	Motl			
SAPIR		Malka		

SAPIR		Manya		
SAPIR		Rivka		
SPEKTOR				entire family
SEKDOREN	Markus			
SKOLSKI				entire family
SKLAR	husband	wife	Eva	
SKRUZ	Berish			
SKRUZ		Frida	Adela	
FALK	Kheskel			
פ Peh				
PAKET	Yaakov	Miryam née SHTIKLER		
PAKET	Michael	Khaya		
PARTER	Martin			entire family
PARIL	Neteh-Simkha			entire family
PODZEMCHER	Manes			entire family
POHORILES		Ela		
POTASH	Iche-Berl			entire family
POIASKES	Yaakov			entire family
FOYERSHAYN				The tailor. Entire family
POLINER	Eliezer	wife	Avraham & Moti	
POLINER	Khanokh			
POLINER	Yosef-Leib	wife	Khaya & Sheindel	
POLINER	Shlomo	Frida	Eliezer & Sheindel	
POLISHCHUK		Pola		
POLAK		Ester		
POLAK	Hershel	Khanche née MARDER		
POLAK	Moshe	Leah	Volf-Sbachyo	
POLAK	Tsvi	Lora née MOTKHES		
PULKES	Benyamin			

PULKES		Miryam		
POPER	R' Yosef	Sara née KAMINER	six children	son in law of the Rabbi from Gur
FUKS	Bernard	Etel née JORNA	two children	
PORTER				entire family
FORMAN	Avraham			entire family
FORMAN		Roza		Roza - mother of Yona-Gafni-Forman
PETRUSHKA	Yisrael			entire family
FICH			Moshe	entire family
FAYERSHTAYN		Ester	Children	Grandmother Cherni
FAYERSHTAYN	Shimon	Ester	Khana'le-Nusya (5 1/2 yrs. old) & Khaim'ke	
PINES	husband	wife	Nusya	
FINKEL				entire family
FINKEL		Ester		
FINKELSHTAYN	Munyo			entire family
FINKELSHTAYN	Melekh			entire family
FINKELSHTAYN		Sofya		entire family
FINKELSHTAYN		Klara		entire family
FINKELSHTAYN				entire family
FEERST	Aharon-Leib			Aharon-Leib the grandfather
FEERST-KLAYN		Tuiba	Itah, Berl & Yosef	
FISHER	Yehoshua			
FISHER	Pitkhia			
FISHER	Tsvi			
FELDMAN				entire family
FLOG-PENLUS	Pinkhas			
FLAYSHMAN	Avraham (Mutsik)			
FLAYSHMAN	Volf (Velvil)			entire family
FLAYSHMAN	Zeev			
FLAYSHMAN		Khava		

FLAYSHMAN		Khana		
FLAYSHMAN		Tsina		
PELKES	Leon		Bernard, Azriel & Tsiril	
PESTES	Eliezer			
PESTES	Efraim-Perets	Khaya-Sara	Bronya, Yafa & Sheindel	
PESTES	Dov-Bernard			
PESTES	Yaakov	wife	Asher, Tsvi & Feiga'le	
PESTES	Yitskhak	Malka	Fanya & Munyo	
PESTES	Mendel	wife		
PESTES		Perla		
PESTES		Klara	Bontsiya & Shenka	
PASTERNAK	Anshel			
PEPPER				entire family
PEPPERMAN	Yoyne			entire family
PEPPERNIK	Avraham		Moshe	
PEPPERNIK	Avraham		Shmuel	
PEPPERNIK	Aharon		Khana, Yetka & Sala	
PEPPERNIK	Aharon	Dina	Yeti	
PEPPERNIK		Eti		
PEPPERNIK		Ita		
PEPPERNIK	Benyamin		Sheindel	
PEPPERNIK		Golda		
PEPPERNIK		Hela		
PEPPERNIK	Volf			
PEPPERNIK		Khaya		
PEPPERNIK		Tonya		
PEPPERNIK	Mondek			
PEPPERNIK	Sender			
PEPPERNIK		Pela		
PEPPERNIK	Reuven			
PEPPERNIK	Shmuel	Khaya		
PEPPERNIK	Shmuel	Rakhel		

PECHNIK	Avraham-Mordekhai	Miryam		
PECHNIK	Barukh-Eliyahu	Malya-Peshya	Gitel, Senya, Feiga, Sheva, Shmuel & two more children	
PECHNIK	Bernard	Pradel		
PECHNIK	David			
PECHNIK		Leah		
PECHNIK		Kahna (née PECHNIK)		entire family
PECHNIK		Mira		
PECHNIK		Pradel	Etel & Dina	
FROINDLIKH	Yitkhak	Guta née FUT		
FROINDLIKH	Maks	Lola née ANDE	Ida & another son	
FRUMER	Avraham			
FRUMER		Adela	Lusya	
FRUMER	David	Braindel		
FRUMER	Mordekhai			
FRUMER		Pnina		
FRUMER				entire family
FROST	Ozer-Yehoshua			
FROST		Tsviya		nurse
FROST		Tsipora		
FROST		Sara		Sara - the mother
FRID				entire family
FRID		Basya		
FRIDMAN		Golda née LUBLIANKER		
FRIDMAN		Hinda		
FRIDMAN		Khaim		
FRIDMAN	Yitskhak (Izyu)		Martselko	son of Izyu and Moshka née LILIAN
FRIDMAN	Meir			entire family
FRIDMAN	Mundziyo			
FRIDMAN	Tsvi			husband of Amalya

				née OLSKER
FRIDMAN		Rakhel née LIFSHITS	Nakhman & Mina	
FRIDMAN	Shlomo	Khaya	Barukh & Lina	
FRIDMAN	Shmuel			entire family
FRIDFELD	Shmuel	Sara		
FRIDFERTIG-ROZENSHTOK	Yisrael	Bronya née FROINDLIKH	Shlomo	
FRISH	Yaakov (Yank'le)			entire family
PERLMUTER	Shaul			
PERELES	Avraham	wife		Avraham - nicknamed "The Russian"
PERMINGER	Dr.			entire family
PARNES	husband	wife	Nusya	
PARNES	Itsyu	Khina née MARGOLIS	Mirko another daughter	
PARNES	Hershel	wife	baby boy	
PARNES		Khana	two small children	
PARNES	Leizer	Roza	Mikhael & Newsya	
PARNES	Mendel	Sliva		
PARNES		Rivka		
PARNES	Shlomo-Salomon	Bat-Sheva née SHPILKA		
FRENKEL	Avraham	Sara née SHEKHTER Khaim		Khaim - a Torah scholar from Narayov
FRENKEL	Ayzik-Mekhel	Dvora née BAUMVALD	Sara	
FRENKEL	Hilel	Dora née SHAPIRA		
FRENKEL	Mendel			
FRENKEL				entire family
FERSTUT	Maks	Hinda née KATSMAN	Munya, Minah & Moshe	
FERCHEP				entire family

FERSHTOT				entire family
צ Tzadik				
TSVIBEL				entire family
TSVILINGER	Aryeh			entire family
TSVAYG				entire family. The father - cantor of the great synagogue in Brody
TSVERLING	Aharon			
TSVERLING	Asher			
TSVERLING		Genya		
CHOP				entire family
TSIMELS	Elazar			
TSIMELS	Betsalel		daughter	
TSIMELS	Dov			entire family
TSIMELS		Khaya	Mikhael	
TSIMELS	L.	Mintsiya		
TSIMELS	Shalom		Yehoshua, Melekh & Khana	
TSIMES	Yehoshua (Shiye)			entire family
TSIN	Birel			entire family
TSIN	Motl		Izyu, Dov, David, Yisrael, Leon & Reizel	Motl's brothers, sisters and sister in law. Entire family
TSINKER	Izyu			entire family
TSINKER				entire family
TSELER	Oscar	wife	Nusya	
ק Kof				
CHACHKES	Adolf	Klara		
CHACHKES-LAMM		Khaya	Avraham, Khaya & Yitskhak	
CHACHKES	Dr. Mendel-Leib			entire family
CHERMAK				entire family

CHERNITS	Pesakh	wife	Berta, Zisl & Tsvi	
KAUFMAN	Volf	Rakhel née ORDENTLIKH	Ginye, Dina, Leon & Moshe	
KAUFMAN	husband	wife	Lenya	
KALIR	Leon			entire family
KANDEL				entire family
KACHER	Volf			entire family
KACHER	Munyo			entire family
KOBER				entire family
KVARTNER				entire family
KVECHKA				entire family
KUTIN	Moshe	Khana (Khanche) née Wachs		Khana - based on grandson's Yad Vasehm testimony
KOL				entire family
KOLER	Shmuel	Khay'ka	Hela	
KUPERBERG	Yaakov			
KUPERBERG	Yitskhak	Bunya		
KUPERBERG	Munyo			
KUPERVASER				entire family
KUPERSHTAYN		Miryam née GELBER		
KUPERMAN				entire family
KUCHAN				entire family
KOCHER	Maks			entire family
KOKOSH				entire family
KORTEN	Izyu			entire family
KORIN		Helena née SHMIRER		
KORIN		Helena née SDOVNIK		
KORIN		Zelda		
KORIN		Yosef		
KORIN		Yeshayahu		
KORKHIN	Mordekhai (Motke)	wife née HOKHBERG	Drizya, Velvel, Yolek & Polah	

KOREN	Vilyu			entire family
KOREN				entire family
KORSOVER	Avraham			
KORSOVER	Moshe			
KORSOVER	Pini			
KORSOVER		Shoshana		
KORSOVER				entire family. Soda manufacturer
KIZELSHTAYN	Zisha			entire family
KAYNITS	Moshe-Khana			
KINEWVER				entire family
KLUGE	Bernard			
KLUGHAUFT	Efraim	wife	Miryam	
KLAYN				entire family
KLING	Benyamin			entire family
KLEFER (or KLEPER / KELPER)				entire family. Restaurant owner
KELER				entire family
KENDEL	Gdalyahu		two daughters	
KNOPF		Gitah	Shmuel (Malik)	
KNOPF	Milek			
KNOPF		Siana		
KNOPF	Frank			
KNOPF	husband	Rozya	Gita'le, Meilekh & Kubush	
KNOPF	husband	wife	Djonek Lusya	
KANCHUKER		Ester		
KANCHUKER	Zindel	Rakhel née FEERST	Zusia, Meir & Mendel	
KANCHUKER		Khaya	Dina, Khaya, Miryam-Manya, Pinkhas & Shimon	
KANCHUKER	Musia (IMANUEL)	Rakhel	Zusia, Meir & Mendel	
KANCHUKER	Menakhem-Mendel		Bat-Sheva, Volf, Zusia & Meir	
KANCHUKER	Moshe	Khaya	Dina, Sara &	

			Ester-Etl	
KANCHUKER	Pinkhas	Khaya	Manya-Miryam	Pinkhas from Podkamin
KANCHUKER	Shimon	Sara	Manya	
KANCHUKER		Sara		
KANER		Malka		
KANAREK				entire family
KRAUZA	Noakh			entire family
KRAFT				entire family
KARABAN	Munyo			brother in law of Sara AURBAKH
KROTOGILOV	Moshe	Khana	Yaakov	entire family
KROIZNER	husband	wife née KATSMAN		
KROKHMEL				entire family
KRONBERG	Leib-Mota'le			entire family
KRONLAND	Khaim			
KRISTIAMPULER	Yosef	Sheindel	Feige'le	
KRISTIAMPULER				entire family
KRAMM	Menakhem	Sheindel	Genk (13 yrs. old)	
KREMENITSER	Yosef			
KREMENITSER	Yitskhak	Beilah		
KREMENITSER		Pepka		
KRASNE	Yisrael	Rakhel née KTSMAN	two children	
KARPAN		Rivka		mother of the family
KARPAN	Itamar	wife	two children	
KARPAN	husband	Bluma née KARPAN		
KARPAN	Khaim	wife	four children	
KARPAN	husband	Tova née KARPAN	five children	
KARPAN	Yisrael	wife	two daughters	
KARPAN	Moshe	wife		
KARPAN	husband	Mina née KARPAN	two children	
KARPAN	Nakhum	wife	son	

ר Resh				
RAUKH		Manya née KATS	Vikah	
RABINOVITS		Brakha	Eliyahu (Elu)	entire family
REDVONTSER	Volfish			
RAHAT	Leib	Perl née LANDAU	Sheinda'le	
RUBINSHTAYN	Natan	Shprintsa	Leah, Moshe & Simkha	
RUBINSHTAYN	Ozer	Ester	Mordekhai	
ROGOVSKA		Penka		
ROGOVSKI				entire family
ROGEN		Khantsiya		
RAVEH	Moshe	Dabusha	Khava	
RAVEH	Sheia	Sheva	Gusta	Sheia from Monstryy
ROZEBLUM	Ayzik			
ROZEBLUM	Moshe			
ROZEBLUM	Simkha	Melah (or Malah)	Avraham, Buni, Beni & Khana	
ROZEBLUM				entire family
ROZENGARTEN	Todros (Tadek)			
ROZENFELD	Henyu	Ruiza		entire family
ROZENFELD		Khasya		
ROZENFELD	Yokl			
ROZENFELD	Mendel			
ROZNER	Shlomo	Leah	Sabina	
ROT	Avraham			
ROT	Velvil			
ROT	Yona	Sharloti	Regina & Sara	
ROT	Mordekhai	Yetka	Moshe & Peppi	
ROT	Nisan	Zusya		
ROT		Frida		
ROT		Regina		
ROTAUG		Malka	Khaim, Khasya, Toil (or Tvil) & Leah	
ROTHAU		Rivka		

ROTHAU		Ronya		
ROTHAU		Shifra		
ROTHAUS	Shmuel	Khina née STOIYANOVER	two children	
ROTENBERG	Hersh	Malka née DINER	Yekhiel	
ROTENBERG		Lola		
ROTENBERG	Lazal	Tauba née PARNES	Ghina, Mikahel & Feiga	
ROTENBERG	Mikhael	Bat-Sheva née BURNSHTAYN		
ROTENBERG		Rivka		
ROTENBERG			Lusya	entire family. Husband - pharmacist
ROTSHTAYN		Betti		
ROTSHTAYN	Yaakov			
ROTSHTAYN	Natan			
ROTSHTAYN	Pesakh			
ROTSHTAYN	Reuven			
ROTSHTAYN		Rakhel		
ROIZMAN				entire family
RIZEL	Mordekhai (Motra)	Leah née KVARTNER	Eliyahu (Elu), Donya, Peppe & Reizel'le	
REIZEL				entire family
RAYBER	Gdalyahu	Khana	Khava'le, Yoel, Leah'le, Moshe & Shlomo	
RAYZETS				entire family
RAYZER	Osvald			
RAYZER	Yaakov			
RAYNHOLD	Izyu			
RAYNERT	Moshe	Etka née BRAUN	Manya	
RAYF	Efraim			
RAYF		Bina		
RAYF	Benyamin	Shprintsi	Bina & Khana	
RAYF		Khana		
RAYF		Leah		

RAYF	Moshe			
RAYTSFELD	Milek			
RIKHTER				entire family
RISMAK				entire family
REKHT				entire family. Owners of a fruit store
REMRET	Hersh'ele			
RAPOPORT		Aydela		
RAPOPORT	Hers'ele			
RAPOPORT				entire family
RATS		Tima		entire family
ש Shin				
SHARF				entire family
SHVAB				entire family
SHVADRON	Markus			
SHVADRON	Professor	wife		
SHVADRON				entire family
SHVARTS	Berish	Frida		
SHVARTS	Hesyu			entire family
SHVARTS		Frida		
SHVARTS	Simkha			
SHVARTSVALD		Etli		
SHVARTSVALD	Yosef	Ester	Edjya & two more sons	
SHVARTSVALD	Mordekhai	Gita	Yosef & Endziya	
SHVARTSVALD			two daughters	entire family
SHVEAGER	Eliezer	Roza née BADIYAN		
SHVAYBISH	Shmuel (Milek)			
SHVELER				entire family
SHVARTSMAN	Herman	Pninah		
SCHOTTLAENDER				entire family
SHUSTER	Leib	Feigeh née OKIN	Asher	
SCHOR	Ichyu			entire family

SCHOR	Moshe	Tuiba née MEIR		
SCHOR		Klara		
SHURTS				entire family
SHTARK				entire family
SCHTOK				entire family
SHTAYNER	Yosef (Yosyu)			entire family
SHTAYNER	Yisrael			entire family
SHTAYNER		Mirel-Leah née MAYZLER		
SHTAYNER			son	engineer
SHTAYNER	Shmuel (Shmil)	Dina	Visya & Renya	
SHTIFTER				entire family
SHTIPEL	Avraham			
SHTIPEL	Shmuel	Slomia née GOLDBERG		
SHTIPEL				entire family
SHTIKLER		Dvora		
SHTIKLER		Khana		
SHTIKLER		Peppi		
SHTELTSER		Khava (Khava'le)		
SHTELTSER	Yaakov (Yanka'le)			
SHTRAYBER				entire family
SHTERN	Yaakov	Hentsiya née STOIYANOVER	son	
SHTERN	Leib			entire family
SHTERN	Lipa			
SHTERN			Yehuda	entire family
SHEIN		Perl née RASHMAN		
SHIKHTER	Tsvi		Beila & Lena	
SHIMEL				entire family
SHKHTER	Leon (Lunek)	Betka	Zuzya	
SHEKHTMAN	Metri			entire family
SHEKHNER	Rakhel			
SHEKHNER	Shlomo			
SHELEV (or SHLAV)	Moshe-Neteh			entire family

SHLINGER	Eliezer			
SHLINGER	Aryeh (leib)			
SHLINGER	Berko	wife	Gizya	
SHLINGER		Golda		
SHLINGER	Yaakov	Simah née HOKHBERG	Yermiyahu & Malka	
SHLINGER	Yaakov	Sima née KRAMM	Eliezer, Yitskhak, Meir & Areyh	
SHLINGER	Yitskhak (Izyu)			
SHLINGER	Yermiyahu (Yarom)	Adela née HOKHBERG	Rivka	
SHLINGER		Malka		from Lechia
SHLINGER	Meir			
SHLINGER				entire family (from Ponikovitsa)
SHLAYFER				entire family
	R' Shlomo			entire family. Shlomo - Melamed in “Talmud Torah”
SHMUSHKIN	Avraham	Matya (Matel) née EPSHTAYN	Naftali-Herts, Manya & Efraim	
SHMIDER	Dr.			Physician
SHMIRER	Hersh		Sheindel'la	
SHENBAUM		Roza née ETTINGER		
SCHNOR	Moshe			entire family
SHNAYDER	Yaakov-Leib			
SHNAYDER	Yaakov-Moshe	Ettah née VASERMAN		
SHNAYDER	Leon			entire family
SCHPAK	Yaakov (Kuba)			
SHPIGEL	Mendel			
SHPIGEL		Rakhel		
SHPIVAK				entire family
SHPILMAN				entire family
SHPILKEH	David	Khaya-Hinda	Avraham,	

			Yaakov, Ester, Feiga, Yehoshua & Menik	
SHPILKEH	Lazar			entire family
SHPILKEH	Moshe	Rivka née PIGLER (or FIGLER)	children	
SHPILKEH		Feigeh née VILDER	daughter	
SHPILKEH		Tsipora	David	
SHPILKEH	Shmuel	Leah-Bilha née CHACHKES	Avraham & David	
SHAPIRA	Khaim-Noakh	Sara née MELES	David	
SHAPIRA		Yokheved	Bilha, Yekhtetsi, Yaakov & Yosef	
SHAPIRA	Yaakov			
SHAPIRA		Lolla		
SHAPIRA	Lazar			
SHAPIRA	Molek			Lawyer
SHAPIRA	Mekhel			
SHAPIRA	Moshe	wife	two children	
SHAPIRA		Risha	Zalman, Mendel, Ada, Pinkhas, Feiga & Sara	
SHAPIRA				Community leader (Parnas). Entire family
SHEPS	Meir	wife	Izyu	
SHPETS	Leon	Rakhel	Khay'ke, Yose'le, Sara'le & two more children	
SHPURH	Khaim			entire family
SHPRUKH	Khanokh			
SHPRUKH-POZNER	Yitskhak	Selah née PLATNER		
SHPRUKH-POZNER	Moshe	wife	Yosef & Munyo	
SHPRUKH	Reuven			
SHPRUKH-POZNER			Barukh, Yosef, Shelna & Volf	

SHPREKHER		Khaya née HALBERTAL		
SHFRAN				entire family
SHATS				entire family
SHCHUPAK	Khaim	wife née KTSMAN		
SHRAGA	Bernard			painters. Bernard's brother
SHRAGA	Yosef	Sam	baby boy	
SHARGA	Moshe	wife née FRIDMAN	daughter	
SHRAGA	Shlomo			
SHARGEL		Riva		
SHRAYBSHTAYN	Moshe	Zisli née STOIYANOVER	Feiga'le	
SHARLOVSKI		Gusta née DISHEL		

[Page 420]

Brody Youths who fought the Nazis in Various Fronts, Killed During the Years 1939-1945

Transliterated by Moshe Kutten

Surname	First name(s)	Additional names and remarks
AURBAKH	Rodolf (Rudek)	
BERGER	Yosef	Partisan. young brother
GLAYKER	Mordekhai (Mota'le)	
GROSSFELD	Moshe	
DRUBICHER	Shmaryahu	
HERTSBERG	Aryeh-Leib	in Denyepro-Petrovsk front
VAYS	Izyu	
ZAYDENVORM	Hersh	
ZILBERBERG	Yitskhak	
TLOMEK	Leon	
LINDER	Yaakov	Partisan
MIKOLINTSER	Yosef	
MARGALYOT	Kopel	
STOYANOVER	Khaim	Partisan
PODNIK		
PESTES	Herman	
FRIDMAN	Isasskhar (Isar)	

ROGOVSKI	Nakhum (Nunek)	
ROZENGARTEN	Todzyo	
SHTAYNER	Yosef	son of Kalman and Froda née BUKHBINDER
FOYERSHTAYN		engineer

[Page 421]

Former Brody Residents Who Passed Away in Israel

Translated by Moshe Kutten

Note: Due to the fact that Hebrew lacks vowels, names may have been spelled inaccurately. In many cases the name was spelled according to the most frequent spelling found on JewishGen databases. The Hebrew Transliteration ANSI Standard (Z39.25-1975) used by JewishGen was used when possible.

Surname	**Given name**	**Note**
ETTINGER	Yosef (Yosyu)	
OKIN-ACKER	Yehoshua	
ETTINGER	Yitzkahk (Izyu)	
ACHTENTUCH	Lusya	née LUTZ-ROSENFELD
ACHTENTUCH	Tzvi	
ALTMAN	Mina	
ACKER-MALES	Lina	
AKSELROD	Manes	
BER	Israel	
BRAUN	Israel (Siunyu)	
BRAUN	Leah	
BRAUN	Mordekhai	
BARLES	Regina	

BRENDWEIN	Prof. Yerakhmiel (Milek)	
GOLDIG-RUBIN	Sara	
GUTERMAN	Pnina	née PECHNIK
GUTERMAN	Shmuel	
GELBER	Dr. Natan-Michael	
GLADSHTEIN	Dosya	
GALILI-HENDELSMAN	Shmuel	
GEMERSHMIDT	Avraham	
GASTHALTER	Uri	
GRINER	Benyamin	
GRINSHTEIN	Sonya	née MONDSHTEIN
DAGAN	Z'enya	née POILSHCHUK
DOICHER	Izyu	
DOICHER	David	
DISTENFELD	Akiva	
DOICHER-DROR	Gershon	
HORN	Dr. Karol	
HALPRIN	Gedalia	
HALPREN	Moshe	
HAMERMAN	David	

HENDELSMAN-HADAS	Shaul	
HENZEL	Shmuel	
HARI	Khaim	
HERMELIN	Arie (Leib)	
HERMELIN	Shalom	
HERNIK	Kalman	
WGMAN	Israel	
WEISS	Dr. Khaim-Mordekhai	
WEINSHTOCK	Israel	
WILDER	Khava	
WASERMAN	Rabbi Moshe	
VIRSOLANSKI-MEIR	Batya	
ZAUBER	Yitzkhak	
ZAUBER	Shimon	
ZOHAR	Genia	
ZUKHMAN	Nesya	
ZUKHMAN-NESYAHU	Yehoshua	
ZUKHMAN	Shalom-Arie	
Z'ORNE	Klara	
Z'ORNE-ZOHAR	Frida	

ZIGELBOIM-TREIBER	Genya	
ZEIDENWORM	Kalman	
ZINGER	Mendel	
ZINGER	Manya	
ZINGER	Shmuel	
ZELIGBOIM	Lorka	
KHUDEK	Peretz	
KHARASH	Khaim-Mordekhai	
KHARASH	Yehoshua	
KHARASH	Imanuel	
KHARSH	Klara	née GOLDSHTEIN
TENENBAUM	Nakhman	
TENENBAUM	Shalom	
TARTAKOVER	Arie	Engineer
Prof. TARTAKOVER	Khaim	
YAROM-SHPIGEL	Moshe	
KAHANA	Otek	
KAHANA	David	From Ramat Yokhanan

KAHANA	Mondek	
KAHANA	Manya	
LAUFER	Fanya	née Z'ORNE
LEVAVI	Sonya	née SCHTOK
LIBERBAUM	Yosef	
LIBERBAUM	Miryam	née DISHEL
LIBERMAN-LEVRIN	Yosef	
LIBERMAN	Yekhiel	
BEICHER	Gershon	
BEICHER-LIDSKI	Ester	née LAMM
LEVAI	Pesya	
LEINER-PARVARI	Yosef	
LIPSKER	Martin	
LAMM	Yitzkhak	
LAMM	Ronya	née PECHNIK
LAMM	Frida	née DOICHER
LAMM	Shmuel	
LANDOU-MEDINI	Yosef	
LANDU	Yisaskhar	
LERNER-NAOR	Naftali	
LESHNOVER	Frida	

LESHNOVER	Rivka	
MEIR-VOROBLANSKI	Batya	
MEIR	Pinkhas	
MEIR	Shmuel	
MAGID	Khava	
MEIZER	Shoshana	
MENKES	Yosef-Dov	
MARDER	Tonya	
MARSH	Shonyo	
NOIGEBOR	Mundek	
SAPIR		Worked in Israel Power Company
DAGAN	Z'enya	née POLISHCHUK
POLK	Hersh	
PONIKOVER		
POPPER	Dr. Tzvi Arye	
FUKS	Etil	née Z'ORNE
PORTER	Yehoshoa (Holesh)	
PURMAN-GFANI	Yona	
PETROSHKA-KATZ	David	

FRIDMAN	Mendel	
FRIDAMN	Amalya	
FREIFELD		Engineer
PARNES	Avraham	
FRANTZUZ	Yehuda	
FRENKEL	Yulek	
CHUP	Zenvil	
TZIMELS	Hersh	
TZIMEND	Mordekhai-Motl	
TZIN	Benyamin	
CHERNITZ	Sonya	
KOVALSKI	Rivaka	née LESHNOVER
KORIN	Zeev	
KORNITZ-BIRENTZWEIG	Gusta	
KELER	Yona	
KENDEL	Yitzkhak	
KANCHUKER	Arie-Leib	
KANCHUKER	Dvora	
KARPEN	David	
KARPEN	Yetti	

RAVEH	Aharon	
RAVEH	Khana	
RAVEH	Tema	
RAVEH	Menashe	
ROZENBLUM	Elieazer	
ROZENBLUM	Aleksander	
ROZENBLUM	Dov	
ROZENBLUM	Moshe	
ROZENBLUM	Reizel	
ROZENBLUM	Shlomo	
ROZENBLUM	Khanokh (Henyu)	
ROZENFELD	Rakhel	
ROTHAUG	Refael	
ROT	Khana	
ROT	Sara	née HENDELSON
ROTAUG-RON	Shmuel	
ROTENBEG	David	
ROTENBEG	Stephan	
REIZER	Fredrick	
REINRET	Elieazer	
REINRET	Natan	
REISS		
SCHVATZ	Guner-Guni-Tzvi	

SCHVATZ-SHKHORI	Tzvi	
SHAKHAR	Yosef	
SCHTOK-SADAN	Avraham (Umek) Yair	
SCHTOK-SADAN	Prof. Dov	
SCHTOK-SADAN ha'KOHEN	Khaim Tzvi	
SCHTOK-SADAN	Meshulam	
SCHTOK-SADAN	Nisan	
SCHTOK-SADAN	Selka	Nisan's Wife
SHPIGEL	Frida	née LESHNOVER
SHAPIRA	Ada	
SHAPIRA	Feibl	
SHAPIRA	Simkha	

[Page 426]

Former Brody Residents and their Offsprings Who Fell in Israel's Campaigns

Transliterated by Moshe Kutten

ATERMAN	Shmuel	Son of Pnina Pitchnuk	Reserve service 1980
BUKHEN	Alexander	Son of Lola and Yosef Bukhen	War of Independence, 1948
GUTERMAN	Shmuel		November 6th, 1980
GEMERSHMIDT	Shmuel	Son of Miriam and Avraham	Reserve service
HURVITZ	Nakhum	Son of Miriam and Yosef	War of Independence July 7, 1948
HEITLER-TAL	Amir	Son of Hela Weintraub	Golan Heights, Yom Kippur War
HENZEL	Yehoshua (Sheike)		Arab Riots 1938-9
HERMELIN	David	Son of Leah and Khayim	Yom Kippur War
WORKER	Yisrael		Independence War, July 16, 1948
ZEIDENWORM	Amnon		In action
KATZ	Eyal-Shmuel	Son of Rakhel	Six Day War
MAZER	Dan	Son of Sonia and Yaakov	Reserve service December 2, 1981
SADAN	Tzvi (Tze-Beh)	Son of Keila and Avraham-Yair	Yom Kippur War

KLANBER	Arie-Dov	Son of Berta Margolis	Navy ship “Eilat”, War of Attrition
ROZENBLUM	Yigal	Son of Yoav, Grandson of Moshe	Golan Heights, Yom Kippur War

[Page 427]

After the Holocaust in Germany – a group of Brody's Holocaust survivors, on their way to the memorial ceremony in Munich

[Page 428]

Brody people meeting in "Yad Vashem", Jerusalem

Brody people meeting on Mount Carmel, Haifa

[Page 429]

Memorial for the Brody community
in the "Martyrs Forest" in the Jerusalem corridor

The memorial forest for the Brody community

[Page 53 - English][Page 59* - Polish][Page 433 - Hebrew][Page 438 - Yiddish]*

We, Polish Jews...

(My, Zydzi Polscy)

by Julian Tuwim

To my Mother in Poland
or to her beloved Shadow

[Editor's note: The ellipsis dots that appear throughout this piece appear also in the translation published in An Eternal Light: Brody, in Memoriam.]

...And immediately I can hear the question: "What do you mean – *WE*?" The question I grant you is natural enough. Jews to whom I am wont to explain that I am a Pole have asked it. So will the Poles, to the overwhelming majority of whom, I am and shall remain a Jew. Here is my answer to both.

I am a Pole because I want to be. It's nobody's business but my own. I certainly have not the slightest intention of rendering account, explaining, or justifying it to anyone. I do not divide Poles into pure-stock Poles and alien-stock Poles. I leave such classification to pure and alien-stock advocates of racialism, to domestic and foreign Nazis. I divide Poles just as I divide Jews and all other nations into the intelligent and the fools, the honest and the dishonest, the brilliant and the dull-witted, the exploited and the exploiters, gentlemen and cads. I also divide Poles into Fascists and anti-Fascists. Neither of these groups is, of course, homogeneous; each shimmers with a variety of hues and shades. But a dividing line certainly does exist, and soon will become quite apparent. Shades may remain, but the color of the dividing line itself will both brighten and deepen to a marked degree.

I can say that in the realm of politics I divide Poles into anti-Semites and anti-Fascists. For Fascism means always anti-Semitism. Anti-Semitism is the international language of Fascism.

2

If, however, it comes to explaining my nationality, or rather my sense of national belonging, then I am a Pole for the most simple, almost primitive reasons. Mostly rational, partly irrational, but devoid of any "mystical" flourishes. To be a Pole is neither an honor nor a glory nor a privilege. It is like breathing. I have not yet met a man who is proud of breathing.

[Page 54]*

I am a Pole because it was in Poland that I was born and bred, that I grew up and learned; because it was in Poland that I was happy and unhappy; because from exile it is to Poland that I want to return, even though I were promised the joys of paradise elsewhere.

A Pole – because, due to some tender prejudice which I am unable to justify by any logic or reason, I desire after death to be absorbed and dissolved into Polish soil and none other.

A Pole – because I have been told so in Polish in my own paternal home, because since infancy I have been nurtured in the Polish tongue; because my mother taught me Polish songs and Polish rhymes; because when poetry first seized me, it was in Polish words that it burst forth; because what in my life became paramount – poetical creation – would be unthinkable in any other tongue no matter how fluent I might become in it.

A Pole – because it was in Polish that I confessed to the quiverings of my first love, and in Polish that I babbled of its bliss and storm.

A Pole – also because the birch and willow are closer to my heart than palms and citrus trees, and Mickiewicz and Chopin dearer than Shakespeare and Beethoven. Dearer for reasons which again I'd be at a loss to explain.

A Pole – because I have taken over from the Poles quite a few of their national faults. A Pole – because my hatred of Polish Fascists is greater than my hatred of Fascists of other nationalities. And I consider that particular point as a strong mark of my nationality.

Above all, a Pole – because I want to be.

3

"All right," someone will say, "granted you are a Pole. But in that case, why 'we JEWS'?" To which I answer: BECAUSE OF BLOOD. "Then racialism again?" No, not racialism at all. Quite the contrary.

There are two kinds of blood: that inside of veins, and that which spurts from them. The first is the sap of the body, and as such comes under the realm of physiologists. Whoever attributes to this blood any other than biological characteristics and powers will, in consequence, as we have seen, turn towns into smoking ruins, will slaughter millions of people, and at last, as we shall yet see, bring carnage upon his own kin.

The other kind of blood is the same blood but spilled by this gang-leader of international Fascism to testify to the triumph of his gore over mine, the blood of millions of murdered innocents, a blood not hidden in arteries but revealed to the world. Never since the dawn of mankind has there been such a flood of martyr blood, and the blood of Jews (not Jewish blood, mind you) flows in widest and deepest streams. Already its blackening rivulets are flowing together into a tempestuous river. AND IT IS IN THIS NEW JORDAN THAT I BEG TO RECEIVE THE BAPTISM OF BAPTISMS: THE BLOODY, BURNING, MARTYRED BROTHERHOOD OF JEWS.

[Page 55]*

Take me, my brethren, into that glorious bond of Innocently Shed Blood. To that community, to that church I want to belong from now on.

Let that high rank – the rank of the Jew Doloris Causa – be bestowed upon a Polish poet by the nation which produced him. Not for my merit, for I can claim none in your eyes. I will consider it a promotion and the highest award for those few Polish poems which may survive me and will be connected with the memory of my name – the name of a Polish Jew.

4

Upon the armbands which you wore in the ghetto the star of David was painted. I believe in a future Poland in which that star of your armbands will become the highest order bestowed upon the bravest among Polish officers and soldiers. They will wear it proudly upon their breast next to the old Virtuti Militari. There also will be a Cross of the Ghetto – a deeply symbolic name. There will be the Order of the Yellow Patch, denoting more merit than many a present tinsel. And there shall be in Warsaw and in every other Polish city some fragment of the ghetto left standing and preserved in its present form in all its horror of ruin and destruction. We shall surround that monument to the ignominy of our foes and to the glory of our tortured heroes with chains wrought from captured Hitler's guns, and every day we shall twine fresh live flowers into its iron links, so that the memory of the massacred people shall remain forever fresh in the minds of the generations to come, and also as a sign of our undying sorrow for them.

Thus a new monument will be added to the national shrine.

There we will lead our children, and tell them of the most monstrous martyrdom of people known to the history of mankind. And in the center of this monument, its tragedy enhanced by the rebuilt magnificence of the surrounding city, there will burn an eternal fire. Passersby will uncover their heads before it.

And those who are Christians will cross themselves.

Thus it will be with pride, mournful pride, that we shall count ourselves of that glorious rank which will outshine all others – the rank of the Polish Jew, we who by miracle or by chance have remained alive. With pride? Let us rather say: with contrition and gnawing shame. For it was bestowed upon us for the sake of your torment, your glory, Redeemers!

[Page 56]*

...And so perhaps I should not say “we Polish Jews,” but “we ghosts, we shadows of our slaughtered brethren, the Polish Jews.”...

5

We Polish Jews ...We, everliving, who have perished in the ghettos and camps, and we ghosts who, from across seas and oceans, will some day return to the homeland and haunt the ruins in our unscarred bodies and our wretched, presumably spared souls.

We, the truth of the graves, and we, the illusion of living; we, millions of corpses and we, a few, perhaps a score of thousands of quasi non-corpses; we, that boundless brotherly tomb; we, a Jewish burial ground such as was never seen before and will never be seen again.

We, suffocated in gas-chambers and turned into soap – a soap that will not wash clean the stains of our blood nor the stigma of the sin the world has perpetrated upon us.

We, whose brains spattered upon the walls of our miserable dwellings and the walls under which we were stood for mass execution solely because we were Jews.

We, the Golgotha upon which an endless forest of crosses could be raised. We, who two thousand years ago gave humanity a Son of Man slaughtered by the Roman Empire, and this one innocent death was enough to make Him God. What religion will arise from millions of deaths, tortures, degradations and arms stretched wide in the last agony of despair?

We Abies, we Kikes, We Sheenies[1] whose names and nick-names will some day exceed in dignity those of Achilles, Boleslaus the Brave, and Richard Coeur-de-Lion.

We, once more in the catacombs, in the manholes under Warsaw pavements, splashing in the stink of sewers to the surprise of our companions – the rats.

We, rifle in hand upon barricades, amidst the ruins of our homes bombed from the sky above; we – soldiers of honor and freedom.

[Page 57]*

"Kike, go and fight!"[2] He did, Gentlemen, and laid down his life for Poland.

We, who made a fortress of every threshold while house after house crashed about us.

We, Polish Jews growing wild in forests, feeding our terrified children on roots and grass; we crawling, crouching, bedraggled and unkempt, armed with an antique shotgun obtained by some miraculous feat of begging and bribing.

"Have you heard the one about the Jewish game-keeper? It's a riot. The Jew fired; and by golly if he didn't wet his pants from fright! Ha! Ha!"

We, Jobs, we Niobes, mourning the loss of hundreds of thousands of our Jewish Urszulkas.[3]

We, deep pits of broken, crushed bones and twisted, welted bodies.

We – the scream of pain! A scream so shrill that the most distant ages shall hear it. We – the Lament, the Howl, we – the Choir chanting a sepulchral El Male Rachamim whose echo will be passed from one century to the next.

We – history's most glorious heap of bloody manure with which we have fertilized the Polish soil so that the bread of freedom may be sweeter for those who will survive us.

We, the macabre remnants, we – the last of the Mohicans, the pitiful survivors of slaughter whom some new Barnum may well exhibit throughout the world, proclaiming upon multicolored billboards: "Super Show! The biggest sensation of the World! Genuine Polish Jews. Alive!" We, the Chamber of Horrors, Schreckenskammer, Chambre des Tortures! "Nervous persons better leave the audience!"

We, who sit and weep upon the shores of distant rivers, as once we sat on the banks of the rivers of Babylon. All over the world does Rachel bewail her children, and they are no more. On the banks of the Hudson, of the Thames, of the Euphrates and the Nile, of the Ganges and Jordan we wander, scattered and forlorn, crying: "Vistula! Vistula! Vistula! Mother of ours! Grey Vistula turned rosy not with the rosiness of dawn but that of blood!"

[Page 58]*

We, who will not even find the graves of our mothers and children, so deep are the layers, so widely spread all over the country in one huge burial ground. There will be no one sacred plot upon which to lay our flowers; but even as a sower sows grain so shall we fling them in a wide gesture. And one, maybe, will find the spot.

We, Polish Jews ...We, the legend dripping with tears and blood. A legend, perhaps, fit only to be told in Biblical verses: "graven with an iron pen and read in the rock forever" (Job 19. 24). We – the Apocalyptical stage of history. We – Jeremiah's Lamentations:

..."The young and the old lie on the ground in the streets: my virgins and my young men are fallen by the sword; thou hast slain them in the day of thine anger; thou hast killed, and not pitied."...

..."They have cut off my life in the dungeon, and cast a stone upon me. Waters flowed over my head, then I said, I am cut off! ...I called upon thy name, O Lord, out of the low dungeon ...O Lord, thou hast seen my wrong: Judge thou my cause ...Render unto them a recompense, O Lord, according to the work of their hands! Give them sorrow of heart, thy curse unto them. Persecute and destroy them in anger from under the heavens of the Lord!" (Jeremiah, 25. 14; Lamentations, 3. 55-66).

* * *

A huge and still growing ghost-skeleton looms over Europe. From his empty eyesockets blazes the fire of dangerous wrath, and his fingers are clutched in a bony fist. It is He – our Leader, our Dictator who shall dictate our rights and our demands.

Translated by Mrs. R. Langer, first published in *Free World*, New York, July 1944.

Translator's notes

1. The original here consists of a string of names and nicknames for Jews which were common in Polish.
2. In the original: "Jojne, idz na wojne!" – "Jonah, go to war!" – a well-known Polish rhyme which mocks the Jews for their lack of military aptitude.
3. Urszulka – the daughter of the famous Polish poet Jan Kochanowski (1530-1584) who died in her youth. Her father's collection of elegies upon her death Treny (1580 – "Dirges") is very famous in the literary and cultural traditions of Poland. In the original English translation, "Jewish Urszulkas" was rendered as "little ones".

Aerial photographs of Brody

These photographs are from the Records of the Defense Intelligence Agency Record 373, Captured German World War II photographs available from the National Archives and Records Administration II Cartographic Section.

Nowy Cmentarz Żydowski
Cmentarz Katolicki
JAZŁOWCZYK
FOLWARKI MAŁE
ZAMEK
WAŁY SZPITALINE
GETTO
SMÓLNO
Stary Cmentarz Żydowski
TARGOWICA (Park Miejski)
SUCHOWÓLKA
STARE BRODY
Dwór Schnella
SZWABY
FOLWARKI WIELKIE
Stacja Towarowa
Stacja Dworzec Kolejowa
Do Lwowa Przez Krasne
Linia Kolejova Równe - Lwów
Do Radziwiłowa
PLAN MIASTA BRODY
1 old synagogue
2 new synagogue
3 jewish municipality house
4 jewish school
5 jewish hall
6 orphanage
7 cinema "palas"
8 home for aged
9 jewish hospital
10 musical association
11 new cemetry
12 old cemetry
13 catholic church
שרטוט: יוסף פרבר (ליינר)
SKRESLIL:PARWARI JÓZEF
(LEINER)

Map of Brody

Brody, Ukraine
National Archives and Records Administration
Cartographic Section, RG ~ 373 ~ GX 12399 ~ SD 91

Legend

1. Ruins of Old Synagogue
2. Zamek (Castle)
3. Leszniowska Street leading to new Jewish cemetery and Catholic cemetery
4. Rynek (town square)
5 Railway
6. Stare Brody (old town of Brody)
12. Old Jewish Cemetery

Brody, Ukraine, German Military Aerial Map, 1944

National Archives and Records Administration,

Cartographic Section, RG~373 ~ GX 12399 ~ SD 91.

Aerial photograph (without arrows)

Name Index

Prepared by Ami Elyasaf

צ **Tzadik**

INDEX

Using The Page Numbers Of This Translation

When using this index for names, please check all possible alternate spellings because transliteration of the names from Hebrew and Yiddish is not consistent between translators and may differ from those the reader is familiar with.

The previous section, starting on page 654, was not included in this index because that index was prepared using the page numbers in the original Yizkor Book and are not the same as in this translation.

A

B

H

L

N

O

T

U

V

W

Y

Z

www.ingramcontent.com/pod-product-compliance
Lightning Source LLC
Chambersburg PA
CBHW082009150426
42814CB00005BA/271